THE HIBBERT LECTURES,

1887.

THE HIBBERT LECTURES, 1887.

LECTURES

ON THE

ORIGIN AND GROWTH OF RELIGION

AS ILLUSTRATED BY THE RELIGION OF THE

ANCIENT BABYLONIANS.

BY

A. H. SAYCE,

FELLOW AND LATE SENIOR TUTOR OF QUEEN'S COLL., AND DEPUTY-PROFESSOR OF COMPARATIVE PHILOLOGY, OXFORD; HON. LL.D. DUBLIN.

THIRD EDITION.

WIPF & STOCK · Eugene, Oregon

Wipf and Stock Publishers
199 W 8th Ave, Suite 3
Eugene, OR 97401

Lectures on the Origin and Growth of Religion, Third Edition
As Illustrated by the Religion of the Ancient Babylonians
The Hibbert Lectures, 1887
By Sayce, A. H.
Softcover ISBN-13: 978-1-6667-5680-7
Hardcover ISBN-13: 978-1-6667-5681-4
eBook ISBN-13: 978-1-6667-5682-1
Publication date 8/30/2022
Previously published by Williams and Norgate, 1891

This edition is a scanned facsimile of the original edition published in 1891.

PREFACE.

A WORD of apology is needed for the numerous repetitions in the following chapters, which are due to the fact that the chapters were written and delivered in the form of Lectures.

I cannot guarantee the exactness of every word in the translations of the cuneiform texts given in them. The meaning of individual words may at times be more precisely defined by the discovery of fuller materials, even where it has been supposed that their signification has been fixed with certainty. The same fate has befallen the interpretation of the Hebrew Scriptures, and is still more likely to befall a progressive study like Assyrian.

How rapidly progressive the latter is, may be gathered from the number of contributions to our knowledge of Babylonian religion made since the following Lectures were in the hands of the printer. Prof. Tiele, in a Paper entitled, "De Beteekenis van Ea en zijn Verhouding tot Maruduk en Nabu," has tried to show that Ea was originally connected with the fire; Mr. Pinches has published a late Babylonian text in the *Babylonian Record*, from which it appears that the *esrâ*, or "tithe," was paid to the temple of the Sun-god not only by individuals, but also by towns; and Dr. Jensen, in the *Zeitschrift für Assyriologie* (ii. 1), has made it probable that the *azkaru* of the hymn translated on pp. 68, 69, was the feast of the new moon.

Certain abbreviations are used in the following pages. W. A. I. means the five volumes of *The Cuneiform Inscriptions of Western Asia,* published by the Trustees of the British Museum; D. P. denotes "determinative prefix;" and the letters D.T., R., M., S. and K., refer to tablets marked accordingly in the British Museum. "Unnumbered" texts mean tablets which had not been catalogued at the time when I copied them. Words written in capitals denote ideographs whose true pronunciation is unknown.

A. H. SAYCE.

QUEEN'S COLL., OXFORD,
 June 4*th,* 1887.

CONTENTS.

LECTURE I.
INTRODUCTORY.

PAGE

Difficulties of the subject—Character and age of the materials—Modification of earlier views—Rise of Semitic culture in the court of Sargon of Accad, B.C. 3700—His conquest of Cyprus—Intercourse with Egypt—Earlier culture of pre-Semitic Chaldæa—Connection between Babylonian and Hebrew religion—Two periods of Babylonian influence upon the Jews—Origin of the names of Moses, Joseph, Saul, David and Solomon—Resemblances between the Babylonian and Jewish priesthood and ritual—Babylonian temples and sabbaths—Human sacrifice—Unclean meats 1

LECTURE II.
BEL-MERODACH OF BABYLON.

Cyrus a worshipper of Bel-Merodach—View of the priesthood about his conquest—Merodach the supreme Bel or Baal of Babylon—Comparison between him and Yahveh—Babylonian religion characterised by localisation—Temple of Bel—Doctrine of the resurrection—Merodach originally the Sun-god of Eridu—Nebo the divine prophet of Borsippa—Assur of Assyria—His origin—His resemblance to Yahveh of Israel 85

LECTURE III.
THE GODS OF BABYLONIA.

General character of Babylonian religion—Ea the Culture-god—The pre-Semitic monuments of Tel-loh (B.C. 4000)—Early trade with India—Ea as god of the sea—The pre-Semitic deities creators, the Semitic deities fathers—Two centres of Babylonian culture, Eridu on the coast and Nipur in the north—Mul-lil, "the lord of the ghost-world," the god of Nipur—Mul-lil the older Bel, confused with Merodach the younger Bel—Other gods: Adar, the Moon-god, the Sun-god, &c.—The Moon-god of Harran—The goddesses of Semitic Babylonia mere reflections of the male deities—Anu, Nergal, and the Air-god—Rimmon and Hadad—Doctrine of the origin of evil—The seven wicked spirits 130

LECTURE IV.
TAMMUZ AND ISTAR; PROMETHEUS AND TOTEMISM.

The descent of Istar into Hades—Tammuz-Adonis the slain Sun-god—Originally of pre-Semitic Eridu—The world-tree—The tree of life and the tree of knowledge—The amours of Istar—Istar, primitively the goddess of the earth, identified with the evening-star—In the west, as Ashtoreth, identified with the moon—Of pre-Semitic origin—The orgies of Istar-worship—The purer side of her worship—Istar the Artemis and Aphroditê of the Greeks—Answers of the oracle of Istar to Esar-haddon—The dream of Assur-bani-pal—The Semitic gods of human form, the pre-Semitic of animal form—Early Chaldæan totems—The serpent—The Babylonian Prometheus and his transformation into a bird—"The voice of the Lord"—The power of the name—Excommunication: the Chaldæan fate—The Plague-god—The angel of destruction seen by David 221

LECTURE V.
THE SACRED BOOKS OF CHALDÆA.

The Chaldæan Rig-Veda—The magical texts—The penitential psalms—The hymns to the Sun-god of Sippara—Relative ages of the collections—The service-books of the temples—Accadian the sacred language of the Semitic Babylonian priesthood—Shamanism—Gradual evolution of the gods—Creation of the state-religion and the hierarchy of the gods—Degradation of the spirits of the earlier faith—Consciousness of sin—Views of the future state—The mountain of the world—Hades and heaven 315

LECTURE VI.
COSMOGONIES AND ASTRO-THEOLOGY.

Babylonian cosmological systems—Tiamat, the dragon of the deep, personifies chaos and is slain by Merodach—The creation in days—Anticipations of Darwin—Sabaism and Babylonian astronomy—The priest becomes an astrologer—Late date of the system—Worship of rivers and mountains—Babylonian Beth-els and the pillars of the sun 367

APPENDIX I. 413
„ II. Mr. G. Smith's Account of the Temple of Bel 437
„ III. The Magical Texts 441
„ IV. Hymns to the Gods 479
„ V. The Penitential Psalms 521
„ VI. Litanies to the Gods 532
INDEX OF WORDS 541
INDEX 545

THE
RELIGION OF THE ANCIENT BABYLONIANS.

Lecture I.

INTRODUCTORY.

It was with considerable diffidence that I accepted the invitation of the Hibbert Trustees to give a course of Lectures on the Religion of the Ancient Babylonians. The subject itself is new; the materials for treating it are still scanty and defective; and the workers in the field have been few. The religion of the Babylonians has, it is true, already attracted the attention of "the Father of Assyriology," Sir Henry Rawlinson, of the brilliant and gifted François Lenormant, of the eminent Dutch scholar Dr. Tiele, and of Dr. Fritz Hommel, one of the ablest of the younger band of Assyrian students; but no attempt has yet been made to trace its origin and history in a systematic manner. The attempt, indeed, is full of difficulty. We have to build up a fabric out of broken and half-deciphered texts, out of stray allusions and obscure references, out of monuments many of which are late and still more are of uncertain age. If, therefore, my account of Babylonian religion may seem to you incomplete, if I am compelled at times to break off in my story or to have recourse to conjecture, I must crave your indulgence and ask you to remember the difficulties of the task. To open up new ground is never an easy matter, more especially when the field of research is vast; and a new discovery may at any moment overthrow the theories we have formed, or give a new complexion to received facts.

I may as well confess at the outset that had I known all the difficulties I was about to meet with, I should never have had the courage to face them. It was not until I was committed beyond the power of withdrawal that I began fully to realise how great they were. Unlike those who have addressed you before in this place, I have had to work upon materials at once deficient and fragmentary. Mine has not been the pleasant labour of marshalling well-ascertained facts in order, or of selecting and arranging masses of material, the very abundance of which has alone caused embarrassment. On the contrary, I have had to make most of my bricks without straw. Here and there, indeed, parts of the subject have been lighted up in a way that left little to be desired, but elsewhere I have had to struggle on in thick darkness or at most in dim twilight. I have felt as in a forest where the moon shone at times through open spaces in the thick foliage, but served only to make the surrounding gloom still more apparent, and where I had to search in vain for a clue that would lead me from one interval of light to another.

The sources of our information about the religion of the ancient Babylonians and their kinsfolk the Assyrians are almost wholly monumental. Beyond a few stray notices in the Old Testament, and certain statements found in classical authors which are for the most part the offspring of Greek imagination, our knowledge concerning it is derived from the long-buried records of Nineveh and Babylon. It is from the sculptures that lined the walls of the Assyrian palaces, from the inscriptions that ran across them, or from the clay tablets that were stored within the libraries of the great cities, that we must collect our materials and deduce our theories. Tradition is mute, or almost so; between the old Babylonian world and our own a deep gulf yawns, across which we have to build a bridge by the help of texts that explorers have disinterred and scholars have painfully deciphered. But the study of these texts is one of no ordinary difficulty. They are written in characters that were once pictorial, like the hieroglyphs of Egypt, and were intended to express the sounds of a language wholly different from that of the Semitic Babylonians and Assyrians, from whom most of our inscriptions come. The result of these two facts was two-fold. On the one hand, every character had more than one value when used phonetically to denote a syllable; on the other hand, every character could be employed ideographically to represent an object or idea. And just as simple ideas could thus be represented by single characters, so compound ideas could be represented by a combination of characters. In the language of the primitive inhabitants of Babylonia, the world beyond the grave was known as Aráli, and was imaged as a dark subterranean region where the spirits of the dead kept watch over hoards of unnumbered gold. But the word Aráli was not written phonetically, nor was it denoted by a single ideograph; the old Chaldean chose rather to represent it by three separate characters which would literally mean "the house of the land of death."

When the Babylonians or Assyrians desired that what they wrote should be read easily, they adopted devices which enabled them to overcome the cumbersome obscurity of their system of writing. A historical inscription, for example, may be read with little difficulty; it is only our ignorance of the signification of particular words which is likely to cause us trouble in deciphering its meaning. But when we come to deal with a religious text, the case is altogether different. Religion has always loved to cloak itself in mystery, and a priesthood is notoriously averse from revealing in plain language the secrets of which it believes itself the possessor. To the exoteric world it speaks in parables; the people that knoweth not the law is accursed. The priesthood of Babylonia formed no exception to the general rule. As we shall see, it was a priesthood at once powerful and highly organised, the parallel of which can hardly be found in the ancient world. We need not wonder, therefore, if a considerable portion of the sacred texts which it has bequeathed to us were intentionally made difficult of interpretation; if the words of which they consisted were expressed by ideographs rather than written phonetically; if characters were used with strange and far-fetched values, and the true pronunciation of divine names was carefully hidden from the uninitiated multitude.

But these are not all the difficulties that beset us when we endeavour to penetrate into the meaning of the religious texts. I have already said that the cuneiform system of writing was not the invention, but the heritage, of the Semitic Babylonians and Assyrians. The Semites of the historical period, those subjects of Sennacherib and Nebuchadnezzar who were so closely allied in blood and language to the Hebrews, were not the first occupants of the valleys of the Tigris and Euphrates. They had been preceded by a population which in default of a better name I shall term Accadian or Proto-Chaldean throughout these Lectures, and which was in no wise related to them. The Accadians spoke an agglutinative language, a language, that is to say, which resembled in its structure the languages of the modern Finns or Turks, and their physiological features, so far as we can trace them from the few monuments of the Accadian epoch that remain, differed very markedly from those of the Semites. It was to the Accadians that the beginnings of Chaldean culture and civilisation were due. They were the teachers and masters of the Semites, not only in the matter of writing and literature, but in other elements of culture as well. This is a fact so startling, so contrary to preconceived ideas, that it was long refused credence by the leading Orientalists of Europe who had not occupied themselves with cuneiform studies. Even to-day there are scholars, and notably one who has himself achieved success in Assyrian research, who still refuse to believe that Babylonian civilisation was originally the creation of a race which has long since fallen into the rear rank of human progress. But unless the fact is admitted, it is impossible to explain the origin either of the cuneiform system of writing or of that system of theology the outlines of which I have undertaken to expound.

Here, then, is one of the difficulties against which the student of Babylonian religion has to contend. We have to distinguish the Accadian and the Semitic elements which enter into it, as well as the mixture which the meeting of these elements brought about. We have to determine what texts are Accadian, what are Semitic, what, finally, are due to a syncretic admixture of the two. What makes the task one of more than ordinary difficulty is the fact that, like Latin in the Middle Ages, the dead or dying Accadian became a sacred language among the Semitic priesthood of a later period. Not only was it considered necessary to the right performance of the ritual that genuinely old Accadian texts should be recited in their original language and with a correct pronunciation, but new texts were composed in the extinct idiom of Accad which bore the same linguistic relation to the older ones as the Latin compositions of the mediæval monks bear to the works of the Latin fathers. Unfortunately, in the present state of our knowledge, it is sometimes impossible to tell to which of these two classes of texts a document belongs, and yet upon the right determination of the question may depend also the right determination of the development of Babylonian religion.

The Accadian element in this religion is productive of yet another difficulty. As we shall see, a large proportion of the deities of the Babylonian faith had their first origin in the beliefs of the Accadian people. The names by which they were addressed, however, were usually written ideographically, not phonetically, after the fashion of the Accadian scribes, and the reading of these names is consequently often uncertain. Even if a gloss happens to inform us of the correct reading of one of these names, it by no means follows that we thereby know how to read its later Semitic equivalent. The Semites continued to represent the names of the gods by the same ideographs that had been used by their Accadian predecessors, but in most cases they naturally gave them a different pronunciation. Even now, when the study of Assyrian has so far advanced that the Hebrew lexicographer is able to call in its help in determining the meaning of Hebrew words, and when an ordinary historical inscription can be read with almost as much facility as a page of the Old Testament, we are still ignorant of the true name of one of the chief Assyrian divinities. The name of Adar, commonly assigned by Assyriologists to the Assyrian war-god, has little else to rest upon except the fact that Adrammelech or "king Adar" was the divinity in whose honour the men of Sepharvaim burnt their children in the fire, according to the second book of Kings (xvii. 31).[1] And yet the name is one which not only constantly occurs in the Assyrian inscriptions, but also enters into the name of more than one Assyrian king. Can there be a better illustration of the difficulties which surround the student

---

[1] Lehmann (*De Inscriptionibus cuneatis que pertinent ad Samas-sumukin*, p. 47) has made it probable that Adrammelech represents the goddess Adar-malkat, "Adar the queen," who seems to be identified with Â or Anunit, the goddess "of births" (*kunê*, W. A. I. ii. 57, 14), and to correspond to the Semitic goddess Erûa, "the begetter." In this case the name of Sennacherib's son, Adrammelech, must be considered to be corrupt. Erûa, however would be an Aramaic and not a Babylonian form, if it is a Semitic word; the Babylonian is Eritu, which is given in K 4195, 6, as a name of Istar. In W. A. I. ii. 54, 60, and S 1720, 2 Eru, "the handmaiden" (W. A. I. v. 19,43), is an Accadian title of Zarpanit.

of Babylonian religion, as well as of the extent to which he is deserted by classical tradition?

As with the name which we provisionally read Adar, so also is it with the name which we provisionally read Gisdhubar. Gisdhubar was the hero of the great Chaldean epic, into the eleventh book of which was woven the story of the Deluge; he had been the fire-god of the Accadians before he became the solar hero of Semitic legend; and there are grounds for thinking that Mr. George Smith was right in seeing in him the prototype of the Biblical Nimrod. Nevertheless, the only certain fact about his name is that it ended in the sound of *r*. That it was not Gisdhubar or Izdubar, however, is almost equally certain. This would be merely the phonetic reading of the three ideographs which compose the name, and characters when used as ideographs were naturally not read phonetically.[1]

I have not yet finished my enumeration of the difficulties and obstacles that meet the inquirer into the nature and history of Babylonian religion on the very threshold of his researches. The worst has still to be mentioned. With the exception of the historical inscriptions which adorned the sculptured slabs of the Assyrian

---

[1] Hommel (*Proc. Soc. Bib. Arch.* Ap. 1866, p. 119) believes that he has found the true reading of the name, and a proof of its correspondence with the Semitic Nimrod, in W. A. I. iv. 2. 21, 22., 23. 3. 26, 27, where the Semitic Namratsit answers to the name of an Accadian divinity which may be read Gi-isdu-par-ra or Gis-du-par-ra. But from S 949, *Obv.* 6, where the Sun-god is called *bil namratsit*, it is clear that *namratsit* is merely personified difficulty, being the feminine of the common adjective *namratsu*, "difficult." The Accadian divinity, therefore, is the goddess of difficulty, and can have no connection with a male Fire-god. Her name should probably be read Gi-ib-bir-ra, a derivative from *gib*, the Accadian form of *gig*, "difficult."

palaces or were inscribed on clay cylinders buried at the angles of a royal building, our documentary materials consist entirely of clay tablets covered with minute characters. In Assyria, the tablets were baked in the kiln after being inscribed; for this purpose holes were made in the clay to allow the escape of superfluous moisture, and the fear of fracture prevented the tablets from being of a great size. In the more southern climate of Babylonia, the tablets were generally dried in the sun, the result being the disintegration of the clay in the course of centuries, the surface of the brick being sometimes reduced to powder, while at other times the whole brick has been shivered into atoms. But apart from the records of "the banking firm" of the Egibi family, which carried on its business from the time of Nebuchadnezzar and his predecessors to that of Darius Hystaspis, we possess as yet comparatively few of the tablets that once stocked the libraries of Babylonia and must still be lying buried beneath the ground. The main bulk of our collection comes from the great library of Nineveh, which occupied one of the upper rooms in the palace of Assur-bani-pal at Kouyunjik. It stood within the precincts of the temple of Nebo,[1] and its walls were lined with shelves, on which were laid the clay books of Assyria or the rolls of papyrus which have long since perished.[2] The library

---

[1] W. A. I. ii. 36, 27: "I placed (the old tablets and papyri) in the inner chamber of the temple of Nebo, his lord, which is in Nineveh." The *bit namari*, or "observatory," on the contrary, was the "tower" of the temple of Istar, whose construction and dimensions are described in an interesting but unfortunately mutilated text (S 1894). Its breadth, we are told, was $154\frac{1}{2}$ cubits.

[2] For the papyrus, frequently mentioned in the colophons of Assur-bani-pal's tablets, under the name of GIS-LI-KHU-ŚI, or "grass of guid-

consisted for the most part of copies or editions of older works that had been brought from Babylonia, and diligently copied by numerous scribes, like the "proverbs of Solomon which the men of Hezekiah, king of Judah, copied out."[1] The library had been transferred from Calah by Sennacherib towards the latter part of his reign,[2] but the larger portion of the collection was got together by Assur-bani-pal, the son of Esar-haddon, and the Sardanapallos of the Greeks. He was the first, indeed we may say the only, Assyrian monarch who really cared for literature and learning. His predecessors had been men of war; if they established libraries, it was only from imitation of their more cultivated neighbours in Babylonia, and a desire to remain on good terms with the powerful classes of scribes and priests. But Assur-bani-pal, with all his luxury and love of display—or perhaps by reason of it—was a genuine lover of books. When rebellion had been quelled in Babylonia, and the Babylonian cities had been taken by storm, the spoil that was most acceptable to the Assyrian king were the written volumes that their libraries contained.

---

ing," see my remarks in the *Zeitschrift für Keilschriftforschung*, ii. 3, p. 208. Another ideographic name was GIS-ZU, "vegetable of knowledge" (W. A. I. ii. 36, 11). The Assyrian name was *aru*, literally "leaf," R 2, iii. *Rev.* 7. GIS-LI-KHU-ŚI was pronounced *liu* or *livu* in Assyrian, the Hebrew *luakh*, of which the Assyrian *lavu* is another form.

[1] Prov. xxv. 1.

[2] Nebo-zuqub-yukin, who was chief librarian from the 6th year of Sargon (B.C. 716) to the 22nd year of Sennacherib (B.C. 684), does not seem to have quitted Calah. So far as we know, the first work written under his direction had been a copy of a text of the standard work on astrology, "The Illumination of Bel," which had been brought from Babylon to the library at Calah.

No present could be sent him which he valued more than some old text from Erech or Ur or Babylon. But naturally it was the works which related to Assyria, or to the special studies of its royal masters, that were most sought after. The Assyrian cared little for the annalistic records of the Babylonian kings, or for the myths and legends which enveloped the childhood of the Babylonian cities and contained no reference to things Assyrian; it was only where the interest of the story extended beyond the frontiers of Babylonia, or where the religious texts held a place in the ritual of the Assyrian priesthood, that it was thought worth while to transport them to a northern home. If the theology was Assyrian as well as Babylonian, or if a legend was as popular in Assyria as it had been in Babylonia, or if, finally, a branch of study had a special attraction for Assyrian readers, the works embodying these subjects were transferred to the library of Nineveh, and there re-edited by the Assyrian scribes. Hence it is that certain sides of the old theology are represented so fully in Assyrian literature, while other sides are not represented at all; hence, too, it is that the drawers of the British Museum are filled with tablets on the pseudo-science of omens which have little save a philological importance attaching to them.

The library was open, it would seem, to all comers, and Assur-bani-pal did his utmost to attract "readers" to the "inspection" and study of the books it contained. But the literary age of Assyria was short-lived. Even before Assur-bani-pal died, the mighty empire he had inherited was tottering to its fall. Egypt had been lost to it for ever; Babylonia was clamouring for independence; and the semi-barbarous nations of the north and east were threatening its borders. Ere the century closed, Nineveh was taken by its enemies, and its palaces sacked and destroyed.

The library of Kouyunjik shared in the common overthrow. Its papyri and leathern scrolls were burned with fire, and its clay books fell in shattered confusion among the ruins below. There they lay for more than two thousand years, covered by the friendly dust of decaying bricks, until Sir A. H. Layard discovered the old library and revealed its contents to the world of to-day. His excavations have been followed by those of Mr. George Smith and Mr. Hormuzd Rassam, and the greater portion of Assur-bani-pal's library is now in the British Museum. It is out of its age-worn fragments that the story I have to tell in this course of Lectures has been mainly put together.

But the sketch I have given of its history is sufficient to show how hard such a task must necessarily be. In the first place, the library of Nineveh was only one of the many libraries which once existed in the cities of Assyria and Babylonia. Its founders never aimed at completeness, or intended to deposit in it more than a portion of the ancient literature of Babylonia. Then, further, even this literature was not always copied in full. From time to time the text is broken off, and the words "lacuna" or "recent fracture" appear upon the tablet. The original text, it is clear, was not perfect; the tablet which was copied had been injured, and was thus no longer legible throughout. Such indications, however, of the faultiness of the *editio princeps* are a good proof that the Assyrian scribes did their best to reproduce it with accuracy, and that if they failed to do so it was through no fault of their own. But they did fail sometimes. The Babylonian forms of the cuneiform characters are often hard to read, and there was no standard official script in Babylonia such as there was in Assyria. Education was not in the hands of a single class, as was the case in the latter country; most Babylonians could read and write, and consequently the forms of handwriting found upon their monuments are almost as numerous as in the modern world. Hence it is that the Assyrian copyist sometimes mistook a Babylonian character, and represented it by a wrong equivalent.

The most serious result, however, of the fact that the library of Nineveh mainly consisted of terra-cotta tablets, broken and scattered in wild confusion when the city was destroyed, still remains to be told. The larger proportion of the texts we have to use are imperfect. Many of them are made up of small fragments, which have been pieced together by the patient labour of the Assyrian scholars in the British Museum. In other cases, only a fragment, not unfrequently a minute fragment, of a text has been preserved. Often, therefore, we come across a text which would seem to throw an important light on some department of Assyrian thought and life if only we had the clue to its meaning, but the text is broken just where that clue would have been found. This fragmentary character of our documents, in fact, is not only tantalising to the student, but it may be the cause of serious error. Where we have only fragments of a text, it is not impossible that we may wholly misconceive their relation and meaning, and so build theories upon them which the discovery of the missing portions of the tablet would overthrow. This is especially the case in the province of religion and mythology, where it is so easy to put a false construction upon isolated passages, the context of which must be supplied from conjecture. We know from experience what strange interpretations have been imposed upon passages of the Bible that have been torn from their context; the student of Babylonian religion must therefore be forgiven if the condition in which his materials have reached him should at times lead him astray. Moreover, it must be remembered that the fragmentary condition of our texts makes the work of the decipherer much harder than it would otherwise be. A new word or an obscure phrase is often made perfectly intelligible by the context; but where this fails us, all interpretation must necessarily be uncertain, if not impossible.

There is yet another difficulty connected with our needful dependence upon the broken tablets of Assur-bani-pal's library—a difficulty, however, that would not be felt except by the student of Babylonian religion. None of the tablets that are derived from it are older than the eighth century before our era; how then are we to determine the relative ages of the various religious or mythological documents which are embodied in them? It is true that we are generally told to what library of Babylonia the original text belonged, but we look in vain for any indication of date. And yet an approximately accurate chronology is absolutely indispensable for a history of religion and religious ideas. If, indeed, we could explore the Babylonian libraries themselves, there would be a better chance of our discovering the relative antiquity of the documents they may still contain. But at present this is impossible, and except in a few instances we have to be content with the copies of the older documents which were made by the Assyrian scribes.

I am bound to confess that the difficulty is a very formidable one. It was not until I had begun to test the theories hitherto put forward regarding the development of Babylonian religion, and had tried to see what could be fairly deduced from the texts themselves, that I realised how formidable it actually was. There is only one way of meeting it. It is only by a process of careful and cautious induction, by noting every indication of date, whether linguistic or otherwise, which a text may offer, by comparing our materials one with another, and calling in the help of what we have recently learnt about Babylonian history—above all, by following the method of nature and science in working from the known to the unknown—that it is possible to arrive at any conclusions at all. If, therefore, I shall seem in the course of these Lectures to speak less positively about the early development of Babylonian theology than my predecessors in the same field have done, or than I should have done myself a few years ago, let it be borne in mind that the fault lies not in me but in the want of adequate materials. It is useless to form theories which may be overthrown at any moment, and which fail to explain all the known facts.

So far, I fear, I have done little else than lay before you a dreary catalogue of the difficulties and obstacles that meet the historian of Babylonian religion at the very outset of his inquiry. If the picture had no other side, if there were little or nothing to counterbalance the difficulties, we might as well admit that the time for investigating the theological conceptions of the ancient Babylonians and Assyrians had not yet come, and that we must be content to leave the subject where it was left by Sir H. Rawlinson nearly thirty years ago. Fortunately, however, this is not the case. Mutilated and broken as they are, we still have texts sufficient to enable us at all events to sketch the outlines of Babylonian theology—nay, from time to time to fill them in as well. The Babylonians were not content with merely editing their ritual and religious hymns or their myths about the gods and heroes; they also compiled commentaries and explanatory text-books which gave philological and other information about the older religious literature; they drew up lists of the deities and their various titles; they described the temples in which their images were placed, and the relation of the different members of the divine hierarchy one to another. They even showed an interest in the gods of other countries, and the names given by neighbouring nations to divinities which they identified with their own are at times recorded. It is true that many of the sacred texts were so written as to be intelligible only to the initiated; but the initiated were provided with keys and glosses, many of which are in our hands. In some respects, therefore, we are better off than the ordinary Babylonian himself would have been. We can penetrate into the real meaning of documents which to him were a sealed book. Nay, more than this. The researches that have been made during the last half-century into the creeds and beliefs of the nations of the world both past and present, have given us a clue to the interpretation of these documents which even the initiated priests did not possess. We can guess at the origin and primary meaning of rites and ceremonies, of beliefs and myths, which the Babylonians knew of only in their later form and under their traditional guise. To them, Gisdhubar, the hero of their great epic, was but a champion and conqueror of old time, whose deeds were performed on the soil of Babylonia, and whose history was as real as that of the sovereigns of their own day. We, on the contrary, can penetrate beneath the myths which have grown up around his name, and can discover in him the lineaments of a solar hero who was himself but the transformed descendant of a humbler god of fire.

In spite, however, of the aids that have been provided for the modern student among the relics of the great library of Nineveh, his two chief difficulties still remain: the fragmentary character of his materials and his ignorance of the true chronology of the larger portion of them.

This last is the most serious difficulty of all, since recent discoveries have so enlarged our ideas of the antiquity of Babylonian civilisation, and have so revolutionised the views into which we had comfortably settled down, that our conclusions on the development of Babylonian religion must be completely modified. At the risk, therefore, of making this first Lecture a dull and uninteresting one, and of seeming to wander from the subject upon which I have been called to speak, I must enter into some details as to the early history of the population among whom the religious system revealed to us by the cuneiform inscriptions first originated and developed.

Until very lately, Assyrian scholars had fancied that the rise and early history of Babylonia could be already traced in its main outlines. By combining the statements of classical authors with the data furnished by such early monuments as we possessed, a consistent scheme seemed to have been made out. About three thousand years before our era, it was supposed, the smaller states which occupied the fertile plain of Babylonia were united into a single monarchy, the capital of which was "Ur of the Chaldees," the modern Mugheir, on the western side of the Euphrates. The whole country was at this period under the domination of the Accadians, though the Semitic nomad and trader were already beginning to make their appearance. It was divided into two provinces, the northern called Accad, and the southern Sumer or Shinar, in which two separate, though closely allied, dialects were spoken. Now and again, however, the two provinces were independent of one another, and there were even times when the smaller states comprised in them successfully re-asserted their former freedom. About 2000 B.C., the Accadian was gradually superseded by the Semite, and before long the Accadian language itself became extinct, remaining only as the sacred and learned language of religion and law. The rise of Semitic supremacy was marked by the reigns of Sargon I. and his son Naram-Sin, who established their seat at Accad, near Sippara, where they founded an important library, and from whence they led military expeditions as far westward as the Mediterranean Sea. The overthrow of Sargon's dynasty, however, was soon brought about through the conquest of Babylonia by Khammuragas, a Kossæan from the mountains of Elam. He made Babylon for the first time the capital of the country, and founded a dynasty whose rule lasted for several centuries. Before the Kossaean conquest, the Babylonian system of religion was already complete. It emanated from the primitive Accadian population, though it was afterwards adopted and transformed by their Semitic successors. It was originally Shamanistic, like the native religions of the Siberians or Lapps. The sorcerer took the place of the priest, magical incantations the place of a ritual, and innumerable spirits the place of gods. By degrees, however, these earlier conceptions became modified; a priesthood began to establish itself; and as a necessary consequence some of the elemental spirits were raised to the rank of deities. The old magical incantations, too, gave way to hymns in honor of the new gods, among whom the Sun-god was specially prominent, and these hymns came intime to form a collection similar to that of the Hindu Rig-Veda, and were accounted equally sacred. This process of religious development was assisted by the Semitic occupation of Babylonia. The Semites brought with them new theological conceptions. With them the Sun-god, in his two-fold aspect of benefactor and destroyer, was the supreme object of worship, all other deities being resolvable into phases or attributes of the supreme Baal. At his side stood his female double and reflection, the goddess of fertility, who was found again under various names and titles at the side of every other deity. The union of these Semitic religious conceptions with the developing creed of Accad produced a state-religion, watched over and directed by a powerful priesthood, which continued more or less unaltered down to the days of Nebuchadnezzar and his successors. It was this state-religion that was carried by the Semitic Assyrians into their home on the banks of the Tigris, where it underwent one or two modifications, in all essential respects, however, remaining unchanged.

Now there is much in this neat and self-consistent account of Babylonian religion which rests on the authority of the cuneiform documents, and about which therefore there is no room for dispute. But the inferences which have been drawn from the facts presented by these cuneiform documents, as well as the general theory by which the inferences have been compacted together into a consistent whole, are, it must be remembered, inferences and theory only. Owing to the fragmentary nature of the evidence, it has been necessary to supplement the deficiencies of the record by assumptions for which there is no documentary testimony whatever. The dates which form the skeleton, as it were, of the whole theory, have been derived from Greek and Latin writers. While certain portions of the scheme have been definitely acquired by science, since they embody monumental facts, other portions are destitute of any other foundation than the combinatory powers of modern scholars. The scheme, therefore, must be regarded as a mere working hypothesis, as one of those provisional theories which science is constantly compelled to put forward in order to co-ordinate and combine the facts known at the time, but which must give way to other hypotheses as new facts are discovered which do not harmonise with the older explanations. It not unfrequently happens that a hypothesis which has served its purpose well enough by directing research into a particular channel, and which after all is *partially* correct, may be overthrown by the discovery of a single new fact. Such has been the fate of the theory as to the development of Babylonian religion which I have been describing above.

The single fact which has shaken it to its very foundations is the discovery of the date to which the reign of Sargon of Accad must be assigned. The last king of of Babylonia, Nabonidos, had antiquarian tastes, and busied himself not only with the restoration of the old temples of his country, but also with the disinterment of the memorial cylinders which their builders and restorers had buried beneath their foundations. It was known that the great temple of the Sun-god at Sippara, where the mounds of Abu-Habba now mark its remains, had been originally erected by Naram-Sin the son of Sargon, and attempts had been already made to find the records which, it was assumed, he had entombed under its angles. With true antiquarian zeal, Nabonidos continued the search, and did not desist until, like the Dean and Chapter of some modern cathedral, he had lighted upon "the foundation-stone" of Naram-Sin himself. This "foundation-stone," he tells us, had been seen by none of his predecessors for 3200 years. In the opinion, accordingly, of Nabonidos, a king who was curious about the past history of his country, and whose royal position gave him the best possible opportunities for learning all that could be known about it, Naram-Sin and his father Sargon I. lived 3200 years before his own time, or 3750 B.C.

The date is so remote and so contrary to all our preconceived ideas regarding the antiquity of the Babylonian monarchy, that I may be excused if at first I expressed doubts as to its accuracy. We are now accustomed to contemplate with equanimity the long chronology which the monuments demand for the history of Pharaonic Egypt, but we had also been accustomed to regard the history of Babylonia as beginning at the earliest in the third millennium before our era. Assyrian scholars had inherited the chronological prejudices of a former generation, and a starveling chronology seemed to be confirmed by the statements of Greek writers.

I was, however, soon forced to re-consider the reasons of my scepticism. The cylinder on which Nabonidos recounts his discover of the foundation=stone of Naram-Sin was brought from the excavations of Mr. Hormuzd Rassam in Babylonia, and explained by Mr. Pinches six years ago. Soon afterwards, Mr. Pinches was fortunate enough to find among some other inscriptions from Babylonia fragments of three different lists, in one of which the kings of Babylonia were arranged in dynasties, and the number of years each king reigned was stated, as well as the number of years the several dynasties lasted. An Assyrian copy of a similar list had been already discovered by Mr. George Smith, who, with his usual quickness of perception, saw that is must have resembled the lists from which Bêrôssos, the Greek historian of Chaldaea, drew the materials of his chronology; but the copy was so mere a fragment that the chronological position of the kings mentioned upon it was a matter of dispute. Happily this is not the case with the principal text published by Mr. Pinches. It had been compiled by a native of Babylon, who consequently began with the first dynasty which made Babylon the capital of the kingdom, and who seems to have flourished in the time of Nabonidos. We can check the accuracy of his statements in a somewhat curious way. One of the other two texts brought

INTRODUCTORY. 23

to light by Mr. Pinches is a schoolboy's exercise copy of the first two dynasties mentioned on the annalistic tablet. There are certain variations between the two texts, however, which show that the schoolboy or his master must have used some other list of the early kings than that which was employed by the compiler of the tablet; nevertheless, the names and the regnal years, with one exception, agree exactly in each. In Assyria, an accurate chronology was kept by means of certain officers, the so-called Eponyms, who were changed every year and gave their names to the year over which they presided. We have at present no positive proof that the years were dated in the same way in Babylonia; but since most Assyrian institutions were of Babylonian origin, it is probable that they were. At all events, the scribes of a later day believed that they had trustworthy chronological evidence extending back into a dim antiquity; and when we remember the imperishable character of the clay literature of the country, and the fact that the British Museum actually contains deeds and other legal documents dated in the reign of Khammuragas, more than four thousand years ago, there is no reason why we should not consider the belief to have been justified.

Now the annalistic tablet takes us back reign by reign, dynasty by dynasty, to about the year 2400 B.C. Among the monarchs mentioned upon it is Khammuragas, whose reign is placed 112 years later (B.C. 2290).[1] Of Sargon

---

[1] As the reign of Khammuragas lasted 55 years, its end would have been about B.C. 2235. This curiously agrees with the date arrived at (first by von Gutschmidt) for the beginning of the Babylonian era. If the Latin translation can be trusted (Simplicius, *ad Arist. de Cœlo*, 503 A), the astronomical observations sent by Kallisthenes from Babylon to Aristotle in B.C. 331 reached back for 1903 years (i.e. to B.C. 2234).

and his son Naram-Sin, however, there is no trace. But this is not all. On the shelves of the British Museum you may see huge sun-dried bricks, on which are stamped the names and titles of kings who erected or repaired the temples where they have been found. In the dynasties of the annalistic tablet their names are as much absent as is the name of Sargon. They must have belonged to an earlier period than that with which the list of the tablet begins, and have reigned before the time when, according to the margins of our Bibles, the flood of Noah was covering the earth, and reducing such bricks as these to their primæval slime. But the kings who have recorded their constructive operations on the bricks are seldom connected with one another. They are rather the isolated links of a broken chain, and thus presuppose a long period of time during which their reigns must have fallen. This conclusion is verified by another document, also coming from Babylonia and also first published by Mr. Pinches. This document contains a very long catalogue of royal names, not chronologically arranged, as is expressly stated, but drawn up for a philological purpose—that of explaining in Assyrian the Accadian and Kossæan names of the non-Semitic rulers of Babylonia. Though the document is imperfect,

---

Bêrôssos, according to Pliny (N. H. vii. 57), stated that these observations began at Babylon 490 years before the Greek era of Phorôneus (B.C. 1753), i.e. B.C. 2243, though Epigenes made it 720 years (B.C. 2473). Babylon, according to Stephanos of Byzantium (s. v.), was built 1002 years before the date (given by Hellanikos) for the siege of Troy (B.C. 1229), which would bring us to B.C. 2231, while Ktêsias (ap. Georg. Synk.) made the reign of Bêlos, or Bel-Merodach of Babylon, last for 55 years from B.C. 2286 to 2231. The correspondence of the reign of the Bêlos of Ktêsias with the reign of Khammuragas is at least curious.

it embodies about sixty names which do not occur on the annalistic tablet, and must therefore be referred to an earlier epoch than that with which the latter begins.

But these names, like the majority of those stamped on the bricks from the ancient temples, are not of Semitic but of Accadian origin. If, then, the Accadian domination preceded the rule of the Semitic Babylonians, the long array of sovereigns to whom they belonged must have reigned before the age of the Semitic rulers of Accad, Sargon and Naram-Sin. This, however, is a conclusion from which the historian will needs recoil. The long space of 1300 years which intervened between the time of Sargon and that of the dynasty of Khammuragas cannot have been wholly filled with Semitic princes who have left no monument behind them. We seem compelled to acknowledge that the Semitic rule in Babylonia was not achieved once for all. The struggle between the older and younger population of the country was not determined by a single battle or a single reign. The dynasty which followed that of Khammuragas bears for the most part Accadian names, and may therefore be regarded as marking an Accadian revival. Before the age of Khammuragas the same event may have often happened. Now it was a dynasty sprung from a Semitic settlement that acquired the supremacy in Babylonia; at other times the ruler of a city which still held out against the Semite succeeded in establishing his power over the whole country. In the dynastic tablet the immediate predecessor of Khammuragas is a Semite bearing the Semitic name of Sin-muballidh, and yet we learn from the inscriptions of Khammuragas himself that he had made himself master of Chaldæa by the overthrow of the Accadian prince Rim-Agu. Moreover, whatever might have been the original character of the Semitic occupation of Babylonia, from the time of Sargon I. downwards it was of a more or less peaceable nature; Accadians and Semites mingled together, and from the mixture sprang the peculiar civilisation of Babylonia, and the peculiar type of its people.

Sargon himself was a monarch whom both Accadian and Semite delighted to honour. Myths surrounded his infancy as they surrounded the infancy of Kyros, and popular legend saw in him the hero-prince who had been deserted in childhood and brought up among squalid surroundings, until the time came that he should declare himself in his true character and receive his rightful inheritance.[1] He was born, it was said, of an unknown

---

[1] Sargon may be the Thilgamos of Ælian, transmitted in a Persian dress, and the legend about him is evidently that connected by Agathias (ii. 25, 15) with Bêletarês (? Tiglath-Pileser), who is stated to have been the gardener of the former king, Bêlokhos or Beleous, and the founder of a new dynasty. In the Epic of Gisdhubar the name of the gardener wooed by Istar is given as Isullanu the gardener of Anu. The text giving the legend of Sargon, as published in W. A. I. iii. 4, 7, is as follows:

1. "Sargon, the mighty king, the king of Accad (am) I.
2. My mother (was) a princess; my father I knew not; the brother of my father dwells in the mountain.
3. (In) the city of Azupiranu, which is built on the bank of the Euphrates,
4. (my) mother, the princess, conceived me; in a secret place she brought me forth;
5. she placed me in a basket of reeds; with bitumen my exit (gate) she closed;
6. she gave me to the river, which drowned me not.
7. The river carried me along; to Akki the irrigator it brought me;
8. Akki the irrigator in the goodness of (his) heart lifted me up;
9. Akki the irrigator reared me as (his own) son;

father; as Mars had wooed the mother of the founder of Rome, so some god whom later tradition feared to name had wooed the mother of the founder of the first Semitic empire. She brought forth her first-born "in a secret place" by the side of the Euphrates, and placed him in a basket of rushes which she daubed with bitumen and entrusted to the waters of the river. The story reminds us of Perseus launched upon the sea with his mother Danaë in a boat, of Romulus and Remus exposed to the fury of the Tiber, and still more of Moses in his ark of bulrushes upon the Nile. The Euphrates refused to drown its future lord, and bore the child in safety to Akki "the irrigator," the representative of the Accadian peasants who tilled the land for their Semitic masters. In this lowly condition and among a subjugated race

---

10. Akki the irrigator made me his gardener,
11. (and in) my gardenership did Istar love me.
12. For 45 (?) years I ruled the kingdom.
13. The men of the black-headed race I governed, I (organised).
14. Over rugged mountains in chariots of bronze I rode.
15. I (governed) the upper mountains;
16. I (ruled) the rulers of the lower mountains.
17. To the sea-coast (?) three times did I advance; Dilmun sub-(mitted);
18. The fortress of the goddess of Hades (Dur-AN-Kigal) bowed....
19. I destroyed ....
20. When the king who comes after me in future (days)
21. (shall govern) the men of the black-headed race;
22. (shall ride) over the rugged mountains in chariots (of bronze),
23. shall govern the upper mountains (and rule) the kings
24. of the lower mountains; (to) the sea-coast (?)
25. shall advance three times; (shall cause Dilmun to submit);
26. (when) the fortress of the goddess of Hades shall bow; from my city of Accad. ....."

Ti-ti-sal-lat (?) seems to mean "the sea-coast" of the Mediterranean; cp. *Tit-num*, the Accadian name of Phœnicia, as well as Dhi-dhi, another Accadian name of the same country (W. A. I. ii. 51, 19).

Sargon was brought up. Akki took compassion on the little waif, and reared him as if he had been his own son. As he grew older he was set to till the garden and cultivate the fruit-trees, and while engaged in this humble work attracted the love of the goddess Istar. Then came the hour of his deliverance from servile employment, and, like David, he made his way to a throne. For long years he ruled the black-headed race of Accad; he rode through subjugated countries in chariots of bronze, and crossed the Persian Gulf to the sacred isle of Dilmun. The very name the people gave him was a proof of his predestined rise to greatness. Sargon was not his real title. This was Sarganu, which a slight change of pronunciation altered into Sargina, a word that conveyed the meaning of "constituted" or "predestined" "king" to his Accadian subjects. It was the form assumed in their mouths by the Semitic *Sarru-kinu*, and thus reminded them of the Sun-god Tammuz, the youthful bridegroom of Istar, who was addressed as *ablu kinu* or "only son," as well as of Nebo "the very son" (*ablu kinu*) of the god Merodach.[1] Sargina, however, was not the only name by which the king was known to them. They called him also *Dádil* or *Dádal*, a title which the Semitic scribes afterwards explained to mean "Sargon, the king of constituted right (*sar-kinti*), deviser of constituted law, deviser of prosperity," though its true signification was rather "the very wise."[2]

---

[1] Upon the inscription of "Sar-ga-ni, the king of the city, the king of Accad," see Pinches, *Proc. Soc. Bib. Arch.* June 1886, p. 244. Sarganu has the same origin as the Biblical Serug.

[2] W. A. I. ii. 48, 40 and 32, where (with the earlier Sumerian pronunciation *tal-tal* or *tatal*) it is a title of Ea as the god of "wisdom.'

But in spite of the atmosphere of myth which came to enshroud him, as it enshrouded the persons of Kyros, of Charlemagne, and of other heroes of popular history, Sargon was a historical monarch and the founder of a really great empire. The British Museum actually possesses an inscribed egg of veined marble which he dedicated to the Sun-god of Sippara, and the seal of his librarian Ibni-sarru is in the hands of M. Le Clercq of Paris. What may be termed the scientific literature of the library of Nineveh makes frequent reference to him, and we learn that it was for the great library which he established in his capital city of Accad that the two standard Babylonian works on astronomy and terrestrial omens were originally compiled. The work on astronomy was entitled "The Observations of Bel,"[1] and consisted of no less than seventy-two books, dealing with such matters as the conjunction of the sun and moon, the phases of Venus, and the appearances of comets. It was translated in later days into Greek by the historian Bêrôssos; and though supplemented by numerous additions in its passage through the hands of generations of Babylonian astronomers, the original

---

When applied to Sargon, the title was ideographically expressed by repeating the character for "king," in order to denote that he was "the king indeed." One of the earliest of the monarchs whose names are found at Tel-loh is called Taltal-kur-galla, "the wise one of the great mountain."

[2] Or perhaps "The Illumination of Bel (Mul-lil)," Namar-Bili. See my paper on "The Astronomy and Astrology of the Babylonians," in the *Tr. Soc. Bib. Arch.* iii. 1 (1874). Later copyists mistook the title for a proper name, and accordingly referred the compilation of the work to a certain Namar-Bili. Up to the time of Bêrôssos, however, it was remembered that the god Bel himself was its traditional author, and the work is sometimes quoted as simply "Bel" (e.g. W. A. I. iii. 52, 27).

work contained so many records of eclipses as to demonstrate the antiquity of Babylonian astronomy even in the remote age of Sargon himself. But besides our knowledge of Sargon's patronage of learning, we also know something about the civil history of his reign. A copy of its annals has come down to us. We gather from these that he was not only successful in overthrowing all opposition at home, he was also equally successful abroad. His first campaign was against the powerful kingdom of Elam in the East, where he overthrew the enemy and mutilated their slain. Next he turned to the West, laying his yoke on Syria, and subjugating "the four quarters" of the world. Then the rival kings of Babylon and other Chaldæan cities felt his power; and out of the spoil of the vanquished he built the city of Accad and gave it its name. From this time forward his attention was chiefly devoted to the West. Year after year he penetrated into Syria, until at last, we are told, "he had neither equal nor rival;" he crossed the Mediterranean to the island we now call Cyprus, and "in the third year," at the bounds of the setting sun, his hands conquered all peoples and his mouth decreed a single empire. Here on the shores of Cyprus the great conqueror erected images of himself, and then carried the booty of the island to the opposite coast of Asia. Such a glimpse into the history of what became afterwards a Grecian sea, when as yet no Greeks had made their way to their later home, is startling to those whose conceptions of authentic history have been limited by the narrow horizon of the classical world. Its trustworthiness, however, has been curiously verified by a discovery made by General de Cesnola in the treasure-vaults of a Kyprian temple among the ruins of the ancient Kurion. Here, among other hæmatite cylinders of early Babylonian origin, he found one the first owner of which describes himself as a "servant" or "worshipper" of "the deified Naram-Sin."[1] Naram-Sin was the son and successor of Sargon, and it is not likely that he would have received divine honours after the fall of the dynasty to which he belonged. The fact that the cylinder was discovered in Cyprus seems to show that even after Sargon's death a connection continued to exist between Cyprus and the imperial power of Babylonia. Naram-Sin, however, was more bent on the conquest of Magána, or the Sinaitic Peninsula, than upon further campaigns in the West. Sinai, with its mines of turquoise and copper, had been a prize coveted by the Egyptians ever since the age of the Third Dynasty, and one of the first efforts of the rising rival power on the banks of the Euphrates was to gain possession of the same country. Naram-Sin, so runs the annalistic tablet, "marched to the land of Magána; the land of Magána he conquered, and overcame its king."

The land of Magána was already known to the inhabitants of Babylonia.[2] The earliest Chaldæan monuments

---

[1] See my paper in the *Trans. Soc. Bib. Arch.* v. 2 (1877).

[2] Oppert, Lenormant and myself have long since shown that Magan originally denoted the Sinaitic peninsula, and Delattre has recently made it clear (*L'Asie occidentale*) that Melukhkha, which is constantly associated with Magan, was the desert district immediately to the south of the Wâdiel-'Arish. Assur-bani-pal transfers the name of Magan to the neighbouring land of lower Egypt, while Melukhkha is used for Ethiopia or Meroë by Sargon and his successors. The name of Magan, however, was probably used from the first in an extended sense, since a list of reeds (W. A. I. v. 32. 64, 65) describes the *sippatu*, or "papyrus," Heb. *sûph*, as "the reed of Magan" (Makkan in Assyrian). The early date to which a knowledge of the plant went back is evidenced

yet discovered are those which have been excavated at Tel-loh in southern Chaldæa by a Frenchman, M. de Sarzec, and are now deposited in the Louvre. Some of them go back almost to the very beginnings of Chaldæan art and cuneiform writing. Indeed, the writing is hardly yet cuneiform; the primitive pictorial forms of many of the characters are but thinly disguised, and the vertical direction they originally followed, like Chinese, is still preserved. The language and art alike are Proto-Chaldæan : there is as yet no sign that the Semite was in the land. Among the monuments are seated figures carved out of stone. The stone in several instances is diorite, a stone so hard that even the modern workman may well despair of chiselling it into the lineaments of the human form. Now an inscription traced upon one of the figures tells us that the stone was brought from the land of Magan. Already, therefore, before the time of Sargon and the rise of Semitic supremacy and civilisation, the peninsula of Sinai was not only known to the

---

by its having an Accadian name, *gizi*, "the flowering reed" (borrowed by Semitic Babylonian under the form of *kisu*). That Magan or Magána was a mountainous country appears from a bilingual hymn to Adar, which mentions "the mountain of Magána" (W. A. I. iv. 13, 16); and in W. A. I. ii. 51, 17, while Melukhkha is described as "the country of turquoise," Magan is described as "the country of bronze." It is possible that the name of Magan or Magána is derived from *mafka*, which signifies in old Egyptian "the turquoise" of the Sinaitic mines. In an early Babylonian geographical list (W. A. I. iv. 38. 13, 14), Magan and Melukhkha are associated with the Babylonian seaport of Eridu, which throws light on "the ships" of Magan and Melukhkha mentioned in W. A. I. ii. 46. 6, 7, immediately after "the ships of Dilmun." The trading ships of Eridu would have touched first at Dilmun, then at Magan, and finally at Melukhkha. For a Babylonian country or mountain (!) of Magan, such as some scholars have dreamed of, there is not a particle of evidence.

inhabitants of Chaldæa, but blocks of stone were transported from it to the stoneless plain of Babylonia, and there made plastic under the hand of the sculptor. I have already alluded to the fact that the quarries of Sinai had been known to the Egyptians and worked by them as early as the epoch of the Third Dynasty, some 6000 years ago. Is it more than a coincidence that one of the most marvellous statues in the world, and the chief ornament of the Museum of Bulâq, is a seated figure of king Khephrên of the Fourth Dynasty, carved out of green diorite, like the statues of Tel-loh, and representing the monarch in almost the same attitude? The Babylonian work is ruder than the Egyptian work, it is true; but if we place them side by side, it is hard to resist the conviction that both belong to the same school of sculpture, and that the one is but a less skilful imitation of the other. The conviction grows upon us when we find that diorite is as foreign to the soil of Egypt as it is to that of Babylonia, and that the standard of measurement marked upon the plan of the city, which one of the figures of Tel-loh holds upon his lap, is the same as the standard of measurement of the Egyptian pyramid-builders—the kings of the fourth and two following dynasties.[1]

Egyptian research has independently arrived at the conclusion that the pyramid-builders were at least as old as the fourth millennium before the Christian era. The great pyramids of Gizeh were in course of erection, the hieroglyphic system of writing was already fully deve-

---

[1] The cubit of 20·63, quite different from the later Assyro-Babylonian cubit of 21·6. See Flinders Petrie in *Nature*, Aug. 9, 1883, p. 341.

loped, Egypt itself was thoroughly organised and in the enjoyment of a high culture and civilisation, at a time when, according to Archbishop Usher's chronology, the world was being created. The discoveries at Tel-loh have revealed to us a corresponding period in the history of Babylonia, earlier considerably than the age of Sargon of Accad, in which we seem to find traces of contact between Babylonia and the Egyptians of the Old Empire. It would even seem as if the conquests of Naram-Sin in Sinai were due to the fall of the Sixth Dynasty and the overthrow of the power of the old Egyptian empire. For some centuries after that event Egypt is lost to history, and its garrisons and miners in the Sinaitic peninsula must have been recalled to serve against enemies nearer home.

If there is any truth in the arguments I have been using, we may now, I think, accept with confidence the date assigned to Sargon of Accad by Nabonidos, strange as it may appear to read of expeditions undertaken by Babylonian kings against Cyprus and Sinai at so remote an epoch. Important results will follow from such a conclusion for the history of Babylonian religion. We shall have time enough for the slow absorption of Accadian religious ideas into the uncultured Semitic mind, for the gradual transformation they underwent, and for the development of those later forms of belief and practice to which the main bulk of our materials relate. We can now trace in some measure the modes in which Accadian and Semite acted and re-acted upon one another, as well as the chief periods at which the influence of the one or of the other was at its height.

The monuments of Tel-loh carry us back to a pre-

Semitic era. The deities they commemorate are Proto-Chaldæan, and we may gather from them some idea of Proto-Chaldæan religion in the heyday of its power. Babylonia was still divided into a number of petty states, which were, however, at times united for a while under a single head, and each state had its own peculiar cult. Gradually the encroaching Semite dispossessed the older dynasties and came to form an upper class, first of soldiers and traders, and then of priests also, throughout the land. It was in northern Babylonia probably that he made his influence first felt. Here, at any rate, the kingdom was founded which culminated in the brilliant reigns of Sargon of Accad and his son Naram-Sin. Before this, the old culture of the non-Semitic population had been fully absorbed by the Semitic intruders. The intercourse between the two races was already for the most part a peaceful one. The great mass of the older people were contented to till the ground, to irrigate the fields, and to become the serfs of their Semitic lords. But inter-marriages must have often taken place; members of the same family bear sometimes Accadian, sometimes Semitic names, and the same king, whether Accadian or Semite, issues his edicts in both languages. The cuneiform system of writing was handed on to the Semites while still in an incomplete state. New values and meanings were given to the signs, new characters and combinations of characters were devised, and in writing Semitic words the old ideographic usage of the Accadian script continued to be imitated. The process was aided by the patronage afforded to literature in the court of Sargon. Here Semitic and Accadian scribes vied with one another in compiling new texts and in making the old ones accessible to Semitic learners. An artificial literary dialect sprang up, the basis of which was Semitic, but into which Accadian words and phrases were thrown pêle-mêle. By way of revenge, the Accadian texts which emanated from the *literati* of the court were filled with Semitic words and expressions. Sometimes they were the work of Semites writing in a foreign language, sometimes of Accadians who were living in an atmosphere of Semitic life and thought.

What happened in the case of the language must have happened also in the case of religion. We know that many of the gods of the later Babylonian faith have Accadian names, and that the ideas connected with them betray a non-Semitic origin; we may therefore expect to find Accadian religious conceptions accommodated to those of the Semite, and Semitic conceptions so closely intertwined with Accadian beliefs as to make it impossible for us now to separate them. How far this is the case I hope to point out in a future Lecture.

The fall of the dynasty of Sargon may have brought with it a temporary revival of Accadian supremacy. At any rate, the Semitic element always remained strongest in northern Babylonia: in southern Babylonia it seems to me not impossible that one of the numerous dialects of the old language may have lingered down to the time of Nebuchadnezzar or Nabonidos. But even in northern Babylonia the Semitic element was not pure. It mainly represented the dominant class, and not the people as well, as was the case in Assyria. The result is that the Babylonian presents us with a moral and intellectual type which is not genuinely Semitic. To convince ourselves of this fact, it is only necessary to compare the

Babylonian with his neighbour the Assyrian. The Assyrian has all the characteristics of the Semite. His hooked nose and angular features proclaim his origin on the physical side as unmistakably as his intensity, his ferocity, his love of trade and his nomadic habits proclaim it on the moral side. The Babylonian, on the other hand, was square-built and somewhat full-faced, an agriculturist rather than a soldier, a scholar rather than a trader. The intensity of religious belief which marked the Assyrian was replaced in him by superstition, and the barbarities which the Assyrian perpetrated in the name of Assur and loved to record in his inscriptions were foreign to his nature. If the Assyrian was the Roman of the ancient East, the Babylonians were the Chinese.

Nevertheless, the contrast of type displayed by the two nations must have been the growth of centuries, and due to that absorption of one race by another of which Ireland furnishes so familiar an example. The Semites of Babylonia—the Babylonians, as I will henceforth call them—and the Assyrians must once have been the same people. Assyrian and Babylonian differ only as two English dialects differ, and are therefore known by the common name of Assyrian; and it was from Babylonia that the Assyrians derived their system of writing, the greater part of their literature, their religion and their laws. It is true that some of this may have been borrowed in later times when the two kingdoms existed side by side, or when Babylonia became the appanage of its ruder but more warlike neighbour; the main bulk, however, like the language, must have been the heritage which the ancestors of Sennacherib and Sardanapallos carried with them into their northern home. The religions of Babylonia and Assyria must be treated together; we shall find, indeed, that in certain particulars they disagree; but these particulars form no portion of their essential character; they are merely unessentials which can be put aside without injury to our view of the main facts.

But, it will be asked, what interest can the religions of Babylonia and Assyria have for us, much more an inquiry into their nature and origin? They have long since perished, like the people who professed them, and have left no apparent traces of their influence upon the nations about whom we know and care most. The Greeks and Romans concerned themselves so little with these Eastern barbarians as neither to read nor to preserve the only Greek history of Chaldæa which was written by a native and professed to be derived from native accounts; we owe the fragments we have of it to the apologetic zeal of Christian controversialists. Still less would it appear that these old people of Babylonia and Assyria can have had any influence upon the world of to-day, or have served to mould the ideas and the society of modern Europe. Such questions may be asked, and until lately it would have been hard to answer them.

And yet a moment's consideration might have shown that there was one nation at all events which has exercised, and still exercises, a considerable influence upon our own thought and life, and which had been brought into close contact with the religion and culture of Babylonia at a critical epoch in its history. The influence of Jewish religion upon Christianity, and consequently upon the races that have been moulded by Christianity, has been lasting and profound. Now Jewish religion was intimately bound up with Jewish history, more intimately perhaps than has been the case with any other great religion of the world. It took its colouring from the events that marked the political life of the Hebrew people; it developed in unison with their struggles and successes, their trials and disappointments. Its great devotional utterance, the Book of Psalms, is national, not individual; the individual in it has merged his own aspirations and sufferings into those of the whole community. The course of Jewish prophecy is equally stamped with the impress of the national fortunes. It grows clearer and more catholic as the intercourse of the Jewish people with those around them becomes wider; and the lesson is taught at last that the God of the Jews is the God also of the whole world. Now the chosen instruments for enforcing this lesson, as we are expressly told, were the Assyrian and the Babylonian. The Assyrian was the rod of God's anger,[1] while the Babylonish exile was the bitter punishment meted out to Judah for its sins. The captives who returned again to their own land came back with changed hearts and purified minds; from henceforward Jerusalem was to be the unrivalled dwelling-place of "the righteous nation which keepeth the truth."

Apart, therefore, from any influence which the old religious beliefs of Babylonia may have had upon the Greeks, and which, as we shall see, was not so wholly wanting as was formerly imagined, their contact with the religious conceptions of the Jewish exiles must, to

---

[1] Is. x. 5.

say the least, have produced an effect which it is well worth our while to study. Hitherto, the traditional view has been that this effect exhibited itself wholly on the antagonistic side; the Jews carried nothing away from the land of their captivity except an intense hatred of idolatry, more especially Babylonian, as well as of the beliefs and practices associated therewith. Now and then, it is true, some bold spirit, like Bishop Warburton, may have ventured to propound the paradox that the doctrine of the resurrection was first learnt by the Jews in Babylonia, but it was treated generally as a paradox, and of late years, if admitted at all, was considered a proof of the influence not of the Babylonians but of their Persian conquerors.

The traditional view had no facts to build upon except such conclusions as it could draw from the Old Testament itself. To-day all this is changed. We know something now about the deities whom the Babylonians worshipped, about the rites and ceremonies they practised, and about the religious ideas they entertained. The result of this knowledge is to show us that the Jews did not live in the midst of the Babylonians for seventy years without borrowing from them something more than the names of the months. Nay more; it shows us that the language of the Babylonian conquerors was not the so-called Chaldee, which is really an Aramaic dialect, but a language more closely resembling that of the exiles themselves. It is true that a Jew could not have understood a Babylonian, any more than a Welshman can understand a Breton, but it was very easy for him to learn to understand. Assyrian, that is to say the language of Babylonia, is on the whole more nearly related to Hebrew than it is to any other member of the Semitic family of speech.

But it was not only through the Babylonian exile that the religious ideas of the Babylonian and the Jew came into contact with each other. It was then, indeed, that the ideas of the conquering race—the actual masters of the captives, who had long been accustomed to regard Babylonia as the home of a venerable learning and culture—were likely to make their deepest and most enduring impression; it was then, too, that the Jew for the first time found the libraries and ancient literature of Chaldæa open to his study and use. But old tradition had already pointed to the valley of the Euphrates as the primæval cradle of his race. We all remember how Abraham, it is said, was born in Ur of the Chaldees, and how the earlier chapters of Genesis make the Euphrates and Tigris two of the rivers of Paradise, and describe the building of the Tower of Babylon as the cause of the dispersion of mankind. Now the Hebrew language was the language not only of the Israelites, but also of those earlier inhabitants of the country whom the Jews called Canaanites and the Greeks Phœnicians. Like the Israelites, the Phœnicians held that their ancestors had come from the Persian Gulf and the alluvial plain of Babylonia. The tradition is confirmed by the researches of comparative philology. Many of the words which the Semites have in common seem to point to the neighbourhood of Babylonia as the district from which those who used them originally came, and where they called the fauna and flora of the country by common names. Their first home appears to have been in the low-lying desert which stretches eastward of Chaldæa—

on the very side of the Euphrates, in fact, on which stood the great city of Ur, the modern Mugheir. Here they led a nomad life, overawed by the higher culture of the settled Accadian race, until a time came when they began to absorb it themselves, and eventually, as we have seen, to dispossess and supersede their teachers.

The tribes which travelled northward and westward must, we should think, have carried with them some of the elements of the culture they had learnt from their Accadian neighbours. And such, indeed, we find to be the case. The names of Babylonian deities meet us again in Palestine and the adjoining Semitic lands. Nebo, the Babylonian god of prophecy and literature, has given his name to towns that stood within the territories of Reuben and Judah, as well as to the Moabite mountain on which Moses breathed his last; Anu, the Babylonian god of heaven, and his female consort Anatu, re-appear in Beth-Anath, "the temple of Anatu," and Anathoth, the birth-place of Jeremiah; and Sinai itself is but the mountain of Sin, the Babylonian Moon-god.[1]

We may thus assume that there were two periods in the history of the Jewish people in which they came under the influence of the religious conceptions of Babylonia. There was the later period of the Babylonish

---

[1] That this is the true derivation of the name of Sinai and of the desert of Sin is plain now that we know that the district in question was possessed by Aramaic-speaking tribes whose kinsfolk spread eastward to the banks of the Euphrates, and who were allied in blood to the population of Moab and Canaan, where the names of Babylonian deities were not unfrequent. The name of Sin, the Moon-god, is met with in an Himyaritic inscription, and a god who thus found his way to southern Arabia would be equally likely to find his way to northern Arabia.

exile, when the influence was strong and direct; there was also the earlier period, when the amount of influence is more hard to determine. Much will depend upon the view we take of the age of the Pentateuch, and of the traditions or histories embodied therein. Some will be disposed to see in Abraham the conveyer of Babylonian ideas to the west; others will consider that the Israelites made their first acquaintance with the gods and legends of Babylonia through the Canaanites and other earlier inhabitants of Palestine. Those who incline to the latter belief may doubt whether the fathers of the Canaanitish tribes brought the elements of their Babylonian beliefs with them from Chaldæa, or whether these beliefs were of later importation, due to the western conquests of Sargon and his successors. Perhaps what I have to say in my subsequent Lectures will afford some data for deciding which of these conflicting opinions is the more correct.

Meanwhile, I will conclude this Lecture with a few illustrations of the extent to which the study of Babylonian religion may be expected to throw light on the earlier portions of Scripture. We have already noticed the curious parallelism which exists between the legend of Sargon's exposure in an ark of bulrushes and the similar exposure of the great Israelitish leader Moses on the waters of the Nile. The parallelism exists even further than this common account of their infancy. Sargon of Accad was emphatically the founder of Semitic supremacy in Babylonia; he was the great lawgiver of Babylonian legend; and to him was assigned the compilation of those works on astrology and augury from which the wise men of the Chaldæans subsequently derived their lore. Moses was equally the legislator of the Israelites and the successful vindicator of Semitic independence from the exactions of Egyptian tyranny, and future generations quoted the books of the Hebrew law under his name. As we have seen, Sargon was a historical personage, and popular tradition merely treated him as it has treated other heroes of the past, by attaching to him the myths and legends that had once been told of the gods.

Now the name of the great Hebrew legislator has long been a puzzle and a subject of dispute. In the Hebrew Old Testament it is connected with the Hebrew verb *masháh*, " to draw out," not, indeed, in the sense that Moses was he who had been drawn out of the water, for this would not be grammatically permissible, though Pharaoh's daughter puns upon the idea (Exod. ii. 10), but in the sense of a leader who had drawn his people out of the house of bondage and led them through the waves of the sea. The translators of the Septuagint, on the other hand, living as they did in Egypt, endeavoured to give the word an Egyptian form and an Egyptian etymology. With them the name is always Μωυσῆς, which Josephos tells us is derived from the Egyptian words *mô*, " water," and *usés*, " saved from the water."[1] But this etymology, apart from other imperfections, depends upon the change the translators of the Septuagint have themselves made in the pronunciation of the name. Modern Egyptian scholars, equally willing to find for it an Egyptian derivation, have had recourse to the Egyptian *messu* or *mes*, " a son." This word, it is true, when occurring in proper names is usually combined with the

---

[1] *Antiq.* ii. 9. 6; *Cont. Ap.* i. 31.

name of a deity; Rameses, for example, the Sesostris of the Greeks, being written in the hieroglyphics Ra-messu, "born of the Sun-god." But it is conceivable that we might occasionally meet with it alone, and it is also conceivable, though not very probable, that the daughter of the Egyptian king would assign to her adopted child the simple name of "son." It is much less conceivable that such an Egyptian name would be that by which a national hero would be afterwards known to his Semitic countrymen. It is difficult to believe that the founder of the Israelitish people would have borne a title which the Israelites did not understand, and which could remind them only of that hated Egyptian land wherein they had been slaves.

Josephos has preserved an extract from the Egyptian historian Manetho, which relates the Egyptian version of the story of the Exodus as it was told in the second century before our era. In this it is stated that the earlier name of Moses was Osarsiph, and that he had been priest of Heliopolis or On. Here it is evident that Moses and Joseph have been confounded together. The name of Joseph, who married the daughter of the priest of On, has been decomposed into two elements, the first of which is the divine name Jeho, and this has been changed into its supposed Egyptian equivalent Osar or Osiris. It is clear that, whatever might have been his opinion about the name of Joseph, Manetho had no doubt that that of Moses was purely Israelitish. It was not until he had become the Israelitish lawgiver and had ceased to be an Egyptian priest that Osarsiph took the name of Moses.

But Moses finds no satisfactory etymology in the

pages of the Hebrew lexicon. It stands alone among Hebrew proper names, like Aaron and David. We do not hear of any other persons who have borne the name. If, therefore, it is Semitic, it must belong to an older stratum of Semitic nomenclature than that preserved to us in the Old Testament. We must look to other branches of the Semitic stock for its explanation.

There is only one other branch of the Semitic family whose records are earlier than those of the Hebrews. Arabic literature begins long after the Christian era, when Jewish and Greek and even Christian names and ideas had penetrated into the heart of the Arabian peninsula. The Arabic language, moreover, belongs to a different division of the Semitic family of speech from that to which Hebrew belongs. To compare Arabic and Hebrew together is like comparing Latin with modern German. There is, however, one Semitic language which has the closest affinities to Hebrew, and this is also the language of which we possess records older than those of the Hebrew Scriptures. I need hardly say that I am referring to Assyrian.

Now the Assyrian equivalent of the Hebrew *Mosheh*, "Moses," would be *mâsu*, and, as it happens, *mâsu* is a word which occurs not unfrequently in the inscriptions. It was a word of Accadian origin, but since the days of Sargon of Accad had made itself so thoroughly at home in the language of the Semitic Babylonians as to count henceforth as a genuinely Semitic term. *Mâsu* signified as nearly as possible all that we mean by the word "hero."[1] As such, it was an epithet applied to more

---

[1] *Mâsu*, "hero," has of course no connection with *mâsu*, "double," on which see Jensen, in the *Zeitschrift für Assyriologie*, i. 3, pp. 259,

than one divinity; there was one god more especially for whom it became a name. This god was the deity sometimes called Adar by Assyrian scholars, sometimes Nin-ip, but whose ordinary name among the Assyrians is still a matter of uncertainty. He was a form of the Sun-god, originally denoting the scorching sun of midday. He thus became invested with the sterner attributes of the great luminary of day, and was known to his worshippers as "the warrior of the gods." The title of *Mâsu*, however, was not confined to Adar. It was given also to another solar deity, Merodach, the tutelar god of Babylon and the antagonist of the dragon of chaos, and was shared by him with Nergal, whose special function it was to guard and defend the world of the dead. But Nergal himself was but the sun of night, the solar deity, that is to say, after he had accomplished his daily work in the bright world above and had descended to illuminate for a time the world below.

It will thus be seen that the name of *mâsu*, "the hero" or "leader," was in a peculiar sense associated with the Sun-god, the central object of primitive Semitic worship. But it seems to have had another signification which it is difficult to bring into connection with the ideas of leadership and war. The character which represented

260. In W. A. I. iii. 70, 167, *mâsu* is rendered by *asaridu*, "firstborn" or "leader" (in l. 171 by *ellu* and *ibbu*, "illustrious"). Some might perhaps see a reference to the other meaning of *mâsu* ("twin") in the close association of Moses and Aaron. There is no difficulty about the equivalence of the sibilants in the Hebrew and Assyrian words, since the Hebrew *shin* corresponds with the Assyrian *s* in proper names which, like Asshur, belong to the earlier period of Hebrew intercourse with Babylonia, and in words which are not proper names it always corresponds. The name of Aaron, I may add, seems to find its root in the Assyrian *aharu*, "to send."

the idea of *mâsu* or "hero," also represented the idea of "a collection of books."[1] With the determinative of personality prefixed, it further denotes "a scribe" or "librarian." It is at least remarkable that Moses the Hebrew legislator was also the unwearied scribe to whom Hebrew tradition referred the collection of its earliest documents and the compilation of its legal code.

But it was in the signification of "hero" that the Assyrian *mâsu* made its way into astrology, and was thus carried wherever a knowledge of Chaldæan astrological lore was spread. The Accadians had pictured the sky as the counterpart of the rich alluvial plain of Babylonia in which they dwelt. In the remote age to which their first observations of the stars reached back, the sun still entered the zodiacal constellation known to us as Taurus at the time of the vernal equinox. It is in consequence of this fact that the constellation is even yet called by us Taurus, "the bull." The sun was likened by the old Accadian star-gazers to a ploughman yoking his oxen to his glittering plough; nay, he was even likened to an ox himself; and the title given to Merodach the Sun-god when he passed through the twelve zodiacal signs was Gudi-bir, "the bull of light." Hence it was that the ecliptic was termed "the yoke of heaven," bound as it were upon the neck of the solar bull; that the first of the zodiacal signs, the opener of the primitive Accadian year, was called "the directing bull," "the bull who guides" the year; and that two prominent stars received the names of "Bull of Anu" and "Bull of Rimmon." But as in the Babylonian

---

[1] See W. A. I. ii. 48. 25, 26, where *mas* is explained by *kissu sa musarê*.

plain below, so too in the plain of heaven above, there were sheep as well as oxen. The seven planets were "the seven bell-wethers," and by their side was another group of seven stars, entitled "the *lu-mâsi*" or "sheep of the hero."[1] The first of these was "the star of the wain;" and among them were reckoned the star of "the eagle," the symbol of the meridian sun, the star of the goddess Bahu, "the pure wild heifer" of the gods, and the star "of the shepherd of the heavenly herds," the hero "who fights with weapons." The last-mentioned star is Regulus, and in his Greek name of Boôtês, "the herdsman," we may see a lingering echo of the Accadian story which made its way through the hands of the Phœnicians to Greece. Boôtês, however, was not originally the "hero," one of whose flock he was himself held to be. *Mâsu*, the "hero" of the astronomers, could only have been the sun.

It is not more strange that a name thus intimately associated with the religious and astrological beliefs of Babylonia should have found its way to the west, than that names like Nebo and Sin, which are similarly religious and astrological, should have done so too. Moses, it will be remembered, died on the summit of Mount Nebo in sight of the "moon-city" Jericho. Now Nebo,

---

[1] Jensen has shown that *mâsi* in this combination was further used in the sense of "twins," the stars composing the "lu-mâsi" being grouped as twins. It is an example of the obliteration of the original signification of an epithet by a secondary one. "The sheep of the hero," the Accadian *lu-mas*, became the Semitic *lu-mâsi*, "the twin oxen," *lu* being an Assyrian word for "ox." The "seven *lu-bad*," or "old sheep," shows, however, what the primitive meaning of *lu* must have been.

as we shall see, was the prophet-god of Babylon and Borsippa, the offspring of the Sun-god Merodach, and the patron of writing and literature. He also figured among the stars. Together with the stars of Istar and Nergal, he was accounted one of the seven "heroes" or *mâsu*. As Nebo was the interpreter of Merodach, so in the language of astrology his star was itself a *mâsu* or solar hero. Sin was the Babylonian name of the Moon-god. We learn from a Himyaritic inscription that his name had been carried into southern Arabia, and there is therefore no reason why it should not have been imported into northern Arabia as well. And we seem to meet with it in the name of the wilderness of Sin, to which Moses conducted the children of Israel when they had first left Egypt, before they arrived at Mount Sinai. Sinai itself can scarcely signify anything else than the mountain sacred to the Moon-god; and we can therefore well believe that a shrine of Sin may have existed upon it, and pilgrims have made their way to the sanctuary long before the Israelites demanded their "three days' journey into the wilderness to sacrifice to the Lord" (Exod. viii. 27).

It is possible that the name of Joseph, like that of Moses, may receive its explanation from Babylonia. Already at the time when the book of Genesis was written, its original meaning seems to have been forgotten. An alternative etymology is there proposed (xxx. 23, 24), from *âsâph*, "to take away," and *yâsâph*, "to add;" while in the Psalms (lxxxi. 6) another derivation is suggested, which would connect it (as was afterwards done by Manetho) with the sacred name of the

God of Israel.[1] Now Joseph was not only the father of the Israelitish tribes of Ephraim and Manasseh, he was also a deity worshipped by the older inhabitants of Canaan. More than two centuries before the date assigned by Egyptologists to the Exodus, the great Egyptian conqueror Thothmes III. inscribed upon the walls of the temple of Karnak the names of the cities captured by him in Palestine. Among them are Yaqab-el, "Jacob the God," and Iseph-el, "Joseph the God." We are therefore tempted to think that the expression "the house of Joseph" may have belonged to an earlier period than that in which it was applied to the tribes of Ephraim and Manasseh; that, in fact, like Beth-el, "the house of God," it was once used by the Canaanites in a literal sense. Now Beth-el, we are told, the older name of which was Luz, was taken by the house of Joseph, and became in later times one of the two great sanctuaries of the northern kingdom. What if Beth-el had itself been the more ancient "house of Joseph;" what if "the house of the god" and "the house of Joseph" had in Canaanitish days been one and the same? The question may receive an answer if we turn for it to the Assyrian inscriptions. Here we find *asipu* or *asip* used in the sense of "a diviner." The word was actually borrowed by the Aramaic of Daniel under the form of *ashsháph*;[2]

---

[1] Manetho (ap. Joseph. *cont. Ap.* i. 28) states that the original name of Moses was Osarsiph, and that he had been a priest of Heliopolis or On. Osar-siph is simply Joseph, Osar or Osiris bein substituted for Jeho (Jo) or Jahveh. Joseph, it will be remembered, married the daughter of the priest of On.

[2] We should have expected a *samech* instead of a *shin;* the word, however, must have been borrowed, since we do not meet with it elsewhere in the Old Testament. By the side of *asipu* we find *isippu*, the

in old Hebrew and Phœnician, its form would have more nearly approached that of *Joseph*. The *asipu* or "diviner" plays a considerable part in the religious literature of Babylonia, and the very phrase *bit assaputi*, "the house of the oracle," is actually met with. A god who seems to be Bel in his character of delivering oracles through the voice of the thunder is called "the hero who prophesies" or "divines uprightly." Although, therefore, it is a point which cannot be proved at present, it appears nevertheless probable that the name of Joseph was originally identical with the Babylonian *asipu*, "the god of the oracle;" and that long before the Israelitish house of Joseph took possession of Luz, it had been a house of Joseph in another sense and the sanctuary of a Canaanitish oracle.[1]

But whether or not we are to look to Babylonia for an explanation of the name of Joseph, there is little doubt that the Babylonian pantheon throws light on the names of the three first kings of Israel. Some years ago I endeavoured to show in the pages of the *Modern Review* (January, 1884), that the names by which they are known to history, Saul and David and Solomon, were not the names they received in childhood, but names subsequently applied to them and current among the people. As regards the name of Solomon, we are actually told that this was the case; his original name— the name given by the Lord through Nathan—was

---

name of a particular class of priests whose duties were confined to soothsaying. It was from this word that the character which denoted "speech" derived its value of *isip*. *Siptu*, "incantation," was *en* in Accadian.

[1] Cf. Gen. xliv. 5

INTRODUCTORY. 53

Jedidiah, which was changed into Solomon, "the peaceful one," when his father had "peace from all his enemies," and had surrounded his new capital of Jerusalem (perhaps the city of "peace") with a single wall.[1] That David's first name was El-hanan (or Baal-hanan) has long been suspected, since it is stated in one passage that Elhanan the son of a Bethlehemite "slew Goliath the Gittite, the staff of whose spear was like a weaver's beam,"[2] while the feat is elsewhere ascribed to David; and at the head of the thirty mighty men of David is placed Elhanan the son of Dodo of Bethlehem, where we should probably read "Elhanan who is Dodo" or David.[3] Saul, too, is presumably of similarly popular origin, the name *Saul*, "the one asked for," being singularly appropriate to a king for whom, we are told, the people had "asked." Now there is a curious parallelism between the three first kings of Israel and the three last kings of Edom enumerated in the 36th chapter of Genesis, where we have, I believe, an extract from the state-annals of the Edomites. Saul had "vexed" the Edomites,[4] and David had completed the conquest; but the accession of Solomon and the murder of Joab brought with them almost imme-

---

[1] 2 Sam. xii. 24, 25. The verses should be rendered: "She bare a son and his name was called Solomon; and the Lord loved him, and sent by the hand of Nathan the prophet and called his name Jedidiah, because of the Lord."

[2] 2 Sam. xxi. 19, where Ya'arê, Yâ'ur or Yâ'ir, seems to be a corruption of Jesse, and *oregim*, "weavers," has been repeated from the following line. The text was already corrupt before the compilation of 1 Chron. xx. 5.

[3] 2 Sam. xxiii. 24. As thirty names follow that of Elhanan, he cannot himself have been one of the thirty, and being ranked with them must have been their head.

[4] 1 Sam. xiv. 47; see, too, xxii. 9.

54   LECTURE I.

diately the successful revolt of Edom under Hadad, who had married the sister of Pharaoh's queen.[1] In strange accordance with this, we find that the three last Edomite kings mentioned in the list in Genesis were Saul, Baal-hanan and Hadar—a name which must be corrected into Hadad, as in Hadarezer for Hadadezer. The kings of Edom seem to have had a predilection for assuming the names of the divinities they worshipped. We have among them Hadad, the son of Bedad (or Ben-Dad), Hadad and Dad being, as we learn from the cuneiform inscriptions, titles of the supreme Baal in Syria, whose attributes caused the Assyrians to identify him with their own Rimmon; and Hadad was followed by Samlah of Masrekah or the "Vine-lands," in whose name we discover that of a Phœnician god recorded in a recently found inscription as well as that of the Greek Semelê.[2]

---

[1] 1 Kings xi. 19—25.

[2] See the letters of Dr. Neubauer and myself in the *Athenæum* of Sept. 12 and Sept. 26, 1885. As the worship of Dionysos, the Wine-god, had been borrowed by the Greeks from the East, it had long been assumed that the name of Semelê must be of Phœnician extraction; but it was only in 1884 that a Phœnician inscription was found in a bay to the west of the Peiræos containing the name Pen-'Samlath ("the face of 'Samlath"). The first king of Edom mentioned in Gen. xxxvi. is Bela the son of Beor, that is, Bileam or Balaam the son of Beor. Dr. Neubauer has shown that Balaam is Bil-'am, "Baal is Am(mi)," the supreme god of Ammon (as we have learned from the cuneiform inscriptions), whose name enters into those of Jerobo-am and Rehobo-am. An Assyrian mythological tablet (W. A. I. ii. 54, 65) informs us that Emu (עם) was the Nergal of the Shuites on the western bank of the Euphrates. The words with which the list of the Edomite kings is introduced ("These are the kings that reigned in the land of Edom before there reigned any king over the children of Israel") are of course an addition by the Hebrew excerptist. It will be noticed that the father of the last king in the list, Hadad II. (Hadar), is not mentioned, while, contrary to the almost universal practice of the Old Testament,

We need not be surprised, therefore, if the name of Saul also turns out to be that of a divinity. We are told that Saul came from "Rehoboth of the river" Euphrates; and since Rehoboth means the public squares and suburbs of a capital city, and is consequently used of Nineveh in the book of Genesis (x. 11), we must look for the Rehoboth of the Euphrates in Babylon. Now one of the principal names under which the Sun-god was known at Babylon was Savul or Sawul, which in Hebrew characters would become Saul. In Saul, accordingly, I think we may see a Babylonian deity transported to Edom and perhaps also to Palestine.

Hadad occupied a higher position than Saul. He was, as I have said, the supreme Baal or Sun-god, whose worship extended southward from Carchemish to Edom and Palestine. At Damascus he was adored under the Assyrian name of Rimmon, and Zechariah (xii. 11) alludes to the cult of the compound Hadad-Rimmon in the close neighbourhood of the great Canaanitish fortress of Megiddo. Coins bear the name of Abd-Hadad, "the servant of Hadad," who reigned in the fourth century at Hierapolis, the later successor of Carchemish, and, under the abbreviated form of Dáda, Shalmaneser speaks

---

the names of his wife and mother-in-law are given. This is explained by 1 Kings xi. 19, where we are told that he was married to the sister of Tahpenes the Egyptian queen. Mr. Tomkins is probably right in identifying Tahpenes with the name of the frontier-fortress which was known to the Greeks as Daphnæ, and is now called Tel-Défeneh, so that the introduction of the name into the text of the book of Kings would be a marginal gloss. Mehetab-el and Me-zahab are apparently the Semitic substitutes of Egyptian names such as the Egyptian monuments have made us familiar with. Me-zahab would presuppose an Egyptian Nub, and Mr. Tomkins ingeniously suggests that Genubath, the name of the son of Hadad, represents the Egyptian Ka-nub-ti.

of "the god Dáda of Aleppo" (Khalman). The abbreviated form was that current among the nations of the north; in the south it was confounded with the Semitic word which appears in Assyrian as *dadu*, "dear little child." This is the word which we have in Be-dad or Ben-Dad, "the son of Dad," the father of the Edomite Hadad; we have it also in the David of the Old Testament. David, or Dod, as the word ought to be read, which is sometimes written Dodo with the vocalic suffix of the nominative, is the masculine corresponding to a Phœnician goddess whose name means "the beloved one," and who was called Dido by the writers of Rome. Dido, in fact, was the consort of the Sun-god, conceived as Tammuz, "the beloved son," and was the presiding deity of Carthage, whom legend confounded with Elissa, the foundress of the city. In the article I have alluded to above, I expressed my conviction that the names of Dodo and David pointed to a worship of the Sun-god, under the title of "the beloved one," in southern Canaan as well as in Phœnicia. I had little idea at the time how soon my belief would be verified. Within the last year, the squeeze of the Moabite stone, now in the Louvre, has been subjected to a thorough examination by the German Professors Socin and Smend, with the result of correcting some of the received readings and of filling up some of the lacunæ. One of the most important discoveries that have been thus made is that the Israelites of the northern kingdom worshipped a Dodo or Dod by the side of Yahveh, or rather that they adored the supreme God under the name of Dodo[1] as well as under

---

[1] Written דודה in the Moabite text, where *hê* elsewhere takes the place of the Hebrew *waw*.

that of Yahveh. Mesha, the Moabite king, in describing the victories which his god Chemosh had enabled him to gain over his Israelitish foes, tells us that he had carried away from Ataroth "the *arel* (or altar) of Dodo and dragged it before Chemosh," and from Nebo "the *arels* (or altars) of Yahveh," which he likewise " dragged before Chemosh." Here the *arel* or "altar" of Dodo is placed in parallelism with the *arels* of Yahveh; and it is quite clear, therefore, that Dodo, like Yahveh, was a name under which the deity was worshipped by the people of the land. I have suggested that Dod or Dodo was an old title of the supreme God in the Jebusite Jerusalem, and that hence Isaiah (v. 1), when describing Jerusalem as the tower of the vineyard the Lord had planted in Israel, calls him Dôd-i, "my beloved." We can easily understand how a name of the kind, with such a signification, should have been transferred by popular affection from the Deity to the king of whom it is said that "all Israel and Judah loved him" (1 Sam. xviii. 16).

That Solomon was a divine name we have the express testimony of the cuneiform inscriptions for asserting. Sallimmanu, "the god of peace," was a god honoured particularly in Assyria, where the name of more than one famous king (Shalman-eser) was compounded with it. As the name of Nineveh was ideographically expressed by a fish within a basin of water,[1] while the name itself was connected in popular etymology with

---

[1] The ideograph also represented the name of the goddess Ninâ—a word which means "the Lady" in Sumerian—who was the daughter of Ea the god of Eridu (W. A. I. iv. 1, 38). There was a city or sanctuary in Babylonia of the same name (K 4629, *Rev.* 8), which explains the statement of Ktêsias that Nineveh stood on the Euphrates (ap. Diod. ii. 3).

the Assyrian *nunu*, "a fish," it is possible that the cult of Sallimman or Solomon in Assyria was due to the fact that he was a fish-god, perhaps Ea himself. In a list of the gods whose images stood in the numerous temples of Assyria (W. A. I. iii. 66, *Rev.* 40), mention is made of "Sallimmanu the fish, the god of the city of Temen-Sallim (the foundation of peace)." His worship was carried westward at a comparatively early period, and in the age of Shalmaneser II. the royal scribe at Sadikan, now Arban on the Khabûr, was named Sallimmanu-nunu-sar-ilani, "Solomon the fish is king of the gods."[1] So, too, in the time of Tiglath-Pileser III. (B.C. 732) the Moabite king was Salamanu or Solomon, a plain proof both that the god was known in Moab, and also that in Moab, as in Israel, the name of the god could be applied to a man.

If a gleam of light has thus been cast by the monuments of Assyria and Babylonia upon the names of the earlier kings of Israel, it is but feeble in comparison with the illustrations they afford us of the ritual and religious practices recorded in the Old Testament. The ritual texts, fragmentary as they are, are numerous among the *débris* of Assur-bani-pal's library, and the references we find from time to time in the historical inscriptions to religious rites and ceremonies give us tantalising glimpses into the service and ceremonial of the Assyro-Babylonian priesthood.

---

[1] On a cylinder now in the British Museum. The inscription runs : "The seal of Muses-Adar the scribe, the son of Adar-esses the scribe, the son of Sallimanu-nun-sar-ilani the scribe." Sir A. H. Layard discovered winged bulls at Arban, inscribed with the words, "The palace of Muses-Adar." For a representation of the seal, see George Smith's *Chaldean Genesis* (ed. Sayce), p. 97.

INTRODUCTORY. 59

In Assyria the king himself performed many of the functions of a high-priest. Like Solomon of Israel, he could offer sacrifice and pour out libations to the gods. Assur-ris-ilim is entitled "the appointed of the divine father (Bel), the priest (*śangu*) of Assur;"[1] Assur-natsir-pal calls himself "the appointed of Bel, the priest (*śangu*) of Assur, the son of Tiglath-Adar the appointed of Bel, the priest of Assur, the son of Rimmon-nirari the appointed of Bel, the priest of Assur;"[2] Sargon is similarly "the appointed of Bel, the exalted priest (NU-ES) of Assur," as well as "the high-priest (*pateśi*) of Assur;" while Nebuchadnezzar designates himself "the worshipper of Merodach, the supreme high-priest (*pateśi*), the beloved of Nebo."[3] But the union of the two offices was by no means necessary. In the far-off pre-Semitic age there were kings of Tel-loh as well as *pateśis* or high-priests of Tel-loh, and the kings did not take the title of high-priest, while the high-priests did not take the title of king. The earliest records of Assyria went back to a period when as yet there were no kings, but only "high-priests of Assur;"[4] and among the objects brought from Babylonia by Dr. Hayes Ward is a barrel-shaped weight of green basalt, on which we read: "the palace of Nebo-sum-esir the son of Dakur, the high-priest (*pateśi*) of Merodach." A distinction is carefully drawn between "the king" and "the high-priest" in the imprecation against the Vandals of the future attached to an old historical text in the Accadian language,[5] and the poet who embodied the Cuthæan legend of the crea-

---

[1] W. A. I. iii. 3, 12. [2] W. A. I. iii. 3, 39.
[3] W. A. I. i. 53, i. 5. [4] W. A. I. i. 15. 62, 63.
[5] W. A. I. iv. 12. 36, 37.

tion in his verses concludes by saying: "Thou, whether king, high-priest, shepherd or any one else whom God shall call to rule the kingdom, I have made for thee this tablet, I have inscribed for thee this record-stone, in the city of Cutha, in the temple of 'Sulim."[1] Ktêsias, therefore, was justified in making a high-priest of his Babylonian Belesys—a name, by the way, which appears in the inscriptions, under the form of Balaśu, as that of a Babylonian prince in the time of Tiglath-Pileser III.[2] The Semitic title of the high-priest (*nisakku* or *issakku*) indicates that his main duty was to pour out libations

---

[1] *Patesi* and NU-ES are rendered by the Assyrian *nisakku* and *issakku*. These have nothing to do with an Accadian *nês*, as Lotz supposed, much less with *nisu* and *ish*, "a man," as Guyard suggested, but are merely derivatives from the verb *nasaku*, "to pour out a libation," which occurs in the eleventh tablet of the Epic of Gisdhubar (col. vi. l. 4). *Patesi* should probably be read *khattesi* or *khüttesi*, since the country of that name is written indifferently PA-SE-KI and PA-TE-ŚI-KI (W. A. I. ii. 53, 13). The substitution of *śi* (*śig*) for *patesi* or *khattesi* in the penitential psalm (W. A. I. iv. 21, 45) seems due to a blunder of the Semitic scribe, who read the first character (*pa*) as *śig* (see v. 19, 55). NU-ES, "the man of the temple," is a compound ideograph of Semitic invention, which originated when false analogy had caused the termination *akku* to be regarded as a separate suffix, so that the root of *nisakku* was supposed to be *nis* or *nês*. The old rendering of *patesi* by "viceroy" rested on a mistake; the word always has reference to the worship of a god. The Nebu-sum-esir mentioned in the text, for instance, was not the viceroy of a king, but "the high-priest of Merodach," who lived at Babylon by the side of the king. The analogy of *nisakku* has created *sakkanakku*, "a high-priest," from *sakanu*, which is borrowed from the Accadian *sagan* (W. A. I. iii. 70, 40), the Zôganês of Bêrôssos.

[2] Arbakês is equally the name of a Median chief mentioned by Sargon, and Sargon himself may be the Akraganês whom Ktêsias makes the last king but one of Assyria. As Schrader points out (*Keilinschriften und Geschichtsforschung*, p. 516), in the time of Ktêsias, Belesys was the Persian governor of Syria and Assyria, and Arbakes of Media (Xenophon, *Anab.* vii. 8, 25).

in honour of the gods, and the phrases in which the word occurs show that he was attached to the cult of the supreme god of the country in which he lived. At Babylon it was Merodach from whom the high-priest received his title; at Nineveh it was Assur.

Under the high-priest several classes of subordinate priests were ranged. There was the *śangu*, for example, whose title interchanges at times with that of the high-priest himself. The *śangu* properly signified one who was "bound" or attached to a particular deity or his sanctuary, who was his slave and bondsman. The name may therefore be compared with that of the Levites, if the latter, too, are those who were "attached" to special places of worship. At Nineveh there was a *śangu* attached to the harem which was under the protection of Istar, as well as one who was entitled "the strong *śangu*," and who may accordingly be regarded as one of the chief priests.[1]

By the side of the *śangu* stood the *pâsisu* or "anointer," whose duty it was to purify with oil both persons and things. The cleansing of objects by anointing them with oil was considered a matter of great importance; even the stone tablets and foundation-stones of a building are ordered to be cleansed in this way. The use of "pure water" for washing the hands and other parts of the body occupies a conspicuous place in the ritual texts, and in one of them we read the following instructions in regard to a person who is undergoing purification:[2]

---

[1] W. A. I. ii. 31. 60, 61. The remains of the palace discovered by Layard at Arban (the ancient Sadikan) belonged, according to the inscription on the bulls, to "Muses-Adar the priest" (*śangu*).

[2] W. A. I. iv. 26, 40 *sq*.

"Pure water give him to drink, and pour out the water over the man; remove the root of the saffron (?),[1] and offer pure wine and pure yeast, and place on the heart the fat of a crane[2] which has been brought from the mountains, and anoint the body of the man seven times."

Another class of priests were the *kali*, a word borrowed by the Semites from the Accadian *kal*, "illustrious." The *kalu* was also termed *labaru*, "the elder," a word again borrowed from the Accadian *labar*, which in Sumerian appears in the earlier form of *lagar*.[3] In the epic of Gisdhubar, where Ea-bani(?) is describing the land of Hades which he is doomed to enter, the *lagaru* and the *pâsisu*, or "anointer," are mentioned along with the *isippu*, or "soothsayer," and the *makhkhu*, or "great one," from the Accadian *makh*, in which Prof. Delitzsch sees the "mag" or "(Rab-)mag" of the Old Testament.[4] "(In the house, O my friend), which I must enter," Ea-bani is made to say, "(for me) is treasured up[5] a crown (among those who wear) crowns, who from days of old have ruled the earth, (to whom) Anu and Bel have given names of renown. Glory have they given to the shades of the dead;[6] they drink the bright waters.

---

[1] *Kurkanê;* in Accadian, *kur-gi-in-na*.   [2] *Kurkê;* Chaldee, *kurk'yâ*.

[3] See Zimmern, *Bab. Busspsalmen*, p. 28, note 2. I may add that the *kali* are the Galli or eunuch-priests of the Kappadokian goddess, their Assyrian name having been borrowed along with the religious rites over which they presided.

[4] The *makhkhu* must have represented a subdivision of the *isippi*, since in W. A. I. ii. 51, 55, the word is the equivalent of *essepu*, "the priest of the god *Nibatu*." Cp. W. A. I. ii. 33, 31.

[5] *Kummuśu; kamâśu* means "to keep oneself," not "to bow" (as Zimmern and Lyon).

[6] *Katsuti* and *katsâti*, literally "fleshless ones;" compare *rĕphaim* in Is. xiv. 9. The ideograph translated *kutstsu* (W. A. I. iv. 15, 38) is

INTRODUCTORY. 63

In the house, O my friend, which I must enter dwell the lord[1] and the *lagaru*, dwell the soothsayer (*isippu*) and the *makhkhu*, dwell the anointing priest of the abysses of the great gods, the god Etannâ and the god Ner. (There dwells) the queen of the earth Nin-ki-gal; (there the Lady) of the field, the scribe of the earth, bows before her; (there she . . .) and makes answer in her presence."[2]

"The abysses" or "deeps" of the great gods is an expression which requires explanation. The temples of Babylonia were provided with large basins filled with water and used for purificatory purposes, which resembled "the sea" made by Solomon for his temple at Jerusalem, and were called *apsi*, "deeps" or "abysses."[3] It was with these "deeps" that the *pâsisu* or "anointing priest," whose office it was to purify and cleanse, was specially concerned. The basins doubtless stood in the open air, in the great court within which the temple itself was erected.

---

also rendered *surpu*, from *rapû*. The passage reads, *dih(u) suruppû . . . kutstsu*, "lunacy, wasting fever . . . consumption." A synonym of *katsutu* is *tarpu* (Accadian *dimme*, "spectre"), the Hebrew *teraphim* (see Neubauer in the *Academy*, Oct. 30, 1886).

[1] Zimmern thinks that *enu*, "lord," denoted a class of priests; but this is unlikely, unless we suppose the word to be borrowed from the Accadian *en*, "an incantation" (Assyrian *siptu*). As, however, the Assyrians formed *enitu*, "lady" (W. A. I. iii. 4, 55), from *enu*, this supposition is improbable.

[2] Haupt, *Nimrodepos*, pp. 17, 19. In 19, 47, we must read *dupśarrat*, "female scribe."

[3] The ceremonies attending the construction of a bronze bull intended to support one of these seas, are described in W. A. I. iv. 23, No. 1. The "sea" is stated to have been placed "between the ears of the bull" (line 17).

LECTURE I.

The description of E-Saggil, the temple of Bel-Merodach at Babylon, which has been translated by Mr. George Smith,[1] states that here at least there was a second court, that of "Istar and Zamâmâ," besides the great court. Within the latter was another walled enclosure, built in the form of a square, and containing the great *ziggurrat*, or "tower," as well as the temples and chapels of a large number of deities. This agglomeration of sacred edifices was due to the fact that the temple of Bel was a Babylonian Pantheon where the images and cult of the manifold gods of Chaldæa were gathered together. Where the temple was dedicated to one divinity only, there was of course only one building.

In one particular, however, the temple of Bel-Merodach differed from that of every other Babylonian temple with which we are acquainted. This is in its orientation. Its sides face the four points of the compass, whereas in the case of the other temples it is the corners that do so. The cause of this departure from the usual canons of Babylonian sacred architecture has still to be discovered.

Within, the temple bore a striking likeness to that of Solomon. At the extreme end was the *paráku*, or "holy of holies," concealed by a curtain or veil from the eyes of the profane.[2] Here, according to Nebuchadnezzar, was "the holy seat, the place of the gods who determine destiny, the spot where they assemble together (?),[3] the shrine (*parak*) of fate, wherein on the festival of Zagmuku at the beginning of the year, on the eighth and the eleventh days, the divine king of heaven and earth, the

---

[1] See Appendix II.   [2] Hence the name *paráku*, Heb. *parocheth*.
[3] So **Flemming**, *Die grosse Steinplatteninschrift Nebukadnezars*, p. 37.

INTRODUCTORY.

lord of the heavens, seats himself, while the gods of heaven and earth listen to him in fear (and) stand bowing down before him."[1] Here, too, Herodotos tells us (i. 183), was a golden image of the god, with a golden table in front of it like the golden table of shewbread in the Jewish temple.[2]

The little chapel of Makhir, "the god of dreams," discovered by Mr. Hormuzd Rassam at Balawat, near Mosul, gives us further information about the internal arrangement of the shrine. In this, Mr. Rassam found a marble coffer containing two stone tablets which recorded Assur-natsir-pal's victories and the erection of the chapel. The coffer and its contents remind us forcibly of the Israelitish ark with its "two tables of stone" (1 Kings viii. 9). Before the coffer, at the north-west of the chamber, was an altar of marble ascended by five steps, where another stone tablet was disinterred similar to those in the coffer. The gates that led to this temple of Makhir were coated with plates of embossed bronze, which are now in the British Museum. The great temple of Bel-Merodach at Babylon was adorned in a more

---

[1] W. A. I. i. 54, ii. 54—62.

[2] There seems to be evidence that the institution of the shewbread was known in Babylonia. In a fragment of a bilingual phrase-book (K 4207) we read (lines 8, 9), (Acc.) *mulu sagar-an-tug-a ê-gûr al-mur-ra-in-u-ne*, which is translated *birûta bit agurri ipallas*, "the food-provider looks down upon the house of brick." (For *ipallas*, see W. A. I. iv. 17, 26, where the corresponding Accadian verb appears as *ide-minin-barren*.) In W. A. I. ii. 44, 74, *birutu* is the rendering of the Accadian *śur* (KI-GAL), out of the ideographic representation of which the Semitic scribes by an erroneous reading formed the word *kigallu*. Now in W. A. I. iv. 13, 12, we find *ina kisal-makhkhi kigalla lâramâta*, "on the high altar mayest thou found a place of feeding," i.e. a table of shewbread.

F

costly way. Its cedar-work was overlaid by Nebuchadnezzar with gold and silver, while its furniture, like that of Solomon's temple, was of "massive gold."

The coffer of the little temple of Imgur-Bel, or Balawat, resembled in form the arks, or "ships" as they were termed, in which the gods and their symbols were carried in religious processions.[1] It thus gives us a fair idea of what the Israelitish ark of the covenant must have been like. It, too, was a small shrine of rectangular shape, carried by means of staves passed through rings at its four corners. It is somewhat curious that the Assyrian ark should have assumed this shape. The name by which it went to the last was that of "ship," a proof that it was originally in the form, not of an ark, but of a ship. The same transformation is observable in the Biblical account of the Deluge as compared with that of the cuneiform inscriptions; here also "the ship" of the Babylonian version has become "an ark." But the fact that the arks of the Babylonian gods were once ships points to a period when the first who made use of them were dwellers by the sea-shore. We are referred back to the ancient Chaldæan city of Eridu, on the shores of the Persian Gulf, from whence, as we shall see hereafter, the religion and religious ceremonies of pre-Semitic Babylonia had once spread. The gods of Eridu were water-gods, and, like the deities of Egypt, had each his sacred ship. These ships occupied an important place in the Babylonian ritual; they all had special names,

---

[1] In Layard's *Monuments of Nineveh*, pl. 65, the images of the gods are represented as standing upon platforms (or boats?) which are carried on men's shoulders, two men supporting one end of each platform and two men the other.

INTRODUCTORY. 67

and were the visible abodes of the divinities to whom they belonged. Let us listen, for instance, to an old hymn that was recited when a new image of the god was made in honour of "the ship of enthronement," the *papakh* or "ark" of Merodach:

> "Its helm is of cedar (?) wood ....
> Its serpent-like oar has a handle of gold.
> Its mast is pointed with turquoise.
> Seven times seven lions of the field (Eden) occupy its deck.
> The god Adar fills its cabin built within.
> Its side is of cedar from its forest.
> Its awning is the palm (?) wood of Dilvun.
> Carrying away (its) heart is the canal.
> Making glad its heart is the sunrise.
> Its house, its ascent, is a mountain that gives rest to the heart.
> The ship of Ea is Destiny.
> Nin-gal, the princess (Dav-kina), is the goddess whose word is life.
> Merodach is the god who pronounces the good name.
> The goddess who benefits the house, the messenger of Ea the ruler of the earth, even Nan-gar (the lady of work), the bright one, the mighty workwoman of heaven, with pure (and) blissful hand has uttered the word of life:
> 'May the ship before thee cross the canal!
> May the ship behind thee sail over its mouth!
> Within thee may the heart rejoicing make holiday!'"[1]

The hymn was an heirloom from Sumerian Eridu. It had come down from the days when Merodach was not as yet the god of Babylon, but was the son of Ea, the water-god of Eridu. It is written in Accadian, and no Semitic translation is attached to it; it is even possible that some of the expressions used in the hymn had ceased to be intelligible to the priests of E-Saggil who recited it.[2] At all events, the references to the ship of the deity

---
[1] W. A. I. ii. 25, 9—32.
[2] I need hardly observe that the Sumerian word *êgur*, "side," *êmur* (*ŏwŭr*) in the northern dialect of Accad, has nothing to do with the

were no longer applicable in the Semitic age of Babylon. The *mâ* or "ship" of the pre-Semitic Sumerians had then become the *papakhu* or "ark" of the Semites; helm and oar and mast had alike disappeared, and it was no longer required to sail across the sacred canals of the temples, but was carried on the shoulders of men.

The festivals at which such arks were borne in procession were naturally numerous in a country where divinities innumerable were adored. The festival of ZAG-MU-KU, mentioned by Nebuchadnezzar as having been held at Babylon at the beginning of the year, is possibly the Sakæan feast of the classical writers, when a slave was dressed in the robes of a king.[1] The service at the temple of Bel-Merodach which was opened by the hymn in honour of his ark, was accompanied by another specially commemorating the festival itself:[2]

"The day the (image of the) god has been made, he has caused the holy festival[3] to be fully kept.

Semitic *igaru*, "a heap" ("wall"), though the scribes of Semitic Babylonia afterwards confounded the two words together.

[1] The month, however, does not agree in the case of the two feasts. Athenæos (*Deipn.* xiv.) says: "Bêrôssos in the first book of his Babylonian History states that in the 11th month, called Lôos, is celebrated the feast of Sakæa, for five days, when it is the custom that the masters should obey their servants, one of whom is led round the house, clad in a royal robe, and called Zoganês." The Zoganês was the Accadian *sagan*, borrowed as *sakanu* by Semitic Babylonian (W. A. I. iii. 70, 40, ii. 51, 31), probably from *saga*, "head." *Sakkanakku*, "high-priest," is a derivative.

[2] W. A. I. iv. 25, 39 *sq.*

[3] *Azkaru*, "commemoration-feast." The corresponding Accadian *udu-sar* is "a day of commemoration;" in W. A. I. iv. 23, 1, *sar* alone is rendered *isinnu*, "festival." In K 2107, 14, it is translated *sipat*, "an incantation" or hymn; hence we read in a fragment (R 528): "At dawn (repeat) a hymn in the presence of Merodach, (then) four hymns to Ea the holy god of Eridu." Then follow the incantations or hymns.

The god has risen among all lands.
Lift up the (nimbus of) glory, adorn thyself with heroism, O hero
    perfect of breast,
bid lustre surround this image, establish veneration.
The lightning flashes; the festival appears like gold;[1]
in heaven the god has been created, on earth the god has been
    created!
This festival has been created among the hosts of heaven and earth.
This festival has issued forth from the forest of the cedar-trees.
The festival is the creation of the god, the work of mankind.
Bid the festival be fully kept for ever;
according to the command of the valiant golden god.[2]
This festival is a sweet savour even when the mouth is unopened,
(a pleasant taste) when food is uneaten and water un(drunk)."

No better idea can be formed of the number and variety of the Babylonian feasts than by reading a hemerology of the intercalary month of Elul, where we find that every day is dedicated to one or other of the gods, and certain rites and ceremonies prescribed for each.[3] We

---

[1] In the Assyrian translation, "brilliantly."

[2] Accadian: "Pronounce for ever the festival completed, through the creative message of the valiant golden god;" Assyrian: "In perpetuity for ever cause (the festival) to be complete, by the command of the same god (who) brought (it) about."

[3] With this hemerology may be compared the following liturgical fragment (K 3765):
2. On the 9th day there is no going forth; to the sun and moon his offerings (*nindabut*) he makes.
3. On the 10th day .... there is no going forth....
4. On the 11th day to the sun and moon his offerings he makes; the man (is pure) as the Sun-god.
5. On the 12th day to the sun and moon his offerings he makes; an eclipse takes place; there is harm (boded to his) house.
6. On the 13th day to the moon his offerings he makes. To the moon he ....; the man approaches the moon in prayer.
7. On the 14th day to the sun and moon he does not present his sin-offering (*mukhibilti*); 'receive my prayer' he does not say. The moon and the sun draw near to Anu.

learn from the colophon that it was the seventh of a series of tablets which must have furnished the Babylonian with a complete "saints' calendar" for the whole year. So careful was he not to lose an opportunity of keeping holiday in honour of his deities, that even the intercalary months, which were rendered necessary from time to time by the frequent disorder of the calendar, were included in the series. Besides the festivals of the regular Elul, there were consequently the festivals of a second Elul whenever the priests deemed it needful to insert one in the calendar. Hence, as the regular Elul was the sixth month of the year, our tablet is the seventh of the series.

"The month of the second Elul. The first day (is dedicated) to Anu and Bel. A day of good luck. When during the month the moon is seen, the shepherd of mighty nations[1] (shall offer) to the moon as a free-will offering[2] a gazelle without blemish.... he shall make his free-will offering to the Sun the mistress of the world, and to the Moon the supreme god.[3] He offers sacrifices. The lifting up of his hand finds favour (*magir*) with the god.

The second day (is dedicated) to the goddesses [the two Istars]. A lucky day. The king makes his free-will offering to the Sun the mistress of the world, and the Moon the supreme god. Sacrifices he offers. The lifting up of his hand he presents to the god.

---

8. On the 15th day to the sun and the moon he makes his offerings. The sun and the moon behold his offerings. His sin-offering he does not present; 'receive my prayer' he does not say. On this day, during the day he approaches the sun in prayer. There is no going forth. On this day his wife is pregnant."

[1] This title refers us to the age of Kkammuragas as the period when the work was composed.

[2] *Nindabu*, Heb. *nĕdhâbhâh*. The Accadian equivalent is "the dues of the goddess."

[3] The fact that the Sun is here a goddess shows that the hemerology has no connection with Sippara. It may have originated in Ur.

INTRODUCTORY.   71

The 3rd day (is) a fast-day,[1] (dedicated) to Merodach and Zarpanit. A lucky day. During the night, in the presence of Merodach and Istar, the king makes his free-will offering. He offers sacrifices. The lifting up of his hand finds favour with the god.

The 4th day (is) the feast-day[2] of Nebo (the son of Merodach). A lucky day. During the night, in the presence of Nebo and Tasmit, the king makes his free-will offering. He offers sacrifices. The lifting up of his hand he presents to the god.

The 5th day (is dedicated) to the Lord of the lower firmament and the Lady of the lower firmament. A lucky day. During the night, in the presence of Assur[3] and Nin-lil, the king makes his free-will offering. He offers sacrifices. The lifting up of his hand finds favour with the god.

The 6th day (is dedicated) to Rimmon and Nin-lil. A lucky day. The king (repeats) a penitential psalm and a litany. During the night, before the east wind, the king makes his free-will offering to Rimmon. He offers sacrifices. The lifting up of his hand he presents to the god.

The 7th day is a fast-day, (dedicated) to Merodach and Zarpanit. A lucky day. A day of rest (Sabbath). The shepherd of mighty nations must not eat flesh cooked at the fire (or) in the smoke. His clothes he must not change. White garments he must not put on. He must not offer sacrifice. The king must not drive a chariot. He must not issue royal decrees. In a secret place the augur must not mutter. Medicine for the sickness of his body he must not apply.[4] For making a curse it is not fit. During the night the king makes his free-will offering before

---

[1] *Nubattu*, borrowed from the Accadian *nu-bad*, "incomplete." The Assyrian equivalent is *yum idirtu*, "day of mourning," W. A. I. ii. 32, 13. The third of the month Ab was the *nubat* of Merodach, according to Assur-bani-pal.

[2] *Yum* AB-AB. AB-AB is stated to be equivalent to *epu* in S 1720, 16, for which Zimmern's signification of "cooking food" is probably correct, since the next line of the tablet speaks of "the house of the dark flesh of Ea." Sargon laid the foundations of his new city on this day (according to his cylinder, line 59).

[3] The Assyrian scribe has here substituted "Assur" for the original Mul-lil of the text.

[4] Literally, "he must not bring medicine to his disease of body;" see *Zeitschrift für Keilschriftforschung*, ii. 1, pp. 2—4. Lotz translates, but wrongly, "magus ægroto manum suam ne applicato."

Merodach and Istar. He offers sacrifice. The lifting up of his hand finds favour with the god.

The 8th day (is) the feast of Nebo. A lucky day. During the night the shepherd of mighty nations directs his hand to the sacrifice of a sheep. The king makes his vow to Nebo and Tasmit. He offers sacrifice. The lifting up of his hand he presents to the god.

The 9th day (is dedicated) to Adar and Gula. A lucky day. During the night, in the presence of Adar and Gula, the king makes his free-will offering. He offers sacrifice. The lifting up of his hand he presents to the god.

The 10th day (is dedicated) to the Mistress of the lower firmament and the divine Judge.[1] A lucky day. During the night, in the presence of the star of the chariot and the star of the son of Istar, the king makes his free-will offering. He offers sacrifice. The lifting up of his hand finds favour with the god.

The 11th day is the completion of the meal-offering[2] to Tasmit and Zarpanit. A lucky day. When the moon[3] lifts up (its) crown of moonlight, and (its) orb rejoices, the king makes his free-will offering to the moon. He offers sacrifice. The lifting up of his hand finds favour with the god.

The 12th day is the gift-day of Bel and Beltis. A lucky day. The king makes his free-will offering to Bel and Beltis. He offers sacrifices. The lifting up of his hand finds favour with the god.

The 13th day (is sacred) to the Moon the supreme god. A lucky day. The moon lifts up (its) crown of moonlight towards the earth. On this day assuredly the king makes his free-will offering to the Sun-god the mistress of the world, and the Moon the supreme god. He offers sacrifice. The lifting up of his hand finds favour with the god.

The 14th day (is sacred) to Beltis and Nergal. A lucky day. A Sabbath. The shepherd of mighty nations must not eat flesh cooked on the fire (or) in the smoke. The clothing of his body he must not change. White garments he must not put on. He must not offer sacrifice. He must not drive a chariot. He must not issue royal

---

[1] The divine judges were twenty-four stars associated with the Zodiac, twelve being north and twelve south, according to Diodôros (ii. 30). See W. A. I. ii. 58, 17, iii. 66, 1—9, 16, 22.

[2] *Maniti*, Heb. *minkhâh*. There was another word *manitu*, "a couch" (W. A. I. ii. 23, 57).

[3] *Arkhu*, as in Hebrew, one of the few instances in which the word is used in Assyrian.

decrees. (In) a secret place the augur must not mutter. Medicine for the sickness of his body he must not apply. For making a curse it is not fit. In the night the king makes his free-will offering to Beltis and Nergal. He offers sacrifice. The lifting up of his hand finds favour with the god.

The 15th day (is sacred) to the (Sun the) Lady of the House of Heaven. (A day for) making the stated offering¹ to Sin the supreme god. A lucky day. The king makes his free-will offering to Samas the mistress of the world, and Sin the supreme god. He offers sacrifice. The lifting up of his hands finds favour with the god.

The 16th day (is) a fast-day to Merodach and Zarpanit. A lucky day. The king must not repeat a penitential psalm. In the night, before Merodach and Istar,² the king presents his free-will offering. He offers sacrifice. The lifting up of his hands finds favour with the god.

The 17th day (is) the feast-day of Nebo and Tasmit. A lucky day. In the night, before Nebo and Tasmit, the king presents his free-will offering. He offers sacrifice. The lifting up of his hands finds favour with the god.

The 18th day (is) the festival (*isinnu*) of Sin and Samas. A lucky day. The king presents his free-will offering to Samas the mistress of the world, and Sin the supreme god. He offers sacrifice. The lifting up of his hands finds favour with the god.

The 19th day (is) the white³ day of the great goddess Gula. A lucky day. A Sabbath. The shephed of mighty nations must not eat that what is cooked at the fire, must not change the clothing of his body, must not put on white garments, must not offer sacrifice. The king must not drive (his) chariot, must not issue royal decrees. The augur must not mutter (in) a secret place. Medicine must not be applied to the sickness of the body. For making a curse (the day) is

---

¹ *Nikaŝu*, W. A. I. v. 11, 4, as corrected. Here the Accadian and Sumerian equivalents are given of the Semitic *nindabu*, "a free-will offering" (*nâdab*), *taklimu*, "offering of shewbread," *kistu*, "a tributary offering," and *nikaŝu*, "a stated offering" or "korban" (Ass. *kirbannu*), *nindabu* and *taklimu* being alike translations of the Accado-Sumerian "dues of the goddess."

² Istar is here identified with Zarpanit.

³ *Ippû*, which like its synonym *ellu* (Heb. *hâlal*, comp. *hillûlîm*, Lev. xix. 24), has the secondary meaning of "holy." Compare the Latin "dies candidus."

not suitable. The king presents his free-will offering to Adar and Gula. He offers sacrifice. The lifting up of his hands finds favour with the god.

The 20th day (is) a day of light,[1] the gift-day of Sin and Samas. A lucky day. The king presents his free-will offering to Samas the mistress of the world, and Sin the supreme god. He offers sacrifice. The lifting up of his hand finds favour with the god.

The 21st day (is the day for) making the stated offering to Sin and Samas. A lucky day. A Sabbath. The shepherd of mighty nations must not eat flesh cooked at the fire or in the smoke, must not change the clothing of his body, must not put on white garments, must not offer sacrifice. The king must not drive (his) chariot, must not issue royal decrees. The augur must not mutter (in) a secret place. Medicine must not be applied to the sickness of the body. For making a curse (the day) is not suitable. At dawn the king presents his free-will offering to Samas the mistress of the world, and Sin the supreme god. He offers sacrifice. The lifting up of his hand finds favour with the god.

The 22nd day (is the day for) making the stated offering to (Sin and) Samas. (It is) the festival of the (Sun the) mistress of the Palace. A lucky day. The king presents his free-will offering to Samas the mistress of the world, and (Sin the supreme god). He offers sacrifice. The lifting up of his hand finds favour with the god.

The 23rd day (is) the festival of Samas and Rimmon. A lucky day. The king presents his free-will offering to Samas and Rimmon. He offers sacrifice. The lifting up of his hand finds favour with the god.

The 24th day (is) the festival of the Lord of the Palace and the Mistress of the Palace. A lucky day. The king presents his free-will offering to the Lord of the Palace and the Mistress of the Palace. He offers sacrifice. The lifting up of his hand finds favour with the god.

The 25th day (is) the processional day[2] of Bel and Beltis of Babylon. A lucky day. In the night the king presents his free-will offering to Bel before the star of the Foundation, and to Beltis of Babylon before the star of the Chariot. He offers sacrifice. The lifting up of his hand finds favour with the god.

The 26th day (is the day) of the establishment of the enclosing wall

---

[2] Probably the ideographic mode of representing *ippû.*

[1] *Sadhakhu,* literally "marching."

INTRODUCTORY. 75

of Ea the supreme god. A lucky day.[1] The king must repeat (?) a penitential psalm whatever (?) he may present. That day at nightfall he makes a free-will offering to Ea the supreme god. He offers sacrifice. The lifting up of his hand finds favour with the god.

The 27th day (is the day) of the chase[2] of Nergal (and) the festival of Zikum. A lucky day. The king presents his free-will offering to Nergal and Zikum. He offers sacrifice. The lifting up of his hand finds favour with the god.

The 28th day (is sacred) to Ea. (It is) the day of the resting of Nergal. A lucky day. A Sabbath. The shepherd of great nations must not eat flesh cooked at the fire or in the smoke, must not change the clothing of his body, must not put on white garments, must not offer sacrifice. The king must not drive a chariot. He must not issue royal decrees. (In) a secret place the augur must not mutter. Medicine for the sickness of the body must not be applied. For making a curse (the day) is not suitable. To Ea the supreme god (the king) presents (his free-will offering). He offers sacrifice. The lifting up of his hand finds favour with the god.

The 29th day (is) the day of the resting of the Moon-god. The day when the spirits of heaven and earth are adored. A lucky day. The king presents his free-will offering to Sin the supreme god. He offers sacrifice. The lifting up of his hand finds favour with the god.

The 30th day (is sacred) to Anu and Bel. A lucky day. The king presents his free-will offering to Anu and Bel. He offers sacrifice. The lifting up of his hand finds favour with the god.

The 2nd month of Elul from the 1st to the 30th day, if the king restores either his god or his goddess or his gods who have been expelled, that king has the divine colossus as his god.

In the second Elul the king of the country gives a name to the temple of the god. Whether he builds a shrine (or) .... his heart is not good.

---

[1] *Nadû amari* (SUB E-MUR, like *ingar*, Ass. *igaru*, "an enclosing wall," W. A. I. ii. 15, 36).

[2] *Me-lul-ti*, "park" or "chase;" see W. A. I. i. 7, B 2; 82. 8—16, 1, Rev. 6, where *esemen* is the Accadian, and *melulti sa Istari* the Assyrian, equivalent of KI-E-NE-DI-INNANA; S 704, 21 ("they enclosed the place of *melulti*"); K 161, Rev. iii. 7, where *melulti* is in parallelism with *tarbatsi*, "stall," *suburi*, "cote," *sukulli*, "stable," *sigari*, "cage," *irriri*, "lair," and *irsi*, "bed;" S 526. 23, 25 ("the place of the *melulti* thou dost not plant, thou dost not cause the little ones to come out of the place of the *melulti*").

76 LECTURE I.

In the second Elul the king restores the sacrifice (*makhru*).

[Beginning of the next tablet of the series]:—The month Tisri (is sacred) to Samas the warrior of mankind. (These are) the commandments of Bel-khummu (the priest) on the first day (sacred) to Anu and Bel.

[Colophon.]—The 8th tablet (of the series beginning) 'The Moon the lord of the month.' The possession of Assur-bani-pal, the king of multitudes, the king of Assyria."

One of the most interesting facts that result from this hemerology is, that the Sabbath was known to the Babylonians and Assyrians. Its institution must have gone back to the Accadian epoch, since the term used to represent it in the text is the Accadian *udu khulgal*, "an unlawful day," like the Latin "dies nefastus," which is rendered by *sulum*, or "rest-day," in Assyrian.[1] Semitic Babylonian, however, possessed the term Sabbath as well, and a vocabulary explains it as being "a day of rest for the heart."[2] Like the Hebrew Sabbath, it was

---

[1] W. A. I. iii. 56, 53.

[2] W. A. I. ii. 32, 16, *yum nukh libbi* = *sabattuv*. In the new edition of the *Encyclopædia Britannica*, the reading *sabattuv* in this passage is called a "textual emendation" made by Delitzsch. This, however, is a mistake. It is the reading of the original tablet, and the published text was corrected by myself long before Delitzsch re-examined the original. The *Encyclopædia Britannica* makes another strange statement in describing the Hebrew Sabbath as a day "of feasting and good cheer." It was, on the contrary, a day of rest (Gen. ii. 2, 3 ; Ex. xx. 10), "the holy day" on which the Jew was forbidden to do his own pleasure—"not doing thine own ways, nor finding thine own pleasure, nor speaking thine own words" (Is. lviii. 13)—in exact conformity with the regulations of the Babylonian Sabbath. The compiler of the text (W. A. I. ii. 32) in which *sabattuv* is explained as "a day of rest of the heart," evidently regarded the word as derived from the Accadian *sa-bat*, "heart-resting," and he certainly had in support of his view the similar term *nubattu*, from the Accadian *nu-bat*. The Assyrian verb *sabatu* is given as a synonym of *gamaru*, "to complete," in W. A. I. v. 28, 14.

observed every seventh day, and was obviously connected with the seventh-day periods of the moon.

But there were two respects in which it differed from the Hebrew institution. Among the Israelites, "the Sabbaths" and "the new moons" were separate from one another; among the Babylonians, they coincided in so far as the Sabbath fell on the first day of the lunar month. Consequently, since the month consisted of thirty days, the last week contained nine days. In the second place, the 19th of the intercalary Elul was also a Sabbath. Why it should have been so I cannot pretend to say.

Besides the stated festivals and Sabbaths, extraordinary days of thanksgiving or humiliation were ordained from time to time. In the closing years of the Assyrian empire, when her foes were gathering around her, the last king, Esarhaddon II., prayed to the Sun-god that he would "remove the sin" of his people, and ordered the *khal*, or "prophet," to prescribe "the legal solemnities (*mesari isinni*) for a hundred days and a hundred nights," from the 3rd of Iyyar to the 15th of Ab.[1] So, too, Assur-bani-pal tells us, that after suppressing the revolt in Babylonia and removing the corpses that had choked the streets of the Babylonian cities, "by the command of the augurs (*isipputi*)" he "purified their shrines and cleansed their chief places of prayer. Their angry gods and wrathful goddesses he soothed with supplications and penitential psalms. He restored and established in peace their daily sacrifices, which they had discontinued, as they had been in former days."[2]

The sacrifices and offerings of the Babylonians and

---

[1] K 4668, 2, 3.   [2] W. A. I. v. 4, 86 *sq.*

Assyrians closely resembled those of the Israelites. Like the latter, they were divided into sacrifices of animals, such as oxen, sheep or gazelles, and offerings of meal and wine. Wine was poured over the victim or the altar. When the effeminate Assur-bani-pal had slaughtered a *battue* of caged lions, he "set up over them the mighty bow of Istar, the lady of war, presented offerings over them, and made a sacrifice of wine over them."[1] An old magical text prays that "the sick man may be purified by sacrifices of mercy and peace," or "peace-offerings," as the translators of our Bible would have expressed it.[2] But although the Assyrian kings are fond of boasting of their exploits in massacreing or torturing their defeated enemies in honour of Assur, we find no allusions in the inscriptions of the historical period to human sacrifice. That human sacrifices, however, were known as far back as the Accadian era, is shown by a bilingual text (K 5139) which enjoins the *abgal*, or "chief prophet," to declare that the father must give the life of his child for the sin of his own soul, the child's head for his head, the child's neck for his neck, the child's breast for his breast. The text not only proves that the idea of vicarious punishment was already conceived of; it also proves that the sacrifice of children was a Babylonian institution. In the great work on astronomy called "The Observations of Bel,"[3] we are told that "on the high-places the son is burnt."[4] The offering was consequently by fire, as in Phœnicia.

---

[1] W. A. I. i. 7. [2] W. A. I. ii. 18. 53, 54.
[3] W. A. I. iii. 60, 162.
[4] *Arur*, connected with *arurti*, "the lightning," an epithet of Rimmon. Delitzsch renders it "earthquake," in curious disregard of the

INTRODUCTORY. 79

The sacrifices were accompanied, sometimes by hymns or incantations, sometimes by prayers. The prayers were all prescribed, and a large number of them have been preserved. Here are some examples of them:[1]

"At dawn and in the night (the worshipper) shall bow down (*ikammiś*) before the Throne-bearer and shall speak as follows: 'O Throne-bearer, giver of prosperity, a prayer!' After that he shall bow down to Nusku and shall speak thus: 'O Nusku, prince and king of the secrets of the great gods, a prayer!' After that he shall bow down to Adar and shall speak thus: 'O Adar, mighty lord of the deep places of the wells, a prayer!' After that he shall bow down to Gula and shall speak thus: 'O Gula, mother, begetter of the black-headed race, a prayer!' After that he shall bow down to Nin-lil and shall speak thus: 'O Nin-lil, mighty goddess, wife of the divine Prince of Sovereignty, a prayer!' After that he shall bow down to Mul-lil and shall speak thus: 'O lord exalted, establisher of law,[2] a prayer!' For three days at dawn and at night, with face and mouth uplifted, during the middle watch, the diviner (*asip*) shall pour out libations."

The best idea, however, of what a Babylonian religious service was like, may be gathered from the instructions given to the priest who watched in the temple of Bel-Merodach at Babylon on the night of the first day of the new year.[3] Part of his duty was to repeat a hymn, the first fourteen lines of which were alternately in Accadian and Semitic. Curiously enough, however, there was no

---

character both of Rimmon and of the plain of Babylonia. The word corresponds with the Heb. *khârar*. M. Ménant has pointed out several instances in which a human sacrifice is represented on early Babylonian cylinders (*Catalogue de la Collection de Clercq*, i. pp. 18, 112 *sq*. In pl. xix. No. 181, is a ruder copy of a scene of human sacrifice depicted on an early Babylonian cylinder procured by Dr. Max Ohnefalsch-Richter in Cyprus).

[1] W. A. I. iv. 61, 19 *sq*.

[2] Literally, "secret wisdom" (82. 8—16, 1, *Obv.* 23), with which Delitzsch compares the Heb. *thorâh*.

[3] W. A. I. iv. 46, 47. The published text is very incorrect.

connection between the Accadian and the Semitic verses; while the Semitic lines were addressed to Bel-Merodach of Babylon and Borsippa, the Accadian portion had to do with "a god of the sanctuary," whose only resemblance to Bel was that he is entitled "the lord of the world." The Accadian verses are thus evidently a heirloom from a distant past, possibly from the pre-Semitic days of Babylon itself, and it is more than probable that the meaning was but little understood by the Semitic priests. This is how the text begins:

"In the month Nisan, on the second day[1] and the first hour (*kasbu*) of the night, the priest[2] must go and take the waters of the river in his hand; he must enter into the presence of Bel, and, putting on a robe in the presence of Bel, shall address to Bel this hymn:[3]

'O Bel, who in his strength has no rival,
O Bel, king of blessedness, Bel (the lord) of the world,[4]
Seeking after the favour of the great gods,
Bel, who in his glance has destroyed the strong,[5]
Bel (the lord) of kings, light of mankind, establisher of trust;[6]
O Bel, thy sceptre is Babylon, Borsippa is thy crown!
The wide heaven is the habitation of thy liver!
O lord, thine is the revelation, (and) the interpretations of visions;
O father (?) of lords, thee they behold the father of lords;

---

[1] It must be remembered that the Babylonians, like the Jews, reckoned the day from evening to evening.

[2] The Accadian title Uru-gal, "the chief watcher," is used. The title perhaps had reference to the nightly watch kept in the sanctuary of Merodach in the tower of E-Saggil.

[3] I omit the Accadian lines of the hymn, as I am unable to translate them fully.

[4] The preceding Accadian line is: "O lord of the blessed sanctuary, lord of the world!"

[5] The preceding Accadian line reads: "What is the lord (doing) now? the lord is resting."

[6] The preceding Accadian line has: "The god of the sanctuary of mankind, the god who holds the sanctuary of man."

INTRODUCTORY. 81

thine is the glance, (and) the seeing of wisdom;[1]
they magnify (?) thee, O master of the strong;
they adore (?) thee, O king (and) mighty prince;
they look up to thee, show unto them mercy;
cause them to behold the light that they may tell of thy righteousness.
O Bel (lord) of the world, light of the spirits of heaven, utterer of blessings,
who is there whose mouth murmurs not of thy righteousness
or speaks not of thine exaltation and celebrates not thy glory?
O Bel (lord) of the world, who dwellest in the temple of the Sun,
reject not the hands that are raised to thee;
Show mercy to thy city Babylon,
to E-Saggil thy temple incline thy face,
grant the prayers of thy people the sons of Babylon!'"[2]

---

[1] Or "law;" *zimat urtuv*, for which see W. A. I. v. 28, 92, and iv. 15, 48 (where *urta* is the Accadian *amma*, which is *terit* in iv. 28, 23).

[2] With this text must be compared another (unmarked at the time I copied it), which is interesting as referring to the oracle established within the "shrine" or "holy of holies" (*parak*) of the temple of Bel: "(4) Like Bel in the shrine of the destinies the prophecy shall be uttered (*ittaspu*), this shall be said: (5) 'Bel has come forth; the king has looked for me (*yuqá'a*); (6) our lady (*bilit-ni*) has come forth; the king has looked for thee; (7) the lord of Babylon has issued forth; the whole (*gamli*) of the world is on his face. (8) Zarpanit the princess has issued forth; his mouth has gone to meet her (?) (*illaku sana pi-su*). (9) Tasmit has issued forth; he has gone to meet her (?). (10) Place the herbs in the hands of the goddess of Babylon; (11) O *aśśinnu* (eunuch-priest) [place] the flute (GI-BU), O seed-planter [place] the seed; (12) purify me (*ellê-a*), purify me, and (13) fill Babylon with pure splendour, O Nin-lil, when thou pardonest the world (*kullat tamtsi*).' (14) O Bel who (art) in the shrine, surrounded by the river (*śikhir nahri*), (this) shall be said: (15) 'O Mul-lil my lord (*ama*) in Nipur I saw thee; (16) O my shepherd when I saw thee in the temple of Sin the first-born, (17) I . . . thy foot and . . thy hand.'" The first three lines, which are mutilated, run as follows: "(1) . . . king of the *aśśinnu* listen; (2) . . . in the house of the supreme chief (*ab-makh*) I saw you my lord (*amur-kunu ama*). (3) . . . he is bright and I saw thee."

LECTURE I.

Various special dresses were worn during the performance of the religious ceremonies, and ablutions in pure water were strongly insisted on. Seven, too, was a sacred number, whose magic virtues had descended to the Semites from their Accadian predecessors. When the Chaldæan Noah escaped from the Deluge, his first act was to build an altar and to set vessels, each containing the third of an ephah, by sevens, over a bed of reeds, pine-wood and thorns. Seven by seven had the magic knots to be tied by the witch,[1] seven times had the body of the sick man to be anointed with the purifying oil.[2] As the Sabbath of rest fell on each seventh day of the week, so the planets, like the demon messengers of Anu, were seven in number, and "the god of the number seven" received peculiar honour.

Along with this superstitious reverence for the sacred number, went a distinction of the animal world into clean and unclean, or rather into food that it was lawful and

---

[1] W. A. I. iv. 3. 5, 6.
[2] W. A. I. iv. 26, 49. The deluge was said to have lasted seven days; three groups of stars—the *tikpi* or "circles" (?), the *masi* or "double stars," and the *lu-masi* or "sheep of the hero," were each seven in number; the gates which led to Hades were also seven; Erech is called the city of "the seven zones" or "stones" (W. A. I. ii. 50, 55—57); and, as Lotz reminds us, seven fish-like men ascended out of the Persian Gulf, according to Bêrôssus, in order to teach the antediluvian Babylonians the arts of life. Similarly we read the following prayer in M 1246, 5—12. "Incantation.—O strong (goddess), the violent (*samrata*), the furious of breast (*nadrata irta*), the powerful, thou beholdest (*paqata*) the hostility of the enemy; who that is not Ea has quieted (thee) (*sa la Ea mannu yunakh*)? who that is not Merodach has pacified (thee)? May Ea quiet (thee), may Merodach pacify thee! (Conclusion of) the spell. Incantation.—Make this prayer seven times over the thread (*napsiti*); stretch (it) around his name (*ema sum-su*), and live (DIL-ES)." In O 535. 10, 14, DIL-ES is interpreted *bulludh*.

unlawful to eat. The distinction may have gone back to an age of totemism; at all events, it prevailed as extensively among the Babylonians and Assyrians as it did among the adherents of the Mosaic Law. In one of the penitential Psalms, the author expresses his contrition for having "eaten the forbidden thing;" and if Jensen is right in seeing the wild boar in the *sakhu* of the texts, its flesh was not allowed to be eaten on the 30th of the month Ab, nor, like that of the ox, on the 27th of Marchesvan.[1] The very mention of the *khumzir*, or domestic pig, is avoided in the Semitic Babylonian and Assyrian inscriptions, and reptiles were accounted as unclean as they were among the Jews.[2] It is true that there are indications that human flesh had once been consumed in honour of the spirits of the earth, as Prof. Maspero has lately shown must also have been the case in pre-historic Egypt, and a bilingual hymn still speaks of "eating the front breast of a man;"[3] but such bar-

---

[1] "Das Wildschwein in den assyrisch-babylonischen Inschriften," *Zeitschrift für Assyriologie*, i. 3, pp. 306 *sq*. I may add here that circumcision was known to the Babylonians as it was to the Jews. In a magical text (W. A. I. ii. 17, 63) it was termed *arlu*, the Heb. *ârêl*, which is used in Hebrew and Arabic in a precisely opposite sense; but the ideographic equivalents of the Babylonian word ("the shaping of the phallus") show what its signification in Assyrian must be.

[2] K (unnumbered), 20.

[3] K 4609. So in S 477. ii. 5, "the flesh of a man" is mentioned along with "the flesh of the gazelle," "the flesh of the dog," "the flesh of the wild boar," "the flesh of the ass," "the flesh of the horse," and "the flesh of the wild ass," and "the flesh of the dragon" (*bisbis*), all of which it was unlawful to eat. In S 1720, 17, mention is made of "the house of the dark (DIR) flesh of Ea," where the idea may be similar to that of the Egyptian texts in which the *ka* or "double" of the dead is described as feasting on the gods. Cp. also an unnumbered tablet containing a hymn to the god Tutu: *sagata ina samami ina ma-*

barous practices were but dimly-remembered reminiscences of a barbarous past, and were never shared in by the Semites. It is equally true that medicine laid contributions on the most unclean articles of food, including snakes, the tongues of "black dogs" and even ordure; but those who swallowed the compounds prescribed by the medical faculty were those who had already lost their faith in the old beliefs of the people, and had substituted the *recipe* of the doctor for the spells of the exorcist and the ritual of the priest. The practice of medicine has often been accused of antagonism to religion; whatever may be the case in these modern days, the theology of ancient Babylonia harmonised but badly with the prescriptions of its medical school.[1]

---

tati nisi tabarri surbata-ma [*ina*] *irtsitiv siru* KHAR-MES-*sunu* [*ta*]*barri siru dukhdhû tabarri atta*, "Thou art exalted in heaven; in the world thou feedest on mankind; thou art princely in the earth, the flesh of their hearts thou eatest, the flesh in abundance thou eatest."

[1] See my articles on "An Ancient Babylonian Work on Medicine" in the *Zeitschrift für Keilschriftforschung*, ii. 1, 3.

Lecture II.

BEL-MERODACH OF BABYLON.

In an inscription upon a clay cylinder brought from Babylonia seven years ago, Cyrus is made to declare that the overthrow of Nabonidos, the last independent Babylonian monarch, was due to the anger of Bel and the other gods. Nabonidos had removed their images from their ancient sanctuaries, and had collected them together in the midst of Babylon. The priests maintained that the deed had aroused the indignation of Merodach, "the lord of the gods," who had accordingly rejected Nabonidos, even as Saul was rejected from being king of Israel, and had sought for a ruler after his own heart. It was "in wrath" that the deities had "left their shrines when Nabonidos brought them into Babylon," and had prayed Merodach, the divine patron of the imperial city, to "go round unto all men wherever might be their seats." Merodach sympathised with their wrongs; "he visited the men of Sumer and Accad whom he had sworn should be his attendants," and "all lands beheld his friend." He chose Cyrus, king of Elam, and destined him by name for the sovereignty of Chaldæa. Cyrus, whom the Hebrew prophet had already hailed as the Lord's Anointed, was thus equally the favourite of the supreme Babylonian god. "Merodach, the great lord, the restorer of his people," we are told, "beheld with joy the deeds of his vicegerent who was righteous in hand and heart. To his city of Babylon he summoned his march, and he bade him take the road to Babylon; like a friend and a comrade he went at his side." A single battle decided the conflict: the Babylonians opened their gates, and "without fighting or battle," Cyrus was led in triumph into the city of Babylon. His first care was to show his gratitude towards the deities who had so signally aided him. Their temples were rebuilt, and they themselves were restored to their ancient seats.

With all the allowance that must be made for the flattery exacted by a successful conqueror, we must confess that this is a very remarkable document. It is written in the Babylonian language and in the Babylonian form of the cuneiform syllabary, and we may therefore infer that it was compiled by Babylonian scribes and intended for the perusal of Babylonian readers. Yet we find the foreign conqueror described as the favourite of the national god, while the last native king is held up to reprobation as the dishonourer of the gods. It is impossible not to compare the similar treatment experienced by Nebuchadnezzar and the native Jewish kings respectively at the hands of Jeremiah. The Jewish prophet saw in the Chaldæan invader the instrument of the God of Judah, just as the Babylonian scribes saw in Cyrus the instrument of the god of Babylon; and the fall of the house of David is attributed, just as much as the fall of Nabonidos, to divine anger.

It is true that the reasons assigned for the divine anger are not the same in the two cases. But the cause of the indignation felt by the gods of Chaldæa against

Nabonidos offers a curious illustration of the words addressed by the Rab-shakeh of Sennacherib to the people of Jerusalem. "If ye say unto me," he declared, "we trust in the Lord our God; is not that he whose high-places and whose altars Hezekiah hath taken away, and hath said to Judah and Jerusalem, ye shall worship before this altar in Jerusalem?" The destruction of the local cults, the attempt to unify and centralise religious worship, was to the Rab-shakeh, as it was to the Babylonian scribes, and doubtless also to many of the Jews in the time of Hezekiah, an act of the grossest impiety.

An annalistic tablet, drawn up not long after the conquest of Babylonia by Cyrus, hints that before making his final attack on the country, the Elamite prince had been secretly aided by a party of malcontents in Chaldæa itself. It is at all events significant that as soon as the army of Nabonidos was defeated, the whole population at once submitted, and that even the capital, with its almost impregnable fortifications, threw open its gates. The revolts which took place afterwards in the reigns of Dareios and Xerxes, and the extremities endured by the Babylonians before they would surrender their city, prove that their surrender was not the result of cowardice or indifference to foreign rule. The great mass of the people must have been discontented with Nabonidos and anxious for his overthrow.

The anger of Merodach and the gods, in fact, was but a convenient way of describing the discontent and anger of an important section of the Babylonians themselves. Nabonidos did not belong to the royal house of Nebuchadnezzar; he seems to have raised himself to the throne by means of a revolution, and his attempt at centralisation excited strong local animosities against him. Religion and civil government were so closely bound up together, that civil centralisation meant religious centralisation also; the surest sign that the cities of Babylonia had been absorbed in the capital was that the images of the gods whose names had been associated with them from time immemorial were carried away to Babylon. The cities lost their separate existence along with the deities who watched over their individual fortunes.

The removal of the gods, however, implied something more than the removal of a number of images and the visible loss of local self-government or autonomy. Each image was the centre of a particular cult, carried on in a particular temple in a particular way, and entrusted to the charge of a special body of priests. It was no wonder, therefore, that the high-handed proceedings of Nabonidos aroused the enmity of these numerous local priesthoods, as well as of all those who profited in any way from the maintenance of the local cults. Most of the cities which were thus deprived of their ancestral deities were as old as Babylon; many of them claimed to be older; while it was notorious that Babylon did not become a capital until comparatively late in Babylonian history. The Sun-god of Sippara, the Moon-god of Ur, were alike older than Merodach of Babylon. Indeed, though in the age of Nabonidos the title of Bel or "lord" had come to be applied to Merodach specially, it was known that there was a more ancient Bel—Belitanas, "the elder Bel," as the Greeks wrote the word—whose worship had spread from the city of Nipur, and who formed one of the supreme triad of Babylonian gods.

Up to the last, Babylonian religion remained local. It was this local character that gives us the key to its origin and history, and explains much that would otherwise seem inconsistent and obscure. The endeavour of Nabonidos to undermine its local character and to create a universal religion for a centralised Babylonia, was deeply resented by both priests and people, and ushered in the fall of the Babylonian empire. The fundamental religious idea which had underlain the empire had been the supremacy of Merodach, the god of Babylon, over all other gods, not the absorption of the deities of the subject nations into a common cult. The policy of Nabonidos, therefore, which aimed at making Merodach, not *primus inter pares*, but absolute lord of captive or vassal deities, shocked the prejudices of the Babylonian people, and eventually proved fatal to its author. In Cyrus, accordingly, the politic restorer of the captive populations and their gods to their old homes, the priests and worshippers of the local divinities saw the pious adherent of the ancient forms of faith, and the real favourite of Merodach himself. Merodach had not consented to the revolutionary policy of Nabonidos; he had, on the contrary, sympathised with the wrongs of his brother gods in Babylonia and throughout the world, and had thus deserted his own city and the renegade monarch who ruled over it.

In all this there is a sharp contrast to the main religious conception which subsequently held sway over the Persian empire, as well as to that which was proclaimed by the prophets of Judah, and in the reforms of Hezekiah and Josiah was carried out practically by the Jewish kings. The Ahura-mazda whom Dareios invokes on the rock of Behistun is not only the lord of the gods, he is a lord who will not brook another god by his side. The supreme god of the Persian monarch is as absolute as the Persian monarch himself. In the Persian empire which was organised by Dareios, centralisation became for the first time a recognised and undisputed fact, and political centralisation went hand-in-hand with religious centralisation as well. In Judah, a theocracy was established on the ruins of the old beliefs which had connected certain localities with certain forms of divinity, and which found such naive expression in the words of David to Saul (1 Sam. xxvi. 19): "They have driven me out this day from abiding in the inheritance of the Lord, saying, Go, serve other gods." The destruction of the high-places and the concentration of the worship of Yahveh in Jerusalem, was followed by the ever-increasing conviction that Yahveh was not only a jealous God who would allow none other gods besides Himself; He was also a God who claimed dominion over the whole world.

Now it was precisely this conception which the Babylonians, at least as a people, never attained. Nebuchadnezzar may invoke Merodach as "the lord of the gods," "the god of heaven and earth," "the eternal, the holy, the lord of all things," but he almost always couples him with other deities—Nebo, Sin or Gula—of whom he speaks in equally reverential terms. Even Nabonidos uses language of Sin, the Moon-god, which is wholly incompatible with a belief in the exclusive supremacy of Merodach. He calls him "the lord of the gods of heaven and earth, the king of the gods and the god of gods, who dwell in heaven and are mighty." Merodach was, in fact, simply the local god of Babylon. Events had raised Babylon first to the dignity of the capital of Babylonia, and then of that of a great empire, and its presiding deity had shared its fortunes. It was he who had sent forth its people on their career of conquest; it was to glorify his name that he had given them victory. The introduction of other deities on an equal footing with himself into his own peculiar seat, his own special city, was of itself a profanation, and quite sufficient to draw upon Nabonidos his vindictive anger. The Moon-god might be worshipped at Ur; it was out of place to offer him at Babylon the peculiar honours which were reserved for Merodach alone.

Here, then, is one of the results of that localisation of religious worship which was characteristic of Babylonia. Nabonidos not only offended the priests and insulted the gods of other cities by bringing their images into Babylon, he also in one sense impaired the monopoly which the local deity of Babylon enjoyed. He thus stirred up angry feelings on both sides. Had he himself been free from the common belief of the Babylonian in the local character of his gods, he might have effected a revolution similar to that of Hezekiah; he had, however, the superstition which frequently accompanies antiquarian instincts, and his endeavour to make Babylon the common gathering-place of the Babylonian divinities was dictated as much by the desire to make all of them his friends as by political design.[1]

---

[1] It must be remembered that the attempt of Nabonidos was essentially different from the mere gathering of the gods of Babylonia into the great temple of Merodach, which Nebuchadnezzar had made a kind of Chaldæan Pantheon. Here they assumed a merely subordinate place they were the attendants and servitors of the god of Babylon, and their

Now who was this Merodach, this patron-god of Babylon, whose name I have had so often to pronounce? Let us see, first of all, what we can learn about him from the latest of our documents, the inscriptions of Nebuchadnezzar and his successors. In these, Merodach appears as the divine protector of Babylon and its inhabitants. He has the standing title of Bilu or "lord," which the Greeks turned into Βῆλος, and which is the same as the Baal of the Old Testament. The title is frequently used as a name, and is, in fact, the only name under which Merodach was known to the Greeks and Romans. In the Old Testament also it is as Bel that he comes before us. When the prophet declares that "Bel boweth down" and is "gone into captivity," he is referring to Merodach and the overthrow of Merodach's city. To the Babylonian, Merodach was pre-eminently "the Baal" or "lord," like the Baalim or "lords" worshipped under special names and with special rites in the several cities of Canaan.

The temple or "tomb" of Bêlos, as it was also called by the Greeks, was one of the wonders of the world. Hêrodotos, quoting probably from an earlier author, describes it in the following terms:

"The temple of Zeus Bêlos, with bronze gates which remained up to my time, was a square building two furlongs every way. In the middle

---

shrines and chapels were ranged humbly round his lofty tower. As Nebuchadnezzar himself says, they here "listened to him in reverence and stood bowing down before him." Nabonidos, on the other hand, endeavoured to transplant the local cults of the deities, along with their time-honoured images, to the capital city, to place them there on a footing of equality with Merodach, and so to defraud him of his privileges; while at the same time he removed the other deities from the localities where alone they could be properly adored.

of the temple was a tower of solid masonry, a furlong in length and breadth, and upon this tower another tower had been erected, and upon that again another, and so on for eight towers. And the ascent to them was by an incline which wound round all the towers on the outside. About the middle of the incline are a resting-place and seats, where those who ascend may sit and rest. In the topmost tower is a large shrine, within which is a large and well-appointed couch, with a golden table at its side. But no image is set up there, nor does any one pass the night there except a single woman, a native of the country, whom the god selects for himself from among all the inhabitants, as is asserted by the Chaldæans, the priests of the god. They further say, though I cannot believe it, that the god himself visits the shrine and takes his rest upon the couch.... There is another shrine below belonging to this Babylonian temple, and containing a great statue of Zeus [Bêlos] of gold in a sitting posture, and a great golden table is set beside it. The pedestal and chair of the statue are of gold, and, as the Chaldæans used to say, the gold was as much as 800 talents in weight. Outside the shrine is a golden altar. There is also another great altar upon which full-grown sheep are sacrificed, for upon the golden altar only sucklings are allowed to be offered. Upon the larger altar also the Chaldæans burn each year a thousand talents of frankincense at the time when they keep the festival of the god. In this part of the temple there was still at that time a figure of a man twelve cubits high, of solid gold."

It is clear from this description that the great temple of Babylon resembled a large square enclosure formed by huge walls of brick, within which rose a tower in eight stages. Below the tower was a shrine or temple, and outside it two altars, the smaller one of gold for special offerings, while the larger one was intended for the sacrifice of sheep as well as for the burning of incense.[1]

We learn a good deal about this temple from the inscriptions of Nebuchadnezzar, which show that although

---

[1] Similarly in Solomon's temple there were two altars, one for larger and the other for smaller offerings (1 Kings viii. 64).

Hêrodotos was correct in his general description of the building, he has made mistakes in the matter of details. The temple itself stood on the east side of Babylon, and had existed since the age of Khammuragas (B.C. 2250), and the first dynasty which had made Babylon its capital. It bore the title of E-Sagila or E-Saggil, an Accadian name signifying "the house of the raising of the head."[1] Its entrance also bore the Accadian title of Ka-khilibu, which Nebuchadnezzar renders "the gate of glory." He says of it: "Ka-khilibu, the gate of glory, as well as the gate of E-Zida within E-Sagila, I made as brilliant as the sun. The holy seats, the place of the gods who determine destiny, which is the place of the assembly (of the gods), the holy of holies of the gods of destiny, wherein on the great festival (Zagmuku) at the beginning of the year, on the eighth and the eleventh days (of the month), the divine king (Merodach), the god of heaven and earth, the lord of heaven, descends, while the gods in heaven and earth, listening to him with reve-

---

[1] *Nasû sa resi* (W. A. I. ii. 26, 59); also *saqû sa risi*, "top of the head" (W. A. I. ii. 30, 3), and *risân elatum*, "of the lofty head" (ii. 30, 14). In W. A. I. ii. 15, 45, *saggil* is rendered by the Assyrian *zabal*, the Heb. *zĕbûl*, which is used of Solomon's temple in 1 Kings viii. 13, where, as Guyard has shown, the translation should be "house of exaltation." In W. A. I. ii. 7, 26, it is rendered by the Assyrian *dinânu;* and in ii. 7, 52, and 28, 42, *gar saggilla* is rendered by *śukkurutu* and *pûkhu*, both of which mean "an enclosed place" or "locked-up shrine," accessible only to the chief priest. In M 242, 11, *dinanu*, which probably means "a stronghold," is the equivalent of *gar saggil;* and in S. 949, *Rev.* 4, we read: "My shrine (*pukhu*) which Ea has made . . . . my stronghold(?) (*dinanâ*) which Merodach has created." In the list of Babylonian kings in which the meaning of their names is explained, Es-Guzi appears as the earlier Sumerian title of E-Saggil. *Guzi*, like *saggil*, is interpreted *saqû sa risi* and *nasû sa resi* (W. A. I. ii. 30, 4; 26, 58).

rential awe and standing humbly before him, determine therein a destiny of long-ending days, even the destiny of my life; this holy of holies, this sanctuary of the kingdom, this sanctuary of the lordship of the first-born of the gods, the prince, Merodach, which a former king had adorned with silver, I overlaid with glittering gold and rich ornament."[1] Just within the gate was the "seat" or shrine of the goddess Zarpanit, the wife of Merodach, perhaps to be identified with that Succoth-benoth whose image, we are told in the Old Testament, was made by the men of Babylon.[2]

E-Zida, "the firmly-established temple," was the chapel dedicated to Nebo, and derived its name from the great temple built in honour of that deity at Borsippa. As Nebo was the son of Merodach, it was only fitting that his shrine should stand within the precincts of his father's temple, by the side of the shrine sacred to his mother Zarpanit. It was within the shrine of Nebo, the god of prophecy, that the *parakku*, or holy of holies, was situated, where Merodach descended at the time of the great festival at the beginning of the year, and the divine oracles were announced to the attendant priests. The special *papakha* or sanctuary of Merodach himself was separate from that of his son. It went by the name of E-Kua, "the house of the oracle,"[3] and probably contained the

---

[1] See Flemming, *Die grosse Steinplatteninschrift Nebukadnezars ii.* (Göttingen, 1883).

[2] For a description of the great temple of Babylon, see George Smith's account of the inscription concerning it quoted in the Appendix.

[3] Bit-assaputi, for which the Semitic translator in W. A. I. ii. 15, 4, erroneously gives *ussabi*, through a confusion of *kua*, "oracle," with *kue*, "to sit." In ii. 15, 5, *assaputu*, or "oracle," is given as a rendering of the Accadian *namga* or *nagga* (AN) *Kua*, "the oracle of the god

LECTURE II.

golden statue of Bel mentioned by Hêrodotos. Nebuchadnezzar tells us that he enriched its walls with "glittering gold." Beyond it rose the stately *ziggurat*, or tower of eight stages, called E-Temen-gurum, "the house of the foundation-stone of heaven and earth." As was the case with the other towers of Babylonia and Assyria, its topmost chamber was used as an observatory. No temple was complete without such a tower; it was to the Babylonian what the high-places were to the inhabitants of a mountainous country like Canaan. It takes us back to an age when the gods were believed to dwell in the visible sky, and when therefore man did his best to rear his altars as near to them as possible. "Let us build us a city and a tower," said the settlers in Babel, "whose top may reach unto heaven."

The Babylonian Bel, accordingly, was Merodach, who watched over the fortunes of Babylon and the great temple there which had been erected in his honour. He was not the national god of Babylonia, except in so far as the city of Babylon claimed to represent the whole of Babylonia; he was simply the god of the single city of Babylon and its inhabitants. He was but one Baal out of many Baalim, supreme only when his worshippers were themselves supreme. It was only when a Nebuchadnezzar or a Khammuragas was undisputed master of Babylonia that the god they adored became "the prince of the gods." But the other gods maintained their

---

Kua." In ii. 62, 41, *mâ Kua* is explained to be "the ship of Merodach." *Kua* is represented ideographically by the character KHA, which was pronounced *kua* when signifying "to proclaim" (*nabu*) or "announce an oracle." Merodach was entitled Kua as "god of the oracle" whose "prophet" and interpreter was Nebo. For *asapu* and *asipu*, "the diviner" or "oracle-giver," see above, p. 51.

separate positions by his side, and in their own cities would have jealously resented any interference with their ancient supremacy. As we have seen, Nabonidos brought upon himself the anger of heaven because he carried away the gods of Marad and Kis and other towns to swell the train of Merodach in his temple at Babylon.

We can now therefore appreciate at its true value the language of Nebuchadnezzar when he speaks thus of his god:

"To Merodach, my lord, I prayed; I began to him my petition; the word of my heart sought him, and I said: 'O prince that art from everlasting, lord of all that exists, for the king whom thou lovest, whom thou callest by name, as it seems good unto thee thou guidest his name aright, thou watchest over him in the path of righteousness! I, the prince who obeys thee, am the work of thy hands; thou createst me and hast entrusted to me the sovereignty over multitudes of men, according to thy goodness, O lord, which thou hast made to pass over them all. Let me love thy supreme lordship, let the fear of thy divinity exist in my heart, and give what seemeth good unto thee, since thou maintainest my life.' Then he, the first-born, the glorious, the first-born of the gods, Merodach the prince, heard my prayer and accepted my petition."[1]

Once more:

"To Merodach, my lord, I prayed and lifted up my hand: 'O Merodach, (my) lord, first-born of the gods, the mighty prince, thou didst create me, and hast entrusted to me the dominion over multitudes of men; as my own dear life do I love the height of thy court; among all mankind have I not seen a city of the earth fairer than thy city of Babylon. As I have loved the fear of thy divinity and have sought after thy lordship, accept the lifting up of my hands, hearken to my petition, for I the king am the adorner (of thy shrine), who rejoices thy heart, appointed a royal priest, the adorner of all thy fortresses. By thy command, O Merodach, the merciful one, may the temple I have built endure for ever, and may I be satisfied with its fulness.'"[2]

---

[1] From the East India House Inscription, Col. i. 52—ii. 5.
[2] Col. ix. 45—x. 5.

Here Merodach, it will be observed, though "lord of all that exists," is nevertheless only the first-born of the gods. There were gods older than he, just as there were cities older than Babylon. He could not therefore be absolute lord of the world; it was only within Babylon itself that this was the case; elsewhere his rule was shared with others. Hence it was that while Nebuchadnezzar as a native of Babylon was the work of his hands, outside Babylon there were other creators and other lords. This fact is accentuated in an inscription of Nabonidos, belonging to the earlier part of his reign, in which Merodach is coupled with the Moon-god of Ur and placed on an equal footing with him.

One of the epithets applied by Nebuchadnezzar to Merodach is that of *riminu*, or "merciful." It is indeed a standing epithet of the god. Merodach was the intercessor between the gods and men, and the interpreter of the will of Ea, the god of wisdom. In an old bilingual hymn he is thus addressed:[1] "Thou art Merodach, the merciful lord who loves to raise the dead to life." The expression is a remarkable one, and indicates that the Babylonians were already acquainted with a doctrine of the resurrection at an early period. Merodach's attribute of mercy is coupled with his power to raise the dead. The same expression occurs in another of these bilingual hymns, which I intend to discuss in a future Lecture.[2] The whole hymn is addressed to Merodach, and was doubtless used in the religious services of E-Sagila. The beginning and end are unfortunately lost. Where the hymn first becomes legible, we read:

---

[1] W. A. I. iv. 19. 1. 11 [2] W. A. I. iv. 29, 1.

"(Thou art) the king of the land, the lord of the world!
O first-born of Ea, omnipotent over heaven and earth.[1]
O mighty lord of mankind, king of (all) lands,
(Thou art) the god of gods,
(The prince) of heaven and earth who hath no rival,
The companion of Anu and Bel (Mul-lil),
The merciful one among the gods,
The merciful one who loves to raise the dead to life,
Merodach, king of heaven and earth,
King of Babylon, lord of É-sagila,
King of E-Zida, king of E-makh-tilla (the supreme house of life),
Heaven and earth are thine!
The circuit of heaven and earth is thine,
The incantation that gives life is thine,
The breath[2] that gives life is thine,
The holy writing[3] of the mouth of the deep is thine:
Mankind, even the black-headed race (of Accad),[4]
All living souls that have received a name, that exist in the world,
The four quarters of the earth wheresoever they are,
All the angel-hosts of heaven and earth
(Regard) thee and (lend to thee) an ear."

It is impossible to read this hymn without being struck by the general similarity of tone that exists between it

---

[1] Accadian, "filling heaven and earth."

[2] *Ivat*, Heb. *Khavváh*, or "Eve."

[3] *Musaru*, perhaps the "Musaros Oannês" of Bêrôssos. Ea, the god of the deep and of the city of Eridu, was the Oannês of Bêrôssos, and not only the god of wisdom and author of Babylonian culture, but himself a writer of books (see W. A. I. iv. 55, 7), which proceeded as it were out of his mouth.

[4] The precise meaning of this expression, which is frequent in the hymns, is uncertain. It may refer to the custom of wearing long black hair, though in this case we should have expected the phrase to be "black-haired" rather than "black-headed." As, however, M. Dieulafoy's excavations on the site of Susa have brought to light enamelled bricks of the Elamite period on which a black race of mankind is portrayed, it may mean that the primitive Sumerian population of Chaldæa was really black-skinned.

and another hymn which is addressed to the Sun-god. Let us hear what the latter has to say to us:[1]

> "O lord, the illuminator of darkness, thou that openest the face of the sick!
> Merciful god, planter of the lowly, supporter of the weak,
> Unto thy light look the great gods,
> The spirits of the earth all behold thy face.
> The language of hosts as one word thou directest,
> Smiting their heads they behold the light of the midday sun.
> Like a wife thou behavest thyself, cheerful and rejoicing,
> Yea, thou art their light in the vault of the far-off sky.
> In the broad earth thou art their illumination.
> Men far and wide behold thee and rejoice.
> The mighty gods have smelled a sweet savour,
> The holy food of heaven, the wine (of the sacrifice) ....
> Whosoever has not turned his hand to wickedness ....
> They shall eat the food (he offers, shall receive the sacrifice he makes ?)."

Like Merodach, the Sun-god also is "the merciful god." Like Merodach, too, it is to him that gods and men alike turn their gaze. Even the power of Merodach of raising the dead to life is ascribed to him. A hymn to Samas the Sun-god begins with the following words:

> "O Sun-god, king of heaven and earth, director of things above and below,
> O Sun-god, thou that clothest the dead with life, delivered by thy hands,
> Judge unbribed, director of mankind,
> Supreme is the mercy of him who is the lord over difficulty,
> Bidding the child and offspring come forth, light of the world,
> Creator of all thy universe, the Sun-god art thou."[2]

May we not conclude, then, that originally Merodach also was a solar deity, the particular Sun-god, in fact, whose worship was carried on at Babylon?

---

[1] W. A. I. iv. 19, 2.   [2] S 947, *Obv.* 3—8.

The conclusion is verified by the express testimony of the ritual belonging to Merodach's temple E-Sagila. Here we read that

"In the month Nisan, on the second day, two hours after nightfall, the priest must come and take of the waters of the river, must enter into the presence of Bel; and putting on a stole in the presence of Bel, must say this prayer: 'O Bel, who in his strength has no equal! O Bel, blessed sovereign, lord of the world, seeking after the favour of the great gods, the lord who in his glance has destroyed the strong, lord of kings, light of mankind, establisher of faith! O Bel, thy sceptre is Babylon, thy crown is Borsippa, the wide heaven is the dwelling-place of thy liver.... O lord of the world, light of the spirits of heaven, utterer of blessings, who is there whose mouth murmurs not of thy righteousness, or speaks not of thy glory, and celebrates not thy dominion? O lord of the world, who dwellest in the temple of the Sun, reject not the hands that are raised to thee; be merciful to thy city Babylon, to E-Sagila thy temple incline thy face; grant the prayers of thy people the sons of Babylon.'"[1]

Nothing can be more explicit than the statement that E-Sagila, the temple of Merodach, was also the temple of the Sun. We thus come to understand the attributes that are ascribed to Merodach and the language that is used of him. He is "the light of the spirits of heaven," even as the Sun-god, in the hymn I quoted just now, is "the illuminator of darkness" whose face is beheld by the spirits of the earth. The wide heaven is naturally his dwelling-place, and he raises the dead to life as the sun of spring revivifies the dead vegetation of winter.

The part that he plays in the old mythological poems, in the poems, that is, which embody the ancient myths and legends of Babylonia, is now fully explained. One of the most famous of these was the story of the combat between Merodach and Tiamat, the dragon of darkness

---

[1] W. A. I. iv. 46. For a fuller account of this hymn, see above, p. 80.

and chaos. Merodach advances to the fight armed with a club and bow which Anu had placed in his hand and which subsequently became a constellation, as well as with his own peculiar weapon which hung behind his back. It was shaped like a sickle, and is the ἅρπη or *khereb* with which Greek mythology armed the Asiatic hero Perseus. The struggle was long and terrible. Tiamat opened her mouth to swallow the god, but he thrust a storm-wind down her throat, and the monster was burst asunder, while her allies fled in terror before the victorious deity. The combat is represented in stone in one of the Assyrian bas-reliefs now in the British Museum. There we can see the demon as she appeared to the Assyrians, with claws and wings, a short tail, and horns upon the head. When we remember the close parallelism that exists between this conflict of Merodach with Tiamat, and the war recorded in the Apocalypse between Michael and "the great dragon," it is difficult not to trace in the lineaments of Tiamat the earliest portraiture of the mediæval devil.

Another myth in which Merodach again appears as champion of the bright powers of day in their eternal struggle against night and storm, is the myth which describes in but thinly-veiled language the eclipse of the moon. We are there told how "the seven wicked spirits, the seven ministers of storm and tempest, who had been created in the lower part of heaven," assailed the Moon-god as he sat in his appointed seat. His comrades, the Sun-god and the Evening Star whom "Bel" had enjoined to share with him the sovereignty of the "lower heaven" or visible sky, fled from before the coming attack, and Sin, the Moon-god, was left alone to face his enemies. But

"Bel" beheld "the eclipse" of the lord of night, and Merodach was sent to rescue him and restore once again the light of the moon. Arrayed in "glistening armour," with a helmet of "light like fire" upon his head, he went forth accordingly against the powers of darkness, and the battle ended in his favour, like that against the dragon.

The Bel of this legend, who has settled the places of the Sun and the Moon in the sky, is not the Babylonian Bel, but the older Bel of Nipur, from whom Merodach, the Bel of Babylon, had afterwards to be distinguished. The Accadian original of the poem belongs to a very early epoch, before the rise of Babylon, when the supreme Bel of the Semitic inhabitants of Babylonia was still the god whom the Accadians called Mul-lilla, "the lord of the lower world." This Bel or Mul-lilla fades into the background as the Semitic element in Babylonian religion became stronger and the influence of Babylon greater, though the part that he played in astronomical and cosmological lore, as well as his local cult at Nipur, kept his memory alive; while the dreaded visitants of night, the demoniac *lilu* and *lilat* or *lilith*, from the lower world, preserved a faint memory of the spirits of which he had once been the chief. One by one, however, the attributes that had formerly attached to the older Bel were absorbed by the younger Bel of Babylon. It was almost as it was in Greece, where the older gods were dethroned by their own offspring; in the Babylonia of Nebuchadnezzar and Nabonidos, it was the younger gods—Merodach, Sin and Samas—to whom vows were the most often made and prayer the most often ascended. Such was the latest result of the local character of Babylonian worship: the younger gods were the gods of the younger Babylonian cities, and the god of Babylon, though he might be termed "the first-born of the gods," was in one sense the youngest of them all.

The title, however, "first-born of the gods" was of the same nature as the other title, "prince of the world," bestowed upon him by his grateful worshippers. It meant little else than that Babylon stood at the head of the world, and that its god must therefore be the first-born, not of one primæval deity, but of all the primæval deities acknowledged in Chaldæa. According to the earlier faith, he was the first-born of Ea only. Ea was god of the deep, both of the atmospheric deep upon which the world floats, and of that watery deep, the Okeanos of Homer, which surrounds the earth like a coiled serpent. All streams and rivers were subject to his sway, for they flowed into that Persian Gulf which the ignorance of the primitive Chaldæan imagined to be the ocean-stream itself. It was from the Persian Gulf that tradition conceived the culture and civilisation of Babylonia to have come, and Ea was therefore lord of wisdom as well as lord of the deep. His son Merodach was the minister of his counsels, by whom the commands of wisdom were carried into practice. Merodach was thus the active side of his father Ea; to use the language of Gnosticism, he was the practical activity that emanates from wisdom.

Ea, however, was not the god of Babylon, nor was his name of Semitic origin. He watched over the destinies of "the holy city" of Eridu, now Abu-Shahrein, which stood in early days on the very shores of the Persian Gulf. How Merodach came to be regarded as his son we can only guess. Perhaps Babylon had been a colony of Eridu; perhaps it was from Eridu that the culture associated with the name of Ea first made its way to Babylon. We must be content with the fact that from time immemorial Merodach had been the firstborn of Ea, and that therefore between Eridu and Babylon a very close connection must have existed in pre-historic times.

Was Merodach himself an Accadian or a Semitic deity? The names of the kings belonging to the first dynasty of Babylon are mostly Semitic; it might therefore be supposed that the deity they worshipped was Semitic also. And so undoubtedly was the Merodach of the historical age, the great Bel or Baal of Babylon. But we must remember that the foundation of Babylon went back into the dim night of the past far beyond the era of its first dynasty of Semitic kings, and that its very name was but a translation of the older Ka-dimira, "gate of the god." The temple of Merodach, moreover, bore, up to the last, not a Semitic, but an Accadian designation. As we shall see, along with the older culture the Semitic settlers in Babylonia borrowed a good deal of the theology of the Accadian people, modifying it in accordance with their own beliefs, and identifying its gods and demons with their own Baalim. It would not be surprising, then, if we found that Merodach also had once been an Accadian divinity, though his attributes, and perhaps also his name, differed very considerably from those of the Semitic Bel. Even after the Romans had identified their Saturn with the Kronos of the Greeks, the essential characteristics of the two deities remained altogether different.

In the legend of the assault of the seven evil spirits

upon the Moon—a legend which, unlike the hymns to Merodach, goes back to the pre-Semitic epoch—the god whom the Semitic translator has identified with Merodach is called in the Accadian original Asari-uru-duga, "the chief who does good to man." He receives his title from the fact that, like the Semitic Merodach, he is the son of Ea, from whom he conveys to mankind the charms and philtres and other modes of healing and help which a belief in sorcery invented. But there is little that is solar about him. On the contrary, he is distinguished from the Sun-god; and if he fights against the storm-demons with his helmet of light, it is because he is one of the bright powers of day who benefit mankind. The fire-god is his minister, but he is himself little more than the personified agency who carries the wisdom of Ea to gods and men. It is in this way that he is regarded as the god of life: the spells taught him by Ea are able, if need be, to recover the sick and raise even the dead to life. Hence he receives the title of Asari-nam-tila, "the chief of life." The title, however, was justified only by the creed of the sorcerer, not yet by the worship of the solar Bel, the "merciful" lord.

Whether the name Maruduk (Merodach) were Accadian or Semitic in origin, I cannot say. If it is Semitic, it has so changed its form that its etymology is no longer recognisable. It may be merely a Semitic transformation of the Accadian Uru-dug, "benefactor of man;" in any case, its origin was already forgotten in the days when the Babylonians first began to speculate on the derivation of their words. When first we meet with it in Semitic texts, it is expressed by two ideographs, which read Amar-ud, "the heifer of day." This is a punning reference to the old Accadian notion of the sky as a ploughed field through which the Sun drew the share in his annual journey. Under this aspect, the Sun was termed by the Accadians Gudibir, "the bull of light;" hence when Merodach became a Sun-god, he was identified with the ancient Gudibir, and astrology taught that he was one and same with each of the twelve zodiacal signs.[1]

We have thus been able, in spite of the imperfection of our documents, to trace the history of the patron-god of Babylon from the time when he was as yet merely the interpreter of the Accadian Ea, merely a water-spirit rising with the dawn out of the Persian Gulf, to the time when he became the Semitic Sun-god Bel, and eventually the head of the Babylonian Pantheon. But we have seen at the same time that up to the last he remained essentially local in character; if he was lord of the other gods, it was only because the king of Babylon was lord also of other cities and lands. It is not until

---

[1] Halévy has proposed to see in the name of Maruduk the Semitic *mar-utuki*, "the lord of demons." This, however, is worse than the Assyrian play upon the name, and takes no account of the fact that *maru* in Assyro-Babylonian means only "son," never "lord," and that *utuki* contains a *t* and not a *d*. In W. A. I. ii. 48, 34, the Sun-god, it is true, is called Utuki, but this word has nothing to do with *udu*, "the day," but is the Accadian *utuk* or "spirit." The Sun-god, in fact, was addressed as "the great spirit." If a conjecture is permitted, I would propose to see in Maruduk a Semitised form of the Accadian Muru-dug, "he who benefits man," the Aśari of the full title being omitted. *Muru*, whence *uru*, "man," is a dialectic side-form of *mulu*. But the vowel of the first syllable of Maruduk creates a difficulty, and since the Babylonians had forgotten the origin of the name, it is not likely that we shall be more successful than they were in discovering it. Perhaps Delitzsch is right (*Wo lag das Paradies*, p. 228) in seeing in Maruduk *mar-Urudug*, "the son of Eridu." At all events, Merodach is called "the son of Eridu" in W. A. I. iv. 8, 41, and other places. Maruduk is frequently contracted into Marduk.

Babylonia ceases to be an independent power that this local conception of the great Babylonian divinity tends to disappear. At Babylon, Cyrus, the foreigner from Elam, becomes the favourite and the worshipper of Bel-Merodach, and the priests of Merodach even pretend that he had been the god's favourite before he came to Babylon as its master and conqueror. Although, therefore, it is only in Babylonia that Merodach is the god of Cyrus, as he had been the god of Nebuchadnezzar, the fact that Cyrus was not a Babylonian necessarily enlarged the old conception of Bel and gave to him a universal character. From this time onwards, Merodach was more and more the god, not of the Babylonians alone, but of all men everywhere; when the Greek kings of Asia caused inscriptions to be written in the Babylonian language and writing, Merodach takes the place of Zeus, and, as the grandson of Aua or Eôa, "the dawn," is identified with the Memnon of Homeric story.[1]

---

[1] In the cuneiform inscription of Antiokhos Sôtêr, published by Strassmaier in the *Verhandlungen des fünften Orientalisten-Congresses*, ii. 1, pp. 139—142, Merodach is called (l. 20) "the offspring of the god who is the son of Aua" (*Abil Aua*). In lines 34—36, Nebo is called "the son of E-Saggil, the first-born of Aśari the chief (*ristu*), the offspring of the god who is the son of Aua the queen." Here Aua is represented as a goddess, and since her son was the father of Merodach, she must correspond to the goddess Zikum of the early texts. Halévy, confounding her with Ea, has gone on to identify Ea with the Hebrew Yahveh—an identification which, it is needless to say, is phonetically impossible. Aua is obviously the Greek Eôa, either the accusative of Ἡώς or the feminine of the corresponding adjective. From the time of Ktêsias, Memnôn, the son of the goddess Eôs, had been made an Assyro-Babylonian prince, and the resemblance of the name of Ea to Eôs may have suggested the idea of associating him with Merodach, the lord of Babylon. Teutamos, with his double Teutæos, the king by whom, according to Ktêsias, Memnôn was sent to the help of Priam, is simply "the man of the sea" or *tavtim*, the name by

But already before the age of Cyrus there was one portion of the Assyro-Babylonian world in which the narrower local view of Merodach had perforce disappeared. This was Assyria. The local gods of Babylonia had been carried into Assyria by its Semitic settlers, or else introduced into the cultivated circle of the court by the literary classes of later days. Merodach was necessarily among the latter. Certain of the Assyrian kings, or at least their scribes, invoke Merodach with the same fervour as the kings of Babylon. Shalmaneser II. calls him "the prince of the gods," just as a pious Babylonian would have done; and the monarchs of the second Assyrian empire, who were crowned at Babylon as the German princes were crowned at Rome, consider themselves placed by the act under the patronage of the Babylonian god.[1] Although, therefore, the earlier Assyrian kings avoid the mention of Merodach, and the introduction of his name into a specifically Assyrian inscription is due either to the affectation of learning or to a claim to the throne of Babylon, the very fact that the name was introduced altered the conception under which

---

which the sea-coast of Babylonia, with its capital Eridu, was known. Aua has, of course, nothing to do with the god Au, "the wind," a title of Rimmon, which forms part of the proper name Au-nahdi (K 344. 6).

[1] To "take the hand of Bel" was equivalent to recognition as king of Babylon. Possibly it denoted that the person who performed the ceremony had entered the holy of holies in which the image of Bel-Merodach stood—an act permitted only to the high-priest or the king in his office of high-priest (*sakkanaku*). The *sakkanaku* is sometimes identical with the king, sometimes distinguished from the king (e.g. W. A. I. i. 64. ix. 64), and the *sakkanaku* of Babylon was a special title (thus Esarhaddon calls himself "*sakkanaku* of Babylon," but "king of Sumer and Accad," W. A. I. i. 48, No. 6). Like *sangu*, the word expressed servitude to the god.

Merodach was regarded, and loosened the bonds of his connection with a particular locality. In Assyria at least, Bel-Merodach was as much a universal god as the older gods of the celestial hierarchy.

This transformation of his nature was aided by the inevitable confusion that arose between Bel-Merodach and the older Bel. To such an extent was this confusion carried, that we find Assur-bani-pal describing Merodach as "Bel, the son of Bel." When such a statement could be made in the learned court of Assur-bani-pal, it is clear that to the ordinary Assyrian "the son of Ea" of ancient Babylonian belief had been absorbed into the solar Bel, the supreme divinity of the southern kingdom.

Even at Babylon, however, Merodach did not stand alone. He shared his divine honours, as we have seen, with his wife Zarpanitu and his son Nebo. The old Accadian cult seems to have had a fancy for trinities or triads, originating perhaps in the primary astronomical triad of the Sun-god, the Moon-god and the Evening Star. The Accadian triad usually consisted of male deities. The Semites, however, as I hope to point out in the next Lecture, introduced a new idea, that of sex, into the theology of the country. Every god was provided with his female reflection, who stood to him in the relation of the wife to the husband. Baal, accordingly, had his female reflex, his "face" as it was termed, Bilat or Beltis. By the side of the Baal of Babylon, therefore, stood Beltis, "the lady" by the side of her "lord." Her local name was Zarpanitu, which a punning etymology subsequently turned into Zir-banitu, "creatress of seed,"[1] sometimes written Zir-panitu, with an obvious

---

[1] So in S 1720, 23 (AN) *Zi-ir-ba-ni-tuv*, W. A. I. ii. 67, 12.

play on the word *panu*, or "face." Zarpanitu was of purely Semitic origin. But she was identified with an older Accadian divinity, Gasmu, "the wise one,"[1] the fitting consort of a deity whose office it was to convey the wishes of the god of wisdom to suffering humanity. The Accadian goddess, however, must originally have stood rather in the relation of mother than of wife to the primitive Merodach. She was entitled "the lady of the deep," "the mistress of the abode of the fish," and "the voice of the deep."[2] Hence she must have ranked by the side of Ea, the fish-god and "lord of the deep;" and in the title "voice" or "incantation of the deep," we may see a reference to the ideas which caused Ea to become the god of wisdom, and brought the fish-god Oannes out of the Persian Gulf to carry culture and knowledge to the inhabitants of Chaldæa. In the roar of the sea-waves, the early dwellers on the shores of the Gulf must have heard the voice of heaven, and their prophets and diviners must have discovered in it a revelation of the will of the gods. It is not surprising, therefore, if Zarpanit was specially identified with the goddess Lakhamun, who was worshipped in the sacred island of Dilmun, or with the goddess Elagu, whose name was revered in the mountains of Elam.[3]

---

[1] W. A. I. ii. 48, 37. The Accadian *gasam* is translated *mudû, enqu*, in 82. 8—16, 1, *Obv.* 19.

[2] W. A. I. ii. 54. 62, 55, 57. Other titles were "the lady of the city of Kurnun," though "the goddess Kurnun" was identified with Tasmit (W. A. I. ii. 48, 39), and Eru or Erua (W. A. I. ii. 54. 60, 59, S 1720, 2). It is probable that she was identified with Nina the fish-goddess, the daughter of Ea.

[3] W. A. I. ii. 54. 58, 65. The name is probably connected with that of the cosmogonic deities Lakhma and Lakhama, with the same

LECTURE II.

In Semitic days, Zarpanit, the inheritor of all these old traditions and worships, fell from her high estate. She ceased to be the goddess of wisdom, the voice of the deep revealing the secrets of heaven to the diviner and priest; she became merely the female shadow and companion of Merodach, to whom a shrine was erected at the entrance to his temple. Her distinctive attributes all belong to the pre-Semitic epoch; with the introduction of a language which recognised gender, she was lost in the colourless throng of Ashtaroth or Baalat, the goddesses who were called into existence by the masculine Baalim.

Zarpanit, however, had something to do with the prominence given to Nebo in the Babylonian cult. Nebo, the son of Merodach and Zarpanitu, had, as we have seen, a chapel called E-Zida within the precincts of the great temple of his father. E-Zida, "the constituted house," derived its name from the great temple of Borsippa, the suburb of Babylon, the ruins of which are now known to travellers as the Birs-i-Nimrúd. Borsippa, it would seem, had once been an independent town, and Nebo, or the prototype of Nebo, had been its protecting deity. In the middle of the city rose E-Zida, the temple of Nebo and Nana Tasmit, with its holy of holies, "the supreme house of life," and its lofty tower termed "the house of the seven spheres of heaven and earth." It had been founded, though never finished, according to Nebuchadnezzar, by an ancient king. For long centuries it had remained a heap of ruin, until restored by Nebuchadnezzar, and legends had grown up thickly around

---

termination as that which we find in the name of Dilmun or Dilvun itself.

it. It was known as the *tul ellu*, "the pure" or "holy mound," and one of the titles of Nebo accordingly was "god of the holy mound."[1]

The word Nebo is the Semitic Babylonian Nabiu or Nabû. It means "the proclaimer," "the prophet," and thus indicates the character of the god to whom it was applied. Nebo was essentially the proclaimer of the mind and wishes of Merodach. He stood to Merodach in the same relation that an older mythology regarded Merodach as standing to Ea. While Merodach was rather the god of healing, in accordance with his primitively solar nature, Nebo was emphatically the god of science and literature. The communication of the gifts of wisdom, therefore, which originally emanated from Ea, was thus shared between Merodach and his son. At Babylon, the culture-god of other countries was divided into two personalities, the one conveying to man the wisdom that ameliorates his condition, the other the knowledge which finds its expression in the art of writing.

This division was due to the local character of Babylonian religion which I have tried to bring into relief. When Babylon became the centre of the Babylonian monarchy, Borsippa was already its suburb. But the suburb had a past life and history of its own, which gathered round its great temple and the god who was worshipped there. When, therefore, Borsippa was ab-

---

[1] W. A. I. ii. 54, 71. Anu was "the king of the holy mound," but in M 602, 14, Lugal-girra, who was identified with Nergal, is brought into connection with it. In the legend of the Tower of Babel (K 3657. ii. 1), reference is made to the "divine king of the holy mound." "The king who comes forth from the holy mound" was one of "the three great" or secret "names of Anu" (W. A. I. iii. 68, 19), while "the goddess of the holy mound" was Istar (iii. 68, 27).

sorbed into Babylon, its god was absorbed at the same time; he became one of the triad worshipped by the pious Babylonian, and was accounted the son of the god of the larger city. But he still retained the proud title of *bilu asaridu*, " the first-born Baal;"[1] and it is possible that the true signification of the name of his sanctuary is not "the constituted house," but "house of the constituted" or "legitimate son."[2] Up to the last, moreover, Nebo maintained all his local rights. He was domesticated, it is true, in Babylon, but he continued to be the god of Borsippa, and it was there that his true and original temple lifted its tower to the sky.[3]

We have only to glance over the titles which were given to Nebo to see how thoroughly the conception of "the prophet" was associated with that of "the writer." He is not only "the wise," "the intelligent," "the creator of peace," "the author of the oracle;"[4] he is also "the creator of the written tablet," "the maker of writing," "the opener" and "enlarger of the ear."[5] Assur-bani-pal is never weary of telling us, at the end of the documents his scribes had copied from their Babylonian originals, that "Nebo and Tasmit had given him broad ears (and) endowed (him) with seeing eyes," so that

---

[1] W. A. I. ii. 60, 30 (K 104). Under this title he was identified with En-zag of Dilmun (W. A. I. ii. 54, 66), whose name occurs in an inscription found by Capt. Durand in the islands of Bahrein (Jrl. R. A. S. xii. 2, 1880). *Zag*, it seems, signified "first-born" in the language of Dilvun. The proper name of the god of Dilvun to whom the title was given was Pâti (K 104), or Wuati (W. A. I. ii. 54, 67), as it is also written.

[2] See Tiele, *De Hoofdtempel van Babel en die van Borsippa* (1886).

[3] Borsippa is called "the second Babylon (Din-Tir)," K 4309, 23.

[4] W. A. I. ii. 60, 33. [5] W. A. I. ii. 60. 34, 45, 44.

he had "written, bound together and published the store of tablets, a work which none of the kings who had gone before had undertaken, even the secrets of Nebo, the list of characters as many as exist." In the literary dialect of the Semitic epoch, Nebo went by the Accadian name of *dim-sar*, "the scribe," and the ideograph by which he is sometimes denoted was regarded by the Semitic literati as signifying "the maker of intelligence" and "the creator of writing."[1]

These, however, were not the only titles that Nebo bore. He was also "the bond of the universe," and "the overseer of the angel-hosts of heaven and earth."[2] The latter office might be explained as derived from his duties as scribe of the gods; but it is hard to discover what connection there could be between the first title and his association with literature. Light is thrown upon it, however, by the fact that the *ziggurrat* or tower of his temple at Borsippa had the name of "the house of the seven bonds of heaven and earth." The seven "bonds" seem to represent the seven planets, or rather their stations; the tower was in seven stages, and each stage was painted so as to symbolise the colours symbolical of the several planets. Nebo must, therefore, have once been an elemental god, or at all events a god connected with the chief of the heavenly bodies. We know that Babylonian astronomy made him the presiding deity of the planet Mercury, just as it made Merodach the presiding deity of Jupiter; but it cannot have been in reference to this that the tower of his

---

[1] W. A. I. ii. 60. 43, 45.

[2] W. A. I. ii. 60. 31, 28. The Accadian equivalent of the first is Â-ûr, "father of the bond."

temple was dedicated to the seven heavenly spheres. Nebo cannot well have been one of the seven himself in the conception of its builders; he must rather have been the universe in which the seven spheres were set.

We shall thus reach the true explanation of the ideograph by which he was commonly denoted, and which has been translated "the maker of wisdom," "the creator of writing," by the Semitic scribes. But such translations are mere glosses. The ideograph signifies nothing more than "maker" or "creator," and points to a time when the local god of Borsippa was something more than the son of Merodach and the patron of the literary class. He was, in the belief of his worshippers at Borsippa, the supreme god, the creator of the world.

Now there are traces of an old Accadian notion of the universe according to which "the deep" was a flowing stream which surrounded the earth like the Okeanos of Homer. It was sometimes compared to a snake, sometimes to a rope, and was then called "the rope of the great god." The spirit or deity who personified it was Innina.[1] (In)nina seems to be the divinity who in later days was assumed to have given a name to Nineveh, and the name is to be explained as meaning "the god Nin,"

---

[1] W. A. I. ii. 51, 45—49, where "the river of the snake" is described as being also "the river of the rope of the great god," "the river of the great deep," "the river of the sheepcote of the ghost-world," and "the river of Innina." In 82. 8—16, 1, *Obv.* 5, *innana* is given as the Accadian pronunciation of the ideograph denoting "a goddess," the initial syllable being only a weakening of the determinative AN, "divinity." Nina and Nana are merely dialectic forms of the same word, which in the genderless Accadian meant indifferently "lord" and "lady," though more usually "lady." Nina seems to have been the pronunciation of the word at Eridu, Nana at Erech. At all events Nina was the daughter of Ea.

or "the divine lord," just as Innana means "the goddess Nana," "the divine lady." It will be remembered that the worship of Nana was associated with that of Nebo in his temple at Borsippa. The name of Borsippa itself, moreover, is sometimes written in a punning fashion by the help of ideographs which would read in Accadian Bat-śi-aabba, "the fortress of the horn of the sea," as if it had once been held to stand on a "horn" or inlet of the Persian Gulf. It is therefore possible that Innina may have been the primitive Nebo of Borsippa, and that, like the Ea of southern Babylonia, he may have been regarded as himself the great "deep." If so, we should have an explanation of his title "the bond" or "rope of the universe," that ocean-stream, in fact, which seemed to bind together the heavens and the earth. It seems to be the same as "the bond" or "rope of the world" commemorated by Accadian mythology (W. A. I. ii. 29, 62), in curious parallelism to "the golden cord" of Homer (*Il.* viii. 19), which Zeus offered to let the other gods hang from heaven to earth, in the vain endeavour to drag him down from the upper end of it.

How the old demiurgic god of Borsippa, the symbolisation of the deep which wound like a rope round the nether world, became the prophet-god Nebo of the Semites, is difficult to understand. There is apparently no connection between them. The prophet-god of the Accadians was Tutu, the setting sun, who is said to "prophesy before the king." The legends, however, which attached themselves to the name of Ea show that the Accadians associated together the ideas of wisdom and of that primordial deep of which the Persian Gulf was the visible manifestation; in so far, therefore, as the primitive god of Borsippa was the deep, he might also have been considered to have been the author of knowledge and intelligence. Indeed, as creator of the universe he must have been credited with a certain degree of wisdom.

It is possible, however, that the mediation between the demiurge of Borsippa and the Semitic Nebo was due to a confusion of the latter with an entirely different god named Nuzku. Nuzku probably signified in Accadian "the brilliance of the daybreak;" at all events he was a solar deity, one of whose titles was "lord of the zenith;" and in the cuneiform texts his name is often used to denote the zenith, or *elat same*, "height of heaven," as it was called in Assyrian, in opposition to the god of the horizon.[1] Now the ideograph which denoted "the daybreak," and was frequently used to represent the name of Nuzku, happened also to denote a leaf; and since the Accadians had written upon the leaves and rind of the papyrus before they began to write on clay, it was employed with a certain determinative to denote the stylus or pen of the scribe. Hence Nuzku, the god of the zenith, became also Khadh, the god of the scribe's pen.

Nuzku, however, does not appear to have belonged originally to Borsippa. He is entitled "the messenger" or "angel of Mul-lil,"[2] the older Bel; and it was only

---

[1] See W. A. I. ii. 48, 55. The phrase is frequent, "From the horizon (the god Ur) to the zenith (the god Nuzku)." In ii. 54, 73, the god Ur is identified with Nebo; hence Nebo and Nuzku will have been regarded as two different phases of the Sun-god, Nebo being the Sun of the dawn, and Nuzku the Sun of midday.

[2] W. A. I. ii. 19, 56. In R 2. 1, 159, 5, Nuzku is called "the supreme messenger of E-kur." The amalgamation of Nebo and Nuzku was no doubt aided by the fact that while Nuzku was thus the mes-

when the older Bel of Nipur became merged in the younger Bel-Merodach of Babylon, that Nuzku followed the fortunes of his master and was himself domesticated in the city of the younger Bel. When the transformation was finally completed, three separate deities found themselves united in the divine patron of the literary class.[1]

Wherever the literary class went, Nebo their patron went with them. Nebo consequently became less local in character than the other divinities of the pantheon, a result that was further encouraged by the absorption of his city of Borsippa into the larger Babylon. It is not surprising, therefore, that Nebo showed a greater tendency to migration than the older and more definitely localised deities of Babylonia. A knowledge of Babylonian letters and learning was accompanied by a knowledge of the

---

senger of Mul-lil the older Bel, Nebo was the prophet and messenger of Merodach the younger Bel. The confusion between the two Bels led necessarily to a confusion between their two ministers.

[1] Up to the last, however, the priesthood of Babylon remembered that Nebo and Nuzku were originally different divinities. In the great temple of Merodach there was a separate chapel for Nuzku by the side of the great tower. Nuzku originally appears to have come from Nipur, and to have been identified with Nebo when the latter came to share with Merodach his solar character. But originally the local god of Borsippa, who as the supreme deity of the place was worshipped by the inhabitants as the creator of the universe, was not the Sun-god, but the power which bound the universe together. As this was the ocean-stream which encircled the horizon and was the home of the rising sun, it was not difficult to confound it with the morning sun itself. It seems strange that Nuzku, the messenger of "the lord of the ghost-world," and as such the morning-grey, should have come to represent the zenith; but the same transference of meaning meets us in the Assyrian verb *napakhu*, which properly refers to the rising sun, but is also used of the zenith. That Nuzku, "who goes on the left of the companions of the king," was primarily the Fire-god is expressly stated in K 170, *Rev.* 5.

Babylonian god of letters and learning. In Assyria, Nebo was honoured as much as he was in Babylonia itself. The Assyrian kings and scribes might be silent about the name of Merodach, but the name of Nebo was continually in their mouths.[1] His name and worship passed even to the distant Semitic tribes of the west. The names of places in Palestine in which his name occurs, proves that the god of prophecy was adored by Canaanites and Moabites alike. Moses, the leader and prophet of Israel, died on the peak of Mount Nebo, and cities bearing the name stood within the borders of the tribes of Reuben and Judah. When the Israelites entered upon their literary era, the old name of *roeh*, or "seer," was exchanged for the more literary one of *Nĕbî*, or "prophet."

The Semites of Babylonia provided Nebo with a wife, Tasmitu, "the hearer." She helped to open and enlarge the ears which received the divine mysteries her husband's inspiration enabled his devout servants to write down. The revolution which transferred the learning of the Babylonians from the Accadians to the Semites, transferred the patronage of the literary class from the old god Ea to his younger rivals Nebo and Tasmit.

I have dwelt thus long on the nature and history of the three deities who shared together the great temple of Babylon, partly because our materials in regard to them are less imperfect than is the case with many of the other gods, partly because they illustrate so well the essentially local character of Babylonian religion. It is

---

[1] In the prayer to Assur, K 100, *Rev.* 18, Nebo is called "the messenger of Assur," who thus takes the place of Merodach of Babylon.

this which gives to it its peculiar complexion and furnishes the key to its interpretation. In so far as the worship of Nebo forms an exception to the general rule, it is an exception which bears out the old legal maxim that the exception proves the rule. The worship of Nebo was less local than that of other divinities, because he was specially worshipped by a class which existed in each of the local centres of the country. He alone was the god of a class rather than of a locality. Babylonian history began with separate cities, and centralisation was never carried so far as to break up the local usages and cults that prevailed in them. In the eyes of the people, the several deities remained to the last a body of equals, among whom the god of the imperial city presided, simply because he was the god of the imperial city. If Ur had taken the place of Babylon, the Moon-god of Ur would have taken the place of Bel-Merodach. The gods of Babylonia were like the local saints of Catholic Europe, not like the Greek hierarchy of Olympus, ruled by the despotic nod of Zeus.

The Semites of Babylonia thus closely resembled their brother Semites of Canaan in their fundamental conception of religion. As the Canaanite or Phœnician had "lords many," the multitudinous Baalim who represented the particular forms of the Sun-god worshipped in each locality, so too the gods of Semitic Babylonia were equally multitudinous and local—Merodach, for example, being merely the Bel or Baal of Babylon, just as Melkarth (Melech-kiryath) was the Baal of Tyre. But the parallelism extends yet further. We have seen that the rise of the prophet-god in Babylonia marks the growing importance of literature and a literary class, just as the beginning of a literary age in Israel is coeval with the change of the seer into the prophet. Now the literary age of Israel was long preceded by a literary age among their Phœnician neighbours, and its growth is contemporaneous with the closer relations that grew up between the monarchs of Israel and Hiram of Tyre. What Israel was in this respect to the Phœnicians, Assyria was to Babylonia. The Assyrians were a nation of warriors and traders rather than of students; their literature was for the most part an exotic, a mere imitation of Babylonian culture. In Babylonia, education was widely diffused; in Assyria, it was confined to the learned class. We must remember, therefore, that in dealing with Assyrian documents we are dealing either with a foreign importation or with the thoughts and beliefs of a small and special class.

This is the class from whom we have to gain our knowledge of the form of religion prevalent in Assyria. It is wholly Babylonian, with one important exception. Supreme over the old Babylonian pantheon rises the figure of a new god, the national deity of Assyria, its impersonation Assur. Assur is not merely *primus inter pares*, merely the president of the divine assembly, like Merodach; he is their lord and master in another and more autocratic sense. Like the Yahveh of Israel, he claims to be "king above all gods," that "among all gods" there is none like unto himself. In his name and through his help the Assyrian kings go forth to conquer; the towns they burn, the men they slay, the captives they take, are all his gifts. It is to destroy "the enemies of Assur," and to lay their yoke upon those who disbelieve in his name, that they lead their armies into other lands;

it is his decrees, his law, that they write upon the monuments they erect in conquered countries. The gods of Babylonia are invoked, it is true; their old Babylonian titles are accorded to them; they are called upon to curse the sacrilegious in the stereotyped phrases of the ancient literature; but it is Assur, and Assur alone, to whom the Assyrian monarch turns in moments of distress; it is Assur, and Assur alone, in whose name he subdues the infidel. Only the goddess Istar finds a place by the side of Assur.

It is not difficult to account for all this. In passing from their native homes to Assyria, the Babylonian deities lost that local character which was the very breath of their existence. How far they owe their presence in Assyrian literature to the literary class, how far they had been brought from Babylonia in early days by the people themselves, I am not prepared to say. One fact, however, is clear; in becoming Assyrian the Babylonian gods have lost both their definiteness and their rank. The invocations addressed to them lack their old genuine ring, their titles are borrowed from the literature of the southern kingdom, and their functions are usurped by the new god Assur. It is almost pitiable to find Bel-Merodach invoked, in phrases that once denoted his power above other deities, by the very kings who boast of their conquests over his people, or who even razed his city to the ground. The Assyrian, in fact, occupied much the same position as an Israelite who, while recognising the supremacy of his national God, thought it prudent or cultivated to offer at the same time a sort of inferior homage to the Baalim of Canaan.

At the outset, Assur was as much a purely local divinity

as Bel-Merodach of Babylon. He was the god of Assur (now Kaleh-Sherghat), the primitive capital of the country. But several causes conspired to occasion him to lose this purely local character, and to assume in place of it a national character. The capital of Assyria was shifted from Assur to Nineveh, and the worship of Assur, instead of remaining fixed at Assur, was shifted at the same time. Then, moreover, the importation of Babylonian deities had broken the close connection which existed in the mind of a Babylonian between the deity and the city where he was worshipped; to the Assyrian, Bel-Merodach was no longer peculiarly the patron-god of Babylon; his other attributes came instead to the front. Assyria, furthermore, from the time it first became an independent kingdom, formed an homogeneous whole; it was not divided into separate states, as was so often the case with Babylonia. A national feeling was consequently permitted to grow up, which the traditions of the old cities of Chaldæa and the frequent conquest of the country by foreigners prevented from developing in the south. Perhaps, too, the composite origin of Assur himself had something to do with the result.

The name of Assur is frequently represented by a character which among other ideographic values had that of "good." The name was accordingly explained by the Assyrians of the later historical age as "the good god," with a reference perhaps to their own words *asiru*, "righteous," and *asirtu*, "righteousness." But this was not the original signification either of the name or of the character by which it was expressed. The god so denoted was one of the primæval deities of Babylonian cosmology who bore in Accadian the title of Ana sar (An-sar), "the god of the hosts of heaven," or simply Sar, "the upper firmament." It was believed that *Ana sar* was the male principle which, by uniting with the female principle (*Ana*) *ki-sar*, "(the goddess of) the earth (and) the hosts of heaven," produced the present world. It was to this old elemental deity that the great temple of E-sarra was dedicated, whose son was said to be the god Ninip or Adar.

A fragment of Babylonian cosmogomy has been preserved to us by Damascius, a writer of the sixth century, who had access to older materials now lost. Here Ana-sar and Ki-sar are called Ἀσσωρὸς and Κισσαρὴ, and we are told of them that they were the offspring of the primæval Lakhma and Lakhama, and the progenitors of the three supreme gods, Anu, Mul-lil and Ea. The worship of these primæval divinities had been rooted in Assyria from an early period; probably the earliest Semitic emigrants from the south found it already established there. It was inevitable that before long a confusion should grow up between the name of the god An-sar or Assôr, and that of the city of Assur in which he was adored. But the city of Assur had nothing to do with the god. The name seems to be a corruption of the Accadian A-usar, or "water-bank," first corrupted by its Semitic inhabitants into Assur and then into Asur, with a possible reference to the word *asurra*, "the bed (of a river)."[1]

---

[1] The attempt has been made to show that the names of the god and of the country ought to be distinguished from one another by writing the first with *ss* and the second with a single *s*. The Assyrians, however, wrote both alike, sometimes with *ss*, sometimes with *s*; and the fact that the name of the country is often expressed by attaching the determinative affix of locality to the name of the god proves that they were not conscious of any difference, phonetic or otherwise,

The confusion between Assôr the god and Assur the city had the effect of identifying the god with his city more closely than could be the case with the divine patron of a Babylonian town. The city of Assur was itself a god: offences against the city were offences against the god; the enemies of the city were the enemies also of the god. The instinct, however, of regarding the deities they worshipped as individuals, was too deeply implanted within the mind of the Semites to allow either this fact, or the further fact that the god himself was originally a mere elemental one, to obliterate his individual and anthropomorphic character. Though Assur was the personification of the city, he was also its Baal or lord.

The transference of the centre of power from Assur to Nineveh made the anthropomorphic side of Assur's nature still more prominent. He represented now the whole nation and the central power which governed the nation. He was thus the representative at once of the people and of the king in whose hands the government of the people was centred. Assyria became "the land of the god Assur," belonging to him in much the same way as the city of Babylon belonged to Bel-Merodach. But whereas Bel-Merodach was the Baal of a particular city only, Assur was, like the Yahveh of Israel, the national god of a race.

There was yet another respect in which Assur resembled the Yahveh of Israel. There was no goddess Assurîtu by the side of Assur, as there was an Anatu by the

---

between the two. In such a matter we cannot be wiser than our Assyrian teachers.

side of Anu, a Beltis by the side of Bel.[1] If, in imitation of Babylonian usage, Bilat or Beltis is sometimes addressed as the consort of Assur, it is simply a literary affectation; Assur was not a Bel or Baal, like Merodach. Bilat is a Babylonian goddess; she is properly the wife of the older Bel, in later times identified with Zarpanit. There is no indication that Assur had a "face" or reflection; he stands by himself, and the inspiration received from him by the Assyrian kings is received from him alone. When a female divinity is invoked along with him, it is the equally independent goddess Istar or Ashtoreth.

We possess a list of the deities whose images stood in the temples of Assur at Assur and Nineveh.[2] At the head of each list the name of Assur is thrice invoked, and once his name is followed by that of Istar. There was, in fact, a special form of Istar, under which she was worshipped as "the Istar of Nineveh;" but the form was purely local, not national, arising from the existence there of a great temple dedicated to her. There was no national goddess to place by the side of the national god.

Assur consequently differs from the Babylonian gods, not only in the less narrowly local character that belongs to him, but also in his solitary nature. He is "king of all gods" in a sense in which none of the deities of Babylonia were.[3] He is like the king of Assyria himself,

---

[1] If Istar is sometimes called Assuritu, "the Assyrian," the adjective is always a mere title, and never becomes a proper name (see W. A. I. v. 1, 65). Like the title "Istar of Nineveh," it serves only to distinguish the Assyrian Istar from the Istar of Arbela.

[2] W. A. I. iii. 66.

[3] The following prayer or hymn (K 100) illustrates the way in which the learned *literati* of Assur-bani-pal's court sought to make good the

brooking no rival, allowing neither wife nor son to share in the honours which he claims for himself alone. He is

---

deficiencies of their national god, and to connect him with the deities of Babylonia:

1. "A prayer to Assur the king of the gods, ruler (*li*) over heaven and earth,
2. the father who has created the gods, the supreme first-born (of heaven and earth),
3. the supreme *muttallu* who (inclines) to counsel,
4. the giver of the sceptre and the throne.
5. (To) Nin-lil the wife of Assur, the begetter (*takkat*), the creatress of heaven (and earth),
6. who by the command of her mouth . . . .
7. (To) Sin the lord of command, the uplifter of horns, the spectacle of heaven,
8. who for delivering the message (has been appointed).
9. (To) the Sun-god, the great judge of the gods, who causes the lightning to issue forth,
10. who to his brilliant light . . . .
11. (To) Anu the lord and prince, possessing the life of Assur the father of the (great) gods.
12. (To) Rimmon the minister (*gugal*) of heaven and earth, the lord of the wind and the lightning of heaven.
14. (To) Istar the queen of heaven and the stars, whose seat (is exalted).
15. (To) Merodach the prince of the gods, the interpreter (BAR-BAR) of the spirits of heaven and (earth).
16. (To) Adar the son of Mul-lil, the giant (*gitmalu*), the first-born . . . .
17. fixed and . . . .
18. (To) Nebo the messenger of Assur (An-sar) . . . .
19. (To) Nergal the lord of might (*abari*) and strength (*dunni*), who . . . .
20. (To) the god who marches in front, the first-born . . . .
21. (To) the seven gods, the warrior deities . . . .
22. the great gods, the lords (of heaven and earth)."

On the obverse, little of which is left, mention is made of "the image of the great gods," "as many as (dwell) in the midst of the stone," and "at the opening of their holy mouth" they are asked to befriend the king "himself, his princes (*maliki*), their name and their seed."

essentially a jealous god, and as such sends forth his Assyrian adorers to destroy his unbelieving foes. Wifeless, childless, he is mightier than the Babylonian Baalim; less kindly, perhaps, less near to his worshippers than they were, but more awe-inspiring and more powerful. We can, in fact, trace in him all the lineaments upon which, under other conditions, there might have been built up as pure a faith as that of the God of Israel.

Lecture III.

THE GODS OF BABYLONIA.

In my last Lecture I have been obliged to some extent to anticipate the conclusions to which a survey of the older literature of Babylonia will lead us. I have had to refer more than once to the older gods of the land, and to point out that the Babylonian deities of the later inscriptions are only in part of purely Semitic origin, in part adaptations of earlier Accadian divinities. They are characterised, however, by one common feature; they are all alike local, belonging to the cities where their cults were established as literally as the temples in which they were adored. Merodach might, indeed, be invoked elsewhere than at Babylon, but it was only as god of Babylon that he would hear the prayer. In Assyria alone we find another order of things, more analogous to that which meets us among the Israelites; in Babylonia the gods are local Baalim as fully as they were in Phœnicia. What differences may have existed between the religious conceptions of the Phœnicians and Babylonians in this respect were but superficial, due mainly to the fact that the Phœnician cities were never amalgamated into a single empire, while Babylon succeeded in imposing its authority upon its sister towns.

There are two especially of the older gods whose names

THE GODS OF BABYLONIA. 131

have frequently recurred. These are Ea and the original Bel. Let me speak of Ea first.

Ea, as we have already seen, was the god not only of the deep, but also of wisdom. Ancient legends affirmed that the Persian Gulf—the entrance to the deep or ocean-stream—had been the mysterious spot from whence the first elements of culture and civilisation had been brought to Chaldæa. Bêrôssos, the Chaldæan historian—so at least his epitomiser Alexander Polyhistôr declared—had reported them as follows:

"At Babylon there was a great resort of people of various races who inhabited Chaldæa, and lived in a lawless manner like the beasts of the field. In the first year there appeared in that part of the Erythræan sea which borders upon Babylonia, a creature endowed with reason, by name Oannes, whose whole body (according to the account of Apollodôros) was that of a fish; under the fish's head he had another head, with feet also below similar to those of a man subjoined to the fish's tail. His voice, too, and language were articulate and human; and a representation of him is preserved even to this day.

"This being was accustomed to pass the day among men, but took no food at that season; and he gave them an insight into letters and sciences and arts of every kind. He taught them to construct houses, to found temples, to compile laws, and explained to them the principles of geometrical knowledge. He made them distinguish the seeds of the earth, and showed them how to collect the fruits; in short, he instructed them in everything which could tend to soften manners and humanise their lives. From that time, nothing material has been added by way of improvement to his instructions. Now when the sun had set, this being Oannes used to retire again into the sea, and pass the night in the deep, for he was amphibious. After this there appeared other animals like Oannes, of which Bêrôssos proposes to give an account when he comes to the history of the kings. Moreover, Oannes wrote concerning the generation of mankind, of their different ways of life, and of their civil polity."[1]

---

[1] Eusebios (*Chron.*), Cory's translation: "The other animals like Oannês," according to Abydenos (ap. Euseb. *Chron.* i. 6, Mai), were Annêdotos in the time of Amillaros, the third antediluvian king, called

A native fragment of the legend has, it is probable, been accidentally preserved among a series of extracts from various Accadian works, in a bilingual reading-book compiled for the use of Semitic students of Accadian. It reads thus:

> "To the waters their god has returned;
> into the house of (his) repose the protector descended.[1]
> The wicked weaves spells, but the sentient one grows not old.
> A wise people repeated his wisdom.
> The unwise and the slave (*literally* person) the most valued of his master forgot him;
> there was need of him and he restored (his) decrees (?)"[2]

The exact etymology of the name which appears under

Amelôn by Apollodôros, Euedôkos, Eneugamos, Eneubulos and Anêmentos in the time of Daôs (? Tammuz) the shepherd, and Anôdaphos in the time of Euedôreskhos. Apollodôros makes "the Musaros Oannês, the Annêdotos," appear in the time of Ammenôn the successor of Amelôn, another Annêdotos in the time of Daonos the shepherd, and Odakôn in the time of Euedôreskhos. A comparison of Anôdaphos and Odakôn shows the true reading to have been Anôdakôn, i.e. "Anu and Dagon (Dagan)," who are constantly associated together by Sargon, and who says of them that he had "written the laws (not "immunitas," as Winckler) of Harran by the will of Anu and Dagon." Annêdotos seems to be a Greek compound, "given by Anu." In any case, some of the successors of Oannês appear to have been derived from the legends of Erech, the city of Anu, and not, like the original Oannês, from Eridu. With the exception of the first, who is made a Babylonian, the antediluvian kings come either from Larankha, which, as we learn from the Deluge-tablet, is a corrupt reading for Surippak near Sippara, or from Panti-bibla, a Greek translation of "the country of tablets" or "books," a title given to the Accad of Sargon, according to W. A. I. ii. 51, 8. We may infer from this that the whole story of the antediluvian kings had its origin at Sippara.

[1] *Iggillum* (which does not signify "a cry of woe," as Jeremias supposes) is explained by *natsiru*, "the defender," in W. A. I. v. 28, 72. Magiru, "the obedient one," is called his throne-bearer in W. A. I. iii. 68, 7, where the Iggillum is identified with Ea.

[2] W. A. I. ii. 16. 57—71.

the Greek dress of Oannês has not yet been ascertained. Lenormant thought that it represented *Ea-khan*, "Ea the fish." But whether or not this is the case, it is certain that Oannês and Ea are one and the same. Ea, as we have seen, not only had his home in the waters of the Persian Gulf, he was also the culture-god of primitive Babylonia, the god of wisdom, the instructor of his worshippers in arts and science. An old Babylonian sermon on the duty of a prince to administer justice impartially and without bribes, declares that if "he speaks according to the injunction (or writing) of the god Ea, the great gods will seat him in wisdom and the knowledge[1] of righteousness."[2] Ea was, moreover, like Oannês, represented as partly man and partly fish. Sometimes the fish's skin is thrown over the man's back, the head of a fish appearing behind that of the man; sometimes the body of the man is made to terminate in the tail of a fish. A gem in the British Museum, on which the deity is depicted in the latter fashion, bears an inscription stating that the figure is that of "the god of pure life." Now "the god of pure life," as we are expressly informed by a rubrical gloss to a hymn in honour of the demiurge Ea (*Obv.* 5), was one of the names of Ea.

The name Ea, which is transcribed Aos by Damascius, signifies "a house," or rather "belonging to a house."[3]

---

[1] *Tudat*, to be distinguished from *Tudâtu*, "offspring," W. A. I. ii. 29, 69.

[2] W. A. I. iv. 55, 7. In a penitential psalm (W. A. I. iv. 61, 27), "the writing of Ea" is referred to as "giving rest to the heart."

[3] *Ea* is translated "house," W. A. I. ii. 15, 42; iv. 16, 48. Conversely the god Ea is represented by (AN) *E*, "the god of the house,"

Ea was therefore originally the "house-god"—a designation which it is difficult to reconcile with his aquatic character. Possibly his worship goes back to a time when the inhabitants of the coast of the Persian Gulf lived in pile-dwellings like those of Switzerland or the British Islands; possibly it belongs to a later period, when the old marine god had become the household deity of those who received his benefits and believed him to be the source of their culture. He was symbolised, it would seem, by a serpent;[1] and to this day the Zulus believe that the spirits of their ancestors are embodied in certain harmless snakes which frequent their homes. However this may be, the primæval seat of the worship of Ea was the city of *Eridu*, now represented by the mounds of Abu Shahrein on the eastern bank of the Euphrates, and not far to the south of Mugheir or Ur.

Eridu is a contracted form of the older Eri-duga, or "good city," which appears in the non-Semitic texts of northern Babylonia as Eri-zêba, with the same meaning. The place was thus a peculiarly holy spot, whose sanctity was established far and wide throughout the country. But it was not a holy city only. It is often termed,

in iv. 6, 47. This seems to be the form which has given rise to the A-os of Damascius. In O-annes the initial is due to the contraction of *ü-a*.

[1] See above, p. 116. Among the symbols of the gods on contract-stones, the serpent occupies a prominent place. According to W. A. I. ii. 59, 21, the snake-god was Serakh, the god of corn and "spirit of E-śara," whose name signified "the treading of corn" (v. 17. 31, 32), and who is called "the overseer" or "assembler of the gods of heaven and earth" (K 4415, *Rev.* 10). On the other hand, in an unnumbered fragment (M, line 10), "a snake in thy bed" (*asurra-ki*) is invoked as a curse.

more especially in the sacred texts, "the lordly city,"[1] and we are told that one of its titles was "the land of the sovereign." In historical times, however, Eridu had sunk to the condition of a second-rate or even third-rate town; its power must therefore belong to that dimly remote age of which the discoveries at Tel-loh have enabled us to obtain a few glimpses. There must have been a time when Eridu held a foremost rank among the cities of Babylonia, and when it was the centre from which the ancient culture and civilisation of the country made its way.[2]

Along with this culture went the worship of Ea, the god of Eridu, who to the closing days of the Babylonian monarchy continued to be known as Eridúga, "the god of Eridu." At the period when the first elements of Chaldæan culture were being fostered in Eridu, the city stood at the mouth of the Euphrates and on the edge of the Persian Gulf. If the growth of the alluvium at the mouths of the Euphrates and Tigris has always been the same as is the case at present (about sixty-six feet a year), this would have been at the latest about 3000 B.C.; but as the accumulation of soil has been more rapid of late, the date would more probably be about 4000 B.C. Already, therefore, the cult of Ea would have been established, and the sea-faring traders of Eridu would have placed themselves under his protection.

It will be noticed that the culture-myths of Babylonia,

---

[1] NUN-KI, pronounced Nunpê, according to 82. 8—16, 1, *Obv.* 21. EN-KI, another title of Eridu, means "land of the lord."

[2] The decay of Eridu was probably due to the increase of the delta at the head of the Persian Gulf, which made it an inland instead of a maritime city, and so destroyed its trade.

like the culture-myths of America, bring the first civiliser of the country from the sea. It is as a sea deity that Oannês is the culture-hero of the Chaldæans; it is from the depths of the Persian Gulf that he carries to his people the treasures of art and science. Two questions are raised by this fact. Was the culture of Babylonia imported from abroad; and was Ea, its god of culture, of foreign extraction?

The last great work published by Lepsius[1] was an attempt to answer the first of these questions in the affirmative. He revived the old theory of a mysterious Cushite population which carried the civilisation of Egypt to the shores of Babylonia. But to all theories of this sort there is one conclusive objection. The origin of Babylonian culture is so closely bound up with the origin of the cuneiform system of writing, that the two cannot be separated from each other. Between the hieroglyphics of Egypt, however, and the primitive pictures out of which the cuneiform characters developed, there is no traceable connection. Apart from those general analogies which we find in all early civilisations, the script, the theology and the astronomy of Egypt and Babylonia show no vestiges of a common source.

Nevertheless, there is now sufficient evidence to prove that at the very dawn of the historic period in Babylonia, maritime intercourse was being carried on between this country on the one hand and the Sinaitic Peninsula and India on the other. The evidence is as startling as it is curious.

The statues discovered by M. de Sarzec at Tel-loh,

---

[1] Introduction to his *Nubische Grammatik* (1880).

which may be roughly dated about 4000 B.C., remind every traveller who has been in Egypt of the great diorite statue of king Khephren, the builder of the second pyramid of Gizeh, which is now in the Bûlak Museum. The execution, indeed, is infinitely inferior; but the attitude, the pose, the general effect, and to a certain extent the dress, are remarkably alike. What is more, some of the Tel-loh statues are carved out of hard diorite stone. Now one of the inscriptions that accompany them affirms that the stone was brought from the land of Magan; and though in later times Magan was used to denote Lower Egypt, Dr. Oppert and myself have long ago pointed out that originally it signified the Sinaitic Peninsula. Ever since the epoch of the Third Dynasty, Egyptian garrisons had held possession of the Peninsula, and Egyptian miners had quarried there; and as the age of the fourth Egyptian Dynasty corresponds with the age which we must assign to the statues of Tel-loh, it would seem that as far back as six thousand years ago stone was conveyed by sea from the quarries of Sinai to Egypt and Babylonia, and that a school of sculpture had already arisen in that part of the world. What clinches the matter is the fact observed by Mr. Petrie, that the unit of measurement marked on the plan of the city which one of the figures of Tel-loh carries upon its lap, is the same as the unit of measurement employed by the Pyramid builders.[1]

In an opposite direction we may infer that Chaldæan traders had also made their way to the western coast of India. Apart from the existence of teak in the ruins of

---

[1] See above, p. 33.

Mugheir, an ancient Babylonian list of clothing mentions *sindhu*, or "muslin," the *sadin* of the Old Testament, the σινδών of the Greeks. That σινδών is merely "the Indian" cloth has long been recognised; and the fact that it begins with a sibilant and not with a vowel, like our "Indian," proves that it must have come to the west by sea and not by land, where the original *s* would have become *h* in Persian mouths.[1] That *sindhu* is really the same word as σινδών is shown by its Accadian equivalent, which is expressed by ideographs signifying literally "vegetable cloth."

This intercourse with other countries, and the influence which a school of sculpture in the Sinaitic Peninsula appears to have exercised upon the Babylonians, must necessarily have had much to do with the early development of Chaldæan culture, even though it were indigenous in its origin. It therefore becomes possible that Ea, the deity with whom the introduction of such a culture is associated, may also have come from abroad. At present, however, there is no proof of this, though it is quite possible that some of his features are foreign; and it is even possible that the primitive Shamanistic worship of spirits, which, as we shall see hereafter, originally characterised the religion of the Accadians, first became a worship of the god Ea through foreign influence, other spirits afterwards passing into gods when the example had once been set.

Ea, however, was not merely a god of the sea. The Persian Gulf, which formed the entrance to the ocean-

---

[1] Supposing, of course, that Iranian tribes were already settled to the east of Babylonia. In W. A. I. v. 28. 19, 20, *sindhu* is explained to be *sipat Kurri*, "cloth of Kur," and *addu*, "a veil."

THE GODS OF BABYLONIA.

stream that encircled the world, was fed by the great river on which Eridu stood. Ea accordingly was a river-god as well as a sea-god; he is entitled not only "the king of the deep," but "the king of the river"[1] also. Out of the mixture of the two arose the conception of the encircling ocean, and the further title, "god of the river of the great snake."[2] Ea was thus emphatically a water-god, the deity who presided over the watery element wherever it was found, and whose home was in the waves of the Persian Gulf.

Ea had a consort who was not at all like the Semitic goddesses we have been considering in the last Lecture. She was no pale reflexion of a male divinity, no Anat or Beltis or Zarpanit, differing from her husband only in the grammatical suffix of her name; but a genuine and independent deity, whose powers were co-extensive with those of Ea. She was known as Dav-kina or Dav-ki, "the lady of the earth," and personified the earth just as Ea personified the water. Water and earth—these were the two elements out of which the old inhabitants of Eridu believed the world to have been formed. It was the theory of Thalês in its primitive shape; the water-god at Eridu took the place occupied by the Sky-god in other cities of Babylonia. He was in fact addressed, not only as "lord of the earth," but also as "lord of heaven and earth," "the master of all created things," "the ruler of all the world," "the god of the universe," "the prince of the zenith" of heaven.[3] There is no room here for the Anu or Sky-god of northern Babylonian theology.

---

[1] W. A. I. ii. 55, 23.   [2] W. A. I. ii. 56, 27.
[3] W. A. I. ii. 58, No. 5.

Not only, then, the elements of culture and civilisation, but the created universe itself proceeded out of that watery abyss, that "deep," as it is called in our translation of the Book of Genesis, which was at once the home and the visible form of Ea. Ea was the demiurge, and a hymn exists in which he is addressed as such under each of his many titles. Thus he is invoked as "the god of pure life" "who stretches out the bright firmament, the god of good winds, the lord of hearing and obedience, creator of the pure and the impure, establisher of fertility, who brings to greatness him that is of small estate. In places difficult of access we have smelt his good wind. May he command, may he glorify, may he hearken to his worshippers. O god of the pure crown, moreover, may all creatures that have wings and fins be strong. Lord of the pure oracle who giveth life to the dead, who hath granted forgiveness to the conspiring gods, hath laid homage and submission upon the gods his foes. For their redemption did he create mankind, even he the merciful one with whom is life. May he establish and never may his word be forgotten in the mouth of the black-headed race (of Sumir) whom his hands created. As god of the pure incantation may he further be invoked, before whose pure approach may the evil trouble be overthrown, by whose pure spell the siege of the foe is removed. O god who knowest the heart, who knowest the hearts of the gods that move his compassion, so that they let not the doing of evil come forth against him, he who establishes the assembly of the gods (and knows) their hearts, who subdues the disobedient.... May he (determine) the courses of the stars of heaven; like a flock may he order all the gods.

THE GODS OF BABYLONIA. 141

May he exorcise the sea-monster of chaos; her secrets may he discover(?) and destroy for evermore. Mankind may he raise to length of days, and may he overthrow mischief(?) for future time. Since (their) places he created, he fashioned, he made strong, lord of the world is he called by name, even father Bel. The names of the angels[1] he gave unto them. And Ea heard, and his liver was soothed, and he spake thus: 'Since he has made his men strong by his name, let him, like myself, have the name of Ea. May he bear (to them) the bond of all my commands, and may he communicate all my secret knowledge through the fifty names of the great gods.' His fifty names he has pronounced, his ways he has restored; may they be observed, and may he speak as formerly. Wise and sentient, may he rule triumphantly. May father to son repeat and hand them down. May he open the ears of both shepherd and flock."[2]

The fracture which has destroyed the middle part of the hymn makes it difficult to connect together the earlier and latter portions of the poem. The poet, however, evidently wishes to show that the demiurge Bel of northern Babylonia is one and the same with the demiurge

---

[1] Or "spirits of heaven," called Igigi in Assyrian, perhaps from *agâgu*, "to be powerful." The name is ideographically expressed by the determinative of divinity followed by "twice five." Jensen, however, has shown (*Zeitschrift für Assyriologie*, i. 1), that whereas the Anúnaki or "spirits of earth" were denoted by the numeral 8 (Accadian *uśa*), the Igigi were denoted by the numeral 9 (Acc. *isimu*). It is difficult to follow his further combinations, which would connect them with the *ribu* of W. A. I. ii. 35, 37 (expressed ideographically by AN-NUN-GAL, "the great divine princes"), as well as with *ra'hebu*, the Heb. Rahab.

[2] The text has been published by George Smith in the *Transactions of the Society of Biblical Archæology*, iv. 2, and by Delitzsch in his *Assyrische Lesestücke*.

Ea of the south. It is one of the many attempts that were made in later days to harmonise and identify the various local deities of Chaldæa to whom in different localities the same attributes were assigned. The task was rendered easier by the numerous names, or rather titles, which the several deities bore. Here Ea is accredited with no less than fifty—all, too, transferred to him from the other "great gods;" and it is by a knowledge of them that the secret wisdom of Ea is communicated to both gods and men. In Babylonia, as in most primitive communities, the name was regarded as identical with the thing which it signified; hence the mystic importance attached to names and the leading part they played in exorcisms and charms.

How a water-god became the demiurge seems at first sight obscure. But it ceases to be so when we remember the local character of Babylonian religion. Ea was as much the local god of Eridu as Merodach was of Babylon, or Assur of Assyria. His connection with the water was due to the position of Eridu at the mouth of the Euphrates and on the shore of the sea, as well as to the maritime habits of its population. In other respects he occupied the same place as the patron-deities of the other great cities. And these patron-deities were regarded as creators, as those by whose agency the present world had come into existence, and by whose hands the ancestors of their worshippers had been made.

This conception of a creating deity is one of the distinguishing features of early Babylonian religion. Mankind are not descended from a particular divinity, as they are in other theologies; they are created by him. The hymn to Ea tells us that the god of Eridu was the creator of the black-headed race—that is to say, the old non-Semitic population whose primary centre and starting-point was in Eridu itself. It was as creators that the Accadian gods were distinguished from the host of spirits of whom I shall have to speak in another Lecture. The Accadian word for " god" was *dimer*, which appears as *dingir*, from an older *dingira*, in the southern dialect of Sumer. Now *dimer* or *dingir* is merely "the creator," formed by the suffix *r* or *ra*, from the verb *dingi* or *dime*, " to create." A simpler form of *dimer* is *dime*, a general name for the divine hierarchy. By the side of *dime*, *dim*, stood *gime*, *gim*, with the same meaning; and from this verb came the Sumerian name of Istar, Gingira.[1] Istar is said to have been the mother of mankind in the story of the Deluge, and as Gula, "the great" goddess, she is addressed in a prayer as " the mother who has borne the men with the black heads."[2] It was in consequence of the fact that he was a creator that Ea was, according to Accado-Sumerian ideas, a *dingir* or " god."

In the cosmology of Eridu, therefore, the origin of the universe was the watery abyss. The earth lay upon this like a wife in the arms of her husband, and Dav-kina accordingly was adored as the wife of Ea. It was through

---

[1] W. A. I. ii. 48, 29. There was another *dimme*, or more properly *dimma*, meaning " weak," the Assyrian *tarpu*, from *rapû* (W. A. I. v. 29, 71). *Tarpu* is the Hebrew *teraphim*, which, as Dr. Neubauer has pointed out, must be connected with the Rephaim, or "shades of the dead," and hence "prehistoric people," and signify the images of dead ancestors. *Dimma*, " weak," being confounded with *dimme*, " creator," by the Semites, caused the ideograph which denotes "a spirit" to acquire the (Assyrian) value of *rap*, from *rappu*, a synonym of *katsutu*, "the shade of the dead."

[2] W. A. I. iv. 61, 27.

her that the oracles of Ea, heard in the voice of the waves, were communicated to man. Dav-kina is entitled "the mistress of the oracular voice of the deep," and also "the lady who creates the oracular voice of heaven."[1] The oracles delivered by the thunder, the voice of heaven, thus became the reflex of the oracles delivered through the roaring of the sea.

We may see here an allusion to the doctrine of a watery abyss above the sky, of "the waters above the firmament," that is, of which we read in Genesis. The sky must have been looked upon as but another earth which floated on the surface of an ocean-stream just as did the nether earth itself. Hence in the theology of Eridu there was no room for a god of the sky. The visible sky was only Dav-kina in another form.

We can now understand why it was that in the theology of Eridu the Sun-god was the offspring of Ea and Dav-kina. The name that he bore there was Dumuzi or Tammuz, "the only-begotten one," of whom I shall have much to say in the next Lecture. At present I need only remark that he was the primæval Merodach; the Sun-god born of Ea who was called Merodach by the Babylonians was called Tammuz (Dumuzi) by the people of Eridu. Perhaps Merodach is after all nothing more than "the god from Eridu." That he came originally from Eridu we have already seen.

---

[1] W. A. I. ii. 55. 56, 59. Perhaps the latter title should rather be rendered "the lady of heaven whence the oracular voice is created." In line 55, *me-te*, which is usually the equivalent of *simatu*, "ornament," takes the place of *me*, just as in K 4245, *Rev.* 4, 5, where (AN) *me sag-L* and *me-te-sag-L* follow one another, *sag* being explained by *ristû* and *pani*, *L* by the god Mul-lil, and AN *me sag* by NIR.

THE GODS OF BABYLONIA. 145

The author of the hymn to the demiurge identifies Ea with "father Bel." As "the lord of heaven and earth," Ea was indeed a Baal or Bel to the Semites, to whose age the hymn belongs. But the particular Bel with whom the poet wishes to identify him was Mul-lil, the supreme god and demiurge of Nipur (the modern Niffer). In a list of the titles of Ea, we find it expressly stated that he is one with "Mul-lil the strong."[1] But such an identification belongs to the later imperial age of Babylonian history. Mul-lil was primitively a purely local divinity, standing in the same relation to his worshippers at Nipur that Ea stood to his at Eridu.

Mul-lil signifies "the lord of the ghost-world." *Lil* was an Accado-Sumerian word which properly denoted "a dust-storm" or "cloud of dust," but was also applied to ghosts, whose food was supposed to be the dust of the earth, and whose form was like that of a dust-cloud. The Accadian language possessed no distinction of gender, and *lil* therefore served to represent both male and female ghosts. It was, however, borrowed by the Semites under the form of *lillum*, and to this masculine they naturally added the feminine *lilatu*. Originally this *lilatu* represented what the Accadians termed "the handmaid of the ghost" (*kel-lilla*),[2] of whom it was said that the *lil* had neither husband nor wife;[3] but before long *lilatu* was confounded with the Semitic *lilâtu*, "the night," and so became a word of terror, denoting the night-demon

---

[1] W. A. I. ii. 55, 20.

[2] In W. A. I. iv. 16. 19-20, the Assyrian has "servant of the ghost" (*ardat li[li]*) for the Accadian *kiel údu-kára*, "servant of the light-coverer," while *kiel lilla* is rendered by *lilatu*.

[3] W. A. I. ii. 17, 30.

L

who sucked the blood of her sleeping victims. In the legend of the Descent of Istar into Hades, the goddess is made to threaten that unless she is admitted to the realm of the dead she will let them out in the form of vampires to devour the living. From the Semitic Babylonians the name and conception of Lilatu passed to the Jews, and in the book of Isaiah (xxxiv. 14) the picture of the ghastly desolation which should befall Idumæa is heightened by its ruined mounds being made the haunt of Lilith. According to the Rabbis, Lilith had been the first wife of Adam, and had the form of a beautiful woman; but she lived on the blood of children whom she slew at night.

The "lord of the ghost-world" extended his sway over this nether earth also. He is therefore entitled "the lord of the world," as well as "king of all the spirits of the earth."[1] According to one version of the story of the Deluge, it was he who caused the waters of the flood to descend from heaven, and who designed the destruction of all mankind. "When Mul-lil," we are told, "approached and saw the ship (of Xisuthros), he stood still and was filled with wrath against the gods and the spirits of heaven.[2] 'What soul has escaped therefrom?' (he cried). 'Let no man remain alive in the great destruction.'" It was then that Ea came forward with words of wisdom, and protested against this attempt of Mul-lil to confound the innocent with the guilty.

---

[1] W. A. I. i. 9, 3.

[2] We seem to have here a mythological reminiscence of the fact that Mul-lil had originally been the god of the lower world and its hosts of spirits, and that he was consequently in opposition to the gods of light and the spirits of the upper air.

"Let the sinner alone bear his sin; let the evil-doer bear his own iniquity." And though the wrathful god was pacified, so that Xisuthros and his companions were allowed to escape from their threatened death, the rescued hero did not forget the evil intentions of Mul-lil; but when inviting the other gods to his sacrifice after his descent from the ark, he specially excepted the god of Nipur. "Let the (other) gods come to my altar, but let Mul-lil not come to the altar, since he did not act considerately, but caused a deluge and doomed my people to destruction."

In these quotations I have called the god by his old Accadian name, Mul-lil.[1] But long before this account of the Deluge was composed, even though in its present form it probably reaches back more than 2000 years before the Christian era, the Accadian Mul-lil had become the Semitic Bel. His primitive attributes, however, still adhered to him. He was still the god of the lower world, whose messengers were diseases and nightmares and the demons of night, and from whom came the plagues and troubles that oppressed mankind. In a magical text (W. A. I. iv. 1. 5, 6), Namtar, the plague-demon, is called "the beloved son of Mul-lil"—standing, in fact, in the same relation to Mul-lil that Tammuz does to Ea, and in the next line Mul-lil's wife is asserted to be Nin-ki-gal or Allat, "the queen of the mighty land" of Hades.

This magical text, however, is a good deal older than

---

[1] Mul-lil was also known as En-lil in one of the Accado-Sumerian dialects. En-lil was contracted into Illil according to W. A. I. v. 37, 21, which explains the Ἴλλινος of Damascius (for which we should read ΙΛΛΙΛΛΟΣ).

the time when the Semites adopted and transformed the deities of the Accadians, or at all events it expresses the ideas of that earlier period. When the god of Nipur became Semitic, his character underwent a change. As the supreme deity of the state he was necessarily a Baal, but the Semitic Baal embodied very different conceptions from those which were associated with the Accadian Mul-lil. It is true that, as I have just pointed out, his primitive attributes still clung to him, but they were superadded to other attributes which showed him to be the supreme Sun-god of Semitic worship. That supreme Sun-god, however, revealed himself to his worshippers under two aspects; he might be either the beneficent god who gave life and light to the world, or he might be the fierce and wrathful sun of summer who scorches all nature with his heat, and sinks at night, like a ball of glowing metal, into the darkness of the under-world. Necessarily it was rather under the latter aspect that the Mul-lil of Nipur became the Semitic Bel.

This is the Bel whose cult was carried to Assyria, and whose name is mentioned frequently in the inscriptions of Nineveh, where among other titles he bears that of "father of the gods." This is a title which he received, not in virtue of his primitive character, but because he had become the Semitic Bel. He was distinguished from the younger Bel of Babylon, Bel-Merodach, as Βελιτανὰς or Βολαθήν (*Bêl-êthân*), "the older Baal,"[1] when Babylon became the imperial city, and its Bel claimed to be the father and head of the Babylonian gods. But the dis-

---

[1] Comp. Baudissin, *Studien zur semitischen Religionsgeschichte*, i. p. 274. A god *Bel-labaru*, "the older Bel," is mentioned in the inscriptions of Assyria, who may be a form of Mul-lil.

THE GODS OF BABYLONIA. 149

tinction, as might be expected, was not always observed, and the older and younger Bel are sometimes confounded together. The confusion was rendered the more easy by the fact that the wife of the Bel of Nipur was addressed as Bilat, and thus was undistinguished in name from Beltis of Babylon. But she was in reality, as we have seen, the queen of Hades, Nin-ki-gal as the Accadians called her, or Allat as she is named in the Semitic texts.[1] Allat is interpreted "the unwearied;"[2] like the Homeric epithet of Hades, ἀδάμαστος, "the inflexible" divinity who ceases not to deal on all sides his fatal blows. Her proper title, however—that, at least, under which she had originally been known at Nipur—was Nin-lil, "the lady of the ghost-world."[3] It is under this name that Assur-banipal addresses her (W. A. I. ii. 66) as "the mistress of the world, whose habitation is the temple of the library" (i.e. the temple of Istar at Nineveh).[4] As Allat, the

---

[1] In a magical text (W. A. I. ii. 18, 40) Nin-ki-gal is called the wife of Nin-azu; but that Nin-azu is merely a title of Mul-lil is shown by W. A. I. ii. 57, 51, where "the star of Nin-azu" is identified with Adar. In W. A. I. ii. 59, 35, the wife of Nin-azu is termed Nin-NER-DA.

[2] R 204, ii. 9, *allattum* = *nu-kusu*.   [3] W. A. I. ii. 19, 6.

[4] Ê-barbar; see W. A. I. iii. 3, 40. For the meaning of *barbar*, "a library," cp. W. A. I. ii. 48, 26. The word is a re-duplicated form of *bar* or *bára*, "to reveal," hence used in the senses of "white" (W. A. I. iv. 21, 5) or "visible" (W. A. I. iv. 6, 46), and "an oracle" (W. A. I. iv. 19, 48). The compound ideograph BAR-BAR is interpreted *tabbak rimka*, "the outpouring of a libation," in S 924, 7, and Rm. 2. 11. 149, 4, and *mási*, "a hero," in W. A. I. iv. 21. 30, 32. With the latter signification it was read *mas-mas*, which is a title of Merodach (K 100, 15, K 48, *Obv.* 18). Since, however, Merodach is called "the lord of BAR-BAR-*ti*" in K 2546, *Rev.* 1, it is clear that the two senses of the compound ideograph were played upon, as the reading here must be *sip-ti*, "an oracle." Between the time of Sennacherib and

goddess of Hades, she was a much-dreaded and formidable figure, who is described in the legend of the Descent of Istar as inflicting upon her sister-goddess all the pains and diseases which emanated from her demoniac satellites. The unfortunate Istar, stripped of her clothing and adornments, is held up to the scorn of the lower world; and Namtar, the plague-demon, is ordered by Allat to smite her with maladies in the eyes, in the sides, in the feet, in the heart, in the head, and, in short, in all the limbs. Throughout the legend Namtar appears as the messenger of the infernal queen.

It is thus clear that, just as Eridu in southern Babylonia was the primitive seat of the worship of the Chaldæan culture-god and of the civilisation with which his name was connected, Nipur in northern Babylonia was the original home of a very different kind of worship, which concerned itself with ghosts and demons and the various monsters of the under-world. It was, in fact, the home of that belief in magic, and in the various spirits exorcised by the magician, which left so deep an impression upon the religion of early Babylonia, and about which I shall have to speak in a future Lecture. The analogy of Eridu would lead us to infer, moreover, that it was not only the home of this belief, but also the source from which it made its way to other parts of the country. In the pre-historic age, Eridu in the south and Nipur in the north would have been the two religious centres of Babylonian theology, from whence two wholly different streams of religious thought and influence spread

---

Assur-bani-pal, the library of Nineveh seems to have been transferred from the temple of Istar to that of Nebo; see above, p. 9.

and eventually blended. The mixture formed what I may call the established religion of Chaldæa in the pre-Semitic period.

That this conclusion is not a mere inference is shown by the monuments discovered at Tel-loh. Tel-loh was geographically nearer to Eridu than to Nipur, and its theology might therefore be expected to be more largely influenced by that of Eridu than by that of Nipur. And such, indeed, is the case. Temples and statues are dedicated to Ea, "the king of Eridu," and more especially to Bahu, a goddess who occupied a conspicuous place in the cosmological legends of Eridu. But Mul-lil, the god of Nipur, appears far more frequently in the inscriptions of Tel-loh than we should have anticipated. Nin-kharsak, "the mistress of the mountain," and "mother of the gods," in whom we may see a local divinity, is associated with him as wife; and Nin-girśu himself, the patron god of Tel-loh, is made his "hero" or "champion." So close, indeed, is the connection of the latter with Mul-lil, that the compilers of the mythological tablets, in a latter age, identified him with the "warrior" god of Nipur, Adar the son of Mul-lil.

Adar, or Ninep, or Uras—for his name has been read in these various fashions, and the true reading still remains unknown[1]—played a conspicuous part in Babylonian, and

---

[1] The only form out of these three which is monumentally established is Uras. Uras is given as the pronunciation of the second ideograph in the name of the god (W. A. I. iii. 70, 203—207, ii. 54, 34); and in W. A. I. ii. 57, 31, Uras is expressly stated to be the name of NIN-IP, as "god of light" (*uddanê*, see ii. 62, 36, where there is a play on the Assyrian *baru*, "fat,". and *baru*, "to reveal"). From *uras* the Assyrians borrowed their *urasu*, "a mourning veil" (v. 28, 60). IP and NIN-IP were two primæval deities who in Accadian cosmology

more especially Assyrian theology. He was regarded as emphatically the warrior and champion of the gods, and as such was naturally a favourite object of worship amongst a nation of warriors like the Assyrians. Indeed, it may be suspected that the extent to which the name of the older Bel was reverenced in Assyria was in some measure due to the favour in which his son Adar was held. In the inscriptions of Nineveh, the title of "hero-god" (*masu*) is applied to him with peculiar frequency; this was the characteristic upon which the Assyrian kings more particularly loved to dwell. In Babylonia, on the other hand, Adar was by no means so favourite a divinity. Here it was the milder and less warlike Merodach that took his place. The arts of peace, rather than those of war, found favour among the Semitic population of the southern kingdom.

Originally, like Merodach, Adar had been a solar deity. We are distinctly told that he was "the meridian sun,"[1] whose scorching heats represented the fiercer side of Baal-worship. But whereas Merodach was the sun conceived of as rising from the ocean-stream, Adar was the sun

---

represented the male and female principles, but the genderless character of the Accadian *nin*, "lord" or "lady," caused the Semites to change NIN-IP into a god and identify him with IP, that is, "Anu who listens to prayer" (ii. 54, 35). As *u* signified "lord" in Accadian, it would seem that they further identified the first syllable of U-ras with the *nin* of Nin-Uras. Hence "the Assyrian king," Horus of Pliny (N. H. xxx. 51, cp. xxxvii. 52), who discovered a cure for drunkenness, as well as the Thouras of Kedrênos (Hist. 15, 16, cp. Suidas and the Paschal Chron. p. 68), who is called the Assyrian Arês and made the son of Zames or Samas. The reading Adar is derived from the Biblical Adrammelech, but it is quite certain that it is false, and I have retained it in the text only on account of its employment by other Assyriologists.

[1] W. A. I. ii. 57. 51, 76 (where he is identified with Mermer).

who issues forth from the shades of night. His wife accordingly is "the lady of the dawn."[1] Like all solar deities in Babylonia, an oracle was attached to his shrine. His name is explained to mean "the lord of the oracle,"[2] and one of his titles was "the voice" or "oracle supreme."[3] It was on this account that later mythologists identified him with Nebo,[4] though between the Sun-god of Nipur and the prophet-deity of Borsippa there was originally no sort of connection. On the other hand, it must have been his solar character that gave rise to the two curious titles of "lord of the date"[5] and "lord of the pig."[6] The latter title was naturally dropped in the Semitic period of Chaldæan history.

Adar bears the same relation to Mul-lil that Merodach bears to Ea. Each alike is the son and messenger of the

---

[1] W. A. I. ii. 59, 10.

[2] W. A. I. ii. 57, 17. It is clear that the compiler of the mythological list here interpreted *baru*, the equivalent of *uras*, in the sense of "a revelation" or "oracle," and read his title in Assyria not as Masu, "a hero," but as Baru, "the oracular god." It illustrates the same play upon the ideographic writing of the god's name as that which we find in BAR-BAR or MAS-MAS for Merodach.

[3] W. A. I. ii. 57, 26.   [4] W. A. I. ii. 57, 18.

[5] W. A. I. ii. 57, 28.

[6] W. A. I. ii. 57, 39. In K 161, i. 8, one of the remedies prescribed for disease of the heart is *siru* AN *Nin-pes*, "swine's flesh." Rimmon, when worshipped as Mâtu (Martu), was also known as *khumuntsir*, the Accadised form of the Semitic *khumtsiru*, "a pig" (W. A. I. iii. 68, 70). The title "lord of the pig" connects Adar with the Arês of Greek mythology, who in the form of the wild boar slew the Sun-god Tammuz; while the title "lord of the date"—the chief fruit of Babylonia—reminds us of Cain, who was "a tiller of the ground." Under the name of Baru, Adar was identified with iron, since the name of "iron" was denoted in Accadian by *bar*, "the shining" (see W. A. I. v. 30, 52), which was written with the determinative of divinity, indicative of the meteoric origin of the first iron worked in Babylonia.

older god. But whereas the errands upon which Merodach is sent are errands of mercy and benevolence, the errands of Adar are those that befit an implacable warrior. He contends not against the powers of darkness, like Merodach, for the father whose orders he obeys is himself the ruler of the powers of darkness; it is against mankind, as in the story of the Deluge, that his arms are directed. He is a solar hero who belongs to the darkness and not to the light.

It is thus that one of his brothers is "the first-born" of Mul-lil, Mul-nugi, "the lord from whom there is no return."[1] Mul-nugi is the lord of Hades, the god who is called Irkalla in the legend of the Descent of Istar, and out of whose hands there is no escape. It may be that he is but another form of the Moon-god, since the Moon-god, we are told, was also the eldest son of Mul-lil. But the name by which the Moon-god went at Nipur was one that signified "the god of glowing fire."[2] It is curious to find the mythologists identifying this "god of glowing fire" with Adar; but the error was natural; both alike were sons of Mul-lil, and both alike represented the great orbs of heaven.

---

[1] See the Deluge-tablet, col. i. l. 17. In W. A. I. iii. 68, 7, he is called "the throne-bearer of Mul-lilla," and he would therefore seem to have been one of "the throne-bearers" of the Deluge-tablet (col. ii. 45) who "went over mountain and plain" carrying destruction with them. Irkalla seems to be a Semitic form of a Proto-Chaldæan word. In W. A. I. v. 16, 80, *irkallum* is the rendering of the Accadian *kesda*, "an enclosure" (comp. ii. 29, 63); and since the queen of Hades was known as Nin-ki-gal, "the lady of the great country," while *uru-gal* or *eri-gal*, "the great city," was the Accadian designation of Hades or the tomb (W. A. I. ii. 1. 191; 30. 13), it is possible that Irkalla represents an earlier Eri-galla.

[2] W. A. I. ii. 57, 56.

THE GODS OF BABYLONIA. 155

The chief seat, however, of the worship of the Moon-god was not Nipur but Ur (the modern Mugheir). Here stood the great temple the ruins of which were partially explored by Loftus. Already in the oldest documents that have come from thence, the god to whom the temple was consecrated is identified with the Moon-god of Nipur. Already he is termed "the first-born of Mul-lil." The spread of the cult of Mul-lil, therefore, and of the magic which it implied, must have made its way as far south as Ur in a very remote age. But we have no reason for believing that the Moon-god of Ur and the Moon-god of Nipur were originally one and the same. Each Babylonian town, large and small, had its own local Moon-god, whose several names are recorded on a broken tablet.[1] The forms under which the Moon-god was worshipped in Babylonia were as numerous as the forms of the Sun-god himself.

What seems yet more singular to the comparative mythologist is that, according to the official religion of Chaldæa, the Sun-god was the offspring of the Moon-god. Such a belief could have arisen only where the Moon-god was the supreme object of worship. It is a reversal of the usual mythological conception which makes the moon the companion or pale reflection of the sun. It runs directly counter to the Semitic Baal-worship. To the Semite the Sun-god was the lord and father of the gods; the moon was either his female consort, or, where Semitic theology had been influenced by that of Chaldæa, an inferior god.

But the belief was thoroughly in harmony with a theology which admitted Mul-lil and his ghost-world to

---

[1] W. A. I. ii. 57, 56 *sq.*

LECTURE III.

the highest honours of the pantheon. With such a theology it was natural that the sun should be regarded as issuing forth from the darkness of night. And the moon was necessarily associated with the night. Indeed, in one passage[1] the Moon-god is actually identified with the plague-demon Namtar, who was, as we have seen, the messenger of the queen of hell. Moreover, the Babylonians were a nation of astronomers. Their astrology was closely allied to their magic, and the lofty towers of their temples were used for the observation of the sky. It is not wonderful, therefore, that the cult of the moon should occupy a foremost place in their creed, or that the moon should be conceived as a male and not as a female divinity.

It was at Ur, however, that the Moon-god was placed at the head of the divine hierarchy, and it was from Ur that the ideas spread which caused him to be addressed as "the father of the gods." At Ur, in fact, he held the same place that Mul-lil held at Nipur; but while Mul-lil seems to have represented the dark sky of night, the Moon-god was the luminary which shed light upon the darkness. He was known at Ur as Nanak or Nannar,[2]

---

[1] W. A. I. ii. 57, 79. Unfortunately, the name of the city where this was the case is lost. The "Lady who decides destiny," who is identified with the impersonal "Mistress of the gods" of Semitic worship (W. A. I. ii. 55, 8), introduces us to a wholly different conception, and the later softening of the plague-demon into a mere instrument of destiny.

[2] The reading is given by 82. 8—16. 1, *Obv.* 3. Nannakos was supposed to be an antediluvian king who predicted the flood (Zen. 6, 10, Steph. Byz. s.v. ’Ικόνιον); the name, like the legend of the ark at Apameia or of Sisythes (Xisuthros) at Hierapolis (Membij), probably came into Asia Minor through the medium of the Hittites. Compare the claim of the Arkadians to be προσέληνοι (Scol. Aristoph. *Nub.* 398).

a name which the Semites by a popular etymology afterwards connected with their word *namaru*, "to see;" so that we find Nabonidos addressing the Moon-god of Harran as "the light of heaven and earth" (*nannari same u irtsitim*). In later days, both Nanak and Nannar, like other of the Babylonian gods, passed into heroes and human kings. Nannakos was transported into Phrygia, and Nannaros became a satrap of Babylonia under the Median monarch Artaios—a personage, it need hardly be observed, unknown to actual history. The Persian legend, as handed down by Ktêsias, is as follows:[1]

"There was a Persian of the name of Parsondês,[2] in the service of the king of the Medes, an eager huntsman, and active warrior on foot and in the chariot, distinguished in council and in the field, and of influence with the king. Parsondês often urged the king to make him satrap of Babylon in the place of Nannaros, who wore women's clothes and ornaments, but the king always put the petition aside, for it could not be granted without breaking the promise which his ancestor had made to Belesys. Nannaros discovered the intentions of Parsondes, and sought to secure himself against them, and to take vengeance. He promised great rewards to the cooks who were in the train of the king, if they succeeded in seizing Parsondes and giving him up. One day, Parsondes in the heat of the chase strayed far from the king. He had already killed many boars and deer, when the pursuit of a wild ass carried him to a great distance. At last he came upon the cooks, who were occupied in preparations for the king's table. Being thirsty, Parsondes asked for wine; they gave it, took care of his horse, and invited him to take food—an invitation agreeable to Parsondes, who had been hunting the whole day. He bade them send the ass which he had captured to the king, and tell his own servants where he was. Then he ate of the various kinds of food set before him, and drank

---

[1] I quote from the English translation of Duncker's *History of Antiquity*, v. pp. 298 *sq*.

[2] The name of Parsondês is probably taken from the important town of Parśindu, among the mountains of the Namri, on the high-road to Ekbatana (W. A. I. i. 21. 69, 70).

abundantly of the excellent wine, and at last asked for his horse in order to return to the king. But they brought beautiful women to him, and urged him to remain for the night. He agreed, and as soon as, overcome by hunting, wine and love, he had fallen into a deep sleep, the cooks bound him and brought him to Nannaros. Nannaros reproached him with calling him an effeminate man, and seeking to obtain his satrapy; he had the king to thank that the satrapy granted to his ancestors had not been taken from him. Parsondes replied that he considered himself more worthy of the office, because he was more manly and more useful to the king. But Nannaros swore by Bel and Mylitta that Parsondes should be softer and whiter than a woman, called for the eunuch who was over the female players, and bade him shave the body of Parsondes, and bathe and anoint him every day, put women's clothes on him, plait his hair after the manner of women, paint his face, and place him among the women who played the guitar and sang, and to teach him their arts. This was done, and soon Parsondes played and sang better at the table of Nannaros than any of the women. Meanwhile the king of the Medes had caused search to be made everywhere for Parsondes; and since he could nowhere be found, and nothing could be heard of him, he believed that a lion or some other wild animal had torn him when out hunting, and lamented for his loss. Parsondes had lived for seven years as a woman in Babylon, when Nannaros caused an eunuch to be scourged and grievously maltreated. This eunuch Parsondes induced by large presents to retire to Media and tell the king the misfortune which had come upon him. Then the king sent a message commanding Nannaros to give up Parsondes. Nannaros declared that he had never seen him. But the king sent a second messenger, charging him to put Nannaros to death if he did not surrender Parsondes. Nannaros entertained the messenger of the king; and when the meal was brought, 150 women entered, of whom some played the guitar, while others blew the flute. At the end of the meal, Nannaros asked the king's envoy which of all the women was the most beautiful and had played best. The envoy pointed to Parsondes. Nannaros laughed long and said, 'That is the person whom you seek,' and released Parsondes, who on the next day returned home with the envoy to the king in a chariot. The king was astonished at the sight of him, and asked why he had not avoided such disgrace by death. Parsondes answered, ' In order that I might see you again and by you execute vengeance on Nannaros, which could never have been mine had I taken my life.' The king promised him that his hope should not be deceived, as soon as he came to Babylon. But

THE GODS OF BABYLONIA. 159

when he came there, Nannaros defended himself on the ground that Parsondes, though in no way injured by him, had maligned him, and sought to obtain the satrapy over Babylonia. The king pointed out that he had made himself judge in his own cause, and had imposed a punishment of a degrading character; in ten days he would pronounce judgment upon him for his conduct. In terror, Nannaros hastened to Mitraphernês, the eunuch of greatest influence with the king, and promised him the most liberal rewards, 10 talents of gold and 100 talents of silver, 10 golden and 200 silver bowls, if he could induce the king to spare his life and retain him in the satrapy of Babylonia. He was prepared to give the king 100 talents of gold, 1000 talents of silver, 100 golden and 300 silver bowls, and costly robes with other gifts; Parsondes also should receive 100 talents of silver and costly robes. After many entreaties, Mitraphernês persuaded the king not to order the execution of Nannaros, as he had not killed Parsondes, but to condemn him in the penalty which he was prepared to pay Parsondes and the king. Nannaros in gratitude threw himself at the feet of the king; but Parsondes said, 'Cursed be the man who first brought gold among men; for the sake of gold I have been made a mockery to the Babylonians.'"

After this thoroughly characteristic example of the way in which Persian euhemerism turned the mythology of their neighbours into fictitious history, it requires an effort to go back to the sober facts of the old cuneiform tablets. Nannaros, or Nannar, however, was originally no satrap of a Median king, but the supreme god of Ur, in whose honour hymns were composed and a ritual performed similar to that carried on in honour of Merodach at Babylon. Thanks to the piety of the chief scribe of Assur-bani-pal, Istar-sum-esses, one of these hymns has been preserved to us in an almost complete state. The Accadian original is accompanied by an interlinear Semitic translation, both of which the chief scribe claims to have accurately reproduced. The hymn runs thus:[1]

---

[1] W. A. I. iv. 9. The translation given by Dr. Oppert of this hymn in his *Fragments mythologiques* is full of errors, and frequently mistakes the meaning of the lines.

1. "Lord and prince of the gods who in heaven and earth alone is supreme!
 2. Father Nannar, lord of the firmament, prince of the gods!
 3. Father Nannar, lord of heaven,[1] mighty one, prince of the gods!
 4. Father Nannar, lord of the moon,[2] prince of the gods!
 5. Father Nannar, lord of Ur, prince of the gods!
 6. Father Nannar, lord of the Temple of the mighty Light, prince of the gods!
 7. Father Nannar, who biddest the crowned disk to rise, prince of the gods!
 8. Father Nannar, who makest the crowned disk[3] fully perfect, prince of the gods!
 9. Father Nannar, who sweeps away with a blow invincible, prince of the gods!
10. Strong ox, whose horn is powerful, whose limbs are perfect, whose beard is of crystal, whose member is full of virility;
11. Its fruit is generated of itself; its eye is bent down to behold (its) adornment; its virility is never exhausted.
12. Merciful one, begetter of the universe, who founds (his) illustrious seat among living creatures.[4]
13. Father, long-suffering and full of forgiveness,[5] whose hand upholds the life of all mankind!
13 Lord, thy divinity like the far-off heaven fills the wide sea with fear.
14. On the surface of the peopled earth he bids the sanctuary be placed, he proclaims their name.
15. Father, begetter of gods and men, who causes the shrine to be founded, who establishes the offering.
16. Who proclaims dominion, who gives the sceptre, who shall fix destiny unto a distant day.[6]

---

[1] The Semitic translator has mistaken the sense of the original and supposed that the god Anu was intended by the poet. Hence he identifies the Moon-god with Assôros (the firmament) and Anu.

[2] Here again the translator has erroneously rendered "the lord Sin."

[3] Here the translator has completely mistaken the sense of the original and has rendered "royalty"!

[4] Such seems to be the meaning of the Semitic translation. The original is: "among men far and wide he erects the supreme shrine."

[5] The Accadian is literally, "long-suffering in waiting."

[6] So in the translation. The original is: "who gives the sceptre to those whose destiny is fixed unto a distant day."

THE GODS OF BABYLONIA. 161

17. First-born, omnipotent, whose heart is immensity, and there is none who may discover it.[1]
18. Firm are his limbs (?); his knees rest not; he opens the path of the gods his brethren.
19. (He is the god) who makes the light from the horizon to the zenith of heaven, opening wide the doors of the sky, and establishing light (in the world).
20. Father, begetter of the universe, illuminator of living beings .... sender of....
21. Lord, the ordainer of the laws of heaven and earth, whose command may not be (broken).
22. Thou holdest the rain and the lightning,[2] defender of all living things; there is no god who hath at any time discovered thy fulness.
23. In heaven who is supreme? Thou alone, thou art supreme.
24. On earth who is supreme? Thou alone, thou art supreme.
25. As for thee, thy will is made known in heaven, and the angels bow their faces.
26. As for thee, thy will is made known upon earth, and the spirits below kiss the ground.
27. As for thee, thy will is blown on high like the wind; the stall and the fold[3] are quickened.
28. As for thee, thy will is done upon the earth, and the herb grows green.
29. As for thee, thy will is seen in the lair[4] and the shepherd's hut; it increases all living things.
30. As for thee, thy will hath created law and justice, so that mankind has established law.
31. As for thee, thy will is the far-off heaven, the hidden earth which no man hath known.[5]

---

[1] In the original: "his heart is far-extended: none shall describe the god."

[2] The order is reversed in the Semitic translation.

[3] *Rîtu u maśkitum*, which are explained in 79. 7-8. 5. Other renderings of U-A given in this tablet are *epiru*, "dust;" *subat nakri*, "the seat of a stranger;" and *zaninu*, "the nourisher." For *rîtu*, see K 4872. 54, 7; it is a derivative from the root of *rieu*, "a shepherd."

[4] *Tarbatsu*; the first syllable has been omitted in the printed text.

[5] The original Accadian is literally: "they will extend (as) heaven, it stretches below (as) earth, there are none who can record (it)."

32. As for thee, who can learn thy will, who can rival it?
33. O lord, in heaven (is thy) lordship, in the earth (is thy) sovereignty; among the gods thy brethren a rival thou hast not.
34. King of kings, of whose .... no man is judge, whose divinity no god resembles.

[The next three lines are too broken for translation.]

38. Look with favour on thy temple!
39. Look with favour on Ur (thy city).
40. Let the high-born dame ask rest of thee, O lord.
41. Let the free-born man, the .... ask rest of thee, O lord!
42, 43. Let the spirits of heaven and earth (ask rest of thee), O lord!"

[The last few lines are destroyed.]

COLOPHON.—" Like its old copy copied and published.

Tablet of Istar-sum-esses, chief scribe of Assur-bani-pal, the king of legions, the king of Assyria, and son of Nebo-zir-csir, chief of the penmen."

As the original language of this hymn is the Accadian of northern Babylonia, and not the Sumerian of the south, it would seem that the priesthood and population of Ur were derived from the north, and not from the geographically nearer region of which Eridu was the head. This will explain the relationship they discovered between their own supreme deity and the god of Nipur. Ur was either a northern colony or had become incorporated in the northern kingdom,[1] and its local god accordingly became the first-born of Mul-lil. It is possible that the hymns of which I have just given a specimen were influenced by Semitic ideas; at all events, throughout the northern part of Chaldæa, wherever the Accadian dialect of the north was spoken, a strong

---

[1] This latter is the more probable explanation, since the Accadian of the hymn is really that artificial language which grew up in the court of Sargon.

Semitic element seems to have existed in the population from an early period; and of Ur of the Casdim we are specially told that it was the birth-place of the Semitic Abraham.

Now Abraham, it will be remembered, migrated from Ur to Harran, in northern Mesopotamia. The distance between the two cities appears considerable, and yet there was a very real connection between them. Like Ur, Harran also was a city of the Moon-god, and the temple of the Moon-god in Harran rivalled that at Ur. Nay, more; Harran was as closely connected with Babylonian history and religion as was Ur itself. Its name recurs in early Babylonian texts, and is indeed of Accadian origin, *Kharran* being the Accadian word for "road," and denoting the city which lay on the great highway from Chaldæa to the west. The mythologists of Babylonia entitled the planet Mercury "the spirit of the men of Harran;"[1] and Nabonidos boasts of his restoration of "the temple of the Moon-god in Harran, in which from time immemorial the Moon-god, the mighty lord, had placed the seat of the goodness of his heart." Gems show us what the image of the god was like. It was a simple cone of stone, above which blazed the star of the moon, such as we see depicted on the seals and monuments of Assyria and Babylonia. Sargon couples together Assur and Harran, whose ancient customs he claims to have restored, and declares that he had "spread his shadow over Harran, and by the will of Anu and Dagon had written (again) its laws." Shalmaneser III. and Assur-bani-pal had rebuilt the temple of the Moon-

---

[1] W. A. I. iii. 67, 28.

god there which bore the Accadian name of E-Khulkhul, "the house of rejoicing," and neither they nor Nabonidos seem to have had any doubt that the Moon-god worshipped therein was the same as the Moon-god worshipped in Assyria and Babylonia.

Whether this were primitively the case must remain an open question. It is more probable that the Moon-god of Harran was originally as much a local divinity as the Moon-god of Ur, unless, indeed, Harran had been itself the foundation of the kings of Ur in their early campaigns to the west. But the leading place won by Ur at the time when its kings made themselves masters of the whole of Babylonia, caused the Moon-god of Ur to supplant the Moon-gods of the other cities of the country, just as the rise of Babylon caused Merodach to supplant the other Sun-gods of Chaldæa. With the growth of the Semitic power in Babylonia, the influence of the Moon-god of Ur became greater and more extensive. Nannar was now invoked as Sin—a name which at first appears to have denoted the orb of the moon only[1] —and the name and worship of Sin spread not only in Babylonia, but in other parts of the Semitic world. His name has been found in an inscription of southern Arabia, and Sinai itself, the sacred mountain, is nothing more than the sanctuary "dedicated to Sin." It may be that the worship of the Babylonian Moon-god was brought to the peninsula of Sinai as far back as the days when the sculptors of Tel-loh carved into human shape the blocks of diorite they received from the land of Magan.

---

[1] Whether the name of Sin is of Accadian or Semitic origin must at present remain an open question. At all events, I cannot believe that it is a Semitic corruption of an Accadian Zu-en.

However this may be, the Moon-god of Ur, like the city over which he presided, took primary rank among the Babylonians. His worshippers invoked him as the father and creator of both gods and men. It is thus that Nabonidos celebrates his restoration of the temple of Sin at Harran: "May the gods who dwell in heaven and earth approach the house of Sin, the father who created them. As for me, Nabonidos, king of Babylon, the completer of this temple, may Sin, the king of the gods of heaven and earth, in the lifting up of his kindly eyes, with joy look upon me month by month at noon and sunset; may he grant me favourable tokens, may he lengthen my days, may he extend my years, may he establish my reign, may he overcome my foes, may he slay my enemies, may he sweep away my opponents. May Nin-gal, the mother of the mighty gods, in the presence of Sin, her loved one, speak like a mother. May Samas and Istar, the bright offspring of his heart, to Sin, the father who begat them, speak of blessing. May Nuzku, the messenger supreme, hearken to my prayer and plead for me."

The moon existed before the sun. This is the idea which underlay the religious belief of Accad, exact converse, as it was, of the central idea of the religion of the Semites. It was only where Accadian influence was strong that the Semite could be brought in any way to accept it. It was only in Babylonia and Assyria and on the coasts of Arabia that the name of Sin was honoured; elsewhere the attributes of the Moon-god were transferred to the goddess Istar, who, as we shall see hereafter, was originally the evening star. But in Babylonia, Sin became inevitably the father of the gods. His reign extended to the beginning of history; Sargon, as the representative of the Babylonian kings and the adorer of Merodach, speaks of "the remote days of the period of the Moon-god," which another inscription makes synonymous with "the birth of the land of Assur."[1] As the passage I have quoted from Nabonidos shows, Sin was more particularly the father of Samas and Istar, of the Sun-god and the goddess of the evening star.

But who was this Sun-god who was thus the offspring of Sin? The Sun-gods of Babylonia were as numerous as its Moon-gods; each city had its own; who then was the Samas who was so specially the son of the Moon-god of Ur? The answer is not very easy to give. Geographical considerations would lead us to think of the Sun-god of Larsa, the modern Senkereh. Larsa was near Ur, though on the opposite bank of the river, and its temple of the Sun had been famous from pre-Semitic times.

---

[1] *Tsibit Assuri*, W. A. I. iii. 11. ii. 32. Oppert is right against George Smith and Lenormant in holding that *adi Sin* in the first-quoted passage (*Khors.* 110) cannot be a proper name, Adi-Ur (!). A fragmentary tablet (quoted on p. 62 of George Smith's *Chaldean Genesis*, ed. Sayce) contained a legend about the foundation of the city of Assur and its two temples, E-Sarra, the temple of Adar, and E-Lusu. We read (line 6): "The god Assur (AN KHI) opened his mouth and says; to the god Khir . . . (he speaks): 'above the deep (*elinu apsi*) the seat (of Ea), before (*mikhrit*) E-Sarra which I have built, below the shrine (*asrata*) I have made strong, let me construct E-Lusu the seat of (the god . . .), let me found (*lusarsid*) within it his fortress . . . when (the god) ascends from the deep thou didst prepare a place (that was still) unfinished . . . thou didst establish in Assur (D. P. PAL-BAT-KI) the temples of the great gods . . . .' to his father Anu even to him (*a[na s]asu*) (he spoke): 'The god . . . has (appointed?) thee over whatsoever thy hand has made, whatever thy (hand) possesses; over the earth that thy hand has made, whatever (thy hand) possesses; the city of Assur whose name thou hast given (*sa tazkura sum-su*), the place (which) thou hast made exalted for ever' (*tanîdi darîsam*)."

But there is a special reason which makes it probable that the Sun-god of Larsa was the deity whose father was Sin. The temple of Sin at Ur, the ruins of which are still in existence, had been founded by Ur-Bagas, the first monarch of united Babylonia of whom we know. His monuments have been met with at Mugheir, at Larsa, at Warka, at Niffer, and at Zerghul; and his bricks show that he was the founder—or more probably the restorer—not only of the great temple of the Moon-god at Ur, but also of those of the Sun-god at Larsa, of Mul-lil at Nipur, and of Anu and Istar at Erech. Under his rule, therefore, the unity of the empire found its religious expression in the union of the worship of the Moon-god of Ur with that of the Sun-god of Larsa. As the dominant state, Ur necessarily stood to Larsa and Erech in the relation of a metropolis, and its god thus became the progenitor of the gods of Larsa and Erech. The Sun-god of Larsa, like the Istar of Erech, became accordingly the child of Nannar or Sin.

It was as Kur(?)-nigin-gára, "the god who makes the palace (of the setting sun)," that the Sun-god of Larsa seems to have been known to his worshippers in pre-Semitic days.[1] But when the Accadian was superseded by the Semite, his special name was merged in the general title of Samsu or Samas, "the Sun." He became the Baal of Larsa, who differed but little, save in the name by which he was addressed, from the other Baalim of Babylonia.

The fame of the Samas of Larsa, however, was obscured at an early period by that of the Samas of Sippara. Sip-

---

[1] W. A. I. ii. 60, 12.

para in historical times was pre-eminently the city of the Sun-god. It was there that Ê-Bábara, "the house of lustre," the great temple of the Sun-god,[1] had been erected in days to which tradition alone went back, and it was around its shrine that Semitic sun-worship in Babylonia was chiefly centred. Sippara and its immediate neighbourhood had been the seat of early Semitic supremacy in Chaldæa. It was, it is true, of pre-Semitic foundation; its primitive name Zimbir would show this, like the name of E-Bábara itself; and we know that Samas had once been worshipped within its walls under the Accadian title of Bábara or Birra. But in these remote days Sippara was probably an insignificant town; at all events, the memory of later ages knew of Sippara only in connection with the empire of Sargon of Accad and the Semitic version of the story of the Deluge.[2]

In the Old Testament, Sippara appears as a dual city— Sepharvaim, "the two Sipparas." One of these has been discovered in the mounds of Abu-Habba by Mr. Hormuzd Rassam, who has brought from it a monument on which

---

[1] The temple of the Sun-god at Larsa was also known as E-bábara (W. A. I. i. 65, 42); its *ziggurrat* was called "the house of the bond of heaven and earth" (ii. 50, 19).

[2] According to Bêrôssos, Xisuthros had written a history of all that had happened before the deluge and buried the books at Sippara, where they were disinterred after the flood by his directions. The legend seems to have been based partly on a popular etymology which connected Sippara with *sipru*, "a book" (Heb. *sepher*), partly on the fact that the whole district was termed "the country of books," in consequence of its being the seat of the library of Sargon, whose city of Accad formed a part of the double Sippara. That the story of the deluge emanated in its present form from Sippara is indicated not only by the legend of the burial of the books, but also by the fact that the hero of it was "a man of Surippak," a small town close to Sippara.

is carved a curious image of the divine solar disk. The other has been found by Dr. Hayes Ward in the mounds of Anbar, an hour's distance from Sufeirah and the Euphrates. The fragment of a geographical tablet seems indeed to mention no less than four Sipparas—Sippara proper, Sippara of the desert, Sippara "the ancient,"[1] and Sippara of the Sun-god;[2] but since the historical texts know of two only—Sippara of Anunit and Sippara of Samas—it is best to regard the three first names as alike denoting the same place, Sippara of Anunit, the modern Anbar. It must have been from this Sippara that the Euphrates received its title, "river of Sippara," since Abu-Habba is seven miles distant from the present bed of the stream.

In the close neighbourhood of this double Sippara, Sargon built or restored the city to which he gave a name, and from which the whole of northern Babylonia received its title of Accad. It is called Agadhé in the non-Semitic texts, Accad (Akkadu) in the Semitic; though whether the name is of Semitic or non-Semitic origin cannot at present be decided. Sargon's patronage of literature, and the celebrated library he founded in Accad, caused the district to be known as "the region of books."[3] A popular etymology afterwards connected the name of Sippara itself with *sepher*, "a book," and the city accord-

---

[1] *Ul-dua* rendered by *tsâtu*, W. A. I. iv. 13, 24, and *kiśittu*, v. 21, 14, K 4874. *Obv.* 21, 22 (*udu ul-dua udu ul-dua-lil = ki-śi-it-ti tsa-a-ti*); comp. K 4171. *Rev.* 9, 23, 28 (UDU UL-DUA-*u supar pî sa Enuva* SAL SAKH).

[2] Hayes Ward, *Proceedings of the American Oriental Society*, Oct. 1885.

[3] W. A. I. ii. 51, 8.

ingly appears in the fragments of Bêrôssos as Pantibibla, or "Book-town."

With the spread and fame of the empire of Sargon, the worship of Samas spread and became famous also. The empire and the cult were alike Semitic; wherever the Semite planted himself, the Sun-god was worshipped under some form and name. The extent, therefore, of the worship of the Sun-god of Sippara marks the extent and power of Sargon's kingdom. The older Samas of Larsa was eclipsed by the new deity; henceforward Sippara, and not Larsa, was the chief seat of the adoration of Samas in Babylonia. It is to Sippara in all probability that the hymns addressed to the Sun-god belong. They are the product of an age of new ideas and aspirations. They represent the meeting and amalgamation of Semitic and Accadian thought. The scribes and poets of Sargon's court were partly Semites, partly Accadians; but the Semites had received an Accadian education, and the Accadians had learnt the language and imitated the style of their Semitic masters. Though the originals of most of the hymns are written in the old language of Accad— a language that had become sacred to the Semites, and in which alone the gods allowed themselves to be addressed—the thoughts contained in them are for the most part Semitic. We have no longer to do with a Mul-lil, a lord of ghosts and demons, nor even with an Ea, with his charms and sorceries for the removal of human ills, but with the supreme Baal of Semitic faith, the father and creator of the world, who was for his adorer at the moment of adoration the one omnipotent god. It is thus that we read:[1]

---

[1] W. A. I. iv. 19, 2.

"To be recited.[1]—1. Lord, illuminator of the darkness, opener of the sickly face,
2. Merciful god, who setteth up the fallen, who helpeth the weak,
3. Unto thy light look the great gods,
4. The spirits of earth all gaze upon thy face;[2]
5. The language of hosts as one word thou directest,
6. Smiting their head they look to the light of the midday sun.[3]
7. Like a wife, art thou set, glad and gladdening.
8. Thou art the light in the vault of the far-off heaven.
9. Thou art the spectacle of the broad earth.
10. Men far and near behold thee and rejoice.
11. The great gods have smelt the sweet savour (of the sacrifice),
12. the food of the shining heaven, the blessings (of the gods).
13. He who has not turned his hand to sin (thou wilt prosper),
14. he shall eat thy food, (he shall be blessed by thee)."

1.[4] "Mighty lord, from the midst of the shining heaven is thy rising;
2. O Sun-god, valiant hero, from the midst of the shining heaven is thy rising;
3. In the enclosure of the shining heaven is the weapon of thy falchion.
4. Where in the shining heavens is thy palace (*kummi*)?[5]
5. In the great gate of the shining heavens, when thou openest (it),

---

[1] EN, i.e. *siptu*, which at the commencement of these Semitic texts no longer means so much "an incantation" as part of a service which must be "recited" by the priest. Though some of the hymns may go back to the time of Sargon, others, at all events in their present form, must be considerably later.

[2] "Head," in the Accadian original.

[3] In the Semitic translation, simply "the Sun-god." The Accadian original is literally, "they make obeisance of their head, and gazing, O light of the midday sun."

[4] W. A. I. iv. 17.

[5] (*K*)*ummi*-(*ka*). *Kummu*, which properly means "a palace," is used specially of the palace of the Sun-god into which he returns at sunset. Hence it is denoted in Accadian by the three ideographs "hole-sun-below."

6. in the highest (summits) of the shining heavens, when thou passest by,
7. (the angels?) joyfully draw near to thee in prayer....
8. (The ministers?) of the queen of the gods attend thee with rejoicing.
9. The .... for the repose of thy heart daily attend thee.
10. The .... of the hosts of the earth zealously regard thee.
11. The (hosts) of heaven and earth attend thee, even thee.
   [The next few lines are too imperfect to be translated.]
18. With a bond are they united together straitly, (they that) are with thee.
19. The divine man[1] on behalf of his son attends thee, even thee, at the head.[2]
20. (*Worshipper.*)—The lord has sent me, even me.
21. The great lord Ea has sent me, even me.
22. (*Priest.*)—Attend and learn his word, enjoin his command.
23. Thou in thy course directest the black-headed race (of Accad).
24. Cast on him a ray of mercy and let it heal his sickness.
25. The man, the son of his god,[3] has committed sin and transgression.
26. (*Worshipper.*)—His limbs are sick, sick and in sickness he lies.
27. O Sun-god, utter thy voice at the lifting up of my hands.[4]
28. (*Priest.*)—Eat his food, receive his sacrifice, show thyself his god.
29. By thine order let his sin be pardoned, his transgression removed.
30. Let his sickness quit his body (?), and let him live.
31. May he live like the king!
32. On the day that he lives (again) may he reverence thy supremacy.

---

[1] Does this refer to the first man, like the Yima-Kshaêta of the Zend-Avesta?

[2] So in the Semitic translation. The original has "alone" (*usués*).

[3] A common phrase in the bilingual poems, denoting the close attachment of the worshipper to his deity. There is no connection between this idea and that embodied in the phrase, "the sons of God" (Gen. vi. 2), or even in the statement that Adam was "the son of God" (Luke iii. 38). But compare the expression, "a son of God," in Dan. iii. 25.

[4] In the original: "May the Sun-god look at the lifting up of my hand."

THE GODS OF BABYLONIA. 173

33. Like a king may thy judgment adjudge.[1]
34. Me also, the magician, thy servant, may thy judgment adjudge.
35. *Conclusion (of the hymn). When the sun is up*
36. *(this is) to be recited.*[2]—I have cried to thee, O Sun-god, in the midst of the glittering heaven;
37. in the shadow of the cedar thou dwellest, and
38. thy feet are set on the bright verdure of the herb.
39. The word inclines towards thee, it loves thee as a friend.
40. Thy brilliant light illumines all men.
41. Overthrower of all that would overthrow thee, assemble the nations,
42. O Sun-god, for thou art he who knoweth their boundaries.
43. Destroyer of the wicked, who inspirest the explanation[3]
44. of signs and evil omens, of dreams and baneful vampires,[4]
45. who turnest evil into good, who destroyest men and countries
46. that devote themselves to baneful sorceries, I humble myself(?) before thee.
47. Of bright corn-stalks their images I have fashioned
48. who have practised magic and devised the binding spell.
49. Terrify their heart and they are filled with dejection,
50. and abide thou, O Sun-god, the light of the mighty gods.
51. With the utmost of my breath let me rejoice.
52. May the gods who have created me take my hands;
53. Purify my mouth, direct my hands,
54. do thou also direct, O lord of the light of hosts, O Sun-god the judge."

---

[1] KA (determinative of speech) *síla khen-síle.* For *síla* (= *saladhu sa* [*ameli*]), see W. A. I. ii. 39, 14. Comp. W. A. I. iv. 12. 31, 32, and 29. 16—18, where *síla* is rendered *dalili.* Tiglath-Pileser I. calls himself *dalil ili rabi ana dalali*, "judging according to the judgment of the great gods." Delitzsch (Lotz's *Tiglath-Pileser*, p. 149) and Zimmern (*Busspsalmen*, p. 74) have entirely missed the true meaning of the expression.

[2] The following incantation is in Semitic-Assyrian only, and was probably appended to the old hymn in the time of Assur-bani-pal.

[3] *Namtablê.*

[4] Also called "(female) devourers of men," W. A. I. ii. 32, 77. Comp. the legend of the Descent of Istar into Hades, line 19.

1.[1] "Incantation.—O Sun-god, from the foundation of the sky thou comest forth (*takhkhar*),
2. a god whose journeying none can (rival),
3. a god who setteth at rest his father's heart.
4. Ea (*Nu-dimmud*) has enlarged for thee (thy) destiny among the gods.
5. The seat (*sulit*) of the earth (he has filled) into thy hand.
6. The fear of thy divinity (overwhelms) the world.
7. From the . . . . the gods are born (?).
8. The Sun-god from the midst of heaven rises."

In the closing days of the Babylonian monarchy, Nabonidos, after restoring the temple of the Sun-god at Sippara, addresses him in the following words: "O Samas, (mighty lord) of heaven and earth, light of the gods his fathers, offspring of Sin and Nin-gal, when thou enterest into E-Babbara, the temple of thy choice, when thou inhabitest thy everlasting shrine, look with joy upon me, Nabonidos, the king of Babylon, the prince who has fed thee, who has done good to thy heart, who has built thy dwelling-place supreme, and upon my prosperous labours; and daily at noon and sunset, in heaven and earth, grant me favourable omens, receive my prayers, and listen to my supplications. May I be lord of the firmly-established sceptre and sword, which thou hast given my hands to hold, for ever and ever!"

Nabonidos, the Babylonian, the peculiar protégé of Merodach, could not regard Samas with the same eyes as the old poets of the city of the Sun-god. His supreme Baal was necessarily Merodach, whose original identity with Samas had long since been forgotten; and Samas of Sippara was consequently to him only the Baal of another and a subject state. Samas is therefore but one of the

---

[1] S 690, *Obv.*

younger gods, who illuminates his divine fathers in the higher heaven. He shares the power and glory of his fathers only as the son shares the authority of the father in the human family. Nothing can illustrate more clearly the local character of Babylonian religion than this difference between the position assigned to Samas in the hymns and in the inscription of Nabonidos. In the one, he is the supreme god who brooks no equal; in the other, the subordinate of Merodach and even of the Moon-god Sin.

As Semitic influence extended itself in Babylonia, the Sun-god of Sippara came to absorb and be identified with the numerous local solar deities of the Chaldæan cities. It was only where a solar divinity was worshipped by the Semitic race under another name, as at Babylon or Eridu or Nipur, or where the Semites had already adopted another deity as the supreme object of their worship, as at Ur, that this process of absorption and identification did not take place. At times the local divinity became the son of Samas. Thus the Kossæan Sun-god Kit, who had been introduced by the Kossæan conquest, along with other gods like Simalia and Sugamuna, under the Semitised name of Kittum, was made his son,[1] and Makhir, the god of dreams, through an error occasioned by the want of any indices of gender in Accadian, was termed his daughter.[2]

---

[1] W. A. I. ii. 58, 11. The Semitic worshipper no doubt identified the name with his own word *kittum*, "right."

[2] W. A. I. ii. 58, 13. In v. 70. 1. 9. 15, on the contrary, Makhir is a god. He was the god of revelation, since a knowledge of the future was declared through dreams. Hence the Accadian *me-gal-zu*, "knowledge of the oracle," is interpreted *suttu pasaru*, "to explain a

This absence of any marks to denote grammatical gender, which Accadian shared with other agglutinative languages, must have been a sore puzzle and difficulty to the Semite when he first began to worship the gods of his more cultured neighbours. *Nin*, for instance, in Proto-Chaldæan, signifies at once "lord" and "lady," its primary meaning being "the great one." But the whole grammatical thought of the Semite was based upon a difference of gender. Not only were nouns distinguished into masculines and feminines, as in our own Indo-European family of speech; the distinction was further carried into the verb. A masculine without a feminine was as inconceivable to him as the man without the woman, the husband without the wife, the father without the mother. But as in Semitic grammar, so also in the Semitic conception of social life, the male was the source of life and authority, the female being but his weaker double, the pale reflection as it were of the man. The father was the head of the family, the supreme creator was the masculine Bel. This was the exact converse of the ideas that prevailed among the Accadians. Here it was the mother, and not the father, who stood at the head of the family; and in the bilingual texts we find that in the Accadian original the female is always mentioned before the male, while the Semitic translator is careful to reverse the order. Woman in Accad occupied a higher position than she did, or does, among the Semites.

The goddesses of Accad, accordingly, were independent

---

dream" (v. 30, 13), and *kibu sakanu*, "to establish a (divine) message" (v. 30, 14). *Suttu pasaru* may, however, be read *supartu pasaru*, "to explain a command."

beings, like the gods whose equals they were. But it was quite otherwise with the Semitic Babylonians. Except where they had borrowed and more or less assimilated an Accadian goddess, their female deities were simply the complement of their male consorts—little more, in fact, than the grammatical feminines of the gods. We may almost say that they were created by grammatical necessity. The Sun-god, therefore, as we have seen in a former Lecture, was provided with his feminine complement, with his "face" or reflection, as it was sometimes termed.

The Semites gave her the general title of *Bilat matati*, "the lady of the world." It was the title of most of the goddesses. They were seldom deemed worthy of a name of their own; they shone by the reflected light of their consorts; and as the supreme god of the worshipper was Bel, and more especially *Bil matati*, "the lord of the world," his wife was necessarily also Bilat or Beltis, and more especially *Bilat matati*. Sometimes, too, she was called *Bilat ili*, "the lady of the gods," in reference to the fact that the supreme Bel was their lord and master.

One of the Accadian solar divinities with whom the *Bilat matati*, when regarded as the wife of Samas, was identified, was Â or Sirrida.[1] Â had originally been a

---

[1] A bilingual hymn to the Sun-god, which was recited by the priests at sunset, has been translated by Mr. Pinches (*Tr. Soc. Bibl. Arch.* viii. 2) as follows:

"O Sun-god, in the midst of heaven, in thy setting
  may the bolts of the glorious heavens speak peace to thee!
  may the door of the heavens be gracious to thee!
  may Misaru, thy beloved messenger, guide thee!
  At Ê-Parra, the seat of thy lordship, thy greatness shines forth.
  May Â, thy beloved wife, gladly receive thee!

male divinity representing the solar disk, "the light of the sun" (Bir-Utu and Utu-Utu), as he was also entitled in Accadian. But the solar disk, the face as it were of the Sun-god, was his female consort, according to the religious conceptions of the Semites, and among them, therefore, the old Accadian god was transformed into a goddess. Â, or Sirrida, thus became a Semitic goddess, and sank into a colourless representative of the female element in the divinity. The transformation was aided

---

may thy heart take rest!
may the glory of thy godhead be established to thee!
Warrior, hero, sun-god, may they glorify thee!
lord of Ê-Parra, may the course of thy path be true!
O Sun-god, make straight thy path, go the everlasting road to thy rest.
O Sun-god, of the country the judge, of her decisions the director art thou."

The same hymn was also chanted in the morning, with the substitution of "O Sun-god, from the glorious heaven rising," for the first line. It was evidently originally intended for the temple of Samas at Sippara, but came in later times to be used in the worship of Nebo at Borsippa, Nebo being recognised as the local Sun-god of Borsippa.

The original Sumerian form of the name of Â was Sirrigam. In W. A. I. ii. 57. 21—31, we have examples of the various ways in which it might be written: Sir-ri-gâ-ma, Sur-gâ-ma, 'Sir-ga-m, 'Sir-da-m (Accadian), Sir-da (NIR-da), 'Sir-gam with the ideograph of the sun inserted, 'Sir-da-m (where the ideograph of the sun has the phonetic value of da transferred to it). From line 26 it appears that Â was properly a title, meaning "the father." A gloss on line 28 reads Tsab-Utu instead of Bir-Utu, but this is a mistake, since *tsab* was Semitic, and signified "warrior" (*erim* in Accadian) and not "light." Pinches (*Proceedings of the Society of Bib. Archæology*, Nov. 1885) would connect Â with Yahveh; but this, of course, is philologically impossible, while the supposed instances of an Assyrian god Ya are all due to misinterpretation of the texts, and the name of the Edomite king Â-rammu does not prove that the Edomite deity Â was identical with the Babylonian. Oppert's proposal to identify Â with Malik or Moloch finds no support in the monuments.

by the absence of gender in Accadian, to which I have already alluded. Where there were no external signs of gender, and where Nin-Gan, one of the epithets applied to Â, might mean indifferently "lord of light" or "lady of light," it was not difficult to bring it about.

One of the deities partially absorbed by the Sun-god was the ancient god of Fire. Among most primitive peoples, fire is endowed with divine attributes. It moves and devours like a living thing; it purifies and burns up all that is foul; and it is through the fire upon the altar —the representative of the fire upon the hearth—that the savour of the burnt sacrifice ascends to the gods in heaven. But fire is itself a messenger from above. It comes to us from the sky in the lightning-flash, and we feel it in the rays of the noontide sun. The Fire-god tended therefore to become on the one side the messenger and intermediary between gods and men, and on the other side the Sun-god himself.

In pre-Semitic times, however, the Fire-god retained all his primæval privileges and rank. He is still one of the leading gods or "creators" of the pantheon. It is he who controls the lower spirits of earth and heaven, and to whom the prayers of the faithful are addressed. Thus he is celebrated in an old hymn in the following strains:[1]

1. "The (bed) of the earth they took for their border,[2] but the god appeared not,
2. from the foundations of the earth he appeared not to make hostility;

---

[1] W. A. I. iv. 15.

[2] In the Semitic rendering, "(In the bed) of the earth their necks were taken."

3. (to) the heaven below they extended (their path), and to the heaven that is unseen they climbed afar.[1]
4. In the Star(s) of Heaven was not their ministry;[2] in Mazzaroth (the Zodiacal signs)[3] was their office.
5. The Fire-god, the first-born supreme, unto heaven they pursued and no father did he know.
6. O Fire-god, supreme on high, the first-born, the mighty, supreme enjoiner of the commands of Anu!
7. The Fire-god enthrones with himself the friend that he loves.
8. He reveals the enmity of those seven.
9. On the work he ponders in his dwelling-place.
10. O Fire-god, how were those seven begotten, how were they nurtured?
11. Those seven in the mountain of the sunset were born;
12. those seven in the mountain of the sunrise grew up.
13. In the hollows of the earth they have their dwelling;
14. on the high-places of the earth their names are proclaimed.
15. As for them, in heaven and earth they have no dwelling, hidden is their name.
16. Among the sentient gods they are not known.
17. Their name in heaven and earth exists not.
18. Those seven from the mountain of the sunset gallop forth;
19. those seven in the mountain of the sunrise are bound to rest.
20. In the hollows of the earth they set the foot.
21. On the high-places of the earth they lift the neck.
22. They by nought are known; in heaven and earth is no knowledge of them."

Fire was produced in Babylonia, as in other countries of the ancient world, by rubbing two sticks one against the other. The fire-stick, therefore, whose point was ignited by the friction, was regarded with special venetion. The idea of "fire" was expressed by two ideographs (GIS-BAR and GIS-ŚIR) which signified literally "the wood

---

[1] So the Semitic rendering. The original has, "the heaven which has no exit they opened."

[2] Iphtael of *idu*, "to know."

[3] In the original: "the watch of the thirty."

of light." This "wood of light" was exalted into a god. Sometimes it represents Gibil or Kibir, the fire-god, sometimes it is itself worshipped as a divinity under the name of 'Savul (in Semitic, 'Savullu). 'Savul seems to have been adored more particularly in Babylon; at all events he was identified with Merodach as well as with Samas in those later ages when the cult of the Accadian fire-god passed into the cult of the Semitic Sun-god, and his name forms part of that of the Babylonian king 'Savul-sarra-yukin or Saosdukhinos, the brother of Assur-bani-pal. It even made its way into the far west. The names of the kings of Edom preserved in the 36th chapter of Genesis throw a curious light on Edomite mythology, and show that 'Savul of Babylon was worshipped among the mountains of Seir. We are told that Hadad the son of Bedad, Samlah of Masrekah or the "Vine-land," and Saul of Rehoboth by the river Euphrates, succeeded one another. Now Hadad, as we shall see, was the Sun-god of the Syrians, whom the Assyrians identified with their own Ramman or Rimmon; and the name of his father Bedad is simply Ben-Dad, "the son of Dad," another form of Hadad according to the cuneiform inscriptions, and possibly the same as the David of the Hebrews, the Dido, or "beloved one," of the Phœnicians. Samlah of the "Wine-land" is the Semelê of Greek mythology, the mother of Dionysos the Wine-god. Her Phœnician origin has long been recognised, and her name has recently been met with in a masculine form in a Phœnician inscription. Saul of Rehoboth by the river Euphrates is, letter for letter, identical with the Babylonian 'Savul, and his Babylonian origin is further betrayed by the statement that he came from the Euphrates.

LECTURE III.

Rehoboth means merely the "public places" of a city; and when we remember that in the 10th chapter of Genesis (v. 11), Rehoboth ('Ir) is the name applied to the suburbs of Nineveh, it seems probable that in the Rehoboth of the Euphrates we may discover the suburbs of its sister-city Babylon.

Let us now turn back again to Sippara, the city whose Sun-god swallowed up so many of the primæval deities of Accad, like the Kronos of Hellenic myth. By the side of Sippara of Samas, I have said, arose the twin-city of Sippara of Anunit. The final dental shows that Anunit was a female divinity, and shows furthermore that she was of Semitic origin. But it was only as a female divinity that she came from a Semitic source. She was, in fact, the Semitic feminine of Anúna, one of the primordial gods of ancient Accad. Anúna, it would appear, must have been adored in Sippara in pre-Semitic days, and subsequently worshipped for a time by the Semites, who created out of his name his female consort Anunit. Anunit was identified with Istar, and thus survived, while her lord and master, to whom she owed her very existence, passed into almost entire oblivion. For this it is possible to assign a reason. Anúna signifies "the master," and is the masculine correlative of Innina or Inina, the "mistress" of the ghost-world, to whom I have had occasion to refer before.[1] Like Inina, he presided over the lower world, and was consequently the local god of primitive Sippara, who corresponded to the Mul-lil of Nipur. But the name was also a general one,

---

[1] As Innina stands for *an nina*, the vowel of *an*, "divine one," being assimilated to that of Nina, Anuna stands for *an nuna*, "the great god."

THE GODS OF BABYLONIA. 183

and might be applied to any of the deities whom the Accadians regarded as specially endowed with power. Hence it is that in a bilingual hymn the Anúnas of the lower world are called "the great gods;"[1] while another text declares that while "the great gods are fifty in number, the gods of destiny are seven and the Anúna of heaven are five."[2] Besides the five Anúnas of the heaven, there were the more famous Anúnas of the lower world, whose golden throne was placed in Hades by the side of the waters of life. They were called the Anúna-ge, "the masters of the under-world," a term which the Semites pronounced Anúnaki. These Anúnaki were opposed to the Igigi or angels, the spirits of the upper air, and, the real origin of their name being forgotten, took the place of the older Anúnas. In one of the texts I have quoted, the Semitic translator not only renders the simple Anúnas by "Anúnaki," he even speaks of the "Anúnaki of heaven," which is a contradiction in terms.[3]

---

[1] W. A. I. ii. 19, 8. "The Anúnas of the lower world to the upper firmament return." The hymn must be of Semitic origin, as the Accadian version shows Semitic influence. Another hymn (ii. 19. 49, 50) declares that "the Anúnas of the lower world in the hollows I cause to grope like swine." In a hymn in which the Fire-god is identified with Samas, the latter is called "the judge of the Anunnaki" (K 2585, Obv. 9).

[2] K 4629, Rev.

[3] Upon the analogy of Anúnaki, the Semites have added a final guttural to several of the words they borrowed from the Accadians, like *asurraku*, "a bed," from the Acc. *asurra*. Similarly the analogy of *issakku*, "a high-priest," from the Semitic root *nasaku*, "to pour out libations," has called into existence other nouns with final *-akku*. The Accadian *abrik*, "a vizier," borrowed by the Semites under the form of *abrikku* (82. 8—16. Obv. 18), whence the *abhrék* of Gen. xli. 43 helped in the same direction. The adverbs in *-ku* of Zimmern (*Babylonische Busspsalmen*, p. 94), like *martsaku* or *zazaku*, should be read *martsatus* and *zazatus*.

Though Anunit was considered merely a local form of Istar (W. A. I. ii. 49, 12), the great temple of Ulbar[1] —if that is the right pronunciation of the word—which had been erected by Zabu about B.C. 2340, preserved her special name and cult at Sippara, from whence it passed into Assyria. Nabonidos tells us that he restored the temple "for Anunit, the mistress of battle, the bearer of the bow and quiver, the accomplisher of the command of Bel her father, the sweeper away of the enemy, the destroyer of the wicked, who marches before the gods, who has made (his) omens favourable at sunrise and sunset." In calling her the lady of battle and daughter of Bel, Nabonidos identifies her with Istar, an identification which is made even more plain a few lines further on (col. iii. 42, 48—51), where he makes her the sister of Samas and daughter of Sin.

This identity of Anunit and Istar brings Sippara into close connection with Erech, the modern Warka, the city specially consecrated to the goddess of love. Erech, we are told in the story of the plague-demon Nerra,[2] was "the seat of Anu and Istar, the city of the choirs of the festival-girls and consecrated maidens of Istar,"[3] where in Ê-Ana, "the house of heaven," dwelt her priests, "the festival-makers who had devoted their manhood in order

---

[1] The word is found in R 2. i. 10, (b)ennâ UL-BAR-MES AN u KI itkhuzu, "the lights (?) of heaven and earth kept the bond." According to W. A. I. ii. 61, 11, the temple of Ulbar was in Agadhe or Accad, thus identifying Accad with Sippara of Anunit, and suggesting that the first foundations of the temple went back to the time of Sargon, the father of Naram-Sin.

[2] Col. ii. 4 sq.

[3] Kitsriti samkhâtu u kharimâtu sa Istar. For samkhâtu (שמחות), comp. Lev. xxiii. 40, Deut. xii. 18.

that men might adore the goddess, carrying swords, carrying razors, stout dresses and flint-knives,"¹ "who minister to cause reverence for the glory of Istar."² Erech, too, was the city with whose fortunes the legend of Gisdhubar was associated; it was here that he slew the bull Anu had created to avenge the slight offered by him to Istar; and it was here in *Uruk śuburi*, "in Erech the shepherd's hut," that he exercised his sovereignty. Erech is thus connected with the great epic of the Semitic Babylonians, and it is probable that its author, Sin-liqi-unníni, was a native of the place. However this may be, Erech appears to have been one of the centres of Semitic influence in Babylonia from a very early period. The names of the kings stamped upon its oldest bricks bear Semitic names, and the extent to which the worship of Istar as developed at Erech spread through the Semitic world points to its antiquity as a Semitic settlement.

It was not of Semitic foundation, however. Its earliest name was the Accadian Unu-ki or Unuk, "the place of the settlement," of which the collateral form Uruk does not seem to have come into vogue before the Semitic period. If I am right in identifying Unuk with the Enoch of Genesis, the city built by Kain in commemoration of his first-born son, Unuk must be regarded as having received its earliest culture from Eridu, since Enoch was the son of Jared, according to Gen. v. 18, and Jared or Irad (Gen. iv. 18) is the same word as Eridu.³

---

¹ *Nas padhri nas naglabi dupie u tsurri.*
² *Sa ana suplukh kaptat D. P. Istar itakkalu.*
³ *Zeitschrift für Keilschriftforschung,* ii. 4, p. 404, where I further suggest that the name represented by the two varying forms of Methuselakh and Methusael should be Mutu-sa-ilati, "the husband of the

The local god of Erech, however, was not Ea, the god of the river and sea, but Ana, the sky. Thus whereas at Eridu the present creation was believed to have originated out of water, the sky being the primæval goddess Zikum or Zigara, mother alike of Ea and the other gods, at Erech the sky was itself the god and the creator of the visible universe. The two cosmologies are antagonistic to one another, and produced manifold inconsistencies in the later syncretic age of Babylonian religion.

But it was not in Erech alone that the sky was considered divine. Throughout Chaldæa, Ana, "the sky,"

---

goddess," i.e. the Sun-god Tammuz, the husband of Istar. He had a shrine in the forest of Eridu, while Istar was the presiding deity of Erech. Lamech would be the Semitic equivalent of Lamga, a name of the Moon-god, according to ii. 47, 66, when represented by the character which had the pronunciation of *nagar, nangaru,* in Semitic (3. 572). *Naga-r* is probably a dialectic form of Lamga. In S769. 1, 2, the ideograph preceded by AB, "lord" is rendered in the Semitic line by *gurgurru.* Cp. "*Nin-nagar,* the great workman (*nagar*) of heaven," W. A. I. iv. 25, 27. Adah and Zillah, the wives of Lamech, would correspond with the Assyrian *edu* and *tsillu,* " darkness" and " shade." Jabal and Jubal, the sons of Lamech, are merely variant forms of the same word, which is evidently the Assyrian *ablu,* " son" (from *abalu,* " to bring down"), like Abel (as Dr. Oppert long since pointed out). *Ablu* refers us to "the only son" Tammuz (W. A. I. ii. 36, 54), who was "a shepherd" like Jabal and Abel, and whose untimely death was commemorated by the musical instruments of Jubal. In Kypros, in fact, he was known as the son of Kinyras, a name that reminds us of the *kinnôr,* or "harp." Adonis-Tammuz, it was said, was slain by Arês in the form of a boar, and Arês was identified with the Babylonian god Adar or Uras (see above, p. 152), "the god of the pig," whose name (AN-BAR) was used ideographically to denote "iron," in curious parallelism to the fact that Tubal-Cain, the son of Lamech, was the "instructor of every artificer in brass and iron." There are some who would aver that the Tubal-Cain of Genesis is but the double of Cain, and that it was he and not his father Lamech who had slain the "young man" (*yeled,* Assyrian *ilattu,* a title of Tammuz). Adar, it may be noticed, was "the lord of the date," and therefore of agriculture (see above, p. 153).

received worship, and the oldest magical texts invoke "the spirit of the sky" by the side of that of the earth. What distinguished the worship of Ana at Erech was that here alone he was the chief deity of the local cult, that here alone he had ceased to be a subordinate spirit, and had become a *dingir* or "creator."[1]

Of this pre-Semitic period in the worship of Ana we know but little. It is only when he has become the Anu of the Semites and has undergone considerable changes in his character and worship, that we make our first true acquaintance with him. We come to know him as the Semitic Baal-samaim, or "lord of heaven," the supreme Baal, viewed no longer as the Sun-god, but as the whole expanse of heaven which is illuminated by the sun.[2]

How early this must have been is shown by the extension of his name as far west as Palestine. In the records of the Egyptian conqueror Thothmes III., in the 16th century before our era, mention is made of the Palestinian town of Beth-Anath, "the temple of Anat," the female double of Anu. Another Beth-Anath was included within the borders of the tribe of Naphtali (Josh. xix.

---

[1] We must not forget that in many passages in the Proto-Chaldæan literature *ana* denotes simply "the sky," and not a divine being at all, though the Semitic translators, misled by the determinative of divinity with which the word is written, have usually supposed it to represent the god Anu.

[2] Compare the Phœnician account of the creation as reported by Philo Byblius: "Of the wind Kolpia and of his wife Baau (i.e. *Bahu, bohu*), which is interpreted night, were begotten two mortal men, Aiôn and Protogonos so called, and Aiôn discovered food from trees. Those begotten from these were called Genos and Genea (? Kain), and inhabited Phœnicia, and when great droughts came they stretched forth their hands to heaven, towards the sun, for this they supposed to be the only god, the lord of heaven, calling him Beel-samin."

38); and Anathoth, whose name shows us that, besides the Ashtaroth or "Astartes," the Canaanites venerated their local goddesses under the title of "Anats," was a city of the priests. Anah or Anat was the daughter of the Hivite Zibeon and mother-in-law of Esau (Gen. xxxvi. 1, 14), and by her side we hear of Anah or Anu, the son of the Horite Zibeon, who "found the mules (or hot-springs) in the wilderness as he fed the asses of Zibeon his father." But Anu did not make his way westward alone. In the Assyrian inscriptions Anu is coupled with Dagan, "the exalted one,"[1] whose female consort seems to have been Dalas or Salas. Thus Assur-natsir-pal calls himself "the beloved of Anu and Dagon;" and Sargon asserts that he "had extended his protection over the city of Harran, and, according to the ordinance of Anu and Dagan, had written down their laws." Here Dagan or Dagon is associated with Harran, the half-way house, as it were, between the Semites of Babylonia and the Semites of the west. From Harran we can trace his name and cult to Phœnicia. Beth-Dagon was a city of Asher, in the neighbourhood of Tyre and Zidon (Josh. xix. 27), and the fragments of Philôn Byblios, the Greek translator of the Phœnician writer Sankhuniathon, tell us expressly that Dagon was a Phœnician god. That the statement is genuine is made clear by the false etymology assigned to the name, from the Semitic *dâgân*, "corn."[2] But it was

---

[1] W. A. I. iv. 20, 16; 79. 7-8. 68. The Accadian *da* means "summit" (W. A. I. v. 21. 45. 6; ii. 26, 49), and *gan* is the participle of the substantive verb. In W. A. I. iii. 68, 21, Dagon is identified with Mul-lil. For his wife Dalas or Salas, see W. A. I. iii. 68, 22.

[2] "Ouranos, succeeding to the kingdom of his father, contracted marriage with his sister Gê, and had by her four sons, Ilos (El), who

among the Philistines in the extreme south of Palestine that the worship of Dagon attained its chief importance. Here he appears to have been exalted into a Baal, and to have become the supreme deity of the confederate Philistine towns. We hear of his temples at Gaza (Josh. xvi. 21—30) and at Ashdod (1 Sam. v. 1 *sq.*), as well as of a town of Beth-Dagon, and we gather from the account given of his image that he was represented as a man with head and hands.

It is probable that the worship of Anu migrated westward along with the worship of Istar. The god and goddess of Erech could not well be dissociated from one another, and the spread of the worship of the goddess among the Semitic tribes brought with it the spread of the worship of the god also. I am inclined to think that this must be placed at least as early as the age of Sargon of Accad. The worship of Istar found its way to all the branches of the Semitic family except the Arabic; and, as we shall see in a future Lecture, the form of the name Ashtoreth, given to the goddess in Canaan, raises a presumption that this was due, not to the campaigns of the early Babylonian kings, but to the still earlier migrations of the Semitic population towards the west. The old sky-god of the Accadians must have become the Semitic Anu at a very remote period indeed.

But it was the sky-god of Erech only. It does not follow that where the divine Ana, or "sky," is mentioned

---

is called Kronos, and Betylos (Bethel), and Dagon, which signifies corn, and Atlas.... Kronos gave (a concubine of Ouranos) in marriage to Dagon, and she was delivered and called the child Demaroôn.... And Dagon, after he had found out bread-corn and the plough, was called Zeus Arotrios."

in the Accadian texts, the god who became the Semitic Anu is referred to, even though the Semitic translators of the texts imagined that such was the case. There were numerous temples in Chaldæa into whose names the name of the deified sky entered, but in most cases this deified sky was not the sky-god of Erech. It is only where the names have been given in Semitic times, or where the Accadian texts are the production of Semitic *literati* composing in the sacred language of the priests, like the monks of the Middle Ages, that we may see the Anu of the mythological tablets. Without doubt the Semitic scribes have often confounded their Anu with the local sky-god of the ancient documents, but this should only make us the more cautious in dealing with their work.

The original sky-god of Erech denoted the visible sky. He is opposed to the visible earth, and was consequently in most of the Chaldæan cities an inferior deity, subordinate to a Mul-lil, an Ea or a Sun-god, who ruled over the sky and the earth. But when the Accadian Ana became the Semitic Anu, he assumed a more spiritual character. It was no longer the visible heaven that was represented by him, but an invisible one, above and beyond the heaven that we behold. Henceforward "the heaven of Anu" denoted the serene and changeless regions to which the gods fled when the deluge had broken up the face of the lower heaven, and which an Assyrian poet calls "the land of the silver sky." It was to this spiritualised heaven that the spirit of Ea-bani, the friend of Gisdhubar, ascended, and from which he gazed placidly on the turmoil of the earth below; and it was from his seat therein that Anu assigned their places in the lower heaven to Samas, Sin and Istar, the Sun, the Moon and the Evening Star, according to the legend of the seven wicked spirits.

But the spiritualisation of Anu did not stop here. As a Semitic Baal he had become a supreme god, the lord and father of the universe. It was only a step further, therefore, to make him himself the universe, and to resolve into him the other deities of the Babylonian pantheon. We read occasionally in the hymns of "the one god." "The ban, the ban," a poet writes, personifying the priestly sentence of excommunication, like the Ara of Æskhylos or the divine burden of Zechariah (ix. 1), " is a barrier which none may overpass;[1] the barrier of the gods against which they cannot transgress, the barrier of heaven and earth which cannot be changed; the one god against whom none may rebel; god and man cannot explain (it); it is a snare not to be passed which is formed against the evil, the cord of a snare from which there is no exit which is turned against the evil." The conception of Anu, however, as "the one god" was pantheistic rather than monotheistic. The cosmological deities of an older phase of faith were in the first instance resolved into him. In place of the genealogical, or gnostic, system which we find in the account of the Creation in days, we have a pantheistic system, in which Lakhama and the other primæval forces of nature are not the parents of Anu, but are identified with Anu himself.[2] It is easy to conceive how the old deity An-sar, " the upper firmament," with all its host of spirits, might be iden-

---

[1] W. A. I. iv. 16, 1.

[2] W. A. I. ii. 54, 40, "Lakhma is Anu, the god of the hosts of heaven and earth." So in ii. 54, 34, &c., and iii. 69, 1.

tified with him; but when we find Uras also, the Sun-god of Nipur, made one with Anu, "the hearer of prayer," and the eagle-like Alala, the bridegroom of Istar and double of Tammuz, equally resolved into the god of Erech, it is plain that we have to do with an advanced stage of pantheism. This monotheistic, or rather pantheistic, school of faith has been supposed by Sir Henry Rawlinson to have grown up at Eridu; but the fact that it centres round the name of Anu points rather to Erech as its birth-place. How long it flourished, or whether it extended beyond a narrow group of priestly thinkers, we have no means of ascertaining. It is interesting, however, as showing that the same tendency which in Assyria exalted Assur to the position of an all-powerful deity who would brook neither opposition nor unbelief, among the more meditative Babylonians produced a crude system of pantheism. Whatever question there may be as to whether the pure and unmixed Semite is capable of originating a pantheistic form of faith, there can be little doubt about it where the Semite is brought into close contact with an alien race. The difference between the Assyrian and the Babylonian was the difference between the purer Semite and one in whose veins ran a copious stream of foreign blood.

The early importance and supremacy of Erech in Semitic Babylonia caused its god to assume a place by the side of Ea of Eridu and Mul-lil, the older Bel. It is possible that the extension of his cult had already begun in Accadian days. The Ana, or Sky-god, to whom Gudea at Tel-loh erected a temple, may have been the Sky-god of Erech, more especially when we remember the connection that existed between Erech and Eridu on the one hand, and between Tel-loh and Eridu on the other.[1] However this may be, from the commencement of the Semitic period Anu appears as the first member of a triad which consisted of Anu, Bel or Mul-lil, and Ea. His position in the triad was due to the leading position held by Erech; the gods of Nipur and Eridu retained the rank which their time-honoured sanctity and the general extension of their cult had long secured to them; but the rank of Anu was derived from the city of which he was the presiding god. The origin of the triad was thus purely accidental; there was nothing in the religious conceptions of the Babylonians which led to its formation. Once formed, however, it was inevitable that a cosmological colouring should be given to it, and that Anu, Bel and Ea, should represent respectively the heaven, the lower world and the watery element. Later ages likened this cosmological trinity to the elemental trinity of the Sun, the Moon and the Evening Star; and below the triad of Anu, Bel and Ea, was accordingly placed the triad of of Samas, Sin and Istar. But this secondary trinity never attracted the Babylonian mind. Up to the last, as we have seen, Sin continued to be the father of Samas and Istar, and Babylonian religion remained true to its primitive tendency to dualism, its separation of the divine world into male and female deities. The only genuine trinity that can be discovered in the religious faith of early Chaldæa was that old Accadian system which conceived of a divine father and mother by the side of their son the Sun-god.

---

[1] The importation of the worship of Istar into Tel-loh, with her temple of Ê-ana, or "house of heaven," would, however, fully account for the importation of the worship of Anu at the same time.

The Semitic Anu necessarily produced the feminine Anat, and as necessarily Anat was identified with the earth as Anu was with the sky. In this way the Accadian idea of a marriage union between the earth and the sky was adapted to the newer Semitic beliefs. But we must not misunderstand the nature of the adaptation. Anat never became an independent deity, as Dav-kina, for example, had been from the outset; she had no separate existence apart from Anu. She is simply a *Bilat matati*, "a mistress of the world," or a *Bilat ili*, "a mistress of the gods," like the wife of Bel or of Samas; she is, in fact, a mere colourless representation of the female principle in the universe, with no attributes that distinguish her from Anunit or Istar except the single one that she was the feminine form of Anu. Hence it is that the Canaanites had not only their Ashtaroth, but their Anathoth as well, for the Anathoth or "Anats" differed from the Ashtaroth or "Ashtoreths" in little else than name. So far as she was an active power, Anat was the same as Istar; in all other respects she was merely the grammatical complement of Anu, the goddess who necessarily stood at the side of a particular god.

There are still two other gods of whom I must speak before I conclude this Lecture—Nergal, the god of Cutha, and Ramman or Rimmon, the air-god. Nergal occupies a peculiar position. He was the local deity of the town called Gudua, "the resting-place," by the Accadians—a name changed by the Semites into Kutu or Cutha—which is now represented by the mounds of Tel-Ibrahim. For reasons unknown to us, the necropolis of Cutha became famous at an early time; and though the Babylonian kings, like the kings of Assyria and Judah, were buried in their own palaces,[1] it is probable that many of their subjects preferred a sepulchre in the neighbourhood of Cutha.

The original name of the god of Gudua was Nerra or Ner, a word which the Semitic scribes render by *gasru*, "the strong one," and less accurately *namru*, "the bright one."[2] Later legends had much to say about this ancient hero-god. Like Etána, his throne was placed in Hades, where he sat crowned, awaiting the entrance of the dead kings of the earth. But the hero-king of the myths was one and the same with the god whom his primitive worshippers at Gudua made king of *aráli* or Hades. He was, in fact, the personification of death. Hence his title of "the strong one," the invincible god who overpowers the mightiest of mortal things. The realm over which he ruled was "the great city" (*uru-gal*); great, indeed, it must have been, for it contained all the multitudes of men who had passed away from the earth.

Like the city over which he ruled, the god, too, was himself "great." He came, therefore, to be familiarly known as Nergal—Nirwal in the dialect of Accad—"the great Ner," or "hero." A punning etymology connected his name with "the great city" (*uru-gal*), as if it had been Ne(r)-uru-gal, "the Ner of Hades." But he was also "king of Cutha," as well as of "the desert" on

---

[1] See the dynastic fragment published by George Smith in the *Trans. Soc. Bib. Arch.* iii. 2, lines 27, 29, 30, 32, 34, 37.

[2] W. A. I. iv. 9, 36. *Ner* is rendered *namru* in K 4245, *Rev.* 13 (where "the god of the high voice" is said to be *ner*). A play seems to be intended on *gir* (*ngir*), "the lightning-flash," which was *numru* in Assyrian, rendered by *ner* in W. A. I. iv. 5, 15. *Numru* in the Accado-Semitic of northern Babylonia was written in rebus fashion NUM-GIR, i.e. *num-mir*. Nerra was pronounced Ngirra; hence the gloss Irra.

whose borders Cutha stood and where its necropolis was probably situated; while other titles made him "king of heaven," "the king who marches before Anu," "the king Nerra," and "the mighty sovereign of the deep."[1] At Cutha he had been known in pre-Semitic days as Aria, "the founder," and his worshippers had called him Allamu and Almu, the god "who issues forth in might."[2] But his most frequent appellation is U-gur, the god of "the falchion,"[3] and under this name he tended to become separate from Nergal, the god of the tomb, and to be regarded as, like the Sun-god Adar, the champion of the gods.

It was as the death-dealing lord of Hades that Nergal first became "the hero of the gods," "who marches in their front." The metaphor was taken from the champion who, like Goliath, places himself before his comrades and

---

[1] W. A. I. ii. 54, 5. The title "king of heaven" must go back to days when the sky-god of Erech was as yet unknown at Cutha, while the title "great king of the deep" indicates a connection with Eridu. In Phœnicia, we are told, he was known as Sar-rabu, "the great king," and among the Shuites on the western bank of the Euphrates as Emu. Emu is letter for letter the national god of the Ammonites, Ammi, which, as Dr. Neubauer has shown, appears as 'Am in such Hebrew names as Jerobo-am and Rehobo-am.

[2] *Allam-ta-ea.* *Allam* may be connected with *alam*, "an image," which probably has the same root as *alad*, "a colossus," *alal* or *ala*, "a demon," *alala*, "the Sun-god," who was afterwards identified with Anu, and *alim*, "a steer," literally "the strong animal." But the word also seems to have been read 'Sulim (see W. A. I. ii. 61. 72, 73).

[3] W. A. I. ii. 2, 342. As Ugur, the god was also worshipped as "Nergal of the *khâdhi*," or "apparitions" (W. A. I. iii. 67, 70). In later times the name may have been divided into U-gur, "lord of the *gur*," which would then have been confounded with *gur*, "the deep" (in Sumerian), one of the titles of Ea being En-gur, "lord of the deep" (W. A. I. ii. 58, 53).

challenges the enemy to combat. It is thus that we read in the story of the Deluge, when the flood of rain and destruction is described as coming upon the guilty world: "Rimmon in the midst of (heaven) thundered, and Nebo and the Wind-god went in front; the throne-bearers went over mountain and plain; Nergal the mighty removes the wicked; Adar goes in front and casteth down."[1]

As lord of Hades, too, he was made the son of Mul-lil. A hymn (K 5268), the colophon of which tells us that it was composed in Cutha, begins with the words: "Let Nergal be glorified, the hero of the gods, who cometh forth as the strong one, the son of Mul-lil." In the same hymn, Marad is declared to be his city, from which we may infer that Marad was near Cutha. Its protecting divinity, however, was, strictly speaking, Lugal-túda, "the royal offspring," or perhaps "valiant king," a personification of the thunder-cloud and lightning; but it is evident from the hymn that he had been identified with the death-dealing god of Cutha. Of Laz, the wife of Nergal, we know little or nothing. Her name survived as the local divinity of Cutha, but her office and attributes were taken by Allat. Even Nergal himself as the lord of Hades belongs rather to the Accadian than to the Semitic period. Among the Semites he was the hero and champion of the gods, and as such the destroyer of the wicked, rather than the king of death who slays alike the wicked and the good. The sovereignty of Hades had passed out of his hands, and he had become

---

[1] It was in this capacity also that he appears as Nerra, the plague-demon (misread Lubara by George Smith), whose adventures formed the subject of a long poem.

LECTURE III.

the companion of the solar Adar and the warrior of the gods of heaven.

Under his old name of Ner, however, a curious reminiscence of his primitive character lasted down to late times. In the hymns and other poetical effusions, we not unfrequently come across the phrase, "mankind, the cattle of the god Ner." I have already drawn attention to the agricultural nature of early Chaldæan civilisation, and the influence that agriculture had upon the modes of thought and expression of the population. Not only was the sky regarded as the counterpart of the Babylonian plain, and the heavenly bodies transformed into the herds and flocks that fed there, but the human inhabitants of the earth were themselves likened to the cattle they pastured and fed. One of the earliest titles of the Babylonian kings was "shepherd," reminding us of the Homeric ποιμὴν λαῶν, "shepherd of nations;" and in the Epic of Gisdhubar the sovereign city of Erech is termed the *subur*, or "shepherd's hut." Just as the subjects of the king, therefore, were looked upon as the sheep whom their ruler shepherded, so too mankind in general were regarded as the cattle slain by the god of death. They were, in fact, his herd, whom he fed and slaughtered in sacrifice to the gods.[1]

But apart from phrases of this kind, which embalmed the beliefs and ideas of a half-forgotten age, Nergal of Cutha was a decaying godhead. His power waned with

---

[1] So in a fragmentary hymn composed by order of Assur-bani-pal on the occasion of an eclipse of the moon, mankind are called "the people of the black heads, the living assembly (*pukhar napisti*), the cattle (*pul*) of the god Ner, the reptiles (*nammassê*) [whom] thy [governance] has overlooked" (K 2836, *Obv.* 11—13).

the rise and growth of Semitic influence in Babylonia. He thus formed a strong contrast to the god of the air and wind, whose cult belongs essentially to the Semitic period.

The primitive inhabitant of Babylonia paid a special worship to the winds. He beheld in them spirits of good and evil. He prayed for "the good wind" which cooled the heats of summer and brought moisture to the parched earth, and he saw in the storm and tempest, in the freezing blasts of winter and the hot wind that blew from the burning desert, "the seven evil spirits." They were the demons "who had been created in the lower part of heaven," and who warred against the Moon-god when he suffered eclipse. They were likened to all that was most noxious to man. The first, we are told, was "the sword (or lightning) of rain;" the second, "a vampire;"[1] the third, "a leopard;" the fourth, "a serpent;" the fifth, "a watch-dog" (?); the sixth, "a violent tempest which (blows) against god and king;" and the seventh, "a baleful wind." But their power caused them to be dreaded, and they were venerated accordingly. It was remembered that they were not essentially evil. They, too, had been the creation of Anu, for they came forth from the sky, and all seven were "the messengers of Anu their king." In the war of the gods against the dragon of chaos, they had been the allies of Merodach. We read of them that ere the great combat began, the god

---

[1] *Usumgálu*, expressed by ideographs that signify "the solitary monster." It denoted a fabulous beast which "devoured the corpses of the dead" (W. A. I. ii. 19, 62), and was therefore not exactly a vampire, which devoured the living, but corresponded rather to one of the creatures mentioned in Is. xiii. 21, 22, xxxiv. 14.

"created the evil wind, the hostile wind, the tempest, the storm, the four winds, the seven winds, the whirlwind, the unceasing wind." When Merodach had slung forth his boomerang[1] and hit the dragon, "the evil wind that seizes behind showed its face. And Tiamat (the dragon of the sea) opened her mouth to swallow it, but (the god) made the evil wind descend so that she could not close her lips; with the force of the winds he filled her stomach, and her heart was sickened and her mouth distorted." Down to the closing days of the Assyrian empire, the four winds, "the gods of Nipur," were still worshipped in Assyria (W. A. I. iii. 66, *Rev.* 26), and Saru, the Wind-god, is mentioned as a separate divinity in the story of the Deluge.

Among the winds there was one whose name awakened feelings of dread in the mind of every Babylonian. This was the tempest, called *màtu* in Accadian,[2] and *abub* in Semitic. It was the tempest which had been once sent by Bel to drown guilty mankind in the waters of a deluge, and whose return as the minister of divine vengeance was therefore ever feared. As each year brought with it the month of Sebat or January, with its "curse of rain," the memory of that terrible event rose again in the Baby-

---

[1] The word means literally "the cord of a snare." Zimmern therefore thinks of "net," but the sculptures show that a boomerang is meant.

[2] The word is written with the determinative of water A. It is probably a contraction of Martu, since in the name of the god who afterwards came to correspond to the Semitic Ramman, the first syllable is represented by the character which usually has the value of *mar*. But we know from another character which has the same value that the same word could assume in different dialects or periods of Accadian the varying forms of *mal*, *mar* and *mâ*.

lonian mind. Mâtu was a god whose favour had to be conciliated, and whose name accordingly appears on numbers of early cylinders.

But though Mâtu was thus specially identified with the great tempest which formed an era in Babylonian history, it was not forgotten that he was but one of several storm-gods, who were therefore spoken of as "the gods Mâtu."[1] Like the clouds, they were children of the sea, and were thus included in the family of Ea. It is possible that this genealogy was due to the systematising labours of a later day; but it is also possible that the gods Mâtu were primarily adored in Eridu, and that Eridu, and not Surippak, was the original city of the Chaldæan Noah. It is at least noticeable that the immortal home of the translated Xisuthros was beyond the mouth of the Euphrates, near which Eridu was built.

If Eridu were the birth-place of Mâtu, it would explain why the god of the tempest was also the god of the western wind. Elsewhere in Babylonia, the western wind blew from across the desert and brought heat with it rather than rain. But in those remote days, when the northern portion of the Persian Gulf had not as yet been filled up with miles of alluvial deposit, a westerly breeze could still come to Eridu across the water. In a penitential psalm,[2] Mâtu, "the lord of the mountain" (*mulu mursamma-lil*), whose wife, "the lady of the mountain," is mentioned on the monuments of Tel-loh, is invoked along with his consort Gubarra, Ea, "the sovereign of heaven and earth and sovereign of Eridu," Dav-kina, Merodach, Zarpanit, Nebo and Nana—in short, along

---

[1] W. A. I. ii. 56. 41, 42.   [2] W. A. I. iv. 21, 2.

with the gods of Eridu and the kindred deities of Babylon. It is true that the Mâtu of this psalm is not the Mâtu of the west, but of the eastern mountains of Elam; we have seen, however, that more than one Mâtu was worshipped in primitive days, and it is the cradle and starting-point of the name which we are now seeking to discover.

But whether or not Eridu were really the first home of the cult of a god (or gods) Mâtu, it was with the west that he came to be chiefly identified. Titnim, the old Accadian name of the land of Canaan, became the land of Mâtu, which the Semites, who faced the rising sun in their prayers, rendered by *Akharru*, "the hinder country." His worship was carried by Aramæan tribes across the desert to Syria and Damascus. But before this happened, a change had taken place in the character of Mâtu himself. He had ceased to be Accadian and had been transformed into a Semitic god, absorbing into himself at the same time the name and attributes of another deity.

This other deity was the god of the town of Muru, who represented the air, more especially the atmosphere when lighted up by the rays of the sun. His Accadian name was Meri, "the exalted" or "glorious," known also as *Mer-mer*, "the very glorious." He represented what the Semitic Babylonians termed the *saruru*, or "shining firmament." His Accadian name was literally translated into Semitic as Ramânu, "the exalted one," which later generations connected with a root signifying "to thunder," and so wrote Rammânu (for Ramimânu), "the thunderer." The Hebrew Masoretes started yet another false etymology. They identified the word with *rimmon*, "a

THE GODS OF BABYLONIA.   203

pomegranate," and punctuated it accordingly in the passages in which it occurs in the Old Testament. As, however, the form Rimmon has thus become familiar to English ears, while Ramman is of strange sound, it is best to adhere to the Hebraised form of the god's name, in spite of its etymological incorrectness. Rimmon, therefore, and not Raman or Ramman, is the form which I shall employ in these Lectures.[1]

Now Rimmon, as we learn from the books of Kings, was the supreme god of the Syrians of Damascus. He was there identified with the Sun-god Hadad, the all-powerful Baal of the northern Syrian tribes. As far south as the plain of Jezreel, according to Zechariah xii. 11, the worship of Hadad-Rimmon was celebrated, and Hadad-Rimmon is but a compound form which expresses the identity of Rimmon and Hadad. The same fact is made known to us by the Assyrian inscriptions. Not only has Mr. Pinches[2] brought to light a series of four documents belonging to the beginning of the reign of Nabonidos, in which mention is made of a Syrian named Bin-Addu-natanu or Ben-Hadad-nathan, "the son of Hadad has given;" we find also the names of Aramæan chieftains written with the ideographs which denote the Assyrian Rimmon, but pronounced, as variant copies of the texts inform us, as Dadda or Dadi. Thus we read of a North-Arabian prince called Bir-Dáda, and the Ben-Hadad of Scripture appears as Dadá-idri, the Biblical

---

[1] The name of Ramman is preserved in the Sôsarmos of Ktêsias, which represents the Samas (Sawas)-Ramman of the monuments,— a sufficient indication of the way in which the god's name was pronounced in Assyria.

[2] *Guide to the Nimroud Central Saloon,* pp. 92, 93.

Hadad-ezer, in the records of Shalmaneser II. The name made its way to the non-Semitic tribes of the Taurus. A Komagenian sovereign bears the name of Kigiri-Dada, which appears also under the abbreviated form of Giri-Dadi; and Dalilu was a Kaskian or Kolkhian king in the time of Tiglath-Pileser III.; while Dadi was a ruler of Khubuskia, to the south-west of Armenia. That Hadad was adored even in Edom is shown by the names of the Edomite kings, Hadad the son of Bedad, and Hadad the adversary of Solomon.

In Bedad, which stands for Ben-Dad, the exact equivalent of Ben-Hadad, we meet with the same shortened form of the name as that which we find in the Assyrian inscriptions. It is possible, therefore, that it was confused with another title of the Sun-god in Canaan, Dôd or David, "the beloved one," the feminine correlative of which is found in the familiar Dido. Dido was the goddess of Carthage, not unnaturally confounded, by the piety of later ages, with Elissa, the foundress of the city. Like Hadad of Edom, David of Israel will thus have borne a name which the people about him applied to their sovereign god. It may be that those scholars are right who believe that the real name of the sweet psalmist of Israel was El-hanan or Baal-hanan; if so, David will have been a popular title derived from a popular appellation of the Deity. He will thus have shared the fate of his son and successor, whose true name Jedidiah was changed into Solomon—the name of the old Semitic "god of peace"— when David sat at rest within the walls of his new capital, Jerusalem, the city of "peace," and had rest from his enemies on every side.[1]

---

[1] See above, p. 57.

Hadad, Addu or Dadda, never superseded the native name of Ramânu (Ramman) in Babylonia and Assyria, and remained foreign to the last. Ramânu, however, was sometimes addressed as Barqu or Barak, "the lightning;" and it is possible that antiquarian zeal may have also sometimes imposed on him the Accadian title of Meru. He grew continuously in popular favour. In Semitic Babylonia, and yet more in Semitic Assyria, his aid was constantly invoked; and, like Anu, Bel and Ea, he tended as time went on to become more and more national in character. Ramman is one of the least local of Babylonian gods.

This was due in great measure to the nature of his origin. He began as the amalgamation of two distinct deities, the wind-god and the air-god, and the extension of his cult was marked by the absorption into his person of the various deities of the winds adored by the older faith. He continued to grow at their expense. The spirits of the winds and storms sank lower and lower; and while the beneficent side of their operation attached itself to Ramman, there remained to them only that side which was harmful and demoniac.

The evolution illustrates the way in which the Babylonian sought to solve the mystery of evil. The divine powers he worshipped had once been alike the creators of good and the creators of evil; like the powers of nature which they represented, they had been at once beneficent and malevolent. By degrees, the two aspects of their character came to be separated. The higher gods came to be looked upon as the hearers of prayer and the bestowers of all good gifts; while the instruments of their vengeance and the inflictors of suffering and misery upon man were the inferior spirits of the lower sphere. But the old conception, which derived both good and evil from the same source, did not wholly pass away. Evil never came to be regarded as the antagonist of good; it was rather the necessary complement and minister of good. The supreme Baal thus preserved his omnipotence, while at the same time the ideas of pain and injustice were dissociated from him. In his combat with the dragon of chaos, Merodach summons the "evil wind" itself to his assistance; and in the legend of the assault of the seven wicked spirits upon the Moon, they are nevertheless called "the messengers of Anu their king." Nerra, the god of plague and destruction, smites the people of Babylonia on account of their sins by the command of the gods, like the angel with the drawn sword whom David saw standing over Jerusalem at the threshing-floor of Araunah; and in the story of the Deluge it is because of the wickedness of mankind that the flood is brought upon the earth. The powers of darkness are degraded from their ancient position of independence, and either driven, like Tiamat, beyond the bounds of the created world, or reduced to the condition of ministers of divine wrath.

If we would realise how widely removed is this conception of them as the instruments of divine anger from that earlier view in which they are mere elemental powers, in themselves neither good nor evil, we cannot do better than compare these legendary compositions of the Semitic period with the old Accadian hymns that relate to the seven harmful spirits. Let us listen to one, for instance, which probably emanated from Eridu and applied originally to the "Mâtu gods:"

1. "They are the destructive reptiles, even the winds that create evil!
2. as an evil reptile, as an evil wind, do they appear!
3. as an evil reptile, as an evil wind, who marches in front are they!
4. Children monstrous (*gitmalutu*), monstrous sons are they!
5. Messengers of the pest-demon are they!
6. Throne-bearers of the goddess of Hades are they!
7. The whirlwind (*mâtu*) which is poured upon the land are they!
8. The seven are gods of the wide-spread heaven.
9. The seven are gods of the wide-spread earth.
10. The seven are gods of the (four) zones.
11. The seven are gods seven in number.[1]
12. Seven evil gods are they!
13. Seven evil demons are they!
14. Seven evil consuming spirits are they!
15. In heaven are they seven, in earth are they seven!"[2]

Another poet of Eridu, in a hymn to the Fire-god, speaks of the seven spirits in similar language:

---

[1] The Semitic translator misrenders: "gods of the hosts (of the firmament)."

[2] W. A. I. iv. 1. ii. 65—iii. 26. The hymn is interrupted by a magical text, a later portion of it being quoted further on (2. v. 30—59) as follows:

1. "Seven are they, seven are they!
2. In the hollow of the deep, seven are they!
3. (In) the glory of heaven, seven are they!
4. In the hollow of the deep in a palace grew they up! (In the original, "from the hollow .... came they forth").
5. Male they are not, female they are not!
6. They are the dust-storm, the travelled ones (?) are they!
7. Wife they possess not, child is unborn to them.
8. Order and kindliness know they not.
9. They hearken not to prayer and supplication.
10. From the horse of the mountain came they forth.
11. Of Ea are they the foes.
12. The throne-bearers of the gods are they.
13. To trouble the canal in the street are they set.
14. Evil are they, evil are they!
15. Seven are they, seven are they, seven doubly said are they!"

"O god of Fire," he asks, "how were those seven begotten, how grew they up?
Those seven in the mountain of the sunset were born;
those seven in the mountain of the sunrise grew up."

Throughout they are regarded as elemental powers, and their true character as destructive winds and tempests is but thinly veiled by a cloak of poetic imagery. But it will be noticed that they already belong to the harmful side of nature; and though the word which I have rendered "evil," after the example of the Semitic translators, means rather "injurious" than "evil" in our sense of the word, they are already the products of night and darkness; their birth-place is the mountain behind which the sun sinks into the gloomy lower world. In the 22nd book of the great work on Astronomy, compiled for Sargon of Accad, they are termed "the seven great spirits" or *galli*,[1] and it is therefore possible that they had already been identified with the "seven gods of destiny," the Anúna-ge or "spirits of the lower world," of the cult of Nipur.

In their gradual development into the Semite Rimmon, the spirits of the air underwent a change of parentage. Mâtu, as we have seen, was, like his kindred wind-gods of Eridu, the offspring of Ea. But the home of the wind is rather the sky than the deep, and Meri, "the shining firmament," was naturally associated with the sky. When Ana, "the sky," therefore, became the Semitic Anu, Rimmon, who united in himself Mâtu and Meri and other local gods of wind and weather as well, was made his son. It is possible that there was another cause working

---

[1] W. A. I. iii. 62, 12. *Gallu* was a loan-word from the Sumerian *galla*, *mulla* in Accadian.

towards the same result. In Syria, Rimmon was identified with Hadad the Sun-god, and there are indications that in parts of Babylonia also he had at one time a solar character. As Meri (or Meru), he could easily pass into a solar divinity, more especially as the re-duplicated Mer-mer, "the most glorious," was a title of the meridian Sun, who was identified in later days with Adar of Nipur,[1] while it was also the name of Rimmon himself as adored in one of the smaller towns of Chaldæa.[2] We are told, moreover, that Rimmon was the god who had gone under the Accadian appellation of Utu-edína-gúba, "the ever-glowing sun of the desert."[3] The elements, therefore, existed among the Babylonians, as well as among the Aramæans, out of which Rimmon could have been transformed into a solar deity; it was only the stronger non-Semitic influence which caused them to be displaced by the associations and conceptions that confined his sphere to the air. Rimmon, accordingly, among the Babylonians and Assyrians, is the god of winds and cloud, of thunder and lightning, of storm and rain; he is the inundator who is called upon to cover the fields of the impious and unjust with water, and to pour his refreshing streams into a thirsty land. His wife went by the Accadian

---

[1] W. A. I. ii. 57, 76.

[2] W. A. I. ii. 48, 35. "Nebo, the binder of law," is also identified with "the god Mermer" in W. A. I. ii. 60, 37, but this was in reference to Nebo's original character as the god of the visible universe, who bound its several parts together. When *mermer* is explained by *mekhû*, "storm," in W. A. I. v. 11, 46, nothing more is meant than that the *god* Mermer had come to represent the storm. It is an illustration of the caution needed in dealing with the statements of the so-called lexical lists.

[3] W. A. I. ii. 49, 30.

P

name of Sala, "the merciful" (?).¹ As her husband had been identified with "the lord of the mountain," so she too was identified with "the lady of the mountain,"² to whom Gudea had built a temple at Tel-loh. As "lady of the mountain," however, she was more strictly the consort of the Sun-god of Eridu; and a mythological tablet speaks accordingly of a "Sala of the mountains, the wife of Merodach."³ It is to Zarpanit, the wife of Merodach, again, and not to Sala, that Nebuchadnezzar refers, when he tells us how he "built in Babylon the House Supreme, the temple of the lady of the mountain, for the exalted goddess, the mother who had borne" him. Sala and Zarpanit, therefore, must once have been one and the same divinity.

---

[1] The Accadian equivalent of *riminû*, "merciful," is written with the ideographs *sag* or *sa*, "heart," *lal* or *la*, "filling," and *śud* or *śu*, "extending" (W. A. I. iv. 9, 27, &c.). But the final character is probably a determinative only, giving the idea of "long-suffering," in which case we should read *sala* instead of *salaśu*. In W. A. I. iv. 19, 41, the word is apparently written phonetically, as *sag-lil-da*; if so, we must read *saglal* instead of *sala*. The name of the goddess might then be explained as "woman," *sala* having this meaning in Accadian. The name seems to be interpreted "the goddess of reptiles" (*nalsi* and *namse*), as well as "the lady of the place of gold," in W. A. I. ii. 57, 33 (where, by the way, the character DIL has the meaning of "place," which it has in Amardian or "Protomedic," and in GIS-DIL-TE, the ideographic mode of writing *guza*, "a throne"). The mountains, more especially those of the north, were "the land of gold."

[2] W. A. I. ii. 57, 33.

[3] In W. A. I. iii. 67, 34, Sala is stated to be "the wife of Mul-lil in the ghost-world." But this seems to refer only to Mul-lil as the Semitic Bel, a Sun-god who rules among the shades below. It is thus that she is called the wife of Duzu or Tammuz (ii. 57, 34) like Â (ii. 57, 12). She was, in fact, originally the goddess of the Sun, and consequently her connection with Ramman must have been the result of his amalgamation with Mer or Mermer.

Sala was, furthermore, the "lady (or exalted lady) of the desert"—a title which brings to one's recollection the similar title of Rimmon, as "the ever-glowing sun of the desert-land." It is under this title that she is addressed in a penitential psalm, where she is named, not Sala, but Gubára, "the fire-flame," and associated with Mâtu (Matö), "the lord of the mountain."[1] As the other deities invoked along with her are Ea and Dav-kina, Merodach and Zarpanit, Nebo and Tasmit, while the whole psalm is dedicated to Nana, the goddess of Erech, it is clear that the psalm is the composition of a worshipper of Nana and native of Erech, whose gods were the gods of Eridu and those who claimed kindred with them.

We may, therefore, see in the primitive Sala the female consort of the Sun-god of Eridu—the original, in fact, of the Babylonian Zarpanit, who became identified on the one side with the "lady of the mountain," and on the other with the wife of Meri, the "bright firmament" of the starry sky. Her name, Gubára, points to her solar connection, and makes it probable that she was not the moon—which does not seem to have been regarded as a goddess in any part of Babylonia—nor the dawn, but the evening and morning star. This will explain why it is that she was known as the goddess of the mountains, over whose heights Venus arose and set, or as the mistress of wisdom and hidden treasure, or, again, as the goddess of the copper hand.[2] Other mythologies have stories of

---

[1] W. A. I. iv. 21, No. 2.
[2] W. A. I. ii. 57, 35. The Sun-god Savitar is called "the golden-handed" in the Veda, a term explained in later Sanskrit literature by the statement that the hand of the god had been cut at a sacrifice and

a solar hero whose hand has been cut off and replaced by one of gold and bronze, and it is in the light of such stories that the epithet must be explained. We are expressly told that Sala of the copper hand was the wife of Tammuz, the beautiful Sun-god of Eridu;[1] and we know that Tammuz, the son of the River-god Ea,[2] was the spouse of Istar, the evening star. What wonder, then, that her later husband Rimmon should have become the Sun-god of the Syrians, whose untimely death was mourned in the plain of Jezreel, as the untimely death of his double, the Babylonian Tammuz, was mourned by the women of Phœnicia and Jerusalem?

I must reserve the story of Tammuz and Istar for another Lecture. We have almost completed now our survey of the principal deities of Babylonia, of those who in the struggle for existence outdistanced their compeers, and in the official inscriptions of Assyria and later Babylonia appear at the head of the divine hierarchy. Purely local in their origin, their worship gradually extended itself chiefly through the influence of the cities that worshipped them, and absorbed at the same time the local cults that came in their way. The adoption of Accadian forms of worship by the Semites was accompanied by a process of generalisation and systematisation. The religion of Accad was adapted to the religious ideas of the Semites, and was transformed accordingly. The Baalim of the Semite took the place of the *dingirene* or "creators" of the Accadian. The Sun-god assumed a new and impor-

---

replaced by a golden one. The Teutonic Tyr is similarly one-handed, and the Keltic Nuad with the silver hand offers a close parallel to the Chaldæan goddess with the copper hand.

[1] W. A. I. ii. 57, 34.   [2] W. A. I. ii. 56, 31.

tant place. Wherever the Semite was wholly triumphant, wherever he succeeded in founding an empire, as at Sippara and Babylon, the Sun-god acquired undisputed sway. Wherever the older population maintained its ground, as at Nipur or Eridu, the older deities, leavened and transformed though they may have been by Semitic thought, still continued to hold their own. In places like Erech, where Accadian and Semitic influences seem to have long struggled for the mastery, the old sky-god remained indeed in name, but was changed into a Semitic Baal.

But the process of transformation was long, and it needed many centuries before it was complete. We have glimpses out of the distant past of a time when the two populations lived side by side in peace or war, fighting, trading and intermarrying, of Semitic conquerors filling their courts with Accadian scribes and patronising the study of Accadian literature, and of Accadian dynasties rising at times in Semitic states. Babylonia in those days must have afforded a close parallel to Egypt during the centuries of Hyksos dominion. The Semitic invaders of Egypt soon submitted to the spell of the higher culture in the midst of which they found themselves. They borrowed the titles of the Pharaohs; they patronised the learning of their Egyptian subjects; and while asserting the supremacy of their own Baal Sutekh, they yet identified him with the Egyptian Set and adopted the divinities of the Egyptian pantheon. The learned court of an Apepi Ra-aa-user, which produced one of the two treatises on Egyptian geometry that have survived to us, offers a close parallel to the court of a Sargon of Accad, which witnessed the compilation of the standard Babylonian works on astrology and terrestrial omens.

But there was one important difference between Egypt and Babylonia. With the help of Nubian allies, the Egyptians of the south succeeded, after five hundred years of submission, in driving the Semitic stranger from the northern land he had made his own. The older population of southern Babylonia was never so fortunate. The Semite had come into Chaldæa not only as a warrior, but as a trader as well. He had planted himself too firmly in the cities of the north to be ever expelled. In Genesis we see Nimrod, the representative of Semitic domination, establishing his kingdom, not only in Babel and Erech and Accad, but also in Calneh or Kulunu in Shinar (Sumer) of the south. And a time came when Calneh ceased to be the only state of Sumer which acknowledged the supremacy of the foreigner. Eridu itself, the sacred city of an immemorial past, the primal home of Chaldæan culture, became Semitic, and the monarchs of Babylonia assumed the imperial title of kings of Accad and Sumer.

But all this happened long before the age of Khammuragas, with whom the history of the city of Babylon begins. The Babylonia of Khammuragas differs but little from the Babylonia of Nabonidos. The religious system of the country is already fully formed. Nay, more; already in the remote age of Sargon of Accad there are indications that the process of assimilation and absorption had long been at work. The son and successor of Sargon was Naram-Sin, "the beloved of the Moon-god," a sign that the Moon-god of Ur was even now in favour in the court of Accad. In fact, it must have been among the priestly *literati* of Sargon that the union of Accadian and Semitic religious belief took definite shape. It marked the union of the Accadian and Semitic elements in the population under Semitic rule. It is possible that some of the mythological tablets in which an attempt is made to harmonise the deities of the various local cults and to bring them into genealogical order, may go back to this early date. It is more probable, however, that they all belong to that later period when northern and southern Babylonia had long formed an united monarchy.

Unchecked, the tendency of Semitic religious thought would have been to resolve the gods of the popular faith into one supreme Baal, by the side of whom was throned his colourless double or wife. This tendency actually found expression in certain cases. But the cities of Babylonia had too venerable a history to allow their local deities to be thus confounded and lost, and the non-Semitic element in the population, though less and less represented in official documents, placed a check upon it. It was the genealogical theory, resuscitated in after times in the Gnostic doctrine of emanations, which obtained most favour. The gods became a family, and their temples palaces in which attendant spirits ministered to their wants.

At the head of the pantheon stood the trinity of Anu, Bel of Nipur and Ea. The order in which they were ranked indicates the relative periods at which the three gods and the cities which originally worshipped them became the property of the Semitic race. The rise of Babylon, however, brought with it the displacement of the older Bel of Nipur. He was forced to yield to his younger rival Bel Merodach, causing endless confusion to the Babylonian mythologists.

Around the three chief gods were grouped the multitudinous deities which Accadian superstition or Semitic piety had invented and dreamed of. Assur-natsir-pal declares that there were " 65,000 great gods of heaven and earth;" and though we may doubt whether the Assyrian king was not indulging in a little royal exaggeration, it is certain that the task of enumerating them all would have exhausted the most indefatigable of priestly scribes. Besides the numberless minor deities of the towns and villages, there were the divine titles out of which new gods had been evolved; divinities which owed their existence to the linguistic or literary errors of the Semites; and, finally, foreign gods like Kittum and Sumaliya of the Kossæans, or Lagamar of Susa. As if this goodly host were not enough, phrases from the ritual of the temples were elevated to the rank of gods. Ê-Sagil, for instance, the temple of Merodach at Babylon, was deified under the name of "What does my lord eat?" and the spirit of Ê-Sagil was known as "What does my lord drink?"[1] while the divine porters of the temple were termed respectively "the binder of the waters of the god of the sea," and "the giver of water for (purifying) the hand."[2] When we remember how the background of this vast pantheon was filled with the obscure deities and spirits of the ancient Accadian cult, whose names survived in magical charms and exorcisms, while the air above was occupied by the "300 spirits of heaven," and the earth

---

[1] W. A. I. ii. 56. 16, 17.   [2] W. A. I. ii. 56. 18, 19.

below by "the 600 spirits of earth," we begin to realise the force of the expression which made the supreme gods rulers of the "legions" of earth and sky. *Bil kissat*, "the lord of hosts," was a phrase full of significance to the believing Babylonian.

It would be useless to waste our time over deities who never obtained a prominent place in the official hierarchy of the gods, and of whom we know little beyond the names. Now and again, when the Assyrian kings made a triumphal march through Babylonia, they sacrificed to the gods of the cities through which they passed, and we hear of Latarak the son of Anu, of Subulu, or of Utsur-amat-śa; but they probably knew as little about them as we do. It is only from local documents like contracts and boundary-stones that we can expect to learn anything about such deities as Supu of Dêr, and Tug of Kis with the dragon's face, and what we learn will seldom throw much light on Babylonian religion as a whole. When Nebuchadnezzar gathered the gods of Babylonia into his capital in token that the god of Babylon was henceforth lord of all the Chaldæan gods, with two exceptions it is only to deities like Sin and Samas, Rimmon and Gula, that he erected shrines. "The lady of the house of heaven" and "the divine son of the house" are the only divinities whom he mentions that bear unaccustomed names, and they are doubtless merely titles of Beltis and Adar or Nergal.

As long, however, as these multitudinous deities were believed to exist, so long was it also believed that they could injure or assist. Hence come such expressions as those which meet us in the Penitential Psalms, "To the god that is known and that is unknown, to the goddess that is known and that is unknown, do I lift my prayer." Hence, too, the care with which the supreme Baal was invoked as "lord of the hosts of heaven and earth," since homage paid to the master was paid to the subjects as well. Hence, finally, the fact that the temples of the higher gods, like the Capitol at Rome, became gathering-places for the inferior divinities, and counterparts on the earth of "the assembly of the gods" in heaven. That curious product of Mandaite imagination, the "Book of Nabathean Agriculture," which was translated into Arabic by Ibn Wahshiya in the 10th century, sets before us a curious picture of the temple of Tammuz in Babylon. "The images (of the gods)," it tells us, "congregated from all parts of the world to the temple of el-Askûl (Ê-Sagil) in Babylon, and betook themselves to the temple (*haikal*) of the Sun, to the great golden image that is suspended between heaven and earth in particular. The image of the sun stood, they say, in the midst of the temple, surrounded by all the images of the world. Next to it stood the images of the sun in all countries; then those of the moon; next those of Mars; after them the images of Mercury; then those of Jupiter; next of Venus; and last of all, of Saturn. Thereupon the image of the sun began to bewail Tammuz and the idols to weep; and the image of the sun uttered a lament over Tammuz and narrated his history, whilst the idols all wept from the setting of the sun till its rising at the end of that night. Then the idols flew away, returning to their own countries."

The details are probably borrowed from the great temple of pre-Mohammedan Mecca, but they correspond very faithfully with what we now know the interior of one of the chief temples of Babylonia and Assyria to have been like. Fragments have been preserved to us of a tablet which enumerated the names of the minor deities whose images stood in the principal temples of Assyria, attending like servants upon the supreme god. Among them are the names of foreign divinities, to whom the catholic spirit of Babylonian religion granted a place in the national pantheon when once the conquest of the towns and countries over which they presided had proved their submission to the Babylonian and Assyrian gods; even Khaldis, the god of Ararat, figures among those who dwelt in one of the chief temples of Assyria,[1] and whose names were invoked by the visitor to the shrine. The spectacle of such a temple, with the statue or symbol of the supreme Baal rising majestically in the innermost cell, and delivering his oracles from within the hidden chamber of that holy of holies, while the shrines of his wife and offspring were grouped around him, and the statues of ministering deities stood slave-like in front, was a fitting image of Babylonian religion. "The gods many and lords many" of an older creed still survived, but they had become the jealously-defined officials of an autocratic court. The democratic polytheism of an earlier day had become imperial. Bel was the counterpart of his vicegerent the Babylonian king, with this difference, that whereas Babylonia had been fused into an united monarchy, the hierarchy of the gods still acknowledged more than one head. How long Anu and Ea, or Samas and Sin, would have continued to share with Merodach the highest honours of the official cult, we cannot say;

---

[1] W. A. I. iii. 66, *Rev.* 7.

the process of degradation had already begun when Babylonia ceased to be an independent kingdom and Babylon the capital of an empire. Merodach remained a supreme Baal—the cylinder inscription of Cyrus proves so much—but he never became the one supreme god.

Lecture IV.

TAMMUZ AND ISTAR; PROMETHEUS AND TOTEMISM.

Among the mythological poems bequeathed to us by ancient Babylonia is one which, though doubtless based on Accadian materials, has survived to us only in a Semitic form. It recounts the descent of the goddess Istar into Hades in search of the healing waters which should restore to life her bridegroom Tammuz, the young and beautiful Sun-god, slain by the cruel hand of night and winter. The poem is as follows:

1. "To the land whence none return, the region of (darkness),
2. Istar, the daughter of Sin, (inclined) her ear,
3. yea, Istar herself, the daughter of Sin, inclined (her) ear
4. to the house of darkness, the seat of the god Irkalla,
5. to the house from whose entrance there is no exit,
6. to the road from whose passage there is no return,
7. to the house from whose visitors the light is excluded,'
8. the place where dust is their bread (and) their food is mud.
9. The light they behold not, in darkness they dwell,
10. they are clad like birds in a garment of feathers.
11. Over the door and the bolt the dust is scattered.
12. Istar, on arriving at the gate of Hades,
13. to the keeper[1] of the gate addresses the word:
14. 'Opener (keeper) of the waters, open thy gate!
15. Open thy gate that I may enter!

---

[1] Literally "opener" (*pitû* or *muselû*).

16. If thou openest not the gate that I may enter,
17. I will smite the door, the bolt I will shatter,
18. I will smite the threshold and pass through the portals.
19. I will raise up the dead to devour the living,
20. above the living the dead shall exceed in number.'
21. The keeper opened his mouth and speaks;
22. he says to the princess Istar:
23. 'Stay, O lady, thou must not break it down!
24. Let me go and declare thy name to Nin-ki-gal, the queen of Hades.'
25. The keeper descended and declares (her name to Nin-ki-gal [Allat]):
26. 'O goddess, the water thy sister Istar (is come to seek);
27. trying (*batqirtu*) the mighty bars (she has threatened to break open the doors) (?).'
28. When Allat (heard) this (she opened her mouth and says:)
29. 'Like a cut-off herb has (Istar) descended (into Hades);
30. like the lip of a drooping reed[1] she has prayed for (the waters of life).
31. What matters to me her wish? what (matters to me) her anger?[2]
32. (When she says:) this water with (my bridegroom)
33. like food would I eat, like beer would I drink:
34. let me weep for the heroes who have left (their) wives;
35. let me weep for the handmaids whom from the bosom of their husbands (thou hast taken);
36. for the little child let me weep whom thou hast taken ere his days are come.
37. Go, keeper (nevertheless), open for her (thy) gate;
38. Strip[3] her also according to the ancient rules.'
39. The keeper went, he opened for her (his) gate:
40. 'Enter, O lady, let Cutha be glad (at thee);
41. let the palace of Hades rejoice before thee.'

---

[1] See W. A. I. ii. 22, 8. Instead of *sapat*, "lip," Jeremias (*Die Höllenfahrt der Istar*, 1886) reads *sabat*, "cutting off;" but he has misunderstood the reference of lines 29, 30.

[2] Literally, "What has her heart brought me? what has her liver (brought me)?"

[3] *Uppidh*, see W. A. I. ii. 29, 38. This is preferable to my old reading *uppis*, "bewitch."

42. The first gate he made her enter, and shut[1] (it); he threw down the mighty crown of her head.
43. 'Why, O keeper, hast thou thrown down the mighty crown of my head?'
44. 'Enter, O lady, (for) thus are the orders of Allat.'
45. The second gate he made her enter and he shut; he threw away the earrings of her ears.
46. 'Wherefore, O keeper, hast thou thrown away the earrings of my ears?'
47. 'Enter, O lady, (for) thus are the orders of Allat.'
48. The third gate he made her enter and he closed; he threw away the precious stones of her neck(lace).
49. 'Wherefore, O keeper, hast thou thrown away the precious stones of my neck(lace)?'
50. 'Enter, O lady, (for) thus are the orders of Allat.'
51. The fourth gate he made her enter and closed; he threw away the ornaments of her breast.
52. 'Wherefore, O keeper, hast thou thrown away the ornaments of my breast?'
53. 'Enter, O lady, (for) thus are the orders of Allat.'
54. The fifth gate he made her enter and closed; he threw away the gemmed girdle of her waist.
55. 'Wherefore, O keeper, hast thou thrown away the gemmed girdle of my waist?'
56. 'Enter, O lady, (for) thus are the orders of Allat.'
57. The sixth gate he made her enter and closed; he threw away the bracelets of her hands and her feet.
58. 'Wherefore, O keeper, hast thou thrown away the bracelets of my hands and my feet?'
59. 'Enter, O lady, (for) thus are the orders of Allat.'
60. The seventh gate he made her enter and closed; he threw away the cincture of her body.
61. 'Wherefore, O keeper, hast thou thrown away the cincture of my body?'
62. 'Enter, O lady, (for) thus are the orders of Allat.'
63. After that Istar had descended into the land of Hades,
64. Allat beheld her and was haughty before her.

---

[1] Not "unclothe," as Jeremias. *Matsû* means "to shut," "discontinue."

224   LECTURE IV.

65. Istar took not counsel, she besought her with oaths.[1]
66. Allat opened her mouth and says,
67. to Namtar (the plague-demon), her messenger, the word she utters:
68. 'Go, Namtar, (take Istar from) me, and
69. lead her out; sixty times (strike) Istar (with disease):
69. the disease of the eyes (into) her (eyes);
70. the disease of the side (into) her (side);
71. the disease of the feet into her (feet);
72. the disease of the heart into (her heart);
73. the disease of the head strike (into her head);
74. into her, even the whole of her, and into (each limb strike disease).'
75. After that the lady Istar (into Hades had descended),
76. with the cow the bull would not unite (the ass would not approach the female),
77. the handmaid (in the street would not approach the freeman),
78. the freeman ceased (to give his order),[2]
79. (the handmaid ceased to give her gift?).
80. Pap-sukal, the messenger of the mighty gods, bowed his face before (the Sun-god):
81. 'There is woe below,[3] (for all things) are full of destruction (*nadi*).'
82. The Sun-god went; in the presence of Sin his father he (stood),
83. in the presence of Ea the king (his) tears flowed down:
84. 'Istar descended to the earth and has not re-ascended.
85. From the time that Istar has descended to the land of Hades,
86. with the cow the bull will not unite, the ass will not approach the female,
87. the handmaid in the street will not approach the freeman,
88. the freeman has ceased to give his order,
89. the handmaid has ceased to give her (gift?).'
90. Ea in the wisdom of his heart formed (a man);[4]

---

[1] Jeremias, "she threw herself on her." This, however, could hardly be the sense of the shaphel of *lû*, "to come."

[2] Perhaps better with Jeremias: "slept while giving."

[3] *Saplis*; if we read *labis*, we must translate, with Jeremias, "clothed in a dress of mourning." But in this case, it would be difficult to account for the omission of the words of Pap-sukal.

[4] So Jeremias.

91. he created Atsu-su-namir ('His rising is seen'), the androgyne ;[1]
92. 'Go, Atsu-su-namir, towards the gate of Hades set thy face;
93. let the seven gates of Hades be opened before thee;
94. let Allat see thee and rejoice at thy presence,
95. when her heart is at rest and her liver is appeased.
96. Conjure her also by the names of the great gods.
97. Turn thy heads; to the resting-place[2] of the stormy wind set thine ear;
98. the home of the pure one,[3] the resting-place of the stormy wind, let them prepare (?); the waters in the midst let her drink.
99. When Allat heard this
100. she struck her girdle, she bit her thumb:
101. 'Thou hast asked of me a request none should request!
102. Go, Atsu-su-namir, let me injure thee with a great injury![4]
103. May the garbage of the sewers of the city be thy food!
104. May the vessels of the daughters[5] of the city be thy drink!
105. May the darkness of the dungeon be thy habitation!
106. May the threshold be thy seat!
107. May drought and famine strike thine offspring!'
108. Allat opened her mouth and says,
109. to Namtar her messenger the word she addresses:
110. 'Go, Namtar, strike open the firmly-built palace,
111. shatter the thresholds (which) bear up the stones of light;
112. bid the spirits of earth (Anúnaki) come forth and seat them on a throne of gold;

---

[1] *Assinnu* explained as "the female man" or "creature in W. A. I. ii. 32, 22. Zimmern is probably right in connecting the word with *isinu*, "a festival," since the tablet in which it appears seems to enumerate various classes of priests; and in W. A. I. ii. 27, 58, "the man" or "creature of Istar" is called *kalu*, i.e. one of the Galli. Atsu-su-namir may be also read Atsu-sunamir, "Rising, cause to shine" (Shaphael imperative). Dr. Oppert reads Uddusu-namir, "renewal of light," but this would require the form Uddus-namari (or nameri). In an unnumbered text given above (p. 81, note 2), the *assinnu* appears as the eunuch-priest of Bel armed with a flute.

[2] *'Sukhal*, from *sakhalu*, for which see W. A. I. v. 40, 11, and K 161. i. 26. According to George Smith, *sakhalu* is a synonym of *sadakhu*, "to reach."

[3] Jeremias, "(Say,) No, my lady."   [4] See W. A. I. ii. 10, 3

[5] See, however, W. A. I. ii. 22, 20.

113. over Istar pour the waters of life and bring her before me.'
114. Namtar went (and) smote the firmly-built palace,
115. he shattered the thresholds (which) bear up the stones of light,
116. he bade the spirits of earth come forth, on a throne of gold did he seat (them),
117. over Istar he poured the waters of life and brought her along.
118. The first gate he passed her out of and restored to her the cincture of her body;
119. The second gate he made her pass, and restored to her the bracelets of her hands and her feet.
120. The third gate he made her pass, and restored to her the gemmed girdle of her waist.
121. The fourth gate he made her pass, and restored to her the ornaments of her breasts.
122. The fifth gate he made her pass, and restored to her the jewels of her necklace.
123. The sixth gate he made her pass, and restored to her the earrings of her ears.
124. The seventh gate he made her pass, and restored to her the mighty crown of her head.
125. 'If she (i.e. Allat) has not given thee that for which the ransom is paid her, turn back to her again
126. for Tammuz the bridegroom of (thy) youth.
127. Pour over him the pure waters, (anoint him) with precious oil.
128. Clothe him with a purple robe; a ring(?)[1] of crystal let him strike upon (the hand).
129. Let Samkhat (the goddess of joy) enter[2] the liver....'
130. (Before this) the goddess Tillili had taken her jewels,
131. the eye-stones also (which) were unbroken;
132. the goddess Tillili had heard of the death[3] of her brother (Tammuz); she broke the jewels[4] (which she had taken),

---

[1] *Gibu* is not to be read ideographically, as is supposed by Jeremias (who has misunderstood lines 135—137); comp. *gibû* in Strassmaier, p. 227, and *gabû* in K 4223, col. ii. (*ana kharran sarri halak-su gabû la illik*). See, however, the text I have quoted above, p. 81, note 2.

[2] *Linaha;* the word is explained by passages in the legends of the shepherd ENNUN-KA-TI (K 2546, *Obv.* 11), and of Atarpi (col. iii. 47, 57).

[3] *Ikrim;* in W. A. I. v. 50, 62, the verb *ikrimu* is used of the violent "carrying below" of a hero by "the handmaid of a *lilu*" or "demon." Jeremias reads *ikkil*, "cry of woe."

[4] More literally, "jewelled circlet" (*sutartum*); see W. A. I. v. 6, 45.

133. even the eye-stones which were full of the face (of light?),
134. (crying) 'O my brother, the only one, do not destroy me.'
135. In the day that Tammuz bound on me a ring (?) of crystal and a bracelet of turquoise, at that time he bound (them) on me,
136. at that time he bound (them) on me. Let the wailing men and wailing women
137. bind (them) on the funeral pyre, and smell the sweet savour.'
COLOPHON. The property of Assur-bani-pal, king of multitudes, king of Assyria."

The poem throws light upon certain passages both in the Old Testament and in classical authors, and in turn receives light from them. On the one hand, we now know who was that Tammuz in whose honour Ezekiel saw the women of Jerusalem weeping at the gate of "the Lord's house."[1] On the other hand, it is clear that the Tammuz and Istar of the Babylonian legend are the Adônis and Aphroditê of Greek mythology. Like Tammuz, Adônis, the beloved one of Aphroditê, is slain by the boar's tusk of winter, but eventually ransomed from Hades by the prayers of the goddess. It has long been recognised that Aphroditê, the Kyprian goddess of love and war, came to Hellas from Phœnicia, whether or not we agree with Dr. Hommel in seeing in her name a mere etymological perversion of the Phœnician Ashtoreth. Adônis is the Phœnician Adôni, "my lord," the cry with which the worshippers of the stricken Sun-god mourned his untimely descent into the lower world.

The cry was familiar throughout the land of Palestine. In the valley of Megiddo, by the plain of Jezreel, each year witnessed "the mourning for Hadad-Rimmon" (Zech. xii. 11), while hard by Amos heard the men of

---

[1] Ezek. viii. 14.

Israel mourning for "the only son" (Am. viii. 10), and the prophet of Judah gives the very words of the refrain: "Ah me, my brother, and ah me, my sister! Ah me, Adonis, and ah me, his lady!" (Jer. xxii. 18). The words were carried across the western sea to men of an alien race and language. "Cry *ailinon, ailinon!* woe, woe!" says the Greek poet of Athens,[1] and already in Homeric days[2] the dirge was attributed to a mythic Linos whose magic fate was commemorated in its opening words: "O Linos, Linos!" Linos, however, had no existence except in a popular etymology; the Greek *ailinos* is in reality the Phœnician *ai-lênu,* "alas for us!" with which the lamentations for the death of the divine Adônis were wont to begin. Like the refrain quoted by Jeremiah, the words eventually go back to Babylonia, and find their counterpart in the closing lines of the old Babylonian poem I have translated above. When Tillili commences her wail over the dead Tammuz, she cries, like the women of Judah and Phœnicia, "O my brother, the only one!" It was, above all, in the Phœnician town of Gebal or Byblos that the death of Adônis was commemorated. Here, eight miles to the north of Beyrût, the ancient military road led from eastern Asia to the shores of the Mediterranean, and brought from early days the invading armies of Babylonia and Assyria to the coasts and cities of Canaan. Hard by was the river of Adonis, the Nahr Ibrahim of to-day, which rolled through a rocky gorge into the sea. Each year, when the rains and melting snows of spring stained its waters with the red marl of the mountains, the people of Gebal

---

[1] Æskhylos, *Agam.* 121.   [2] *Il.* xviii. 570.

beheld in it the blood of the slaughtered Sun-god. It was then, in the month of Tammuz or June, that the funeral-festival of the god was held. For seven days it lasted. "Gardens of Adonis," as they were called, were planted, pots filled with earth and cut herbs, which soon withered away in the fierce heat of the summer sun—fitting emblems of the lost Adonis himself. Meanwhile, the streets and gates of the temples were filled with throngs of wailing women. They tore their hair, they disfigured the face, they cut the breast with sharp knives, in token of the agony of their grief. Their cry of lamentation went up to Heaven mingled with that of the Galli, the emasculated priests of Ashtoreth, who shared with them their festival of woe over her murdered bridegroom. Adonis, the young, the beautiful, the beloved of Ashtoreth, was dead; the bright sun of the springtide, like the verdure of nature which he had called into life, was slain and withered by the hot blasts of the summer.

In later times, after the revolt of Egypt from the Assyrian king and the rise of the 26th Dynasty, the cult of Adonis at Gebal entered upon a new phase. Egyptian beliefs and customs made their way into Phœnicia along with Egyptian political influence, and the story of Adonis was identified with that of the Egyptian Osiris. As the Sun-god Osiris had been slain and had risen again from the dead, so, too, had the Phœnician Adonis descended into Hades and been rescued again from its grasp. How long, indeed, he had remained in the world below was a matter of doubt. There were some who said that he shared half the year with the goddess of death, and the other half only with the goddess of love; there were others who declared that his year was divided into three—

four months was he condemned to dwell in Hades, four months he was free to live where he might choose, while the other four were passed in the companionship of Ashtoreth, and that it was to Ashtoreth that he devoted his months of freedom. But all agreed that the Sun-god of spring was not compelled to live for ever in the gloomy under-world; a time came when he and nature would alike revive. It was inevitable, therefore, that in the days of Egyptianising fashion, Adonis and Osiris should be looked upon as the same god, and that the festival of Adonis at Gebal should be assimilated to that of Osiris in Egypt. And so it came about that a new feature was added to the festival of Adonis; the days of mourning were succeeded by days of rejoicing; the death of Adonis was followed by the announcement of his resurrection. A head of papyrus came from Egypt over the waves; while, on the other hand, an Alexandrian legend told how the mourning Isis had found again at Gebal the chest in which the dismembered limbs of Osiris were laid.

It is clear that the Babylonian poet who sang of the descent of Istar into Hades had no conception of a festival of joy that followed immediately upon a festival of mourning. Nevertheless, the whole burden of his poem is the successful journey of the goddess into the under-world for the sake of the precious waters which should restore her beloved one to life. Even in Babylonia, therefore, there must have been a season when the name of Tammuz was commemorated, not with words of woe, but with joy and rejoicing. But it could have been only when the fierce heats of the summer were past; when the northern wind, which the Accadians called "the prospering one," began again to blow; and when the Sun-god regained once more the vigour of his spring-tide youth. That there had once been a festival of this kind is indicated by the fact that the lamentations for his death did not take place in all parts of Syria at the same time. We learn from Ammianus that when Julian arrived at Antioch in the late autumn, he found the festival of Adonis being celebrated "according to ancient usage," after the ingathering of the harvest and before the beginning of the new year, in Tisri or October. It must have been in the autumn, too, that the feast of Hadad-Rimmon was observed, to which Zechariah alludes; and Ezekiel saw the women weeping for Tammuz in "the sixth month." Nay, Macrobius[1] even tells us that the Syrian worshippers of Adonis in his time explained the boar's tusk which had slain the god as the cold and darkness of winter, his return to the upper world being his "victory over the first six zodiacal signs, along with the lengthening daylight."

We can draw but one conclusion from all this. The resurrection of Tammuz had once been commemorated as well as his death, and the festivals had been identified, not only with that of the Egyptian Osiris, as at Gebal, but also with those of other Semitic forms of the Sun-god, of Hadad and of Rimmon. When Macrobius states that Adad meant "the only one" in Syrian, he implies that Adad or Hadad—the Sun-god whose festival fell after the harvests of autumn—was identical with Tammuz. In Babylonia, Tammuz was the Sun-god of spring; his foe was the summer heat; his death was mourned in the month of June. If there was another feast in which grief gave place to joy at his restoration to life, it was

---

[1] *Saturn.* i. 21.

separate from that which celebrated his death, and must have taken place at a different time of the year. In its transplantation to the west, however, the cult of Tammuz-Adonis underwent a change. He was identified with other forms of the solar deity; his festivals were merged into theirs; and, except in places like Gebal, where a natural phenomenon prevented the alteration, the anniversary of his death was shifted to the fall of the year. He ceased to be the Sun-god of spring, and became the Sun-god of summer. In the highlands of Syria the summer was not the dangerous foe it was in Babylonia; it was, on the contrary, a kindly friend, whose heats quickened and fostered the golden grain. Winter, and not summer, was the enemy who had slain the god.

The story of Tammuz was not of Semitic invention, however much it may owe, in the form in which we know it, to Semitic imagination. The month of Tammuz was called in the Accadian calendar "the month of the errand of Istar," a clear proof that the legend of the Descent of the goddess into Hades was already known. Nor is the name of Tammuz itself of Semitic origin. The Semites did not agree about the precise form which it should assume, and it is probable that the form (Tammuz) which prevailed in the west was due to a "popular etymology." At all events, the Assyro-Babylonian form is not Tammuz, but Duzu, itself contracted from Duwuzu, and a fair representative of the original Accadian Dumu-zi or Duwu-zi, "the son of life." The word was interpreted by the Semites as meaning the "offspring," "the only son;"[1] but it may be merely a shortened form of the name Dumu-zi-apzu, "the son of the spirit of the deep."

---

[1] W. A. I. ii. 36, 54.

The "spirit of the deep" is of course Ea, as is expressly stated in a mythological tablet,[1] where Dumu-zi-apzu is given as the name of one of his six sons. How early the designation must be, is shown by the fact that Ea appears in it as not yet a god, but as a spirit only. We are carried back to the first dawn of Chaldæan religious belief. The name was translated by the Semites "Timmuz (or Dimmuz) of the flood" (W.A.I. ii. 47, 29), and the solar character of the deity was indicated by writing his name with ideographs that signified "the maker of fire" (*tim-izi*).[2] But this very mode of writing the name, which probably grew up in the court of Sargon of Accad, proves that already the name had lost its last element. The "son of the spirit of the deep" had become "the son of life," "the only son" of the god Ea. It is thus that a mythological tablet gives "the River-god," who is but Ea under another title, a single son Duzi,[3] where the name has assumed its contracted Semitic form, and is written with ideographs that mean "the heart of life."[4]

---

[1] W. A. I. ii. 56, 33—38.

[2] *Tim-izi*, or Dim-izi, is a good example of what Halévy has termed the rebus. As in several other cases, notably that of the Fire-god Gibil, the two elements of the name are transposed in writing (*Izi-tim* instead of *Tim-izi*). The tablet in which the name is explained is a commentary on an old astrological text, giving explanations of the rare words and ideographs contained in the text. The text may have emanated from the court of Sargon at Accad. *Izi* is given as the pronunciation of the Accadian word for "fire" in 82. 8—16. 1. *Rev.* 15.

[3] W. A. I. ii. 56, 31.

[4] The spelling may have originated at Accad. At all events, both Â, the wife of the Sun-god of Sippara, and Sala, "of the mountain of gold," are called the wives of Duzu in W. A. I. ii. 57. 12, 34. It is possible that in W. A. I. ii. 54. 8, 9, we ought to read Duzu and Dazu; if so, the two primordial principles, the male Duzu and the female

We have just seen that the pronunciation Timmuz was once known to the Babylonian scribes. But it never found its way into the language and literature of the country. The medial labial became a semi-vowel; and the attempt to give a Semitic colouring to the word by hardening the initial consonant, never succeeded in expelling the pronunciation which their Accadian neighbours had made familiar to the Semites of Babylonia. The case, however, was different in other portions of the Semitic world. Here there was no Accadian population to prevent the Semitised form from holding full sway, and it was accordingly as Tammuz (or Timmuz) that the name passed to the west. It is probable that the intermediaries were those Aramæan tribes who stretched across the desert from the borders of Babylonia to the fields of Syria, and were known in after days under the comprehensive title of Nabathæans. At any rate, the worship of Tammuz could not have been introduced into Palestine by the Assyrian conquests, as has been suggested; had it been so, the name of the god would have had a different form. Nor again, had such been the case, could we have explained the early prevalence of the cult of Adonis in Phœnicia and Cyprus,[1] and the traces that it left even upon Homeric Greece. The name and story of Tammuz must have come to Phœnicia in those remote times when it was whispered that "Kronos" or Ea had

---

Dazu, will be here identified with Anu (and Anat). What makes this the more likely is that a few lines further Alala and Tillili are also identified with Anu and Anat.

[1] The name of Tamassos, the city in whose neighbourhood were the famous copper-mines of the island, perhaps preserved a recollection of the name of Tammuz. It is called Tametsi by Esar-haddon.

taken Yeûd,[1] his "only begotten son," and arraying him in royal robes had sacrificed him on an altar in a season of distress.[2]

Greek mythology itself knew the name of Tammuz as well as that of Adonis. Theias or Thoas[3] was not only the Lemnian husband of Myrina and the king of the Tauric Khersonese who immolated strangers on the altars of Artemis, he was also king of Assyria and father of Adonis and his sister Myrrha or Smyrna. In the Kyprian myth the name of Theias is transformed into Kinyras; but, like Theias, he is the father of Adonis by his daughter Myrrha. Myrrha is the invention of a popular etymology;[4] the true form of the name was Smyrna or Myrina, a name famous in the legendary annals of Asia Minor. Myrina or Smyrna, it was said, was an Amazonian queen, and her name is connected with the four cities of the western coast—Smyrna, Kymê, Myrina and Ephesos—whose foundation was ascribed to Amazonian heroines. But the Amazons were really the warrior priestesses of the great Asiatic goddess, whom the Greeks called the Artemis of Ephesos, and who was in origin the Istar of Babylonia modified a little by Hittite influence. It was she who, in the Asianic cult of Attys or Hadad, took the place of Istar and Aphroditê; for just as Attys himself was Tammuz, so the goddess with whom he was associated was Istar. At Hierapolis, which succeeded to the religious fame and beliefs of the ancient Hittite city of

---

[1] Assyrian *edu*, "only one."   [2] Philo Bybl. p. 44.

[3] Thoas is practically identical with the Ssabian Ta'uz. For Theias, the Assyrian king, see Apollod. iii. 14, 4; Tzetzes, *ad Lykoph.* 91.

[4] The Aramaic *marthâ*, "mistress," or the Assyrian *martu*, "daughter," may have assisted the etymology; compare the Biblical name Miriam.

Carchemish, the name under which the goddess went seems to have been Semiramis,[1] and it is possible that Semiramis and Smyrna are but varying forms of the same word. However this may be, in the Kyprian Kinyras who takes the place of Theias we have a play upon the Phœnician *kinnôr*, or "cither," which is said to have been used in the worship of Adonis. But its real origin seems to be indicated by the name of Gingras which Adonis himself bore.[2] Here it is difficult not to recognize the old Accadian equivalent of Istar, Gingira or Gingiri, "the creatress."[3]

The fact that Tammuz was the son of Ea points unmistakably to the source both of his name and of his worship. He must have been the primitive Sun-god of Eridu, standing in the same relation to Ea, the god of Eridu, that Adar stood to Mul-lil, the god of Nipur. It is even possible that the boar whose tusk proved fatal to Adonis may originally have been Adar himself. Adar, as we have seen, was called the "lord of the swine" in the Accadian period, and the Semitic abhorrence of the animal may have used it to symbolise the ancient rivalry between the Sun-god of Nipur and the Sun-god of Eridu.[4] Those who would see in the Cain and Abel of Scripture the representatives of elemental deities, and who follow Dr. Oppert in explaining the name of Abel by the Babylonian *ablu*, "the son," slightly transformed by a popular etymology, may be inclined to make them the Adar and Tammuz of Chaldæan faith.

---

[1] Lucian, *De Dea Syria*, 33, 39.
[2] *Athen.* iv. 174, xiv. 618.
[3] W. A. I. ii. 48, 29; K 170. *Rev.* 7 (AN-*gi-ri*).
[4] See above, p. 153.

TAMMUZ AND ISTAR. 237

As mother of Tammuz, Dav-kina, the wife of Ea, had a special name. She is called Tsirdu, or ʼSirdu[1]—a word in which I believe we may see the Assyrian *śurdu*, "a falcon." Now it will be remembered that ʼSirrida, also written ʼSirdam, and pronounced ʼSirgam, ʼSirrigal or ʼSirrigâ, ʼSurgâ and Nirda,[2] in the different dialects of pre-Semitic Chaldæa, was a title of Â, the wife of the Sun-god of Sippara or Accad. As we are told that a temple of Tammuz existed at Accad, where it was known by the double name of "the tower of mighty bulk" and "the shrine of observation,"[3] it would seem that the worship of Tammuz had been transported from Eridu to the capital of Sargon at the time when the culture of southern Babylonia made its way to the north, and the empire of Sargon was fusing the civilisation and religion of the country into a single whole. It was then that the Sun-god of Eridu and the Sun-god of Accad would naturally be identified together, and that the wife of Samas of Accad should become the goddess whom mythology represented as at once the wife and the mother of Tammuz.

But the primitive home of Tammuz had been in that

---

[1] W. A. I. ii. 59, 9. As she seems to be identified with Istar in the same passage, we may conclude that the compiler of the mythological list regarded her as equally the mother and the wife of Tammuz.

[2] W. A. I. ii. 57. 11, 24, 23, 21, 22, 26. In line 26 the name of Â is also written phonetically by means of the ideograph for father (*â*). In lines 30, 31, ŚIR-UT-KAN and ŚIR-UT-AM must each be read ʼSirdam (or ʼSirudam). See above, p. 178.

[3] W. A. I. ii. 50. 10, 11. It would appear from this that the *parâku*, or "shrine," was, like that of Bel-Merodach at Babylon, in the highest chamber of the *ziggurat*, or "tower," from whence observations of the sky could be made.

238   LECTURE IV.

"garden" of Edin, or Eden, which Babylonian tradition placed in the immediate vicinity of Eridu.[1] The fragment of an old bilingual hymn has been preserved, which begins in the following way:

1. "(In) Eridu a stalk[2] grew over-shadowing; in a holy place did it become green;
2. its root ([*sur*]*sum*) was of white crystal which stretched towards the deep;
3. (before) Ea was its course in Eridu, teeming with fertility;[3]
4. its seat was the (central) place[4] of the earth;
5. its foliage (?) was the couch of Zikum (the primæval) mother.
6. Into the heart of its holy house which spread its shade like a forest hath no man entered.
7. (There is the home) of the mighty mother who passes across the sky.
8. (In) the midst of it was Tammuz.
10. (There is the shrine ?) of the two (gods)."

The description reminds us of the famous Ygg-drasil

---

[1] Hence his mother (and wife) is called "the lady of Edin" (W.A.I. ii. 59. 10, 11.

[2] See K 165, 22 (U-QI *gesdin*), "the stalk of a grape." QI ($=lamma$) *tur* is the Assyrian *epitâtu*, "a small stalk" (W. A. I. ii. 41. 52, 56). U-QI is also explained as *ritu sitehu*, "a growing slip" (W.A.I. ii. 41, 8). We are reminded of the old story of Jack and the Bean-stalk as well as of the Polynesian tree which enables the climber to ascend into the heavenly land. The mother of Tammuz was called "the (mistress) of the vine" (W. A. I. ii. 59, 11). Hommel (*Die Semitischen Völker*, p. 406) very ingeniously reads the "QI-tree" as *gis-kin*, in Accadian *mus-kin*, from which he derives the Assyrian *musukkanu* or *mussikannu*, "a palm." But the Semitic rendering is not *ukkanu*, as he reads, but *kiskanu*, from the Accadian *giskin*. The palm was the sacred tree of Babylonia, and Adar was "lord of the date."

[3] The original seems to be literally, "while (before Ea) it went ($=$grew), Eridu was richly fertile."

[4] This appears to be the meaning of the line, the site of the tree being regarded as, like Delphi among the Greeks, the $\delta\mu\phi\alpha\lambda\delta s$ of the earth. The Sumerian equivalent of "earth" is SI-MAD, which must be read *mad* (W. A. I. v. 38, 59) with the determinative prefix.

of Norse mythology, the world-tree whose roots descend into the world of death, while its branches rise into Asgard, the heaven of the gods. The Babylonian poet evidently imagined his tree also to be a world-tree, whose roots stretched downwards into the abysmal deep, where Ea presided, nourishing the earth with the springs and streams that forced their way upwards from it to the surface of the ground. Its seat was the earth itself, which stood midway between the deep below and Zikum, the primordial heavens, above, who rested as it were upon the overshadowing branches of the mighty "stem." Within it, it would seem, was the holy house of Davkina, "the great mother," and of Tammuz her son, a temple too sacred and far hidden in the recesses of the earth for mortal man to enter. It is perhaps a reminiscence of this mystic temple that we find in the curious work on "Nabathæan Agriculture," composed in the fourth or fifth century by a Mandaite of Chaldæa, where we are told of the temple of the sun in Babylon, in which the images of the gods from all the countries of the world gathered themselves together to weep for Tammuz.[1] What the tree or "stalk" was which sprang

---

[1] Ibn Wahshîyah, the translator of the *Nabathæan Agriculture* of Kuthâmi into Arabic, adds that he had "lit upon another Nabathæan book, in which the legend of Tammuz was narrated in full; how he summoned a king to worship the seven (planets) and the twelve (signs of the Zodiac), and how the king put him to death, and how he still lived after being killed, so that he had to put him to death several times in a cruel manner, Tammuz coming to life again after each time, until at last he died; and behold, it was identical with the legend of St. George that is current among the Christians." Abû Sayid Wahb ibn Ibrahim, in his calendar of the Ssabian festivals, says under the month Tammuz: "On the 15th of this month is the festival of the weeping women, which is identical with Ta'uz, a festival held in honour

up like the bean-stalk of our old nursery tale, is indicated in the magical text to which the fragment about it has been appended.[1] In this, Ea describes to Merodach the means whereby he is to cure a man who is possessed of the seven evil spirits. He is first to go to "the cedar-tree, the tree that shatters the power of the incubus, upon whose core the name of Ea is recorded," and then, with the help of "a good *masal*" or phylactery which is placed on the sick man's head as he lies in bed at night, to invoke the aid of the Fire-god to expel the demons. It is the cedar, therefore, which played the same part in Babylonian magic as the rowan ash of northern Europe, and which was believed to be under the special protection of Ea; and the parallel, therefore, between the ash Ygg-drasil of Norse mythology and the world-tree of the poet of Eridu becomes even closer than before.

Long after the days when the hymns and magical texts of Eridu were composed, the mystic virtues of the cedar were still remembered. A tablet which describes

---

of the god Ta'uz. The women weep over him, (telling) how his lord slew him, and ground his bones in a mill, and scattered them to the winds; and they eat nothing that has been ground in a mill, but only soaked wheat, vetches, dates, raisins and the like" (Chwolson's *Die Ssabier*, ii. p. 27).

[1] W. A. I. iv. 15. *Rev.* 10—13. It is pretty clear from the sculptures that the sacred tree of the Babylonians was the cedar, which was subsequently displaced by the palm; so that Hommel's view, which sees a palm in "the stalk" of Eridu, may still be maintained. On the other hand, in W. A. I. ii. 59. *Rev.* 10, "the divine Lady of Eden" is called "the goddess of the tree of life" in the Accadian of north Babylonia, "the goddess of the vine" in the Sumerian of south Babylonia. It is clear from this that the sacred tree was also conceived of as the vine. According to the Old Testament, it will be remembered, there were two sacred trees in the garden of Eden.

the initiation of an augur, and states how he must be "of pure lineage, unblemished in hand and foot," speaks thus of the vision which is revealed to him before he is "initiated and instructed in the presence of Samas and Rimmon in the use of the book and stylus" by "the scribe, the instructed one, who keeps the oracle of the great gods:" he is made to descend into an artificial imitation of the lower world, and there beholds "the altars amid the waters, the treasures of Anu, Bel and Ea, the tablets of the gods, the delivering of the oracle of heaven and earth, and the cedar-tree, the beloved of the great gods, which their hand has caused to grow."[1] It was possibly the fragrance of the wood when lighted for sacrificial purposes that gave the tree its sacred character.

But the cedar was something more than a world-tree. It was employed, as we have seen, in incantations and magic rites which were intended to restore strength and life to the human frame. It was thus essentially "a tree of life," and the prototype and original of those conventional trees of life with which the walls of the Assyrian palaces were adorned. Those who have visited the Assyrian collection of the British Museum will remember the curious form which it generally assumes, as well as the figures of the two cherubs which kneel or stand before it on either side. At times they are purely human; at other times they have the head of a hawk and hold a cone—the fruit of the cedar—over the tree by whose side they stand.

It is possible that, as time went on, another tree became

---

[1] K 2486, *Obv.* 2—4. A fragment of a duplicate of this text is published in W. A. I. ii. 58, No. 3.

confounded with the original tree of life. The palm was from the earliest period characteristic of Babylonia; and while its fruit seemed to be the stay and support of life, the wine made from it made "glad the heart of man." Date-wine was largely used, not only in Babylonian medicine, but in the religious and magical ceremonies of Babylonia as well. It is not at all improbable, therefore, that the later Babylonian tree of life, with its strange conventional form, was an amalgamation of two actual trees, the cedar and the palm. It is even possible that while one of them, the cedar, was primarily the sacred tree of Eridu, the other was originally the sacred tree of some other locality of Chaldæa.

What gives some colour to this last suggestion is, that in later Babylonian belief the tree of life and the tree of knowledge were one and the same. The text which describes the initiation of a soothsayer associates the cedar with "the treasures of Anu, Bel and Ea, the tablets of the gods, the delivering of the oracle of heaven and earth." It was upon the heart or core of the cedar, too, that the name of Ea, the god of wisdom, was inscribed. And it was wisdom rather than life, the knowledge of the secrets of heaven and the magical arts that benefit or injure, which the priesthood of Babylonia and the gods they worshipped kept jealously guarded. Only the initiated were allowed to taste of its fruit. In this respect, consequently, there was a marked difference between the belief of the Babylonians and the account which we find in the earlier chapters of Genesis.

We can trace the first steps by which the name and worship of Tammuz made their way from Eridu northwards. In the same part of Babylonia, a few miles only to the north, lie the mounds of Tel-loh, which have yielded to French enterprize the earliest monuments of Chaldæan art we as yet possess. We learn from them that the god of Tel-loh was Nin-girśu. It was in honour of Nin-girśu that the kings who reigned at ´Sirgulla built and adorned their chief temples; and in the inscription of Sukal-duggina (?) he is brought into association with the god of Nipur and entitled "the valiant warrior of Mul-lil." Nin-girśu was, in fact, "the lord of Girśu," the native name, probably, of Tel-loh. When the cult of Mul-lil found its way to Girśu, the god of Girśu necessarily entered into relation with him; and as "the lord of Girśu" seems to have been a Sun-god, he took the place of Adar and became "the valiant warrior of Mul-lil." It was on this account that the mythologists subsequently identified Adar and Nin-girśu.[1] In Accad, however, an earlier identification had been discovered, in whose justification, it is probable, more might have been said. After the establishment of the worship of Tammuz in Sippara, and the introduction of the divinities of southern Babylonia into the north, Tammuz came to be addressed there as Mul-Merśi or En-Merśi, the Accadian or North-Chaldæan form of Nin-girśu. In forgetfulness of the real origin of the name, the Semitic scribes of Sargon and his successors seem to have interpreted the title as if it meant "lord of the horned crown," the head-dress worn by the Babylonian kings. A broken text, which was probably the compilation of a bilingual Semite, breaks out into these words:[2] "O Merodach, go, my

---

[1] W. A. I. ii. 57, 74.

[2] W. A. I. iv. 27, 6, completed from S 1208, which reads *akala* instead of *akali* in line 17 (W. A. I. 57). *Mir-śi* is found in an unnum-

son, take the hand of the white offspring of Mul-Merśi (Tammuz); lull the plague of the sick man to rest; change his heart; assist the man;[1] grant the spell of Ea; the offspring of his heart whom thou hast taken away and the strong food of the man restore (to him)." "The white offspring of Mul-Merśi" is perhaps an equivalent of a common phrase in these old texts: "the man the son of his god." It represents that close relationship which was supposed to exist between the Babylonian and the god he worshipped, and which the Egyptian symbolised by the assumption of an identity between himself and the divine being. But whereas the pantheistic Egyptian believed in his absorption into the divinity, the pious Babylonian, who regarded his gods as creators and generators, called himself their son.

The worship of the Sun-god of Eridu had embodied other elements before it reached northern Babylonia, besides those which resulted in the identification of Tammuz and Nin-Girśu. It was probably as Nin-Girśu that he became the patron and lord of the green marsh-plants which flourished in the neighbourhood of Tel-loh; it was as Nin-girśu that he was adored as the son of Ea the river-god, rather than of Ea the god of the deep; and it was from the story of his untimely death that he came to be the Nergal of southern Chaldæa, the Sun-god of winter and night who rules, like Rhadamanthos, in the

---

bered bilingual fragment belonging to the series K (*Obv.* 6) : *bit sa mirśi.* For Mul-merśi, see W. A. I. ii. 59, 8. *Girśu* seems to mean the "bank" of a river. At all events, in S 1366, *Obv.* 3, 4, the Accadian *me-ir-śi gu id* UD-KIP-NUN-KI-LIL-*ma* is rendered by the Semitic *ina girśé sa Puratti*, "on the bank of the Euphrates."

[1] The Semitic is literally, "put the man into the hand;" the Accadian, "take the hand of the man."

lower world. But he was more than this. The Chaldæans were a people of agriculturists and herdsmen; their monarchs were addressed as "shepherds;" and just as Abel in the Old Testament is "a keeper of sheep," so, too, Tammuz in Babylonia was accounted a shepherd. This is how an old Accadian hymn speaks of him (W. A. I. iv. 27, No. 1):

> "O Tammuz, shepherd and lord, bridegroom of Istar the lady of heaven,
> lord of Hades, lord of the shepherds' cot,[1]
> the green corn[2] which in the meadow[3] has not drunk the water,
> its progeny in the desert is not green of leaf;
> the acacia (?) tree which in the canal is planted not,[4]
> the acacia (?) tree whose foundation is taken away ;
> the grain[5] which in the meadow has not drunk the water."

The poem is written in the artificial dialect which sprang up in the court of Sargon, and it probably emanated from the city of Accad.[6] It may have been one of the dirges chanted in commemoration of the death of Tammuz, the shepherd who was cut off like the unwatered corn, or the tree from beneath whose roots the soft soil of the canal slips away.

The story of Tammuz of Eridu did not stand alone. There were other cities of Babylonia which knew of a hapless Sun-god cut off in the prime of his life, or perish-

---

[1] *Tul*, i.e. "tel" or "mound." [2] Aram, *bina*.
[3] Comp. Jensen, *Z. f. K.* ii. 16.
[4] For *erisu*, "to be planted," see W. A. I. v. 24, 12.
[5] W. A. I. ii. 33, 73, compared with v. 21, 7, 8.
[6] The Accadian is Semitised and the Semitic is Accadised. Thus in the Accadian we have *simba* for *siba*, "shepherd," the Semitic *tul*, and *gu* from the Semitic *qu*; in the Semitic, *musarê*, a derivative from the Accadian *sar*, "grass," *radi*, borrowed from the Accadian *rat* (more correctly *radh*, W. A. I. ii. 38, 18), and *gu* instead of *qu*.

ing through love of a heartless goddess. But in these legends, it would appear, the goddess herself was the cause of the hero's death; so far from venturing into the glooms of Hades for the sake of her youthful bridegroom, it was she who had herself lured her lover to his destruction. This was the light in which Istar was represented at Erech, and this was the interpretation put there upon the name of the Accadian month of the Errand of Istar. The fate of the suitors of Istar is glanced at in the sixth book of the Epic of Gisdhubar.

1. "For the favour of Gisdhubar the princess Istar lifted the eyes;
2. '(Look up), Gisdhubar, and be thou my bridegroom!
3. I am thy vine,[1] thou art its bond;
4. be thou my husband and I will be thy wife.
5. I will give thee a chariot of crystal and gold,
6. whose pole is of gold and its horns are of glass,[2]
7. that thou mayst yoke (thereto) each day the mighty coursers.
8. Enter our house in the gloom of the cedar.
9. When thou enterest our house
10. let (the river) Euphrates kiss thy feet.
11. Let kings, lords (and) princes (bow) beneath thee!
12. The tribute of the mountain and the plain let them bring thee as an offering.
13. (In the folds?) let thy flocks bring forth twins;
14. (in the stables) let the mule seek (its) burden;
15. let thy (horse) in the chariot be strong in galloping;
16. let (thine ox) in the yoke have no rival.'
17. (Gisdhubar) opened his mouth and speaks,
18. (he says thus) to the princess Istar:
19. '(I will leave) to thyself thy possession,
20. (in thy realm are) corpses and corruption (?),
21. . . . . disease and famine.

[The next seven lines are too mutilated to be translated.]

29. The wind and the blast hold open the back-door (of thy palace).
30. The palace is the destroyer of heroes.

---

[1] *Sabi.* Haupt reads *inbi*, "fruit."
[2] *Elmesu;* see W. A. I. iv. 18, 42, and ii. 30, 42.

31. A deceitful (?) mouth are its hidden recesses
32. A destructive (?) portent are its columns.
33. A girdle of dark cloth are its columns.
34. Of white stone is the construction (*musab*) of the stone fortress.
35. As for me, 'tis the mouth of the land of the enemy.
36. A devouring flame (?) is its lord.
37. Never may I be (thy) bridegroom for ever!
38. Never may a god make thee joyous.
39. Go, and let me tell (the story) of thy enslavements
40. of those into whose hands thou puttest no ransom.
41. To Tammuz the bridegroom (of thy youth) thou didst look;
42. year after year with weeping didst thou cling to him.
43. Alala, the eagle, also didst thou love;
44. thou didst strike him and break his wings;
45. he remained in the forest; he begged for his wings.
46. Thou didst love, too, a lion perfect in might;
47. seven by seven didst thou tear out his teeth, seven by seven.
48. And thou didst love a horse glorious in battle;
49. he submitted himself; with spur and whip didst thou cling to him;
50. seven leagues didst thou cling to him galloping;
51. in his trouble and thirst didst thou cling to him:
52. to his mother the goddess 'Silili with tears didst thou approach.
53. Thou didst love also the shepherd Tabulu,
54. who continually poured out for thee the smoke (of sacrifice).
55. Every day was he slaughtering for thee the victims;
56. thou didst bring him forth and into a hyena didst change him;
57. his own sheep-cote drove him away
58. and his own dogs tore his wounds.
59. Moreover, thou didst love Isullanu[1] the gardener of thy father,
60. who was ever raising for thee costly trees.
61. Every day had he made bright thy dish.
62. Thou didst take from him (his) eye and didst mock him:
63. 'O my Isullanu, come, let us eat thine abundant store,
64. and bring out thy hand and dismiss all fear of us.'
65. Isullanu says to thee:
66. 'As for me, what dost thou ask of me?
67. O my mother, thou cookest not (and) I eat not;

---

[1] In W. A. I. iii. 68, 23, Isullanu is called by his Accadian name of Si-śigśig or Si-śimśim, "he who makes green the living things."

68. the food I have eaten are garlands and girdles;
69. the prison of the hurricane is (thy) hidden recess.'
70. Thou didst listen and (didst impose) punishment;
71. thou didst strike him; to bondage thou didst (assign him);
72. and thou madest him sit in the midst of (a tomb?).
73. I will not ascend the height; I will not descend to the (depth);
74. and yet thou lovest me that thou (mayest make) me as they are.'
75. When Istar (heard) this,
76. Istar was enraged and (mounted up) to heaven.
77. Moreover Istar went before Anu (her father),
78. before Anu she went and she (says):
79. 'O my father, Gisdhubar has kept watch on me;
80. Gisdhubar has counted my garlands,
81. my garlands and my girdles.'"

Like Potiphar's wife, Istar thus accuses Gisdhubar of doing the exact contrary of what he really had done. The portion of the tablet which contained the conversation between her and Anu is broken, but enough remains to show that she eventually persuaded him to punish the hero. Anu accordingly created a divine bull of monstrous size; but without much result, as Gisdhubar and his friend Ea-bani succeeded in destroying the animal and dragging its body in triumph through the streets of Erech. With Gisdhubar and the divine bull of Anu, however, we are not at present interested. What concerns us just now is the list given by Gisdhubar of the unhappy victims of Istar's coquetry. Of the first, Tammuz, there is but little said. Even Sin-liqi-unnini, the author of the Epic of Gisdhubar, could find but little in the story of Tammuz which could throw discredit on the goddess. The next mentioned is Alála, "the eagle." Now the eagle is stated to be "the symbol (*tsalam*) of the noon-tide sun;" and that Alála, whose name is of Accadian origin signifying "the great Spirit," has solar connections, is indicated not only by the fact that his consort Tillili is the sister of Tammuz in the legend of the Descent of Istar, but also from the compound title *Alála alam*, "Alála of the image."[1] In one of the local cosmogonies of Chaldæa, however, he and his consort took the place of Assoros and Kissarê, the primordial heavens and earth. Like them, he was resolved into Anu by the monotheistic school;[2] and a text associates both him and Tillili with the cosmogonic deities Lukhma and Lakhama, "the gods who are immanent in the heaven and in the earth."[3] Who the lion and the horse were we do not yet know; we hear of "a god of lions" (W.A.I. iii. 66, 34), and one of the Assyrian names of the month Sebat was "the month of 'Silili" (K 104, *Rev.*). In the shepherd Tabulu, however, we have the double of the shepherd Tammuz himself. The name reminds us of Abel and Tubal-Kain, more especially when we remember that it is but a *tiphel* formation—so common in Assyrian—from the simpler *abalu*. His fate recalls that of the hunter Aktæôn, torn by his own dogs through the anger of

---

[1] W. A. I. ii. 54, 12.

[2] W. A. I. ii. 54, 11. In W. A. I. iii. 66, 15, we have (AN) *Sam-su* (AN) *alam;* comp. ll. 18, 20, 26.

[3] D. T. 122, 17—20. Laban(?)-same, "the brick foundation of heaven" is also mentioned in the same text. Nabonidos, when describing the rebuilding of the temple of the Moon-god at Harran, says that he set about it "by the commission (not "work," as Latrille) of the god Laban (?), the lord of foundations and brick-work" (*libnâti*, W. A. I. v. 64. i. 53), and that on either side of the eastern gate of the building he placed "two Lukhmu gods who sweep away my foes." Laban is mentioned (W. A. I. iii. 66, 6) among the gods whose images stood in the temple of Anu at Assur, and it is probable that he was of foreign importation. According to Genesis, Harran was the home of Laban. The name would mean "the white one." "The god of the Foundation" (*ûr*) is mentioned in 79. 7-8. 68. This was the horizon of heaven as opposed to the zenith or Nebo.

Artemis, the Asianic representative of the Babylonian Istar. Isullanu, the gardener of Anu, is probably the mythic prototype of the historical Sargon of Accad, whom later legend turned into a gardener beloved by the goddess Istar. As it was upon the famous king of Accad that the old myth was fastened, it is possible that Isullanu had been the representative of Tammuz at Accad before the cult of the god of Eridu had been introduced there from the south.

But who, all this while, was the goddess, whom one legend made the faithful wife enduring even death for her husband's sake, while another regarded her as the most faithless and cruel of coquettes? I have already spoken of her as the goddess of love, and such, indeed, she was to the Babylonian or Assyrian of later days. In the story of her descent into Hades, her residence in the lower world is marked by all cessation of intercourse between male and female in the animal creation, as well as among the gods of heaven. It was this feature of the story which caused it to find its way into the literature of another people, and to survive the days when the clay tablets of Assyria and Babylon could still be read. We find it serving to point a moral in the pages of the Talmud. We are there told how a pious rabbi once prayed that the demon of lust should be bound, and how his petition was granted. But society quickly fell into a state of anarchy. No children were born; no eggs even could be procured for food; and the rabbi was at length fain to confess that his prayer had been a mistaken one, and to ask that the demon should again be free.

But though a moral signification thus came to be read into the old Babylonian myth, it was a signification that was originally entirely foreign to it. Prof. Tiele has clearly shown that the legend of Istar's descent into Hades is but a thinly-veiled description of the earth-goddess seeking below for the hidden waters of life, which shall cause the Sun-god and all nature with him to rise again from their sleep of death.[1] The spirits of earth, the gnomes that guard its treasures below, watch over the waters, and not until they are led forth and placed on their golden throne can their precious treasure be secured. It is the earth who loses her adornments, one by one, as she passes slowly downward into the palace-prison of the infernal goddess, and it is the earth who is once more gladdened at spring-time with the returning love of the youthful Sun-god.

Istar, then, must primitively have been the goddess of the earth, and the bride of Tammuz at Eridu must accordingly have been his mother Dav-kina. This alone will explain the persistent element in the myth as it made its way to the Greeks, according to which the mother of Tammuz was also his sister. Istar, Tillili, Dav-kina, were all but different names and forms of the same divinity. We have just seen that Tillili, at all events, was the primordial earth.

What Istar was primitively, however, will not explain what she became in those later ages of Babylonian history to which our monuments belong. Her origin faded more and more into the background; new elements entered into her character; and she absorbed the attributes and functions of numberless local divinities. The Istar of Assur-bani-pal or Nabonidos was the inheritress of cults

---

[1] *Actes du sixième Congrès internationale des Orientalistes*, ii. 1, pp. 495 *sq.*

and beliefs which had grown up in different localities and had gathered round the persons of other deities.

The Istar of the historical period is essentially Semitic. But let me not be misunderstood. What is Semitic in her nature is an after-growth, which cannot be explained unless we assume that it has grown out of non-Semitic elements. The Semitic superstructure presupposes a non-Semitic basis. It is only thus that we can explain both the name of Istar and the striking difference that exists in regard to her character between the Semites of Babylonia and those of the west. It is only where the Semite had come into contact with the Accadian that we find the name and worship of Istar at all. We look in vain for it among the Arabs of central Arabia, among the descendants of those who parted from their Semitic brethren of the north before they were affected by the culture of primæval Babylonia. We find the name of Aththor, it is true, on the southern coast of Arabia; but we find there also the name of the Babylonian Moon-god Sin, and other traces of the influence which Babylonian trade could not fail to exert in comparatively late days. Inland, Istar remained unknown.

All attempts to discover a Semitic etymology for the name have been unavailing. And there is a good reason why they should be so. The name itself bears evidence to its non-Semitic origin. We find it in its earliest form in Babylonia; and here, though it denotes the name of a female goddess, it is unprovided with that grammatical sign of the feminine—the dental suffix—which marks the names of other genuinely Semitic goddesses. Belit, Zarpanit, Anat, Tasmit, all show by their termination their source and meaning; and Istar, without that termination, in spite of its meaning, shows equally plainly what its source must be. As the name travelled further to the west, away from its old associations with Chaldæa, the grammatical instincts of the Semites could no longer be held in check, and Istar was transformed into the Ashtoreth of the Old Testament and the Phœnician monuments, the Astartê of the Greeks. Even in Babylonia and Assyria, when Istar became the representative of all other female divinities, and the name passed into a common term signifying "a goddess," the Semitic feminine suffix was attached to it. But the suffix was attached to it only when it was thus used, no longer as a proper name, but as one of the words of the Semitic dictionary; whenever it still retained its ancient sense and denoted a specific deity, it retained also its ancient genderless appearance. As a foreign name, it continued to the last a stranger in the province of Semitic grammar.

We can thus understand why it was that the Semites sometimes changed the old Chaldæan goddess into a male divinity. On the Moabite Stone, Mesha declares that he dedicated Nebo of Israel to Istar-Kemosh, "to Istar who is the god Kemosh;" and an astronomical tablet[1] informs us that Dilbat, the planet Venus, which, as we shall see, was the primitive Istar, is "a female at sunset and a male at sunrise," the word employed for male being a curiously artificial coinage, such as "maless" would be in English. In fact, the tablet goes on to add that Venus was not only a male by reason of her identification with the morning star, she was also the rising Sun-god himself, and thus "a male and the offspring (of a male);"

---

[1] W. A. I. iii. 53. 30—39.

while at sunset she was the god Adar, and thus "an androgyne and the offspring (of an androgyne)." After this, we are told that "Venus at sunrise is Istar of Accad by name," while at sunset she is "Istar of Erech by name;" at sunrise she is "Istar of the stars," at sunset *bilat ili*, "the mistress of the gods." The doubt as to whether Istar were male or female was the same as that which was felt by the Semites in regard to other Accadian deities.[1] Where there was no grammatical indication, where the same word might mean "master" or "mistress" according to the context, the zealous but half-educated Semitic neophyte might well be forgiven the mistakes he sometimes made in his adoption and adaptation of the older divinities. It was thus that the ambiguity of the Accadian *nin*, which signified at once "lord" and "lady," led him at times to transform the god Adar into a goddess; and I have already pointed out in an earlier Lecture how in like manner the god A became the wife of the Sun. But that a similar doubt should hang over the sex of Istar proves more plainly than anything else the non-Semitic origin of her name and character.[2]

When, however, we come to look closely into this character, we shall find here also clear traces of a non-

---

[1] In W. A. I. ii. 35, 18, we are told that the god Tiskhu was "Istar of Erech;" and yet in ii. 57, 35, Tiskhu appears as the equivalent of Adar as "god of libations." But it must be remembered that the Semites were doubtful about the sex of Adar. On the other hand, Iskhara, another name of Istar (ii. 49, 14 ; K 4195, 7), is said to be a male deity whose wife was Almanu or (Al)manâti (Strassmaier, 3901).

[2] That the Phœnicians also knew of a male Istar is perhaps indicated by the Greek myth which made Európa the wife of Asterios, the king of Phœnician Krêtê.

Semitic descent. In the first place, Istar is distinguished from the other goddesses of the Semitic world by her independent nature. She is not the mere reflexion of the male divinity, like Anat or Beltis or Zarpanit; in so far as she is Istar, she is placed on an equal footing with the male deities of the pantheon. In this respect she stands in marked contrast to the goddesses of the pure Semitic faith, and to the purely Semitic conception of the divine government of the world. She holds equal rank with the Sun-god Baal; Babylonian mythology, in fact, makes her his sister, and treats her as if she were a god. We may even say that she takes rank before him, at all events in early times, in conformity with the old Accadian custom of setting the woman before the man, but in flagrant violation of the contrary practice of the Semitic race. So far, indeed, from being the double and shadow of the god, Istar is rather the divinity who gives life and substance to her divine lovers. Tammuz himself is but "the bridegroom" of Istar; it was only for the sake of Istar that his name was held in honour. Istar, in short, is an anomaly in the Semitic pantheon; she is there as a goddess who masquerades in the garb of a god.

Away from Accadian influences, in the Phœnician lands of the west, the character, like the name, of the goddess was more closely accommodated to Semitic ideas. Istar had become Ashtoreth, and Ashtoreth had put on the colourless character of the Semitic goddess. Hence it was that, just as Baal became the common designation of the male deity, Ashtoreth was the common designation of the female. By the side of the Baalim stood the Ashtaroth—those goddesses whose sole right to exist was the necessity of providing the male divinity with a consort. Ashêrah, the southern Canaanitish goddess of fertility, alone retained some of the independence of the Babylonian Istar.

In the second place, there is a very important difference between the Istar of Babylonia and the Ashtoreth of Phœnicia. Ashtoreth was the goddess of the moon; Istar was not. It was in the west alone that Astartê was

> "Queen of heaven with crescent horns;
> To whose bright image nightly by the moon
> Sidonian virgins paid their vows and songs."

It was in the west alone that the shrine was erected to Ashtoreth Karnaim,[1] "Ashtoreth of the double horn;" and Greek legend described the wandering Astartê, under the name of Eurôpa, crossing the celestial sea on the bull that Anu had created for her so long before to punish the disdainful Gisdhubar. In Babylonia and Assyria, however, Istar and the moon were separate one from another. The moon was conceived of as a god, not as a goddess, in conformity with pre-Semitic ideas; and the Moon-god Sin was never confounded with the goddess Istar. It must have been the same wherever the worship of Sin extended, whether in Harran in the north or in Yemen and the Sinaitic desert in the south. But the worship never made its way to Canaan. Sin failed to establish himself there, and the moon accordingly remained the pale mirror and double of the mightier Baal. The Semites of Phœnicia were too distant from the cultured kingdoms of the Euphrates to allow their religious instincts to be overridden and transformed. The name and cult of Istar were indeed introduced among them,

---

[1] Gen. xiv. 5, where the word is wrongly punctuated "Ashteroth."

but a new interpretation was given to both. Istar sank to the level and took the place of the older goddesses of the Canaanitish faith.

Perhaps you will ask me what is the meaning of the name of Istar? This, however, is a question which I cannot answer. The Babylonians of the historical age do not seem to have known what was its origin, and it is therefore quite useless for us to speculate on the subject. Its true etymology was buried in the night of antiquity. But its earliest application appears to have been to the evening star. This is the oldest signification that we can assign to the word, which by the way, it may be noticed, does not occur in any of the Accadian texts that we possess.[1]

The legend of the assault of the seven wicked spirits upon the moon tells us pretty clearly who the goddess Istar was primarily supposed to be. Mul-lil, it is said, "had appointed Sin, Samas and Istar, to rule the vault of heaven," and, "along with Anu, had given them to share the lordship of the hosts of heaven. To the three of them, those gods his children, he had entrusted the night and the day; that they cease not their work he urged them. Then those seven, the wicked gods, darted upon the vault of heaven; before Sin, the god of light, they came in fierce attack; Samas the hero and Rimmon the

---

[1] From which we may infer that the name originated in one of the smaller cities of the country. It is possibly a side-form of Iskhara, Is-tar and Is-khara being alike compounds of *is*. The suffix -*ra* or -*r* is common in Proto-Chaldæan, and the Semitic spelling of the first syllable (with '*ain*), like that of the first syllable of *Anu*, points to its having originally been *as*. Istar appears as *Esther* in the book of Esther, where Mordechai, it may be noted, is a derivative from Merodach.

warrior turned and fled; Istar set up a glittering throne by the side of Anu the king, and plotted for the sovereignty of heaven."[1] Thus once more the mythologist gives the goddess an unfavourable character, though it is easy to see what the story means. When the moon is eclipsed, the evening star has no longer any rival in the sky; it shines with increased brilliancy, and seems to meditate ruling the night alone, in company only with the heaven itself.

Already, before the days of Sargon of Accad and the compilation of the great Babylonian work on astronomy, it had been discovered that the evening and morning stars were one and the same. Not only, therefore, was Istar the evening star, the companion of the moon; she became also the morning star, the companion and herald of the sun. It was thus that she assumed the attributes and titles of a male deity, since Dun-khud-e, "the hero who issues forth at daybreak," was both a god and the morning star. As the morning star, therefore, Istar was a god and the successor of a god, so that it is not wonderful if the bewildered Semite, who found no visible sign of gender in the name of the divinity he had adopted, should sometimes have regarded Istar as the masculine form of Ashtoreth. Some of the early Accadian titles of Istar belong to her as the star of the morning, though the title of "Lady of Rising,"[2] given her as "the wife

---

[1] W. A. I. iv. 5, 60—79.

[2] W. A. I. ii. 54, 20. As "Lady of the dawn" she was called Bis-bizi, a re-duplicated form, apparently, of *bis* or *pes*, which is rendered by *mamlu* (W. A. I. iv. 69, 33; 21, 66), a synonym of *allallu* (ii. 31, 65) and *rahâbu* (ii. 35, 35). Compare *pes*, "a pig." *Rahâbu* is the Hebrew *rahab*, "the crocodile" as a symbol of Egypt, and denoted in Assyrian "a sea-monster." Hence George Smith seems to have been right in

of Anu" (W. A. I. ii. 54, 15), would apply equally to the evening star.

In making her the wife of the Sky-god, the mythologists were only expressing in another way what the poet of the legend of the seven evil spirits had denoted by saying that Istar set up her throne by the side of Anu. More usually, however, the relation between Istar and Anu was regarded as a genetic one; she was the daughter, rather than the wife, of the Sky.[1] At times, again, she is called the daughter of the Moon-god, the Moon-god being here the larger body which begets the smaller star. It is possible that these different views about her descent are derived from different centres of worship; that which made her the daughter of Sin having its origin in Ur, while that which made her the daughter of Anu emanated from Erech. At any rate, her connection with the Moon-god seems to have been the more popular view in Semitic times.

As a planet, Istar's ordinary name was the Accadian Dilbat, or "Announcer." One of the smaller cities of Babylonia had the same name, and was probably the chief seat of the worship of the goddess under this particular form. It is obvious that the name must have been originally applied not to the evening but to the morning star. It was only as the announcer of day and the herald of the sun that Venus could be the Accadian representative of the Semitic Nebo. The other mes-

---

identifying the *bis-bis* or "dragon" Tiamat with Rahab, since *is bis-bis* is interpreted *turbuhtu* (W. A. I. ii. 32, 9), "the locust-swarm of the sea," according to ii. 5, 4.

[1] Both at Erech and Tel-loh her temple was called E-Ana, "the temple of the Sky."

sengers of the gods were male; and in Semitic times the fact that there had once been a female messenger was forgotten. The name of Dilbat, it is true, remained, but only as the name of a star; the place of Istar as the herald of the Sun-god was taken, at Babylon at all events, by Nebo.

It is possible that the records of the city of Dilbat, if ever they are recovered, will show us that this was the primal home of the name of Istar itself, and the centre from which it first spread. If so, however, it was little more than the primal home of the goddess's name. The real source and centre of the worship of Istar at the dawn of the historical period, the starting-point from which it was handed on to the Semites and became overlaid with Semitic beliefs and practices, was not Dilbat, but Erech. In the days when Erech had been a leading state, when the cult of the Sky-god had been carried by its people to other parts of the Eastern world, the cult of Istar also had been carried with it. Wherever the worship of Anu had gone, the worship of Istar, the daughter of Anu, went too. But the Istar of Erech was originally known by a different name. She was Nána, "the lady," a title which does not appear to have been replaced by the name of Istar until after the beginning of the Semitic period. At all events the common title of the goddess in the Accadian texts is Nána; the word Istar is never found in them. As Nána,[1] "the lady," she continued to be known at Erech down to the most recent times. It was the famous image of Nana that the Elamite

---

[1] As the name is always written in combination with the prefix of divinity, the compound character was called In-Nána, for Au-Nána (see above, p. 116).

invader Kudur-nankhundi had carried off 1635 years before the generals of Assur-bani-pal recovered it in the sack of Shushan, and late texts draw a distinction between Nana and Istar. Thus in a tablet of exorcisms, the patient is told to address "Istar, Nana and Kasbâ,"[1] and an augural tablet is careful to distinguish between Nana and "Istar the queen" (*milkatu*).[2]

It was, in fact, easy to identify a goddess who bore so general a name as that of "the lady" with any other female divinity. At Borsippa, for instance, Nana was made one with an otherwise unknown deity 'Sutitil (?), "the goddess who quickens the body." A text copied for Assur-bani-pal from a tablet originally written at Babylon, contains part of a hymn which had to be recited "in the presence of Bel-Merodach when he had seated himself (*ittasbu*) in the house of sacrifice (*akitum*) in the beginning of Nisan." The latter portion reads as follows:

"(O Bel, why) dost thou not take thy seat in Babylon? In E-Saggil is set thy dwelling-place. 'His is the . . . .' they have not said to thee, and Zarpanit has not cried to thee. O Bel, why dost thou not take thy seat in Borsippa? In E-Zida is set thy dwelling-place. 'O Nebo, I am here,' they have not said to thee; Nana the goddess who quickens the body has not cried to thee. O Bel, why dost thou not take thy seat in Kis? In E-Dubba (the house of libation) is set thy dwelling-place. 'O Zamama,[3] why dost thou not take thy seat?'

---

[1] K 3464, 18.

[2] K 220, *Obv.* 4, 13. The divine names in this tablet follow in this order: Istar of Babylon, Nana, Kani-surra, the god of Kibib, Nebo, Tasmetu, Gula, 'Sakin of E-Ana, Samas, Sala, Istar the queen, Nergal (Ugur), Rimmon, Zamama, Mul-lil.

[3] Zamama (in Sumerian Zagaga) was the Sun-god of Kis (W. A. I. ii. 60, 7; 61, 52), and was consequently identified with Adar by the mythologists (W. A. I. ii. 57, 70). On a contract-stone he is symbolized by an eagle, which is said to be "the image of the southern sun

Bahu, the queen of Kis, has not cried to thee. O Bel, why dost thou not take thy seat in Cutha? In E-'Sulim [SIT-LAM] is set thy dwelling-place. 'O Nergal (Ugur), why dost thou not take thy seat?' Laz and the goddess Mamit have not said unto thee. 'O my pure one,' they have not cried unto thee."[1]

It will be noticed that in this hymn, while Nana has ceased to be the special goddess of Erech and has become the goddess of Borsippa, she is ranked with Bahu of Kis and Laz and Mamit—that terrible "Ban" which even the gods must obey—who presided over Cutha. Laz disappeared almost entirely from the pantheon of later Babylonia, and was remembered only by antiquarians, except perhaps in Cutha itself;[2] but the name of Bahu remained better known. Bahu probably was the Gurra of Eridu, the great mother "deep" which was the home of the seven evil spirits,[3] and represented the waters of the abyss in their original chaotic state before they were reduced to order by the creator Ea.[4] She seems to have been the Bohu of Genesis, the Baau of the Phœnician

---

of Kis." We gather also from W. A. I. ii. 57, 53, that he was symbolised (like Alála) by the eagle.

[1] *Unnumbered;* a few lines are quoted by Strassmaier, 6049.

[2] Yet in 2 Kings xvii. 30, "the men of Cuth" are said to have "made Nergal" only, from which we may infer that the ordinary population even of Cutha had forgotten the special name of their ancient goddess.

[3] W. A. I. iv. 15, 5.

[4] Zikum and Zigarum or Zikúra are the names of Gurra when regarded as the whole body of chaos out of which the heaven and the earth were formed (W. A. I. ii. 48. 26, 27). Zigarum or Zikúra stands for Zi-Gúra, "the spirit of Gúra." Cp. Gen. i. 2. If the king of Telloh whose name reads Ur-Bahu is to be identified with the well-known Chaldæan monarch Ur-Bagas or Ur-Zikum, the identity of Bahu and Zikum would be certain. Bahu is of Semitic origin, but was borrowed by the Accadians at an early period.

Sanchuniathon, whose Greek interpreter identifies her with the night and makes her the mother of the first mortal men. The Semitic Bohu, however, was no deity, much less a goddess; the word signified merely "emptiness," and was thus a quite unsuitable rendering of the old Accadian Gurra, "the watery deep." There is little reason for wonder, therefore, that the recollection of what Bahu had primitively been should have faded out of the memories of the Semitic Babylonians. As the gods of the Accadians had become Baalim, so Bahu, like the other goddesses of primæval Chaldæa, was swept into the common vortex of Ashtaroth. She became the wife of the Sun-god of Kis (W. A. I. iii. 68, 63), and, when he was identified with the Sun-god of Nipur, of Adar also (K 133, 21). She thus passed into Gula, "the great goddess," who, though carefully distinguished from both Bahu and Nana in the earlier texts, ended in the Semitic period by becoming confounded with both. She was originally the local goddess of Niśin,[1] and had the titles of "lady of the evening," "lady of the house of death," "lady of life and death." In one of the prayers prescribed for recitation in the temple of Merodach at Babylon, she is invoked as "the mother who has begotten the black-headed race (of Accadians)." She thus takes the place that is occupied by Istar in the story of the Deluge, who is there made to declare that "I have begotten my people," and is called Rubat, the Assyrian equivalent of the Accadian Gula. In fact, it is pretty clear from the local titles of Gula that she must once have been the evening star; and we can therefore under-

---

[1] W. A. I. ii. 67, 31.

stand why it is that on the one hand she is termed "the wife of the southern sun,"[1] and on the other hand is made the consort of Adar by the mythologists. She forms the common meeting-point of the various local deities of Chaldæa who were connected with the Sun-god; Bahu, Â, Sala, all alike are Gula, "the great one;" and Gula is but the Accadian original of Rubat, the Semitic Istar. In this way we may explain the statement that Gula is "the heaven" (W. A. I. v. 31, 58), the sky of the evening which was ruled by the evening star.

But it is also quite possible that, as Hommel thinks, one of the elements which went to make up the character of the later Istar was a goddess of the sky who corresponded to the Sky-god of Erech. If so, this might well have been Gula, whose assimilation to Istar would have been assisted by the close relation existing between Anu and Nana. However that may be, the Istar of the Semitic period inherited the attributes of Dav-kina, the goddess of the earth. The bride of Tammuz of Eridu was not the Istar of Erech, not the Istar of the evening star, but a goddess of the earth. At Eridu, the goddess of the earth was Dav-kina, his own mother, and we can thus trace to its primitive home those forms of the myth of Adônis which made his mother his sister as well. In Cyprus, the Phœnicians called him Gingras, and declared that Kinyras was his father's name. Kinyras, however, is but a popular perversion of Gingras, slightly changed in pronunciation so as to remind the speaker of the Phœnician *kinnôr*, "the zither," just as Kenkhrêis, the wife of Kinyras, is again but Gingras in an Hellenised

---

[1] W. A. I. i. 70. 4, 5.

form. Now the title of Gingras seems to bear the marks of its origin upon its face. It is the old Accadian Gingiri, or Gingira, which we are told was the Accadian name of Istar.[1] Gingiri, however, meant nothing more specific than "goddess." It was the feminine equivalent of the masculine *dingir*, and, like *dingir*, signified "creator." The "great" goddess of southern Babylonia was thus the creator of the world just as much as the god who stood by her side.

The identification of Istar and Gingira simplified the process whereby the worship of the goddess spread through Babylonia. Each city had its own Gingira, or "creatress;" each city, therefore, gave a welcome to its own Istar. When the empire of Sargon had transported the deities of southern Chaldæa to Accad, Istar naturally accompanied her bridegroom Tammuz. Whether the Semitic colouring which the worship of Istar received was given to it now for the first time at Accad, or whether it had already been received at Erech, we have no means of determining. The fact remains that from henceforth Istar became a Semitic goddess; her cult was almost

---

[1] W. A. I. ii. 48, 29. The ideographs of which it is a gloss read Sar-sar, a name of Ea, according to ii. 55, 54. Perhaps therefore we should look to Eridu as the source of the name, where Ea and Davkina would be grouped together as "the gods Sar-sar," corresponding to the An-sar and Ki-sar of another system of cosmogony. However, the words explained in the portion of the text which gives the gloss Gingira seem to belong to a document that emanated from the court of Sargon of Accad; see ll. 40, 47, and the astronomical notices. In the early Accadian inscriptions Gingira has the more correct form Gingiri (written GINGI-*ri*). The mode of writing the name proved very convenient for the Semites, who regarded it as expressing their Ista-ri (instead of Istar or Istaru), as well as for the people of Van in after times, who employed it to denote the name of their own goddess 'Sari (instead of 'Saris). See also above, p. 143.

purely Semitic in character, and the two great centres of her worship were the Semitic cities of Erech and Accad.

Her worship was a reflexion of that worship of nature which underlay the Semitic conception of Baalism. The fierce passions excited by an Eastern sun found their expression in it. Prostitution became a religious duty, whose wages were consecrated to the goddess of love. She was served by eunuchs and by trains of men and boys who dressed like women and gave themselves up to women's pursuits. Istar, in fact, had ceased to be the "pure" goddess of the evening star. The other elements in her hybrid character had come to the front, aided by the Semitic conception of the female side of the divinity. She was now the fruitful goddess of the earth, teeming with fertility, the feminine development of the life-giving Sun-god, the patroness of love. The worshipper who would serve her truly had to share with her her pains and pleasures. Only thus could he live the divine life, and be, as it were, united with the deity. It was on this account that the women wept with Istar each year over the fatal wound of Tammuz; it was on this account that her temples were filled with the victims of sexual passion and religious frenzy, and that her festivals were scenes of consecrated orgies. As the worship of the goddess spread westward, the revolting features connected with it spread at the same time. The prophets of Israel denounce the abominations committed in honour of Ashtoreth and Baal within the sacred walls of Jerusalem itself; the Greek writers stand aghast at the violations of social decency enjoined as religious duties on the adorers of the oriental Aphrodité; and Lucian himself —if Lucian indeed be the author of the treatise—is shocked at the self-mutilation practised before the altar of the Syrian goddess of Hierapolis. From Syria, the cult, with all its rites, made its way, like that of Attys-Adonis, to the populations beyond the Taurus. At Komana in Kappadokia, the goddess Ma was ministered to by 6000 eunuch-priests, and the Galli of Phrygia rivalled the priests of Baal and Ashtoreth in cutting their arms with knives, in scourging their backs, and in piercing their flesh with darts. The worship of the fierce powers of nature, at once life-giving and death-dealing, which required from the believer a sympathetic participation in the sufferings and pleasures of his deities, produced alternate outbursts of frenzied self-torture and frenzied lust.

There was, however, a gentler side to the worship of Istar. The cult of a goddess who watched over the family bond and whose help was ever assured to the faithful in his trouble, could not but exercise a humanising influence, however much that influence may have been sullied by the excesses of the popular religion. But there were many whose higher and finer natures were affected only by the humanising influence and not by the popular faith. Babylonia does not seem to have produced any class of men like the Israelitish prophets; but it produced cultivated scribes and thinkers, who sought and found beneath the superstitions of their countrymen a purer religion and a more abiding form of faith. Istar was to them a divine "mother," the goddess who had begotten mankind, and who cared for their welfare with a mother's love. It is true that they seem to have preferred addressing her by some other name than that which was polluted by the Galli and their female comrades; it was to Gula, rather than to Istar or Rubat, that the priest of Bel was told to pray; and the translators of the penitential psalms turn the Nana (Innana) of the Accadian original into *istaritu*, "the goddess," instead of Istar. But if questioned, they would have said that the goddess to whom their petitions and praises were addressed was indeed Istar, and that Gula and Nana and Milkat were but various names under which the same deity was adored. The people, it is true, may have regarded the goddesses of Babylonia as separate divinities, even as the peasant of Spain or Italy may to-day regard his local Virgins as distinct each one from the other; the educated Babylonian knew them to be but one—divers forms of the godhead, but no more. In fact, he did not scruple to translate by the common name of Istar the several names under which the chief goddess of Babylonia went in the old Accadian hymns. It is thus that we read in one of these:

> "The light of heaven, who blazeth like the fire, art thou,
> O goddess (*istaritum*), when thou fixest thy dwelling-place in the earth;
> thou who art strong as the earth!
> Thee, the path of justice approaches thee
> when thou enterest into the house of man.
> A hyæna, who springs to seize the lamb, art thou!
> A lion, who stalks in the midst, art thou!
> By day, O virgin, adorn the heaven!
> O virgin Istar, adorn the heaven!
> Thou who art set as the jewelled circlet of moonstone[1] adorn the heaven!

---

[1] *Subî*, from the Accadian *suba*, the Assyrian equivalent of which was (*aban*) *yarakhu* (W. A. I. ii. 40, 59). In the legend of the Descent of Istar (p. 227) the *sutartum* or "jewelled circlet" belongs to Tillili, and is composed of "eye-stones." The Suba was the name of a god (ii. 58, 46),

Companion of the Sun-god, adorn the heaven!
'To cause enlightenment to prevail[1] am I appointed, alone[2] am I appointed.
By the side of my father the Moon-god[3] to cause enlightenment to prevail am I appointed, alone am I appointed.
By the side of my brother the Sun-god to cause enlightenment to prevail am I appointed, alone am I appointed.
My father Nannaru has appointed me; to cause enlightenment to prevail am I appointed.
In the resplendent heaven to cause enlightenment to prevail am I appointed, alone am I appointed.
In the beginning was my glory, in the beginning was my glory.
In the beginning was I a goddess (*istaritum*) who marched on high.
Istar[4] the divinity of the evening sky am I.
Istar the divinity of the dawn am I.
Istar the opener of the bolts of the bright heaven is my (name of) glory.
My glory extinguishes the heaven, it spoils the earth.
The extinguisher of the heaven, the spoiler of the earth is my glory.
That which glows in the clouds of heaven, whose name is renowned in the world, is my glory.
As queen[5] of heaven above and below may my glory be addressed.
My glory sweeps[6] away the mountains altogether.

---

and of a river which was consecrated to Tammuz (ii. 50, 12). As the god Suba is stated to be a form of the Sun-god, like Ilba, he is doubtless to be identified with Tammuz as "god of the Moon-stone."

[1] In the Accadian, "the gift of light."

[2] *Gitmalu.* The word has no connection with *gamâlu*, "to finish," and means "sole," "unique" (as here, where the Accadian equivalent signifies "going alone"). The statement in W. A. I. iv. 69, 76, that *gitmalu* is the Accadian *sar*, "big," is derived from the secondary sense of *gitmalu* as "monstrous" or "gigantic."

[3] Mistranslated in the Assyrian, which has wrongly construed the Accadian postpositions.

[4] In the original Accadian, "mistress of the sky."

[5] In the original, "the unique monster" (*usugal*).

[6] The Assyrian translation misrenders: "I sweep away."

270 LECTURE IV.

Thou art[1] the mighty fortress of the mountains, thou art their mighty bolt, O my glory.'

May thy heart rest, may thy liver be tranquil.[2]
O lord (Bel) Anu the mighty one, may thy heart be at rest.
O lord (Bel), the mighty mountain Mul-lil, may thy liver be tranquil.
O goddess (*istaritum*), lady of heaven, may thy heart be at rest.
O mistress, lady of heaven, may thy liver be tranquil.
O mistress, lady of E-Ana, may thy heart be at rest.
O mistress, lady of the land of Erech, may thy liver be tranquil.
O mistress, lady of the land of the city of precious stones,[3] may thy heart be at rest.
O mistress, lady of the mountain of mankind,[4] may thy liver be tranquil.
O mistress, lady of the temple of the pasturage of mankind, may thy heart be at rest.
O mistress, lady of Babylon, may thy liver be tranquil.
O mistress, lady of the name of Nana, may thy heart be at rest.
O lady of the temple, lady of spirits, may thy liver be tranquil.
(COLOPHON.)—Tearful supplication of the heart to Istar.
Like its old copy written and published. Palace of Assur-banipal, king of Assyria."

But Istar was not merely the goddess of love. By the side of the amorous goddess there was also a warlike one. The Syrian goddess who migrated westward was a war-

---

[1] The Assyrian mistranslates : " I am."
[2] The concluding litany probably belongs to a later period than the rest of the hymn, to which it has been attached, and is of the age when Erech and Babylon were the leading cities of Chaldæa.
[3] " The city of Sula." " The river of Sula " is called " the river of Tammuz" or of Suba in W. A. I. ii. 50, 12.
[4] Kharsag-kalama, the name of a temple at Kis (W. A. I. ii. 61, 15), or 'Sabu (v. 12. 49, 50), also called *kapar ri'i*, " the village of the shepherd," or *kapar garradi*, " the village of the warrior" Tammuz (ii. 52. 66, 67).

rior as well as a bride. Among the Hittites and their disciples in Asia Minor, she was served not only by Galli, but by Amazons—warrior priestesses—as well. The Artemis of Ephesos, her lineal descendant, was separated by a wide gulf from the Aphroditê of Cyprus. Both Artemis and Aphroditê were alike the offspring of the same Babylonian deity, but in making their way to Greece they had become separated and diverse. The goddess of the Hittites and of Asia Minor preserved mainly her fiercer side; the goddess of Phœnician Cyprus her gentler side. Both sides, however, had once been united in the Istar of Chaldæa. The Greek myths which recounted the story of Semiramis recorded the fact. For Semiramis is but Istar in another guise. As Istar was called "queen" by the Assyrians, so is Semiramis the queen of Assyria; as Semiramis deserts Menôn for Ninos or Nineveh, so did Istar desert her old haunts for her later temple at Nineveh. The dove into which Semiramis was changed was the bird sacred to Istar. Her passion for her son Ninyas, "the Ninevite," whom another version of the myth names Zames or Samas, is an echo of the passion of Istar, the Dav-kina of Eridu, for Tammuz the Sungod. The warrior-queen of Assyria, in fact, was the great Babylonian goddess in her martial character.

While the gentler-mannered Babylonians preferred to dwell upon the softer side of Istar, the Assyrians, as was natural in the case of a military nation, saw in her mainly the goddess of war and battle. Like Babylonia, with its two centres of her worship at Erech and Accad, Assyria also had its two great sanctuaries of Istar at Nineveh and Arbela. That she should have had no famous temple in

Assur,[1] the old capital of the kingdom, shows clearly the comparatively late development of her cult. Doubtless the earliest inhabitants of the Assyrian cities had brought with them the name and worship of Istar, but it could only have been long afterwards that it attained its final celebrity. Indeed, we can trace its progress through the historical inscriptions until it culminates in the reign of Assur-bani-pal.

There was a particular cause for this gradual development which was connected with the warlike attributes of the Assyrian Istar. The Assyrians were an essentially Semitic people. Their supreme goddess accordingly was that vague and colourless Bilit ili, "the mistress of the gods," who sat as a queenly shadow by the side of Bel. They had none of those associations with the older Accadian goddesses, with their specific names and functions, which the natives of the Babylonian cities possessed; apart from Istar, the evening star, there was no goddess among them who could claim a more independent position than that of a Bilit ili. Assur himself had no special consort, like Zarpanit at Babylon or even Â at Accad.[2] Except Istar, therefore, the Assyrian pantheon was destitute of a goddess who could assert her equality with the gods.

But the name of Istar, supported as it was by the

---

[1] Tiglath-Pileser I. speaks of building one there along with temples of Martu and of Bel-labaru, "the old Bel" (Col. vi. 86, 87). He gives Istar the title of *Assuriti*, "Assyrian," not "Assurite."

[2] Tiglath-Pileser III. once mentions Seruha apparently as the consort of Assur (Lay. 17, 15), but this is in connection with his occupation of Babylonia.

traditions, the sacred teaching and the literature the Assyrians had brought from Babylonia, sufficed to keep alive a recollection of the fact that such female divinities had once been recognised. Accordingly, while Istar on the one hand tended to be merged into the vague and general Bilat ili, on the other hand she absorbed their attributes into herself. With the increasing fame of her shrines at Nineveh and Arbela, and the rise of Nineveh as the capital of the country, the second process went on rapidly. Istar, therefore, while still preserving her individuality, took upon herself all the offices and attributes of Beltis, the wife of the Sun-god. The ancient myths which had made her the bride of Tammuz and Alala, and her identification with Â in Semitic Accad, had already paved the way. It was thus that the fiercer aspect of the Sun-god as a warrior, first reflected on his consort, the Bilat ili, became transferred to the Assyrian Istar. Istar of Arbela was primarily a militant deity, the bearer of the bow of war. If the Assyrians were to have a goddess at all, a deity with an independent character and position of her own, it was necessary that she should be a goddess of war. The earlier kings of Assyria, Rimmon-nirari I., Tiglath-Pileser I., Assur-natsir-pal and his son Shalmaneser II., pay her but slight attention, invoking her only at the end of their list of gods; and when they address her, it is as "the lady of onset, the strengthener of battle," "the lady of battle and war," "the chieftainess of heaven and earth who makes perfect the face of the warriors." Even Sargon and Sennacherib are chary of their references to her; while Tiglath-Pileser III. in Babylonia sacrifices to Nana of Erech

T

rather than to Istar,[1] and Shalmaneser II. distinguishes between the military goddess Istar and Beltis (Nin-lil), "the wife of Bel, the mother of the (great) gods." But with Esar-haddon all is changed Oracles of encouragement and prophecies of victory pour in for him from the priestesses and priests of the temple of Istar at Arbela; Istar declares herself to be his mistress, "who will do battle with the enemies before (his) feet." She promises to give his foes into his hand: "Fear not, O Esar-haddon," is the prophecy delivered through the mouth of the priestess Bayâ, "I am thy strong Baal, I devise the might[2] of thy heart: I am jealous[3] as thy mother, for thou hast given me power; the sixty great gods, my strong ones, shall protect thee; the Moon-god shall be on thy right hand, the Sun-god on thy left." Another oracle is even more explicit:

"I am Istar of Arbela, O Esar-haddon, king of Assyria; in Assur, in (Nineveh), in Calah, in Arbela, long days and everlasting years will I give to Esar-haddon my king. I am the lover of thy limbs,[4] thy nurse and (thy guardian) am I. For long days and everlasting years thy throne I have established in earth and heaven the mighty. For my veil of gold in the midst of heaven I am jealous. I will cause the light which clings to it to shine before the face of Esar-haddon, king of Assyria, like the crown of my head, (and) behind his feet. Fear not, O king, I have spoken with thee, I have not withheld myself (?)

---

[1] Similarly Sennacherib (W. A. I. i. 43, 31—33) speaks of "the Sun-god of Larsa, the Lady of Rub-esi (?), the Lady of Erech Nana, the goddess Utsura-amatsa, the Lady of Life, the god Kasdinnam, the goddess Kassitu, and Nergal." Kassitu probably means "the Kassite" or Kossæan goddess; in Kasdinnam we may see an Aramæan form of the Biblical Kasdim.

[2] Literally, "strong beams of wood."

[3] *Akharidi*, akin to *khardatu*, "solicitude."

[4] "Testicles," according to Haupt.

(from thee). (Thy) foeman shall cease to be. The river, in despite of opposition, I will cause thee to cross. O Esar-haddon, the faithful son, son of Beltis, ... with my hands do I make an end of thy foes."

Assur-bani-pal inherited his father's devotion to Istar, as well as her care and protection. It was, however, upon Istar of Nineveh, "the queen of Kidmur,"[1] rather than upon Istar of Arbela, that his attention was more particularly bestowed. Nineveh was for him "the supreme city of Istar," and it was "by the command of Assur and Istar" that his wars were undertaken, and by their help that they were crowned with success. When Teumman of Elam threatened the empire with invasion, he went into the temple of the goddess, and, like Hezekiah when he received the letter of Sennacherib, knelt there at the feet of his deity, and laid before her the scornful message of the Elamite king The whole passage in which Assur-bani-pal describes his conduct at this moment of danger is a striking parallel to what we read in the Old Testament concerning the Jewish monarch.

"When Teumman," says Assur-bani-pal, "strengthened himself in Elam, in the assembly of his forces, I looked to Istar who looks on me. I obeyed not the command of his rebellious mouth, I surrendered not the fugitives (he had demanded). Teumman devised evil, (and) the Moon-god devised for him omens of evil; in the month Tammuz, an eclipse during the morning watch obscured the lord of light and the sun was darkened; and as he rested, so too did I rest for three days, that the regnal years of the king of Elam might be ended and his country destroyed. (Thus did) the Moon-god (give) me his command, which may not be altered. .... In the month Ab, the month of the appearance of the star of the Bow, the festival of the glorious queen the daughter of Bel (Mul-lil), in order to worship her, the great (goddess), I stayed in Arbela, the chosen city of her heart. Of the invasion

---

[1] Also written *Kidimuri*, K 11, 35. It was the name of the part of the palace set apart for the royal harem.

of the Elamite, who marched godlessly, they reported to me as follows: 'Teumman says thus and thus of Istar,' and they reported the tenor of his message that he would not depart until he had gone against Assur-bani-pal to make war. On account of this threat which Teumman had uttered, I prayed to the exalted one, Istar; I wept before her, I bowed beneath her, I did honour to her divinity, (and) she came with favour to me. 'O lady of Arbela,' I prayed, 'I am Assur-bani-pal, the creation of thy hands (and the creation of Assur), the father who created thee, that I might restore the shrines of Assyria and complete the fortresses of Accad. .... I seek after thy courts, I go to worship (thy divinity); and now he, Teumman, king of Elam, who values not the gods, has come up to (make war). Thou art the lady of ladies, the terror of conflict, the lady of war, the queen of the gods, ... who in the presence of Assur, the father that created thee, utterest blessings. In the .... he hath desired me .... to make glad the heart of Assur and to give rest to the liver of Merodach. .... As for Teumman, king of Elam, who has sinned (grievously) against Assur (the king of the gods), the father that created thee, and against Merodach thy brother and companion .... and (against) me, Assur-bani-pal, whom (thou hast desired) to give rest to the heart of Assur and (Merodach), he has gathered his army, has made ready for war, has asked his soldiers to march to Assyria; do thou that art the archer of the gods, strike him down like a weight in the midst of the battle, and smite him as a tempest of evil wind.' My lamentable supplication did Istar hear, and 'Fear not,' she said; she caused me to overflow with (joy of) heart: 'For the lifting up of thy hands which thou hast lifted up, for thine eyes (that) are filled with tears, I have compassion.' In that very hour of the night when I prayed to her, a certain seer slept, and he dreams a prophetic (?) dream. A revelation during the night Istar revealed to him (which) he repeated to me thus: 'Istar who dwells in Arbela entered, and right and left was a quiver uplifted. She held a bow in her hand; she drew a heavy falchion to make war; her countenance was wrathful. Like a fond mother she speaks with thee, she cries to thee. Istar, the exalted of the gods, appoints thee this message: 'Thou entreatest to gain victory; the place lies before thee; I am coming!' Thou shalt answer her thus: To the place to which thou goest with thee let me go! The lady of ladies even she declares to thee thus: I will defend thee that thou mayest dwell in the sacred precincts of Nebo:[1] eat food, drink wine, keep festival, glorify my divinity; when I have gone, this

---

[1] See W. A. I. ii. 29, 18. The library of Kouyunjik seems intended.

message shall be accomplished. I will cause the desire of thy heart to prevail; thy face shall not grow pale, thy feet shall not stumble, thy beauty (?) shall not fade. In the midst of battle, in her kindly womb she embosoms thee and embraces thee on every side. Before her a fire is kindled (fiercely) to overcome thy foes."[1]

Istar is here represented in human form, with a quiver on either shoulder and a bow in the hand. This, in fact, is the ordinary fashion in which Assyrian art portrayed the warlike goddess. But Assyrian art was not peculiar in thus depicting the goddess of love and war. In the older art of Babylonia, of which that of Assyria was but a modification, the deities of the popular faith were all represented in human shape. The oldest cylinders of Semitic Chaldæa agree in this respect with the bas-reliefs of the palaces of Nineveh. It is only the demons and inferior spirits, or mythical personages like Ea-bani, the friend of Gisdhubar, who are portrayed as animals, or as composite figures partly human and partly bestial. Ea alone, in his character of "god of life,"[2] is given the fish's skin, and even then the skin is but thrown over his back like a priestly cloak. The composite monsters, whose forms Bêrôssos saw painted on the walls of the temple of Bêlos, were the brood of chaos, not of the present order of the world. The legend of the creation preserved by the priests of Cutha declares that the creatures, half men and half birds, which were depicted in sacred art, were suckled by Tiamat, the dragon-like personification of anarchy and chaos. Their disappearance marked the victory of light over darkness, of the gods of heaven over the Titanic monsters of an extinct

---

[1] G. Smith's *Assur-bani-pal*, pp. 117—126.
[2] On an early cylinder in the British Museum.

age. The deities of Babylonia were emphatically human; human in character and human in form. They stood in marked contrast to the animal-headed gods of Egypt, and harmonised with the Semitic belief that made the deity the father of the human race, who had created man in his own image. Even in pre-Semitic days, Chaldæan art had already followed the same line of thought, and had depicted its divinities in the likeness of men; but in pre-Semitic days this was a tendency only; it was not until the Accadian came in contact with the Semite that he felt the full force of the Semitic conception, and allowed his ancient deities of light and life to take permanently upon them the human shape.[1]

For there are many indications that it had not always been so. The very fact that the divine beings who in the Semitic era were relegated to the realms of chaos or the inferior world of subordinate spirits, were to the last represented as partly bestial in form, proves pretty clearly that the Babylonians had once seen nothing derogatory to the divine nature in such a mode of representation.

---

[1] The fact that the gods of Babylonia were represented in human form leads us to expect to find also the converse fact, the apotheosis of men. Our expectation is fulfilled, at any rate as regards the earlier period of Semitic Babylonia. A hæmatite cylinder, found by Gen. di Cesnola in Cyprus, gives Naram-Sin, the son of Sargon, the invader of the island, the title of god, and on the bricks of Amar-Agu or Buru-Sin of Ur (W. A. I. i. 5, xix.) the divine title is prefixed to the royal name. It is significant that this deification of the monarch is coeval with the rise of Semitic supremacy, and that it never took firm hold of the religious faith of the people. At all events, there is no trace of it from the time of Khammuragas downwards. It is true that the Kassite sovereign Agu-kak-rimê (cir. B.C. 1630) claims to be descended from the god Sugamuna (W. A. I. v. 33. i. 4); but Agu-kak-rimê was neither a Semite nor a Sumerian, and to claim descent from a god is not the same as claiming to be a god oneself.

The winged bulls who guarded the approach to the temple and protected it from the invasion of evil spirits, or the eagle-headed cherubs who knelt on either side of the sacred tree, were survivals of a time when "the great gods of heaven and earth" were themselves imaged and adored in similar form. The same evidence is borne by the animals on whose backs the anthropomorphic deities are depicted as standing in later art. When the gods had become human, there was no other place left for the animals with whom they had once been so intimately connected. The evidence, however, is not borne by art alone. The written texts aver that the gods were symbolised by animals, like the Sun-god of Kis, whose "image" or symbol was the eagle. It is these symbols which appear on the Babylonian boundary-stones, where in the infancy of Assyrian research they were supposed to represent the Zodiacal signs.

That they were originally something more than mere symbols is expressly indicated in the myths about the goddess of love. Gisdhubar taunts her with her treatment, not only of Alála, the eagle, but also of the horse and the lion, whose names are not given to us. Here, at any rate, popular tradition has preserved a recollection of the time when the gods of Babylonia were still regarded as eagles and horses and lions. We are taken back to an epoch of totemism, when the tribes and cities of Chaldæa had each its totem, or sacred animal, to whom it offered divine worship, and who eventually became its creator-god. Not less clear is the legend of the first introduction of culture into the valley of the Euphrates. Oannes, or Ea, it was ever remembered, had the body of a fish, and, like a fish, he sank each night into the waters of the Persian Gulf when the day was closed which he had spent among his favoured disciples of Eridu. The culture-god himself had once been a totem, from which we may infer how long it was before totemism disappeared, at all events from southern Babylonia, where the contact with Semitic thought was less strong and abiding than was the case further north.

We can learn a good deal about this totemism from the old ideographic representations of the names of the chief deities. They are like fossils, embodying the beliefs of a period which had long passed away at the date of the earliest monuments that have come down to us. The name of Ea himself affords us an example of what we may find. It is sometimes expressed by an ideograph which signifies literally "an antelope" (*dara* in Accadian, *turakhu* in Assyrian, whence perhaps the Biblical name of Terah).[1] Thus we are told that Ea was called "the antelope of the deep," "the antelope the creator," "the antelope the prince," "the lusty antelope;"[2] and the "ship" or ark of Ea in which his image was carried at festivals was entitled "the ship of the divine antelope of the deep."[3] We should, indeed, have expected that the animal of Ea would have been the fish rather than the antelope, and the fact that it is not so points to the conclusion that the culture-god of southern Babylonia was an amalgamation of two earlier deities, one the divine

---

[1] *Turakhu* is the Arabic *arkhu*, "an antelope," and is a tiphel formation from the Assyrian verb *arákhu*, "to run quickly." The word has no connection with the Accadian *dara*. Friedrich Delitzsch long ago suggested that it represented the Biblical Terah (*Assyrische Studien*, i. p. 51).

[2] W. A. I. ii. 55, 27—30.   [3] W. A. I. ii. 62, 39.

antelope, and the other the divine fish. Perhaps it was originally as the god of the river that Ea had been adored under the form of the wild beast of the Eden or desert. There was yet another animal with which the name of Ea had been associated. This was the serpent. The Euphrates in its southern course bore names in the early inscriptions which distinctly connect the serpent with Ea on the one hand, and the goddess Inniná on the other. It was not only called "the river of the great deep"— a term which implied that it was a prolongation of the Persian Gulf and the encircling ocean; it was further named the river of the *śubur lilli*, "the shepherd's hut of the lillu" or "spirit," "the river of Innína," "the river of the snake," and "the river of the girdle of the great god."[1] In-nina is but another form of Innána or Nâna, and we may see in her at once the Istar of Eridu and the female correlative of Anúna. Among the chief deities reverenced by the rulers of Tel-loh was one whose name is expressed by the ideographs of "fish" and "enclosure," which served in later days to denote the name of Ninâ or Nineveh. It seems clear, therefore, that the pronunciation of Nina was attached to it; and Dr. Oppert may accordingly be right in thus reading the name of the goddess as she appears on the monuments of Tel-loh. Nina, consequently, is both the fish-goddess and the divinity whose name is interchanged with that of the snake.[2] Now Nina was the daughter of Ea, her eldest

---

[1] W. A. I. ii. 51, 45—49.

[2] In W. A. I. iv. 1. 33, 38, In-nána is mentioned along with Nina, but, as Hommel has already pointed out (*Vorsemitische Kulturen*, p. 360), this magical text includes older and newer elements, the mention of In-nána belonging to the later portion of the text.

daughter being described in a text of Tel-loh as "the lady of the city of Mar," the modern Tel Id, according to Hommel, where Dungi built her a temple which he called "the house of the jewelled circlet" (*sutartu*). This latter epithet recalls to us the Tillili of the Tammuz legend as well as the Istar of later Babylonia. In fact, it is pretty clear that Nina, "the lady," must have been that primitive Istar of Eridu and its neighbourhood who mourned like Tillili the death of Tammuz, and whose title was but a dialectic variation of that of Nana given to her at Erech.

After this, it is not difficult to disentangle the primitive relation that existed between the totems of the antelope, the fish and the serpent, at Eridu. Ea was the antelope as god of the river; as god of the deep he was Oannes the fish. His daughter was denoted by a compound ideograph which represented her birth from the residence of the fish-god, though she was herself one of the poisonous reptiles that swarmed in the marshes at the mouth of the Euphrates. It was in this way that the serpent became connected with the god of wisdom, "more subtil than any beast of the field" which had been created in the land of Edina.

It is now possible to explain the allusions in an old Accadian poem, in which Merodach (?) is made to describe his weapon of war. After comparing it with "the fish of seven fins," he goes on to say: "The tempest (*mâtu*) of battle, my weapon of fifty heads (I bear), which like the great serpent of seven heads is yoked with seven heads, which like the strong serpent of the sea (sweeps away) the foe."[1] Here the serpent is regarded as essen-

---

[1] W. A. I. ii. 19, 11—18.

tially a serpent of the sea, and in its seven heads we may see the primitive conception of its divine power. The "evil spirits" were seven in number also, like the spirits of the earth, and the mythical fish which may be the totem of the fish-god is provided with seven fins.[1] The destructive character of the great serpent is naturally insisted on. Doubtless the serpent-god of the primitive Sumerian was morally of a negative nature, or else regarded as injuring only his enemies, while he did good to those who propitiated him. But this early serpent-worship faded away with the transformation of the totem into an anthropomorphic deity. The goddess Nina ceased to retain her serpentile attributes, and after the era of the monuments of Tel-loh passed almost entirely out of memory; while the serpent became, what indeed he always seems to have been in genuine Semitic belief, the incarnation of wickedness and guile. We read in the bilingual lists of "the evil serpent," "the serpent of darkness;"[2] and it is probable that the imagination of a later time confounded this serpent of darkness with the dragon Tiamat, the leader of the powers of night and chaos. It was a curious process of development which eventually transformed the old serpent-goddess, "the lady Nina," into the embodiment of all that was hostile to the powers of heaven; but, after all, Nina had sprung from the fish-god of the deep, and Tiamat is herself "the deep" in a Semitic dress.

At times Ea was regarded as a gazelle[3] rather than

---

[1] W. A. I. ii. 19, 65.

[2] W. A. I. ii. 24. 10, 12. The "evil serpent" is called "the monstrous (*russû*) serpent of the sea" in W. A. I. ii. 19, 17.

[3] *Elim* in Accadian, *ditanu* in Assyrian (W. A. I. ii. 6, 7; 59, 5;

as an antelope. It was thus that he was entitled "the princely gazelle," "the lusty gazelle," "the gazelle who gives the earth" (W.A.I. ii. 55. 31—33); and Merodach as his son is termed Aśari-elim, "the mighty one of the gazelle-god." A hymn which celebrates Merodach under a number of his archaic names, declares that he is "Aśari-elim, the mighty prince, the light (of the gods), the director of the laws of Anu, Bel (Mul-lil) (and Ea)."[1] The gazelle, however, was more correctly appropriated to Mul-lil of Nipur, who was specially called "the gazelle-god."[2] We may infer, accordingly, that the gazelle had once been the totem of Nipur, and the representative of its god of the under-world. It was, indeed, a peculiarly sacred animal. We find it repeatedly on the early Chaldæan cylinders, sometimes being offered in sacrifice to a deity, sometimes simply standing at his side as a symbol. It frequently takes the place of the goat, which was also sacred, and as such was exalted into the Zodiacal sign of Capricornus. Since Tebet, the tenth month, corresponds to the sign of Capricornus and was dedicated to Pap-sukal, it is possible that Pap-sukal, "the messenger of the gods," was himself the goat-god. At any rate, there was a deity called Uz,[3] the Accadian word for a goat; and a

---

iv. 70, 55). The position of the name in the list of animals (W. A. I. ii. 6, 7), shows what species of animal must be meant. *Lulim*, "a stag," seems to be a re-duplicated form of the same word. Both *lulim* and *elim* are said to be equivalent to *sarru*, "king."

[1] K 2854, 5, 6. In line 10, Merodach is apparently identified with the god Tutu, of whom it is said that "he confronts their life" (BA-AN-TE *ana napisti-sunu*). In the first line he is called Aśari, *sabis zalmat kakkadi*, "nourisher(?) of the black-headed race." Comp. W. A. I. ii. 55, 69.

[2] W. A. I. iv. 70, 55; ii. 59, 5.

[3] In W. A. I. ii. 48, 34, the archaic Babylonian form of the character

curious piece of sculpture on a stone tablet found by Mr. Rassam in the temple of the Sun-god at Sippara describes "Sin, Samas and Istar," as being "set as companions at the approach to the deep in sight of the god Uz."[1] The "crown of the Sun-god" is further said to be the *uz*, or "glory," of the eyes, with a play upon the resemblance of the Semitic word *uzzu*, "glory," to the Accadian *uz*, "a goat." The god Uz himself is depicted as sitting on a throne, watching the revolution of the solar disk, which is placed upon a table and slowly turned by means of a rope. He holds in his hand a ring and bolt, and is clad in a robe of goats' skin, the sacred dress of the Babylonian priests. It reminds us of "the skins of the kids of the goats" which Rebekah put upon Isaac in order that he might receive his father's blessing. The milk of the goat appears in the liturgical texts along with other offerings to the gods; thus we read in a hymn:[2]

"The milk of a light-coloured[3] goat which in a pure feeding-place
the shepherd of Tammuz[4] has reared,

Uz is glossed by Utuki, "the (great) spirit," and explained to be synonymous with the Sun-god. As the document or documents upon which this tablet is a commentary seem to have been a product of the court of Sargon at Accad, we may infer that Uz, "the goat," was a title of the Sun-god of Sippara. The mythical "goat with six heads" is referred to in a bilingual text (W. A. I. iv. 30, 11).

[1] W. A. I. v. 60. *Timi* here means "companions," from *emu*, "to make like." The common word *birit* has nothing to do with either *birit*, "chain," or *birtu*, "a citadel," but is from *barû*, "to see."

[2] W. A. I. iv. 28, 3.

[3] *Asundu*, Accadian *śig-śiga*, "the long-horned," rendered *banu*, or "light-coloured," in W. A. I. iv. 24, 11; ii. 6, 32. The species of goat was called *zur* (Semitised into *surru*) in Accadian (W. A. I. ii. 2. 284, 285, compared with 21. 41).

[4] Not "the shepherd Tammuz," which would require the converse order of words.

the milk of the goat let the shepherd give thee with his pure hands. Mingle (it) in the middle of the skin of a suckling[1] yet unborn. Let the god Azága-śúga,[2] the supreme goat of Mul-lil, with his pure hands cause (it) to be eaten.
Merodach the son of Eridu has given the charm;
O Nin-akha-kúda,[3] lady of the purely-gleaming water, make the worshipper pure and bright!"

Here the divine goat is associated with Mul-lil, and perhaps we may therefore conclude that it was specially adored at Nipur. The inference is not certain, however,

[1] *Uniki,* Accadian QAR-US, in a liturgical fragment (S 712, 5) we read of "the wool (or hair) of a QAR-US yet unborn;" and in S 2073, R. 9, mention is made of "the flesh of the QAR."

[2] "The god of far-reaching purity" or perhaps "the distant gleam"(?). *Súga,* however, may represent *śíga,* "the horned one." In W. A. I. ii. 4, 662, *śigga* is written *śiqqa,* and in 6, 5, *seqa,* and rendered by the Assyrian *atudu,* "he-goat." In W. A. I. iii. 68, 12—14, Azaga-śuga (śud), the wife of Rimmon, is called the milch-kid of Mul-lil, and the names of its two shepherds are given in lines 36, 37.

[3] Nin-akha-kúda is invoked in other magic formulæ : so in W. A. I. iv. 15, 39, it is said of the sick man, "May Nin-akha-kudda seize upon his body and rest upon his head!" and in Haupt's *Keilschrifttexte,* ii. 26, she is mentioned along with Bahu and Gula. In W. A. I. ii. 58. 48, 49, we read of "the pure water of Ea, the purely-gleaming water of Nin-akha-kudda, the water of the pure hand, of the pure deep," where the goddess is associated with Ea and the deep; and in D.T. 57. *Obv.* 14—16, we have "the spell of Ea and Merodach, the spell of Damu and Gula, the spell of Nin-akha-kudda." Similarly in 1266. 12, 13, an invocation is addressed to "Nin-akha-kuddu, Nin-kurra, [En-nu-]gi the son of Nin-si-nagar-bu, and Nin-zadim." In K 4195, 12, Nin-akha-kuddu is identified with Iskhara or Istar. In M 192, 4 *sq.,* "the daily food" is enumerated of Mul-lil, Ea "the king of the deep," "the divine king of the gods and the queen (of the gods)," Samas "the lord of crowns, the decider of (destiny)," "the god who prospers all above and below," Merodach, Adar "the first-born of Mul-lil," Nin-akha-kuddu, Nin karratim and Istar. Nin-akha-kudda means "the lady who divides the rising (fresh) water" as appears from the statement in W. A. I. iii. 68, 40, that she was "the lady of the rising waters (*a-khad*) of Ea." The following line shows that Agubba, "the purely-gleaming water" (*sunqu* in Assyrian), was also deified.

as the text belongs to that later period when the cities and deities of Babylonia had been brought into union with one another.

I have already alluded to the fact that the Sun-god of Nipur was connected with the pig. Adar was "lord of the swine," and the swine would therefore seem to have once been a totem of the city in which he was worshipped. Nothing could show more clearly that Babylonian totemism belongs to the pre-Semitic history of the country, and the conclusion is supported by the large place occupied by the dog in what I may call the zoological mythology of Chaldæa. In Semitic times the dog was as distasteful to the Babylonians as he was, and is, to the Semitic inhabitants of other parts of the world. We have a proof of this in a prayer against the powers of evil, in which we read:

"(From) the baleful fetter, the fetter which injures the feet.... the dog, the snake, the scorpion, the reptile, and whatsoever is baleful, the possession of the heart, the possession (of the body, may Merodach preserve us)."[1]

The dog is avoided by the earlier art of Assyria; and even in Babylonia, where a particular and much-esteemed breed existed, almost the only representation of the animal that is known is on a terra-cotta plaque of the Sassanian period.[2] Nevertheless, there was a time when the Baby-

---

[1] K (unnumbered), 19—21, *buanu limnu buanu naptsu sa sepa*.... UR-KU *tsir* GIRTAB *nammas(tuv) û nin limnu tsibit libbi tsibit (zumri)*.

[2] See the illustration of a "Terra-cotta Tablet from Babylon, representing an Indian dog," in Layard's *Nineveh and Babylon*, p. 527. In Assyria, it is not until we come to the time of Assur-bani-pal that we find the dog represented in the bas-reliefs. The five clay figures of dogs, with their names inscribed upon them, now in the British Museum, belong to the same monarch. The names are (1) Epar tallik epus nabakha, "He ran and barked;" (2) Musetsu limnuti, "the producer

lonian dog was otherwise regarded. Merodach and the dog were brought into connection with one another. The beneficent god of later Babylonian religion owned four divine hounds, named Ukkumu, "the seizer," Akkulu, "the devourer," Iksuda, "the capturer," and Iltebu, "the pursuer."[1] We may suspect that the dogs were not always sent on errands of mercy, and that originally they had been devastating winds who followed in the track of a death-dealing god. An incantation begins with the words: "O Merodach, the lord of death, thy hand establishes the house of light,"[2] where perhaps we have a tradition of the age when Merodach was not as yet the god who raises the dead to life, but the god of death only. At all events, the hounds appear in no favourable character in the fragment of a legend which related to the shepherd Matsarat-pi-baladhi (?).[3] After a reference to Rimmon, the shepherd's heart is told to rejoice because of the message sent him by Ea through the lips of Merodach. "(Ea) has heard thee," it is said to him; "when the great dogs" assault thee, then "Matsarat-pi-baladhi, shepherd of the flock, seize them from behind and lay them down. Hold them and overcome them. Strike their head, pierce (*nihi*) their breast. An expedition they are gone; never may they return! With the wind

---

of mischief;" (3) Dayan rits-su, "the judge of his companions;" (4) Munasiku gari-su, "the biter of his foes;" (5) Kasid âbi, "the seizer of enemies." See Houghton on "The Mammalia of the Assyrian Sculptures" in the *Trans. Soc. Bib. Arch.* v. 1.

[1] W. A. I. ii. 56, 22—25. Iltebu may be derived from *lahbu*, "to be violent."

[2] R 2. 11. 153. *Rev.* 7, 8.

[3] K 2546. The name is written ENNUN-KA-TI, "watch of the mouth of life."

may they go, with the storm above it! Take their road and cut off their going. Seize their mouth, seize their mouth, seize their weapons! Seize their teeth (*sut*), and make them ascend, by the command of Ea, the lord of wisdom; by the command of the Sun-god, the lord of all that is above; by the command of Merodach, the lord of revelation" (*bar-bar-ti*). The recitation of this curious legend formed part of a religious ceremony, and was ordered to be followed by the triple repetition of a prayer "before the god Azag-śuga." This god, as we have seen, was primarily a goat, and it was no doubt on this account that a portion of an old poem about a shepherd who had driven away the dogs from his flock was introduced into the service. The poem, however, like the service, transports us to Semitic days; the dog has become a hateful creature, and what divinity he has is of a demoniac character.

Unlike the dog, the ox remained in honour among the Babylonians, and the mythologists accordingly did not wholly forget that one at least of "the great gods" had once been identified with this animal. An early geographical list calls Dapara, "the mountain of the Bull-god," the country of crystal;[1] and that this was to be sought in southern Babylonia is indicated by the name of the Uknu, the river of "crystal." There is some evidence that the primitive Bull-god was Merodach himself. Ea and his wife had each two divine "bulls" attached to them, those of Ea being named "the god of the field of Eden" and "the god of the house of Eden."[2] These bull-gods must be distinguished from the colossal figures,

---

[1] W. A. I. ii. 51, 13.   [2] W. A. I. ii. 56, 59—62.

the winged bulls, that guarded the entrance to a temple.¹ We may speak of the latter as "Assyrian bulls," but such was never their name among either Babylonians or Assyrians. To them they represented divine beings, the gods or genii of the household, in fact, but not bulls. The face was wanting which was needed to transform the colossus into an image of the animal. The human head showed that the creature was endowed with humanity as much as Ea-bani, the friend of Gisdhubar, whose body terminated in the legs of a goat, but who was nevertheless in all respects a man. The bull-like body of the divine guardians of the household symbolised strength, at all events to the Semitic Babylonian, who persistently paraphrased the Accadian word for "bull," when used as a proper name, by words that denoted "hero" and "strong one." The winged bulls and the divine bulls of Eridu were not one and the same, however much the imagination of a later day may have tended to confound them together.

The fact that the two great deities of Eridu were thus attended by a body-guard of divine bulls, makes us inclined to connect the Bull-god of Dapara very closely indeed with the city of Eridu. We need not be astonished, therefore, at finding Merodach entitled in early astronomical literature Gudi-bir, "the bull of light." The sky, as we have seen, was regarded as a second Babylonian plain, over which the sun ploughed his way along the ecliptic or "furrow of heaven." The pole-star was called

---

[1] In Accadian, *alad* and *lamma*; in Assyrian, *sêdu*, *buhidu* and *lamassu*. The last word seems to have been borrowed from the Accadian *lamma* in its primitive form (*lamas*). *Alad* is "the spirit," from *ala*, with the suffix *d(a)*.

its "yoke,"[1] and Jupiter, the nearest of the planets to the ecliptic, was known as Lubat-Gudibir, "the wether" or "planet of the Bull of Light." The Bull of Light, therefore, was himself the ploughman of the celestial fields, the Sun-god who trod his steady path through the heavenly signs, like the patient ox who dragged the plough through the fields below. It was as the Sun-god, moving through the twelve Zodiacal signs of the year, that Merodach, it is asserted, was known by this particular name.

Now the explanation of the name of Gudibir as Merodach, the Sun-god, comes from a tablet which seems to have been a philological commentary on the astronomical works compiled for the court of Sargon of Accad. We know that Sargon's patronage of science produced the great standard Babylonian work on astronomy and astrology, in seventy-two books, which went under the name of the "Observations of Bel." It was translated into Greek by the Chaldæan historian Bêrôssos, and large portions of it, including a table of contents, are among the tablets found on the site of the library of Kouyunjik. In the course of centuries it had undergone a large amount of interpolation and addition; marginal glosses had crept into the text, and new paragraphs had been inserted recording the observations that had been made

---

[1] Or rather, perhaps, the constellation of Draco generally, *a Draconis* being at the time the pole-star. The star (or constellation) was called MU-BU-KHIR-DA in Accadian, which the Semitic astronomers paraphrased by "the star of Anu, the arbiter (*mamit*) of heaven" (W. A. I. ii. 47, 16), and more literally "the yoke of heaven" (v. 18, 24). The Accadian (or rather Sumerian) is probably to be read *guśir kesda*, "yoke of the enclosure." *Giśra* and *giśrara*, *giśśa*, *giśśilla* and *gunirra*, are given as dialectical forms of the Accadian word for "yoke" (W. A. I. v. 18. 17, 19, 20, 21; 15, 28).

by the astronomers and astrologers of Babylonia during the whole length of the historical period. In the form, therefore, in which it was edited for the library of Nineveh, it was very different from the original work that had been composed by the orders of Sargon. Old and new matter had been mixed up in it, and the enlargements introduced into it had probably nearly doubled its original size. But the original work was itself a compilation of records and observations that had been made during an untold number of previous years. These records and observations had for the most part been written in Accadian; the result being that, although the astronomy of the Chaldæans, as we know it, is purely Semitic in form and character, many of its technical terms are non-Semitic, as well as the names of the celestial bodies. Hence it is that we find a remarkable inconsistency between certain facts reported by the astronomical tablets and the astronomical system which they set before us. This astronomical system is based upon the assumption that the sun enters the first point of the constellation Aries at the time of the vernal equinox. The system must therefore have come into existence later than the 26th century before the Christian era, when Aries first became the starting-point of the Zodiacal signs. But the signs themselves were named, and the path of the sun through them was mapped out, when the vernal equinox still coincided with the sun's entrance, not into Aries, but into Taurus. The whole pre-Semitic nomenclature of the Zodiacal signs, and the months of the year that correspond to them, rests on the supposition that the Zodiacal bull ushers in the vernal year. Its Accadian name was "the directing Bull," the bull that directs the course of the year; and the sign which faced it, the Scorpion of a later age, was correspondingly termed the star "that is opposite to the foundation" of the year.

We can now understand why the Sun-god Merodach, whom even the astronomers of the historical period continued to identify with the typical constellations of the twelve months of the year,[1] should have been entitled "the Bull of Light" in the primitive astronomical records. He was, in fact, the celestial bull who ploughed the the great furrow of the sky, and from whom the first sign of the Zodiac borrowed its name. We may see in him the prototype of that famous bull of later legend whom Anu created in order to avenge upon Gisdhubar the slight offered by the latter to Istar. The Sun-god eventually became the monster slain by a solar hero. Such are the results of time working upon the half-forgotten beliefs and tales of an earlier age.

While in some instances the old totemistic conceptions were evaded by the degeneration of a god into a mere animal, in others the reverse process took place, the bestial element being eliminated from the nature of the god. It was thus that "the divine storm-bird" of the ancient Accadian faith passed into the god Zu of the Semitic epoch. "The divine storm-bird" was a ravenous bird of prey, of large size and sharp beak, who darted on its spoil and devoured the flesh. The Semitic Babylonians identified it with their Zu, partly because *zu* signified a

---

[1] W. A. I. iii. 53, 2. In Nisan, the first month, he was accordingly identified with Dun-kun-e, "the hero of the rising dawn," or Mercury, who is elsewhere called "the prince of the men of Harran" (iii. 67, 28), in consequence of the cult that was carried on there. In Adar, the last month, he was "the fish of Ea" or Pisces. "The Bull of heaven" (Gud-ana) is mentioned in iii. 53, 56

"stormy wind," partly because a species of vulture was called by the same name. But the conception of the tempest as a bird which rushes on its prey is common to many mythologies. In Aryan mythology the storm-cloud appears under the varying forms of the eagle, the woodpecker, and the robin redbreast, the sacred bird of Thor; while in Chinese folk-lore the storm-bird is "a bird which in flying obscures the sun and of whose quills are made water-tuns." The roc of the Arabian Nights, with its wings ten thousand fathoms in width, and its egg which it was a sin in Aladdin to wish to take from the place where it hung, is but an echo of the Chinese storm-bird. It is in the nest of the storm-bird that the tempest is brewed; it swoops upon the earth with the rush of his wings, and the lightning itself is but the gleam of his flight. Even a poet of to-day instinctively speaks of the curlews as "dreary gleams about the moorland flying over Locksley Hall."

"The divine storm-bird" was known as Lugal-banda, "the lusty king," and was the patron deity of the city of Marad, near Sippara. He brought the lightning, the fire of heaven, from the gods to men, giving them at once the knowledge of fire and the power of reading the future in the flashes of the storm. Like Prométheus, therefore, he was an outcast from the gods. He had stolen their treasures and secret wisdom, and had communicated them to mankind. In Babylonia, as in Greece, the divine benefactor of primitive humanity was doomed to suffer. The knowledge and the artificial warmth man has gained are not the free gifts of the gods; they have been wrenched from them by guile; and though man has been allowed to retain them, his divine friend and benefactor is condemned to punishment. The culture-god of totemistic Marad is thus a very different being from the culture-god of Eridu; both, indeed, are clad in animal form; but whereas the fish-god of Eridu is the willing and unhindered communicator of civilisation, whose successor, Merodach, becomes a god of light and healing, the bird-god of Marad is a pariah among his divine brethren, hunted out of heaven by the great gods, and wresting from them by craft man's future knowledge of good and evil. It was only in the later syncretic age, when these uglier facts of the earlier mythology were glossed over or forgotten, that the divine "bull" was described as "the offspring of the god Zu" (W. A. I. iv. 23, 19).

The scribes of Assur-bani-pal have preserved for us the mutilated copy of a bilingual poem, or part of a poem, which recounted the flight of Zu to the mountain of 'Sabu or Kis. It begins thus:[1]

"Lugal-tudda (fled) to the mountain a place remote
In the hill of 'Sabu he (dwelt).
No mother inhabits it and (cares for him).
No father inhabits it and (associates) with him.
No priest[2] who knows him (assists him).
He who (changed) not the resolution, even the resolution of his heart,
in his own heart (he kept) his resolution.
Into the likeness of a bird was he transformed,
into the likeness of Zu the divine storm-bird was he transformed.
His wife uplifts the neck.[3]
The wife of Zu, the son of Zu, may he cause them to dwell in a cage,

---

[1] W. A. I. iv. 14, No. 1.
[2] *Kal*, "the gallus-priest" in the Accadian. The Semitic version has *aqru*, "noble."
[3] Assyrian *tu(lle)*; see W. A. I. iv. 15, 41.

296   LECTURE IV.

even the god of the river-reeds (Enna) and the goddess the lady
of the basket of river-reeds (Gu-enna).[1]
From his mountain he brought (her),
as a woman fashioned[2] for a mother made beautiful,[3]
the goddess of plants,[4] as a woman fashioned for a mother made
beautiful.
Her paps[5] were of white crystal;
her thighs[6] were bathed in silver and gold.
    [Here follow many mutilated lines.]
On (his) head he placed a circlet;
.... on his head he set a coronal
(when) he came from the nest of the god Zu.
(In a place) unknown in the mountain he made his tomb."

It will be seen that the identity of the god Zu with a bird is explained in accordance with the ideas of a modern time. It has become a transformation voluntarily undergone by the deity, for the sake, as it would seem, of securing a beautiful bride. The old faith of totemism is

---

[1] Nin-Gu-enna was resolved into the Semitic *Bilat-ili* (W. A. I. ii. 55, 11); but according to W. A. I. iii. 67, 56, she was peculiarly the *uluk*, or "spirit of the temple of Mu . . ." The Gu-enna, or guardian of the river, was the title of an officer (K 177, 30).

[2] Not "clever," as Lyon.

[3] In the Semitic translation: "a mother who has been appointed for beauty."

[4] In the Accadian original, Nin-ka-śi. Her nine sons are enumerated in W. A. I. iii. 68, 25—32, the eldest being 'Siriś, "the goddess of plants," herself! Among the others are "the god of the pure tongue," "the god of the strong tongue," "the god of the beautiful tongue," "the god of the palate of the fat mouth," and "the god who is not powerful." Nin-ka-śi should probably be read Nin-gu-śiga, "lady of the full mouth."

[5] Accadian *kakkul*. The Assyrian *mazu* is the Hebrew מזה, and means "to suck," not "to pour out," as Zimmern supposes. *Namzitum* is also found in K 161. iii. 24, and R 358, 4 (where it signifies "a bowl").

[6] Comp. W. A. I. ii. 1, 175, and 41, 53. The Accadian seems to be [lam-śi-]di.

thus changing into a fairy-tale. But there were other stories which remembered that the transformation of the god was not the voluntary act it is here represented to have been. A long but broken text explains why it was that he had to take refuge in the mountain of ′Sabu under the guise of a bird of prey. We learn that Zu gazed upon the work and duties of Mul-lil; " he sees the crown of his majesty, the clothing of his divinity, the tablets of destiny, and Zu himself, and he sees also the father of the gods, the bond of heaven and earth. The desire to be Bel (Mul-lil) is taken in his heart; yea, he sees the father of the gods, the bond of heaven and earth; the desire to be Bel is taken in his heart: 'Let me seize the tablets of destiny of the gods, and the laws of all the gods let me establish (*lukhmum*); let my throne be set up, let me seize the oracles; let me urge on the whole of all of them, even the spirits of heaven.' So his heart devised opposition; at the entrance to the forest where he was gazing he waited with his head (intent) during the day. When Bel pours out the pure waters, his crown was placed on the throne, stripped from (his head). The tablets of destiny (Zu) seized with his hand; the attributes of Bel he took; he delivered the oracles. (Then) Zu fled away and sought his mountains. He raised a tempest, making (a storm)."

Then Mul-lil, "the father and councillor" of the gods, consulted his brother divinities, going round to each in turn. Anu was the first to speak. He "opened his mouth, he speaks, he says to the gods his sons: '(Whoever will,) let him subjugate Zu, and (among all) men let the destroyer pursue him (?).' (To Rimmon) the first-born, the strong, Anu declares (his) command, even to him: ... 'O Rimmon, protector (?), may thy power of fighting never fail! (Slay) Zu with thy weapon. (May thy name) be magnified in the assembly of the great gods. (Among) the gods thy brethren (may it destroy) the rival. May incense (?) (*etarsi*) be offered, and may shrines be built! (In) the four (zones) may they establish thy strongholds. May they magnify thy fortress that it become a fane of power in the presence of the gods, and may thy name be mighty?' (Rimmon) answered the command, (to Anu) his father he utters the word: '(O my father, to a mountain) none has seen mayest thou assign (him); (never may) Zu play the thief (again) among the gods thy sons; (the tablets of destiny) his hand has taken; (the attributes of Bel) he seized, he delivered the oracles; (Zu) has fled away and has sought his mountains.'" Rimmon goes on to decline the task, which is accordingly laid upon another god, but with like result. Then Anu turns to Nebo: "(To Nebo), the strong one, the eldest son of Istar, (Anu declares his will) and addresses him: ... 'O Nebo, protector (?), never may thy power of fighting fail! (Slay) Zu with thy weapon. May (thy name) be magnified in the assembly of the great gods! Among the gods thy brethren (may it destroy) the rival! May incense (?) be offered and may shrines be built! In the four zones may thy strongholds be established! May they magnify thy stronghold that it become a fane of power in the presence of the gods, and may thy name be mighty!' Nebo answered the command: 'O my father, to a mountain none hast seen mayest thou assign (him); never may Zu play the thief (again) among the gods thy sons! The tablets of destiny his hand has taken; the attributes of

Bel he has seized; he has delivered the oracles; Zu is fled away and (has sought) his mountains.'" Like Rimmon, Nebo also refused to hunt down and slay his brother god, the consequence being, as we have seen, that Zu escaped with his life, but was changed into a bird, and had to live an exile from heaven for the rest of time.

The "divine storm-bird," however, who invested himself by stealth with the attributes of Mul-lil, and carried the knowledge of futurity to mankind, served to unite the two species of augury which read the future in the flight of birds and the flash of the lightning. The first species was but a branch of the general pseudo-science which discovered coming events from the observation of animals and their actions, while the second species was closely allied to the belief that in the thunder men heard the voice of the gods. The old belief marked its impress upon Hebrew as well as upon Assyro-Babylonian thought. "The voice of thy thunder was in the whirlwind," says the Psalmist;[1] and nothing can show more clearly what must once have been the Canaanitish faith than the poetic imagery of another Psalm (xxix.): "The voice of the Lord is upon the waters; the God of glory thundereth; the Lord is upon many waters. The voice of the Lord is powerful; the voice of the Lord is full of majesty. The voice of the Lord breaketh the cedars; yea, the Lord breaketh the cedars of Lebanon. . . . The voice of the Lord shaketh the wilderness; the Lord shaketh the wilderness of Kadesh. The voice of the Lord maketh the hinds to calve, and discovereth the forests." In the Talmud, "the voice of the Lord" has become the *bath qôl*,

---

[1] Ps. lxxvii. 18.

or "daughter of the voice," a supernatural message from heaven which sometimes proceeded from the Holy of Holies, sometimes, like the δαιμόνιον of Socrates, assumed the form of an intuition directing the recipient as to his course in life.[1]

This prophetic voice of heaven was heard in the thunder by the Accadians as well as by the Semites. I have already noticed that the Accadians believed the sounds of nature to be divine voices, from which the initiated could derive a knowledge of the future. At Eridu it was more especially the roar of the sea in which the Sumerian priest listened to the revelations of his deities, and this perhaps was the oracle through which Oannes had spoken to men. In the rival city of northern Babylonia, where the supreme god presided over the realm of the dead, and not over the waters of the sea, the divine voice came to men in the thunder. By the side of Mul-lil, the lord of the ghost-world, stood Mul-me-sarra (Wül-mö-sárä), "the lord of the voice of the firmament." Mul-me-sarra, in fact, was but Mul-lil himself in another form, and hence, as lord of Hades, was the author, not only of the thunder, but of subterranean noises as well. It is thus that he is addressed in a hymn, which is, however, not older than the Semitic period:[2]

---

[1] See Dr. S. Louis in the *Proceedings of the Society of Biblical Archæology*, Ap. 6, 1886, pp. 117, 118.

[2] K 48. It is probably quite late, but embodies earlier ideas. There is no Accadian text attached to it. On the reverse, which is almost entirely destroyed, mention is made of "six hymns" to Samas, Merodach and Anu, besides other hymns to Merodach which had to be recited on the north side of the altar, and a hymn or hymns to Nusku on the east side of it. "Altogether," it is stated, "there are fifteen hymns (to be said) on the north and east sides. On the west, nine

"'O lord of the voice of the firmament, lord of the earth, prince of Hades,
lord of the place[1] and the mountain from whence none returns, even the mountain of the spirits of earth,
ordainer of the laws of the earth, the mighty bond of heaven and earth,
mighty lord, in whose absence Nin-girśu will not direct in garden and canal, will not create the crop (*appuna*);
lord of the fetter (*umasi*), who in his might rules the earth,
strengthening the broad (earth), holding the bolts of the lower world,
giving sceptre and reign to Anu and Mul-lil;
by thy command let the foundation-stone of this place last long before thee at all seasons;[2]
like the seat of thy lordship let it be a judgment-hall on earth.
Upon it may Anu, Bel and Ea firmly establish the throne."

Perhaps Mul-me-sarra is also the deity who is addressed in another hymn[3] as "the warrior-god (Erimmu), the bright one, the sword (or lightning) of Istar," and of whom it is said: "May he give thee rest with kindly hand (*rittu*), may he rain life and tranquillity upon thee with his hand!" Under the name of Iskhara, Istar herself was called "the sword" or "lightning of heaven," and as such was identified with the constellation of the Scorpion;[4] and the hand of the goddess Bunene is entitled "the inundator of the lightning," that of the Elamite god Lagamar being "the inundator of the earth,"

---

hymns to Assur, Mul-me-sarra, the Sun of midday, Laz(?), and the Hero-god (Dun) who quiets the heart, Bel of cattle, the Lady of cattle, Bel of the pure mound (Birs-i-Nimrud), (and) the Lady of the pure mound. Offer sacrifices, lay reeds which have been cut up, offer food and oil; let the hand of the prince take honey and butter, the food of the god of revelations (BAR-BAR), and recite the following."

[1] *Asri*, possibly for *asari*, "destruction," here.
[2] Or, perhaps, "all the cardinal points" (IM-KAK-A-DI).
[3] R 2. 111. 150. *Obv.*   [4] K 4195, 8—10.

and that of the god of impurity "the inundator of the crown (?)."[1]

The voices heard by the Babylonian in nature, however, were not a whit more sacred to him than the inarticulate voice which found expression in the name. Like all primitive peoples, the Chaldæans confounded the person and the name by which he was known. The name, in fact, was the personality, and whatever happened to the name would happen equally to the personality. Injury could be done to a person by using his name in a spell; and, similarly, to pronounce the name of a deity compelled him to attend to the wishes of the priest or exorcist. As among the ancient Egyptians, the secret names of the gods—many of them heirlooms from a primæval age, whose actual meaning was forgotten—were not only especially holy, but also especially efficacious. Names, consequently, like the persons or things they represented, were in themselves of good and evil omen; and the Babylonian would have sympathised with the feeling which made the Roman change Maleventum into Beneventum, or has caused the Cape of Storms to become the Cape of Good Hope. Whether this superstition about names was of purely Semitic origin, or whether it was shared in by the Accadians, we have no means of determining at present; the analogy of other races, however, in a corresponding stage of social development would lead us to infer that the superstition was the independent possession of Accadians and Semites alike. At all events, it was deeply imprinted upon the Semitic mind. The sacredness attached to the name of the God of Israel

---

[1] K 220, *Rev.*

among the later Jews, and the frequent employment of the name for the person of the Lord, bear witness to the fact. When Moses was ordained to his mission of leading his people out of Egypt and forming them into a nation, it was prefaced by what was henceforth to be the sacred and national name of their God.

There were names of good fortune and names of evil fortune,[1] and special significance was attached to a change of name. Three successive usurpers of the throne of Assyria—Pul, Ululâ or Ilulaios, and the father of Sennacherib—all discarded their old names on the successful accomplishment of their usurpation. Pul and Ululâ adopted those of the two famous monarchs of the older Assyrian dynasty, Tiglath-Pileser and Shalmaneser, retaining their original designations only in Babylonia, where the names they had adopted were associated with ideas of hostility and invasion; while Sargon, who claimed to be lord of Babylonia as well as of Assyria, identified himself with the past glories of the ancient kingdom by taking the name of Sargon of Accad. The adoption of these time-honoured names of itself conferred legitimacy upon the new claimants of the throne; along with the name they inherited the title and the claim to veneration of those who had borne them. It must have been for a similar reason that Esar-haddon's name, according to Sennacherib, was changed to that of Assur-etil-yukin-abla, "Assur the hero has established the son," "for affection's sake,"[2] though the prince preferred to retain his earlier appellation of Esar-haddon or Assur-akh-

---

[1] W. A. I. v. 27, 49—52.

[2] *Ki ruha*, W. A. I. iii. 16, 3. Possibly the change of name was occasioned by the death of an elder brother.

iddina, "Assur has given the brother," after his accession to the throne. We are reminded of the records of the Jews, from which we learn that Jedidiah became the Solomon of later history, and the Pharaoh of Egypt "turned the name" of Eliakim into Jehoiakim.

The preservation of their names was a matter about which the kings of Babylonia and Assyria were especially anxious. Terrible curses are denounced against those who should destroy or injure "the writing of their names," and substitute their own names instead. On the other hand, the gods are invoked to allow the names of the kings to last "for ever," or to "guide their names aright." Even captured cities have their names altered in token of conquest, and it is possible that the scrupulous care with which the names of foreign potentates are recorded in the Assyrian annals, as well as the interest shown by both Babylonians and Assyrians in the languages of their neighbours, had to do with the peculiar respect they paid to the name.

In the ancient hymns, the phrase, "mankind, whatsoever be their name," is of frequent occurrence, and seems to signify that as the special favours of the gods could be showered only on those whose names were recited, a vague and general expression of the kind would avoid the difficulty of enumerating by its own name each division of the human race. So, too, when the author of a penitential psalm speaks of a god or goddess whom he "knew not," it is probable that he is thereby deprecating the wrath of some offended deity with whose name he is unacquainted.[1] A hymn to the creator calls upon him

---

[1] A fragment from the great medical work (M. 1101, *Obv.* 3—14), in which the patient is allowed his choice of a practitioner's receipt or

under his various names to direct the laws of the world, to raise the dead to life, to overthrow the wicked and hostile, and to guide the stars of heaven, and puts into the mouth of Ea the following words: "Since his name has made his offspring strong, let his name be Ea even as mine is; all the bonds of my laws may he carry (to them); all my secret wisdom may he bear away, through the fifty names of the great gods." After this, it is said, his hearers "pronounced his fifty names and wrote down his precepts."[1] As "the great gods" were fifty in number,[2] the ascription of their fifty names to the creator was equivalent to identifying him with all of them. When they lost their names, they lost their individual personality as well.

Closely connected with the mystical importance thus assigned to names was the awe and dread with which the curse or excommunication was regarded. Once uttered with the appropriate ceremonies, the binding of knots and the invocation of divine names, it was a spell which even the gods were powerless to resist. In Assyrian it

---

a charm, makes this pretty clear. The whole passage runs: "Cut up some eyebright (?), the slice of a bird, the tongue of a dog, the plant that grows in the plain, the flesh of the *daslum*, and the golden *kakis* of the sheep (*kakis lunum khuratsi*, a species of grebe, according to Houghton), and compound these six ingredients: (or make a *khutesitiya* of herbs, offer beer, and repeat a spell seven times to the heart:) drink the mixture in wine; continue drinking (it) for three days, and on the fourth day your health will be restored. (This is) the spell: 'Thou, whoever he is, who like a road has determined the path,' (which) repeat in addition: 'The god, whoever he is, who like a road has determined the path, like long-drawn brandings (*kê sadduti*) he has loved my *ganni*.'"

[1] See above, p. 141.
[2] K 4029, *Rev.*

was called the *mamit*, in Accadian the *šabba*,[1] and was naturally considered to be divine. In Accadian, Mami had been a goddess;[2] the borrowed Assyrian deity, therefore, assumed the Semitic feminine termination. In the tenth book of the Epic of Gisdhubar, the goddess Mammetu, as her name is there spelt, is called "the maker of fate" who "has fixed the destinies" of mankind, "along with" the spirits of the earth; "she has established death and life, but the days of death are unknown."[3]

Mamit thus bore a striking resemblance to the Fate of the Romans and the Atê of the Greeks. Like Atê, her operations were usually conceived of as evil. Just as Namtar, the plague-demon, was also the personification of doom and destiny, so too Mamit was emphatically the concrete curse. If she established life as well as death, it was only because the term of life is fixed by death; death, and not life, was the real sphere of her work. Hence the *mamit* was known among the Accadians as the (*nam-*) *eríma* or "hostile doom;" and though Anu, as we have seen, might as the pole-star be called "the *mamit* of heaven," it is in no friendly guise that the *mamit* is presented to us in the magical texts. It was,

---

[1] In Sumerian, *šagga*, from an earlier *šangua*, perhaps connected with *šanga*, "a bond," whence the Semitic *šanaqu*, "to bind." A special class of priests, "attached," like the Levites, to particular sanctuaries, took their name from *šanga*.

[2] W. A. I. ii. 51, 55, "Mami the queen." "The river of Mami the queen" seems to have been near Cutha, since both it and "the river of the companion of Mami" come between "the river of the fortress of Nergal" and "the river of the place of ascent of Laz." In K 220, *Obv.* 27, the goddess Mamiti is mentioned immediately before Nin-gur, "the lady of the abyss."

[3] Haupt, *Babylonische Nimrodepos*, p. 66. The Accadian equivalents of "the maker of fate" are given in W. A. I. v. 9, 10.

in fact, like the power of excommunication in the Middle Ages, the most terrible weapon that could be used by the priestly exorcist. For the power of invoking the aid of the goddess Mamit by pronouncing the curse was completely in his hands. All that was needed was the performance of certain rites and the repetition of certain words. Armed with the magic wand,[1] he could lay the terrible excommunication on the head of his enemy, and cause it to issue forth from the body of his friend. " Let the *mamit* come forth that I may see the light," is one of the petitions we meet with in the tablets;[2] and Tiglath-Pileser I. states that after his conquest of the kings of Nahri he "freed them, prisoners and bound as they were, in the presence of the Sun-god (his) lord, and made them swear to be his servants from henceforth and for ever, under pain of the curse (*mamit*) of (his) great gods."[3]

In the hymns the *mamit* occupies a conspicuous place. Thus we read:

"The river-god is bright like the digger of the ground. The curse (flies) before him; its cry (is) like that of a demon.[4] All the land glows like the height of the sunset-horizon. May the sun at his rising remove the darkness, and may there never be gloom in the house. May the curse go forth to the desert, to a pure place. O spirit of heaven, conjure the curse; O spirit of earth, conjure it!—The formula for undoing the curse when the water of the river surrounds a man."[5]

---

[1] Called *gilgillum* in Assyrian, "the reed of doom" in Accadian (W. A. I. ii. 24. 2, 3). In a ritual text (1266, 1—6) the worshipper is ordered to come into the presence of Ea, and, turning his face to the rising sun, to "place the point (GIR) of the reed of the free-will offerings and the reed of the priests (*qan nindabi qan urugalli*), the implements (*unut*) of the gods as many as exist, the implements of the sons of the people."

[2] W. A. I. iv. 7, 7.   [3] W. A. I. i. 13. Col. v. 12—16.

[4] In the Accadian, "the monstrous beast."

[5] W. A. I. iv. 14, No. 2.

Another hymn begins in the following way:

"O curse, curse, the boundary that none can pass! The limit of the gods (themselves) against which they may not transgress! The limit of heaven and earth which altereth not! The unique god against whom none may sin![1] Neither god nor man can undo (it). A snare not to be passed through, which is set for evil. Whether an evil *utuk*, or an evil *alu*, or an evil *ekimmu*, or an evil *gallu*, or an evil god, or an evil incubus, or a *labartu*, or a *labatsu*, or an *akhkharu*, or a *lilu*, or a *lilat*, or the maid of a *lilu*, or the evil plague-demon, or a disease-bringing *asakku*, or a bad sickness, which has set its head towards the dropping[2] water of Ea, may the snare of Ea seize it! which has stretched its head against[3] the wisps of Nirba (the Corn-god), may the lasso of Nirba bind it! Against the limitation (of the curse) it has transgressed. Never may (the limitation) of the gods, the limitation of heaven and earth, depart from it. (The limitation of the great) gods it reverences not. May (the lasso of) the great gods bind it! May the great gods curse it! May they send back (the demon) to (his) home! The home of (his) habitation may they cause him to enter! As for him who has turned to another place, to another place, a place invisible, may they bring him! As for him who has turned into the gate of the house, the gate of a place from whence there is no exit may they cause him to enter! As for him who has stationed himself in the door and bolts, in the door and bolts may they bind him with bonds from which there is no release! As for him who has blown (?) into the threshold and socket, who into threshold and hinge has crept, like water may they pour him out, like a cup may they shatter him, like a quarry-stone may they break him to pieces! As for him who has passed across the beam, his wings may they cut! As for him who has thrust his neck into the chamber, may they twist his neck!"[4]

This is a fair sample of the incantations by means of which the Babylonians believed that they could free

---

[1] The Assyrian plays upon another meaning of the Accadian word, and renders, "whom none may humble." Jensen is mistaken in considering the Assyrian word to stand for *musepilu*.

[2] "Tidal" seems to be meant. In W. A. I. iv. 3. 15, 16, *izarruru* is interchanged with *inattuku*, "spits out," as a rendering of *biz-biz-ene* (alternate renderings being, "thy weapon is the great monster [*usum-gallu*] which from its mouth spits out the breath" or "drips blood").

[3] Assyrian, "drips upon."   [4] W. A. I. iv. 16, No. 1.

themselves from the demoniac agencies that surrounded them. The power of the *mamit* was such that the gods themselves could not transgress it, and the *mamit* was accordingly invoked to protect the mortal from the demons of plague and sickness. But the plague itself might be regarded as a *mamit* or "doom" inflicted by heaven upon the guilty earth. Such is the view taken in the following fragment, which I once compared with the Biblical account of the destruction of Sodom and Gomorrah. Perhaps the doom of Sennacherib's host may furnish a closer parallel:[1]

> "A darkness came from the middle of the deep,
> The doom des(cended) from the midst of the heaven,
> The sword (mowed down) the earth like grass;
> Towards the four winds the flash (went) overthrowing like fire.
> It sickened the men of the city, it tortured their bodies.
> In city and land it caused lamentation; small and great[2] (alike) it (smote).
> Freeman and handmaid it bound; with wailing it filled (them).
> In heaven and earth like a storm-cloud it rained; it made a prey.
> To the place of supplication of their god they hastened and raised high the voice.
> They received his mighty (aid) and like a garment it concealed (them).
> They . . . . him and the poison (was expelled?).
> . . . . (they embraced) his feet.
> [The next line is completely destroyed].
> . . . . his body was tried.
> (In lamentation) he smites[3] his breast."

The Babylonian, at all events in early times, did not

---

[1] W. A. I. iv. 9, No. 1.

[2] In the Accadian original the order is reversed: "great and small."

[3] *Udannis;* cf. S 949, *Rev.* 17, *ina kûri u sakparim ramani udannis,* "with scourges and in expiation I beat myself." Zimmern misreads *utannis,* "he weakens."

hold a very consistent theory about the origin of disease. On the one hand, all sickness was ascribed to demoniacal possession; the demon had been eaten with the food, or drunk with the water, or breathed in with the air, and until he could be expelled there was no chance of recovery. But, on the other hand, a pestilence, an epidemic, which swept over a whole country, was regarded with the same feelings of awe-struck veneration as the greater gods themselves. It was believed to be an instrument in their hands for punishing the sins and shortcomings of mankind. As we shall see, the same theory was held by the authors of the penitential psalms in respect of maladies that attacked some single individual only; but it was the general persuasion when a wide-reaching calamity like a plague afflicted the country. The plague consequently was held to be a divine being who was sent by the gods, like the storm or the deluge, to take vengeance on men for their misdeeds.

But this plague-god could be viewed under two aspects. Under the older one he was Namtar, the plague-demon, who was the minister of the gods of the lower world and the arbiter of human fate. In Semitic times the minister of divine anger approached more nearly the Jewish conception of the angel of death. He was himself a god, and had under his command not only the " seven gods," but also a special messenger, Isum or Itak, " the street-traverser."[1] Isum was represented by the colossi which

---

[1] On a cylinder in the possession of Dr. Huggins; also in W. A. I. iv. 2. 23, 24, where the word "traverser" is represented by *nagir*, and the Accadian name of Isum—'Sig-sagga, " the head of destruction"—is given. Like the seven evil spirits, Isum was regarded as having the form of a whirlwind.

stood at the approach to a temple;[1] his master's name was Nerra (Nera), who, as we have seen, was one and the same as Nergal, the god of the dead. Nerra, "the warrior of the gods," as he is termed, appears in an old legend, first brought to light by Mr. George Smith, as bringing death and desolation upon the states of Babylonia, apparently in consequence of their evil-doing. "Anu had heard" the report of the seven gods who had, perhaps, been sent to investigate what was going on upon the earth. Accordingly he summoned Nerra; "Let thy hands march," he said, "since the inhabitants of the country have seditiously broken their bond;[2] and I have set thy heart to cause desolation;[3] thou shalt strike the people of the black heads unto death with the desolation (?) of the god Ner; may thy weapons be their sword of destruction, and let thy hands go!"[4]

Babylon is one of the first cities to feel the destroying sword of the Chaldæan angel of death. It is besieged by its foes, and during the siege, the sword, the famine and the plague are let loose in its streets. Mul-lil is represented as looking on, and at last saying in "his heart:"

"Nerra is crouching at his great gate among the corpses of the noble and the slave: Nerra is crouching at the gate; thou hast set his seat (there). Their foes have besieged the men of Babylon,[5] and thou art

---

[1] W. A. I. ii. 50, 10.

[2] *Ki sa nisi dadme khubur-sina* KA-KA *imkhatstsu.*

[3] *Ublá-va libba-ka ana sakan kamarri. Kamarri* is not "snare" here.

[4] *Zalmat-kakkadi ana sumutti taqqud puqu* AN *Ner; lu kakki-ka* IZ-GIR-*ti-sunu-va lilliku idáka.*

[5] The same siege of Babylon may possibly have been referred to in a tablet (S 2037), of which the ends only of a few lines remain. They begin thus: (1) ... "he lamented; (2) .... he cried out; (3) ... seize me; (4) ... Babylon is taken."

their curse. Thou didst bind them with chains (?) and didst fix the doom (?), O warrior Nerra. Thou didst leave one and go forth against another. The form of a dog dost thou assume and enterest into the palace. The people saw thee; their weapons were broken. The heart of the high-priest, the avenger of Babylon, is full of valour; when he urged on his troops to take the spoil of the enemy, before the people he has done wickedness. In the city to which I shall send thee thou shalt fear no man, shalt reverence none; small and great slay together, and leave not the youngest of the evil race. Thou shalt spoil the first that come to Babylon, the people of the king which is gathered together and entered into the city, shaking the bow and setting up the spear, auxiliaries who have transgressed against Anu and Dagon; thou shalt set up their weapons; like the waters of the storm shalt thou give their corpses to the open places of the city; thou shalt open their treasures (?) and bid the river carry them away."[1]

Merodach mourned over the doom pronounced against his city, and apparently with some effect; for after a good many broken and lost lines, the tablet goes on to describe the despatch of the terrible plague-god to Erech, "the seat of Anu and Istar, the city of the choirs of the festival-makers and consecrated maidens of Istar," who "dreaded death," for the nomad ʼSuti of the desert had combined against their state. The eunuch-priests were now compelled to bow the face before another deity than the peaceful Istar, who "cried and was troubled over the city of Erech." Eventually, however, Nerra was "quieted" by "Isum his councillor, the illustrious god who goes before him," " and the warrior Nerra spake thus: 'Sea-land against sea-land, ʼSumasti against ʼSumasti, the Assyrian against the Assyrian, the Elamite against the Elamite, the Kossæan against the Kossæan, the Kurd against the Kurd, the Lullubite against the Lullubite, country against country, house against house, man against

---

[1] M 55, col. 1, 4—26.

man, brother against brother, let them destroy one another, and afterwards let the Accadian come and slay them all, and fall upon their breasts.'[1] The warrior Nerra (further) addresses a speech to Isum, who goes before him : 'Go, Isum, incline all thy heart to the word thou hast spoken.' (Then) Isum sets his face towards the land of the west; the seven warrior gods, unequalled, sweep (all things) away behind him. At the land of Phœnicia, at the mountains, the warrior arrived; he lifted up the hand, he laid it on the mountain; the mountain of Phœnicia he counted as his own soil."

In thus marching to the west, the minister of the Babylonian god of death approaches the country in which another angel of pestilence was seen by the king of Israel. "By the threshing-floor of Araunah the Jebusite," David had beheld the angel of the Lord "stretching out his hand upon Jerusalem to destroy it." As in Babylon, so too in Israel, the plague had been a visitation for the sins of man. It was the instrument of God's anger wielded by the hands of his angel-minister. That same angel-minister had once before stood before Balaam, and with a drawn sword in his hand had threatened the Syrian prophet with death. He was not a demon from the lower world, like the old Chaldæan plague-spirit Namtar; he was not the inexorable law of destiny, before whom even the gods had to submit their wills; but a member of the celestial hierarchy, the messenger of a beneficent God. He came to destroy, but it was to destroy the guilty. The sins of man, and not the malevolence or passionless law of a supernatural being, brought death

---

[1] Comp. Is. xix. 2—4.

and suffering into the world. The Babylonian legend of Nerra, like the records of the Old Testament, tells the same tale as the Babylonian story of the Deluge.

So remarkable an agreement, on the one hand, between the religious conceptions of Semitic Babylonia and Israel, and, on the other, their equally remarkable contrast to the older Accadian doctrines embodied in the plague-demon Namtar and Mamit the goddess of fate, can be explained in only one way. Even if the fact stood alone, and we had no knowledge of the earlier history of Chaldæa, we should be forced to conclude that while the later population of Babylonia belonged to the same race as that which inhabited Palestine, it was essentially different from the race which had formulated the older beliefs. The Semitic belief, in fact, stands out in striking contrast to beliefs which betrayed no consciousness of human sin, and the necessity of finding in this an explanation of malevolent action on the part of the gods above. The difference between the plague-god of Cutha and the agencies which had once been imagined to work evil to mankind, is a difference that cannot be bridged over by any theory of development; it is necessarily due to a difference of race.

Lecture V.

THE SACRED BOOKS OF CHALDÆA.

To François Lenormant, whose untimely death was an irreparable loss to the progress of Assyrian research, belongs the merit of first describing and defining the sacred books of ancient Babylonia. With the keenness of perception that characterised him, he pointed out two main collections of Babylonian sacred texts; one containing magic incantations and exorcisms; the other, hymns to the gods. The magical texts obviously belong to an earlier and less advanced stage of religious belief than the hymns; they presuppose, in fact, a sort of Shamanism, according to which each object and power of nature has its *zi* or "spirit," which can be propitiated only by a sorcerer-priest and certain magical rites; while the hymns, on the other hand, introduce us to a world of gods, and their language from time to time approaches a high level of spiritual expression. The collection of hymns Lenormant very happily named the Chaldæan Rig-Veda, and to them he subsequently added a third collection, consisting of penitential psalms which in many respects resemble the psalms of the Old Testament. All three collections are generally composed in both Accadian and Semitic Babylonian, the Semitic Babylonian being a translation of the presumably older Accadian text which is written line by line above it. It was natural to suppose that what has happened in the case of other sacred books happened also in Babylonia; that the magical texts were first collected together, the collection subsequently acquiring a sacred character; and that a similar process took place in the case of the hymns. The whole work would have been complete before the culture and literature of the Accadians were handed on to the Semites: in this way the preservation of the Accadian originals would be accounted for, the very words of the primitive documents and their correct pronunciation having come to be looked upon as sacred and inspired; while the Semitic interlinear translation served, like the Aramaic Targums of the Old Testament, to assist the priests in understanding the object of their recitations. As time went on, the religious beliefs which underlay the magical texts became so far removed from those of a later age that the texts themselves gradually passed into the background, the collection of hymns taking more and more their place as pre-eminently the Babylonian Bible.

The theory as thus stated is at once simple and probable. But although in its main outlines it is no doubt correct, further research has shown that its simplicity is due to the imperfection of the materials upon which Lenormant had to work, and that it will have to be very considerably modified before all the facts now known to us are accounted for.

In the first place, there are numerous magical texts which are later, and not older, than many of the hymns. Nothing is more common than to find a magical text breaking off into a hymn or a fragment of a hymn the recitation of which forms part of the spell or ceremony.

A large number of the hymns that have come down to us are thus embedded in the magical documents of which they form an integral part. The hymn to the seven evil spirits, for instance, quoted in a former Lecture, is really a portion of one of the most famous of the magical texts. In such instances there can be no question that the hymn is older than the text in which it is found. Moreover, it is difficult to distinguish the hymns when used in this way from similar poetical addresses to divine beings, which, so far from being especially sacred, were employed as spells in medical practice.

Thus in a great work on Babylonian medicine, fragments of which I have published and explained,[1] receipts for the cure of diseases, which scarcely differ from those that would be prescribed to-day, are mingled with charms and spells for driving away the demons of sickness. The sick man, in fact, was given his choice between a scientific treatment and a recourse to the old system of the primitive "medicine-man;" and it was left to his faith or superstition to determine whether he would employ the regular practitioner or his spiritual predecessor the exorcist-priest. Thus in the middle of a list of various medicines, carefully prepared from different ingredients and mixed with date-wine or water, we find an alternative spell, which the patient was instructed to "place on the big toe of the left foot," and there cause it to remain. The spell was as follows:

"O wind, my mother, wind, wind, ruler of the gods art thou, wind among the storm-gods!

---

[1] *Zeitschrift für Keilschriftforschung*, ii. 1, 3.

Yea, thou makest the water[1] to stream down (*tutsitsa*), and with the gods thy brothers liftest up the stream (*etsits*) of thy wisdom."

Now these two verses are introduced by a word which was read *en* in Accadian, *siptu* in Assyrian, and had the meaning of "spell" or "incantation." The same word introduces also a certain number of the hymns to the gods, and thus throws light on the object of their quotation and use. They were, in fact, spells, and the sacredness with which they were invested was due to the fact that they were so.[2]

We now have an explanation of two further facts which would otherwise be puzzling. On the one hand, by the side of the hymns to the gods there exist texts which agree with the hymns in form and character, but differ from them in being addressed, like the medical spell I have just quoted, to an inferior order of supernatural beings. On the other hand, the place of a hymn may be taken by a legendary poem or a portion of a legendary poem. The transformation of the god Zu into a bird, which I cited in the last Lecture, is an example of this. If the legendary poem had to do with the divine powers who were to be invoked or whose wrath had to be deprecated, its use as a spell was as efficacious as that of a hymn. Our own folk-lore shows that nothing comes amiss to the inventor of popular spells; the Lord's Prayer or a verse from the Bible are as serviceable in

---

[1] Literally, "the urine," which indicates the object of the spell.

[2] The hymns to the Sun-god of Sippara, composed by Semitic priests, form, however, an exception to this rule. The introductory word *siptu* with them merely means "to be recited," its old signification having come in time to take this meaning upon itself.

THE SACRED BOOKS OF CHALDÆA. 319

curing disease or in removing the curse of a witch as the most time-honoured combination of unintelligible words.

The relation between the magical texts and the hymns of ancient Babylonia is now, therefore, clear. In many cases, at least, the hymns formed part of the magical texts; they were the mystical incantations around the recitation of which the rites prescribed in the texts were intended to revolve. The magical text was not complete without the repetition of a form of words as well as a direct appeal to the names of certain supernatural beings; and the form of words was in many instances furnished by hymns to the gods or analogous kinds of composition.

It is not only the magical texts, however, in which we find the hymns embedded and prefaced by the significant word *siptu*, "incantation." They are still more numerous in the ritual texts—in the texts, that is to say, which describe the religious ceremonies the Babylonian was called upon to perform. These ceremonies had for the most part the same end and object as the magical texts; they were not so much a communion with the deities of heaven, as an attempt to compel them by particular rites and words to relieve the worshipper from trouble, or to bestow upon him some benefit. Divine worship, in short, was a performance rather than an act of devotion, and upon the correctness of the performance depended entirely its efficacy. The mispronunciation of a single word, the omission to tie a knot at the right moment, would invalidate the whole ceremony and render its repetition necessary. The ritual, therefore, was a sort of acted magic, and it is consequently not surprising that the hymns should play the same part in it as they did in the incantations of the magical texts.

It follows from all this that many of the magical texts are, like the ritual texts, later than many of the hymns. The fact must necessarily introduce some modification into Lenormant's theory of the origin of the sacred books of Chaldæa.

In the second place, not only the hymns, but even the magical texts are at times composed in Semitic Babylonian only. There is no trace of an Accadian original of any kind whatever. And not only is this the case, but these purely Semitic hymns occasionally glide into what is neither more nor less than unadulterated magic. Here is a specimen of one, which begins with an address to the Sun-god full of deep feeling and exalted thought, and finally passes into an incantation equally full of dull bathos and debasing superstition:[1]

> "O Sun-god, king of heaven and earth, director of things above and below,
> O Sun-god, thou that clothest the dead with life, delivered by thy hands,
> Judge unbribed, director of mankind,
> the mercy is supreme of him who is the lord over difficulty (*bit namratsit*),
> bidding son and offspring to come forth, light of the world,
> creator of all thy universe, the Sun-god art thou!
> O Sun-god, when the ban (*mamit*) for many days
> is bound behind me and there is no deliverer,
> expulsion of the evil and of the sickness of the flesh is brought about (by thee);
> among mankind, the flock of the god Ner, whatever be their names, he selects me:

---

[1] S 949, *Obv.* The upper part of the tablet is lost. All that remains of it are the two last lines: "He clothes with life, and to the blessed hands of my god and my goddess for grace and life entrust me." Then comes a line of separation, and the hymn to Samas is introduced by the word *siptu*.

THE SACRED BOOKS OF CHALDÆA. 321

after trouble fill me with rest,
and day and night I will stand undarkened.
In the anguish of my heart and the sickness of my flesh I was
    bowed down.
O father supreme, I am debased and walk to and fro.
With scourges[1] and in expiation I beat myself.
My littleness (?) I know not, the sin I have committed I knew not.
I am small and he is great;
The walls of my god may I pass.
O bird, stand still and hear the hound!
O Sun-god, stand still and hear me!
Overpower the name of the evil ban that has been created,
whether the ban of my father, or the ban of my begetter,
or the ban of the seven branches of the house of my father,
or the ban of my family and my slaves,
or the ban of my free-born women and concubines,
or the ban of the dead and living, or the ban of the adult (?) and
    the suckling,
or the ban of my father and of him who is not my father.
For father and mother I pronounce the spell; and for brother and
    child I pronounce the spell.
For friend and neighbour I pronounce the spell, and for labourer
    and workman I pronounce the spell.
For the field thou hast made and thy pasturage I pronounce the
    spell.
May the name of my god be a father where there is no justice.
To mankind, the flock of the god Ner, whatever be their names,
    who are in field and city,
speak, O Sun-god, mighty lord, and let the evil ban be at rest."

---

[1] *Kûri;* so in W. A. I. iv. 7, 4 : " the incantation is laid as a scourge
(*kûru*) upon his back." The Accadian equivalent was *lûba* (sometimes
written with the determinative prefix AL, W. A. I. v. 16. 24, 25), which
is also translated by the Assyrian *sidhtum* (Heb. *shôdh*). *Sadi* was
another Accado-Sumerian equivalent (iv. 1, 42). The word is expressed
ideographically (" cord-hand-cutting," and " cutting cord") in v. 14.
54, 55, where we also find mention of " the scourge," *sa ina tabqirti
nadû,* " which is used in penal examination" (Heb. *biqqoreth*). The
ideographic equivalent of the latter is " rope-length (*śarda*)-making."
Rappu is further the Assyrian rendering of the ideographic compounds
" rope-skin-cutting" and " rope-hand-cutting" (v. 14. 57, 58).

Here the hymn to the Sun-god is made a vehicle for removing the ban or "curse" that has fallen on the sick man. The beliefs which produced the magical texts must still have been active, although the hymn belongs to a late period of Babylonian history; the old doctrine of an inexorable fate, even if degraded into a belief in the witch's art, still existed along with the worship of a god who restored the dead to life and was "supreme in mercy to those that were in trouble." We have only to turn to our modern newspapers to discover how slowly such primæval beliefs die out, and how long they may linger among the uneducated and superstitious by the side of the most exalted faiths and the mightiest triumphs of inductive science. The fact that one text is magical, while another contains a hymn to the deity, does not of itself prove the relative ages of the two documents.

Then, thirdly, it has become increasingly manifest that a good many of the so-called Accadian texts are not Accadian in their origin. As I pointed out several years ago,[1] the old Accado-Sumerian language was learned by the Semitic Babylonians as Latin was learned by the mediæval monks, and for much the same reasons. It was the language of the oldest sacred texts; it was also the early language of law; and both priests and lawyers were accordingly interested in its preservation and use. What happened to Latin in the Middle Ages had already happened to Accadian in Babylonia. The monks spoke and wrote in a language which was Latin indeed, but which had lost its classical purity; monkish Latin was full of modern words and idioms, and its grammar was not

---

[1] *Babylonian Literature*, pp. 64, 71, 72.

always scrupulously accurate. On the other hand, it contributed multitudes of words, and even forms of expression, to the languages of every-day life that were spoken around it, and the words were frequently modified to suit the pronunciation and genius of the languages that borrowed them, just as the modern words which monkish Latin had itself adopted were furnished with classical terminations and construed in a classical fashion. The case was precisely the same in ancient Chaldæa. Here, too, there was a monkish Accadian, both spoken and written, some of which would have shocked the Accadian speakers of an earlier age. The *literati* of the court of Sargon of Accad had been partly Accadian, partly Semitic; the Accadian scribes wrote and spoke Semitic, the Semitic scribes wrote and spoke Accadian. The result was necessarily a large amount of lending and borrowing upon both sides, and the growth of an artificial literary language which maintained its ground for centuries. The way for the rise of this artificial dialect had already been prepared by the long contact there had been between the two chief languages of primitive Chaldæa. When two languages thus exist side by side—like Welsh, for example, by the side of English— they will borrow one from another, the language of superior culture and organisation being that which exerts the greatest influence. The pupils will imitate the speech of their masters in art and science even if, as in the case of Greece and Rome, the masters in art and science are the subjects in political power.

From a very early epoch, therefore, possibly before the separation of the Semitic family, the old agglutinative dialects of Chaldæa had been influencing their Semitic neighbours. The work carried on at the court of Sargon was accordingly but a continuation of an older process. But it was distinguished from the older process in two ways. It was the work of cultivated men, working upon literary models with a definite object in view. It was, moreover, a work that was carried on under Semitic patronage and supremacy, with the necessary result that in the new artificial language the influence of Semitic thought and speech upon the decaying speech of pre-Semitic Accad tended constantly to become greater. The Accadian texts, which were first composed by Semitic scribes, and subsequently handed down through generations of Semitic copyists, could not fail to show their origin and history plainly stamped upon their face.

And such is actually the case as regards a good many of the texts which in the early days of Accadian study could not be distinguished from the genuine productions of Accadian writers. It was as yet impossible to separate classical from monkish Accadian; to determine whether the Semitic text were a translation of an older Accadian one, or whether the Accadian was a literary rendering of a Semitic original. Even now, with all the progress that has been made during the last few years in our knowledge of the pre-Semitic dialects of Chaldæa, it is not always easy to decide the question. It is not enough to show that the Accadian text contains Semitic words or idioms. The words may have been introduced by copyists; while what we imagine to be Semitic idioms may really be imitations of earlier Accadian modes of speech, borrowed when the ancestors of the Semitic family still lived together in their tents by the western banks of the Euphrates. Apart from the monuments of Babylonia and Assyria, we have no records of Semitic speech which reach back even approximately to that remote epoch when the dialects which afterwards became the languages of Assyria, of Aram and of Phœnicia, were still spoken within the limits of a single community, and when that community was still leading the life of the Bedouin of to-day. It is always possible that words and forms of expression which we believe to be distinctively Semitic may, after all, have had an Accadian origin; before this can be settled, it will be necessary to exhume more monuments which, like those of Tel-loh, belong to the pre-Semitic era, and to subject the non-Semitic language in which they are written to a searching examination.[1]

Enough now, however, is known about the characteristic features of pure and unadulterated Accado-Sumerian to enable us to assign most of the hymns and magical texts to their true origin, and to determine whether their parentage is Semitic or Accadian. Not unfrequently the conclusions which have been arrived at on philological grounds are confirmed by the contents of the texts. Texts which refer to Semitic deities or to Semitic sanctuaries disclose at once their real age and source. It is equally impossible to refer to an early date compositions which breathe a philosophical spirit, or are in accord with the Semitic conceptions of the divine government of the world. The only question is, to how

---

[1] Arabic is of little assistance in settling the question, since our knowledge of it is so recent that it is impossible to say in many cases whether the lexical and idiomatic points of agreement between it and the North Semitic languages may not be due to borrowing. Aramæan tribes have lived in immediate proximity to the original speakers of Arabic from very early times, and must have lent many words, if not idioms, to their neighbours.

late a period such compositions belong; whether, for example, the account of the Creation in days, which bears so curious a resemblance to the first chapter of Genesis, goes back to the epoch of Khammuragas, or is, as I believe, a product of the age of Assur-bani-pal.

But even when we have determined the relative date and origin of a particular composition, our difficulties are by no means over. An ancient literature like that of Babylonia must necessarily contain comparatively little that is original. Most of the works that have come down to us are based on older literary productions, and are often mere centos of earlier compositions. The great Epic of Gisdhubar is little more in its present form than a redaction of earlier poems relating to the Hêraklês of Erech. It is full of episodes like that of the Deluge, which have no very close connection with the main subject of the work. And the episode itself may be pieced together out of more than one earlier poem. Thus the story of the Deluge shows clear traces of having been compounded out of at least two older narratives, in one of which the catastrophe was ascribed to the Sun-god, in the other to Bel (Mul-lil). The Descent of Istar into Hades, again, begins with a description of the infernal world, which, with a few slight differences of expression, is found again in the sixth book of the Epic; a comparison of the two passages goes to show that the authors of both have alike copied the description from an earlier source. The Descent of Istar, indeed, abounds with passages which are plainly borrowed from other poems, and whose richly poetical language stands out in marked contrast to the dull and prosaic character of their setting; while its concluding lines have little connection with what precedes them, and are obviously an extract from a separate work. The authors of the penitential psalms are fond of adding to their productions a litany of varying length, in which the names of certain divinities are invoked; the litany was a common possession which existed in an independent form, and had been handed down from an early period. Even the hymns are sometimes put together out of older materials, like certain of the Old Testament psalms; not only do the same phrases and lines recur, but whole passages as well. It is the same with the magical texts. Here, too, we have repetitions and borrowing; here, too, we have older fragments incorporated into later texts.

It will be seen from this how much remains to be done before the sacred books of ancient Babylonia can be made fully to tell their tale, and to what an extent the first theory about their origin and history must require modification. In its main outlines, nevertheless, the theory first sketched by the brilliant insight of Lenormant still continues true; it is only in its details that it needs correction and improvement.

The magical texts formed the earliest sacred literature of Chaldæa. This fact remains unshaken. They reach back to a period when the Semitic conception of a supreme Baal was utterly unknown—when, indeed, there was no definite conception of a god at all. The "creating" deity of later Accadian belief had not yet emerged from the religious consciousness of the Chaldæan. The inhabitant of Babylonia was as yet in the purely Shamanistic stage of religious development. The world about him was peopled by supernatural powers, each of which was to him a *zi* or "spirit." But it was not a spirit in our sense of the word, nor in the sense in which the term was used by the Semitic scribes of a later day. The zi was simply that which manifested life, and the test of the manifestation of life was movement. Everything that moved, or seemed to move, was endowed with life, for only in this way could primitive man explain the fact. He himself moved and acted because he had life; life, therefore, was the cause of movement. Hence the objects and forces of nature were all assigned a zi or spirit. The arrow that flew through the air, the stone that struck and injured, the heavenly bodies that moved across the sky, the fire that blazed up from the ground devouring all that fell in its way, had all alike their spirits. The spirits were as innumerable as the objects and forces which surrounded the Chaldæan, and as mysterious and invisible as his own spirit or life.

In this phase of faith the moral element was wholly wanting. The Chaldæan had not yet entered the Garden of Eden, and eaten of the tree of the knowledge of good and evil. The visible things of nature may benefit or injure; but their benefits and injuries seem altogether capricious and accidental, entirely independent of the actions and thoughts of man. The same stone which has killed a man to-day may help to build his son's house to-morrow; the fire which scorches to death will also cook the food to sustain life. In each event, all seems determined by blind chance; the spirits of nature may live and move, but they have no passions, no emotions. If their invisible spirits are to be influenced, it must be by other means than appeals to their love, their anger, their jealousy or their pride.

Shamanism accordingly implies, not a priesthood, but

a body of "medicine-men," or exorcists, who know the spells whereby the spirits of nature can be compelled either to cease from injuring or to ill-treat the foe. Whether the medicine-men of primæval Chaldæa had to undergo any initiatory course of training, or whether the profession were open to all alike, we do not know; our records do not reach back to the remote period of pure Shamanism, the magical texts being merely survivals which in their present form belong to a later time.

It is this class of exorcists, however, which distinguishes the early Shamanism of Chaldæa from what Dr. Tylor has termed simple Animism. Shamanism, is, in fact, organised Animism; Animism controlled and regulated by a body of exorcists who take the place of the priesthood of a higher cult. It was doubtless the existence of disease which first called this body of exorcists into being. The prevention and cure of disease is the main object of the magical texts and incantations. Disease was looked upon, as it still is in many parts of the uncivilized world, as possession by a malevolent spirit. Just as an external wound might be caused by a piece of stone or metal, so it was inferred an internal malady must be caused by an invisible agent of a similar kind—that is, by the spirit of the stone or metal. The same means that were adapted for getting rid of the visible stone and metal would be suitable for getting rid of their invisible spirits. There is no evidence to show that the exorcists of Chaldæa ever professed to extract pieces of actual stone or metal from the body of the sick, like the medicine-men of Australia or America; but they claimed by their spells to expel the spirits which enabled these pieces of stone and metal to afflict and injure. Listen, for instance, to the opening words of the great collection of Chaldæan magical texts:

"The evil god, the evil demon, the demon of the field, the demon of the mountain, the demon of the sea, the demon of the tomb, the evil spirit, the dazzling fiend, the evil wind, the assaulting wind which strips off the clothing of the body like an evil demon, — conjure, O spirit of heaven! conjure, O spirit of earth!.... That which is misformed, that which is diseased, that which is racked (with pain), even a diseased muscle, a constricted muscle, a swollen muscle, an aching muscle, a painful muscle, a broken muscle, an injured muscle,—conjure, O spirit of heaven! conjure, O spirit of earth!

The sickness of the entrails, a sick heart, faintness of the heart, disease, disease of the bile, headache, violent vomiting, a broken blood-vessel (?), disease of the kidneys, difficult miction, painful sickness which cannot be removed, a dream of ill omen,—conjure, O spirit of heaven! conjure, O spirit of earth!

Him who is the possessor of the likeness of another, the evil face, the evil eye, the evil mouth, the evil tongue, the evil lips, the evil breath, —conjure, O spirit of heaven! conjure, O spirit of earth!....

The painful fever, the virulent fever, the fever which quits not a man, the fever-demon who leaves not (the body), the fever unremovable, the baleful fever,—conjure, O spirit of heaven! conjure, O spirit of earth!

The painful plague, the virulent plague, the plague which quits not a man, the plague-demon who leaves not (the body), the plague unremovable, the baleful plague,—conjure, O spirit of heaven! conjure, O spirit of earth!"

The exorcisms for driving away the spirits of disease gradually introduced a moral element into the character of the old spirits of nature. But the moral element was wholly on the dark side. The spirits of disease were essentially evil and malevolent. In so far as human passions could be ascribed to them, the passions were those of the wicked, not of the good. The worship of the spirits of nature thus tended to become a religion of fear.

Side by side, however, with the growing belief in the malevolence of the spirits of nature, there existed the totemism of which I have spoken in the last Lecture. Animals, as well as other objects, had each their special spirit, and these spirits naturally shared the feelings and passions which moved the animals to which they belonged. The sacred animals were regarded as moral agents, like men; the ox, whose labours benefited mankind, protected his worshipper from the attacks of evil; while the fish which supplied the inhabitants of Eridu with food, also brought to them the elements of culture and civilisation. In this way the Shamanism of earlier and ruder times began to pass into a higher form of creed; the exorcist approximated more and more to the priest, and the spells he used tended to recognise the distinction between good and evil in the world of spirits as well as in the world of men.

It was at this point that cosmogonic speculations first exercised an influence upon the religion of the Chaldæan states. The Babylonian began to generalise and to sum up his individual impressions of outward phenomena in wider and more abstract ideas. Earth and heaven took the place of the individual objects and forces whose sphere of action was in the one or the other; the spirits of these separate phenomena were subordinated to the spirits of the earth and the sky. The stereotyped conclusion of the old Accadian exorcism, as we have just heard, is, "Conjure, O spirit of heaven! conjure, O spirit of earth!" The earth out of whose bosom the agriculturist received the bounties of life, the heavens from which the fertilising rain and dew dropped upon the ground, and the rays of the sun warmed all nature into activity, became the supreme powers whose spirits dominated over all others and demanded the reverence of man.

Unlike the malevolent spirits of disease, the great cosmogonic spirits were essentially beneficent; the moral conceptions of Chaldæan faith were enlarged by the belief in the existence of good as well as of evil spirits, and the superiority of the good to the evil. It was an immense step in advance, and it corresponds with the time when the religious literature of Babylonia first commences with the oldest surviving magical texts. The earliest portions of the latter belong to the age when the crude Shamanism of the past had been tempered and modified by the first beginnings of a theory of the world.

From this point onward we can trace the further development of the older creed. The struggle between good and evil had already begun in the mind of the Chaldæan thinker. The supernatural beings he worshipped were now divided, for the most part, into two hostile camps. On the one side stood the demons of disease and nightmare; on the other, the great cosmogonic powers of earth and heaven. It is true that the terrible spirits of disease, who loved the darkness of night and the solitary places of the wilderness, were not yet consciously conceived as demons, but the moment was not far off when such would be the case. Light and darkness now stood opposed to one another in the spiritual as well as in the physical world. The old medicine-man was fast becoming a priest.

The introduction of cosmological ideas and speculations into Chaldæan religion brought with it two results. First of all, there grew out of it the conception of creating gods. We have already had occasion to observe the essential distinction that existed between the Accadian and Semitic conceptions of the universe: with the one, all things were made; with the other, they were begotten. The Semitic Baal was a father; the Accadian divinity a creator. According to the Semite, the heavens and the earth were carved out of a pre-existent chaos; according to the Accadian, the heavens and the earth were themselves primordial powers, maintaining an eternal struggle with the chaos of darkness and anarchy. The temporary triumph of chaos means the irruption of anarchy into the fair order of nature—the destructive hurricane, the devastating tempest, the darkening eclipse. The return of light and sunshine, of bright skies and germinating seeds, marks the victory gained over the encroaching forces of the lower world.

The earth and the sky became the first creators, the first gods. It is they who create all the good things which man enjoys below, including man himself. The spirit of the earth and the spirit of the heaven thus developed into creating gods. But it was before the old habits of thought and expression could be quite eradicated from the Chaldæan mind. The spirits which had developed into gods were themselves provided with spirits; there was a spirit of Ea and Dav-kina, of Ana and Mul-lil, as well as of water and earth, of heaven and hell. When the gods took upon them human shape, these spirits were regarded as similar to the spirits of individual men; and the functions and attributes of the human spirit were reflected upon the spirits of the gods. At the outset, however, it was with the animal and not with the human world that the new gods were associated. They were, in fact, confounded with the old totems. Just as the heavenly bodies, which seemed to move of their own accord like living beings, were identified with the sacred animals, so too the spirits of earth and heaven, of water and air, to whom a creative power had been given, were similarly identified with them. The god was a beast before he became a man, and the spirit that moved him was that of the brute.

In the second place, the deification of the spirits of earth and heaven necessarily brought with it the deification of other spirits which resembled them in character and power. The test of supernaturalism—of the existence of a spirit—was the power of movement possessed by an object or a force of nature; this power now became itself the supernatural being, the god or spirit. The spirit of the moon, for example, developed into a god; but the god was abstracted from the visible moon itself, and identified with the creative force of the lunar orb which manifested itself in motion. The new god might in turn be abstracted from the creative force, more especially if he were assimilated to the sacred steer; in this case the creative force would become his spirit, in no way differing, it will be seen, from the spirit that was believed to reside in man.

We have now reached the culminating point of the old Accadian religion. Spirits innumerable still exist, but they are controlled and overawed by creative gods. The gods represent the order and law of the universe embodied by the *sabba*, or "fate," to which even the gods themselves must submit. Over against them are the malevolent spirits of disease, of chaos and of darkness; while beside them are other spirits which still retain their primitive character of moral indifference, neither good nor bad, though some might approximate more to the good and others to the bad. But gods and spirits alike were amenable to the spells and exorcisms used by the sorcerer-priest, for a priest he had now become. By his magical words he could remove the sickness which was caused by demoniac possession, or bewitch the person and the property of his enemy; he could compel the gods to listen to his petition and to perform his commands. In his hands and on his lips was the power of the terrible *sabba*, which even the gods were forced to obey. The sorcerer was still the intermediary between mankind and the spiritual world.

But, as I have just said, he had lost much of his old character. Among the spells he employed were hymns which imply a more advanced cult than that of mere magic. Indeed, the very conception of a creative deity necessarily brought with it a service of praise and adoration and the formation of a fixed ritual. A beneficent god required another kind of worship than that which was appropriate to the non-moral spirits of Shamanism. When the spirit of heaven became Anu, temples were raised in his honour, and the worshippers who entered them required something else than that the priest should "conjure" the object of his cult. We leave the era which witnessed the rise of the magical texts, and enter on the era of the hymns.

The Penitential Psalms, of which I shall speak further on, frequently have a sort of litany attached to them, written in Accadian only, and invoking the aid of certain deities under their pre-Semitic names or titles. The litany was an old heirloom, selections from which were taken by the authors of the psalms and added to their compositions. One of those translated by Dr. Zimmern[1] concludes as follows:

> "O my god, the lord of prayer, may my prayer address thee!
> O my goddess, the lady of supplication, may my supplication address thee!
> O Matö (Mâtu), the lord of the mountain, may my prayer address thee!
> O Gubarra, lady of Eden, may my prayer address thee!
> O lord of heaven and earth, lord of Eridu, may my supplication address thee!
> O Merodach (Asar-mulu-duga), lord of Tin-tir (Babylon), may my prayer address thee!
> O wife of him, (the princely offspring (?) of heaven and) earth, may my supplication address thee!
> O (messenger of the spirit) of the god who proclaims (the good name), may my prayer address thee!
> O (bride, first-born of) Uras(?), may my supplication address thee!
> O (lady, who binds the hostile (?) mouth), may my prayer address thee!
> O (exalted one, the great goddess, my lady Nana), may my supplication address thee!
> May it say to thee : '(Direct thine eye kindly unto me).'
> May it say to thee : '(Turn thy face kindly to me).'
> (May it say to thee : 'Let thy heart rest.')
> (May it say to thee : 'Let thy liver be quieted.')
> (May it say to thee : 'Let thy heart, like the heart of a mother who has borne children, be gladdened.')
> ('As a mother who has borne children, as a father who has begotten a child, let it be gladdened')."

The litany belongs to a period considerably later than that which witnessed the rise and first collection of the magical texts. It is written in the Accadian dialect of north Babylonia, which exhibits the old Sumerian of the south in an advanced stage of decay, and further shows traces of contact with a Semitic language. The deities

---

[1] From Haupt's *Akkadische Keilschrifttexte*, pp. 116 *sq.*

whose names are invoked belong to different parts of Babylonia, and point to a time when not only the separate states of Chaldæa had begun to recognise a common pantheon, but when northern and southern Babylonia had already been united into a single empire. Nevertheless, the litany is earlier than the age of Sargon of Accad and the supremacy of the Semitic population. Though Merodach has already migrated from Eridu to Babylon, still referred to under its old Accadian name of Din-Tir, the Sun-god of Sippara and Accad is altogether unknown. There is no allusion to either city or to the divinities they adored. Nana herself, the queen of Erech, is not yet known as Istar, and the Tasmit of a later day is "the bridal goddess, the first-born of Uras."

We are still, therefore, lingering on the verge of the pre-Semitic epoch. The Semite may be in the land, but the official religion does not as yet recognise him. The difference, however, between the religious ideas of the litany and those which inspired the old magical texts is immense. A whole age of religious development lies between them. The fundamental conception of the preceding period, it is true, still survives; the deities must be influenced by the spoken word of their worshipper. But the spoken word has ceased to be the spell or incantation; it has become a prayer and supplication. Its efficacy depends no longer on the exorcisms of a medicine-man, but on the faithful petitions of the worshipper himself. And along with this change in the nature of the cult has gone a corresponding change in the divine beings to whom the cult is dedicated. They have become gods, bound together in a common brotherhood, like the brotherhood of the cities over whose fortunes they preside.

Babylonia possesses not only gods; it possesses a pantheon, an Olympus, as well.

It was, of course, only among the more cultivated classes that this newer and higher conception of the divine government of the world was likely to be found. The masses, doubtless, still clung to their old superstitions, their old Shamanism. The formation of magical texts, therefore, never ceased. The older texts continued to be interpolated until their antiquity at last threw such a halo of holiness around them that it was considered impious to tamper with their words. Other texts of a similar character were composed, which in course of time came to receive as much reverence as the more ancient collection. Far down into Semitic times, exorcisms and incantations continued to be written, and to receive the *imprimatur* of the official priesthood. They even entered largely into the ritual of the temples. But the sanctity attached to them became fainter and fainter as years went on. Although the sorcerer maintained his ground among the uneducated multitude, like the witch in modern times, the spells with which he served himself were simply means for curing the bite of a scorpion, and such-like necessities of popular medicine. They were dissociated from the worship of the gods and degraded to vulgar uses. Even in medicine the cultivated Babylonian gentlemen preferred to employ the drugs prescribed by scientific practitioners; the spells were left to the ignorant and superstitious. The old collections of magical texts, indeed, remained among the sacred books of the nation; but this was on account of their antiquity, and not because they any longer expressed the religious feelings of the day. The litany at the end of the penitential psalms marks the beginning of a new era in religious thought.

This era is represented by the hymns to the gods. Dr. Hommel has pointed out that the hymns fall into two main classes. There are, firstly, the hymns which show no trace of contact with the magical texts, and, secondly, other hymns which are either partly magical in character or else are introduced by the significant word *en (siptu)*, "incantation." These latter hymns emanate for the most part from Eridu and its neighbourhood, and bring Merodach before us as carrying out the behests of his father Ea for the good of man. Most of them, moreover, are dedicated to those older divinities who, like Gibil the fire-god, were eclipsed by the more human deities of the later cult. But the division must not be pressed too far. The introductory *en*, "incantation," merely indicates that the hymn is of sufficiently early date to be incorporated in a magical text, or that it was selected as a spell, like the Lord's Prayer or the fragments of Latin which have served the same object in modern times. It is of importance, however, to observe whether the hymn is of a semi-magical character, like that to the Fire-god which I have quoted in a former Lecture, or whether it was originally altogether independent of the use to which it has been put. In the first case, we may confidently assign it to the period when Eridu was still the religious capital of Chaldæa, and the faith of the people was only emerging out of its earlier Shamanistic phase. In the other case, where the hymn itself is free from all taint of magic and Shamanistic superstition, we may as confidently ascribe it to a later date. Its precise age will depend upon that of the text in which it is embodied. If the latter is one of those late survivals which proved how deeply rooted the belief in magic and witchcraft was among the lower strata of the population, the hymn or fragment of the hymn which is incorporated in it may be of almost any period. To determine its age more exactly, we must have recourse to the language in which it is written and the other indications of date it may contain. Sometimes these may point to an early epoch, at other times to a comparatively recent one.

The hymns to the Sun-god of Sippara afford a fixed point of departure for settling the relative antiquity of the hymns. They form a separate class by themselves, and were part of the daily service performed by the priests in the temple of Samas. It is plain, therefore, that they had been collected for liturgical use, and had been invested with a sacred character. There were hymns that had to be recited at sunrise and sunset, or on the special festivals held in honour of the god. The individual hymns had doubtless been composed on different occasions and at different times, and it is possible that they had been revised and altered more than once before they were put together as a single whole. But whatever may have been the respective ages of the individual hymns, they were all alike of Semitic origin. They all belong to the epoch when Sippara and Accad were ruled by Semitic princes, and were a centre and focus of Semitic influence. It is true that the hymns are provided with an Accadian text, which is followed, line by line, by the Semitic rendering, as is the case with the other bilingual texts of early date. But it is equally true that the Accadian text is really a translation of the Semitic. It may have been made by Accadian scribes; it may have been made, and more probably was made, by Semitic scribes, like the Accadian texts which emanated from the library of Assur-bani-pal; but it is not original. The Semitic words and idioms it contains bear witness to its secondary character. There is only one period in the history of Sippara, of which we know, to which such a work is attributable. This is the age of Sargon and his son Naram-Sin. The pre-Semitic epoch of northern Babylonia was but just passing away; the sacred texts, the hymns to the gods, the older incantations, were all in the agglutinative language of the first inhabitants of the country. Though the ancient Sun-god of Sippara had become the Semitic Samas, it was natural to suppose that he would be better pleased with the language in which the spirits and deities of Chaldæa had been addressed than with the vulgar speech of every-day life. Like the monk of the Middle Ages, accordingly, who composed his prayers and hymns in Latin, the priest of Samas addressed his god in the older and more sacred tongue. The sentiment, the expression, might be Semitic, but the form in which it must be clothed before it could be acceptable to the divinity was Accadian.

In a later age there was no longer the same strong motive for assimilating the hymns to the Sun-god to those addressed to the more purely Accadian deities of Babylonia. The Semitic language became first literary and then a fit vehicle of devotion. Not only were magical texts written in it, but hymns also, without any endeavour to render them into the obsolete Accadian. Assur-bani-pal, antiquarian as he was, thinks it no sin to publish hymns to Nebo and Samas in Semitic only, and the invocations addressed to the gods by Nebuchadnezzar and his successors are in the same Semitic language as the rest of their inscriptions. The translation of the hymns to Samas into Accadian presupposes a time when the Accadian influence was still powerful, and when Accadian was still believed to be the language of the gods.

If, then, we can assign the hymns to Samas of Sippara to the age of Sargon of Accad, it becomes more easy to find an approximate date for the hymns to the other great gods of Babylonia. Like the hymns to Samas, we must suppose them to have belonged to different collections employed liturgically in the chief temples of Chaldæa. We know, indeed, that this was the case as regards the hymns addressed to Bel-Merodach of Babylon. With few exceptions they are bilingual, in Accadian and Semitic; and in the larger number of them the Accadian text is the original. Where this is the case, and the hymns belong to the sanctuaries of northern Babylonia, we may consider them older than the age of Sargon. As the ancient language of the country continued to be spoken in southern Babylonia long after his time, the same conclusion cannot be drawn in regard to the hymns employed there, but it is probable that the majority of them are quite as early as those of the north.

How far they have come down to us in their original condition and form it is hard to say. In some instances we can show that they have been modified and interpolated, and analogy would lead us to suppose that such was generally the case. Nor is it possible to determine at present whether the collections of sacred hymns used in the different temples of Babylonia were formed into a single whole, and thus constituted a sort of Babylonian Rig-Veda, as Lenormant conjectured. It is very probable, however, that the unification of the country brought with it a unification of the sacred books used in its several temples, and that the copies of the hymns we possess were not made by the scribes of Assur-bani-pal from the hymn-books of different sanctuaries, but from a common hymn-book in which the special collections had been grouped together.

At the same time, if such a common hymn-book ever existed, it must have contained selections only from the hymn-books of the individual sanctuaries. One of the few hymns to Nergal, for instance, which we possess, was, we are told, copied from the service-book of Cutha,[1] and this is by no means an isolated example of the kind. On the other hand, the hymns—or more usually the fragments of hymns—which are incorporated in the magical texts, perhaps imply the existence of a sacred volume which was in common use among the priestly schools of Babylonia. This is a point which it must be left to future research to decide.

But whether or not such an authorised collection of hymns existed for the whole of Chaldæa, it is certain that a considerable number of the hymns were composed when the chief cities of Babylonia and their presiding deities had been, as it were, confederated together. The matter is, indeed, complicated by our ignorance of the extent to which the hymns have been altered and interpolated before their present text was finally fixed; on the whole, however, it seems pretty evident that Ana, Mul-lil and Ea, had already been linked together in a divine brotherhood, and that the other "great gods" had been assigned their places in a common pantheon,

---

[1] K 5268, *Rev.* 12.

before a considerable proportion of the hymns had been composed. A distinct advance had thus been made beyond the religious conceptions of the litany of the penitential psalms; not only are the gods of different cities invoked side by side, but they are now connected together in the bonds of a single family. The family system, in fact, has taken the place of a system of mere co-ordination.

Now the family system implies an entire change in the conception of the gods themselves. They cease to be creators; they become fathers and children. Along with this change necessarily goes another. The gods become human. The last vestiges of primitive totemism fade away, and Merodach is no longer "the bull of light," the son of "the antelope of the deep," but an anthropomorphic god, standing in the same relation to Ea that a human son stands to his human father. Babylonian religion had long been tending to regard the gods as supernatural men; the introduction of the family relation completed the work.

The work, however, in its final form bears clear marks of artificiality. The whole family system, in which the deities of different states are each given a definite position, must have been deliberately built up. Family relationships may grow up naturally among the divinities worshipped in the same locality or in the colonies sent out by a mother-state; where these relationships are found existing among divinities, originally independent and each adored as supreme in its own primitive seat of worship, they must belong to an artificial system, and be the product of intentional arrangement. Religion, in the hands of its official representatives in Chaldæa, had not only passed out of the sphere of simple and spontaneous belief, it had become organised and reflective—a subject to be discussed and analysed, to be arranged and methodised.

Can all this have been the natural and uninterrupted development of the old pre-Semitic Shamanism? With François Lenormant, I think not. Between the religion of the magical texts, of the earlier semi-magical hymns and of the litanies on the one side, and the religion of the later hymns on the other, there seems to me to be an almost impassable gulf, which can be bridged over only by the assumption of an intrusive foreign element. What this element must have been we know already. The Semitic nomads of the western desert in the days of their barbarism had come into contact with the cultured kingdoms and people of the valley of the Euphrates. At first they were content to be pupils; eventually they became masters themselves. The amalgamation of the two races produced the Babylonian population of later times, and along with it the history, the civilisation and the religion of a subsequent era. Bêrôssos expressly notes that Babylonia was the home of different races; he might have added that it was the home also of different faiths.

The Semite sat at the feet of his Accadian Gamaliel when the crude Shamanism of the latter had passed into a higher phase of religion, and the creator-gods had been evolved out of the spirits of the earlier creed. He adopted the gods, but at the same time he adapted them to his own notions concerning the divine government of the world. They became Baalim, so many manifestations of the supreme deity whose children we are, and who exhibits himself to us in the solar energy. The old goddesses, with the exception of Istar, sank to the rank of Ashtaroth and "mistresses of the gods," mere companions and doubles of the male divinity.

Now, as I have already tried to point out, the keystone of Semitic belief was the generative character of the deity. A language which divided nouns into masculines and feminines, found it difficult to conceive of a deity which was not masculine and feminine too. The divine hierarchy was necessarily regarded as a family, at the head of which stood "father Bel." If the gods of Accad were to be worshipped by the Semite, they must first conform to the requirements of his religious conceptions, and allow themselves to be grouped together as members of a single family. All that stood outside the family were servants and slaves—the hosts of heaven and earth who performed the behests of their masters, and carried the messages of Baal to all parts of the universe. The rest of the supernatural world, if such existed, was relegated to the domain of the enemy; it comprised the empire of chaos and night, which, like the gods of foreign nations, might at times invade the realms of the Baalim, only, however, to be beaten back once more into the outer darkness. The empire of chaos, however, was really a stranger to genuine Semitic belief; it was a legacy left by the Accadians, which was assimilated and adapted by the Semites as best they could. Where the Semitic faith existed in its full purity, Satan, the adversary, himself was but an angel and minister of the Lord, and the supreme god was the creator alike of good and evil, of light and darkness.

The rise of Sun-worship at Sippara, the prominence given to the solar element in Babylonian religion generally, the obliteration of the older gods whose attributes could not be harmonised with those of a Sun-god, and the identification of deity after deity with the solar Baal, was again the result of the introduction of Semitic ideas into the religion of Chaldæa. Perhaps the most striking transformation ever undergone by any object of religious faith was the conversion of Mul-lil, the lord of the ghost-world, into a Bel or Baal, the god of light and life. Such a transformation could not have been produced naturally; it needed the grafting of new religious conceptions upon an older cult; it is a sudden change, not a development.

Equally hard to explain, except by calling in the aid of a foreign religious element, is the degradation of the spirits of the primitive faith into demons. We have traced the process whereby certain of these spirits developed into deities, while others of them were invested with a distinctly malevolent character; but they are not yet demons. The evil spirits who brought disease or caused eclipse might be the brood of chaos, and therefore hostile to the gods of light; but they were all the subjects of Mul-lil, and even of the sorcerer and the medicine-man. It was the necessity the Semite was under of accommodating his beliefs to the doctrine of an empire of chaos that turned them into veritable demons, working for evil against the gods in a world of evil of their own. Persian dualism was no new thing in Babylonia; the gods of good and the spirits of evil had been struggling there one against the other since the remote days of Sargon of Accad.[1]

---

[1] Nothing can be more striking than the following expression in a prayer to "Ea, Samas and Merodach, the great gods, the supreme

In what precedes I have, of course, been describing only the official religion of Babylonia, as it is known to us from the sacred literature of the country. It was the religion of the upper classes, of the priesthood and of the court. What the mass of the people may have believed, and how far they may have participated in the official cult, we can only guess. The later magical texts and incantations were condescensions to their necessities and superstitions, like the legends of the gods which formed the subject-matter of popular poetry. The differences that exist to-day between the creed of a Spanish peasant and that of a scientific savant are not greater than those which existed in Babylonia of old between the religion of the multitude and that of the school which resolved the divinities of the popular theology into forms of the one supreme god.

The magical texts and hymns were not the only sacred books possessed by the Babylonians. There was yet a third class of sacred literature—those penitential psalms to which I have so often alluded. The litany frequently attached to them belongs, as we have seen, to the pre-Semitic epoch, though it has been altered from time to time in later ages. The litany, however, is not written, like the magical texts and the majority of the hymns, in the Sumerian dialect of the south, but in the Accadian of the north. Dr. Hommel is perfectly right in calling the Accadian of the north neo-Sumerian; it represents the Sumerian of the early texts in an advanced stage of

---

powers who establish the ban,"—"the sins of my father and my mother I saw not ([sa]abi-ya u ummi-ya khidati ul amrá) . . . from darkness I stepped forth and (became) the soldier of Samas" (*ultu edhuti utsav-va tsab Samas* [*assakin*]), R 278, Obv. 7—9.

decay. But this does not prove that it was spoken at a later period than the Sumerian of the south, or that it is the direct descendant of the latter dialect. There were several dialects of the Accadian or pre-Semitic language of Chaldæa; one of these gave rise to the Accadian of northern Babylonia at a time when the Sumerian dialect in the south still preserved its pristine purity. What hastened the decay of the northern dialect was its contact with Semitic. The Semites established themselves in the northern part of the country long before they settled in the south. The kingdom of Sargon rose and waned at Accad more than a thousand years before Sumerian dynasties ceased to rule in the southern cities. It is not strange, therefore, if the Accadian of the north decayed long before its sister dialect of Eridu, borrowing at the same time Semitic words and modes of expression. It is in this Accadian of the north that the penitential psalms are written. They belong neither to the same age nor to the same city. But they are all distinguished by the same characteristics, which lend to them a striking resemblance to the Psalms of the Old Testament. Let us take one, for example, which has been preserved to us in a fairly complete condition:[1]

"The heart of my lord is wroth; may it be appeased![2]
May the god whom I know not be appeased!
May the goddess[3] whom I know not be appeased!
May the god I know and (the god) I know not be appeased!

---

[1] W. A. I. 4, 10. Zimmern's *Busspsalmen*, pp. 61 *sq.*

[2] Literally, "return to its place."

[3] The Assyrian translation here has *Istar* instead of *Istarit*, which indicates its antiquity. The expression "whom I know not" means "whose name I know not." The author of the psalm is uncertain as to the particular god who has punished him.

May the goddess I know and (the goddess) I know not be appeased!
May the heart of my god be appeased!
May the heart of my goddess be appeased!
May the god and the goddess I know and I know not be appeased!
May the god who (has been violent against me) be appeased)!
May the goddess (who has been violent against me be appeased)!
The sin that (I sinned I) knew not.
The sin (that I committed I knew not).
A name of blessing (may my god pronounce upon me).
A name of blessing (may the god I know and know not) record for me.
A name of blessing (may the goddess I know and know not) pronounce upon me).
(Pure) food I have (not) eaten.
Clear water I have (not) drunk.
The cursed thing[1] of my god unknowingly did I eat;
The cursed thing of my goddess unknowingly did I trample on.
O lord, my sins are many, my transgressions are great!
O my god, my sins are many, my transgressions are great!
O my goddess, my sins are many, my transgressions are great!
O god whom I know and whom I know not, my sins are many, my transgressions are great!
O goddess whom I know and whom I know not, my sins are many, my transgressions are great!
The sin that I sinned I knew not.
The transgression I committed I knew not.
The cursed thing that I ate I knew not.
The cursed thing that I trampled on I knew not.
The lord in the wrath of his heart has regarded me;
God in the fierceness of his heart has revealed himself to me.
The goddess has been violent against me and has put me to grief.
The god whom I know and whom I know not has distressed me.
The goddess whom I know and whom I know not has inflicted trouble.

---

[1] The Assyrian *ikkib*, as Mr. Pinches has pointed out, is borrowed from the Accadian *iv-giba*, "what is harmful." Zimmern quotes Haupt's *Texts*, p. 119 (6 *sq.*), "the handmaid cateth the cursed thing, she has committed the cursed thing." We may compare the words of Gen. ii. 17, "in the day that thou eatest thereof thou shalt surely die."

I sought for help and none took my hand;
I wept and none stood at my side;
I cried aloud and there was none that heard me.
I am in trouble and hiding; I dare not look up.
To my god, the merciful one, I turn myself, I utter my prayer;
The feet of my goddess I kiss and water with tears.[1]
To the god whom I know and whom I know not I utter my prayer.
O lord, look upon (me; receive my prayer!)
O goddess, look upon (me; accept my prayer!)
O god whom I know (and whom I know not, accept my prayer!)
O goddess whom I know (and whom I know not, accept my prayer!)
How long, O god, (shall I suffer?)
How long, O goddess, (shall thy face be turned from me?)
How long, O god whom I know and know not, shall the fierceness (of thy heart continue?)
How long, O goddess whom I know and know not, shall thy heart in its hostility be [not] appeased?
Mankind is made to wander and there is none that knoweth.
Mankind, as many as pronounce a name, what do they know?
Whether he shall have good or ill, there is none that knoweth.
O lord, destroy not thy servant!
When cast into the water of the ocean (?) take his hand.
The sins I have sinned turn to a blessing.
The transgressions I have committed may the wind carry away.
Strip off my manifold wickednesses as a garment.
O my god, seven times seven are my transgressions; forgive my sins!
O my goddess, seven times seven are my transgressions; forgive my sins!
O god whom I know and whom I know not, seven times seven are my transgressions; forgive my sins!
O goddess whom I know and whom I know not, seven times seven are my transgressions; forgive my sins!
Forgive my sins; may thy ban be removed.[2]

---

[1] See W. A. I. v. 19. 35—38; 20. 55; ii. 21. 53; 24. 45.

[2] Zimmern has mistaken the meaning of this passage. In W. A. I iv. 12. 32, 33, *sa-mun-sillalil* is rendered *unakkaru*. KA-TAR (perhaps pronounced *kus*) is "spoken judgment," "excommunication;" thus in

May thy heart be appeased as the heart of a mother who has borne children.
As a mother who has borne children, as a father who has begotten them, may it be appeased!
COLOPHON.—Psalm of 65 lines; a tablet for every god.
Its repetition ensures my peace.[2]
Like its original copied and published: palace of Assur-bani-pal, king of legions, king of Assyria."

It is only necessary to read the psalm to see in it distinct traces of contact on the part of the Accadians with Semitic thought. The god cannot be addressed alone; the goddess necessarily stands at his side. The introspection, moreover, which the psalm reveals is hardly reconcilable with the religious conceptions presupposed by the magical texts and the earlier hymns. The consciousness of sin is a new feature in Chaldæan religion, and belongs to the age that saw the rise of poems like that on the Deluge, which ascribed the sufferings of mankind to their wrong-doing. Hitherto the evil that existed in the world had not been given a moral significance. It was due to the action of malevolent spirits or the decrees of inexorable fate rather than to the wickedness of man, and it was removed by spells and ceremonies which occasioned the interference of the god of wisdom and his son Merodach. At most, it was considered a punishment for offences against the divine order of the

---

1253. *Rev.* 1, 2, we have *ina* KA-GA-*ka lu-ub*(KU)-*ludh* KA-TAR-ZU KA *libbi-ka lusapi*, "by thy word may I live; may I honour thy commandment, the word of thy heart." In W. A. I. iv. 29, 16—18, *dalali*, "exaltation" (not "subject"), is the equivalent of the Accadian UB (for which see ii. 35, 36, *ári* = *tanittu*, "exaltation").

[2] This is the conclusion of the original Accadian colophon. The next line is in Assyrian, and was added by the scribes of Assur-banipal.

world, like the punishments inflicted by human judges for disobedience to the laws. Unassisted by intercourse with Semitic belief, Accadian religion never advanced beyond the idea of vicarious punishment, which grew out of the doctrine of primitive society that demands an eye for an eye and a tooth for a tooth. It is a doctrine that lies at the root of the institution of sacrifice, and it marks the high tide of Accadian faith before the Semite appeared upon the stage.

Along with these indications of Semitic influence, however, the psalm bears equally clear evidence of its Accadian origin. The consciousness of sin is still but rudimentary; the psalmist knows that one of the gods is angry with him because he is suffering pain. He has eaten what has been cursed by heaven, or else has unwittingly trampled on the forbidden thing. In the language of the Polynesians, he has touched what is tabooed, and the curse of heaven accordingly falls upon him. Even when he speaks of his transgressions, he falls into the language of the old magical texts; his sins are seven times seven, that mystical number which was so closely connected with the spirits of earth. The belief in the mysterious power of names, moreover, is still strong upon him. In fear lest the deity he has offended should not be named at all, or else be named incorrectly, he does not venture to enumerate the gods, but classes them under the comprehensive title of the divinities with whose names he is acquainted and those of whose names he is ignorant. It is the same when he refers to the human race. Here, again, the ancient superstition about words shows itself plainly. If he alludes to mankind, it is to "mankind as many as pronounce a name," as many, that is, as have names which may be pronounced.

We must, then, regard the penitential psalms as originating in the Accadian epoch, but at a time when the Accadian population was already profoundly influenced by Semitic ideas. This agrees well with the language and contents of the psalms themselves. They all belong to northern Babylonia, more especially to Erech and Nipur. But there is no reference in them to Sippara and its Sun-god, no trace of acquaintanceship with the empire of Sargon. It would therefore seem that they mount back to an earlier date than the rise of the city of Accad, and may consequently be placed midway between the older hymns and those which were composed in honour of the Sun-god.

But just as the sacred hymns were constantly added to, new hymns being introduced into the ancient collections perhaps as late as the time of Assur-bani-pal, so, too, the number of the penitential psalms was increased from time to time. At first the additions were in Accadian; afterwards they were written in Semitic only, the character of the psalm being at the same time considerably changed. "Vain repetitions" were avoided, and the psalm was more and more assimilated in form to a prayer; on the other hand, forms of expression were borrowed from the semi-magical hymns of Eridu, and a stronger element of superstition gradually entered into the composition of it. Here, for example, is a fragment which I have elsewhere termed a prayer after a bad dream, but which Dr. Zimmern, perhaps more correctly, would entitle a psalm. The tablet which contains it is broken, the beginning and end of the prayer or psalm being consequently lost.¹

"O my god who art violent (against me), receive (my supplication).
O my goddess, thou who art fierce (towards me), accept (my prayer).
Accept my prayer, (may thy liver be quieted).
O my lord, long-suffering (and) merciful, (may thy heart be appeased).
By day, directing unto death that which destroys me,² O my god, interpret (the vision).
O my goddess, look upon me and accept my prayer.
May my sin be forgiven, may my transgression be cleansed.
Let the yoke be unbound, the chain be loosed.
May the seven winds carry away my groaning.
May I strip off my evil so that the bird bear (it) up to heaven.
May the fish carry away my trouble, may the river bear (it) along.
May the reptile of the field receive (it) from me; may the waters of the river cleanse me as they flow.
Make me shine like a mask of gold.
May I be precious in thy sight as a goblet (?) of glass.
Burn up (?) my evil, knit together³ my life; bind together thy altar that I may set up thine image.
Let me pass from my evil, and let me be kept with thee.
Enlighten me and let me dream a favourable dream.
May the dream that I dream be favourable; may the dream that I dream be established.
Turn the dream that I dream into a blessing.
May Makhir the god of dreams rest upon my head.
Yea, let me enter into E-Sagil, the palace of the gods, the temple of life.
To Merodach, the merciful, to blessedness, to prospering hands, entrust me.
Let me exalt thy greatness, let me magnify thy divinity.
Let the men of my city honour thy mighty deeds."

The psalm or prayer, it will be seen, was composed by a native of Babylon, and probably formed part of the

---

¹ W. A. I. iv. 66, No. 2.   ² *Pasdhi.*
³ *Kutstsur;* we may read (with Zimmern) *utsur*, "protect."

ritual used in the service of the great temple of Merodach. In any case it could hardly have been included in the old collection of penitential psalms. These were written in Accadian, and it is not probable that any were admitted among them whose language showed plainly their more recent date. Assur-bani-pal informs us[1] that after putting down the rebellion of his brother, the viceroy of Babylonia, he "pacified the angry gods and wrathful goddesses with a public prayer (*takribti*) and a penitential psalm, restoring and establishing in peace their festivals, which had been discontinued, as they were in former days." As the word for penitential psalm is expressed by the compound ideograph which served to denote it in Accadian, it is possible that on the occasion in question a psalm was selected from the ancient collection; but it is also possible that a new psalm was composed specially for the event.

That such special compositions were not unusual among the Assyrians of Assur-bani-pal's days, is proved by a hymn or prayer on behalf of the king which the compiler of a list of the gods in the chief temples of Assyria has added to his catalogue. It seems to have been intended for use in one of them. Where the text first becomes legible, the hymn reads as follows:[2]

"Joy of heart, production of purity, production of enlightenment (*sukallimtu*), the explanation of what is revealed and concealed (?), reveal to the city of Assur; long days and years unending, a strong weapon, a reign hereafter, names abundant and long, first-born who shall be rulers, adjudge to the king my lord who has given all this to his gods. Habitations (?) many and far-extended adjudge to his people (?). As a man may he live and be at peace. Over kings and princes may he exercise wide empire. May he come to a hoar old age. For the

---

[1] W. A. I. v. 4, 88 *sq*.　　[2] W. A. I. iii. 66, *Rev*. 6 *sq*.

men who pronounce these prayers may the land of the silver sky,[1] oil unceasing and the wine of blessedness, be their food, and a good noon-tide[2] their light. Health to my body and prosperity is my prayer to the gods who dwell in the land of Assyria."

This prayer introduces us to a subject without a discussion of which no description of a religion can be complete. What were the views about a future life entertained by the Babylonians and Assyrians? Was their religion intended for this world only, to avoid evil here and to live happily, or did they look forward to a world beyond the grave, with joys and miseries of its own? The reference to "the land of the silver sky" in the prayer I have just cited would seem to show that Assyrian religion was neither a faith which, like that of the Buddhist, hoped for the annihilation of consciousness, nor yet a faith which, like that of the Greeks of old, saw in the future nothing but a dreary existence in a sunless world, a passage from the world of light and life to the darkness and the night.

But this conclusion would not be in accordance with the testimony of the older texts. The incantations and exorcisms, the semi-magical hymns of Eridu, limit the horizon of their view to the present life. The spirits

[1] We may compare with this expression a phrase in a small fragment (R 528) which runs: "At dawn a hymn (KHIR) before Samas.... four hymns to Ea the pure god of the land of the (silver?) sky.... (beginning with) the incantation: The pure seat."

[2] *Kiriru*, allied to *kararu*, rendered AN-IZI, "divine fire," in W. A. I. iv. 15. 18, 19, where we read, " in the noon-tides of day and night" (i.e. the dead of night). In W. A. I. ii. 47, 61, AN-IZI is translated *urru*, "full day," and in iii. 55. 49, 50, as Jensen points out, we have the four periods of the day enumerated: " On the nineteenth day enter in the morning the presence of Bahu, at noon (AN-IZI) the presence of the supreme god, in the afternoon the presence of Rimmon and in the evening the presence of Istar."

with whom they people the universe are to be dreaded or praised by the living only. The pains man seeks to remove, the blessings he asks for, all cease with death. There is little or no trace of any thought of a world beyond. In the hymns, it is true, Merodach, the benefactor of the human race, is described as raising the dead to life, but the life to which they are raised is the life of the present world. Whatever might have been the sense afterwards attached to the expression, in the early hymns it means nothing more than a belief in the power of spells to restore the dead to life. The recovery of the sick was considered in no way more wonderful than a recovery from a state of trance or from death itself; if the god of wisdom and magic could effect the one, he could equally effect the other.

I do not deny that the primitive Chaldæan may have believed in the continuation of existence after death. The belief in a Mul-lil, a lord of the ghost-world, presupposes this. The lost friends who returned to him in his dreams would have assured him that they had not vanished utterly. But I can find no traces of ancestor-worship in the early literature of Chaldæa which has survived to us. Whatever views the Chaldæan may have entertained about the ghost-world, they were vague and shadowy; it was a subterranean region, inhabited for the most part by spirits who were not the spirits of the dead, but of the objects of nature. They were typified by the spirits of earth, and were all the subjects of Mul-lil.

The ghost-world of Nipur lay beneath the earth. It was here that the golden throne of the Anúnas, the spirits of earth, was erected, hard by the waters of life which they were appointed to guard. When the cult of Nipur and the cult of Eridu were united into one, this underground region was necessarily connected with the great ocean-stream which encircled the earth. Here accordingly was placed the home of the Anúnas, and it became the entrance to the realm of Hades. As primitive Accadian geography, however, identified the Euphrates and the Persian Gulf with the ocean-stream, the approach to Hades passed into Datilla, the river of death;[1] and Xisuthros, the hero of the Deluge, was translated to dwell among the gods beyond the mouth of the Euphrates.[2] This was the land set apart for the immortal deities in the belief of the people of Eridu, for their gods were gods of the sea whose waters washed their shore. The unification of the creeds of Nipur and Eridu thus brought with it an identification of the ghost-world with the world of Ea, of the empire of Mul-lil with the deep over which Ea ruled. The world of the ghosts and the world of the gods were accordingly confounded together, the distinction between them being that whereas the ghosts were still left in their subterranean abodes, Mul-lil was elevated to the world above, there to dwell with Ea and his son Merodach, the god of light. But this upper world of the gods was immediately above the world of the ghosts, and was in fact the passage into it.

This theological geography is perfectly incompatible

---

[1] W. A. I. ii. 62, 50. "The ship of the river Datilla is the ship of the Lady of life and death."

[2] The story here preserves a feature of the original myth. In the time of the composition of the poem, the seat of the gods was regarded as being in heaven, so that the author of the Gisdhubar epic, Sin-liqi-unnini, has admitted a contradiction into his narrative.

with another theory of the abode of the gods, which placed it on the summit of Kharsag-kurkúra, "the mountain of the world." This mountain of the world is declared by Sargon to be the mountain of Arallu or Hades: "The gods Ea, Sin, Samas, Rimmon, Adar and their august wives, who were truly born in the midst of the temple of Kharsag-kurkúra, the mountain of Arallu, have excellently founded glistering sanctuaries and well-wrought shrines in the city of Dur-Sargon."[1] Famous temples were named after it, in Assyria at all events, and its site was sought in the mountainous region of the north-west. An old geographical table tells us that Arallu was the land or mountain of gold,[2] a statement which reminds us of the words of Job (xxxvii. 22), "Out of the north cometh gold," as well as of the Greek legend of the griffins who guarded the hidden gold in the distant north. We find an allusion to the Babylonian myth in the 14th chapter of Isaiah (ver. 13). There the Babylonian monarch is described as having said in his heart: "I will ascend into heaven, I will exalt my throne above the stars of El; I will sit also upon the mount of the assembly (of the gods), in the extremities of the north; I will ascend above the heights of the clouds; I will be like the Most High." Here, in this Chaldæan Olympos, the gods were imagined to have been born and to have their seats; its summit was hidden by the clouds, and the starry firmament seemed to rest upon it. It is possible that it was identified, at any rate in later times, with the mountain on which the ark of the Chaldæan

---

[1] Khors. 155 *sq.* See Delitzsch, *Wo lag das Paradies*, pp. 117—122.
[2] W. A. I. ii. 51, 11.

Noah rested, "the mountain of Nizir," the modern Rowandiz. Rowandiz towers high above its fellows in the Kurdish ranges, and the Babylonian might well believe that its peak had never been ascended by mortal man. If Xisuthros had touched the sacred soil with his ship, he was qualified by the very fact to take his place amid "the assembly of the gods."

"The mountain of the world" was peculiarly sacred among the Assyrians. Perhaps their nearer proximity to the great mountainous chains of the north-west, and their distance from the sea, had made them more ready to adopt the belief which placed the home of the gods in the mountains of the north than beside the waters of the Persian Gulf. It is difficult to tell in what part of Babylonia the belief first arose. If Kharsag-kalama, "the mountain of mankind," the name given to the tower of the chief temple of Kis, is the same as "the mountain of the world," we might discover its cradle in the neighbourhood of Babylon. It will be remembered that in the hymn to the Fire-god the seven spirits of earth are declared to have been born in "the mountain of the sunset," and to have grown up "in the mountain of the sunrise." Here the sun is distinctly regarded as rising and setting behind a mountain; and since there were no mountains on the western side of the Babylonian plain, we must consider the poet to have looked upon the mountain behind which the sun rose and set as one and the same.[1] During the hours of darkness the Sun-god must have

---

[1] I have assumed that the poet's horizon was bounded by the plain of Babylonia. He may, however, have lived after the Babylonians had become acquainted with Palestine, and "the mountain of the sunset" may therefore be the mountainous land of Dhidhi or Phœnicia.

been supposed to have journeyed underneath the earth, traversing, it may be, the realms of Hades on his way. Whether this mountain, which thus fringed, as it were, the sides of the earth, can be connected with "the mountain of the world," I cannot say. In any case, by the side of a belief in a subterranean Hades and a paradise of the gods beyond the mouth of the Euphrates, there was also a belief in a Hades and a paradise which were established on the loftiest of the mountains of the north.

A bilingual Babylonian hymn, which appears to have been connected with Nipur relates to the latter belief. It is thus that it begins:[1]

> "O mighty mountain of Mul-lil, Im-kharsag (the mountain sky), whose head rivals the heavens; the pure deep has been laid as its foundation.
> Among the mountains it lies like a strong wild bull.
> Its horns glisten like the splendour of the Sun-god.
> Like the star of heaven that proclaims (the day) it is full of glittering rays.
> The mighty mother Nin-lilli (the lady of the ghost-world), the reverence[2] of E-Sára (the temple of the hosts of heaven), the glory[2] of E-Kúra (the temple of the hosts of earth), the adornment of E-Giguna (the temple of the city of darkness), the heart of E-Ki-gusúra (the temple of the land of light)."

In this hymn the world-tree of Eridu, whose roots were planted in the deep, has made way for a world-mountain, with its head reaching unto heaven like the tower of Babel, and its feet planted upon the deep. As the conception of the world-tree belonged to Sumir or southern

---

[1] W. A. I. iv. 27, No. 2.

[2] The female and male organs of generation are referred to. As the word for "shame" or "reverence" in the Accadian text is the Semitic *uru*, the text must either belong to the Semitic period or have been revised by Semitic copyists.

Babylonia, so the conception of the world-mountain belongs to Accad or northern Babylonia; it is expressly termed the mountain of Mul-lil, and is identified with Nin-lil, the "reverence of E-Sára," whose son was the Sun-god Adar. It is at least noticeable that one of the hymns to the Sun-god which originated at Sippara begins by declaring that he "rose from the mighty mountain," "from the mountain of the stream," "the place of the destinies."[1]

The introduction of an Olympos into Babylonian mythology must necessarily have modified the conception of the Chaldæan Hades, more especially when we find that Mul-lil, the lord of the ghost-world, was himself associated with it. The world of the gods was separated from the abode of the dead; the latter remained below, while the gods who had once presided there ascended to the upper world. Their places were taken by the god Irkalla and the goddess Allat, originally mere forms of Mul-lil and Nin-lil, but now distinguished from the Bel and Beltis into whom Mul-lil and Nin-lil had been transformed. The addition of the sky-god of Erech to the common pantheon of Babylonia still further tended to divide the two worlds. The Olympos became a ladder

---

[1] W. A. I v. 51, 1—6. Can "the mountain of the stream" have any reference to Gen. ii. 10 ? This mountain of the sun is described in the second column of the ninth tablet of the Epic of Gisdhubar (Haupt, *Babylonische Nimrodepos*) : "When he arrived at the twin (*mâsi*) mountains, where day by day they guard the rising (and setting of the sun), their crown (touched) the massy vault of heaven, below their footing reached to (*kasdat*) Hades; scorpion-men guard its gate, whose terribleness is dread and their appearance death; the greatness of their splendour overthrows the forests. At the rising of the sun and the setting of the sun they guard the Sun-god, and when Gisdhubar saw them, fear and dread took possession of his face."

to the heavens in which the visible deities of light—Samas, Sin and Istar—ruled over the visible firmament, while the other gods dwelt in a yet more remote region of the universe, "the heaven of Anu."

This is the point at which the religious development of Babylonian belief had arrived when the majority of the legendary poems—or at least the older portions of them—were composed. Hades is still the gloomy realm beneath the earth, where the spirits of the dead flit about in darkness, with dust and mud for their food and drink, and from whence they escape at times to feed on the blood of the living. Here the shades of the great heroes of old sit each on his throne, crowned and terrible, rising up only to greet the coming among them of one like unto themselves. The passage to these subterranean abodes is through the seven gates of the world, each guarded by its porter, who admits the dead, stripping him of his apparel, but never allowing him to pass through them again to the upper world. Good and bad, heroes and plebeians, are alike condemned to this dreary lot; a state of future rewards and punishments is as yet undreamed of; moral responsibility ends with death. Hades is a land of forgetfulness and of darkness, where the good and evil deeds of this life are remembered no more; and its occupants are mere shadows of the men who once existed, and whose consciousness is like the consciousness of the spectral figures in a fleeting dream. The Hades of the Babylonian legends closely resembles the Hades of the Homeric poems.

But side by side with this pitiful picture of the world beyond the grave, there were the beginnings of higher and nobler ideas. In the Epic of Gisdhubar, the ghost of

Ea-bani is described as rising like a dust-cloud from the earth and mounting up to heaven, where he lives among the gods, gazing on the deeds that are done below.

"On a couch he reclines and pure water he drinks. He who is slain in battle, thou seest and I see. His father and his mother (support) his head; his wife addresses the corpse. His body in the field (is placed); thou seest and I see. His ghost in the earth is uncovered; of his ghost he has no overnight; thou seest and I see. The food at the edge of the tomb is bewitched (?); the food which is thrown into the street he eats."

Ea-bani, however, was half a god. Gisdhubar, too, who seems to be associated with him in his future lot, was half divine. If while E-bani and Gisdhubar were thus permitted to

"live and lie reclined
On the hills, like gods together, careless of mankind,"

the other heroes of ancient renown, Ner and Etána, were relegated to the shades below, it was because Ner had once been Nergal, the prince of the infernal world, and Etána seems to be the Titan of Bêrôssos who made war against Kronos or Ea. But when the semi-human heroes of epic song had thus been permitted to enter heaven, it could not be long before a similar permission was extended to heroes who were wholly human. Little by little, as the conception of the gods and their dwelling-place became spiritualized, "the mountain of the world" passing first into the sky and then into the invisible "heaven of Anu," the conception of the future condition of mankind became spiritualised also. The doctrine of the immortality of the conscious soul began to dawn upon the Babylonian mind, and along with it necessarily went the doctrine of rewards and punishments for the actions committed in the flesh. The Babylonian was already familiar with the idea of sacrifice for sin and of vicarious punishment; all that remained was to enlarge the horizon of his faith, and to extend his belief in the divine awards for piety and sin to the life beyond the grave. The prayer I quoted just now from the compiler of the list of the gods in the Assyrian temples, proves that some at least of the Assyro-Babylonian people asked their deities for something more than merely temporal blessings. They might pray that their monarch should live "a hundred years,"[1] but they prayed also that they themselves might live "for ever" hereafter in "the land of the silver sky." The world-mountain had followed the fate of the world-tree, and been consigned to the mythologists and the mythologising poets; even the invisible "heaven of Anu" itself had vanished into the deep blue of the visible firmament; above and beyond them all was the true home of the gods and the spirits of the blest, a home towards which the smoke of the altar might ascend, but into whose mysteries none could penetrate till death and the grace of Baal had freed him from the shackles of the flesh.

---

[1] While 60 was the numerical unit of Accadian literature, the Semitic Assyrians made 100 their standard number. The stereotyped form of addressing the monarch accordingly was, "A hundred years to the king my lord; may he live to old age; may offspring be multiplied to the king my lord!" (K 501, 12—16; K 538, 13—16).

Lecture VI.

COSMOGONIES AND ASTRO-THEOLOGY.

More than once I have had to allude to the speculations the Babylonians indulged in regarding the origin of the world. In an early age these speculations naturally assumed a theological form. As the elements themselves were regarded as divine, or at any rate as possessed of a divine spirit, their source and shaping must have been divine also. They were deities who had formed themselves into their present order and appearance, or else they had been so formed by other and superior powers.

In course of time this theological conception became mythological. The elements themselves ceased to be divine, but they represented and symbolised divine beings whose actions produced the existing order of nature. The mythological conception in turn gave way to another, which saw in the elements inert matter created, begotten or moulded by the gods. Lastly, schools of philosophy arose which sought to find in matter the original cause of all things, including even the gods, though they veiled the materialism of their views under a mythological symbolism.

Broadly speaking, the cosmological theories of Chaldæa divide themselves into two main classes, the genealogical and the creative. According to Accadian ideas, the world was created by the gods; the Semite saw in it rather a birth or emanation. A time came, it is true, when the two sets of ideas were harmonised; and by the assumption of a chaos which had existed from "the beginning," and the further assumption that "the great gods" had created the objects we see about us, room was left for the creative hypothesis, while the belief in the birth of the elements one out of the other was at the same time stoutly maintained. The form taken by the combination of the two ideas will be best seen in the latest product of Assyro-Babylonian cosmogonical systems, that which describes the creation of the world in a series of days.

First of all, however, let us read the account given by Bêrôssos of the creation of the world, and professed by him to be derived from the writings of Oannes, that semi-piscine being who rose out of the waters of the Persian Gulf to instruct the people of Chaldæa in the arts and sciences of life. It is pretty certain that Bêrôssos had access to documents which purported to come from the hand of Oannes or Ea, and consequently to deal with events which preceded the appearance of man on the earth. The Chaldæan system of astronomy which Bêrôssos translated into Greek was likewise asserted by him to have been composed by a god, namely Bel; and the fragments of the original work which we now possess show that his assertion was correct, inasmuch as the work bears the title of the Observations of Bel. The inscriptions, moreover, expressly inform us that Ea was not only the god of wisdom, but himself an author. We learn from a tablet, "with warnings to kings against injustice," that if the king "decrees according to the writing of Ea, the great gods will establish him in good report and the knowledge of justice."[1] There is, therefore, no reason to doubt the statement of Bêrôssos that the account of the creation which he gives was extracted from a document that professed to have been inscribed by the god of Eridu himself.

"The following is the purport of what he said : There was a time in which there existed nothing but darkness and an abyss of waters, wherein resided most hideous beings, which were produced by a twofold principle. There appeared men, some of whom were furnished with two wings, others with four, and with two faces. They had one body, but two heads ; the one that of a man, the other of a woman ; they were likewise in their several organs both male and female. Other human figures were to be seen with the legs and horns of a goat ; some had horses' feet, while others united the hind-quarters of a horse with the body of a man, resembling in shape the hippocentaurs. Bulls likewise were bred there with the heads of men ; and dogs with four-fold bodies, terminated in their extremities with the tails of fishes ; horses also with the heads of dogs ; men, too, and other animals, with the heads and bodies of horses and the tails of fishes. In short, there were creatures in which were combined the limbs of every species of animal. In addition to these, there were fishes, reptiles, serpents, with other monstrous animals, which assumed each other's shape and countenance. Of all which were preserved delineations in the temple of Bêlos at Babylon.

The person who was supposed to have presided over them was a woman named Omoroka, which in the Chaldæan language is Thalatth (*read* Thavatth), which in Greek is interpreted Thalassa (the sea) ; but according to the most true interpretation it is equivalent to the Moon. All things being in this situation, Bêlos came and cut the woman asunder, and of one half of her he formed the earth, and of the other half the heavens, and at the same time destroyed the animals within her (in the abyss).

All this was an allegorical description of nature. For, the whole

---

[1] W. A. I. iv. 55. 7, 8. *Sipar* is literally "a message," but as the message was in later times a written one, it signifies "a letter" or "writing." I have translated *sitilti* (for *sitišti*), " good report," on the strength of W. A. I. v. 17, 4—7, and the meaning of its ideographic equivalent, " fatherliness ;" but it may signify " study."

universe consisting of moisture, and animals being continually generated therein, the deity above-mentioned (Bêlos) cut off his own head; upon which the other gods mixed the blood, as it gushed out, with the earth, and from thence men were formed. On this account it is that they are rational, and partake of divine knowledge. This Bêlos, by whom they signify Zeus, divided the darkness, and separated the heavens from the earth, and reduced the universe to order. But the recently-created animals, not being able to bear the light, died. Bêlos upon this, seeing a vast space unoccupied, though by nature fruitful, commanded one of the gods to take off his head, and to mix the blood with the earth, and from thence to form other men and animals, which should be capable of bearing the light. Bêlos formed also the stars and the sun and the moon and the five planets."[1]

The account of the cosmological theories of the Babylonians thus given by Bêrôssos has not come to us immediately from his hand. It was first copied from his book by Alexander Polyhistor, a native of Asia Minor, who was a slave at Rome for a short period in the time of Sulla; and from Polyhistor it has been embodied in the works of the Christian writers Eusêbios and George the Synkellos. It is not quite certain, therefore, whether the whole of the quotation was originally written by Bêrôssos himself. At all events, it evidently includes two inconsistent accounts of the creation of the world, which have been awkwardly fitted on to one another. In one of them, the composite creatures who filled the watery chaos, over which Thavatth, the Tiamat or Tiavat of the inscriptions, presided, were represented as being destroyed by Bel when he cut Thavatth asunder, forming the heavens out of one portion of her body, and the earth out of the other. In the second version, the monsters of chaos perished through the creation of light, and their places were taken by the animals and men produced by the

---

[1] Euseb. *Chron.* i. 4.

mixture of the earth with the blood of Bel. What this blood meant may be gathered from the Phœnician myth which told how the blood of the sky, mutilated by his son Kronos or Baal, fell upon the earth in drops of rain and filled the springs and rivers. It was, in fact, the fertilising rain.

Both versions of the genesis of the universe reported by Bêrôssos agree not only in the representation of a chaos that existed before the present order of things, but also in the curious statement that this chaos was peopled with strange creatures, imperfect first attempts of nature, as it were, to form the animal creation of the present world. In these chaotic beginnings of animal life we may see a sort of anticipation of the Darwinian hypothesis. At any rate, the Babylonian theory on the subject must have been the source of the similar theory propounded by the Ionic philosopher Anaximander in the sixth century before our era. The philosophical systems of the early Greek thinkers of Asia Minor came to them from Babylonia through the hands of the Phœnicians, and it is consequently no more astonishing to find Anaximander declaring that men had developed out of the fish of the sea, than to find his predecessor Thalês agreeing with the priests of Babylonia in holding that all things have originated from a watery abyss.

The fact that Anaximander already knew of the Babylonian doctrine shows that it could not have been suggested to Bêrôssos himself, as we might be tempted to think, by the colossal bulls that guarded the gates, and the curious monsters depicted on the walls, of the temple of Bel. And we are now able to carry the belief back to a period very much earlier than that of Anaximander.

LECTURE VI.

The library of Nineveh contained the copy of a tablet which, according to its concluding lines, was originally written for the great temple of Nergal at Cutha.[1] The words of the text are put in the mouth of Nergal the destroyer, who is represented as sending out the hosts of the ancient brood of chaos to their destruction. Nergal is identified with Nerra, the plague-god, who smites them with pestilence, or rather with Ner, the terrible "king who gives not peace to his country, the shepherd who grants no favour to his people."[2] We are first told how the armies of chaos came into existence. "On a tablet none wrote, none disclosed, and no bodies or brushwood were produced in the land; and there was none whom I approached. Warriors with the body of a bird of the valley, men with the faces of ravens, did the great gods create. In the ground did the gods create their city. Tiamat (the dragon of chaos) suckled them. Their pro-

---

[1] Col. iv. ll. 9 sq. *Atta sarru patesi rium lu nin sanama sa ilu inambu (u) sarruta tebus dup suatu ebus-ka narâ asdhur-ka ina ali* GU-DU-A-KI *ina bit* ŚU-LIM (*i*)*na parak*[LUL] D. P. U-GUR *ezibakka*: "Thou, king, priest-ruler, shepherd, or whatever thou art, whom God shall proclaim to govern the kingdom, for thee have I made this tablet, for thee have I written the record-stone; in the city of Cutha, in the temple of 'Sulim, in the sanctuary of Nergal, have I left it for thee."

[2] *Ana palé minâ ezib anaku sarru la musallimu mati-su û rieum la musallimu ummanu-su ki ustakkan pagri u bûti usetsi salum mati nisi musi mûtu namtar arur-su*: "What have I left for (my) reign? I am a king who gives not peace to his land, and a shepherd who gives not peace to his people; since I have made corpses and produced jungle, the whole of the land and the men I have cursed with night, death and pestilence." *Buti* means "thickets" or "jungle," and corresponds with the Accadian *śag*; see GIS-BA *śag* and GIS-BA-PAL = *bûtum*, W.A.I. ii. 41. 70, 71 (for NAM-BA = *kistu*, cf. v. 11, 3, also *qistu*, "offering"); .... *śag* = *bûtum* ("thickness"), v. 20, 48; *śag* = *bûtum*, v. 29, 56. In 82. 5—22. 196. *Rev.* 8, *buti* is opposed to *dibiri*, "pasture-lands."

geny (*sasur*) the mistress of the gods created. In the midst of the mountains they grew up and became heroes and increased in number. Seven kings, brethren, appeared and begat children. Six thousand in number were their peoples. The god Banini their father was king; their mother was the queen Melili." It was the subjects and the offspring of these semi-human heroes whom the god Ner was deputed to destroy.

It is clear that the legend of Cutha agrees with Bêrôssos in the main facts, however much it may differ in details. In both alike, we have a first creation of living beings, and these beings are of a composite nature, and the nurselings of Tiamat or Chaos. In both alike, the whole brood is exterminated by the gods of light. A curious point in connection with the legend is the description of chaos as a time when writing was as yet unknown and records unkept. Perhaps we may see in this an allusion to the fact that the Babylonian histories of the pre-human period were supposed to have been composed by the gods.

The date to which the legend in its present form may be assigned is difficult to determine. The inscription is in Semitic only, like the other creation-tablets, and therefore cannot belong to the pre-Semitic age. It belongs, moreover, to an epoch when the unification of the deities of Babylonia had already taken place, and the circle of "the great gods" was complete. Ea, Istar, Zamama, Anunit, even Nebo and "Samas the warrior," are all referred to in it. We must therefore place its composition after the rise not only of the hymns of Sippara, but also of the celebrity of the Semitic god of Borsippa. On the other hand, the reference to the *patesi* or priest-king in the concluding lines seems to prevent us from assigning too late a date to the poem. Perhaps we shall not be far wrong in ascribing it to the era of Khammuragas.

Tiamat or Tiavat, the Thavatth of Bêrôssos, is the *t'hôm* or " deep " of the Old Testament, and the word is used in Assyrian, in the contracted form *tamtu*, to denote " the deep sea." It was upon the face of the *t'hôm* or " deep" that " the breath of Elohim" brooded, according to the first chapter of Genesis. The word is not only Semitic, but, in its cosmological signification, of Semitic origin. It has, however, an Accadian descent. The belief that the watery abyss was the source of all things went back to the worshippers of the sea-god Ea at Eridu. But with them the deep was termed *apzu*, which a punning etymology afterwards read *ab-zu*, " the house of knowledge," wherein Ea, the god of wisdom, was imagined to dwell. The Sumerian *abzu* was borrowed by the Semites under the form of *apśu*. The Sumerians had endowed it with a spirit, in accordance with the Shananistic faith of early days, and as such had made it the mother of Ea and of the other gods. But I have already pointed out in a previous Lecture that the *abzu*, or deep, of which Ea was lord, was not only the ocean-stream that surrounded the earth, and upon which the earth floated, like Dêlos in Greek myth; it was also the deep which rolled above the firmament of heaven, through whose windows its waters descended in the days of the deluge. Consequently the mother of Ea was usually known by another name than that of Apzu. She was Zikum or Zigarum, " the heaven" (W. A. I. ii. 48, 26; 50, 27), whom a mythological list describes as " the mother that has begotten heaven and earth" (W. A. I. ii. 54, 18). In the same passage she is declared to be "the handmaid of the spirit of E-kura," the lower firmament or earth; and with this agrees the statement that Zikura, a dialectic form of Zigarum,[1] is the earth itself (W. A. I. ii. 48, 27). But it was not the existing earth or the existing heaven that was represented by Zikum; she was rather the primordial abyss out of which both earth and heaven were produced. Possibly an old myth may have related that she was torn asunder when the present world was made, the upper half of her becoming the sky and the lower half the earth. This at least is what we may gather from the story given by Bêrôssos.

As far back as the days of the priest-kings of Tel-loh, Zikum was honoured in southern Babylonia under the name of Bahu.[2] She was "the daughter of heaven," to whom they had erected a temple at Zerghul. Like Gula, she was "the great mother," and in the era of totemism was known as "the pure heifer." Bau, or Bahu, is the *bohu* of the Old Testament, the Baau of Phœnician mythology, of whom Philôn Byblios informs us that "of the wind Kolpia and of his wife Baau, which is interpreted 'night,' were begotten two mortal men, Aiôn and Pro-

---

[1] Zi-kum, Zi-garum, Zi-kura, are all compounds of *Zi*, "a spirit," and are explained by Zi-(E-)kura, "the spirit of the lower firmament." It is possible that Zi-kum was originally "the spirit of the earth" alone, Ea being the spirit of the deep. Zi-kura and Zi-garum may have different etymologies, since *garum* seems to be connected with *gur*, a Sumerian synomym of *apzu*. In W. A. I. iv. 15, 5, *ê-gur-ra* is rendered by the Assyrian *apsu*. There seems to have been a confusion between Ê-kúra and Ê-gúra.

[2] See Hommel, *Vorsemitische Kulturen*, p. 380. I do not feel quite certain, however, about the identification.

togonos."[1] According to the book of Genesis, the earth created by God in the beginning was "without form and void," the word translated "void" being *bohu* or "chaos." The wind or spirit which the Phœnicians associated with Baau is the Sumerian spirit of the deep, the *Zi Zikum* invoked in the magical texts.[2]

An allusion to the creation of the heavens out of the watery abyss, and the subsequent formation of the earth, is found in a mythological document, where we read: "The heaven was made from the waters; the god and the goddess create the earth."[3] The god and the goddess must of course mean the heaven and the deep, and thus presuppose a cosmological theory inconsistent with that of the rulers of Tel-loh, who entitle Bahu the daughter of the sky. We may gather from this that Bahu and Zikum were not originally the same divinities, and that it was only through a belief that the ocean-stream was fed from heaven that Bahu became identified with it. The Semites, therefore, could not have come into contact with the cosmogony of the Sumerians until after the age of the *patesis* of Zerghul.

But whatever form the old cosmogony may have assumed, the fundamental element in it remained unchanged. The watery abyss was always the primal source of the universe. Whether it was the heaven which first rose out of the deep, and then in combination with the deep produced the earth, or whether the deep

---

[1] Euseb. *Præp. Evang.* i. 10.

[2] So in W. A. I. iv. 1. ii. 36.

[3] K 170, *Obv.* 6, 7. The word "goddess" is phonetically written in Accadian DIN-*gi-ri*, which settles the reading of the form DINGI-*ri* on the early bricks.

itself developed into the heavens and the earth, the deep, and the deep alone, was the first of things to exist. If Bahu, therefore, was ever identified with the deep in the mind of the southern Babylonian, it must have been when the deep had ceased to be the watery abyss of chaos and had become the home of the creator Ea, deriving its waters from the heavens above.

But it is more probable that the identification was due to a total misconception of the true character of Bahu. In the Phœnician mythology as in Genesis, Bohu is simply "chaos," but it is the chaos which existed on earth, not within the waters of the abyss. It represents that pre-human age which, according to the legend of Cutha, witnessed the creation of the monsters of Tiamat. These monsters had their home, their "city," in "the ground;" there was therefore already an earth by the side of the deep. But this earth was the abode of chaos, of Bahu, and had originated, like the sky, out of the waters of the abyss. There were thus two representatives of chaos, the primæval Apzu, the Tiamat of the Semitic epoch, and the secondary Bahu who presided over the chaos of the earth. Later ages failed to distinguish between the two, and Apzu and Bahu thus became one and the same.

But a new distinction now took the place of the older one. Bahu was no longer distinguished from Apzu; she was distinguished, on the other hand, from Tiamat. Bahu became one of the great gods, while Tiamat was left to personate chaos and all the anarchy and evil that proceeded out of chaos. The spirits of earth were transformed into the seven evil demons who had their dwelling in the deep, and the cosmological sundering of the body of Zikum took a mythological shape. It appears in the legendary poems as the struggle between Merodach and the dragon Tiamat, which ended in the rout of Tiamat and her allies, and the tearing asunder of the body of the fiend. The poems are all of the Semitic age; and though the materials upon which they are based doubtless go back to a pre-Semitic era, we have no means at present of determining how much in them belongs to primitive Chaldæa, and how much is the invention of Semitic imagination. That Merodach appears in them as the champion of the gods, proves only that the legends they embody originated in either Eridu or Babylon.

Nothing can show more plainly the wide gulf that lies between the religions of pre-Semitic and Semitic Chaldæa, than the contrast between the Zikum of Eridu, the mother of gods and men, and the wicked Tiamat of the legends, with her misshapen body and malignant mind. In the watery abyss in which the first philosophers of Eridu saw the origin of all things, there was nothing unholy, nothing abhorrent. On the contrary, it was the home and mother of the great god Ea, the primal source of his wisdom and his benevolence towards man. It was from its waters that Oannes had ascended, bringing the light of knowledge and art to the human race. But the watery abyss personified by the Tiamat of the poems belongs altogether to another category. It represents all that is opposed to the present orderly course of the universe; it stands outside and in opposition to the gods of heaven, and is thus essentially evil. Not only has the problem of the origin of evil presented itself to the Babylonian; he has found a solution of it in his dragon of chaos. It is thus that the great fight between Bel and the dragon is described:[1]

> "He (Anu ?) established for him (Merodach ?) also the shrine of the mighty,
> before his fathers for (his) kingdom he founded (it).[2]
> Yea, thou art glorious among the great gods,
> thy destiny has no rival, thy gift-day is Anu;
> from that day unchanged is thy command;
> high and low entreat thy hand;
> may the word that goes forth from thy mouth be established, the unending decision of thy gift-day.
> None among the gods surpasses thy power,[3]
> as an adornment has (thy hand) founded the shrine of the gods;
> may the place of their gathering (?)[4] become thy home.
> 'O Merodach, thou art he that avenges us;
> we give thee the sovereignty, (we) the multitudes of the universe;
> thou possessest (it), and in the assembly (of the gods) may thy word be exalted!
> Never may they break thy weapons, may thine enemies tremble!
> O lord, be gracious to the soul of him who putteth his trust in thee, and destroy (*literally*, pour out) the soul of the god who has hold of evil.'

---

[1] Fragments of an Assyrian copy of the text from the library of Assur-bani-pal at Nineveh were discovered by Mr. George Smith, and published by him in the *Transactions of the Society of Biblical Archæology*, iv. 2, a revised edition of them being subsequently published by Prof. Fr. Delitzsch in his *Assyrische Lesestücke*. They have since been supplemented by a tablet brought by Mr. Hormuzd Rassam from Babylonia, which gives the beginning and end of the text, and shows that it belonged to the fourth tablet of the Creation series. This important tablet has been copied by Mr. Budge, who has been kind enough to allow me the use of his copy. He gave an account of it in the Proceedings of the Society of Biblical Archæology, Nov. 6th, 1883, reserving a complete paper on the subject for the Transactions of the same Society.

[2] These are the last two lines of the third tablet of the Creation series.

[3] Literally, "passes by thy hand."

[4] *'Sagi*, which occurs also in K 2584, 10 (*lilil śagi-sunu*).

LECTURE VI.

Then they placed in their midst by itself his plan ;[1]
they spoke to Merodach their first-born:
'May thy destiny, O lord, go before the gods, and
may they confirm the destruction and the creation of all that is said.
Set thy mouth, may it destroy his plan ;
turn, speak unto him and let him produce again his plan.'[2]
He spake and with his mouth destroyed his plan ;
he turned, he spake to him and his plan was re-created.
Like the word that issues from his mouth, the gods his fathers
    beheld (it) ;
they rejoiced, they approached Merodach the king ;
they bestowed upon him the sceptre (and) throne and reign,
they gave him a weapon unrivalled, consuming the hostile:
'Go' (they said) 'and cut off the life of Tiamat ;
let the winds carry her blood to secret places.'
They showed his path and they bade him listen and take the road.
There was too the bow, his weapon (which) he used ;
he made the club swing, he fixed its seat ;
then he lifted up his weapon, (which) he caused his right hand to
    hold ;
the bow and the quiver he hung at his side ;[3]
he set the lightning before him ;
with a glance of swiftness he filled his body.
He made also a snare to enclose the dragon of the sea.

---

[1] Or "word." It is impossible in a translation to preserve the play upon words in the original. The god of evil (Kingu, the husband of Tiamat) is represented as having uttered a word which becomes a plan or plot: it is this which Merodach is called upon to destroy and re-create.

[2] Literally, "lift up his word."

[3] The arming of Merodach with the bow of Anu in "the assembly of the gods," was the subject of a special poem, of which a fragment is preserved. One of the constellations was named "the Star of the Bow ;" and according to the story of the Deluge (Col. iii. 51, 52), when Xisuthros had left the ark and offered his sacrifice on the peak of Mount Nizir, "Istar (the great goddess) at (her) coming lifted up the mighty shafts (*namzabi*) which Anu had made." That the bow is here referred to seems evident from a passage in a hymn (W. A. I. ii. 19. 7, 8), where allusion is made to "the bow of the deluge," in Accadian *gisme* (GIS-BAM) *mâtu*. The word "bow" is here translated, not by the ordinary Assyrian *midpanu*, but by *qastu*, the Heb. *qesheth*. Comp. Gen. ix. 13—16.

He seized the four winds that they might not issue forth from her,
the south wind, the north wind, the east wind (and) the west wind.
His hand brought the snare near unto the bow of his father Anu.
He created the evil wind, the hostile wind, the storm, the tempest,
the four winds, the seven winds, the whirlwind, the unending wind;
he caused the winds he had created to issue forth, seven in all,
confounding the dragon Tiamat, as they swept after him.
Then Bel lifted up the hurricane (deluge), his mighty weapon.
He rode in a chariot of destiny that fears not a rival.[1]
He stood firm and hung the four reins at its side.
   . . . . unsparing, inundating her covering.
   . . . . their teeth carry poison.
   . . . . they sweep away the learned (?).
   . . . . might and battle.
On the left they open . . . .
   . . . . fear . . .
With lustre and (terror) he covered his head.
He directed also (his way), he made his path descend;
Humbly he set the . . . . before him.
By (his) command he kept back the . . . .
His finger holds the . . . .
On that day they exalted him, the gods exalted him,
the gods his fathers exalted him, the gods exalted him.
Then Bel approached; he catches Tiamat by her waist;
she seeks the huge bulk (?) of Kingu her husband,
she looks also for his counsel.
Then the rebellious one appointed him the destroyer of the commands (of Bel).
And the gods his helpers who marched beside him
beheld (how Merodach) the first-born holds their yoke.
He laid judgment on Tiamat, but she turned not her neck.
With her hostile lips she declared opposition :
   . . . . O lord, the gods swept after thee.
They gathered their (forces) together to where thou wast.
Bel (launched) the deluge, his mighty weapon ;
(against) Tiamat who had raised herself (?) thus he sent it.

---

[1] If Delitzsch's copy is correct, it is possible to extract sense out of the line only by supposing that the negative is misplaced, and that we should read *makhri la galidta*. In W. A. I. iii. 12, 32, *galitti* is used of the "ebbing" sea.

. . . . .

(Against) the gods my fathers thy enmity hast thou directed.
Thou harnesser of thy companions, may thy weapons pierce their
    bodies.
Stand up, and I and thou will fight together.'
When Tiamat heard this,
she uttered her former spells, she repeated her command.
Tiamat also cried out violently with a high voice.
From its roots she strengthened (her) seat completely.
She recites an incantation, she casts a spell,
and the gods of battle demand for themselves their arms.
Then Tiamat attacked Merodach the prince of the gods;
in combat they joined; they engaged in battle.
Then Bel opened his snare and enclosed her;
the evil wind that seizes from behind he sent before him.
Tiamat opened her mouth to swallow it;
he made the evil wind to enter so that she could not close her lips.
The violence of the winds tortured her stomach, and
her heart was prostrated and her mouth was twisted.
He swung the club; he shattered her stomach;
he cut out her entrails; he mastered her heart;
he bound her and ended her life.
He threw down her corpse; he stood upon it.
When Tiamat who marched before (them) was conquered,
he dispersed her forces, her host was overthrown,
and the gods her allies who marched beside her
trembled (and) feared (and) turned their back.
They escaped and saved their lives.
They clung to one another fleeing strengthlessly.
He followed them and broke their arms.
He cast his snare and they are caught in his net.
They recognise the spot (?), they are filled with grief;
they bear their sin, they are kept in bondage,
and the elevenfold offspring are troubled through fear.
The brilliancy (of Bel) the spirits as they march clearly perceived.
His hand lays darkness (upon their host).
At the same time their opposition (fails) from under them,
and the god Kingu who had (marshalled) their (forces)
he bound him also with the god of the tablets (of destiny in) his
    right hand;
and he took from him the tablets of destiny (that were) with him;

COSMOGONIES AND ASTRO-THEOLOGY.

with the string of the stylus[1] he sealed (them) and held the (cover ?) of the tablet.
From the time he had bound and laid the yoke on his foes
he led the illustrious enemy captive like an ox;
the victory of the Firmament (*an-sar*) he laid fully upon (his) antagonists;
Merodach the warrior has overcome the lamentation of Ea the lord of the world.
Over the gods in bondage he strengthened his watch, and
Tiamat whom he had bound he first turned backward;
so Bel trampled on the foundations of Tiamat.
With his club unswung (*la masdi*) he smote (her) skull,
he broke (it) and caused her blood to flow;
the north wind bore (it) away to secret places.
Then his father beheld, he rejoiced at the savour,
he bade the spirits (?) bring peace to himself;
And Bel rested, his body he fed.
He strengthened his mind (?), he formed a clever plan,
and he stripped her like a fish of (her) skin according to his plan;
he described her likeness and (with it) overshadowed the heavens;
he stretched out the skin, he kept a watch,
he urged on her waters that were not issuing forth;
he lit up the sky, the sanctuary rejoiced,
and he presented himself before the deep the seat of Ea.
Then Bel measured the offspring of the deep,
the mighty master established the Upper Firmament (Ê-Sarra) as his image.
The mighty master caused Anu, Bel (Mul-lil) and Ea
to inhabit the Upper Firmament which he had created, even the heavens, their strongholds.
[First line of the 5th tablet]:—He prepared the stations of the great gods.
[COLOPHON]:—One hundred and forty-six lines of the 4th tablet (of the series beginning) : 'When on high unproclaimed.'
According to the papyri of the tablet whose writing had been injured.[2]

---

[1] *Kisibu*, see W. A. I. v. 32, 53.

[2] *Tsullupu*. A fragmentary prayer to Merodach (R 601, *Rev.* 12), in which mention is made of the man who "forsakes (*issir*) the command of Merodach" and of how "Merodach will purify thy sin" (*gillati-*

Copied for Nebo his lord by Nahid-Merodach, the son of the
  irrigator, for the preservation of his life
  and the life of all his house. He wrote and placed (it) in Ê-Zida."[1]

The legend of the great battle between light and darkness thus took the form of a poem addressed to Merodach, and constituted the fourth tablet or book of the story of the creation in days.

This story, which bears a curious resemblance to the account of the creation in the first chapter of Genesis, was first brought to light by Mr. George Smith. The first tablet of the series to which it belongs opens as follows:

"At that time the heaven above had not yet announced,
or the earth beneath recorded, a name;
the unopened[2] deep was their generator,
Mummu-Tiamat (the chaos of the sea) was the mother of them all.
Their waters were embosomed as one,[3] and
the corn-field[4] was unharvested, the pasture was ungrown.
At that time the gods had not appeared any of them,

---

ki Maruduk izakkú), ends with the colophon: (*Bab-)ili kima mustaldir* KHIR *tsullupi*, "(copy of) Babylon; like one who causes an injured text to be written.

[1] This copy seems to have been made in the Persian age, and the text does not appear to be always correct. This would be explained by the statement that the original was injured. Of much older date is a short incantation (M 1246, 3, 4) which concludes with the words: "O lord exalted (and) great, destroy (*apal*) Tiamat, strike (*pudhur*) the unpitying (*la edheru*) evil one."

[2] *La patû*; Delitzsch reads, *ristû*, "the first-born."

[3] S 1140, 8, shows that this is the meaning of *istenis*.

[4] For *gipara*, see W. A. I. v. 1, 48—50 : D. P. *Nirba kán yusakhnapu giparu sippáti summukha inbu*, "the corn-god continuously caused the corn-field to grow, the papyri were gladdened with fruit;" and S 799, 2, *ana gipári eltu erubbi* (Accadian, *mi-para-ki azagga imma-dan-tutu*), "to the holy corn-field he went down." The word has nothing to do with "clouds" or "darkness," as has been supposed.

by no name were they recorded, no destiny (had they fixed).
Then the (great) gods were created,
Lakhmu and Lakhamu issued forth (the first),
until they grew up (when)
An-sar and Ki-sar were created.
Long were the days, extended (was the time, and)
the gods Anu, (Bel and Ea were born).
An-sar and Ki-sar (gave them birth)."

The cosmogomy here presented to us bears evident marks of its late date. The gods of the popular religion not only have their places in the universe fixed, the period and manner of their origin even is described. The elementary spirits of the ancient Accadian faith have passed into the great gods of Semitic belief, and been finally resolved into mere symbolical representatives of the primordial elements of the world. Under a thin disguise of theological nomenclature, the Babylonian theory of the universe has become a philosophic materialism. The gods themselves come and go like mortal men; they are the offspring of the everlasting elements of the heaven and earth, and of that watery abyss out of which mythology had created a demon of evil, but which the philosopher knew to be the mother and source of all things. The Tiamat of the first tablet of the Creation story is a very different being from the Tiamat of the fourth.

The old Semitic confusion between names and things was, however, as potent as ever. Heaven and earth existed not in the beginning because no name had been pronounced in them, and they themselves were nameless. It was the same with the gods. The gods, too, came into being only when they received names. The day on which the names of Lakhmu and Lakhamu were first heard was the day on which they first "issued forth."

I doubt much whether the story in its present form is older than the time of Assur-bani-pal. It is true that a copy of the fourth tablet, originally deposited in the temple of Nebo at Borsippa, is now in the British Museum, but this cannot be earlier than the reign of Nebuchadnezzar; and although the last two words of the first line of the story are quoted in it in an Accadian form, this proves but little. The scribes of Assur-bani-pal's court frequently amused themselves by composing in the old language of Chaldæa, and the introduction of Accadian words into their texts gave them a flavour of antiquity.

However this may be, the cosmogony of the poem eventually found its way into the pages of a Greek writer. Damaskios, an author of the sixth century, has preserved an account of the cosmological system of the Babylonians, which he probably borrowed from some older work.[1] "The Babylonians," he tells us, "like the rest of the barbarians, pass over in silence the one principle of the universe, and they constitute two, Tavthê and Apasôn, making Apasôn the husband of Tavthê, and denominating her 'the mother of the gods.' And from these proceeds an only-begotten son, Mumis, which, I conceive, is no other than the intelligible world proceeding from the two principles. From them also another progeny is derived, Lakhê and Lakhos;[2] and again a third, Kissarê and Assôros; from which last three others proceed, Anos and Illinos and Aos. And of Aos and Davkê is born a son called Bêlos, who, they say, is the fabricator of the world."

---

[1] *De Prim. Princip.* 125, p. 384, ed. Kopp.
[2] So we must read, in place of the Dakhê and Dakhos of the MSS.

There is only one point in which the account of Damaskios differs from that of the cuneiform text. Mumis or Mummu becomes in it the only son of Tavthê and Apasôn, that is to say, of Tiamat and Apśu, "the deep," instead of being identified with Tiamat. He takes the place of the heaven and the earth, which the Assyrian poet represents as born of Apśu and Mummu-Tiamat. The alteration seems to be due to a later Babylonian striving to reconcile the Assyrian cosmological system with the belief that Bel-Merodach was the creator of the visible world. The birth of the gods is thus thrown back beyond the creation of the heavens and the earth; whereas in the Assyrian poem, as in the first chapter of Genesis, the creation of the heavens and the earth is placed in the forefront.

Between the cosmogony we have just been considering and the Babylonian cosmogony reported by Bêrôssos, no reconciliation is possible. In the one, Tiamat is already the teeming mother of strange creatures before Bel Merodach creates the light, and by tearing her asunder forms the heaven and the earth. In the other, Tiamat is the *mummu*, or "chaos," which, in combination with Apśu, "the deep," produces Lakhmu and Lakhamu, from whom Ansar and Kisar, "the hosts of heaven" and "the hosts of earth," are begotten; and then after long ages the gods come into existence, to whom, with Merodach the son of Ea, the origin of all living things is ascribed. The names of Ansar and Kisar have, however, wandered far from their primitive signification. They have come to represent the firmament above and the earth below—not only the visible sky and the visible earth, but also the invisible "heaven of Anu" and the underground world of Hades.

Like Lakhmu and Lakhamu, they were resolved into forms of Anu and his female counterpart Anat by the monotheistic, or rather pantheistic, school to whom I have alluded in a former Lecture. It was to this pantheistic school that the materialistic school of the cosmogonists was most sharply opposed. In the lists in which the views of the pantheistic school find expression, Lakhmu and Lakhamu appear as Lakhma, or Lukhma, and Lakhama, an indication that the names are of non-Semitic origin. It is possible that they denote the element of "purity" presupposed by the creation of the world out of the watery abyss. At all events, they are placed in one of the lists between Du-eri and Da-eri, "the children of the state," and E-kur and E-sarra, "the temples of earth and heaven." Like so many of the Babylonian deities, their names and worship were probably carried to Canaan. Lakhmi seems to be the name of a Philistine in 1 Chron. xx. 5, and Beth-lehem is best explained as "the house of Lekhem," like Beth-Dagon, "the house of Dagon," or Beth-Anoth, "the house of Anat."[1]

It is unfortunate that the Assyrian cosmological poem has reached us only in a fragmentary state. The latter part of the first tablet is lost, and the second and third tablets have not yet been recovered. The first half of the fifth tablet, however, is complete; and as it describes

---

[1] Lakhmu is mentioned but rarely in the inscriptions. His name, however, occurs in K 2866, 18, between those of Gula and Rimmon. Perhaps it is connected etymologically with Lakhamun, the name of Zarpanit in Dilvun.

COSMOGONIES AND ASTRO-THEOLOGY. 389

the creation of the heavenly bodies, we may compare it with the work of the fourth day according to Genesis, more especially as the Assyrian poet assigns to the fourth tablet the overthrow of Tiamat and her hosts. It begins thus:

"(Anu) prepared the (seven) mansions of the great gods;
he fixed the stars, even the twin-stars, to correspond to them;
he ordained the year, appointing the signs of the Zodiac[1] over it;
for each of the twelve months he fixed three stars,
from the day when the year issues forth to the close.
He founded the mansion of the god of the ferry-boat (the Sun-god)
　that they might know their bonds,
that they might not err, that they might not go astray in any way.
He established the mansion of Mul-lil and Ea along with himself.
He opened also the great gates on either side,
the bolts he strengthened on the left hand and on the right,
and in their midst he made a staircase.
He illuminated the Moon-god that he might watch over the night,
and ordained for him the ending of the night that the day may be known,
(saying): 'Month by month, without break, keep watch (?) in thy disk;
at the beginning of the month kindle the night,
announcing (thy) horns that the heaven may know.
On the seventh day, (filling thy) disk,
thou shalt open indeed (its) narrow contraction.[2]
At that time the sun (will be) on the horizon of heaven at thy (rising).'"

The rest of the text is in too mutilated a condition to offer a connected sense, and we may therefore pass on to another fragment which perhaps belongs to the seventh tablet. At all events it records the creation of the animals. "At that time," it declares,

---

[1] *Mizrâta yumazzir.* Oppert and Schrader have misunderstood the expression. *Mizrâta* is the *mazzârôth* of Job xxxviii. 32.

[2] *Sutkhurat meskhir(râti sa pu-)u.*

"The gods in their assembly created (the beasts);
they made perfect the mighty (monsters);
they caused the living creatures of the (field) to come forth,
the cattle of the field, the wild beasts of the field, and the creeping things of the (field);
(they fixed their habitations) for the living creatures (of the field),
(and) adorned (the dwelling-places of) the cattle and creeping things of the city.
(They made strong) the multitude of creeping things, all the offspring (of the earth)."

The lines that follow are too much broken for translation; the only matter of remark which they contain is a statement put into the mouth of some deity that he had "destroyed the seed of Lakhama." Here, therefore, there seems to be a clear reference to the monstrous brood of chaos which the ancient cosmogony of Cutha regarded as the offspring of Tiamat. The place of Tiamat has been taken by the cosmological principle Lakhama, and the crude conceptions of an earlier day have been worked into the philosophical system of the later cosmology.

The Babylonian Genesis, then, it will be seen, is neither simple nor uniform. Its history forms a close parallel to the history of the Babylonian pantheon. Like the pantheon, it is essentially local in character; but the local elements have been combined eventually so as to form that great epic of the Creation whose fragments have come to us from the library of Nineveh. Local, however, as these elements were in their origin, they all agree in certain main particulars. In each case the watery abyss is the primary source of all things; in each case the present creation has been preceded by another. How far these common features are due to the comparative lateness of the documents from which we derive our information we cannot say. For my own part, I suspect that the legend of Cutha originally knew nothing of the sea-serpent Tiamat, the chaotic hosts of which it speaks having been the progeny of the mountains and not of the deep. But in its present form it agrees with all the other Babylonian cosmogonies that have been preserved, in making Tiamat their mother and nurse. The Babylonian of the historical period was firmly persuaded that in the ocean-stream that encircled the world lay the germs of the whole universe.

This belief stands in marked contrast to that prehistoric belief in a "mountain of the world" which survived only in mythology. No doubt the two conceptions could be reconciled by those who undertook the trouble; it was possible to hold that this mountain of the world was not the central shaft around which the earth and heavens were built, but merely the centre of the existing world. If this view was not generally taken, if in Babylonia, hard by the Persian Gulf, the world-mountain was allowed to drop out of sight, it must have been because the ideas associated with it did not readily combine with the cosmological theories of a later day. At any rate, the cosmologies of Babylonia, whatever might be the locality in which they were taught, were all based on the assumption that the watery abyss was the first of things.

This assumption agrees strikingly with the character of the Sumerian culture-god. Ea, the god of Eridu, Oannes who rose out of the Persian Gulf, was primarily a water-god. His home was in the deep; his mother was the watery abyss. We shall not go far wrong if we trace the fundamental doctrine of Chaldæan cosmology to Eridu and its worship of the deities of the deep. Eridu did not communicate to the rest of Babylonia only the seeds of culture or the adoration of Ea, the god of wisdom; it impressed upon all the cosmogonies of Babylonia the stamp of its own, and originated that view of the origin of the world which found its western prophet in the first of Hellenic philosophers. Like so much else that had its primal home in Shinar, it was carried westward to the shores of the Mediterranean. Phœnician cosmology also began with an abyss of waters in which the seeds of all things were begotten;[1] and even the Hebrew writer tells us that "in the beginning," before Elohim "carved out the heavens and the earth," "the earth had been waste and void, and darkness was upon the face of the deep."

It does not seem, however, that the belief in a provisional creation, in the existence of composite animals who perished when the present world came into being, can have emanated from Eridu. At Eridu the deep was not the representative of chaos and confusion; quite the contrary, it was a venerable divinity, the mother of Ea himself. So far, moreover, from the composite animals of mythology being subjects of abhorrence, Oannes, the god of culture, the god of pure life, as the inscriptions term him, was actually one of them. It was he who is described in the fragment of Bêrôssos as half-human, with the tail of a fish.

These composite creatures were really the offspring of totemism and the attempts of a later age to explain the figures which totemism had bequeathed to art and mytho-

---

[1] Euseb. *Præp. Evang.* i. 10; Damaskios, *De Prim. Princip.* 123, p. 381, ed. Kopp.

logy. A place had to be found for the colossal bulls with human heads and eagles' wings, for the hawk-headed cherubs who guarded the tree of life, for "the scorpion-men" who watched the sun at his rising and setting, or for the centaurs, half-man and half-horse, whose forms are engraved on Babylonian boundary-stones, and who passed over to the Greeks through Phœnician hands. Many of these, it is true, were beneficent beings, like the man-headed bulls; but the majority belonged to those spirits of the earth and air against whom the sorcerer-priest had prepared his spells. They had no place or portion in the existing order of the universe; when, therefore, Tiamat had become a cosmological principle, symbolised by the serpent or dragon and opposed to the gods of light, it was easy to banish them all to her domain and to regard her as their mother and nurse.

It may be that this was the work of the priests of Babylon. At any rate, Bel-Merodach is credited with having been their destroyer, as he was also the destroyer of Tiamat herself; and it is difficult to believe that this belief grew up anywhere else than in the city which owned Merodach as its lord. It is certainly noticeable that Bêrôssos refers to the images of the monsters painted in vermilion on the walls of the temple of Merodach when he is describing the strange creatures of the pre-human world.

In the epic of the Creation, whether or not it owes its existence, as I have suggested, to an Assyrian poet of the age of Assur-bani-pal, we may see the final unification of the varying cosmological legends of Babylonia. They are here combined and harmonised together; and though the whole is thrown into a mythological form, as befits the requirements of poetry, its spirit is unmistakably materialistic. In spite of the fragmentary condition in which it has come down to us, it is possible to guess at the order of its arrangement by comparing it with the first chapter of Genesis.

The first tablet or book was occupied with the cosmogony proper and the creation of the gods. The birth of the gods of light necessarily brought with it the creation of the light itself. This would have been followed by a second tablet, in which the creation of the firmament of heaven was described. The gods needed a habitation, and this was provided by the firmament of the sky. A mythological tablet, it will be remembered, states that "the heaven was created from the waters," before that "the god and goddess," or Ansar and Kisar, "created the earth," in exact agreement with the account in Genesis. Here, too, the firmament of the heaven is created out of the waters of the deep on the second day, dividing "the waters which were under the firmament from the waters which were above the firmament," while the earth does not emerge above the surface of the deep until the third day. It is therefore probable that the third tablet of the Assyro-Babylonian epic recounted the formation of the earth. Unlike the Biblical narrative, however, in place of the vegetable creation of the third day, it would seem to have interpolated here the appearance of the brood of chaos. The legend of Cutha declares that when the earth was peopled by them, there were as yet neither "bodies nor brushwood," neither the animal nor the vegetable world of to-day. However this may be, the fourth tablet recorded the great struggle between Merodach and Tiamat, of which no trace appears in the book of Genesis, though we seem to have allusions to a similar conflict in the spiritual world in other parts of the Bible. In Isaiah xxiv. 21, 22, we read "that the Lord shall visit the host of the high ones that are on high, and the kings of the earth upon the earth. And they shall be gathered together, as prisoners are gathered in the pit, and shall be shut up in prison;" while a well-known passage in the Apocalypse (xii. 7—9) tells how "there was war in heaven: Michael and his angels fought against the dragon; and the dragon fought and his angels, and prevailed not; neither was their place found any more in heaven. And the great dragon was cast out, that old serpent, called the Devil, and Satan." The fifth tablet, as we have seen, was concerned with the appointment of the heavenly bodies, the work of the fourth day in Genesis; the sixth probably related the creation of vegetables, birds and fish; and the seventh that of animals and mankind.[1] In two respects, therefore, the epic would have differed from the Biblical account: firstly, in the interpolation of the appearance of the monsters of chaos and of the combat between Merodach and the dragon; and secondly, in making the seventh day a day of work and not of rest.

The epic never succeeded wholly in supplanting what we may regard as the local legend of the Creation current at Babylon. Its cosmogony was indeed known to Da-

---

[1] A passage in one of the magical texts indicates that a similar view as to the creation of the woman from the man prevailed in Babylonia, to that which we read of in the book of Genesis. In W. A. I. iv. 1. i. 36, 37, it is said of the seven evil spirits: "the woman from the loins of the man they bring forth," in conformity with the Semitic belief which derived the woman from the man. This part of the magical text, at all events, must belong to the Semitic period.

maskios, and doubtless suited the philosophic conceptions of the Græco-Roman age far better than the older creation-stories of Babylonia; but it is ignored by Bêrôssos, who collected the materials of his narrative from the priests of Bel-Merodach at Babylon. As one of their order himself, he preferred to give their own version of the creation of the world, rather than a version which was less peculiarly Babylonian, however consonant the latter might be with the opinions of his Greek readers.

The contents of the fifth tablet introduce us to a side of Babylonian religion which occupied an important and prominent position, at all events in the official cult. At the beginning of the present century, writers upon the ancient East were fond of enlarging upon a Sabaistic system of faith which they supposed had once been the dominant form of religion in Western Asia. Star-worship was imagined to be the most primitive phase of Oriental religion, and the reference to it in the book of Job was eagerly seized upon as an evidence of the antiquity of the book. Dupuis resolved all human forms of faith into Zodiacal symbols, and Sir William Drummond went far in the same direction. That the first gods of the heathen were the planets and stars of heaven, was regarded by high authorities as an incontrovertible fact.

The plains of Shinar were held to be the earliest home of this Sabaism or star-worship. The astronomy and astrology of Babylonia had been celebrated even by Greek and Latin authors, and scholars were inclined to see in the "Chaldæan shepherds" the first observers of the heavens. The "astrologers, the star-gazers, the monthly prognosticators" of Babylon, are enumerated in the Old Testament (Is. xlvii. 13); and the small cylinders brought by travellers from Bagdad, with their frequent representations of a star or sun, seemed to leave no doubt that the deities of Babylonia were in truth the heavenly bodies. The decipherment of the cuneiform inscriptions has shown that the belief in Babylonian "Sabaism" was, after all, not altogether a chimæra.

Babylonia was really the cradle of astronomical observations. Long before the lofty *zigurráti* or "towers" of the temples were reared, where the royal astronomers had their stations and from whence they sent their reports to the king, the leading groups of stars had been named, a calendar had been formed, and the eclipses of the sun and moon had been noted and recorded. The annual path of the sun through the sky had been divided into twelve sections, like the twelve *kasbu* or double hours of the day, and each section had been distinguished by its chief constellation or star. It was thus that the Zodiac first came into existence. The names given to its constellations are not only Accadian, but they also go back to the totemistic age of Accadian faith. The first sign, the first constellation, was that of "the directing bull," so named from the solar bull who at the vernal equinox began to plough his straight furrow through the sky, directing thereby the course of the year. The last sign but one was "the fish of Ea;" while midway between the two, presiding over the month whose name was derived from its "facing the foundation" or "beginning" of the year, was the great star of the Scorpion. The fact that the year thus began with Taurus proves the antiquity of the Chaldæan Zodiac, and of the months of thirty days which corresponded to its several signs. From about B.C. 2500 and onwards, the precession of the equinoxes caused Aries, and not Taurus, to be the asterism into which the sun entered at spring-time; the period when Taurus ushered in the year reached back from that date to about B.C. 4700. The Zodiacal circle may therefore have been invented nearly a thousand years before Sargon of Accad was born; and that it was invented at an early epoch is demonstrated by its close connection with the Accadian calendar.

With the Semitic domination of Sargon of Accad, however, Babylonian astronomy entered upon a new phase. To him, tradition ascribed the compilation of the standard work on Babylonian astronomy and astrology called the "Observations of Bel," and afterwards translated into Greek by Bêrôssos. But the edition of the work which we possess presupposes a much later date. Aries, and not Taurus, marks the beginning of the year, and the text contains references to political and geographical facts, some of which are probably not much older than the age of Assur-bani-pal. This is explained by the nature of the work. It was not so much a treatise on astronomy, as on the pseudo-science that had been evolved out of the observations of astronomy. The Chaldæan priests had grasped but imperfectly the idea of causation; their fundamental assumption was "post hoc, ergo propter hoc;" when two events had been noticed to happen one after the other, the first was the cause of the second. Hence their anxiety to record the phenomena of the heavens and the occurrences that took place after each; if a war with Elam had followed an eclipse of the sun on a particular day, it was assumed that a recurrence of the eclipse on the same day would be followed by a recurrence of a war with Elam. In this way a science of astrology was created whose students could foretel the future by observing the signs of the sky.

It is obvious that a work whose object was to connect astronomical observations with current events must have been constantly undergoing alteration and growth. New observations would from time to time be introduced into it, sometimes causing confusion or even omissions in the text. There are instances in which we can detect the presence of observations placed side by side, though belonging to very different periods, or of older records which have been supplemented by the calculations of a later age.[1] In their present form, therefore, the "Observations of Bel" have to be used with caution if we would argue from them to the beliefs and practices of early Babylonia.

But the astrological science, or pseudo-science, which underlies the whole work, shows that even in its earliest form it was a product of the Semitic epoch. Between the attitude of mind presupposed by this pseudo-science, and the attitude of mind presupposed by the magical texts and Shamanistic cult of Sumerian Chaldæa, there lies an impassable gulf. According to the latter, events are brought about by the agency of the innumerable spirits of earth and air, and can be controlled by the spells and exorcisms of the sorcerer; according to the astrologer of Sargon's court, they are natural occurrences, caused and determined by other natural occurrences

---

[1] See the examination of the Venus-tablet (W. A. I. iii. 63), by Mr. Bosanquet and myself in the *Monthly Notices of the Royal Astronomical Society*, xl. 9, pp. 572, 578, where it is shown that a later scribe has interpolated a series of fabricated observations in the middle of an older and genuine record.

which can be discovered and noted by the observer. Out of the astrologer the astronomer could be born; between science and sorcery there can be only an eternal feud.

It does not follow, however, that the pre-Semitic population of Chaldæa took no notice of the phenomena of the sky. Unusual phenomena, such as an eclipse, must necessarily excite the attention of superstitious and half-civilised tribes; and the formation of a calendar, the invention of the Zodiac, and the naming of the principal constellations, show that a rudimentary astronomy was already in existence. Indeed, the "Observations of Bel" not only contain technical terms of Accadian origin, but embody notices of phenomena like eclipses which presuppose a long period of earlier observations. Unless such observations had existed, even the first compilation of the work would have been impossible. It was astrology, not the rudiments of astronomy, for which the Semites of Babylonia can claim the entire credit.

In the "Observations of Bel" the stars are already invested with a divine character. The planets are gods like the sun and moon, and the stars have already been identified with certain deities of the official pantheon, or else have been dedicated to them. The whole heaven, as well as the periods of the moon, has been divided between the three supreme divinities, Anu, Bel and Ea. In fact, there is an astro-theology, a system of Sabaism, as it would have been called half a century ago.

This astro-theology must go back to the very earliest times. The cuneiform characters alone are a proof of this. The common determinative of a deity is an eight-rayed star, a clear evidence that at the period when the cuneiform syllabary assumed the shape in which we know it, the stars were accounted divine. We have seen, moreover, that the sun and moon and evening star were objects of worship from a remote epoch, and the sacredness attached to them would naturally have been reflected upon the other heavenly bodies with which they were associated. Totemism, too, implies a worship of the stars. We find that primitive peoples confound them with animals, their automatic motions being apparently explicable by no other theory; and that primitive Chaldæa was no exception to this rule has been already pointed out. Here, too, the sun was an ox, the moon was a steer, and the planets were sheep. The adoration of the stars, like the adoration of the sun and moon, must have been a feature of the religion of primæval Shinar.

But this primæval adoration was something very different from the elaborate astro-theology of a later day. So elaborate, indeed, is it that we can hardly believe it to have been known beyond the circle of the learned classes. The stars in it became the symbols of the official deities. Nergal, for example, under his two names of Sar-nerra and 'Sulim-ta-ea, was identified with Jupiter and Mars.[1] It is not difficult to discover how this curious theological system arose. Its starting-point was the prominence given to the worship of the evening and morning stars in the ancient religion, and their subsequent transformation into the Semitic Istar. The other planets were already divine; and their identification with specific deities of the official cult followed as a matter of course. As the astronomy of Babylonia became more developed, as the heavens were mapped out into groups of constel-

---

[1] W. A. I. iii. 57, 52.

lations, each of which received a definite name, while the leading single stars were similarly distinguished and named, the stars and constellations followed the lead of the planets. As Mars became Nergal, so Orion became Tammuz.

The priest had succeeded the old Sumerian sorcerer, and was now transforming himself into an astrologer. To this cause we must trace the rise of Babylonian astro-theology and the deification of the stars of heaven. The Sabianism of the people of Harrân in the early centuries of the Christian era was no survival of a primitive faith, but the last echo of the priestly astro-theology of Babylonia. This astro-theology had been a purely artificial system, the knowledge of which, like the knowledge of astrology itself, was confined to the learned classes. It first grew up in the court of Sargon of Accad, but its completion cannot be earlier than the age of Khammuragas. In no other way can we explain the prominence given in it to Merodach, the god of Babylon.

But side by side with this "cunningly-devised" system of theology, the ancient cult of the stars—not as manifestations or symbols of the official gods, but as divine beings themselves—maintained itself not only among the multitude, but among the higher orders as well. The hemerology of the intercalary Elul, enumerating the feasts and fasts of the month and the religious services to be performed on each, states that the tenth day was sacred to the Lady of the Lower Firmament (Bilat-Ekur) and the divine judges of the starry sky, and that offerings and sacrifices should be made during the night of it to two particular stars.[1] Towards the

---

[1] W. A. I. iv. 32, 47.—50. See above, p. 72.

close of the Assyrian empire, we find an Assyrian scribe similarly laying down that the king should offer sacrifices "before the stars, before Assur, before Merodach," and other gods.[1] The stars, be it noticed, here take the first place, even before Assur, the god of Assyria, and Merodach, the god of Babylon, and hold the same rank as the colossal bulls and sacred rivers mentioned by the same author as objects of veneration.[2]

In a country which owed so much to its great rivers as Babylonia, we should naturally expect to find traces of river-worship. And such indeed is the case. But the rivers of Babylonia were not, like the Nile, the bringers of unmixed good. They might indeed be termed "the bearers of fertility," but their destructive floods needed curbing by dams and canals; and "the curse of rain" that descended on the land during the winter months made the rivers also curses instead of blessings. Hence it was that, by the side of the cult paid to the streams, and more especially to the supreme river-god, the divine Euphrates, in whom the people of Eridu had seen the features of Ea, there was a feeling of dread and fear, which prevented the cult from attaining its full development. Nevertheless, an old Accadian text declares that "the name of the man shall perish who destroys the body of a river;"[3] and a Semitic hymn, which is prefaced by the word *siptu*, "incantation," addresses the river (Euphrates?) in words of adoration and respect:[4]

---

[1] W. A. I. iii. 66, *Rev.* 12 *sq.*
[2] W. A. I. iii. 66, *Obv.* 30—33.
[3] W. A. I. ii. 17, 26, completed by Strassmaier.
[4] S 1704, *Rev.*

"Thou, O river, I have made thee![1]
At the time I dug thee, the great gods (were) on thy bank.
Ea, the king of the deep, has created blessings in thy heart.
He has presented his deluge before thee.
Fire, might, brilliance (and) terribleness
have Ea and Merodach presented unto thee.
Judgment (?) hast thou given mankind,
O mighty river, river supreme of limb.[2]
Grant me (to bathe in) the straight course of thy waters.
The (impurity) which is in my body to thy channel carry it, even to the channel.[3]
(Take) it, bear it down into thy stream.
(Deliver) me, and it shall not come nigh my altar.
(Purify) my sin that I may live.
May I glorify (that which the god) has created.
May I exalt (*ludlul*) (thy) spring (*enu*)."[4]

Side by side with this primitive worship of rivers and

---

[1] *Atti, nâru, ebusu kasum.*

[2] *Di(?)ni tenisêti tadin atti nâru rabiti, nâru tsiriti mesrêti.*

[3] *Sa ina zumri-ya basû* (KI-PUR =) *kibir-ki uri-su kibir-ki.*

[4] Here several lines are lost. The text becomes legible again in the fourth line of the obverse, from which it appears that the tablet contains charms against the bites of serpents. The lines which are legible read as follows:

"Save me (*suzibaninni*) from the venom of these serpents.
Myself and my house never may it destroy, never may it poison, never may it approach;
never may it overcome me; may it cross the river, may it pass over my life.
[Lacuna] pouring their poison into my body like the star-coloured bird (*tarri*).
May it mount to heaven like an arrow, pouring forth the *zikhi* of its mission.
May (the serpents), O lord, be far from my body.
May they depart . . . and let me glorify your LUL-GIR.
Let me exalt (*ludlul*) the making of your god, O Ea, Samas and Merodach."

The last line shows that we have here to do with a product of the school of Sippara, as the name of Samas is interpolated between the old god of healing spells and his ministering son.

springs, we find traces of a worship of the mountains. But this worship belonged rather to the days when the early colonists of Chaldæa had not as yet descended from the mountains of the East, and its traces are a survival, assisted perhaps by the conquest of the country in the historical epoch by the Kossæan highlanders. At any rate, in Babylonia itself the primitive cult of the mountains could be carried on only artificially. The sacred mountains of the plain were the mounds which marked the sites of ancient temples, or the towers which rose within them in order that the priest might continue on their summits that close communion with heaven which he had once enjoyed on the high places of the mountaintops. In the story of the Deluge, the mountain peak of Nizir, where the rescued hero of the legend built his altar and poured out his offerings, is called a *ziggurrat*, or temple-tower. Conversely, "the mountain of the world" was the name given to a temple at Calah; and the mountain of 'Sabu, to which the god Zu took his flight, was Kharsak-kalama, "the mountain of mankind," an artificial mound near Kis. The most famous of these sacred tels or mounds, however, was the famous *tilu ellu*, "the illustrious mound," at Borsippa, now represented by the Birs-i-Nimrud. Nebo, to whom the great temple of Borsippa was dedicated, is called its god (W. A. I. ii. 54, 71). One of "the three great" or secret "names of Anu" was that of "the lord who issues forth from the illustrious mound" (W. A. I. iii. 68, 19), in reference to the fact that the Accadian prototype of Nebo was once the universe itself, in which the seven spheres of light were set, and around which the ocean-stream wound like a rope or serpent. When the old god of Borsippa had passed into the Semitic Nebo, the attributes which had formerly connected him with the firmament of heaven were transferred to Anu, the sky-god of the official cult.

A fragmentary tablet, which gives us, as I believe, the Babylonian version of the building of the tower of Babel, expressly identifies it with "the illustrious mound." Here we are told of the leader of the rebellion that when "the thought of his heart was hostile" and he "had wronged the father of all the gods," when "he was hurrying to seize Babylon," and "small and great were mingling the mound," "the divine king of the illustrious mound" intervened, " Anu lifted up (his hand) in front" and prayed "to his father the lord of the firmament." "All day long he troubled" them; "as they lamented on their couch he ended not" their "distress." "In his wrath he overthrows (their) secret counsel; in his (fury) he set his face to mingle (their) designs; he gave the command (?), he made strange their plan."[1] The very word that the Hebrew writer uses in order to explain the origin of the name of Babylon, and which the Authorised Version translates "confound," is here employed of those who "mingled together" the mound, and whose designs were afterwards themselves "mingled" by the god of heaven.

"The illustrious mound" was known as far back as the time when the months of the Accadian year were named. The month which corresponded to the Semitic Tasrit or Tisri, and our September, was "the month of the illustrious mound." It would seem, therefore, that legend had referred the attempt to build the tower whose

---

[1] The text has been published by Mr. Boscawen in the *Transactions of the Society of Biblical Archæology*, v. 1.

head should reach to heaven to the autumnal equinox; at any rate, it is clear that the mound of Borsippa was not only in existence, but was already in a state of ruin when the Accadian calendar was first drawn up.

The sacred mounds of Babylonia, in fact, like the Gilgals of Palestine, appear to have been the sites of older structures which had long fallen into decay, and around which fancy and tradition were allowed to play freely. They had in this way become veritable hills— tumuli, as we should term them in our modern archæological vocabulary—and as such deserved the venerable title of *sadu*, or "mountain." New temples like that of "the mountain of the world" could be named after them, but this did not imply a recollection that the sacred mounds had once been temples themselves. They were rather, like the mountains of the eastern frontier, the everlasting altars of the gods, on whose summits worship could most fittingly be paid to the deities of heaven. And, like the mountains, they were something more than altars; they were themselves divine, the visible habitations of the spirits of the air. It is possible that Prof. Friedrich Delitzsch is right in proposing to see in the Assyrian *sadu*, or "mountain," the explanation of the Hebrew title of the Deity, El Shaddai.[1] At all events, God is compared to a rock in the Old Testament (Deut. xxxii. 15, Ps. xviii. 2), and the worship of sacred stones was widely spread through the Semitic world.

---

[1] Mul-lil is called *kur-gal*, *sadû rabû* in Semitic, "the great mountain," W. A. I. iv. 18, 15; 23, 30; and in v. 44, 41, "the god Kur-gal" is rendered by Bel. In the list of Babylonian kings in which the meaning of their names is explained, the Accadian E-Guzi-kharsag-men is interpreted Ê-Saggil-saddu-ni, " Ê-Saggil is our mountain."

Between the sacred mounds of Babylonia, however, and the sacred stones of Semitic faith, there was a wide difference, answering to a difference in the minds of the two races to whom these separate cults belonged. The sacred stone was a Beth-el, or "house of god;" no habitation of a mere spirit, but the dwelling-place of deity itself. Its sanctity was not inherent; it was sacred because it had been transformed into an altar by the oil that was poured out upon it in libation, or the priest who was consecrated to its service. The worship of these sacred stones was common to all the branches of the Semitic family. The famous black stone of the Kaaba at Mecca is a standing witness of the fact. So firmly rooted was the belief in its divine character among the Arabs of Mohammed's day that he was unable to eradicate it, but was forced to make a compromise with the old faith by attaching to the stone the traditions of the Old Testament. The black stone, though more sacred than any others, did not stand alone. All around Mecca there were similar stones, termed *Anzab*, three of which may still be seen, according to Mr. Doughty, at the gates of the city, where they go by the names of Hobbal, Lâta and Uzza. Northward of Mecca, at Medain-Saleh, the burial-place of the ancient kingdom of the Nabathæans, Mr. Doughty has discovered niches in the rock containing sacred stones. Above one of them is an inscription which shows that the stone was the symbol or habitation of the god Auda (or Aera): "This is the place of prayer which Seruh the son of Tuka has erected to Auda of Bostra, the great god, in the month Nisan of the first year of king Malkhos." Within the last few years, bas-reliefs have been found in Sicily and Tunisia representing persons in the act of adoration before a small triad of stone. We are here on Phœnician territory, and it is not strange therefore that classical writers should speak of the Βαίτυλοι or Beth-els, the meteoric stones which had fallen from heaven like "the image" of Artemis at Ephesos, and were accordingly honoured by the Phœnicians. In the mythology of Byblos, Heaven and Earth were said to have had four sons, Ilos or El, Bêtylos or Beth-el, Dagon and Atlas; and the god of heaven was further declared to have invented the Baityli, making of them living stones.[1] Bethuel is connected with Aram in the Old Testament (Gen. xxii. 21, 22); and we all remember how, on his way to Haran, Jacob awakened out of sleep, saying, "Surely the Lord is in this place," and "took the stone that he had put for his pillows, and set it up for a pillar, and poured oil upon the top of it, and called the name of that place Beth-el." In Palestine, however, the Beth-els were arranged in a circle or Gilgal, rather than singly; the isolated monuments were the cones of stone or the bare tree-trunks which symbolised Ashêrah, the goddess of fertility, and Baal the Sun-god. The sun-pillars and the *ashêrim* meet with frequent mention in the Biblical records; and we may gain some idea as to what the latter were like from the pictures we have on coins and gems of the famous conical stone that stood within the holy of holies in the temple of the Paphian Aphroditê, as well as from the description given of it by Tacitus.[2] On a gem

---

[1] Euseb. *Præp. Evang.* i. 10. Halévy's arguments against the identification of Baitylos and the Beth-el amount to very little.

[2] *Hist.* ii. 2 : "Simulacrum deæ non effigie humana, continuus orbis latiore initio tenuem in ambitum metæ modo exsurgens."

in the British Museum, Sin, "the god of Harran," is represented by a stone of the same shape surmounted by a star. The "pillars of the Sun" were also stones of a like form. When the Phœnician temple in the island of Gozo, whose ruins are known as the Temple of the Giants, was excavated, two such columns of stone were found, planted in the ground, one of which still remains *in situ*. We cannot forget that even in Solomon's temple, built as it was by Phœnician workmen, there were two columns of stone, Boaz and Yakin, set on either side of the porch (1 Kings vii. 21), like the two columns of gold and emerald glass which Herodotos saw in the temple of Melkarth at Tyre (Herodt. ii. 44).

The sacred stones which were thus worshipped in Arabia, in Phœnicia and in Syria, were worshipped also among the Semites of Babylonia. There is a curious reference to the consecration of a Beth-el in the Epic of Gisdhubar. When the hero had been dismissed by the Chaldæan Noah, and his sickness had been carried away by the waters of the sea, we are told that "he bound together heavy stones," and after taking an animal for sacrifice, "poured over it a homer" in libation. He then commenced his homeward voyage up the Euphrates, having thus secured the goodwill of heaven for his undertaking.[1]

---

[1] W. A. I. iv. 51, v. 52. vi. 1—4. The stones or *ashêrim* which had thus been consecrated by oil being poured over them, are frequently mentioned in the Babylonian and Assyrian inscriptions under the name of *kisalli*. *Kisallu* is a word borrowed from the Accadian *ki-zal*, "place of oil" or "anointing," and represented the "altar," so often depicted on Assyrian gems and bas-reliefs, which consisted of an upright post or column, sometimes with an extinguisher-like top. A good representation of three of these columns, of different forms, will be seen on a Phœni-

The homeward voyage of the Chaldæan hero is a reminder that we, too, have finished our survey of Babylonian religion, so far as our present knowledge of it will allow. Two facts in regard to it stand prominently forth; its essentially local character, and its hybrid origin. We cannot understand even its most elementary features unless we bear in mind that it is the product of different races and different political systems. In detail, indeed, it may not always be easy to distinguish between Accadian and Semitic, or between the gods of Eridu and the gods of Babylon; but the main outlines of the picture are clear and distinct, and any attempt to obliterate or forget them will lead only to confusion and error. That the materials are still wanting for a complete history of the rise and development of Babylonian religion, I am only too well aware; but where completeness is unattainable, even an imperfect sketch has its merits and value. And the importance of Babylonian religion to the student of theology need not be pointed out. Apart from its general interest in illustrating the history of religion among one of the few races of mankind who have been the pioneers of civilisation, it has a special interest from its bearing on the faiths of Western Asia, and more especially on that of the people of Israel. If I have not more frequently drawn attention to the latter, it has been due to my desire to keep faithfully to the subject of my Lectures. I have undertaken to treat of Babylonian religion only, not of Semitic religion in general. For such

---

cian gem procured by Dr. Hayes Ward at Bagdad, and published by him in the *American Journal of Archæology*, June 1886, p. 156. They correspond to the "sun-pillars" and *ashêrim*, or symbols of the goddess Asherah, so frequently alluded to in the Old Testament.

a task there are others far more competent than myself; great Arabic or Syriac or Hebrew scholars, who have devoted their lives to the study of one or more of these better-known Semitic tongues. My own studies have of late years lain more and more in the ever-widening circle of Assyrian research; here there is enough, and more than enough, to fill the whole time and absorb the whole energies of the worker; and he must be content to confine himself to his own subject, and by honest labour therein to accumulate the facts which others more fortunate than he may hereafter combine and utilise. This is the day of specialists; the increased application of the scientific method and the rapid progress of discovery have made it difficult to do more than note and put together the facts that are constantly crowding one upon the other in a special branch of research. The time may come again—nay, will come again—when once more the ever-flowing stream of discovery will be checked, and famous scholars and thinkers will arise to reap the harvest that we have sown. Meanwhile I claim only to be one of the humble labourers of our own busy age, who have done my best to set before you the facts and theories we may glean from the broken sherds of Nineveh, so far as they bear upon the religion of the ancient Babylonians. It is for others, whose studies have taken a wider range, to make use of the materials I have endeavoured to collect, and to discover in them, if they can, guides and beacons towards a purer form of faith than that which can be found in the official creeds of our modern world.

APPENDIX.

APPENDIX.

I.

The primitive language and population of Chaldæa have excited so much discussion, and the views held on the subject by Assyriologists have undergone so much modification as their knowledge of the inscriptions has become more extensive and exact, that it is necessary for me to state precisely the conclusions to which, as it seems to me, the evidence now at our disposal would lead us. Others besides Assyrian students are probably aware that the question has aroused more than one fierce controversy; every step in advance has been gained after a good deal of fighting; and not only the name and relationship of the pre-Semitic language of Babylonia, but its priority to the Semitic Babylonian and even its very existence, have been made the subjects of animated discussion. The discussion, it is true, has usually been the result of misunderstandings and errors, of hasty conclusions and misinterpreted facts; but in this respect it has not differed widely from most other discussions in science or theology.

The decipherment of the Assyrian inscriptions had not proceeded far before it became clear that the Assyrian syllabary was not of Semitic origin. This, at least, seemed to the first decipherers the most natural way of accounting for the curious fact that the characters possessed phonetic values which did not correspond to the Semitic words represented by the same characters when used ideographically. The character which denoted "a head," for example, not only possessed the Semitic value of *ris*, but also the non-Semitic value of *sag*. Moreover, the syllabary expressed very imperfectly the sounds of a Semitic language. The distinctive Semitic sounds of *ayin*, *têth* and *tsaddê*, were wanting in it, or else represented defectively. In place of the clear pronunciation of the consonants which distinguishes a Semitic idiom, it was found that surds and sonants were confounded together at the end of a syllable. It appeared evident, therefore, that the syllabary, the pictorial origin of which was soon recognised, must have been invented by a non-Semitic people, and handed on by them to the Semitic populations who inhabited the valleys of the Tigris and Euphrates during the historical period. Dr. Hincks proposed the name of "Accadian" for the old language and its speakers, and Dr. Oppert believed that he saw in it marks of relationship to the languages of the "Turanian" or Ural-Altaic family.

It was not long before this view of the origin of the Assyrian syllabary appeared to find a verification, partly in the discovery of early Babylonian inscriptions written by means of it in a non-Semitic idiom, partly in the "bilingual texts" of Assur-bani-pal's library, in which the words and documents of the old idiom were interpreted by interlinear or parallel translations in Semitic Assyrian. All that remained was to analyse the words and forms of the old language—no easy task, however, when it is remembered that they are for the most part written ideographically, and not phonetically. Dr. Oppert's first essays in this direction were followed by an article of mine in the *Journal of Philology* for 1870, in which I endeavoured to give the first fairly complete sketch of "Accadian" grammar. Three years later this was systematised and extended by the brilliant and inexhaustible pen of François Lenormant.

Dr. Oppert objected to the term "Accadian," which had been adopted from Dr. Hincks by Lenormant, Delitzsch and myself, and proposed instead of it the term "Sumerian." From an early epoch Chaldæa had been divided into two main divisions, called respectively Accad and Sumer; and the monarchs who claimed sovereignty over the whole country entitled themselves accordingly "kings of Sumer and Accad," in contradistinction to those who could claim to be rulers of "the land of Accad" only.[1] To Dr. Haigh belongs the credit of first pointing out that Sumer is the Shinar of the Old Testament;[2] while George Smith, with his usual divinatory instinct, perceived that it must represent southern Babylonia, Accad being the district round the capital city of Accad, or Agadê (formerly read Aganê). George Smith's views, however, were not at first adopted by other Assyriologists, and

---

[1] *Kengi Agade*, misinterpreted in later days to mean "Sumer and Accad."

[2] Halévy's "Rabbinical" etymology of Shinar does not require refutation. Already in Gen. xi. 2, the name of Shinar has been extended to denote the whole of Babylonia, as in Daniel and Zech. v. 11, just as in Micah v. 6, the dominion of Nimrod seems to be extended to Assyria; but in Gen. x. 10, the name is still confined to southern Babylonia, and is therefore used to indicate the southern position of Calneh.

APPENDIX I.

it is only within the last three or four years that newly-found inscriptions have shown them to be correct.

The arguments by which Dr. Oppert supported his proposal were not convincing, and for some time he secured no converts. But the researches of Professor Paul Haupt, one of the ablest and best-trained of the younger band of Assyriologists, threw an entirely new light on the matter. I had noticed (in 1874) the existence of more than one dialect in Proto-Chaldæan, and in a paper on Accadian Phonology (in 1877) had tried to show that our "Accadian" texts contain newer as well as older forms, and that many of them are composed in a language which exhibits all the signs of long decay; but it was reserved for Prof. Haupt to demonstrate scientifically that there were two clearly-marked dialects of Accadian, and to point out the principal characteristics of each. He assumed that the standard dialect, that which preserved the old language in its purest and most archaic form, was the dialect of Accad or northern Babylonia; the second dialect, which he regarded as standing to the other in the relation of a daughter or a younger sister, being the dialect of Sumer or the south. My own view had originally been the converse of this, but Prof. Haupt's arguments brought me over to his side. Subsequently, however, his assumption was attacked by Dr. Hommel; and after a considerable amount of hesitation, I have arrived at the conviction that Dr. Hommel is right.

"The dialect" which Prof. Haupt would make Sumerian and Dr. Hommel Accadian, exhibits the language of early Chaldæa in a decayed and degenerated form. It is largely affected by Semitic influence; not only has it adopted Semitic words, but Semitic idioms as well. These Semitisms, moreover, are partly popular, partly literary in origin; some of them, that is, are manifestly the introductions of a learned class who have imported them into Proto-Chaldæan much in the same way as Greek terms have been imported into English by men of science, or French expressions by *littérateurs*. Now it was in northern Babylonia, and not in the south, that Semitic influence and Semitic supremacy first made themselves felt. It was at Accad that the earliest Semitic empire, that of Sargon, first grew up, and it was there that the first Semitic library was founded under the patronage of a Semitic monarch. Sumer continued much longer under Proto-Chaldæan rule; and it is possible, if not probable, that one or more Proto-Chaldæan dialects continued to be spoken in Sumer down to the days of Nebuchadnezzar himself.

Whether the Semitic name of Accad is derived from the Proto-Chaldæan Agadê, or the Proto-Chaldæan Agadê from the Semitic Accad, we do not know; but it is certain that the importance of the city dates only from the Semitic epoch of Babylonia. The name is represented by a compound ideograph (BUR-BUR) which signifies "a mound," and a gloss informs us that this ideograph was pronounced *tilla*.[1] Sir Henry Rawlinson saw in *tilla* a derivative from *elû*, "to ascend," with the signification of "high-lands;" and I formerly believed that support for this view could be found in the word Accad itself, which I connected with a supposed Proto-Chaldæan *aka*, "to lift up." But this belief was entirely wrong. Accad has nothing to do with *aka*, which means "to love," and *tilla* is the common Assyrian *tillu*, "a *tel*." It signifies the mound on which a city or temple stood, as well as the mound formed by the *débris* of a ruined town. Accad was therefore known as *Tilla*, either because it stood on the site of an earlier pre-Semitic city, or because of the lofty artificial platform on which it was built.

The compound ideograph to which the pronunciation of Tilla was attached was applied by Sargon to the country of Ararat or Armenia. This may have been due to a simple confusion of two geographical names which had nothing to do with one another. In the tablet which gives us the name of Tilla, and which appears to have been intended to explain difficult words in texts emanating from the library of Accad, Tilla is interpreted to mean Urdhu. Since the Euphrates at Sippara was termed the Urudtuv, or "river of bronze" (from the Proto-Chaldæan *urud*, "bronze"[2]), it seems probable that Urdhu is a Semitised form of Urud, a name which we may suppose to have been given to Sippara or Accad and the surrounding district in consequence of the bronze with which their edifices were adorned. The resemblance of Urdhu to Urardhu or Ararat, the Assyrian designation of Armenia, may have led the Assyrian king to transfer an ideograph which properly denoted the north of Babylonia to the mountainous land of Armenia.

However this may be, Dr. Hommel has, I believe, made it clear that the texts whose primitive home can be shown to have been Sumer are in the older and standard Proto-Chaldæan dialect, while those which display a later and more Semitised phase of the language belong primarily to Accad. At the same time, it must not be forgotten that the priests of Accad not unfrequently attempted to write in the archaic and revered language of Sumer; while, on the other hand, texts which originated in Sumer have undergone such extensive modifi-

---

[1] W. A. I. ii. 48, 13.   [2] W. A. I. ii. 48, 47.

cations by repeated revision as to be overlaid with the characteristics of the northern dialect. It is also not impossible that changes similar to those undergone by the old language in Accad may at a later time have overtaken the dialect of the south, so that phonetic peculiarities, which seem to us to belong to Accad, may really belong to the language of Sumer in a later stage of decay.

I must here diverge for a moment in order to emphasise the fact that very few of the earlier texts of Sumer and Accad have come down to us in their original form. With the exception of the contemporaneous inscriptions of the kings of Tel-loh or Mugheir, and perhaps also of the hymns to the Sun-god of Sippara, which were composed in literary "Accadian" at a time when the old language had long become extinct, the earlier literature of Chaldæa has been subjected to alterations and modifications of the most extensive kind. Documents of different age and origin have been pieced together; words, lines, and even whole passages have been freely interpolated; glosses have crept into the text from the margin; the language has been modernised again and again; and the errors of copyists, intentional or unconscious, have made their way into the text. The corruption of the text has been further increased by the imperfect acquaintance of many of the later editors with the pre-Semitic dialects of Chaldæa. This has been a frequent cause of error, and in one case at least has resulted in macaronic verses, the Semitic portion of which has no real connection with the Sumerian.[1] It is true that the scribes were assisted in understanding the earlier texts by commentaries, in which explanations were given of the more difficult words and ideographs; but the explanations of the commentators were not always correct, while the commentaries or so-called "bilingual lists" have themselves suffered from the mistakes and ignorance of later editors. The scrupulous care with which the scribes of Assur-bani-pal copied the tablets brought from Babylonia, noting the places where there was "a lacuna" (*khibi*) or "a recent lacuna" (*khibi essu*), giving alternative characters where the scribe was uncertain as to the Assyrian character to which the Babylonian original corresponded, and at times frankly confessing the inability of the copyist to understand his copy (*ul idi*, "I do not know"), was a growth of comparatively modern date. The Babylonian scribes may have shown the same carefulness for a few centuries before the age of Assur-bani-pal, and efforts may have been made to secure the accurate reproduction of the religious texts as soon as they acquired

---

[1] See above, p. 80.

a sacred character; but for at least two thousand years after the era of Sargon of Accad all the causes of corruption above enumerated were freely at work, and it was just during this period that the larger part of the Babylonian literature we possess assumed its present form. The only wonder is that the non-Semitic portion of it should have been handed down as correctly as it is. It was probably in the time of Khammuragas (B.C. 2300) that the main bulk of it came into existence. There seems to have been a literary revival at that period, not unlike the literary revival in Wales in the 12th and 13th centuries. A considerable number of the older commentaries were probably composed at the time; at all events, the Epic of Gisdhubar and other similar works are in all likelihood to be referred to this date. Under Khammuragas, Babylon became the dominant state in Babylonia, and absorbed the older fame of the Semitic empire at Accad and Sippara; hence it is that the list of Babylonian dynasties begins with the dynasty of Khammuragas, and that while the antediluvian kings of Bêrôssos belong for the most part to Larankha or Surippak, the near neighbour of Accad, the first of them, Alôros, is made a native of Babylon.

But behind the Semitic legends of Accad and Babylon, as may be seen from the foregoing Lectures, lie older non-Semitic legends which speak of the origin of culture and civilisation in Chaldæa. These legends describe it as beginning on the shores of the Persian Gulf and working its way to the cities of the north. This is in complete harmony with what we have found to be the evidence of the native inscriptions. Eridu, the primæval capital of the south, was the first home of the god of culture and healing, and it is with Eridu and its deities that the oldest religious texts are intimately associated. As these texts are in the standard dialect, it would follow that Dr. Hommel is right in regarding it as the dialect of Sumer.

But yet more. The cuneiform system of writing was at the outset pictorial, and its earliest documents would therefore be mainly written with ideographs, and not with phonetic signs. Now this is one of the peculiarities which distinguish the texts of the standard dialect from those composed in the second dialect, and consequently justifies us in assigning them to Eridu and the surrounding district. If once we assume that the standard dialect is that of Sumer, and the secondary dialect that of Accad, everything falls naturally into its place.

The so-called "bilingual lists" sometimes qualify a word or form belonging to the secondary or Accadian dialect by a couple of ideographs which literally mean "the language of woman." This " woman's language" has been supposed to have a grammatical reference, denoting perhaps what we should call a "weak form;" but though grammatical terms were certainly used by the compilers of the lists, it is only those of a more obvious character, such as "singular" and "plural," "masculine" and "feminine;" and I prefer to see in the expression, "woman's language," a reference to one of those numerous cases in which the language of the women and the nursery is distinguished from that of the men. In northern Babylonia, where Semites and non-Semites intermingled from an early period, there would have been reasons in plenty for such an appellation. Semitic wives would not have spoken Sumerian with the same purity as their non-Semitic husbands; while, on the other hand, the dialect of the Sumerian wife would have been regarded by her Semitic husband as essentially a feminine idiom.[1]

That more than one dialect prevailed in Chaldæa before its complete occupation by the Semites, is not only necessary from the nature of things, but is also borne out by facts. Besides the two main dialects of Sumer and Accad, our texts, in spite of the corruption they have suffered, permit us to recognise other sub-dialects, among which may be noted the dialects of Sippara and Eridu. To these must be added the literary dialect which probably grew up in the court of Sargon of Accad, and is distinguished by its incorporation of Semitic words and idioms, as well as by its mixture of archaic and more modern non-Semitic forms. An indication of its date may be found in the Semitic loan-word *gabiri*, "a mountain" (Arabic *jebel*),[2] which had ceased to be used in Assyro-Babylonian long before the age of Khammuragas. Corresponding with this literary Accadian was the literary Assyro-Babylonian whose beginnings also go back to the era of Sargon of Accad. While the language of Accadian literature borrowed Semitic words and expressions, the language of Semitic literature borrowed from Accadian. Where the scribes were either Semites who had learnt Accadian, or else Accadians who had learnt Semitic, this was only

---

[1] The ideographic designation of Sumer in late Assyrian inscriptions, EME-KU, is probably an example of what Halévy has happily termed a rebus, and should be read *emequ—emgu* in Babylonian—that is, "wise" or "secret," in reference to the fact that the old language of Sumer was chiefly employed in later days in the composition of spells. KU was chosen instead of QU, partly because of its resemblance in sound to the Sumerian *kua*, "an oracle," partly because the similarity of the Semitic *asabu*, "to sit," to *asapu*, "to divine," had given the Sumerian *ku*, "to sit," the further signification of "soothsaying."

[2] W. A. I. ii. 50, 56.

natural; and since Chaldæan culture and writing were of Sumerian origin, while most of the religious and other texts were composed in the Sumerian language, it was inevitable that the amount of borrowing on the Semitic side was greater than that on the Accadian side. The technical terms of Sumerian science, or pseudo-science, whether this dealt with magic or with astrology, were introduced into Semitic documents, and the Semitic vocabulary was enriched with words like *asakku*, "fever," and *ribanna*, "a conjunction." As time went on, it seems to have become more and more fashionable to import Accadian or Sumerian words into literary Babylonian, and an imperfect knowledge of the old language not unfrequently assigned to these words a wrong form or a wrong meaning. The most curious errors, however, on the part of the borrowers were caused by the ideographic character of the script. When the cuneiform system of writing was first learned by the Semites, it was still in process of formation. Its pictorial origin was still remembered, and the Semitic scribes considered themselves at liberty not only to create new ideographs by combining two or more together, but even to invent ideographs for which there was no precedent in the Sumerian syllabary. New phonetic values were introduced, derived from the Semitic words which expressed the meaning of the several ideographs, and the characters received new ideographic significations due to the similarity of two Semitic roots, one of which only was the real representative of the ideograph in question. As the second root was often translated back into Accado-Sumerian, and the Accado-Sumerian word so obtained was sometimes used as a phonetic value of the ideograph, the Accado-Sumerian texts which originated under Semitic influence came to be filled with a strange medley of Sumerian and Semitic.

It was in the Semitic texts, however, that literary affectation was carried to the greatest lengths. In the more modern epoch of cuneiform writing, when the dialect of literature and the dialect of every-day life had come to stand more and more apart, the learning of the scribes was displayed in an almost Kabbalistic play upon the characters of the syllabary. Not content with borrowing words and phrases from the Sumerian literature, which had now entered upon a stage analogous to that of monkish Latin, they read the ideographs phonetically, and then imported them bodily into the inscriptions of the Semitic kings. Thus the Sumerians had a word *śur*, signifying "a table of shewbread," and represented by the two ideographs KI-GAL; literally "great place;" and we actually find this KI-GAL, under the Semitic form of *kigallu*, used in the inscriptions of Nebuchadnezzar and his successors, and interpreted to mean "a platform." A large number, however, of these far-fetched and erroneous forms are to be found only in the so-called "bilingual lists," and it is probable that they never made their way into any actual text. The compiler of one of these lists was proud of showing his erudition by heaping words together which only the initiated could understand.

But of course it was not the artificial literary Semitic dialect alone that was indebted to the Sumerian for the enrichment of its vocabulary. Two languages cannot be in contact one with another without mutual borrowing, and the more cultivated language is the one which usually gives more than it takes. The existence of the Sumerian language, therefore, postulates not only a large number of Sumerian loan-words in the Assyro-Babylonian of daily intercourse, but also, as students of the science of language know well, a certain amount of influence upon its structure and grammar. Thus I have long believed that the distinction made in Assyro-Babylonian between the present *asakkin* and the aorist *askun*—a distinction so contrary to the ordinary character of the Semitic verb—is due to the influence of the Sumerian, which possessed a real verb with a present and an aorist; and it is difficult to explain in any other way the order of the Assyro-Babylonian sentence which followed the Sumerian in placing the verb at the end, thus setting at defiance the primary law of Semitic structure. Equally instructive is the comparatively little use made by Assyro-Babylonian of the permansive, which answers to the perfect of the other Semitic tongues. The Semitic perfect could flourish only where the verb expressed condition and not time; a language which had developed real tenses with a temporal signification had but slight need of its employment. In fact, if he did not already know of the existence of Sumerian, the comparative grammarian, like the discoverers of the planet Uranus, would have to presuppose it.

The same would also be the case with the comparative philologist who undertook an examination of the Assyro-Babylonian vocabulary. Not only the literary dialect, but the spoken language as well, contained an enormous number of words, of which we seek in vain for any satisfactory representatives in the other Semitic languages. Now it is a commonplace of scientific philology that when we come across a large residuum of words in a language for which we can find no allied words in the other languages of the same family of speech, we must conclude that a considerable proportion of them have been borrowed from elsewhere. In Greek, Mr. Wharton has shown that, besides 641 words whose foreign origin can be traced, there are about 520 which seem to have no Indo-European etymology, and presumably, therefore, come for the most part from a foreign source ;[1] and what is true of Greek is true also of Semitic Babylonian. The roots preserved by one member of a linguistic family and lost by all its sisters can never be very numerous; the roots—or words—which it has invented are fewer still ; and hence the long list of words peculiar to Assyro-Babylonian points with an unerring hand to borrowing from a foreign source. If we would feel the full force of the argument, we must compare Assyro-Babylonian with Hebrew, to which it bears so close a relationship. The words peculiar to Hebrew, and probably for the most part of foreign extraction, like *har*, "a mountain," are in the proportion of only one to ten when compared with the words peculiar to the language of Semitic Babylonia used, so far as we can judge, in the daily intercourse of the people. Many of the latter we know to be derived from Sumerian, and it is therefore probable that as our knowledge of Sumerian increases we shall find many more which have had the same origin. At the same time it must not be supposed that Sumerian was the only foreign tongue upon which the Semites of Babylonia levied their contributions. At one period or another they were in contact with Elamites, Kossæans, Sutians and the like, and it is only reasonable to conclude that they borrowed something from each. We know, indeed, that they adopted certain of the Elamite and Kossæan deities, and those who adopt deities are likely to adopt other things as well. No Semitic parallel has yet been pointed out for the common Assyro-Babylonian verb *kasadu*, "to possess ;" it is equally difficult to discover for it a Sumerian derivation ; may it not then be a word, not evolved out of the inner consciousness of the Babylonians, nor preserved by them while forgotten by their Semitic brethren, but taken from the language of one of their numerous neighbours ?

There are two facts which make it specially difficult to determine whether a given word peculiar to Assyro-Babylonian, but not discoverable in Sumerian, is really a loan-word or not. The first is our uncertainty as to the primitive home of the speakers of the Semitic parent-speech before its separation into the languages of the north and the south. If, as I believe, this home was in the desert on the western side of the Euphrates, in the immediate proximity of the Sumerian kingdoms of Chaldæa, the parent-speech itself would have been in contact with Sumerian long before one of its dialects developed into the Semitic language of Babylonia, and we should therefore expect to

---

[1] *Etyma Græca*, p. vi.

find traces of Sumerian influence not only in the Semitic languages of the north—Assyro-Babylonian, Phœniko-Hebrew and Aramæan—but in the Semitic languages of the south as well. The second fact is the want of any early monuments of Semitic speech except those composed in the dialects of Babylonia and Assyria. The next oldest monuments are in Phœnician and Hebrew; but the Phœnicians and Hebrews, according to their own traditions, had migrated from Babylonia, and a large part of the literature of the Old Testament belongs to the period of the Babylonish Captivity. We know nothing of Arabic before the fifth century of the Christian era; and who can tell the extent to which it had already been influenced by the Aramaic dialects which had themselves been so long in contact with Babylonia? For these reasons it is somewhat rash to conclude, with Dr. Zimmern, that the occurrence of the same phrase or idiom in an Accadian and a Semitic text necessarily proves that the Accadian text has been composed under Semitic influence. The rashness, indeed, is paralleled by the same scholar's assertion that the interjections *ua* and *â* have been introduced into an Accadian text from Semitic Babylonia. As Professor Friedrich Delitzsch remarks, interjections are much the same all over the world.[1]

But Professor Delitzsch has himself put forward statements which make one wish that Assyriologists would submit to a training in scientific philology. His conception of a root is still that of Ibn Khayyuj, if we may judge from his assertion that the Semitic word for "mother" is derived from the idea of "spaciousness;"[2] and his opinion that the word *ad*, in the sense of "father," is of Semitic origin, is a greater crime against linguistic science than Dr. Zimmern's belief in the peculiarly Semitic character of certain vocalic interjections.[3] It is only necessary to glance over a list of the words for "father" in the various languages of the world, to discover that *ad* or *at* is one of the commonest of titles given by the child to the parent.[4] Professor De-

---

[1] Zimmern, *Busspsalmen*, p. 116.
[2] *The Hebrew Language viewed in the Light of Assyrian Research*, p. 60.
[3] Zimmern, *Busspsalmen*, p. 114.
[4] E.g. in Keltic, Albanian, Turkish, Kirgiss, Moko, Akra, Dacotan. See Buschmann in the *Abhandlungen der Berliner Akademie*, 1852, pp. 391 *sq*. I have often wished that Assyriologists would devote some study to phonetics. A page bristling with diacritical marks may look scientific, but not unfrequently the appearance is greater than the reality. Diacritical marks are objectionable for two reasons, first of all because they cannot be reproduced by an ordinary printing-press, and secondly because they often serve to conceal an ignorance of what the sounds really were which were intended to be

litzsch, however, after turning half the Semitic Babylonian vocabulary into Accadian, has now gone to the opposite extreme, and would transform what is Accadian into Semitic. The cause of both exaggerations is the same. He has put his faith in the so-called syllabaries and bilingual lists rather than in the actual texts which we possess. Far be it from me to disparage either the value of these lists or of the work which has been accomplished by Professor Delitzsch and his pupils. We owe it in great measure to him that the decipherment of Assyrian stands at its present level of scholarship, and the publication of his long-promised but long-delayed Assyrian Dictionary will tend to place the study of Assyrian on the same footing as that of the better-known Semitic languages. But the Leipzig school has, with one or two striking exceptions, been far too one-sided. Archæology, history, religion, mythology, have been neglected in favour of the almost exclusive study of words : words, too, not as bound together in the sentences of untranslated texts, but isolated and apart. Their explanation has been sought in syllabaries and lists of synonyms, rather than in the context of the documents which have come down to us. This excessive devotion to vocabularies has been too often accompanied by a misconception or forgetfulness of the real nature of the "bilingual lists." They are for the most part commentaries upon older texts, made we know not when, and intended to explain the meaning of rare

---

expressed. If the Assyrian *tsaddé* was pronounced *ts*, it is better to write it so than to denote it by a symbol which may mean anything or nothing. Where the two letters belong to different syllables, which is rarely the case in Assyrian, they can be separated by a hyphen (*t-s*). In fact, when the Assyriologists come to represent their diacritical marks by letters to which an intelligible pronunciation can be assigned, I find them flying in the face of phonetic possibilities. It is all very well to represent the simple sibilant of Assyrian by *š*; but this is the symbol chosen by Sievers and other phonologists to express the sound of *sh*, and it is accordingly replaced at times by *sh* by those Assyrian scholars who make use of it. Unfortunately, phonetics prove that the Assyrian sibilant could not have had this value, as Rawlinson and Oppert long ago perceived. A well-known phonetic rule of Assyrian is for a dental followed by the sibilant to become *samech*, the dental being first assimilated to the sibilant. Now *ss* is *samech*, but not *shsh*. The representation of the Assyrian *teth* by *t* is another phonetic error. The Assyrian *teth* had affinities with *daleth* and not with *tau*, as is proved by its frequent interchange with the former, as well as by the fact that the same characters were employed to express the *daleth* and the *teth*. Its pronunciation was in all probability that of the English *dh* (as in *the*). As for the *qoph* (which in Babylonian passed into *g*), palæography and phonetics alike sanction its symbolisation by *q*.

APPENDIX I. 427

or obsolete words, ideographs and expressions. The original text was sometimes in Accado-Sumerian, sometimes in an older form of Semitic Babylonian; while at other times texts in both languages were commented on together by the scribe. In the so-called non-Semitic column of the "bilingual lists," accordingly, we must expect to find not only Accado-Sumerian, but also Semitic words as well as ideographs which may be either of Sumerian or of Semitic origin. Now and then the scribe displays his learning by introducing synonyms or equivalent ideographic combinations, many of which had probably never been used in any real text at all. The mythological lists, which contain a medley of divine names and epithets drawn from sources of all kinds and ages, partly Accado-Sumerian, partly Assyrian, partly purely ideographic, partly even Elamite or Kossæan, afford a good example of the difficulty and danger of trusting implicitly to such guides. It is from this cause that Assyrian has been mistaken for Accadian, Accadian for Assyrian; while ideographs have been read phonetically, and phonetic characters as if they were ideographs. We must never forget that the object of the commentators was not to provide a bilingual vocabulary; the distinction between Accadian and Assyrian was one which they hardly understood. Their task was to explain everything that seemed obscure to the current language of their own time, and consequently obsolete or unusual Semitic words and forms, as well as rare modes of writing otherwise well-known words, stood for them on precisely the same footing as the words of the old dialects of Sumer and Accad. The lists of Semitic synonyms must be studied with equal caution. The Assyrian scribe had not the same fine discrimination as the modern lexicographer; it was sufficient for him to group words together which had the same general sense or could be employed in parallel phrases. Moreover, in these lists he had an excellent opportunity of displaying the extent of his erudition, and it is therefore by no means always certain that all the words included in them were ever used either in literature or in the language of daily life.

Another fact must be remembered which seriously detracts from the value of the "bilingual lists." Where an Accado-Sumerian word is translated by an Assyrian one, the latter has generally been taken by the commentator from what may be termed the authorised translation of the non-Semitic texts. But the Babylonian translator had not the same ideas in regard to translation as a modern scholar. At times, indeed, he was slavishly literal—so literal, in fact, as to contravene the common idiom of Semitic speech; but more usually his rendering was a paraphrase rather than a translation. It was sufficient for him if he gave the general sense of the original, or what appeared to him the general sense; since the notes attached to the bilingual texts given in this volume will show that the translators were not always thoroughly well acquainted with the language they undertook to explain. Hence it is that different Accado-Sumerian words are rendered by the same Semitic equivalent, that Accado-Sumerian verbs are apt to be represented by the same monotonous ideas of "giving" or "placing," and Accado-Sumerian adjectives by the same conceptions of "strong" or "great." Conversely, the same Accado-Sumerian word is made a synonym of different Semitic ones. The result is, that the labours of the Leipzig school have made us acquainted with a prodigious number of Assyrian words all signifying "to go," or "to bind," or "to give," or "to be strong." This is well enough for a beginning, but we naturally wish to know what kind of "going," or "binding," or "giving," is denoted in a particular case.

All this goes to show how needful it is to criticise the native vocabularies, and more especially to control them by the evidence of connected texts, if we would employ them with success. But there is yet a further and important reason for criticism and control. These native vocabularies are not infallible. Not only must we admit mistakes on the part of the original translator and the original commentator; we must admit them also on the part of the later copyists. The Leipzig school has done valuable work by insisting on the necessity of having exact facsimiles of the tablets which have come down to us; but when these facsimiles are made, there is a further necessity for vigorously applying to them the canons of textual criticism. The time is past when we can accept a reading simply because it is found on one of the tablets of Assur-bani-pal's library.

The Semitic character of Assyrian has been recognised from the first; the linguistic relationship of Accado-Sumerian has been a more disputed matter. Dr. Oppert long ago pointed out its agglutinative nature, and endeavoured to connect it with the Turanian or Ural-Altaic family of speech. I followed in the same path in 1870, and have ever since felt convinced, for reasons which I need not here specify, that it would eventually prove to be an early representative of the Ural-Altaic languages, though separated from the existing members of the family by a wide interval of time and space. Lenormant's attempts, however, to demonstrate its affinity with the languages of the Uralic branch were not very successful, and the adverse judgment of Dr. Donner seems to have definitely decided the question against them. These attempts, in fact, brilliant as they were, were nevertheless premature, and, as I said in 1877, until Accado-Sumerian phonology has been determined in its main outlines, it is useless to continue them. Before we can compare Sumerian with other languages, we must first ascertain approximately how it was pronounced, and what changes its pronunciation underwent in the course of centuries.

Thanks to Prof. Haupt and Dr. Hommel, these conditions have now been fulfilled. Our knowledge of Sumerian is still, it is true, imperfect; but we now know enough about it to be able to compare it with other languages with some chance of success. No unprejudiced student of linguistic science can resist the conviction that Dr. Hommel's comparison of the Sumerian grammar and vocabulary with the grammar and vocabulary of the Turko-Tatar languages is founded on a solid basis of fact. Some of his comparisons may indeed be disputable, but this does not affect the net result. He has succeeded in discovering the leading laws of phonetic change between Accado-Sumerian and the modern Turkish dialects, and has thus fulfilled the primary conditions of proof demanded by linguistic science. The structure, the grammar, the phonology, the vocalic harmony and the vocabulary, all go to show that the primitive language of Chaldæa is a remotely ancient representative of the Altaic family of speech. The unexpected resemblances that can be pointed out between such widely-severed members of the same family as Accado-Sumerian on the one side, and the modern Turkish idioms on the other, are a remarkable illustration of the fixity of human language. In this, as in his historical combinations, Dr. Hommel's work has been at once so brilliant and so good, that I cannot refrain from formally expressing my admiration of it. Doubtless he is rash at times, but rashness is the privilege of the pioneer.

After what precedes, it seems hardly necessary to discuss seriously M. Halévy's curious contention that Accado-Sumerian had no existence. Indeed, a writer who maintains that Mugheir is not "Ur of the Chaldees," appears to be beyond the reach of argument. But M. Halévy is not only a good Semitic scholar, he has also a keen eye to the weak points in his adversary's harness, and he has defended and re-modelled his paradox with a perseverance and audacity worthy of a better cause. Started while as yet he was ignorant of Assyrian, it has been supported and preached by him with renewed vigour since his enrolment in the band of Assyriologists. But his arguments and theory have alike changed a good deal during the progress of his Assyrian studies, although his main thesis remains unaltered, that "Accadian is not a language, but a form of writing." His chief arguments, however, have been directed, not towards the demonstration of his own theory, but against the assumptions and assertions of certain Assyriologists. As these assumptions and assertions have too frequently been based on hasty generalisations and imperfectly known facts, their demolition has been a comparatively easy matter; but it has left the chief question at issue—that of the existence of Sumerian—wholly untouched. The early relations between Sumerians and Semites, the period when Sumerian became an extinct language, the pronunciation and meaning of particular Sumerian words—these are all subsidiary questions, the answers to which may be right or wrong without affecting the main point in dispute. The views attacked by M. Halévy are for the most part views which I, at least, have never shared; for years I have maintained that many of the Accadian texts we possess were written by Semites, and that the language of them is comparable to monkish or even "dog" Latin;[1] while M. Halévy will bear me witness that I have myself long ago called his attention to Semitisms in the Accado-Sumerian portion of the bilingual inscriptions. To argue from the presence of these Semitisms that the rest of the texts must be in a strangely deformed kind of Semitic, is an *argumentum per saltum* which, whatever force it may have against the views of other Assyriologists, has certainly never had any force against mine.

Apart from arguments which merely criticise the peculiar historical theories or misreadings of certain writers, I find M. Halévy advancing two only of any apparent weight against the belief that Sumerian was a real language. One of these is, that it is expressed by the same characters as Semitic Babylonian. The statement is not quite exact; but granting that it is, we have only to glance at the numerous languages which make use of the Latin alphabet to discover its weakness. Even within the cuneiform system of writing itself, the Alarodian language of Van is written in the characters of the syllabary of Nineveh. M. Halévy's second argument is more specious, but unfortunately it is not correct. He asserts that the syntax and idioms of the Sumerian sentence are the same as those of the Assyrian sentence. But it is not necessary to translate many of the bilingual hymns before discovering that the Semitic rendering not unfrequently differs a good deal from the Sumerian original; and that even in such small matters of idiom as the order of two parallel words, the Semitic scribe has not cared to disturb the familiar Semitic expression by a literal translation of the Sumerian text. Thus where the Sumerian has "female and male," "day and night," "fire and stones," the Semitic version ostentatiously

---

[1] See, for example, my *Babylonian Literature*, p. 71.

gives "male and female," "night and day," "stones and fire." It is the same disregard of exact rendering which causes different Sumerian words to be represented by the same Semitic one, or the same Semitic word by different Sumerian ones. Nothing, however, can better illustrate the diversity of the syntax of the two languages than the incorporation of the pronouns and the extensive employment of postpositions which meet us in almost every line of a Sumerian text; while the agreement of Assyro-Babylonian and Sumerian in regard to the position of the verb is, as we have seen, one of those contraventions of Semitic structure which indicate the disturbing influence of a foreign idiom on the Semitic language of Babylonia and Assyria.

M. Halévy's own explanation of the phenomena which, in the opinion of other Assyriologists, prove the existence of the Sumerian language, belongs rather to the age of the Kabbalists than to that of linguistic science. It ignores all that we now know of the condition of men in an early stage of culture, as well as of the development of a system of writing. It is neither more nor less than the supposition that the inventors of the Atbash and Kabbala presided over the beginnings of cuneiform writing. It revives the old theory of a secret writing invented by a primitive priesthood, and understood only by the initiated few. Such a theory is inconsistent with the doctrine of evolution ; it inverts the history of writing, and ascribes what is necessarily a very late phenomenon to the first beginnings of a written literature. Men who are laboriously developing a system of writing out of pictorial hieroglyphs, are not the inventors of cipher and "Atbash," or the elaborators of a secret script. A system of writing must have become old and widely used before the idea can arise of evolving out of it a mysterious script whose meaning shall be known only to a few. To refer such a script to a primitive age of culture is to misconceive utterly the conditions of human progress. The student of anthropology can only wonder that a theory of the kind can have been seriously promulgated in this age of scientific knowledge.

M. Halévy does indeed support his hypothesis by appealing to the fact that ideographs are of frequent occurrence in the Semitic inscriptions of Assyria and Babylonia, and that one of the chief difficulties presented by Assyrian proper names arises from their being expressed ideographically. But the fact shows just the contrary of what he would have it prove. No one doubts that the ideographs occurring in a Semitic cuneiform text represent Semitic words, and not a system of secret or "hieratic" writing ; why, then, should they be supposed to represent a system of secret writing when found in texts which do not contain a single phonetically-written Semitic word? If M. Halévy's "hieratic" script had ever existed, we should meet with it in inscriptions of whose Semitic character there is no question. But the best disproof of such a "hieratic" system is the nature of so many of the documents which, according to the Assyriologists, are composed in the Sumerian language. A "hieratic" script would have been used for magical texts and charms, conceivably also for religious literature, but certainly not for historical annals or the legal documents of private individuals. Yet we find historical texts like those of Khammuragas written in this hypothetical secret writing, and—still more wonderful to relate—with a translation in ordinary Semitic Babylonian at the side; while there are numberless deeds relating to the sale of slaves, the loan of money or the purchase of property, composed in the same mysterious script and without any Semitic version attached to them. To believe that such documents are drawn up in a hieratic system of writing requires the robust faith of a mediæval rabbi.

Apart, however, from a certain love of paradox which M. Halévy seems unable to resist, it is probable that this curious theory of a Kabbalistic script as old as the oldest known inscriptions of Chaldæa would never have been started, but for the premature theories, and still more the erroneous readings, enounced by Assyriologists on the subject of Sumerian. The correct reading of Sumerian words is a matter of extreme difficulty, and a considerable number of the readings, given in earlier works on the language, and not unfrequently quoted at second-hand by philological paradoxers in support of their peculiar theories, were mere makeshifts, which had no pretensions to accuracy. What increases the difficulty is that the Semitic scribes, through whom we have to obtain our knowledge of the ancient language of Chaldæa, were often as ignorant as ourselves, and either read phonetically what was really written ideographically, or else substituted a Semitic for the genuine Accado-Sumerian word. It is only gradually that we are acquiring a better knowledge of the Accado-Sumerian vocabulary, and are becoming able to control the statements made by the compilers of the "bilingual lists." Sumerian, it must be remembered, started with pictorial hieroglyphs; it was only by degrees that these came to be used phonetically; and long before the system of writing had attained completeness, it was adopted and further developed by a Semitic population. The cuneiform script is therefore like a palimpsest where the original Sumerian text has been overlaid by a Semitic one; and in order to reach this text, the decipherer must first work his way through what overlays and conceals it. If we would read it rightly, we must divest our minds of the prejudices derived from the study of its later Semitic phase, and endeavour to interpret it by the analogy of similar ideographic systems of writing, like the old Egyptian or the Chinese. It is only in this way that we shall come to understand the principles that have guided its growth. We shall then discover, for instance, that determinatives have played a much more important part in its constitution than the Assyriologists, or indeed the Semitic scribes themselves, have supposed. The determinatives retained by the Semitic syllabary are but a remnant of those that enter into the composition of the old Sumerian ideographs. The ideograph of "water," for example, is not only a determinative in the compound character which signifies "to drink" (*nak*), but also in the word which denotes a "storm" or "deluge" (*mâtu*). Of equal importance with the recognition of this extended use of determinatives, is the recognition of a principle which prevails widely in all pictorial systems of writing. When phonetic values are beginning to attach themselves to the primitive ideographs, an attempt is made to assist the memory in remembering the pronunciation and meaning of a particular word, by writing it in ideographs which denote words whose sound and signification alike recall the word intended to be expressed. Thus "a fetter" was called *saggid* or *sägidä* in Sumerian; but it was represented by the two characters, *su*, "a hand," and *gid*, "to extend," *sugid* being sufficiently near *saggid* in pronunciation, while the idea of "a fetter" was called up by that of "extending the hand."[1] At other times the meaning and pronunciation of an ideograph were defined by coupling it with another, which either gave its pronunciation—in which case the ideograph became a simple determinative, as in A-*pur*, "water"—or else indicated the precise shade of meaning with which it was used. An illustration of the latter mode of combining characters may be taken from the Semitic texts composed in the court of Sargon at an epoch when the cuneiform system of writing was still in process of formation. Here, for example, we find the ideograph of hand—*idu* in Semitic—further defined by the attachment to it of the character which had the phonetic value of GAP, and accordingly reminded the reader of *kap*, "a hand." It is from a neglect of these and similar devices common to all pictorial forms of script, that the Sumerian vocabulary has been filled by Assyriologists with monstrous or hybrid forms. It is only of late that Assyrian students have begun to realise that the characters of an ideographic system of writing are seldom to be read phonetically. When

---

[1] W. A. I. v. 29, 71., 41, 47.

a word is expressed by a combination of characters, its pronunciation can only be recovered either by a gloss or by a comparison of the various modes in which it is written. The error of the Semitic scribes, who read KI-GAL as *kigal* instead of *šur*, has been too often repeated in these latter days.

It cannot be supposed that the criticisms of a scholar so erudite and keen-sighted as M. Halévy should remain wholly barren. In fact, they have helped to further the progress of science, though not exactly in the direction he desired or intended. His earlier objections led to Prof. Schrader's discovery that the characters of the cuneiform script had all been catalogued and named in the Accado-Sumerian period, and that many of the values assigned to them in the third column of the so-called syllabaries are merely Semitised forms of these names. He has himself done much towards forcing his brother Assyriologists to recognise, not only that a goodly number of the Accadian texts belong to the Semitic period and were composed or re-modelled by Semitic scribes, but also that from the first what he has termed the rebus played an important part in the formation of compound ideographs and ideographic expressions. The rebus was always a favourite plaything in the hands of Semitic *littérateurs*, though it attained its greatest proportions in the later ages of cuneiform writing, when the ideograph of "crown" was used to denote *izzu*, "strong," because one of its values was *gir*, which also signified "power," and the name of Darius was written Dari-musu, in order to assimilate it to the Assyrian *daru* and *musu*, "everlasting" of "name." But the theory itself which M. Halévy's "rebus" has been called upon to support, will share the fate of similar curiosities of philological literature, and be classed with Sir William Jones's denial of the existence of Zend, and Dugald Stewart's demonstration that Sanskrit was an invention of the Brahmans, palmed off upon the unsuspecting mind of the modern European.

M. Halévy, however, is not alone in denying to the Sumerians the credit of originating the culture which most Assyriologists ascribe to them. I cannot pronounce an opinion on Prof. De Lacouperie's theory that the ancestors of the Chinese were once in contact, probably in Elam, with the inventors of the cuneiform system of writing, since I am not a Sinologist; though I find it difficult to believe that "the Bak tribes" could have carried not only the forms of the Sumerian ideographs, but also their pronunciation with so little alteration as Prof. De Lacouperie maintains, across nearly the whole length of barbarous Asia. But there are other writers who would substitute for the Sumerians of the inscriptions the shadowy race of Cushites; and since in recent years the Cushite theory has been revived and defended by so great an authority as Lepsius, it is necessary for me to state in a few words why I feel myself compelled to reject it. That Babylonian tradition brought the early civilisation of the country from the waters of the Persian Gulf is perfectly true, and we have seen that the evidence of the monuments tends to corroborate it. It is also perfectly true that there seems to have been intercourse, if not between Chaldæa and Egypt, at all events between Chaldæa and the Sinaitic Peninsula, as far back as the days of the Fourth Egyptian Dynasty, and there is no reason why this intercourse should not have brought with it certain elements of Egyptian art and civilisation. But the cuneiform system of writing was already developed, and the culture of Tel-loh had already entered upon its later stage. There is nothing that would lead us to believe that the beginnings of this writing and culture came to Eridu from abroad.

If Lepsius were right, the primitive hieroglyphs out of which the cuneiform characters were evolved would offer resemblances to the hieroglyphs of Egypt. But this is not the case. With the exception of such obvious symbols as a circle to denote the sun, which occur in every pictorial system of writing, the ideographs of Chaldæa and Egypt have nothing in common. Even the idea of divinity is represented differently in them. In Chaldæa it is expressed by an eight-rayed star; in Egypt, by a stone-headed axe. The existence of the famous "Cushite race," in fact, depends on a misinterpretation of a verse of the Old Testament, eked out by the loose terminology of Greek writers who spoke of "Ethiopians" in the east as well as in the west. The basis of the whole Cushite theory are the words of Gen. x. 8, "And Cush begat Nimrod." Critics, however, have long since agreed that the passage about Nimrod is a later insertion in the ethnographical table of Genesis, and the preceding verses show that in the original text Cush is understood in the same geographical sense as elsewhere in the Old Testament. Properly speaking, Cush denoted Ethiopia or Nubia, and was a name borrowed from the Egyptians, who called that part of the world Kesh; but since the southern coasts of Arabia were peopled by colonies from Ethiopia, it was further extended to them. The regions adjacent to Cush, Phut or Punt on the Somâli coast, Egypt, and even Canaan, with its Philistine emigrants from the Delta, were described as the children of Cush, just as the Libyans or Lehabim were described as the children of Egypt. There is nothing to show that between the geographical Cush of Gen. x. 6, 7, and Cush the father of Nimrod, there is anything more than a similarity of name; for aught we know, the latter may be the Sumerian god of darkness and eclipse, Kus or Kusi. In Gen ii. 13, it is true, a land of Cush is brought into connection with Assyria and Babylonia;[b] but the text here is probably corrupt. Instead of Cush, the original reading was probably Cash, that is Kassi or Kossæans, the vowel *u* having slipped into the *k'thibh* from the *q'ri*. It is possible that the father of Nimrod was also Cash rather than Cush, in which case Nimrod would be a representative of the Kossæans. However this may be, Cush is never found elsewhere in the Bible with any other meaning than that of Nubia or southern Arabia, while the Kusu of the Assyrian inscriptions means Nubia alone. The hypothesis started by Mr. Pinches[2] that the Chaldæans came out of Kappadokia because a Kappadokian district is called Kuśu on an Assyrian tablet, reminds us of the ethnographical speculations of a former age, which identified the Cymry with the Cimbri, and derived them both from Gomer.

For the Cushites, Mr. Bertin would, like M. Halévy, substitute the Semites; only, unlike M. Halévy, he believes that the Semites, after inventing the cuneiform system of writing, handed it over to the Sumerians. But this is to invert the real order of events. The arguments brought forward by Mr. Bertin in support of his thesis tell a contrary tale; the primitive ideographs and their primitive phonetic values are Sumerian and not Semitic. When Mr. Bertin can show that the Semitic *ris* was used by the Sumerians as a phonetic value of the ideograph for "head," while the value of *sag* was not known to the early Semitic texts, it will be time to listen to his theory. Meanwhile we may rest content with the old doctrines, however commonplace they may be, engaged in the less ambitious task of strengthening and testing their foundations, and working out the problems which they still present.

---

[1] The Asshur of verse 14, however, is not Assyria, but the city of Assur. Gihon, which watered Cush, seems to be a Hebraised form of *Gikhinnu*, "a snare," borrowed from the Sumerian *gi-khan* (W. A. I. iv. 22, 31). *Gi-khan* is usually written ŚA-*khan*, with the determinative of "a cord," and ŚA-*khan* (pronounced *gikhan*) is said, in W. A. I. ii. 35, 6, to be a name of the Euphrates. We must not forget that the first syllable of the classical "Kossæan" gives us the vowel *o* instead of *a*. Gikhinnu will have been assimilated to the Hebrew word Gikhôn.

[2] *Proceedings of the Society of Biblical Archæology*, Dec. 6th, 1881.

II.

MR. G. SMITH'S ACCOUNT OF THE TEMPLE OF BEL.*

"I have discovered a Babylonian text, giving a remarkable account of the Temple of Belus at Babylon; and as my approaching departure for Nineveh does not allow me time to make a full translation of the document, I have prepared a short account for your readers, giving the principal points in the arrangement and dimensions of the buildings.

Additional interest attaches to this inscription from the fact that it is the first time any detailed description of a temple has been found in the cuneiform texts; it thus supplies the first information as to the dimensions of the great temples, and it is fortunate that the one described was the most famous in the valley of the Euphrates.

The importance of this temple is well known; it was the grandest religious edifice in the country, the centre of the national worship, and one of the wonders of the capital, Babylon.

This temple was founded centuries before Babylon became the chief city in the state, and retained its fame even down to Roman times. Herodotus and Strabo have given us accounts of the Temple of Belus, the former representing the principal building as one stade in length and breadth, and as consisting of eight stages or towers one above another, forming a pyramid, the highest stage being the sanctuary. Strabo states that this building was a stade in height, a stade being supposed to equal about 600 English feet.

The height given by Strabo for the tower of the Temple of Belus has already been considered very questionable (see Rawlinson's 'Ancient Monarchies,' vol. ii. p. 515), and, now that we have the dimensions of the building, must be rejected.

First, I must remark on the Babylonian measures used, that they are principally the cubit, equal to about 1 foot 8 inches English; and the *gar* or *sa*, equal to 12 cubits, or 20 feet English; but there is another series of numbers used in measuring, consisting apparently of

---

* Athenæum, Feb. 12th, 1876.

numbers of barleycorns arranged in sixties; thus the first number is a length of 11·33·20, which consists of 11 × 3600 + 33 × 60 + 20 barleycorns, in all 41,600 barleycorns, or 1155 feet, 7 inches. The barleycorn was the standard unit of measure among the Babylonians, and for this reason was used sometimes in measures of length without the other terms.

First in the tablet we have the measures of the outer court, called the 'Grand Court,' which is given as 11·33·20 in length (that is, about 1156 feet) and 9· in breadth (that is, 900 feet). There is a calculation as to the area of this court, which I pass over, and come to the next court, called the 'Court of Ishtar and Zamama.' This space is reckoned as 10·33·20 in length (1056 feet) and 4·30 (450 feet) in breadth. There is again here a calculation of area, which I omit.

Round the court were six gates admitting to the temples. There were, 1, the grand gate; 2, the gate of the rising sun (east); 3, the great gate; 4, the gate of the colossi; 5, the gate of the canal; and 6, the gate of the tower-view.

The next division is the space or platform apparently walled, and called a *ki-galli*, *sur*, or *birut*. It is uncertain if this was paved, and its extent is also uncertain. It is stated as a square, three *ku* in length and three *ku* in breadth, but the value of the *ku* is uncertain. The four walls faced the cardinal points, in this agreeing with the other parts, all the buildings having their sides west, north and south.

There were four gates, one in the centre of each side of this division: 1, the gate of the rising sun (east); 2, the southern gate; 3, the gate of the setting sun (west); 4, the northern gate.

Inside stood some building or enclosure, the name of which is damaged. It was 10 *gar* long and 10 *gar* broad (200 feet by 200), connected with the great Ziggurat or tower, which was the inner and crowning edifice of the group. Round the base of the Ziggurat or tower were ranged the chapels or temples of the principal gods, on its four sides, and facing the cardinal points.

On the eastern side stood a sanctuary or temple, 70 or 80 cubits long and 40 cubits broad (117 or 133 feet by 67 feet), with sixteen shrines, the principal being the shrines devoted to the god Nebo and Tasmit his wife. Nebo was considered the eldest son of Bel, the great deity of the temple.

On the northern side stood two temples, one devoted to the god Ea, the other to Nusku. The temple of Ea was 85 cubits long and 30 broad (142 feet by 50 feet), and that of Nusku was a square, 35 cubits each way (58 feet by 58 feet).

On the southern side stood a single temple dedicated to the two great gods, Anu and Bel. This was 70 cubits long and 30 cubits broad (117 feet by 50 feet).

On the western side were the principal buildings, consisting of a double house, with a court between the two wings. On the one side the wing was 100 cubits long and 20 cubits broad (166 feet by 34 feet). On the other side the wing was 100 cubits long and 65 cubits broad (166 feet by 108 feet), and the space between them was 35 cubits wide (58 feet). The building at the back was 125 cubits long and 30 cubits broad (208 feet by 50 feet). I do not properly comprehend the disposition of the buildings on this side, and my description of the position of the western temples must be taken as conjectural. In these western chambers stood the couch of the god, and the throne of gold mentioned by Herodotus, besides other furniture of great value. The couch is stated to have been 9 cubits long and 4 cubits broad (15 feet by 6 feet, 8 inches).

In the centre of these groups of buildings stood the grandest portion of the whole pile, the great Ziggurat, or temple-tower, built in stages, its sides facing the cardinal points.

The bottom or first stage was a square in plan, 15 *gar* in length and breadth, and $5\frac{1}{2}$ *gar* in height (300 feet square, 110 feet high). This stage appears to have been indented or ornamented with buttresses.

The next or second stage of the tower was also square, being 13 *gar* in length and breadth, and 3 *gar* in height (260 feet square, 60 feet high). The epithet applied to this stage is obscure; it had probably sloping sides.

The third stage differs widely from the lower ones, and commences a regular progressive series of stages, all of equal height. It was 10 *gar* in length and breadth, and 1 *gar* in height (200 feet square, 20 feet high).

The fourth stage was $8\frac{1}{2}$ *gar* in length and breadth, and 1 *gar* in height (170 feet square, 20 feet high).

The fifth stage was 7 *gar* in length and breadth, and 1 *gar* in height (140 feet square, 20 feet high). Probably by accident, the dimensions of the sixth stage of the tower are omitted in the inscription, but they can be easily restored in accordance with the others. This stage must have been $5\frac{1}{2}$ *gar* in length and breadth, and 1 *gar* in height (110 feet square, 20 feet high).

On this was raised the seventh stage, which was the upper temple or sanctuary of the god Bel. This building had a length of 4 *gar*, a breadth of 3½ gar, and a height of 2½ gar (80 feet long, 70 feet broad, and 50 feet high).

Thus the whole height of this tower above its foundation was 15 gar, or 300 feet, exactly equal to the breadth of the base; and as the foundation was most probably raised above the level of the ground, it would give a height of over 300 feet above the plain for this grandest of Babylonian temples.

The only ruin now existing at or near Babylon which can be supposed to represent the temple of Belus is the mound and enclosure of Babil, the ruins corresponding fairly with the account of these structures in the Greek authors and in the inscription. The sides of the building face the cardinal points, like those in the inscription; the remains of the two sides of the enclosure now existing indicate a circumference about equal to the Greek measurement, and slightly in excess of that in the inscription; but it must be remembered that the exact length of the Babylonian measures is not known, and there are different opinions even as to the length of the Greek stade, while the present remains of the wall require careful measurement to determine more exactly their length and the dimensions they indicate. On the other side of the Euphrates stands a ruin, Birs Nimroud, also consisting of an enclosure, various temples, and a temple-tower; but this represents the site of the temple of Nebo at Borsippa, and its angles, instead of its sides, face the cardinal points, while not a single one of its known dimensions agrees with the corresponding point in the inscription. The mound of Babil, which is already identified by the best authorities with the temple of Belus, consists now of the lower stage of the tower and the ruins of the buildings round it."

III.

THE MAGICAL TEXTS.

I. (Haupt, *Akkadische und Sumerische Keilschrifttexte*, ii. pp. 82 *sq.*;
W. A. I. ii. 17, 18. Sumerian with Semitic translation in parallel
columns. Also Sumerian text only in R 612.)

Col i. 1. Incantation (*siptu*). The evil (hostile) god, the evil demon (*utuk*),
2. the demon of the field, the demon of the mountain,
3. the demon of the sea, the demon of the tomb,
4. the evil spirit (*sedu*, Heb. *shêd*), the dazzling fiend (*alu*, Sum. *galla*),
5. the evil wind, the assaulting wind,
6. which strips off the clothing of the body as an evil demon,
7. conjure, O spirit of heaven! conjure, O spirit of earth!

8. The (possessing) demon which seizes a man, the demon (*ekimmu*) which seizes a man,
9. the (seizing) demon which works mischief, the evil demon,
10. conjure, O spirit of heaven! conjure, O spirit of earth!

11. The sacred prostitute whose heart is sick, the sacred prostitute of the oracle (?),
12. the sacred prostitute of heaven (Ass. Anu) who rests not,
13. the embryo of the beginning of an incomplete month,
14. the unburied in the earth,
15. who turns not the breast, who lets not the hand fall,
16. the hostile one who smites the head of the mountain,
17. conjure, O spirit of heaven! conjure, O spirit of earth!

18. That which is misformed, that which is unlucky (Ass. unestablished),
19. that which is racked, even a diseased muscle,

APPENDIX III.

20. a constricted muscle,[1] a swollen muscle, an aching (*lit.* shrieking) muscle, a painful muscle,
21. a broken muscle, an evil muscle,
22. conjure, O spirit of heaven! conjure, O spirit of earth!

---

23. Sickness of the entrails, a sick heart, faintness of the heart,
24. sickness, disease of the bile, headache, an evil vomit,
25. a broken blood-vessel (?),
26. disease of the kidneys, difficult miction,
27. painful sickness which cannot be removed,
28. a dream of ill omen,
29. conjure, O spirit of heaven! conjure, O spirit of earth!

---

30. Him who is the possessor of the images of a man,
31. the evil face, the evil eye,
32. the evil mouth, the evil tongue,
33. the evil lip, the evil breath,[2]
34. conjure, O spirit of heaven! conjure, O spirit of earth!

---

35. The nurse,
36. the nurse whose breast is sweet,
37. the nurse whose breast is bitter,
38. the nurse whose breast is wounded,
39. the nurse who has died through a wound of the breast,
40. the pregnant woman whose womb[3] is opened,
41. the pregnant woman whose womb is struck,
42. the pregnant woman whose womb is loosed,
43. the pregnant woman whose womb is unprosperous,
44. conjure, O spirit of heaven! conjure, O spirit of earth!

---

45. The painful fever, the potent fever,
46. the fever which quits not a man,
47. the fever-demon who departs not,
48. the fever unremovable,[4] the evil fever,
49. conjure, O spirit of heaven! conjure, O spirit of earth!

---

[1] *Maškadu*, see W.A.I. v. 21, 8; ii. 28, 14; iv. 16, 11, and Deluge Tablet, iv. 5.

[2] *Ivtu*, Heb. *khavvâh*, not "poison."

[3] *Kirimma*, cf. the Atarpi-legend (iii. 49): *lipalkit kirim-sa, sammu yâ yutsâ-su akalu yâ ihru*, "may its (the field's) womb rebel, may food not come forth from it, may bread not be produced."

[4] "Unassailing" in the Assyrian translation.

50. The painful plague, the potent plague,
51. the plague which quits not a man,
52. the plague-demon who departs not,
53. the plague unremovable, the evil plague,
54. conjure, O spirit of heaven! conjure, O spirit of earth!

---

55. The disease of the appearance which indicates disease,
56. the disease of the shadow [1] (of a man),
57. the disease which departs not, the disease of the form,
58. the disease unremovable, the evil disease,
59. conjure, O spirit of heaven! conjure, O spirit of earth!

---

60. The spittle and breath which are foully formed in the mouth,[2]
61. the expectoration[3] of the spittle which is foully enclosed (in the mouth) [*sallis*],
62. the shaving of the privy parts, the shaving of the body,
63. the cutting of the nails, circumcision,[4] a rag,[5]
64. an old ring, a broken chain,[6]
65. the sipped (water) which is returned from the body,
66. the food which is excreted from the body of a man,
67. the food which is returned in eating,
68. the water which in drinking is spued out,
69. the baleful breath which hides not the dust,
70. even the wind of the desert that departs not,
71. conjure, O spirit of heaven! conjure, O spirit of earth!

---

72. The cincture which is buried (*etsrit*) in the ground,
73. the cloth which is severed from a man's body,
Col. ii. 1. the curse upon the head (which) strikes (?) the earth,
    2. which among the ignorant leads the hand of the man astray,

---

[1] *Katsâti*.

[2] The Assyrian translates, "the product of the mouth and evil breath." "Spittle" is *arsasu* in Assyrian; comp. the Heb. *rasás*.

[3] *Naruqu*, Heb. *rûk*.

[4] *Arlu*, Heb. *'arêl*, where the word has the reverse sense to that which the Accadian text shows it to have had in Assyrian. The corresponding ideographs mean "the shaping of the phallus." That circumcision was practised in early Chaldæa is indicated by the primitive form of the character which denoted a phallus (Amiaud and Méchineau: "Tableau comparé des Ecritures Babylonienne et Assyrienne," No. 74).

[5] *Malu*, Heb. *mĕlâkhim*, Jer. xxxviii. 11, 12.

[6] Comp. W.A.I. v. 47, 13, *laqâ sa isiri ina ur ipti*, "the link of the chain from the penis he unloosed," and the Latin *infibulare*.

APPENDIX III.

   3. the baleful thirst (which . . . .),
   4. the fear[1] of the coming of death (which . . . .),
   5. conjure, O spirit of heaven! conjure, O spirit of earth!

---

   6. Him who is placed in the ground (or laid in) the field,
   7. with his phallus (*purrud*) uncut,
   8. (in) a grave concealed or unconcealed,
   9. the vampire who lies in wait continually,
 10. the destroying one who is unconcealed,
 11. whose head is unconcealed (in) the dust,
 12. the son of the king who is buried in the desert or in the palace,
 13. the mighty one who has been slain by a weapon,
 14. conjure, O spirit of heaven! conjure, O spirit of earth!

---

 15. That I may eat during the day,
 16. that I may drink during the day,
 17. that I may sleep during the day,
 18. that I may satisfy myself during the day,
 19. deliver
 20. O spirit of heaven, (and) conjure, conjure, O spirit of earth!

---

 21. Him who dies from hunger and watching,
 22. him who dies from thirst and watching,
 23. the feaster who in his feasting
 24. his crumbs has not collected,
 25. him whom the flood of a river
 26. has destroyed so that his name perishes,
 27. him who dies in the desert or in the marsh,
 28. him who the Air-god has drowned in the field,
 29. the handmaid of a *lilu* over whom death has no power,
 30. the *lilu* himself who has no wife,
 31. him whose name is remembered,
 32. him whose name is not remembered,
 33, 34. him who rises not from satisfying his hunger,
 35. the noxious breast (of a nurse) at the beginning of an incomplete month,
 36. conjure, O spirit of heaven! conjure, O spirit of earth!

---

 37. May the divine attendant of Pap-sukal,
 38. the creator of the life of the man,

---

[1] *Gilittam;* so in 79. 7-8. 158, *Rev.* 8, *atta naplisa gilittam,* "do thou look on (our) fear."

39. stand in the presence of the Sun-god.
40. May the divine spirit (*sedu*) and the divine colossos (*lamaśśu*), the givers of blessings,
41. alight upon his head.
42, 43. Over his life never may they cease (to watch).
44. Conjure, O spirit of heaven! conjure, O spirit of earth

---

45. The pure figure of gossamer (?)[1]
46. which is placed in the hand of the god of pure eating,
47. that he may rest his eyes upon it,
48. bind it to his right hand :
49. the ring of reverential fear, a pure stone,
50. which has been brought from his country,
51. for the satisfaction (*rikani*)[2] of his eyes,
52. set on the little finger of his right hand :
53. conjure, O spirit of heaven! conjure, O spirit of earth!

---

54. The white cloth, the cloth which is folded double,[3]
55, 56. bind both to the side and to the frame[4] of his couch;
57. the black cloth, the cloth which is folded double,
58. bind upon his left hand.
59. The evil demon, the evil fiend (*alu*), the evil demon (*ekimmu*),
60. the evil *gallu*, the evil god, the evil incubus,
61. the female colossus,[5] the spectre,[6] the vampire,[7]
62. the *lilu*, the *lilat*, the handmaid of the *lilu*,

---

[1] *Kammeda*, cf. " cloth of *kammeda*," W.A.I. iv. 25, 6. The combination of *kamme* with *dim* in the ideographic representation of *dimme*, " ghost" or " female colossus," seems to show that *kammeda* must mean " cloud-like" or " unsubstantial."

[2] *Rikani* (as in line 47, *amur rikani*) is akin to *rikâtu*, by which BAR, " bright," is rendered (W.A.I. ii. 30, 35).

[3] The Assyrian *damû*, "a fold," is borrowed from the Accadian *tabba*. The Accadian *sur(ra)* is rendered by *damû* and *kapalu*, " to fold," in W.A.I. iii. 70, 159. It is here represented by *izkhad* (as in W.A.I. v. 19, 29), which Zimmern reads *itspa* from *etsepu*. For *damu=kilallan*, " double," see W.A.I. v. 15, 44.

[4] In the Accadian, " head" (*sabba*).

[5] *Lamaśtu*, Acc. *dimme*, " creative spirit."

[6] *Labatsu*, Acc. *dimmea* ("that which comes of the *dimme*"), is probably the same as *dimma*, rendered by *ulalu*, W.A.I. ii. 28, 66, with which *ululu*, " a spirit," is connected. Cf. *dim* rendered by *makutu*, " feebleness," W.A.I. ii. 2, 332.

[7] *Ikhkhazu*, literally " the seizer;" Acc. *dimme-gur*.

63. the sorcery,[1] the breathing,[2] the breaking of wind,
64. the sickness, the sickly constitution,
65, 66. their head against his head,
67, 68. their hand against his hand,
69. their foot against his foot,
70. never may they set,
71. never may they turn![3]
72. Conjure, O spirit of heaven! conjure, O spirit of earth!

Col. iii. 1. The god Aśari-elim-núna (Merodach, "the mighty royal steer"),
2. the first-born son of Ea ("the lord of the earth"),
3. glittering water, pure water,
4. holy water, resplendent water,
5, 6. the water twice seven times may he bring,
7, 8. may he make pure, may he make resplendent.
9. May the evil incubus depart;
10. to another place may he betake himself;
11. may the propitious spirit (*sêdu*) (and) the propitious colossus
12. rest upon his body.
13. Conjure, O spirit of heaven! conjure, O spirit of earth!

14. Bind this man with wisps of straw;
15. with wisps of straw which the wind has dried;
16, 17. bind the gate of the court on the right hand and on the left:
18, 19. unriddle the curse and all that is baleful:
20. conjure, O spirit of heaven! conjure, O spirit of earth!

21. Into the house never may they enter;[4]
22. into the house of the living (?) never may they enter;
23. into the house of another's ringed fence never may they enter;
24. into the hollow of a yoke never may they enter;

---

[1] *Kišpu*, in the Acc. "evil breath."

[2] In the Acc. "breath of knowledge."

[3] We learn from a fragment (S 1140) what were the different parts of the body upon which the several kinds of evil spirit were supposed to act: "The evil *ekimmu* attacks his breast; the evil *gallu* attacks his hand; the evil god attacks his foot; those seven have seized (the man) together (*istenis*); his body in another place like consuming fire they (burn)." In S 1366. 2, 10, the *gallu* is the Semitic translation of the Accadian (north Babylonian) *libirri* and *libirra*.

[4] In the Assyrian rendering, "never may he enter."

25. into the hollow of the tomb never may they enter;
26. into (the ....) of the prison (?) never may they enter;
27. into (the ....) of the well (?) never may they enter;
28. into (the ....) of the tomb never may they enter;
29. into (the ....) of the furnace (?) never may they enter;
30. into (the ....) of the son of the Sun-god the glowing (*naplê*) never may they enter;
31. into (the place that is un)illuminated never may they enter;
32. into the shadow never may they enter;
33. into the darkness never may they enter;
34. into the cup (?) never may they enter;
35. into the cup (?) of the libation-bowl never may they enter;
36. into the ravines never may they enter;
37. into the ravines of the mountain never may they enter;
38. into the valley never may they enter;
39. into the vaults of the house never may they enter;
40. into the vaults of the tomb never may they enter;
41. into the body[1] of a man who goes out never may they enter;
42. into the body of a sick man never may they enter;
43. into the shadow of a man's step never may they enter;
44. with his goddess[2] never may they enter;
45. after his goddess never may they enter;
46. into the gate of the house never may they enter;
47. into the doorposts of the house never may they enter;
48. into the door of the house never may they enter;
49. into the bolt of the house never may they enter;
50. into the fastening[3] of the house never may they enter;

---

[1] The Assyrian renders, "with the traveller may he never descend."

[2] Accadian D. P. *śigga-ni*. '*Sigga* is the Sumerian form of which *simma* was the Accadian equivalent: in col. ii. 56, on the contrary, we had the Accadian *sabba*, "head," instead of the Sumerian *sagga*, showing the extent to which this originally Sumerian text has been interpolated by the Accadian scribes of northern Babylonia. If *gisal*, "a ravine" (iii. 36), is Semitic, it will be an example of a Semitic word foisted into the text by the scribes of Accad. Lines 36 and 37, in fact, are mere amplifications of the original line 38.

[3] The Accadian *sakkul* has been borrowed from the Semitic *sikkur*, but the change in the pronunciation shows that the borrowing was on the part of the people, and not of the literary class, and that it probably goes back to an early period. As lines 49 and 50, however, repeat the same statement, it is probable that line 50 is an interpolation. In line 51 the Sumerian *śigar* has, as usual, been confounded by the *litterati* of Sargon's court with the Semitic *sigaru*, "a cage" or "fetter," the Accadian form being *śimar* (W.A.I. iv. 18, 29).

51. into the latch of the house never may they enter;
52. into the border (*tupqat*) of the house never may they enter;
53. into the side of the house never may they enter;
54. into the upper hinge[1] (of the door) never may they enter;
55. into the lower hinge never may they enter;
56. into the upper hole for the hinge[2] never may they enter;
57. into the lower hole for the hinge never may they enter!
58. conjure, O spirit of heaven! conjure, O spirit of earth!

---

59. O female colossus, the daughter of Anu,[3]
60. who declarest[4] the name of the gods,
61. the goddess Innin(a), the heroine (*itillat*)
62. among the (divine) mistresses (*beléti*),
63. the binder of the sickening fever,
64, 65. the glorious spirit (*alitu*) among mankind,
66. the female colossus supreme in might
67. against (those who dare) not face (her);
68. conjure, O spirit of heaven! conjure, O spirit of earth!

---

69. .... the chosen place of the Moon-god
71, 72. *Destroyed.*
73. Conjure, O spirit of heaven! conjure, O spirit of earth!

Col. iv. 1, 2. (Against) the evil (demons) who return,
3. may the prince, Merodach,
4. the prince, the hero of heaven and earth,
5. the first-born of Ea,
6. (reveal) an omen of life,
7. may he alight on the man's head,
8, 9. over his life may he never cease (to watch);
10. conjure, O spirit of heaven! conjure, O spirit of earth!

---

11. May the fire-god (Kibirra) the son of the earth ....
12. (the offspring) of Ea the mighty ....
13. (the lord) of the demons (*utuki*) ....
14. (the minister?) of the great gods ....
15. (the companion?) of the hero Adar ....

---

[1] The Semitic *nukusu* has been borrowed, doubtless by the literary class, from the Accadian *nu-kusu*, "the unresting."

[2] *Tsirri*, borrowed (by the people) from the Accadian *zara*; see W.A.I. iv. 24. 47, 48.

[3] In the original Accadian, "The *dimme*, the son of heaven."

[4] "Understands," *kha(sisu)*, in the Assyrian version.

16. (reveal) an omen for the life (of the man),
17. may he alight upon his head,
18, 19. over his life may he never cease (to watch);
20. conjure, O spirit of heaven! conjure, O spirit of earth!

---

21. May Nin-akha-kudda, the mistress of spells,
22. the spell of Eridu
23. utter with pure mouth;
24. may Bahu the great mother,
25. the generatress of mankind,
26, 27. restore the blessing of health to the body; may Gula
28. with quieting hand the consecrated water, the water which the air has warmed,
29. send into his body;
30. the sickness of the head, the sickness of the mouth, the sickness of the heart,
31. the sickness of the entrails, (the sickness of the eye,)
32, 33. the ebbing sea, the rising sea,
34. the flood, the high-tide,
35. the water of the Tigris, the water of the Euphrates,
36. the mountain of the night, the mountain of the sunrise,
37. the mountain of the centre,[1]
38. may they turn back their breast;
39. conjure, O spirit of heaven! conjure, O spirit of earth!

---

40. May Nin-ki-gal, the wife of Nin-a-zu,
41. set her face towards the place of another;
42. may the baleful demon (*utuk*) depart,
43. may he betake himself to another spot;
44. may the propitious spirit (*sêdu*) (and) the propitious colossus,
45. settle in the man's body;
46. conjure, O spirit of heaven! conjure, O spirit of earth!

---

47. May the god Isum, the mighty lieutenant (*nagiru*),[2] the supreme incubus
48. of the gods, like the god who made him[3]
49. rest upon his head;

---

[1] *Idguruti*, or *idgurti* (W.A.I. v. 26. 15, 22; ii. 46, 54; 2, 294), means "the hollow of a cup," the Sumerian equivalent being *gil*, and the Accadian *dil*. Comp. *adagur*, "a cup," in the story of the Deluge, iii. 47.

[2] Isum was the minister of Nerra, the plague-god.

[3] In the Accadian text, "like the head-god" (*dingir sa-ag-ga*).

50, 51. over his life never may he cease (to watch);
52. conjure, O spirit of heaven! conjure, O spirit of earth!

53. May the sick man by offerings of mercy
54. (and) peace like copper[1] shine
55. brilliantly.[2] To this man
56. may the Sun-god give life.
57. O Merodach ("the great princely steer"), first-born son of the deep,
58. the blessing and the dazzling glory[3] are thine!
59. Conjure, O spirit of heaven! conjure, O spirit of earth!

60. (COLOPHON.) (The next tablet begins:) Spirit of the legions of earth and of the legions of heaven.[4]
The property of Assur-bani-pal, the king of multitudes, the king of Assyria."

II. The 5th tablet of the collection of the Magical Texts (W.A.I. iv. 1, 2).
Col. i. 1. "Incantation.—The storm-like-ghost,[5] the tormentor[6] of all things,

---

[1] *Kêmassi*, a literary loan-word from the Accadian (D. P.) *kâmas*.

[2] In the Accadian, *susubbi lalaghgha-lil*. For *susubbi*, "girdle" or "loins," see W.A.I. v. 15. 30, 43. *Susub* is rendered by the Assyrian *esipu* and *usap*, and *susûbu*, "a girdle," was a literary loan-word in place of the native Semitic *dumsu*. Instead of *susubbi lalaghgha-lil*, the Semitic version has *limmasis*, "may he be polished." Comp. *esipati ekili*, "the harvest (?) of the field," K 61, 5. Comp. W.A.I. iv. 4, 42.

[3] *Tatag-gubbi*, Assyrian *zuhunu*. The Semitic version reverses the order of these two words.

[4] The Semitic version reverses this order, giving, "spirit of (An-)sar and Ki-sar."

[5] *Suruppû*, from *rapû*, "to be weak," Heb. *rĕphâim*. See Zimmern, *Buss-psalmen*, pp. 26, 27. Jensen is wrong in making it "fever." In W.A.I. iv. 15, 38, it means "weakness." The Accadian equivalent signifies "one who is gone to his rest," and, as Zimmern shows, is probably to be read *seddhe* or *séde* (in W.A.I. iv. 15, 38, *seddhe* is translated *kutstsu*, "skinlessness"). From this the Semites would have borrowed their *sêdu* (Heb. *shêd*, see above, p. 441), for which no satisfactory Semitic etymology can be found. *Sêdu* is also the Semitic equivalent of the Accadian *alad*, or "warrior spirit," which along with the *lamma*, or "divine colossus," guarded the entrance to a palace or temple. Zimmern is doubtless right in holding that the collection of Magical Texts was known to the Assyrian scribes under the title of *surpu* in consequence of the first tablet of the series having begun with this word,

[6] See next page.

2. and the demon (*utukku*) who disturbs the disturbers of Anu,
3. the plague-demon (*namtaru*) the beloved son of Mul-lil,
4. the begetter[1] of Nin-ki-gal (the goddess of Hades),
5. above destroy like consumption (*kutstsu*) and below cut down.
6. They are the creation of Hades, even they!
7. Above they roar, below they peep;
8. the bitter breath of the gods are they.
9. The great worms[2] who have been let loose from heaven are they!
10. The mighty ones (*khuśi*, W.A.I. ii. 37, 13, Strass. 3440) whose roar is in the city;
11. who cast down the water of heaven, sons who have come forth from the earth! [*In the Assyrian version*: who disturb the disturbers of Anu, children of the wife of the earth are they.]
12. The lofty beam, the broad beam they encircle like a crown.
13. From house to house they make their way.
14. As for them, the door restrains them not, the bolt turns them not back.
15. Into the door like a snake they glide,
16. into the socket like a wind they blow.
17. The woman from the loins of the man they bring forth;
18. the child from the knees of the man they cause to issue.[3]
19. The freeman from the house of his fecundity they call forth.
20. They are the scourging voice which they bind to the man's back.
21. The god of the man, O shepherd who lookest after the sheep-cote, (is) towards the man

---

which is an equivalent of *suruppu*. From the root *rapû* was formed the Assyrian *tarputu* (W.A.I. v. 38, 27; 40, 35), the Heb. *tĕrâphim*, which Dr. Neubauer has already connected with the root *raphâ*. The worship of the *terâphim* indicates an early ancestor-worship among the Semites.

[6] *Munassir*, see W.A.I. iv. 16, 54; in the Atarpi legend (iii. 56) the Air-god is said to have "ruined" (*issur*) the field.

[1] Here the Assyrian translator has used the feminine *alidti*, hereby getting into a difficulty, as the demon was called "son" (*maru*) in the preceding line.

[2] *Ud-gal*: the *Ud-gallu* is conjoined with the *ur-bat*, or "beast of death," in K 3938, 6, and in S 477, ii. 11, the mention of "the flesh of the *ud-da*" follows that of the flesh of the gazelle, of man, of the dog, of the boar, of the ass, of the horse, and of the wild ass. In R 149, *udda-khul* is "poison." Perhaps the *udda* was a species of serpent. At all events, in W.A.I. v. 41, 6, *umŭ* is the synonym of *nammassu*, "reptile."

[3] Compare S 1366, *Obv.* 5—8: "(The *gallu*) has opened my loins and my wife (has issued forth); he has opened my knees and the child (has been born)."

452 APPENDIX III.

22. whom his god[1] has carried away to the veil.[2]
23. Whether it be a ghost (*dimme*),
24. whether it be a spectre (*dimmea*),
25. whether it be a vampire,
26. whether it be the lord of sickness,
27. whether it be the nurse,
28. whether it be the tear ....
29. whether it be the man ....
30. whether it be the incubus (*utuk*) ....
31. whether it be the handmaid (of the incubus),
32. whether it be the side ....
33. whether it be the day .....
    [The next six lines are too much broken for translation.]
34. whether it be the milk that has descended or the milk that has not descended (?),
35. whether I am hungry,[3] may I eat food,
36. whether I am thirsty, may I drink water,

Col. ii. 1. whether I am insect-bitten (?), let me anoint myself with oil,
2. whether I am stripped (*sedde-tagga*), let me put clothing round my loins.
3. The fever, the curse of the spirits of earth, conjures thee.
4. Baleful is the fever; the curse of the spirits of earth conjures thee.
5. The fever which has approached has confronted the sick man.
6. The fever may the spirit of heaven conjure, may the spirit of earth conjure.
7. Whether it be the spirit of the divine lord of the earths;

---

[1] In the Sumerian, "gods."

[2] *Kurummati*, rendering the Sumerian (KU) *suku*. The determinative shows it to be an article of dress, and in W.A.I. ii. 39, 67, it is stated to have been worn on "the head of a female slave," the Accadian equivalent of *suku* being *söba* (ll. 68–72). The latter is translated *ipru*, "a veil" (ii. 39, 50, *séba* in line 53 being *nalbasu*, "clothing"). Compare *epartum* = *nakhlaptu*, "a veil" (W.A.I. v. 28, 68). Hence "a dark veil" is vaguely rendered *simtu*, "ornament," in W.A.I. v. 16, 17. Xisuthros, in the story of the Deluge, tells his wife to "fold up (*epi*) the veil" of Gisdhubar and place it on his head. The ideographic equivalent of *nindabu*, "a free-will offering," is *suku Innana*, "the veil of the goddess," in reference to the sacrifice of their virginity by the women of Babylonia in honour of Istar. The reference in the text is to a sort of monastic vow, whereby a man placed himself under the protection of the deity, and, as in the case of Gisdhubar, by wearing a veil on his head became proof against all evil spells.

[3] In K 4207, 15 (NIS)LIB-SA-AN-TUK-A (*sagar-tagga*) is rendered by *birâta*.

THE MAGICAL TEXTS. 453

8. whether it be the spirit of the divine lady of the earths;
9. whether it be the spirit of the divine lord of the stars;
10. whether it be the spirit of the divine lady of the stars;
11. whether it be the spirit of the divine lord of seeds;
12. whether it be the spirit of the divine lady of seeds;
13. whether it be the spirit of the god Mul-Da-uhma;[1]
14. whether it be the spirit of the goddess Nin-Da-uhma;
15. whether it be the spirit of the divine lord of the illustrious mound (Birs-i-Nimrud);
16. whether it be the spirit of the divine lady of the illustrious mound;
17. whether it be the spirit of the divine lord of the dayspring of life;
18. whether it be the spirit of the divine lady of the dayspring of life;
19. whether it be the spirit of the divine lord of the voice of the firmament;
20. whether it be the spirit of the divine lady of the voice of the firmament;
21. O spirit, divine lord of the father and mother of Mul-lil, conjure!
22. O spirit, divine lady of the father and mother of Mul-lil, conjure!
23. O spirit of the Moon-god whose ship crosses the girdle (?) of its river, conjure!
24. O spirit of the Sun-god, king and judge of the gods, conjure!
25. O spirit of Istar, who to the command of the spirits of earth alone turns not the head, conjure![2]
26. O spirit of Zikum, mother of Ea, conjure!
27. O spirit of Nina, daughter of Ea, conjure!
28. O spirit of the divine lord (*Accadian*, lady) of growth, shepherd of the pastures, conjure!
29. O spirit of the fire-god, that makest pure (?) thy head towards the earth, conjure!

---

[1] The printed text has, falsely, *Dazarma*.

[2] The three lines 23—25 are evidently an interpolation. They interrupt the context, as the father and mother of the primitive god of Nipur must naturally have been followed by the mother of the primitive god of Eridu— the Moon-god, the Sun-god and Istar, belonging to a wholly different and later theological system—while the alliteration in the Semitic version of the 25th line shows that it must be the original of which the Accadian is a translation. It contains a play upon the name of Istar: "nis *Istari* sa ana kibiti sa Anúnaki *istánu* la iśaru (*istaru*)."

30. O spirit of the lady of the magic wand,[1] throne-bearer of the earth, conjure !
31. O spirit of the seven doors of the earth, conjure !
32. O spirit of the seven bolts of the earth, conjure !
33. O spirit of the opening fire-god, opener of the earth, conjure !
34. O spirit of the strong goddess with the cup of blessing (?), wife of the plague-demon, conjure !
35. O spirit of the pure cloud-spirit, the daughter of the deep, conjure !
36. The man, the son of his god,
37. when[2] he is angry,[3] or when he is violent, or when
38. he eats food, or when he drinks water,
39. the cup (?) of the father above thee, even Mul-lil, thy hand places ;
40. (when) the water of the sea, the waters of the marsh-lands (Merathaim), the water of the Tigris, the water of the Euphrates,
41. the water of the pool, (and) the water of the river fail,
42. to the god he betakes himself, his sceptre he grasps,
43. a seat he sets, he sits down ; he establishes thee . . . .
44. the man, the son of his god, confronts (them, and) they return.
45. Conclusion (of the spell regarding) the evil incubus.

---

46. Incantation.—Destructive reptiles, baleful winds are they !
Col. iii. 1. As a baleful reptile, as a baleful wind do they appear ;
2. as a baleful reptile, (or) a baleful wind do they march in front ;
3. monstrous children, monstrous sons are they ;
4. the messengers of the plague-demon are they !
5. the throne-bearers of Nin-ki-gal (queen of Hades) are they ;
6. a deluge which has been collected upon the land are they ;
7. (they are) the seven gods of the wide-spread heaven,
8. the seven gods of the broad earth,
9. the seven gods confederated together.[4]

---

[1] *Gis Zida*, "the eternal wood." In W.A.I. iv. 25, 12, it seems to mean "a mast." The Lady of the Magic Wand was Allat, the queen of Hades.

[2] *Enna*, to be distinguished from (AN)*enna*, which in R 204, *Obv.* 7, is rendered by *lilû*.

[3] *Ba-ran-tarin*. In K 4874, *Obv.* 19, *ne-tarrin* seems to correspond with *tsirikhum*; cf. *khe-nib-tarré-ne*, rendered *ligazziru*, W. A. I. iv. 16, 65.

[4] The Accadian *ûr-ûrri*, as in K 4874, *Rev.* 9, where AB-KHAL *ûr-ûrri-ene* is rendered by *yarrura tamâti*, "he bound the spell together." Cf. W.A.I. iv. 11, 45. *mu-nib-ûr-ûrri* = *imtanaśśar*.

10. The seven are gods seven in number,[1]
11. seven evil gods are they!
12. Seven evil demons (*lamastuv*) are they!
13. Seven evil consuming spirits (*labatsi*) are they!
14. In heaven are they seven, in earth are they seven!
15. The evil incubus (*utuk*), the evil *alu*, the evil *maskim*, the evil *gallu*, the evil god, the evil succubus,
16. O spirit of heaven, conjure! O spirit of earth, conjure!
17. O spirit of Mul-lil, king[2] of the world, conjure!
18. O spirit of Nil-lil, lady of the world, conjure!
19. O spirit of Uras (Adar), son of Ê-sarra (the temple of the hosts of the firmament), conjure!
20. O spirit of Innana (Istar), lady of the world, illuminator of the night, conjure!
21. when the body of the man, the son of his god,
22. eats food (or) drinks water.

---

23. Incantation.—The plague (*namtar*), the fever[3] which will carry the people away,
24. the sickness, the consumption (*dilibti*) which will trouble mankind,
25. harmful to the flesh, injurious to the body,
26. the evil incubus, the evil *alu*, the evil *maskim*,
27. the evil man, the evil eye, the evil mouth, the evil tongue,
28. from the flesh of the man, the son of his god, may they be expelled, from his body may they be driven forth.
29. Against my body never may they come;
30. my eye never may they injure;
31. against my back never may they go;
32. into my house never may they enter;
33. over the beams of my (house) never may they pass;
34. into the house of my seat never may they descend!
35. O spirit of heaven, conjure! O spirit of earth, conjure!
36. O spirit of Mul-lil, king of the world, conjure!
37. O spirit of Nin-lil, mistress of the world, conjure!
38. O spirit of Uras, mighty warrior of Mul-lil, conjure!
39. O spirit of Nusku, supreme messenger of Mul-lil, conjure!

---

[1] In the Semitic translation, "the seven are gods of multitudes."

[2] In the Semitic version, *bel*, "lord."

[3] *Asakku*, an Assyrian loan-word from the Accadian *a-sig*, "strength-destroying."

40. O spirit of Mul-zu-na (the Moon-god), first-born son of Mul-lil, conjure!

41. O spirit of Innana (Istar), lady of the people (*ummani*), conjure!

Col. iv. 1. O spirit of Rimmon, the king[1] whose shout is good, conjure!

2. O spirit of the Sun-god, the king[1] of judgment, conjure!

3. O spirit of the Anúnas,[2] the great gods, conjure![3]

4. Conclusion (of the spell regarding) the evil incubus.

5. Incantation.—The waster of heaven and earth, the warrior-spirit (*sêdu*) waster of the earth,

6. the warrior-spirit, waster of the earth, whose power is exalted,[4]

7. whose power is exalted, whose step is exalted;

8. the *gallu*, madly-rushing bull, the bull supreme,[5]

9. the bull who runs through the houses,

10. the *gallu* who has no member, are those seven.

11. Mistress they know not.

12. The land like husks they devour.

13. Compassion they know not.

14. Against mankind they rage.

15. The flesh they devour, the seed they sicken, the blood they drink.

16. .... the image of the gods are they.

17. In the house of the god of the holy mound,[6] on the fruit of the god of corn, are they fattened.

18. Demons (*gallu*) are they, filled with wickedness.[7]

19. Devourers of blood, unceasing are they.

20. Cut off from them (their power of) sorcery, and to highland and lowland never may they return.

21. O spirits of heaven, conjure! O spirits of earth, conjure!

---

[1] *Bili*, "lord," in the Semitic version.

[2] In the Semitic version, *Anunnaki*, "the spirits of the lower world."

[3] Lines 41—iv. 2 are interpolations, the original exorcism having emanated from Nipur, and being, therefore, concerned only with Mul-lil and his attendant deities.

[4] *Su-ana*, "of heavenly power," in Accadian, whence the literary name of Babylon, Su-ana-KI, "place of heavenly power."

[5] Paraphrased in the Assyrian rendering by "great *ekimmu*."

[6] The temple of Nebo at Borsippa. We may infer from this that the incantation in lines 5—21 emanated from Babylon.

[7] In the Accadian, "filling the front with witchcraft."

22. Conclusion (of the spell regarding) the evil incubus.

23. Incantation.—The apparition, the apparition, which treads down all things whatever their name;
24. the troublers of the earth, the troublers of the heaven;
25. .... like the heaven not receiving.
[The rest of this incantation is destroyed.]
40. Incantation.—The warriors .... are they.
Col. v. 1. Troublers unique are they,[1] troublers of heaven have they been born.[2]
2. They are whirlwind-like ghosts; travellers are they.
3. Wife they possess not; child they beget not.
4. Lusty offspring they know not.
5. Horses which have come forth[3] from the mountain are they.
6. Unto Ea are they hostile.
7. The throne-bearers of the gods are they.
8. To trouble the canal[4] in the street are they set.
9. Before Nergal the mighty warrior do they go to and fro.
10. O spirit of heaven, conjure! O spirit of earth, conjure!
11. O spirit of the Moon-god, lord over difficulty,[5] conjure!
12. O spirit of Isum,[6] traverser (*nagir*) of the street), drinker up of the water, conjure!
13. To the body of the man come not nor return;
14. before him depart, behind him depart!

15. Conclusion (of the spell regarding) the evil incubus.

16. Incantation.—Seven are they, seven are they,
17. in the hollow of the deep seven they are;
18. gleams of the sky are those seven.
19. In the hollow of the deep, in a palace, they grew up.
20. Male they are not, female they are not.

---

[1] The Semitic translator has made nonsense of this line, rendering it, "whose troublers are unique."

[2] In the Semitic rendering, "troublers of Anu have they been created."

[3] In the Semitic version, "descended."

[4] Accadian *esirra*, perhaps borrowed from the Semitic *isaru*, "to be straight," as conversely the Assyrian *sulu* is a loan-word from the Accadian *sila*, "a cutting" or "canal." As in Holland, "canal" and "street" were synonymous terms.

[5] *Namratsit*. In the Accadian, "god of the throne of light."

[6] Accadian *sig-sagga*, "head-destroying."

21. They are whirlwind-like ghosts; travellers are they.
22. Wife they possess not, child they beget not.
23. Compassion[1] and kindness know they not.
24. Prayer and supplication hear they not.
25. Horses which are bred in the mountains are they.
26. Unto Ea are they hostile.
27. The throne-bearers of the gods are they.
28. To trouble the canal in the street are they set.
29. Evil[2] are they, evil are they!
30. Seven are they, seven are they, seven twice again are they!
31. O spirit of heaven, conjure! O spirit of earth, conjure!

32. Conclusion (of the spell regarding) the evil incubus.

Col. vi. 1. . . . . the evil incubus (*utuk*) is violent;[3]
   2. (that which) is unnamed has begotten him.
   3. that which has not issued forth from a body has begotten him
   4. His hand one sculptured,[4] and made his hand;
   5. his foot one sculptured, and made his foot;
   6. his head one sculptured, and made his head.
   7. For his destiny the meadow of gold (was prepared).
         [Three lines lost.]
  10. The (evil) incubus . . . . may he never enter the house
  11. May the evil incubus remove his seat to another place.
  12. May the prospering incubus (and) the colossus of the land go to and fro!

  13. Conclusion (of the spell regarding) the evil incubus.

  14. Incantation.—The evil incubus, the incubus of the mountain ravine. [The first line of the next tablet.]
  15. Fifth tablet of (the series concerning) the evil incubi."

III. Incantation against madness (W. A. I. iv. 3, 4).
Col. i. 1. "Incantation.—The disease of the head coils (like a serpent) in the desert, like a wind it blows.
   2. Like the lightning it lightens; above and below it has wrought destruction.

---

[1] *Edhira*, from *edheru*, "to spare."   [2] Accadian *śiśśi*.
[3] *Itarus*, iphteal of *arasu*, "to be strong," connected with *ursanu*. It is doubtful whether the corresponding Accadian *rus* is borrowed from *arasu* or *arasu* from *rus*.
[4] Assyrian "cut," Accadian "took."

3. Unfearing its god, like a reed has it cut (the man) off.
4. Its cord (*buani*) like a snare[1] has it wound around (him).
5. It destroys the body of him who has not mother Istar as his guardian.
6. Like a star of the heavens it shoots (*itsarrur*), like water it traverses the night.
7. Against the sick man it turns its front, and like the day it overpowers[2] him.
8. This man it smites, and
9. the man, like one who is faint at heart, staggers;
10. like one whose heart is taken from him, he passes away.
11. Like one who is fallen in the fire, he quivers;
12. like a wild ass inflamed with love, his eyes are filled with mist.
13. With his life it devours the man,[3] to death it binds him.
14. The madness is as a heavy storm whose path there is none that knoweth.
15. Its perfect bewitchment,[4] its bond, there is none that knoweth.
16. Merodach! substance of myself! go, my son![5]
17. With the plant that gladdens life[6] which grows in the desert before him,
18. like the Sun-god when he enters his house, cover the clothing of thy head.
19. With the plant that gladdens life surround it like a covering.[7]
20. At dawn,[8] when the sun has not yet risen,

---

[1] *Gikhinu*, from the Accadian *gikhan* (also written ṠA-*khan*). In W.A.I. ii. 35, 6, we are told that Gikhan (ṠA-khan) was a synonym of the Euphrates, which explains the Gihon of Gen. ii. 13, where the word has been assimilated to the Heb. *gîkhôn*, "a spring."

[2] In the Semitic version *ikhme*, "scorches" (?).

[3] Accadian *uru*.   [4] *Ittu*, "sign," "omen."

[5] Fragments of Accadian from the words put into the mouth of Ea in other magical texts inserted here by way of a charm.

[6] Accadian *khul-til-gillan* (for *gilla*, "to live," see W. A. I. iv. 23, 5), whence the Semitic *khiltalti* (ii. 28. 16), though the latter word may be read *khilpalti*, and compared with the Aramaic *khilpâ*, "sedge." It was a plant that grew on the mountains (ii. 28. 16, 17).

[7] The Semitic translator, in his word-for-word rendering, has here produced an extraordinary violation of Semitic grammar: "(with) the plant that gladdens life cover like [as it were] and enclose"(!).

[8] *Agu-ziga* in Accadian, literally "the hour of the fresh breeze." Thus we have the following hymn (D. T. 57, *Rev.*): (1) "At dawn (*agu-ziga*) the bird proclaims not the fresh breeze (*ziga*); (2) the waters of the deep (*gurra*) his mouth brings not; (3) the lord of strength is unsatisfied (*saga nu-sia*,

APPENDIX III.

21. pluck it from its place.
22. Seize its stem.[1]
23. Take the skin of a suckling that is still ungrown,
24. and bind (with it) the head of the sick man,
25. bind also the neck of the sick man.
26. May (the sickness) of the man's head which is produced in the street[2] be removed;
27. (which) the curse of the wind has borne to him, never may it return to its place!
28. O spirit of heaven, conjure! O spirit of earth, conjure!

[The first 19 lines of the next spell are destroyed; then we read:]
Col. ii. 1. On cries of woe he feasts daily.
2. Merodach! substance of myself! go, my son!
3. Take the skin of a suckling that is still ungrown;
4. let the wise woman bind (it) to the right hand and double it on the left.
5. Bind the knot twice seven times;
6. lay (upon it) the spell of Eridu;
7. bind the head of the sick man;
8. bind the neck of the sick man;
9. bind his life;
10. bind firmly his limbs;
11. approach his bed;
12. pour over him the magical waters;[3]
13. may the disease of the head, like the eye when it rests itself, ascend to heaven.
14. Like the waters of an ebbing (flood), to the earth may it descend.
15. May the word of Ea issue forth.
16. May Dav-kina direct.
17. O Merodach, first-born of the deep, thou canst make pure and prosperous!

18. Incantation.—The disease of the head is fallen on the man;

Ass. *la isbû*); (4) take the green corn (GIS *sunni*, Ass. *binu*) as food (U *innus*, Ass. *patatan*)."

[1] Accadian *ana*, connected with *anu*, "an ear of corn." The ideograph denotes "what grows long." The Semitic rendering *surut* is connected with the Heb. *sâr*, "a vine-shoot."

[2] Or perhaps we should read *sa ina zumur (ame)li basû*, "which is in the body of the man."

[3] Literally, "the waters of the spell."

19. madness, even the disease of the muscle of the neck, has fallen on the man.
20. The disease of the head like a crown coils (around him);
21. the disease of the head, from the rising of the sun to the setting of the sun,
22. unto the disease of the head answers in thunder.
23. In the sea and the broad earth
24. the little crown is the crown that has departed,
25. the crown gigantic (is) its crown.
26. Make broad the ears, O (Merodach) son of Ea!
27. the disease of the head, like an ox, walks with rolling gait.
28. To his father (Merodach) approached and (his) decision[1] reported:
29. 'O my father, the disease of the head is fallen on the man;
30. like a wall .... it is laid upon him.
31. (As with) a weapon .... let me cut off his sickness.'
33. (Ea unto his son Merodach) made reply:
    [Several lines lost:]
39. The sickness of the head, (like) a dove to (its) nest,
40. like a raven to the sky,
Col. iii. 1. like a bird into broad space, let it fly away.
2. To the prospering hands of his god let him be confided.

---

3. Incantation.—The madness is bound in heaven, from the earth it is driven away.
4. The power of the freeman, the master of power, is opened (afresh).
5. The hand of the fruitful handmaid returns not,[2]
6. which is laid on the body of the sick.
7. As for Istar, who rejoices in quietude, one that exists not[3] causes her train[4] to descend from the mountain.
8. To the form of the sick man they approach;[5]
9. she raises a cry of lamentation over the man:
10. 'Who takes (it) away, who gives (him) health?'[6]

---

[1] Accadian *gu-kud*, elsewhere written KA(*gu*)-*kud*.

[2] In the Accadian, "the blessed handmaid turns not back her hand."

[3] In translating "one that exists not" (literally, "none is"), the Semitic scribe has mistaken the meaning of the Accadian *mulu nu-tilla*, "the eunuch."

[4] *Ulmanu*, connected with *alamu*, a synonym of *sadadu*, "to draw."

[5] "He approaches" in the Semitic text.

[6] In the Accadian, "takes away."

11. Even Istar, the daughter of Sin;
12. the mighty father,[1] the son of Mul-lil;
13. (and) Merodach, the son of Eridu.
14. May they give health to the body of the sick man.'
15. The god who adorns the gate (?), who (issues?) the command, has bound his (body).
16. On the butter which is brought from a pure stall,
17. the milk which is brought from a pure sheep-cote,
18. the pure butter of the pure stall lay a spell.
19. May the man, the son of his god, recover;[2]
20. may the man be bright and pure as the butter;
21. may he be white as this milk;
22. like refined (*tsurrupi*) silver may his firm flesh[3] glisten,
23. like copper may it shine as a polished vessel.
24. To the Sun-god, the first-born of the gods, confide his body.
25. May the Sun-god, the first-born of the gods, to the prospering hands of his god confide him.—Incantation.[4]

26. Incantation.—Seizing the face, the middle of the head, of the man who is strengthless and ignorant,
27. like the covering (?) of a man (the disease) conceals;
28. it directs the path of the man who has no god.
29. He carves an image, but encloses not the enclosure.
30. Like a water-snake, like a water-snake the roof of the yard
31. by day casts not a shadow, by night casts not a shadow.
32. Merodach looks on; 'Substance of mine art thou' (says Ea), go, my son!
33. The slice of a snake, *sisi*, *siman*, *abi*,
34. human flesh, *kharkhar*, medicine of the mountains,[5]
35. the seed of the male organ, the herb of Adar, his mouth,
36. the breath of the god of the river of the quarryman,[6] the body of the god of the river of the quarryman,
37. his strong food,
38. mix together and rub into oil,

---

[1] *Pap-sim-nun-bada*, a title of Adar. [2] Literally, "be turned."

[3] Accadian *mubu*, for the older Sumerian *gubbu*.

[4] The references to Istar, Mul-lil and Samas, as well as the linguistic forms, show that this incantation is of very much later date than those of the obverse of the tablet. It probably emanated from Sippara.

[5] These are all medicines used both by the exorcists and by the medical practitioners.

[6] According to W.A I. ii. 62, 40, this deity was "the river-god," Ea.

39. rub on the body with pure hand.

[The following lines are too much broken for translation, like the last incantation of the tablet : then comes the colophon :]

Col. iv. 35. The 9th tablet (of the series beginning :) A spell for diseases of the head : thoroughly complete.

36. The palace of Assur-bani-pal, the king of legions, king of Assyria,
37. who puts his trust in Assur and Nin-lil."

IV. The 16th tablet concerning evil spirits (W. A. I. iv. 5, 6).

Col. i. 1. "The reptiles that creep round and round, the evil gods are they
2. The warrior spirits (*sêdu*) that spare not, who were created in the cloudy vault of heaven, are they.
3. They are they who produce disease.
4. Enlarging (their) evil heads, ... to lay the yoke (upon it they march).
5. Among those seven, the first is a scorpion of rain,
6. The second is a monster (whose) mouth (no) one (can bridle).
7. The third is the lightning-flash, the strong son of . . . .
8. The fourth is a serpent . . . .
9. The fifth is a watch-dog which (rages) against (his foes).
10. The sixth is a rushing (tempest) which to god and king (submits not).
11. The seventh, like a messenger, is the evil wind which (Anu made ?).
12. Those seven are the messengers of Anu their king.
13. In city after city do they cause the rainy wind.
14. The storm that is in heaven they bind together strongly.
15. The fleecy clouds that are in heaven making the rainy wind are they.
16. The rushing blast of the wind which produces darkness on a clear day are they.
17. With baleful wind, with evil wind, they darted forth.
18. The deluge of Rimmon, mighty whirlwinds are they,
19. at the right hand of Rimmon they march.
20. On the horizon of heaven like the lightning (they flash).
21. To impose the yoke they march in front.
22. In the wide heaven, the seat of Anu the king, they set themselves with evil purpose and had no rival.
23. On that day Mul-lil heard of this matter and carried the word to his heart.

APPENDIX III.

24. With Ea, the supreme adviser of the gods, he was king,[1] and
25. had appointed Sin, Samas and Istar to direct the cloudy region of heaven.
26. Along with Anu he had divided among them the sovereignty of the hosts of heaven.
27. Among the three of them, the gods his children,
28. he had divided the night and the day; that they cease not (their work) he urged them.
29. On that day those seven, the evil gods, in the cloudy region of heaven darted forth.
30. In front of Nannar[2] violently they beset the Moon-god.
31. The hero Samas and Rimmon the warrior returned to their quarters;
32. Istar set (her) holy seat with Anu the king, and over the kingdom of heaven is exalted.

Col. ii.   [The first 19 lines are destroyed.]

20. .... (Sin) was troubled and sat in grief;
21. (night and) day in darkness, on the throne of his dominion seated not.
22. The evil gods, the messengers of Anu their king,
23. enlarging (their) evil heads, assisted (one another).
24. Evil they plotted together.
25. From the midst of heaven, like the wind on the land they swooped.
26. Mul-lil beheld the darkness of the hero Sin in heaven.[3]
27. The lord (Bel) says to his messenger Núsku:
28. 'O Núsku, my messenger, carry my word to the deep;
29. the news of my son the Moon-god, who is grievously darkened in heaven,
30. to Ea in the deep convey.'
31. Núsku exalted the word of his lord;
32. to Ea in the deep he went with the message.

---

[1] *Imtalik* means "he was king," not "he took counsel," here, as is shown by its equivalent in the Accadian text (*â-gágá*). The Semitic *parśu*, "adviser," has been adopted in the Accadian version, pointing (like the mention of Sin, Samas and Istar) to the composition of the poem in the Semitic era.

[2] The Accadian text reads, "at the beginning they beset with violence the festival of the Moon-god."

[3] The Accadian imitates the Semitic idiom in this sentence, proving that the Semitic version is the older.

33. To the divine prince, the counsellor supreme, the lord, the sovereign of the world,
34. Núsku conveyed the word of his lord on the other side.
35. Ea in the deep listened to the tale, and
36. he bit his lip, with outcry he filled his mouth.
37. Ea addressed his son Merodach and roars out (*isakhkhats*) the word:
38. 'Go, my son Merodach!
39. Grievous is the eclipse of the son of the festival, the Moon-god;[1]
40. his eclipse in heaven is proceeding.
41. Those seven, the evil gods, the serpents of death,[2] who have no fear,
42. those seven, the evil gods, who swoop (*tebuni*) like the deluge,
43. swoop upon the world like a storm.[3]
44. Before Nannar, the Moon-god violently (they beset);
44. the hero Samas and Rimmon the warrior (return) to their quarters;[4]
45. (Istar plants her holy seat with Anu the king, and over the kingdom of heaven is exalted).'

[Many lines are lost here.]

Col. iii. 31. In the gate of the palace the mask (fold) doubly . . . .
32. In a cloak[5] of many colours, the skin of a suckling still ungrown the skin of an ungrown calf, make supplication.
32. Bind (the magic knots) round the hands and feet of the king, the son of his god;
33. the king, the son of his god, who, like Nannar, the Moon-god, completes the life of the land;
34. like Nannar, the resplendent, his head upholds favour.

[Many lines lost.]

46. . . . . make his . . . . pure and brilliant;
47. . . . . (the evil (god), the evil spirit (*utuk*), the evil *gallu*:
48. . . . . the evil incubus (*maskim*).

---

[1] The Semitic version is different here: "the news is that of my son the Moon-god, who is grievously eclipsed in heaven." The text published by Haupt has, "the son of the prince Nannar."

[2] In the Accadian, "men of death."

[3] In Haupt's text, "they seek the land, upon the world like a storm they swoop."

[4] Lines 26—44 have been published by Haupt in his *Akkadische und Sumerische Keilschrifttexte*, ii. pp. 76, 77.

[5] The Semitic *samlin* (Heb. *simlâh*) has been introduced into the Accadian text. The genuine Accadian equivalent was *sik* (W.A.I. iv. 21, 4).

2 H

49. Never may they enter (the house);
50. never may they approach (the doors) of the palace;
51. never may they approach (the chamber) of the king;
52. never may they surround the . . . .
53. never may they enter the . . . .

[Col iv. containing another incantation against the evil spirits, in which "the spirit of Mul-lil" is invoked and "the spell of Ea" named, is too mutilated for translation.]

Col. v. 36. Conclusion (of the spell) for cursing[1] the evil gods accursed.

37. Incantation.—The huge reed of gold, the pure reed of the marsh,
38. the pure dish of the gods,
39. the reed of the double white cup which determines favour,[2]
40. the messenger of Merodach am I.
41. When I deliver the pure incantation,
42. I lay a foundation of bitumen below in the centre of the gate.
43. May the god of the house dwell in the house!
44. May the propitious spirit (*utuk*) and the propitious god enter the house!
45. May the evil *utuk*, the evil (god), the evil *ekimmu*, the evil *gallu*, and the evil (*alu*),
46. (never approach) the king.
47. O spirit of heaven, conjure! (O spirit of earth, conjure!)

48. Conclusion (of the spell) cursing the evil gods.

[The beginning of the next incantation is lost.]

Col. vi. 1. Never may they enter the palace;
2. never may they approach the king!
3. O spirit of heaven, conjure! O spirit of earth, conjure!

4. Conclusion (of the spell) of the light-coloured goat-skin which is . . . .

5. Incantation.—Evil is the evil man, evil is that man;
6. that man among men is evil, that man is evil;
7. in the bed of a man he places a snake.
8. That man among men lays a snare misleadingly to ensnare (others).

---

[1] *Tarruda*, rendered "to curse" in W.A.I. iv. 16, 39, "to shatter" in iv. 8, 41.

[2] The divining cup is referred to

9. The fear of him is the herald of his cry; the breath of the man destroys.
10. The place of his sickness the evil creeps into; his heart it cuts (in two).
[The following lines are too mutilated for translation.]
17. Conclusion (of the spell) cursing the evil gods.

---

18. Incantation. The Sun-god . . . .
19. The 16th tablet (of the series beginning) 'the evil spirits.'
20. Palace of Assur-bani-pal, the king of legions, the king of Assyria,
21. who has put his trust in Assur and Nin-lil,
22. to whom Nebo and Tasmit
23. have given broad ears,
24. that he might have seeing eyes;
25. the store of written tablets,
26. as regards which, among the kings that have gone before me,
27. there was none who undertook this business;
28. the hidden wisdom of Nebo, the lines of characters as many as singly exist,
29. on tablets I wrote, I connected together, I published, and
30. for the inspection of my readers
31. I placed within my palace.
32. Thine is the kingdom, O Assur, light of the king of the gods!
33. Whoever carries (them) away and his name with my name
34. shall write, may Assur and Nin-lil mightly and violently
35. overthrow him and destroy his name (and) his seed in the land."

V. W.A.I. ii. 51, 1—31, revised by Jensen in the *Zeitschrift für Keilschriftforschung*, ii. 4, pp. 320, 321.

1. [Lost.]
2. "never may they approach . . . his hands.
3. Against such and such a man, the son of his god, may (the evil spirits) never come.
4. Like a dove may he ascend[1] . . . . to his place may he never return.
5. Whatever is evil, whatever is bad, which is in the body of such and such a man,
6. like the water [perspiration] of his body and the purifications (?)[2] of his hands,

---

[1] Comp. D. T. 57, *Obv.* 13, *kima tarri etilli ana same sa* AN *Anum*, "like a dove he ascends to the heaven of Anu."

[2] *Musâti*. In S 1896, *Rev.* 9, we have *rabits musâti*.

7. may he strip off, and may the river carry to the bottom of its bed.
8. The curse, O spirit of heaven, conjure! O spirit of earth, conjure!

---

9. The coal (which) the great gods have polished, on the torch I have kindled:
10. I offer the corn-god, the assembler of the gods of heaven and earth.
11. May the establishers of the fortresses of the great gods station themselves here, and
12. may they promise life to such and such a man, the son of such and such a man, the son of his god.
13. May his god and his goddess remain here, and on this day may they grant him grace.

---

14. Incantation.—The milk of a light-coloured goat I prepare in plenty, and I light the fire.
15. The coal I place, I burn the whole offering.
16. The libation pure and white of Ea, the messenger of Merodach am I.
17. May the gods, as many as I have invoked, produce a flame.
18. May Ea and Merodach never have (wrath), though the god and the goddess are angry.

---

19. (The coal I have kindled), the fire I have quieted, I burn, I increase;
20. the corn-god I have offered; I am great and glorious.
21. May (the god of herbs), the assembler of god and man, deliver from his bond.
22. Like a coal I have blazed, I have quieted the bird:
23. like the fire I have burned, I have increased food;
24. like the corn-god I have offered, I am great and glorious.
25. May the god of herbs, the assembler of god and man, deliver from his bond.
26. Deliver such and such a man the son of his god, and may he be saved.

---

27. Incantation.—The directress ascends, the offspring of the house of the life of the prince.
28. Like its old copy, written and published.
29. Tablet of Adar-sum-tir-su the Zôganês (*sagan*), the librarian: his utterance."

THE MAGICAL TEXTS.

VI. Magical text from Eridu (W.A.I. iv. 15). See p. 179.

Col. i. 1. "The (bed) of the earth was taken for their border, but the god appeared not;[1]
2. he appeared not on the horizon of the earth, making hostility;
3. (to) the heaven below they extended (their path), and to the heaven that is unseen they climbed afar.[2]
4. Among the star(s) of heaven was not their ministry (knowledge); in the watch of the thirty (stars)[3] was their office.
5. The Fire-god, the first-born, supreme, unto heaven they pursued, and no father did he know.
6. O Fire-god, supreme on high, the first-born, the mighty, supreme enjoiner of the commands of Anu![4]
7. The fire-god enthrones with himself the friend that he loves.
8. He reveals the enmity of those seven.
9. On the work he ponders in his dwelling-place.
10. O Fire-god, how were those seven begotten, how were they nurtured?
11. Those seven in the mountain of the sunset were born;
12. those seven in the mountain of the sunrise grew up;
13. In the hollows of the earth they have their dwelling;
14. on the high-places of the earth their names are proclaimed.
15. As for them, in heaven and earth they have no dwelling, hidden is their name.
16. Among the sentient gods they are not known.
17. Their name in heaven and earth exists not.
18. Those seven from the mountain of the sunset gallop forth;
19. those seven in the mountain of the sunrise are bound to rest.
20. In the hollows of the earth they set the foot;
21. on the high-places of the earth they lift the neck.
22. They by nought are known; in heaven and earth is no knowledge of them.
23. To Merodach[5] approach, and this word may he say to thee:
24. 'May he give thee the message[6] for those evil ones, the seven, as many as go straight before thee;

---

[1] A copyist has substituted *la* for *nu*, "not," in the Accadian text.
[2] In the original Accadian, "the heaven that has no exit they opened."
[3] *Matstsarâti*, "the Zodiacal signs," in the Semitic version.
[4] "Heaven" in the Accadian.
[5] Called Aśari in the Accadian text.
[6] *Amma*, for the earlier Sumerian *agga*.

25. he the command of whose mouth is favourable, the supreme judge of heaven.'[1]
26. The Fire-god to Merodach approaches, and this word he speaks to thee;
27. in the canopy of the bed at night he hears this word;
28. to his father Ea he descends into the house and says:
29. 'O my father, the Fire-god flames up at the rising of the sun and their hiding-place approaches.
30. The paths of those seven he knows, and he seeks[2] their quarters in various places.[3]
31. Enlarge the ears, O son of Eridu!'
32. Ea answered his son Merodach:
33. 'My son, those seven dwell in the earth;
34. those seven from the earth have issued forth;

Col. ii. 1. those seven in the earth were born;
2. those seven in the earth grew up.
3. To tread down the sides of the deep have they approached.
4. Go, my son Merodach!
5. Let the fire of the cedar-tree, the tree that destroys the wickedness of the incubus,
6. on whose core the name of Ea is recorded,
7. with the spell supreme, the spell of Eridu, (and) of purity,
8. to foundation and roof[4] let (its fire) ascend, and to the sick man never may those seven approach.
9. Like a wide snare in a wide place outspread[5] the hand:
10. at noon and midnight on his head let it lie;
11. by night let him charm(?)[6] the canal and the street, and by day with his hand.
12. In the night let him place on the couch a sentence (*masal*) from a good book on the sick man's head.'
13. The warrior sends (the message) to his friend:
14. 'May the Fire-god seize that incubus.

---

[1] "Anu" in the Semitic version, which is nonsense.

[2] *Siteh*, iphteal permansive.

[3] In the Accadian, "he turns his head in front" (W.A.I. iv. 21, 29).

[4] In the Semitic version, "to roof and foundation."

[5] Literally, "cause to recline."

[6] *Lunasi;* comp. *itanasa* (W.A.I. iv. 7, 15), which the Accadian equivalent shows must mean "lay a spell upon," or something similar. In the present passage the Accadian *enege* is probably the older form of *enem*, "a word" or "command."

15. The evil ones, those seven, may he carry them away and drive (them) from the man's body.
16. By day smite the incubus unrestingly (?).
17. May the Fire-god, the power supreme, restore his foundation.
18. May Nin-ki-gal, the wife of Nin-aśu-gâ, establish his face to be with good fortune (?).
19. May his madness (and his) faintness . . . vanish away.
20. May Nin-akha-kúda take possession of his body, and rest upon his head.'
21. Such (is) the speech of Nin-akha-kúda,
22. (such is) the spell of Eridu ;
23. pronounce the spell of the deep and of Eridu supreme . . . .
24. May Isum,[1] the leader (*nagir*) of the incubus supreme among the gods, rest upon his head, and in the night protect him.
25. By night and day to the prospering hands of Samas may he consign him. Incantation.

---

26. (In) Eridu[2] a stalk (palm-tree?) grew overshadowing; in a holy place did it become green.
27. Its root was of white crystal, which stretched towards the deep.
28. (Before) Ea was its course in Eridu, teeming with fertility.
29. Its seat was the (central) place of the earth.
30. Its foliage[3] was the couch of Zikum the (primæval) mother.
31. Into the heart of its holy house, which spread its shade like a forest, hath no man entered.
32. (There is the home) of the mighty mother who passes across the sky.
33. (In) the midst of it was Tammuz.
34. .   .   .   .
35. (There is the shrine?) of the two (gods)."

VII. The sixth tablet of the series concerning "the weakening disease," (W. A. I. iv. 7, 8); translated by Jensen, *Keilschrift für Keilschriftforschung*, i. 4, ii. 1.

Col. i. 1. "Incantation.—The evil curse like a demon (*gallu*) has fallen on the man.

---

[1] Accadian *Kun-sagga*. The original text is Sumerian and of an early date, as is shown by forms like *digga*, "to grow" or "flame up;" but it has been modified and interpolated by Accadian and Semitic copyists, who have introduced words like *amma* and *la*, and lines like the concluding one (col. ii. 25).

[2] See p. 238.   (*Ar*)*kit-su*.

2. The voice as a scourge has fallen upon him.
3. The voice ill-boding has fallen upon him,
4. the evil curse, the ban (*mamit*), the madness.
5. The evil curse has cut the throat of this man like a sheep.
6. His god has gone far from his body.
7. His goddess, the giver of counsel, has stationed herself without.
8. The scourging voice like a garment has covered him and bewitched (?)[1] him.
9. Merodach has regarded him.
10. To his father Ea into the house he descends and says:
11. 'O my father, the evil curse like a demon (*gallu*) has fallen on the man.'
12. Twice did he speak to him, and (says):
13. '(What) this man should do I know not; what will give him rest?'
14. (Ea) to his son Merodach made answer:
15. 'O my son, what dost thou not know? what shall I tell you more?
16. O Merodach, what dost thou not know? what shall I add to thy (knowledge)?
17. What I know, thou too knowest.
18. Go, my son, Merodach!
19. Take the man to the house of pure sprinkling, and
20. remove his ban and expel his ban,
21. the evil that troubles his body,
22. whether it be the curse of his father,
23. or the curse of his mother,
24. or the curse of his elder brother,
25. or the curse of the destruction[2] of a man (which) he knows not.
26. May the ban by the spell of Ea
27. like garlic be peeled off,
28. like a date be cut off,
29. like a branch be torn away.'
30. The ban, O spirit of heaven, conjure! O spirit of earth, conjure!

---

31. Incantation.—Like this garlic which is peeled and cast into the fire,
32. the burning flame shall consume (it);
33. in the garden it shall not be planted,
34. in pool or canal it shall not be placed;
35. its root shall not take the earth;

---

[1] See note 6, p. 470. [2] *Sakkastum*, from *sakasu*, "to destroy."

36. its stem shall not grow, and shall not see the sun;
Col. ii. 1. for the food of god and king it shall not be used.
   2. (So) may the guardian-priest[1] cause the ban to depart from him (and) unloose the bond
   3. of the torturing disease, the sin, the backsliding, the wickedness, the sinning,
   4. the disease which exists in my body, my flesh (and) my muscles.
   5. Like this garlic may it be peeled off, and
   6. on this day may the burning flame consume.
   7. May the ban depart that I may see the light.

   8. Incantation.—Like this date which is cut and cast into the fire,
   9. the burning flame shall consume (it),
   10. to its stalk he who plucks (it) shall not restore (it),
   11. for the dish of the king it shall not be used;
   12. (so) may the guardian-priest cause the ban to depart from him (and) unloose the bond
   13. of the torturing disease, the sin, the backsliding, the wickedness, the sinning,
   14. the disease which exists in my body, my flesh (and) my muscles.
   15. Like this date may it be cut, and
   16. on this day may the burning flame consume (it).
   17. May the ban depart that I may see the light.

   18. Incantation.—Like this branch which is torn away and cast into the fire,
   19. the burning flame shall consume (it),
   20. its leaves to the trunk shall not return;
   21. for the work of dyeing it shall not be used.
   22. (So) may the guardian-priest cause the ban to depart from him (and) unloose the bond
   23. of the torturing disease, the sin, the backsliding, the wickedness, the sinning,
   24. the disease which exists in my body, my flesh (and) my muscles.
   25. Like this branch may it be torn away, and
   26. on this day may the burning flame consume (it).
   27. May the ban depart that I may see the light.

   28. Incantation.—Like this wool which is torn and cast into the fire,
   29. may the burning flame consume (it);
   30. to the back of its sheep it shall not return;

---

[1] *Turta*, whence *turtanu*, "commander-in-chief;" cf. W. A. I. ii. 31, 26.

APPENDIX III.

31. for the clothing of god and king it shall not be used.
32. (So) may the guardian-priest cause the ban to depart from him (and) unloose the bond
33. of the torturing disease, the sin, the backsliding, the wickedness, the sinning,
34. the evil which exists in my body, my flesh (and) my muscles.
35. Like this wool may it be torn, and
36. on this day may the burning flame consume (it).
37. May the ban depart that I may see the light.

---

38. Incantation.—Like this goat's hair, which is torn and cast into the fire,
39. the burning flame shall consume (it);
40. to the back of its goat it shall not return,
41. for the work of dyeing it shall not be used.
42. (So) may the guardian-priest cause the ban to depart from him (and) unloose the bond
43. of the torturing disease, the sin, the backsliding, the wickedness, the sinning,
44. the disease which exists in my body, my flesh (and) my muscles.
45. Like this goat's hair may it be torn, and
46. on this day may the burning flame consume (it).
47. May the ban depart that I may see the light.

---

48. Incantation.—Like this dyed thread (which) is torn and cast into the fire,
49. the burning flame shall consume (it),
50. the weaver into a garment shall not weave (it),
51. for the clothing of god and king it shall not be used.
52. (So) may the guardian-priest cause the ban to depart from him (and) unloose the bond
53. of the torturing disease, the sin, the backsliding, the wickedness, the sinning,
54. the disease which exists in my body, my flesh (and) my muscles.
55. Like this dyed thread may it be torn, and
56. on this day may the burning flame consume (it).
57. May the ban depart that I may see the light.

Col. iii. 1. (This) seed of the pea (?)[1] (I cast into the fire),
2. (speaking) thus : (May) a flame that (ceases) not (consume thee),

---

[1] So Halévy (from the Talmudic). The Assyrian word is *upunti*, expressed ideographically by "husk-like plant of the mountain" (KU-KUR-LIL).

3. may the guardian-priest cause the (evil) ban to depart from him
4. (and) unloose the bond of the ban,
5. the torturing disease, the sin, the backsliding, the wickedness, (the sinning),
6. the malady of the heart, the malady of the flesh that (is in my body),
7. the bewitchment,[1] the destruction,[2] the pain,[3] the foul spittle;
8. like the seed of this pea (?) it shall (be consumed) with fire,
9. the son of the gardener shall not plant (it) in the field,
10. in pool or canal it shall not be laid,
11. its root shall not take the ground,
12. its stalk shall not rise on high nor see the sun.
13. Never may the bewitchment be produced in my heart,
14. never may (the destruction) seize the spine,
15. never may (the pain) seize the root of my heart (= *angina pectoris*);
16. may the guardian-priest (cause the ban to depart from it) and unloose the bond.
17. (The torturing disease, the sin, the) backsliding, the wickedness, the (sinning),
18. (the disease which is in my body), my flesh and (my) muscles,
19. (like this seed of the pea may it be destroyed, and)
20. on (this day may) the burning flame (consume it).
21. May the ban depart that I may see the light.

22. Incantation.—On her maiden (Istar) has laid the command (?),
23. Istar[4] has directed (her maiden).
24. The maiden has settled (the man in her bed?);
25. with white thread (and) black thread the rod has folded a snare double upon the distaff,
26. a huge snare, a great snare, a varicoloured snare, a snare that removes the ban.
27. (Against) the curse of the evil ban of mankind,
28. (against) the malediction of the gods,
29. the snare that removes the ban
30. (the man) binds about (his head), his hands and his feet.

---

[1] *Kispu*, ideographically "evil breath."

[2] *Rukhû*, ideographically "breath of violence."

[3] *Rusû*, ideographically "breath of casting down" ($\oplus$ 255). In W. A. I. ii. 29, 34, *pinnaru rusê* is interpreted "the demon who injures the womb."

[4] Nin-lil in the Accadian text.

APPENDIX III.

31. Merodach, the son of Eridu, the prince, with his pure hands breaks (it);
32. may he send the ban of that snare to the desert, a pure place.
33. May the evil ban settle elsewhere.
34. May this man be pure and resplendent!
35. To the prospering hands of his god may he be entrusted!
40. Conclusion (of the spell) for breaking the ban.

---

41. Incantation.—I uplift a vessel large and stately and kindle the fire.
42. I kindle the coal, I burn the whole offering.

Col. iv. 1. The pure pourer of libations to Ea, the messenger of Merodach am I.
2. The coal I have kindled (and) I lull to rest.
3. The fire have I lighted (and) I increase.
4. The whole offering I have offered (and) I glorify.
5. Like the coal I have kindled, I will lull to rest;
6. (like) the fire I have lighted, I will increase;
7. (like) the whole offering I have offered, I will glorify.
8. May the god of herbs, the assembler of god and man,
9. unloose the knot he has knotted.
10. From the knot of the heart may the god and goddess of so-and-so, the son of so-and-so, deliver him.
11. May his backsliding be outpoured on this day.
12. May they forgive him, may they deliver him!

---

13. Incantation.—Rest, O Fire-god the warrior!
14. Along with thee may the mountains (and) rivers rest!
15. With thee may the Tigris and (Euphrates) rest!
16. With thee may the sea (and) the seas rest!
17. With thee may the road (*kharran*) rest, the daughter of the (great) gods!
18. With thee may the plant of the high-place rest, the growth of the height (*suli*)!
19. With thee may the heart of my god and my goddess who are angry rest!
20. With thee may the heart of the god of my city and the goddess of my city who are angry rest!
21. On this day may the heart of my god and my goddess unloose the knot,
22. and may the ban depart from my body!
23. Since thou (enlightenest) the judge with thy light,

24. and (grantest) thy protection to the arbitrator,
25. judge my judgment, decide my decision!

26. [First line of the next tablet:] Incantation.—Wherefore has the locust issued forth from (the heaven)?
27. The (sixth) tablet of the *surpu* (consumption) series.
28. (Like its) copy (written and published).
29. Property of (Assur-bani-pal, king of legions,) king (of Assyria)."

VIII. K 1284, published by Lenormant, *Études accadiennes*, ii. 1, pp. 239 *sq.*

1. "Incantation.—The evil plague-demon burns up[1] the land like fire.
2. The plague-demon like the fever (*asakku*) attacks the man.
3. The plague-demon in the desert like a cloud of dust makes his way.
4. The plague-demon like a foe takes captive the man.
5. The plague-demon like a flame consumes the man.
6. The plague-demon, though he hath neither hands nor feet, ever goes round and round.
7. The plague-demon like destruction cuts down the sick man."

IX. Magical formulæ published by Haupt, *Akkadische und Sumerische Keilschrifttexte*, ii. pp. 77—79.

Obv. 1. "Incantation.—The pure waters ....
2. The waters of the Euphrates whose place is ....
3. The water which in the deep is firmly established.
4. The pure mouth of Ea purifies them.
5. The sons of the deep are those seven.
6. The waters glisten purely, the waters are bright, the waters shine.
7. In the presence of your father Ea,
8. may he be pure, may he be bright, may he shine.
9. May the evil tongue depart elsewhere.
10. Conclusion of the spell.—Before a vessel of pure water repeat the prayer thrice.
11. Incantation. —The river-god is fresh and bright like a wrestler (?).
12. The cry of the ban before him is like (that of) a demon (*alê*).

---

[1] *Ikhimu.* In S 1425. 1, 2, the ideograph is rendered by *iqammû.* The fragment runs: "(The demons) burn up the land like water (?), ... compassion they know not, ... against mankind they rush."

APPENDIX III.

13. All the earth it encloses like the height of the firmament (*simetan*).
14. May the Sun-god at his rising banish its darkness, and never may there be night in the house.

Rev. 1. May the ban depart to the desert (to) a pure place.
2. The ban, O spirit of heaven, conjure! O spirit of earth, conjure!
3. Conclusion of the spell.—For undoing the ban when with the water of the river-god thou assistest him (*tukattar-su*).
4. Incantation.—O Fire-god, the sentient chief who art exalted in the land,
5. the warrior, the son of the deep, who art exalted in the land,
6. O Fire-god, in thy holy fire,
7. in the house of darkness thou settest the light.
8. Of all that is called by a name thou fixest the destiny, and
9. of bronze and lead thou art the mingler (i.e. melter).
10. Of gold and silver[1] thou art the prosperer.
11. Of Nin-ka-śi thou art the companion.
12. Thou art he who turns the breast of the foe at night.
13. May the limbs of the man, the son of his god, be bright!
14. Like the heaven may he be pure!
15. Like the earth may he be bright!
16. Like the midst of heaven may he shine!
17. May the evil tongue (depart) elsewhere!
18. Conclusion of the spell for undoing the ban . . . .

S 504. *Rev.*
1. Incantation.—Land land, land . . . .
2. thine, thine, thine . . . .
3. (is) the mouth, the mouth, the mouth, the mouth . . . .
4. of the lord, the lord, the lord, the lord, the lord, the lord, the lord, ...
5. the unique, the unique, the unique, the unique . . . .
6. unique (among) men . . . .
7. O spirit of heaven, conjure!
8. O spirit of Mul-lil, king of the world, (conjure!)
9. O spirit of Nin-lil, lady of the world, (conjure!)
10. O spirit of Adar, son of Ê-sarra, (conjure!)
11. O spirit of Nergal, king of Cutha, (conjure!)
12. O spirit of the Sun-god, king of Larśa, (conjure!)
13. O spirit of Nusku . . . ."

---

[1] In the Semitic version, "of silver and gold."

IV.

HYMNS TO THE GODS.

I. Hymn to Adar (Haupt, *Akkadische und Sumerische Keilschrifttexte*, ii. No. 10).

1. "The sting of the scorpion (*labi*),[1] the mighty serpent of the god, thou removest, making (its poison) to turn away from the land.
2. Adar, the king, the son of Mul-lil, has caused it to turn into itself.
3. He is the warrior whose lasso overthrows the foe.
4. O Adar, the fear of thy shadow inclines towards the world.
5. He assembles his people in strength to invade the hostile country.
6. Adar, the king, the son of his father, has made them turn the face against distant lands.
7. On the throne of the shrine supreme, even on his seat, is a brilliant light[2] when he lights it up.
8. At the festival they establish him joyfully in his seat.
9. He is the rival of Anu and Mul-lil, he maketh the wine to be good.
10. Bahu supplicates him with a prayer for the king.
11. Adar the lord, the son of Mul-lil, is the determiner of destiny.
12. The time is the weapon of my lord, in the mountain are his ears.
13. The god who binds the hosts of the firmament speaks to the lord, to Adar!
14. 'O lord, a station on high (is thy habitation) . . . .
15. O Adar, thy command changes not . . . .'

16. Anu the lord has created the earth.
17. Adar, the warrior who knows not fear, (has driven away) the pest.
18. The son of the nurse, the unresting, has (suckled) the essence of milk.

---

[1] Not "lion."

[2] Compare the Shekinah of the Hebrew writers, the light which shone over the mercy-seat.

19. O lord, the offspring that knows not a father, the smiter of the mountain,
20. the strong (*darru*) hero, before whom the foe exists not,
21. Adar, manly exalter, who makes joyful his side,
22. O warrior, like a bull, mayest thou strengthen the side.
23. The lord who (grants) pardon to his city (and) action to his mother,
24. has driven the chariot over the mountain, has scattered wide the seed.
25. (Men) altogether have proclaimed his name daily for sovereignty over them.
26. In their midst, like a great wild bull, has he lifted up his horns.
27. The *śu* stone, the precious stone, the strong stone, the snake-stone and the mountain-stone,
28. the warrior—the fire-stone too—their warrior carries away to the cities.[1]
29. The tooth of the worm (*kuśî*) that comes forth from the mountain he binds.
30. To their hand, their city, their god and their land he brings it back."

II. W.A.I. ii. 19. No. 2. Hymn to Merodach.

Obv. 1. "The smiter of the neck, the falchion, the blade that proclaims me Anu,[2] (I bear).
2. That from whose hand the mountain escapes not, the lasso of battle, (I bear).
3. The spear (Sum. *agar*) of the hero, the long shaft of battle, (I bear).
4. The strap which is bound fast to the man, the bow (*qastu*) of the deluge (*abubi*),[3] (I bear).

---

[1] This line is evidently corrupt, and since the Semitic *qarradu* has been introduced into the Accadian text, it must be regarded as an interpolation. The line must originally have run, *uru-sag eri bab-śig-śig*, "the hero has carried to the city."

[2] In the original Accadian, "the blade of my divinity."

[3] Is this an allusion to the "bow" of Gen. ix. 13—16? At any rate the original phrase, "the bow of the deluge," is Accadian (*gisme mâtu*), and the word *gisme*, "bow," is rendered not by the usual Assyrian *midpanu*, but by *qastu*, the Heb. *qesheth*. [For the pronunciation of GIS-BAM, "bow," see W.A.I. ii. 39, 31.] A fragmentary text gives an account of the arming of Merodach with "the bow of Anu" in "the assembly of the gods" before his combat with Tiamat, and one of the constellations was named "the star of the bow."

HYMNS TO THE GODS.

5. Destroying the temples of the foe, the bow and the arrow (*kababa*) (I bear).
6. The deluge of battle, the weapon of fifty heads, (I bear).
7. That which like the monstrous snake bears the yoke on its seven heads (I bear).
8. That which like the strong serpent of the sea (drives?) the foe before it,
9. the overthrower of mighty battle, prevailing over heaven and earth, the weapon of (fifty) heads, (I bear).
10. That whose light gleams forth like the day, the god of the eastern mountain, who binds the hand, (I bear).
11. The establisher of heaven and earth, the god whose hand has no foe, (I bear).
12. The weapon, the terror of whose splendour (overwhelms) the earth,
13. which in my right hand mightily is made to go, (and) with gold and crystal (is covered),
14. (which) is set for the view (of mankind), the god who ministers to life, (I bear).
15. The weapon (which like) .... battles against the hostile land, the weapon of fifty heads, (I bear).

. . . . . .

Rev. 1. Like a bird ....
2. May their habitation be pure!
3. Against the terror of my splendour, which is glorious as Anu, who can stand?
4. I am lord of the tower-like mountains, as high as the winds they look.[1]
5. With a mountain of diamond (?),[2] of turquoise and of crystal, I fill my hand.
6. The spirits of the earth like a swine grope in the hollows.
7. In the mountain, to the hand of my supreme warriorship, I .... my hand.
8. In my right hand the god who binds the hosts of the firmament I bear.
9. In my left hand the god who slays the hosts of the firmament I bear.

---

[1] This is the Semitic paraphrase, the translator having punned upon the resemblance of the Semitic *sâri*, "winds," to the Accadian *sarra*, "the hosts of the firmament." The original Accadian text is literally, "which to the dwelling-place of the hosts of the firmament turn the head."

[2] Literally, "stone of light."

10. The Sun-god of fifty faces, the falchion which proclaims me as Anu, I bear.
11. The hero who destroys the mountain, the Sun-god who lifts not up the offering, I bear.
12. The weapon, which like a monster (*usumgalli*) devours the corpses (of the dead), I bear.
13. The destroyer of the mountain, the glorious weapon of Anu, I bear.
14. The subduer (*musaknis*) of the mountain, the fish with seven fins, I bear.
15. The offspring of battle, the flail of the hostile land, I bear."[1]

III. W.A.I. ii. 19. No. 1. Compared with R 126 (Hymn to Adar).
Obv. 1. "Below in the deep a loud voice is heard (*lit.* taken);
2. the terror of the splendour of Anu in the midst of heaven is the extension of his path.
3. The spirits of the earth, the great gods, urge him on (?).
4. The lord like the deluge descends.[2]
5. Adar, the destroyer of the fortress of the hostile land, descends like the deluge.
6. . . . . the hostelries in the precinct (?) of heaven . . . .
7. (He establishes) his path by the command of Mul-lil, destroying the temple.
8. The hero of the gods who sweeps away the land.
9. To Nippur from afar (*nisis*) he draws not near.
10. Nuzku, the supreme messenger of Mul-lil, receives him in the temple (È-kur).
11. To the lord Adar he addresses words of peace.
12. 'O my king, thou makest warlike deeds perfect (*suklulat*), to thyself give ear.
13. O my king, thou makest warlike deeds (*qarradat*) perfect, to thyself give ear.
14. The terror of thy splendour like a . . . .

Rev. 1. Thy chariot is the voice of its thundering (*ana rigim rimeme-sa*).
2. In thy marching, heaven and earth are its face.
3. To the lifting up of thy hands is the shadow turned.
4. The spirits of the earth, the great gods, return to the winds.[3]

---

[1] It is probable that the places of the obverse and reverse ought to be interchanged.

[2] Literally, "opens the clouds," *iptah*, for which see W.A.I. iv. 23, 11.

[3] This is the Semitic "translation," which, however, is due to bad etymologising on the part of the translator, who has identified the Semitic *sâru*,

HYMNS TO THE GODS.

5. Thy father on his seat thou fearest not.
6. Mul-lil on his seat thou fearest not.
7. The spirits of the earth on the seat of the height of the assembly thou bindest not.
8. May thy father present thee with a gift in the hands of thy warriorship.
9. May Mul-lil present thee with a gift in the hands of thy warriorship.
10. A mighty king is Anu, the first-born of the gods.
11. The creation (*sitkin*) of Mul-lil, the creation of the life of É-kur.
12. (Thou art) the warrior of the mountain who subjugatest,
13. .... the one god will not urge on.'"

IV. R 117.
Obv. 10. "For the lord .... he took and utters the prayer:
11. 'O lord, in thy city (which) thou lovest may thy heart be at rest!
12. O lord Adar, (in the house which) thou lovest may thy heart be at rest!

Rev. 1. In the temple of Nippur, thy city which thou lovest, (may thy heart be at rest!)
2. Into the house of prayer and listening, the seat of the goodness of thy heart, in joy descend.
3. The (handmaid) of thy wife is the servant of Nin-lil.
4. Speak to her from thy heart, speak (to her) from thy liver.
5. Declare (in) the land the goodness of the king unto distant regions.'"

V. K 5001.
1. "O lord, who liftest up the torch (*dipari*), who pursuest swiftly (*mukhammedh*) the foe,
2. who carriest away the land of the disobedient, may thy heart be exalted!
3. Thou who destroyest (*mupalli*) the life of the evil one, may thy heart be exalted!
4. Thou who rainest fire and stones[1] upon the enemy, may thy heart be exalted!"

"wind," and *taru*, "to return," with the Accadian *sarra*, "the hosts of the firmament," and *nam-tar*, "destiny." The Accadian original is really, "as far as the hosts of the firmament determine destiny."

[1] In the Semitic translation, "stones and fire." Compare the account of the destruction of the cities of the plain in Gen. xix. 24: "The Lord rained upon Sodom and upon Gomorrah brimstone and fire."

VI. W. A. I. iv. 11.

Obv. 1. "(The chief shepherd [*damgarru*]) became hostile (*ittakhap*); all the world was troubled.
2. (The lord) of the chief shepherd became hostile; all the world was troubled.
3. He cried in the house (*es*) of Nipur:
4. 'In Ê-kur is the dwelling of the hero of the house of life.'
5. In Sippara he was hostile :
6. 'The temple of Babára is the house of the judge of the world.'
7. In Babylon was he hostile :
8. 'Ê-Saggil is the house of the temple of the resting-place of the world.'
9. In Borsippa did he become hostile :
10. 'In Ê-Zida is the house of the supreme temple of life ;
11. the (temple) of the foundations of heaven and earth is the house of the temple of the antelope of heaven.'
12. His lord sets the offering.[1]
13. (On) a throne of pain he seats himself.
14. His lord behind him delivered not the oracle.
15. Ul-lilli (Mul-lil) descended to the ghosts.
16. With tears he weeps and mourns.
17. In the distance one far off he (sees).
18. (On) his mound a fire (he kindled ?).
19. His god with the reed of weeping . . . .
20. The anointer-priest speaks not.
21. The gallos-priest says not: 'When shall thy heart (be pacified) ?'
22. The anointer comes forth from the (place of) anointing (*kuzbi*).
23. His lord comes forth from the corn-field.
24. The gallu-priest comes forth from his (place of) supplication.
25. His lord sits not down, his mistress sits not down.
26. His lord shouted and rode upon the mountain.
27. His mistress shouted and rode to the mountain.
28. 'The fox is tied by his tail.'[2]
29. Lifting up his voice with the many-coloured bird he answers.
30. His heart is . . . .

Rev. 6. The incantation (in Sippara) is evil.
7. The house of the temple of Babára is evil.
8. The incantation in Babylon is evil.
9. The incantation in Ê-Saggil is evil.

---

[1] In the Semitic version, "trembles."

[2] "Turned round" in the Semitic version.

HYMNS TO THE GODS.

10. The incantation in Borsippa is evil.
11. The incantation in Ê-Zida is evil.
12. In the supreme temple of life it is evil.
13. In the temple of the foundations of heaven and earth it is evil.
14. In the temple of the antelope of heaven it is evil.
15. What is that which is in the heart of my lord?
16. What is there in his ear?
17. What has he perceived with his holy ear?
18. The god has wrought destruction (*sakhluqta*).
19. He has caused the river to carry away (the people).
20. He has caused (the simoom?) of sickness (*pusti*) to come forth from the desert.
21. The (hair?) of the head has been sown as seed in the field.
22. .... he cries out; words he addresses to him:
23. 'O (Mul)-lil and wife (of thee) Nin-lil!
24. His (spouse), the lady of the temple of ....'
25. (To the queen) the divine lady of Nipur he utters the cry.
26. .... the world he completes.
29. .... thou restorest.
30. .... during the night thou completest.
31. .... among the flocks thou art set.
32. .... night by night a watch thou establishest.
33. .... and write the tablet of his blessedness."

VII. W. A. I. iv. 13. No. 1. On the execution of a stone image of Adar.

Obv. 1, 2. "(The god) Adar, the lord, the son of Mul-(lil, who can rival thee?)
3. The strong stone (*usû*), which in my battle (the bow contains),
4. like a glorious eye (is seen).
5. Thy hand thou raisest not ....
6. In sovereignty the lord is alone (supreme).
7. O Adar, the lord, the son of Mul-lil, who can rival (thee)?
8. From the lofty mountains of Elam may it be fetched.
9. From the mountain of Magan (Sinai) may it be brought down.
10. Thou art (as) strong bronze, like the skin (thou art smooth?)
11. I am lord; to the hands of my warriorship mightily I (commit it?).
12. (I am) the king who establishes his name for a life of long days.
13. His image is resplendent unto future days.
14. In the temple of Mul-lil (L) the temple of completion ....
15. a place of drinking (and eating), for beauty (constructed),

16. the lord has made good the stone.
17. For his body has he made its stonework.
18. Adar, the lord, the son of Mul-lil, (drives away ?) the curse of rain.
19. The stone which when it is harmful (?) to me, he . . . .
20. that stone, which for my battle the bow holds (ta[mikh]),[1]
21. mayest thou, when thou ragest like a wild boar, overshadow.
23. It is laid, and according to the message is wrought, to its smallest parts it is made perfect.
24. May he who knows thee bring thee back to the waters.
25. My king has taken the stone of the papyrus for a stone,
26. Adar, the lord, the son of Mul-lil, cuts it not.
27. The opening (of) the ear thou makest holy (tuqdis); mayest thou send terror.

Rev. 1. In the land of the foe, in all the world together, mayest thou proclaim my name.
2. In peace with thee have I walked uprightly.
3. May thy might[2] be hard upon him that is made small.
4. My command in thy body let it guide aright.
5. In the slaughter of the weapon the warrior whom thou slayest is utterly destroyed.
6. On the altar supreme mayest thou lay the table of shewbread (*birutu*)!
7. May one purify the land happily for thee, and establish it in exaltation.
8. My king has taken the mountain-stone for a stone.
9. To its strength he gives answer.
10. Adar the lord, the son of Mul-lil, cuts it not.
11. (He is) the hero exalted, the lifting up of the light of whose eyes is upon other lands.
12. The mountain-stone (it is) which in the hostile land utters strongly (?) (its) cry to you.
13. A woman (?) did not fall (?) into my hand.
14. With the strong I was not weak (*attadhû*).
15. At the foot of thy men thou didst pour out the . . . .
16. May the command of the Sun-god be a command unto thee!
17. Like a judge direct the world aright.
18. He who knows the command, whatever be his name,

---

[1] The hymn must be of some antiquity, since stone arrow-heads are here referred to.

[2] *Rabbut*, Accadian *gurra;* see W.A.I. v. 20, 22.

HYMNS TO THE GODS. 487

19. to the command may he guide thee."

VIII. W. A. I. iv. 13. No. 2.
1. "Thy hand is clean, thy hand is white;
2. may the hands of the gods that accompany thee be clean, may their hands be white!
3. On a pure dish eat pure food.
4. In a pure vessel drink pure water.
5. May the king, the son of his god, give ear to thee for judgment (= at the judgment-seat)."

IX. W. A. I. iv. 14. No. 2.
Obv. 1. "Incantation.—The pure waters . . . .
2. The waters of the Euphrates which in a place . . . .
3. The waters which are for ever collected together[1] in the deep,
4. the pure mouth of Ea has made resplendent.
5. The sons of the deep, those seven,
6. have made the waters resplendent, have made the waters white, have made the waters shine.
7. In the presence of your father Ea,
8. in the presence of your mother Dav-kina,
9. may it be resplendent, may it be white, may it shine.
10. May the evil mouth, unresting, be closed.
11. End of the incantation. Repeat it three times, using pure water.

12. Incantation.—The curse is before him; its cry is like that of a demon;
13. it binds all the world like the zenith of the dawn.
14. The Sun-god at his rising scatters its darkness, and never may there be gloom in the house!

Rev. 1. May the curse depart to the desert, a pure place!
2. The curse, O spirit of heaven, conjure! O spirit of earth, conjure!
3. Conclusion of the incantation for exorcising the evil spell. The earth, O river-god, thou dost surround (*tukattar*).

4. Incantation.—The fire-god (is) the prince (vizier) who is high in the earth,
5. the warrior, the son of the deep, who is high in the earth.
6. O Fire-god, by thy pure fire,
7. in the house of darkness thou makest light.

---

[1] Literally, "firmly established," in the Semitic version.

8. Thou determinest the destiny of all that is called by a name.
9. Of bronze and lead thou art the mingler.
10. Of gold and silver[1] thou art the benedictor.
11. Thou art the companion of the god Nin-guśi.
12. Thou art he that turnest (to flight) the breast of the evil man at night.
13. Mayest thou enlighten the limbs of the man the son of his god.
14. Like heaven may he be pure!
15. Like the midst of heaven may he shine!"

X. W. A. I. iv. 14. No. 3. Hymn to Nebo.

1. "To Nebo the supreme messenger, who binds all things together,
2. the scribe of all that has a name, for thy purity[2] (ascribe) the lordship.
3. The lifter up of the stylus supreme, the director of the world.
4. The possessor of the reed of augury, the traverser of strange (lands),
5. the opener of the wells, the fructifier of the corn,
6. the god without whom[3] the irrigated land (*iku*) and the canal are un(watered),
7. the glorious lord who pours out the oil of anointing and the unguent,
8. hear the prayer, (consider) the supplication!
9. O mighty hero, king (of É-Zida?)."

XI. W. A. I. iv. 18. No. 1. Hymn on the building of Ê-Saggil.

1. "(The god who dwells?) in Babylon has proclaimed its name for ever.[4]
2. .... at the gate of the deep he built the house he loves.
3. (The men) of the city he fills with joy and gladness.
4. Its head like heaven he raised.[5]
5. At the gate of the deep founding the house (with) fear and mercy, for the glory of his godhead he made it march.
6. (O Bel) and Zarpanit, thy holy shrine he founds.

---

[1] The order is reversed in the Semitic version.

[2] The Semitic version seems to have "wisdom."

[3] The Accadian has "the gods without him," but the Semitic translator has mistaken the plural for a singular.

[4] In the Accadian, *zides*, from *zida*, "perpetual."

[5] Comp. Gen. xi. 4.

7. He caused (his guardian priests?) to inhabit the seat of abundance.
8. The .... for its midst he opened.
9. (In the oracle) a favourable destiny he determines (*isama*).
10. (The men of the city joy and) gladness established.
11. .... the goddess (satisfies) the heart with sounds of music day and night."[1]

XII. W. A. I. iv. 18. No. 2. Fragment of a hymn to Merodach.

Obv. 1. "The resting-place of the lord of the supreme temple of life is thy house,
2. Ê-Saggil, the temple of thy lordship, is thy house.
3. May thy city speak to thee of a resting-place: (it is) thy house.
4. May Babylon speak to thee of a resting-place: (it is) thy house.
5. May Anu, the chief, the father of the gods, say to thee: 'When (wilt thou) rest?'
6. May the great mountain (*sadu rabu*), the father of Mul-lil, (say to thee): 'When (wilt thou rest)?'
7. May Zikum, (the mistress) of the house, the mighty mother of Mul-lil, (say to thee): 'When (wilt thou rest)?'
8. May the (spirits of the earth) of Mul-lil, the supreme powers of Anu, (say to thee): 'When (wilt thou rest)?'

. . . . . .

Rev. 1. Look down upon thy temple, look down upon thy city, O lord of rest!
2. Look down upon Babylon and Ê-Saggil, O lord of rest!
3. The scenery of Babylon, the enclosure of Ê-Saggil, the brickwork of Ê-Zida, may he restore to their place!
4. May the gods of heaven and earth say unto thee: 'O lord, be at rest!'
5. Give life to Ansar (Assur)[2] thy shepherd, thy feeder; hear his prayer!
6. Lay well the foundations of the throne of his sovereignty; may he nourish the seed of men unto everlasting days!
7. The lifting up of the hand to Merodach."

XIII. W. A. I. iv. 18. No. 3.
1. "On the seat of the holy of holies of the oracle ....

---

[1] "Night and day" in the Semitic version.

[2] An Assyrian scribe seems to have introduced the name of the old capital city of Assur into the line in place of some deity, probably Tammuz, who is called "the divine son" in the Accadian text.

2. a staff of crystal for .... of the shepherd .... (place in) his hand.
3. Honey, milk and abundance of (corn, give to him).
4. The mountain which bears the offering, even the offering of....
5. The desert (and) the field which bear the offering, even the offering of ....
6. The garden of fruit which bears the offering, even the offering of ....
7. In the right hand of the king the shepherd of his country may the Sun-god be (carried?).
8. In his left hand may the Moon-god be (carried?).
9. May thy prospering spirit (*sêdu*), thy prospering colossos of the lordship and sovereignty of the land, rest upon his body!

10. Conclusion of the spell for a storm (?).

11. Incantation.—The weapon which scatters rays of brilliance, that is made beautiful for kingship,
12. the lofty falchion which has been fitted for the hands of sovereignty,
13. the forceful flash, made for the hand to grasp (*sutaskhar*), there is none who faces.
14. (It is) for the land of the enemy to sweep away the attacking foe.
15. Ea, the king of the deep,
16. answered Nin-gur (?), the chief handmaid of Anu, and the word he takes:
17. 'Go, Nin-gur (?), great handmaid of Anu!
18. In the holy forest of the wood of the locust (?),
19. the great stones, the great stones that are made beautiful with rejoicing,
20. that are fitted to become the body[1] of the gods,
21. the porous stone (*khulal*) of the eyes, the porous stone of the snake's sting, the porous-stone, the turquoise, the crystal,
22. the *gubsu* stone, the precious stone, glass[2] completely doubled,[3]
23. its *sapingu* stone, (and) gold must be taken,
24. to be set on the pure breast of the man for an adornment.

---

[1] "Flesh" in the Assyrian version. Of course, stone images are meant.

[2] *Elmesu*, Accadian *sudam*.

[3] *Antasurra*, explained in W.A.I. ii. 20, 5, by *tsuppuru sa libbi*, "folding of the heart." In W.A.I. iv. 26, 38, it is the equivalent of the Assyrian *zarikhu*.

25. The pure god who is exalted afar, the supreme bull of Mul-lil purifies and enlightens.
26. May the evil prince depart to another place.

27. The great stones, the great stones, the great stones of honour,
28. (the fragment) of crystal, the fragment of crystal,
29. the holy (stones) which are full of beauty and rejoicing, that are fitted to be gazed upon,
30. (which are) the flesh of the gods, very brilliant are they,
31. even the *gubsu* (stone), the eye-stone of Melukhkha and the porous stone!"

XIV. W.A.I. iv. 20. No. 2. Hymn to the Sun-god.
1. "O Sun-god, on the horizon of heaven thou dawnest!
2. The pure bolts of heaven thou openest!
3. The doors of heaven thou openest!
4. O Sun-god, thou liftest up thy head to the world!
5. O Sun-god, thou coverest the earth with the bright firmament of heaven!
6. Thou settest the ear to (the prayers) of mankind;
7. thou plantest the foot of mankind . . . .
8. The cattle of the god (Ner thou enlightenest)."

XV. W.A.I. iv. 20. No. 3. Hymn to Nebo.
1. " . . . . O lord of Borsippa!
2. Thou createst (?) the power, O son of Ê-Saggil!
3. O lord, there is no power that can compare with thy power!
4. O lord, who givest the name to Borsippa,[1] there is no power that can compare with thy power!
5. There is no temple that can compare with thy temple Ê-Zida!
6. There is no city that can compare with thy city Borsippa!
7. There is no place that can compare with thy place Babylon!
8. Thy weapon is the unique monster (*usumgallu*), from whose mouth the breath pours not out (*inattuku*), the blood drips not (*izarruru*).
9. Thy command is unchangeable like the heavens; in heaven thou art supreme!"

XVI. W.A.I. iv. 21. No. 1.
Obv. 1. "At the lifting up of your[2] hands, with a dark blue dress (*tsubatu*) I cover myself.

---

[1] In the Semitic rendering, simply "Nebo."
[2] The Semitic version mistranslates "their."

2. A robe (*samlinna*) of many colours I place in your hands; a cedar-tree whose heart is strong . . . .
3. The barrier I have completely drawn; with clean hands the *sagatstsi* (destroyers ?) I have brought for you.
4. The . . . . of the corn god, the curse of the gods I have brought for you.

. . . . . .

8. Complete the . . . . of the image with two-fold knottings of the image.
9. (Set) the image of the baleful *gallu*-demon on the head of the sick man on the right hand and the left.
10. (Set) the image of Nergal (Lugal-nerra) who has no rival on the enclosure of the house.
11. (Set) the image of 'Sulim-ta-e who has no rival . . . .
12. (Set) the image of Narudu, who (performs) the commands of the great gods, below on the bed . . . .
13. Against all evil that cannot be faced (set) the Honey-god and Latarak in the gate (of the house).
14. To expel all that is evil (set) him who[1] shatters the offspring of evil in front of its gate.
15. (Set) the twin fighters, the *sagatstsi*, in the midst of the gate.
16. (Set) the twin fighters who bind the hand on the threshold of the gate on the right hand and on the left.
17. (Set) the image of the watcher of Ea and Merodach in the midst of the gate on the right hand and on the left.
18. (This?) is the spell of Aśari (Merodach) who dwells in the image . . . .

. . . . . .

Rev. 1. A spell! a spell! He laid on him the curse like the going down of cattle and the coming up of cattle.
2. Ye are the offspring of the pure deep, the children of Ea.
3. Eat what is good, drink honey water, ye are a watch that no evil (happen).

---

4. Like a god he concealed (?) the face of the seven images on (his) hand . . . .
5. Before them (his) foot was stationary, and to the presence of the seven images . . . .

---

[1] Here the Semitic translator, who in the previous line has transferred the Accadian *nu-té* into the Semitic text, has introduced the Semitic relative pronoun *sa* into the Accadian text. The whole text has evidently undergone extensive alterations.

6. of the cedar (and) of the weapons which they lifted up.

7. Incantation.—The slaughterer of the hostile incubus,
8. the presenter of life, the very strong (*mugdhasru*),
9. who turns the breast of the evil one,
10. the protector of the oracle of Mul-lil,
11. the fire-god who sweeps away the foe,
12. the falchion which overwhelms the plague,
13. the dragon (*mamlu*) which shines brightly,[1]
14. the gods seven, the destroyers of hostility.

15. (The god) who makes perfect the barrier of heaven and earth."

XVII. W.A.I. iv. 22. No. 1.

Obv. 1. "(The demon) from Ê-kur has come forth.
2. From the temple of Nipur he has come forth.
3. The female spirit devours with a snake's mouth.[2]
4. He has not overshadowed the . . . . he has not made good the evil.
5. The sickness of night and day is he.
6. His hand is the storm-demon (*alû*), his side is the deluge.
7. His face is that of the god of destruction.
8. His eye is filled with the shadow of the forest.
9. The sole (*muzzulu*) of his foot is the *lullub* tree.[3]
10. May he lift up the muscle as he hurries (it) along.
11. He makes (all) creatures hurry (in fear).
12. Lifting up the body he seizes the . . . .

. . . . .

20. The side like a brick he breaks in pieces.
21. The breast like a snare he tears in two.
22. The ribs like an old ship he shatters.
23. The very heart like a double frame he seizes.
24. The locust he makes lie down like water-cress.
25. The . . . . he divides like an ox.
26. The . . . . he slaughters and the ox he spares not.
27. The ox he slaughters and the wild bull he tames not.
28. He . . . . and makes not perfect his horns.
29. He slaughters (the cows) and makes not their oxen.

---

[1] In the Accadian, "is favourable."

[2] In the Semitic version, simply *pasidhtuv*, "the destroyer."

[3] In Accadian, "the *atu* of the desert," here described as "the tree of the supreme spirit."

30. The cattle of the field he slaughters, and like a cloud of . . . . locusts sweeps along together.
31. Like a bow made ready (*basme*) he fills all that has a name.
32. Merodach beholds him, and
33. to his father Ea into the house he entered and says:
34. 'O my father, the demon of madness has gone forth from Ê-kur.'
35. Twice did he address him, and
36. what the man may do he knows not, or how he may be at rest.

Rev. 1. Ea answered his son Merodach:
2. 'My son, what knowest thou not, what can I teach thee?
3. Merodach, what knowest thou not, what can I teach thee?
4. What I know, thou too knowest.
5. Go, my son Merodach!
6. Take the . . . . of the vault and
7. at the mouth of the twin rivers take the waters, and
8. lay thy holy spell on their waters.
9. Purify (them) with thy pure charm.
10. Sprinkle the . . . . of the man the son of his god.
11. Bind the bond upon his head.
12. Let him be fed abundantly.
13. At the dayspring give the command.
14. In the broad street place (him).
15. Let the madness of his head be removed (from him).
16. May the malady of the head which has descended (*kitmuru*) like the rain (*zunni*) of the night be driven away.
17. May the word of Ea issue forth like the dawn!
18. May Dav-kina direct (it)!
19. May Merodach, the eldest son of the deep, be light and happiness unto thee!"

XVIII. W. A. I. iv. 22. No. 2.

1. "Merodach thine enkindler (?) (*dali*) . . . .
2. in the night he was in grief, in the day he was troubled.
3. And in a dream he sent unto him a warning (*gipilutuv*);
4. revealing (it) in a vision,[1] he did not direct him.
5. The questioner (of the oracle) at the altar (*mussakka*) did not open for him the eye.
6. His sick (neck) was not quiet in the yoke.
7. The . . . . with pure means did not soothe him.

---

[1] The ideograph used in the Accadian text for *biru*, "a vision," is the representative of *biru*, "produce," showing that this text belongs to the Semitic epoch.

8. Like an ox (in) the ..:.. was he.
9. Like a lamb (among) the bricks.... was he confounded, and
10. at the mouth of the camp (was he) laid."

XIX. W. A. I. iv. 23. No. 1.

Col. i. 6. "Seven are the gods the sons of Bel who is the voice of the firmament; they heap up the seat.

7. Twelve are the sons of copper; on the heart of the rim they lay the copper.
8. The rim of the copper is dark (*tekil*).

9. The great bull, the supreme bull, who treads down the pure pasturage,
10. has opened the heart (of it), spreading wide (its) fertility,
11. planting the corn, and beautifying the field;
12. my pure hands has he purified before thee!

13. The mouth of the deep ('the sea') which is between the ears of the bull is made; on the right is it made; a rim of copper I found.
14. On a reed whose head is cut thou shalt press a good reed.

15. The bull, the offspring of the god Zu, art thou!
16. At thy command am I carrying the pails for thee.
17. For ever is the Lady of the eternal tree thy comrade;
18. The great (gods?), who determine the boundaries,
19. who establish (*musim*) the laws of heaven and earth.
20. .... May the rim be watched over, and
21. .... to Bel may he present (*liqdhais*).

22. .... of the bull is made, on the left hand it is made; the rim[1] of copper I found.

23. How long, O lord of shade, shall the shade be a cover?
24. How long, O mighty mountain, father of Mul-lil, who art a shade?
25. O shepherd that determinest destiny, who art a shade, how long?

Col. ii. iii. and iv. are too mutilated for translation.

---

[1] *Lilisu* means the metal band which was laid over a door, like the metal bands that bound together and ran across the gates of Balawât. In this text, therefore, it may denote the "cover" of "the sea" rather than its "rim."

Last line: At the time when thou bringest the bull to the temple of Mummu (Chaos). The work of the gallos-priest."

XX. W. A. I. iv. 26, 1. Hymn to Nergal.
1. "O warrior, the mighty deluge, that sweepest away the hostile land !
2. O warrior of the great city of Hades, that sweepest away the hostile land !
3. O god that comest forth from 'Sulim, that sweepest away the hostile land !
4. O mighty ruler (*am*), illustrious (*nerra*) lord, that sweepest away the hostile land !
5. O lord of Cutha, that sweepest away the hostile land !
6. O lord of the temple of 'Sulim, that sweepest away the hostile land !
7. O gallos-spirit (*libir*) of the divine master of the dawn, that sweepest away the hostile land !
8. O warrior of the god Supulu, that sweepest away the hostile land !
9. the mighty deluge, who has no rival,
10. the uplifter of the weapon, who threshes out opposition !"

XXI. W. A. I. iv. 26. No. 5.
1. "(He traverses) the canal in his march ;
2. (he disturbs ?) the canal in his march ;
3. (he troubles ?) the public square (*ribitu*) when he seeks it ;
4. (he troubles ?) the canal (and) the street in his march.
5. The libation (and) the outpouring he treads down ;
6. in the waters that run not straight he plants the foot.
7. The waters of an unclean hand does he give.
8. The woman whose hand is unpropitious does he receive.
9. The handmaid whose hand is unclean he looks down on.
10. The woman of impurity he embraces."

XXII. W. A. I. iv. 26. No. 2.
1. "The poison of the snake which infects the sheepcote,
2. the poison of the scorpion which cannot be expelled from the man,
3. the poisonous water which descends in the dead of night,
4. the snare which is set at the edge of the forest,
5. the outspread net which is stretched unto the sea,

6. from whose meshes no fish can escape."

XXIII. W. A. I. iv. 26. No. 3. Hymn to Nuzku (as the Fire-god).
1. "The lord who giveth rest to the heart, counsellor of the counsels[1] of the great gods;
2. Nuzku, who giveth rest to the heart, counsellor of the counsels of the gods;
3. (god) of Nipur, who giveth rest to the heart, counsellor of the counsels of the gods;
4. wise prince, the flame of heaven, who giveth rest to the heart, counsellor of the counsels of the gods;
5. the chief Mubarra,[2] the exalted male,
6. who hurls down terror, whose clothing (?) is splendour;
7. the forceful Fire-god (Mubarra), the exalter of the mountain-peaks,
8. the uplifter of the torch, the enlightener of the darkness."

XXIV. W. A. I. iv. 26. No. 4.
1. "Who can escape from thy message (*piridi* or *puridi*)?
2. Thy word is the supreme snare which is stretched towards heaven and earth.
3. It turns to the sea, and the sea dreads it.
4. It turns to the marsh, and the marsh mourns.
5. It turns to the channel[3] of the Euphrates, and
6. the word of Merodach disturbs its bed.
7. O lord, thou art supreme! who is there that rivals thee?
8. O Merodach, among the gods as many as have a name thou art he that coverest them!"

XXV. W. A. I. iv. 26. No. 7.
1. ".... and with a rag (?) which is useless for the body,
2. (and) the water of a pool which the hand has not drawn, fill a cup that is bound with a cord;
3. place in it green corn, pieces of broken (?) cane, horned sugar (?) (*ukhula*) (and) drops of beer,
4. and lay it upon a double ring,
5. and give the man pure water to drink.

---

[1] *Malik milki.*

[2] Accadian (north Babylonian) form of the Sumerian Gubarra, rendered "the Fire-god" in the Semitic version.

[3] Literally, "band."

    6. Pour the water over him, and
    7. remove the womb of a crane, and
    8. compound the pure wine and pure sugar (?);
    9. the fat of a crane which has been brought from the mountains place in it, and
    10. seven times anoint (therewith) the body of the man."

XXVI. W. A. I. iv. 27. No. 4. Hymn to Mul-lil.
    1. "(Of thee), O Mul-lil, mighty is the power,
    2. who upliftest the terror of (thy) splendour, who protectest the day, who castest abroad (thy) majesty,
    3. lord of the morning-star, mighty (is thy) power,
    4. destiny supreme, who hurlest abroad (thy) majesty;
    5. the god of ghosts (Lillum)[1] was the father and mother that begat him, mighty is (his) power;
    6. the lasso that overthrows the hostile land;
    7. the great lord (and) warrior, mighty (is his) power;
    8. the house that exalts itself, which destroys the wicked sorcerer.
    9. Of thee, the lord of Nipur, even of thee, mighty (is) the power,
    10. O lord, the life of the land, the hero (*massu*) of heaven and earth."[2]

XXVII. W. A. I. iv. 27. No. 5. Perhaps a poem on the Deluge.
    1. . . . . (it overthrew?) them like a cup of outpoured wine.
    2. . . . . country to country ran together.
    3. It made the handmaid ascend her chamber (?);[3]
    4. the freeman it made to depart from the house of her trade.
    5. It drove the son from the house of his father;
    6. the doves in their cotes it took.
    7. The bird on its wing it caused to ascend;
    8. it made the swallow fly from his nest.
    9. The ox it slaughtered, the lamb it slaughtered;

---

[1] In the Accadian text, "the man of ghost(s)."

[2] In the Accadian text, "hero of the earth."

[3] *An(a)taki*. The word occurs again in the fragment of a bilingual poem, of which only the ends of the lines are preserved (S 704, 19), and which seems to refer to the deluge. The fragment is as follows (l. 8): " . . . . they made a tempest, ... the waters seized the corpses, ... like (a fisherman?) they caught the fish of the deep, ... they took the *dakkani*, ... they took the fortresses, ... of her chamber (*antaki*) they took, ... in the park of Istar they took, ... the lord of the gods received, ... it concealed him," &c.

10. the great serpents, the evil spirits (*utukku*), were their huntsmen.
11. They .... of the land.
12. In the brickwork of the foundations ....
13. The mountain like a cup that is bound with a cord ....
14. Balum, the mistress of the supreme ones, the mountain of the bond ....
15. The foot to the earth (she set) not.
16. The street of the land (she crossed) not."

XXVIII. W. A. I. iv. 27. No. 6.
1. "The lamb, during the day, which Tammuz[1] (feeds),
2. make to lie down in front of the sick man;
3. remove its heart;
4. place it in the hand of the man.
5. Repeat the spell of Eridu:
6. 'The offspring of his heart thou hast taken away;
7. turn back the food the man has swallowed;
8. expel, pour out, his food, which burns as fire.'[2]
9. Bind a wisp of straw round the man, and
10. repeat the spell of Eridu: 'O spirit of the great gods, conjure
11. the evil incubus (*utuk*), the evil *alu*, the evil demon (*ekimmu*),
12. the phantom (and) the vampire!'"

XXIX. W. A. I. iv. 28. No. 1. Hymn to the Sun-god.
Obv. 1. "O Sun-god, the (supreme) judge of the world art thou!
2. O lord of the living creation, the pitiful one who (directest) the world!
3. O Sun-god, on this day purify and illumine the king the son of his god!
4. Let all that is wrought of evil which is in his body be removed elsewhere!
5. Like the cup of the Zoganes, cleanse him!
6. Like a cup of ghee, make him bright!
7. Like the copper of a polished tablet, let him be made bright!
8. Undo his curse!
9. Until the day when he shall live, the supremacy ....
Rev. 1. With Anu and Mul-lil ....
2. Direct the law of the multitudes of mankind!
3. Thou art eternal righteousness in the heaven!

---

[1] *En-mirśi* in the Accadian text.
[2] Rendered by the Assyrian *kilutu*, "a burning," in 82, 9 (cf. M 602).

4. Thou art justice, even the bond[1] of the ears of the world!
5. Thou knowest right, thou knowest wickedness!
6. O Sun-god, righteousness has lifted up its foot![2]
7. O Sun-god, wickedness has been cut as with a knife!
8. O Sun-god, the minister of Anu and Mul-lil art thou!
9. O Sun-god, the judge supreme of heaven and earth art thou!

XXX. W.A.I. iv. 28. No. 2. Hymn to Rimmon.
8. .... the god, the lord of the deluge.
9. (Rimmon in) his anger has bound for him the heaven.
10. Rimmon in his strength has shaken for him the earth.
11. The mighty mountain, thou hast overwhelmed it.
12. At his anger, at his strength,
13. at his roaring, at his thundering,
14. the gods of heaven ascend to the sky,
15. the gods of earth descend to the earth.
16. Into the horizon of heaven they enter,
17. into the zenith of heaven they make their way."

XXXI. W.A.I. iv. 28. No. 4. (Haupt, *Keilschrifttexte*, p. 182.)
Obv. 1. "Of Babylon the digging up ....
2. Of the city the digging up ....
3. Of Nisin the digging up ....
4. The city whose corn is cut, in baskets (is carried?),
5. has let food be seen where there was no food.
6. She whose husband is a lad says: 'Where is my husband?'
7. The son of the lad says: 'Where is my son?'
8. The handmaid says: 'Where is my brother?'
9. In the city the mother who bears children says: 'Where is my son?'
10. The young girl says: 'Where is my father?'
11. He who resides in the street has driven (them) along.
12. The mean man comes forth, the great man comes forth (to destroy).
13. (From) Nipur the mean man comes forth, the great man comes forth.

---

[1] *Birit*. In W.A.I. iv. 14, 9, the same ideograph SI-GAL is rendered by *berati*, "well," an illustration of the artificial character of the language of the hymns to the Sun-god. The Accadian of this line is: "Justice in heaven, a bond on earth art thou."

[2] "Neck" in the Accadian text.

14. (From) Babylon the mean man comes forth, the great man comes forth.
15. (From) Niśin the mean man comes forth, the great man comes forth.
16. .... he made perfect the dog; he reared the watch-dog (*nadhiru*).
17. .... strength; he made perfect the hyæna.
18. .... he filled the dust-cloud.
19. .... not returning to his place.

. . . . .

Rev. 8. the god .... from the temple came not forth.
9. The goddess of the city of Kur-núna .... from the temple came not forth.
10. The mistress looked not towards her temple.
11. The mistress looked not towards her city.
12. The .... she knows, of the cities none exist.
13. On the mounds of the temple of her commands she prayed.
14. On the foundations of the temple in the city of her holy border she stood not.
15. On the hill of the city of the goddess Kur-núna she sat not.
16. To the pure ear of her city she speaks.
17. To Babylon the evil-doer she speaks:
18. 'My house, the house of my life, has suffered evil ....
19. The temple of Larśa has done ....'"

XXXII. W.A.I. iv. 29. No. I. Hymn to Merodach.

Obv. 1. "(O king) of the land, lord of the world!
2. (O king), first-born of Ea, powerful (over) heaven and earth!
3. .... mighty lord of mankind, king of the world, god of gods!
4. (Prince) of heaven and earth, who has no rival!
5. The companion of Anu and Mul-lil!
6. The merciful one among the gods!
7. The merciful one who loveth to give life to the dead!
8. Merodach, king of heaven and earth!
9. King of Babylon, lord of Ê-Saggil!
10. King of Ê-Zida, lord of Ê-makh-tila ('the supreme house of life')!
11. Heaven and earth are thine!
12. All round heaven and earth is thine!
13. The spell that giveth life is thine!
14. The breath that giveth life is thine!
15. The holy writing of the mouth of the deep is thine!
16. Mankind, even the black-headed race,

17. the living creatures as many as pronounce a name and exist in the earth,
18. the four zones, all that there are,
19. the angels of the hosts of heaven and earth, whatever be their number,
20. (all worship) thee and (lend to thee their) ears.

Rev. 1. Thou art the . . . .
2. Thou art the (good) colossos.
3. Thou art the (god) who givest life (to the dead).
4. Thou art the (god) who makest (the sick) whole,
5. the merciful one among the gods,
6. the merciful one who loveth to restore the dead to life,
7. Merodach, king of heaven and earth together.
8. Thy name I celebrate, thy majesty I declare.
9. Let the gods exalt the memory of thy name, let them magnify and exalt thee!
10. May he expel (*littatstsi*) the sickness of the sick man!
11. The plague, the fever, the sprain (?),
12. the evil incubus (*utuk*), the evil *alu*, the evil *ekimmu*, (the evil) *gallu*,
13. the evil god, the evil succubus,
14. the phantom (and) the vampire,
15. Lilith (and) the handmaid of the ghost (*lilu*),
16. the evil (plague), the fever, and the painful sickness,
17. (along with all) that worketh evil . . . ."

XXXIII. W.A.I. iv. 29. No. 2.

1. "Incantation.—The injurious fever (rages) against the head.
2. The evil plague against the life.
3. The evil *utuk* against the neck.
4. The evil *alu* against the breast.
5. The evil *ekimmu* against the waist.
6. The evil *gallu* against the hand."

XXXIV. W.A.I. iv. 30. No. 1.

Obv. 1. "O glorious one, who art strong as the heaven!
2. Mighty warrior, who art firm as the earth!
3. Who, like the heaven and the earth, art exalted!
4. O warrior, on the day when thou marchest against the land of the enemy!
5. O glorious one who, in difficulty (from which) there seems no exit,

HYMNS TO THE GODS.

6. what is there in the ravine, what is there which thou dost not overcome?
7. What is there in the seas (which) drown (*yumalluqu*) below?
8. The lofty stone thou destroyest on the day when in strength its forces thou smitest.
9. The weak man is among thy weak ones.
10. The gods thou slaughterest with destruction.

Rev. 1. The gods of heaven have set thee to battle.
2. The gods of earth gather themselves together before thee.
3. The spirits of the earth prostrate their faces before thee.
4. The goat with six heads in the mountain contrives death.
5. The storm in the mountain is a destroying sword decreed to it."

XXXV. W.A.I. iv. 30. No. 3.

Obv. 1. "With dark clothing which is the terror of the vampire (*akhkhazu*),
2. the dark cloak, the cloak of splendour, he has covered (*yusakhlip*) the pure body.
3. The evil .... in the fastening of the gate he ....
4. .... a cutting off of the .... along with the weapon ....
5. (With) the knife (*kinazi*) like a lamb (he cut) the strings (?) of thy heart.
6. The (evil) *utuk*, the evil *alu* ....
7. In the body of the man (the son) of his god, the *alu* ....
8. In the shrine of Ea thou dost not stand, thou dost not make the pilgrimage.
9. On the ascent of the temple thou dost not stand, thou dost not make the pilgrimage.
10. Thou dost not say: 'Let me seize on the house!'
11. Thou dost not say: 'Let me seize on the ascent!'
12. Thou dost not say: 'Let me seize on the (shrine)!'
13. O evil *utuk*, depart to distant places!
14. O evil *alu*, descend into the stream!
15. Thy station (*manzaz*) is a place hemmed in.
16. Thy resting-place (*mamid*) is established in the stream."

XXXVI. W.A.I. iv. 30. No. 2, with S 2148. Fragment of a text about the Deluge.

(S 2148) 1. .... binding the goat ....
2. The cow and its youngling (*pupat*) he binds.
3. The goat and its offspring (*lala*) he binds.
4. The cow and its youngling he slaughters.
5. The goat and its offspring he slaughters.

6. Thou didst smite (?) (*tukû*), and I went as a hero who returns not to rest.
7. As the flood of the warrior-god U-azu (the lord of medicine),
8. as the flood of my hero the god Damu.

(W.A.I. iv. 30.) *Obv.* 1. The flood of the (god) . . . .
2. The flood of the god Nangar (the moon), the lord of the bond.
3. The flood of the gallos-spirit (*libir*) . . . .
4. The flood of the god Gudi . . . .
5. The flood of the man of Kharran (the planet Mercury) . . . .
6. The flood of the great unique mother-goddess . . . .
7. The flood of the brother of the mother of the male god.
8. It came, it descended upon the breast of the earth.
9. The Sun-god caused the earth to see the dead, spread the dead over the earth.
10. He was full of lamentation on the day he slaughtered the leader of the ranks.[1]
11. In a month imperfect year by year,
12. to a road that benefits men, that pacifies mankind,
13. for the enclosure of his seat,
14. the hero (descended) to the distant earth which had not been seen.

---

15. When shall that grow up which was bound?[2]
16. My bond has gone forth, it is carried away (?);
17. from the city my bond has gone forth;
18. from the house of the corn-field it has gone forth;
19. the hero of the corn-field has gone forth.

Rev. 1. The flood of the warrior-god U-a(zu).
2. The flood of my hero, the god Damu.
3. The flood of the son my lord, the living (Tammuz).
4. The flood of the god Nangar, the lord of the bond.
5. The flood of the spirit (*libir*), the lord of the *gallu*.
6. The flood of the god Gudi . . . .
7. The flood of the man of Kharran . . . .
8. The flood of the great unique mother (Zikum).
9. The flood of the brother of the mother of the male god.
10. His youth from the sailing ship he (brought out?).
11. His age from the scattering of the corn he (brought out?).
12. His manhood from the storm he (brought out?)."

---

[1] The Accadian text has simply, "the day of destruction" (*û sübbä*).

[2] In the Accadian text, "How long shall the hand be bound? how long shall the hand be bound?"

HYMNS TO THE GODS. 505

XXXVII. W.A.I. iv. 58, 59. A prayer against sins.

Obv. Col. i. 22. "(Along with the father his) son they cut off.
23. (along with) the son (his) father they cut off;
24. (along with) the mother (her) daughter they cut off;
25. (along with) the daughter (her) mother they cut off;
26. (along with) the bridesmaids the bride they cut off;
27. (along with) the bride the bridesmaids they cut off;
28. along with the brother his brother they cut off;
29. along with the friend his associate they cut off;
30. along with the neighbour his neighbour they cut off.
31. They cease not to capture, they pity not the bondage;
32. they let not the light in the prison-house be seen.
33. 'Take him to captivity, and bind him in bondage,' they have said.
34. He knows not (his) sin against the god, he knows not (his) transgression (*ennit*) against the god and the goddess,
35. (yet) the god has smitten,[1] the goddess has departed[2] (from him).
36. Against his god is his sin, against his goddess is his iniquity (*khablat*).
37. (There are) smitings (for the sinner?),[3] there are *ziráti* for the guardian-priest (*urugal.*)
38. (The goddess) has departed (from him); against the great lady (*nin-gal*) has he acted shamefully.

. . . .

44. The rod (*zibanit*) of injustice has taken (*itsbat*) (thee) . . . .
45. The doubled cord of injustice has seized thee . . . .
46. The son has removed (*ittasakh*) what is established, the son has established (what should be removed).
47 In a confederacy of injustice he has confederated thee, for (right and) justice he has not formed a league.
48. He has laid on the yoke and taken up the landmark.
49. He has entered the house of his companions.
50. He has attacked the property of his companions.
51. He has poured out the blood of his companions.
52. He has stripped his companions of their clothing.
53. His bitterness (wickedness) the freeman has left.
54. The freeman, the workman, has raised his family.
55. He has . . . . (his) family (*qinna*) and household (*pukharta*).

---

[1] *Idaz*, akin to *dazâti*, "battles."
[2] *Imtes*, not from *masû*, "to forget," but *mâsu*, Heb. *mûsh*.
[3] Perhaps *bil enni*, "lord of sin."

56. He plants himself where there is no opening.
57. He directs his mouth, (but) his heart is unfaithful.
58. His mouth is sin, his heart is . . . .
Col. ii. 1. His speech (*gábi*) he has uttered . . . .
    2. The faithful man he has pursued (?) . . . .
    3. He has driven away purity . . . .
    4. He has wrought wickedness . . . .

    9. The witch comes behind ;
10. at the side the sorceress passes through ;
11. she who bears not children has done (the deed).
12. To the charm and the sorcery he has put his hand.
13. By the painful sickness (from the food) he has eaten,
14. by the multitude of sins he has committed,
15. by the assembly he has overthrown,
16. by the gathered troops he has broken through,
17. by the words of the god and the goddess he has forgotten,
18. by the promises he has made in his heart and his mouth and has not performed,
19. by the gift (and) the name of his god which he has forgotten,
20. he consecrates himself, he laments, he has drawn back,
21. he has manifested fear, he has spoken contritely,
22. he has purified himself and inclined to the lifting up of the hand.
23. He sets down the dish according to rule ;
24. his god and his goddess feed along with him.
25. He stands in the congregation,[1] and utters the prayer :
26. 'May I be pardoned,'[2] (for) he knew not and was forsworn.
27. He seized and was forsworn.
28. He broke through and was forsworn.
29. With the gift he had given he was forsworn.
30. In life he was forsworn.
31. To the divine colossos his finger he raised.
32. In the divine colossos he has (found) father and mother.
33. The divine colossos (has become to him) the *urugal* and the *nin-gal*.
34. The divine colossos (has restored to him) friend and comrade.
35. The divine colossos (has restored to him) god and companion.

39. The suffering of (his) city . . . .

---

[1] *Sipari*, see W. A. I. ii. 35, 10.
[2] Literally, "may (the Sun-god) deliver!"

40. The word of (his) city ....
41. The cutting off (?) of his city ....
42. At the command thou swearest ....
43. swearing before ....
44. by the rod of affliction thou swearest by, (ask !)
45. by the throne thou swearest by, (ask !)
46. by the dish thou swearest by, (ask !)
47. by the goblet thou swearest by, (ask !)
48. Ask, ask !
49. Ask on the couch !
50. Ask on the seat !
51. Ask at the dish !
52. Ask at the giving of the goblet !
53. Ask at the kindling of the fire !
54. Ask at the fire !
55. Ask when it is aglow !
56. Ask from the tablet and the stylus of the tablet !
57. Ask of the bond and the fetter !
58. Ask at the side of the tame beast !
59. Ask at the side of the wild beast !
60. Ask at the side of the foundation !
61. Ask at the edge of the marsh !
62. Ask at the bank of the river !
63. Ask by the side of the ship, at the helm and at the prow !
64. Ask at the rising of the sun and the setting of the sun !
65. Ask among the gods of heaven (and) the sanctuaries of earth !
66. Ask among the sanctuaries of the lord and the lady (Baal and Beltis) !
67. Ask when thou comest out of the city and when thou goest into the city !
68. Ask when thou comest out of the city-gate and when thou enterest the city-gate !
69. Ask when thou comest out of the city and when thou enterest into the house !
70. Ask in the street !
71. Ask in the temple !
72. Ask on the road !
73. May the Sun-god, the judge, deliver !
74. Deliver, O Sun-god, lord of all that is above and below,
75. director of the gods, king of the world, father (of mankind) !
76. By thy command let justice be accomplished !
77. May he direct his people (*teniset-su*) before him !

78. Deliver, O hero (*masu*) of the gods, compassionate lord, the god (Merodach)!
79. (Deliver), O divine lord of the house, deliver, O (Ea)!
80. (Deliver), O god who art lord . . . .
   .   .   .   .   .   .
82. Deliver, O Suqamuna and Sima(liya)!
83. Deliver, O great gods . . . .
84. Deliver, O fire son of (the Fire-)god!
85. (May) Baal and Beltis (stretch forth) the hand!
86. May Anu and Anat (stretch forth) the hand!
87. May Mul-lil deliver, the king who has created (thee)!
88. May Nin-lil deliver, the queen of Ê-(kur)!
89. May the temple of Ki . . . . deliver, the secret abode of . . . .
90. May the divine lord of the earth deliver, may the divine lady of the earth deliver!
91. May the divine lord of the firmament deliver, may the divine lady of the firmament deliver!
92. May Ea deliver, the king of the deep!
93. May the deep deliver, the habitation of wisdom!
94. May Eridu deliver, may the house of the deep deliver!
95. May Merodach deliver, the king of the angels!
96. May Zarpanit deliver, the queen of Ê-Saggil!
97. May Ê-Saggil and Babylon deliver, the seat of the great gods!
98. May Nebo and Nana deliver in Ê-Zida!
99. May Tasmit deliver, the mighty bride!
100. May the divine judge deliver, the throne-bearer of Ê-Saggil!
101. May the god who pronounces blessings deliver, who causes good fortune to enter!
102. May the fortress of heaven and earth and the house of the mighty bond of the world deliver!
103. May the great god and the goddess Dirituv deliver!
104. May they deliver when (*assû*) thine eye weeps in trouble and the god is not . . . .
105. May the god Yabru and the god Khum(tsi)ru (the swine god) deliver, the illustrious gods!
106. May the stars of the south, of the north, of the east and of the west, (like) winds blow away the name and inscribe its curse (*mamit*)!
107. May Istar deliver in Erech, the shepherd's hut!
108. May the Lady of Ê-Ana (Nana) deliver in Ê-Ana, the robe (of her glory?)!
109. May Anunit deliver in Accad, the city of . . . .

110. May Accad deliver, the house of . . . .

Col. iv. 1. May Iskhara deliver, the mistress of mankind (*dadme*)!
2. May Siduri deliver, the Istar of wisdom, the living colossos!
3. May Nerra, Nergal and Nergalgal deliver!
4. May Laz and Khani and Mulu-duga-nea deliver!
5. May the divine king of the desert (Eden), Latarak and 'Sarrakhu deliver!
6. May Dun and Xisuthros and their monster (*mamlu*) deliver!
7. May Tibul and Sakkut and . . . . and Immeriya deliver!
8. May Sagittarius and the star of stars (Iku) and Sirius and the god . . . . and the god Narudu deliver!
9. May the divine chief of the dawn and Arcturus and the god Na . . . . (deliver)!
10. May all the gods and goddesses whose names (are recorded deliver)!
11. On this day may they (deliver)! . . . .

COLOPHON: Incantation.—' Every curse which has seized upon the king the son of his god.' The second tablet of the *surpu* ('fever') series."

XXXVIII. S 924.; 79. 7-8. 65.

Obv. 1. " He whose body is not directed aright . . . .
2. Merodach (comes);
3. to his father Ea (the word he addresses):
4. ' O my father, the outpouring of the libation, the outpouring he has devised . . . . [1]
5. In water that flows not straight (he has bathed?).
6. In the water of the unclean hand he (washes?).
7. A woman with unlucky hand has approached (him).
8. A handmaid with an unclean hand (has washed him?).
9. A woman who inspires terror has seized (him).
10. A man of an unlucky hand has approached (him).
11. A man of an unclean hand has (washed him?).
12. A man whose body is not directed aright has seized (him).
13. What wilt thou do? as for me . . . .'
14. Ea (answered) his son Merodach:
15. Go, my (son) Merodach; what thou knowest not (I know) . . . .
Rev. 1. The limpid water (*agubbû*) which makes the house of the gods resplendent,

---

[1] The second text here interpolates two fragmentary lines which are not in S 924. The lines are not provided with a Semitic translation, as they are in the second text.

510   APPENDIX IV.

   2. the limpid water (which makes) the temple of the gods (to shine),
   3. the limpid water which cleanses (the begetter?) . . . ."

XXXIX. S 497.

   7. "Incantation.—The water of judgment (NAM-DI), the waters of the oracle . . . .
   8. the spell (*tâ*) of whosoever it be who (knows) Merodach, the son of (Ea),
   9. has purified the house of the land . . . ."

XL. K 2585.

Obv. 8. "May the Lord of justice and righteousness, the director (of mankind),
   9. the judge of the spirits of earth,
   10. the Sun-god, him who enchants me (*kassip*),
   11. him who bewitches me and her who bewitches me (*mustepisti*), may he destroying (*rakhi*)
   12. the enchantment and the image of their breath, breaking their womb (*rusi*),
   13. pass over them so that he may be over them and not . . . .
   14. O Sun-god, may the Fire-god thy companion destroy (them)!
   15. O Sun-god, may the Fire-god enclosing enclose them, even the god of fire . . . .
   16. May the Sun-god melt (?) (*lissub*) their image, may the Fire-god receive their bodies!
   17. May the Fire-god consume (*likabbib*) them, even the god of fire who causes (destruction)!
   18. The Fire-god is wrathful like water.
Rev. 1. May the Fire-god (carry them) to the land whence none return!
   2. The Fire-god who illumines the gloom (*ukli*) of darkness . . . .
   3. The Fire-god (turns?) to the plague-god (*Namtaru*), the messenger of earth.
   4. The Sun-god is he who inspires the breath of those who act (?).
   5. The god who is king of the dead and living (?) (BAD *u* NUN),
   6. along with the god and goddess, has been angry with me.
   7. In the house of the kindling of the altar-flame (*pukhpukhkhu*),
   8. the Sun-god of the mighty mouth, the living one, knows; the goddess Â thus
   9. (or) not thus knows, (but) I know not. Of the exorciser
   10. of him who bewitches me and of her who bewitches me (and) of the destroyer (*rákhi*),

11. their enchantment in the place of thy temple like a branch of wood
12. against these (sorcerers) may they behold; may the god
13. overwhelm them like a goblet, like
14. a . . . . may he injure, may he cut off (?)
15. their life . . . ."

XLI. 79. 7-8. 68.

Col. ii. 4. "Incantation.—O altar son of heaven, may the son of Ea,
5. Merodach, the son of Eridu, purify my hand!
6. May he make pure my mouth, may he make bright my foot!
7. May the evil tongue depart to another place!"

XLII. S 526. Hymn to Nergal.
2. "(In the . . . .) may it be, in thy heart may it be, in thy liver may it be!
3. (In the . . . .) may it be, in thy liver may it be, in thy heart may it be!
4. Among the fat oxen thou enterest not on this side.
5. . . . . thou bringest not out.
6. Among the sheep the . . . . thou enterest not on this side.
7. To the sheep the strong sheep thou bringest not out.
8. O lord, thou enterest not the temple of beer.
9. The clothing (*bursumtu*) of the place of the oracle thou gatherest not together.
10. O lord, the place of sovereignty (*situlti*) thou enterest not.
11. Her, even the servant who knows the word of the oracle, thou seatest not.
12. O lord, the park of Istar thou establishest not.
13. The little ones thou leadest not out of the park of Istar.
14. The place where the bond (*enu*) is fixed thou enterest not.
15. The small child (*mara*) who knows the bond thou bringest not out.
16. The . . . . thou dost not remove, its cow (*lati*) thou dost not destroy.
17. . . . . reclining with evil intent, the offering (*kurbanna*) thou dost not kiss.
18. . . . . in the place of his lord (?) thou dost not smite."

XLIII. K 4874.

Obv. 1. "(O hero whose) power is over the hosts of heaven and earth until future days,
2. . . . . he is good of mouth for exaltation.

3. .... men regard the observation of his token (*itti*).
4. Directing the .... in every fortress he establishes the daily sacrifice.
5. (The man whom) he exalts he leads forth to headship.
6. .... he magnifies the command of his heart.
7. Directing the .... in every fortress he establishes the daily sacrifice.
8. He urges on ([*yumahha*]*ru*) the ending of the deluge.
9. .... he has established justice great and pure, he has reared the cedar.
10. .... Samas and Rimmon, the divine judges.
11. .... (he is) the faithful one who establishes the foundation of the land.
12. .... to future ages, even to future ages.
13. (He is) the .... of the goddess Uban-same (the finger of heaven) the companion of Assôros.
14. .... the .... of the great (gods) am I.
15. .... he has doubled the might of former kings.
16. .... he answered and the wicked woman writes.
17. .... he grants the offering.
18. ..... lifting up the face .... my storm.
19. .... the divine hero of justice has established (*ittaziz*) elsewhere.
20. .... and he bound together (*emâ*) their confederacy.
21. .... his fortress they entered.
22. .... her counsel she repeated.
23. .... his fortress did his onset capture (*idhruddu*).

Rev. 1. ... he founds the shrine.
2. .... he swoops (over) the world, he beholds (*ikhadh*) the confederacy.
3. .... he uplifts not his gift (*kadara*).
4. .... the man whomsoever he has not taken.
5. .... his wife he binds (*yarrura*) with oaths (*tamâti*).
6. .... multitudes submitted to him.
7. .... (if) he is angry, may he be quieted whoever he be.
8. .... the name they behold and his destruction (*saladh*).
9. .... the mountain, the man who utters good words.
10. .... Mul-lil who exhorts (?) the gods.
11. .... the prince, the proclaimer of the cry (?) (*tsirikhum*).
12. .... (spreading) splendour and glory, casting down fear.
13. .... his .... and his lordship."

XLIV. R 2. iii. 150.

Obv. 1. "O warrior-god (*Erimmu*), the shining one, the sword of Istar in strength (*ursi*) which accepts not prayer,
2. may the good prayer soothe thee!
3. May the prayer rain life and quietude upon thee!
4. Raise the cry of the oracle (*sakri*) (at) the dawning of day, like the offspring of a gazelle!
5. O lord of thy mother, thou marchest and turnest for thyself thy marching.
6. Like the waters of a marsh, mayest thou be placid (*lûtaknâta*);
7. like the waters of a pool (*yarkhi*), mayest thou be at rest (*lûnikhâta*).
8. Like the herdsman of the reposing ox, may sleep (?) overtake (?) thee!
9. Hear me and (help me), O stalwart king!
10. Mayest thou spread (*lutsallâta*) (thy) shadow (over me)!"[1]

XLV. Sp. iii. Bertin, *Revue d'Assyriologie*, i. 4. Hymn to the Sun.

1. "O Sun-god, in the midst of heaven, at thy setting,
2. may the enclosure of the pure heaven speak to thee of peace!
3. May the gate of heaven be thy bond!²
4. May the directing god, the messenger who loves thee, direct thy way.
5. In E-Babára, the seat of thy sovereignty, thy supremacy rises like the dawn.
6. May Â,³ the wife whom thou lovest, come before thee with joy!
7. May thy heart take rest!
8. May the glory of thy divinity be established for thee!
9. O Sun-god, warrior hero, may it exalt thee in strength!⁴
10. O lord of Ê-Babára,⁵ as thou marchest, may it direct thy course!
11. Direct thy road, march along the path fixed for thy pavement (*durus*).
12. O Sun-god, judge of the world, the director of its laws art thou!

---

[1] The remainder of the tablet is too mutilated for translation. The final lines are: "when the sun sets thou shalt say thus to the Sun-god: like a father thou wilt draw me to the earth."

² In the Assyrian version, "May the gates of heaven approach thee!"

³ In the Accadian, KU-NIR-DA.

⁴ *Meli-g*, in the Accadian, from *meli* or *meri*, "strength" (W. A. I. iv. 30. 18, 19). The Assyrian version has simply, "may they exalt thee."

⁵ Omitted in the Assyrian version.

13. Conclusion of the spell: When the Sun-god may be the setting sun.
14. The enchanter after the strengthening (?) of his mother.... a prayer.
15. [First line of the next hymn.] O Sun-god that risest in the bright sky!
16. Like its original, copied and published.
17. Tablet of Nebo-damiq, son of Ina-ili-bur....
18. For Nebo his lord, Nebo-baladhsu-iqbi, the son of the man of Ê-Saggil,
19. for the preservation of his life, has caused Nebo-bani-akhi, the son of the man of Ê-Saggil,
20. to write (it), and has placed (it) in Ê-Zida."

XLVI. Pinches, *Texts in the Babylonian Wedge-writing*, p. 15. Alliterative Hymn.

Obv. 5. Monthly (*arkhu*) and yearly may the prince of Ê-Saggil the supreme assist,
6. the strongholds (*arsubbê*) of Merodach and its brickwork may the king assist;
7. (in) the month (?) (*arakh*) of life and the festivals of sacrifice may glad music be sounded;
8. let the four (*arbah*) zones behold his countenance!
9. To those that bring (?) (*arrihi*) his nourishers may he grant life and goodness of heart!

10. Founding (*basimu*[1]) the *enceinte* of the sanctuary, restoring the shrine,
11. Babylon (*Babilu*), the city of multitudes, has he completed as his mighty fortress;
12. (its) property (*basâti*) has he restored, even its vast temples;
13. the daily sacrifices that had been discontinued (*batluti*) he has established as of yore;
14. those who behold (his) mercy and power celebrate (?)[2] his....

Rev. 3. May the fame (*zikir*) of .... mount upon wings!
4. May Zirpanit the princess, the supreme, assist the prince to his sovereignty!

---

[1] *Basamu* means properly, "to make suitable" or "prepare;" hence "a seat." *Basmu*, a species of large serpent (the *usumgal*), has no connection with the root.

[2] *Ipulu*, perhaps connected with *pilu*, "white."

5. May his seed (*ziru*) increase and may his progeny (*nannab*) be numerous!

6. May trouble (*kiru*) never be to him! may he overcome his woes (*nizmat*)!

7. May the blessings (*kirrê*) of happiness and obedience wait upon him daily!

8. Gardens (*kirrit*) of peace and joy of heart may he make for the midst of Babylon!

9. Within (*kirbi*) its temples may the women walk and accomplish his commands!

10. Within Babylon the prosperous exultantly may he establish joy!

11. May its sides (*sutaqut*)[1] be adorned[2] with *zakkal* wood, and may he achieve its exaltation!

12. The exits (*supûti*)[3] of its stronghold may he nourish with the primest oil!

13. The secret chambers (*kuttumme*) of its temples may he fill with unnumbered goods and treasure!

14. As for (*supar*) their deeds . . . .

15. The name (*sum*) of the king . . . ."

XLVII. W.A.I. v. 50, 51. Hymn to the Sun-god.

Obv. Col. i. 1. "Incantation.—O Sun-god, from the great mountain is thy rising;

2. from the great mountain, the mountain of the ravine, is thy rising;

3. from the holy mound,[4] the place of the destinies, is thy rising.

4. To be with heaven and earth (is thy) appearance; from the horizon (thou risest).

5. The great gods (bowing) the face stand before thee.

6. (The spirits obedient?) to (thy) command stand before thee.

7. (Men?) . . . . their . . . . behold thee.

8. . . . . of his four feet.

---

[1] From *equ*, "to wind." In W. A. I. v. 27, 9, *equ* is a synonym of *amamu*, "to bind," *liru*, *sibu*, *rukdu* (?) *khuratsu*. *Sutaqutu* must be distinguished from *sutuqu*, "a passage" (from *etiqu*).

[2] *Itstsamir*, to be distinguished from *tsamaru* (*itsmur*), "to consider," and *zamaru*, "to quit." Perhaps we should read *izzamir*, allied to the Heb. *zimráh*, "music."

[3] Or, perhaps, "those who issue forth from its stronghold."

[4] In the Semitic rendering, "from the mountain" simply.

9. .... are directed towards thee.
10. O Sun-god, who knowest (all things), thine own counsellor art thou!
11. O Sun-god, hero supreme, the lord of heaven and earth art thou!
12. Whatsoever exists in the heart is uttered by (thy) mouth.
13. (Thy) hands bring back to thee the spirits of all men.
14. Wickedness (and) evil-dealing (thou destroyest).
15. Justice and righteousness thou bringest to pass.
16. The wicked man and the injurious (*sagsa*),
17. he who has sworn an oath in ignorance,
18. he who has offered what he has (not) seen,
19. he whom the plague has seized,
20. he whom the fever has bound,
21. he upon whom the evil incubus (*utuk*) has settled,
23. he whom the evil *alu* has concealed in his bed,
24. he whom the evil *ekimmu* has cast down at night,
25. he upon whom the mighty *gallu* has laid the yoke,
26. he whose limbs the evil god has snared (*ispuru*),
27. he, the clothing of whose body the evil succubus has torn away,
28. (he whom) the .... has taken,
29. (he whom) .... has cast down,
30. (he whom) the *akhkhazu* has consumed,
31. he upon whom the handmaid of the *lilu* has cast the eye,
32. the freedman whom the handmaid of the *lilu* has embraced fatally (*ikrimu*),
33. he whom an evil portent has cut off,
34. he whom the ban has bound,
35. he whom the evil mouth has devoted to destruction,
36. (he whom) the evil tongue has cursed,
37. (he whom) the evil eye has ruined (*ikrimu*) utterly,
38. (he whom) the stranger has fettered,
39. (he) whose .... has been poured out for him,—
40. may (all) of them be with thee!

. . . . . .

Col. ii. 27. Incantation.—The fever-demon has overwhelmed like a river-flood,
28. the curse has (cut men off) like a green herb in the desert.
29. In the sea, where is the home (of the fish),
30. the fever has cast its shadow (*tsulillat*) like a garment ....
32. The .... returned to the great waters.
33. In their midst the fire burns, their fish (the fever-demon) consumes.

HYMNS TO THE GODS. 517

34. To heaven his snare he spreads, and
35. the bird of heaven he inundates like the storm.
36. The antelope by its head and its horns is taken.
37. The goat, the chamois of the mountains, their own young chamois, is taken.
38. (The fever-demon) bows the neck of the gazelle (*pagma*) of the desert.
39. He slaughters the cattle of the god Ner in the pasture.
40. The furious (demon) overwhelms the man in his own house.
41. 'O Merodach, substance of mine' (Ea says), 'go, my son!
42. Enclose in the ground the image thou hast founded for his support!
43. Cause to the king to walk over it!
44. Before the Sun-god take his hand!
45. Repeat the spell of the pure hymn!'[1]
46. The waters of his head (pour upon him)!
47. The waters of prophecy....'

Rev. Col. iii. 12. Incantation.—The king who is pure in faithfulness of heart....
13. The oil of the cedar which (grows) in the mountains....
14. Renewing the green fruit, creating the glory of sovereignty,
15. .... of kingship,
16. when thou enterest into the house of libations,
17. may Ea make thee glad!
18. May Dav-kina, the queen of the deep, enlighten thee with her sheen!
19. May Merodach, the great overseer[2] of the spirits of heaven, exalt thy head!
20. The great messenger, the pure one, of Ea has confirmed their deeds for ever (?) in the place where they are established.
21. The exalted gods of heaven and earth establish him.
22. In the great shrines of heaven and earth they establish him.

23. He purifies their border (sanctuary), he makes it white;
24. In his waters the pure are white.
25. The spirits of earth, the great gods, purify themselves.
26. The divine lord of .... the pontiff (*abgal*) of mercy, is the white one of Eridu.
27. The divine lady of .... the pontiff of mercy, is the white one of Eridu.

---

[1] Or "writing" (*muśaru*).   [2] "Priest" in the Accadian text.

APPENDIX IV.

28. He who is the pure mouth[1] of the deep fully accomplishes.
29. He who is clothed with the linen stuffs of Eridu fully accomplishes.
30. In the house of libations before the king Ea they establish him.
31. By the commands[2] of the Sun-god, the great lord of heaven and earth,
32. long may he extend to him life and goodness of heart!
33. The king is the heifer of a pure cow.
34. When thou approachest the house of libations,
35. in thê waters (?) of Merodach of the deep,
36. may the .... of the Sun-god enlighten thee!
37. May the (robe) of royalty clothe him!

. . . . .

44. With the bent sacrificial reed (*suduk*) (make) libations with the hand ....
45. The divine prince, the lord of prophesying ....
46. By his spell of life ....
47. The fish, the bird, the glory of the marsh, the countenance ....
48. Zikum, the mistress of the deep ....

. . . . .

Col. iv. 21. When thou leavest the house of libations,
22. may the spirits (of the earth), the great gods, grant thee long life and goodness of heart.
23. May Adar, the mighty warrior of Mul-lil, be thy helper on the field of battle.
24. When thou comest out of the house of libations,
25. may the propitious *utuk* and the propitious colossos turn to thee in peace.[3]
26. (Though) the *ekimmu* be hostile, and the *alu* hostile, (may) the *utuk* be propitious and the divine colossos propitious.
27. May the spirits (of earth), the great gods, (be propitious).
28. May the Sun-god utter words of blessing unto thee!"

XLVIII. W. A. I. v. 52.

Obv. Col. i. 4. "(O lord) of heaven and earth, divine lord of the star, divine lady of the star!
5. (O lord of Da-)uhma, lady of Da-uhma!

---

[1] In the Semitic version, *asipu*, "augur."

[2] *Kibâti* for *qibâti*, Accadian *gudu*, connected with *gudea*, "the proclaimer."

[3] In the Accadian text, "extend (*khen-dab-sigübös*) the returning of the hand."

HYMNS TO THE GODS. 519

6. (Divine lord) of the holy mound, divine lady of the holy mound!
7. Mother of Nin-lil, father of Mul-lil!
8. Divine lord of the living day, divine lord of Ê-sarra!
9. Concubine of the spirit of heaven, divine lady of the mountain (*kharsagga*)!
10. Sul-kun-ea (Mercury), lord of the dish!
11. Mother of the Corn-god (Serakh), mother of the seven gods!
12. Divine lord and high-priest of Nipur, mighty lord of Nipur!
13. Prophetess (?), divine lady of Nipur!
14. Nappaśi, the lady of . . . .
15. The god whose law is supreme, the incubus of Ê-kur!
16. Mother of the house, 'Sa-dara-nuna ('the bond of the princely antelope')!
17. Serpent-god (Serakh), the incubus of Ê-sarra!
18. The propitious colossos (*lamaśśi*) whose splendour is exalted!
19. Son of the mighty prince, Nannaru the Moon-god!
20. Lord of the white image[1] of the spirit of Sin, wife of Sin!
21. Glorious image supreme, Mul-lil of life!
22. Divine beast of the Moon-god, who traverses the sides of the house!
23. . . . . son of Ê-Saba!

. . . . .

Col. iv. 2. . . . . tears I bore, and who is there that gives me rest?

3. (May thy heart) be still, may thy liver have rest!
4. O supreme judge . . . . may thy heart be still!
5. (O lady) of the temple of Dim-riri, may thy heart be still!
6. O lady who takes away life, may thy heart be still!
7. O lady of Niśin, may thy heart be still!
8. O lady of the mighty temple supreme, may thy heart be still!
9. O lady of the temple of Dim-riri, may thy heart be still!
10. O my lady, my goddess Bahu, may thy heart be still!
11. O concubine and mother, Bahu, may thy heart be still!
12. O Bahu, propitious white image, may thy heart be still!
13. O namer of the evil name, lady of heaven, may thy heart be still!

14. Lamentation of the heart to the divine lady of life and death; lamentation of the heart to the male (divinity) who has created the white image.

---

[1] *Nunuz*, in the Assyrian version *zir*, a word related to *zariru*, "white gold."

15. [First line of next tablet.] Of the evil deluge. The seizer of the name . . . .
16. Sixth tablet (of the series beginning): 'The male (divinity) who has created the white image :' quite complete.
17. To Nebo the mighty (*gitmalu*) son, the overseer of the hosts of heaven and earth,
18. the holder of the papyrus scrolls, the taker of the stylus of the tablets of destiny,
19. the lengthener of the day, the restorer of the dead to life, the establisher of life for men in trouble,
20. the great lord of births (*eri*), Assur-bani-pal the prince, the servant of Assur, Bel and Nebo,
21. the shepherd who feeds the sanctuaries of the great gods, the establisher of their daily sacrifices,
22. the son of Essar-haddon (the king of hosts), the king of Assyria,
23. the grandson of Sennacherib (the king) of hosts, the king of Assyria,
24. for the preservation of his life, the length of his days, the perfecting of his seed,
25. the establishment of the seat of the throne of his royalty, the obedient to his glory and his honour,
26. the presentation of his prayers that the disobedient to him may be given into his hands,
27. (he who knows the purity of Ea, the gallos-priest of secret treasure), the pontiff (*abkallu*),
28. (who has been made to walk that he may give rest to the heart of the great gods),
29. (according to the tablets, the copies of Assyria and) Accad,
30. (on tablets I have written, connected together, published), and
31. (in the inner chamber of Ê-Zida, the temple of Nebo, who is in Nineveh, my lord, I placed).
32. (For the pleasure of Nebo, the king of the hosts of heaven and earth, look with joy upon this chamber, and)
32. (support by day the head of Assur-bani-pal, the worshipper of thy divinity ; grant (his) prayer ;)
33. (decree his life that he may exalt thy great divinity.)"

V.

THE PENITENTIAL PSALMS.

I. W. A. I. iv. 29. No. 5. Haupt, *Keilschrifttexte*, iii. No. 14; Zimmern, *Babylonische Busspsalmen*, i.

Obv. 1. "(Accept) the prostration of the face of the living creature....
2. (I) thy servant ask (thee) for rest.
3. To the heart of him who has sinned thou utterest words of blessing.[1]
4. Thou lookest on the man, and the man lives,
5. O potentate of the world, mistress of mankind!
6. Compassionate one, whose forgiveness is ready, who accepts the prayer.
7. [PRIEST.] O god and mother goddess that are angry with him, he calls upon thee!
8. Turn (thy face) towards him and take his hand!

Rev. 1. Above thee, O god, have I no director.
2. Ever look upon me and accept my prayer.
3. Say, 'How long shall my (heart be wroth)?' and let thy liver be quieted.
4. When, O my mistress, shall thy countenance be turned in pardon?
5. Like a dove I mourn, on sighs do I feast myself.
6. [PRIEST.] (From) woe and lamentation is (his) liver rested;
7. he weeps tears, (he utters) a cry."

II. Haupt, *Akkadische und Sumerische Keilschrifttexte*, iii. No. 15; Zimmern, ii.

Obv. 1. "(Thou that performest) the commands of Bel (Mul-lil), (thou that strengthenest?) the limbs,
2. the point of the sword....

---

[1] Zimmern has misunderstood this passage, taking the noun for the verb, and the verb for the noun. *Temeq-su* is literally, "thou plantest deep in him."

3. thou that createst the gods, that performest the commands of (Bel),
4. thou that producest the herbs, mistress of mankind,
5. creatress of the world, creatress of all that has a form,
6. mother goddess (destroyer of evil), whose hand no god attacks,
7. exalted lady, whose command is mighty!
8. A prayer let me utter; let her do unto me what seems good to her.
9. O my mistress, from the day when I was little much am I yoked unto evil.
10. (Food) I have not eaten; weeping has been my veil.
11. (Water I have not drunk); tears have been my drink.
12. (My heart has rejoiced not); my liver has not been enlightened.
13. .... like a hero I have not walked.

Rev. 1. .... bitterly I mourn.
2. (My transgressions?) are many, my liver is full of anguish.
3. O my mistress, cause me to know what I have done, establish for me a place of rest!
4. Absolve my sin, lift up my countenance!
5. O my god, the lord of prayer, may the prayer address thee!
6. O my goddess, the mistress of supplication, may the supplication address thee!
7. O Mâtu, lord of the mountain, may the prayer address thee!
8. O Gubarra ('the fire-flame'),[1] lady of the border of Eden, may the supplication address thee!
9. O (Ea), ruler of heaven and earth, ruler of Eridu, may the prayer address thee!
10. O Dam-kina, mother of the house supreme, may the supplication address thee!
11. O Merodach (lord of Babylon), may the prayer address thee!
12. His (spouse, the royal bond of heaven) and earth, may the supplication address thee!
13. (O messenger of life), the god (whose good name) is pronounced, may the prayer address thee!

---

[1] Gubarra is the Sumerian (and older) form of the Accadian Mubarra, "the Fire-god" (W. A. I. iv. 26, 39). The ideographic mode of writing the word "fire," GIS-BAR, shows that the original form must have been *gusbarra*, *gus* becoming *mu* (*wu*) as in *mu* from the primitive *gus*, "heaven." *Gus*, "the sky," and *gus-qin*, "the yellow metal" (gold), probably have the same root as *gus*, "fire." Dialectal forms of Gubarra are Kibirra and Gibil. Gubarra, the wife of Mâtu, was subsequently identified with Sala, the wife of Rimmon; and as Kibirra and Gibil were regarded as gods, the female Gubarra dropped out of sight.

14. (O bride, first-born of IP)A, may the supplication address thee!
15. (O mistress of him who binds the mouth of the dog), may the prayer address thee!
16. (O exalted one, Gula, my mistress, even the goddess Nanâ, may the supplication address thee!')
17. ('Regard me with favour,' may it say to thee!)
18. ('Turn thy face towards me,' may it say to thee!)
19. ('May thy liver be quieted,' may it say to thee!)
20. (May thy heart, as the heart of a mother who has borne children, return to its place!)
21. (As a mother who has borne children, as a father who has begotten (them), may it return to its place!)."

III. Haupt, *Akkadische und Sumerische Keilschrifttexte*, iii. No. 19; Zimmern, *Busspsalmen*, No. 3.

1. [PRIEST.] "(Over his face, which for) tears is not lifted up, falls the tear.
2. (Over his feet, on) which fetters are laid, falls the tear.
3. (Over his hand,) which from weakness is at rest, falls the tear.
4. Over his breast, which like a flute pipes forth in cries, falls the tear.
5. [PENITENT.] O my mistress, in the trouble of my heart I raise in trouble the cry to thee; say: 'How long (shall my heart be wroth)?'
6. O my mistress, speak pardon to thy servant; let thy heart be at rest!
7. To thy servant who suffers pain, grant mercy!
8. Turn thy neck unto him, accept his supplication!
9. Be at peace with thy servant with whom thou art angry!

Rev. 1. O my mistress, my hands are bound, yet I embrace thee.
2. To the warrior, the hero Samas, the husband of thy love, grant a pledge that I may walk before thee with a life of long days.
3. My god has made supplication unto thee; may thy heart be at rest!
4. My goddess has uttered a prayer unto thee; may thy liver be quieted!
5. O hero, god of heaven, the husband of thy love, may the prayer address thee!
6. .... O god of uprightness, may the supplication address thee!
7. O .... thy *gallu* supreme, may the prayer address thee!
8. (O Sun-god), the potentate of Ê-Babára, may the supplication address thee!

9. ('Turn thine eye upon me,') may he say unto thee!
10. ('Turn thy face to me,') may he say unto thee!
11. ('Let thy heart be pacified,') may he say unto thee!
12. ('Let thy liver be quieted,') may he say unto thee!
13. (May thy heart, as the heart of a mother who has borne children,) return to its place!
14. (As a mother who has borne, as a father who has begotten,) may it return to its place!
15. (Psalm to) the goddess Â."

IV. W. A. I. iv. 19. No. 3. Zimmern, No. 5.

1. "How long, O my mistress, shall the powerful stranger (consume thy land)?
2. In thy chief city Erech has famine come.
3. In Ê-UL-BAR, the house of thy oracle, is blood poured out like water.
4. On all thy lands has he laid the fire, and like smoke has outpoured (it).
5. O my mistress, greatly am I yoked to evil.
6. O my mistress, thou hast surrounded me and hast appointed me to pain.
7. The strong enemy, like a solitary reed, has cut me down.
8. No message have I received; myself have I not understood.
9. Like a field, day and night do I mourn.
10. I, thy servant, bow myself before thee.
11. May thy heart be quieted; may thy liver be appeased!
12. .... lamentation; may thy heart be pacified!"

V. W. A. I. iv. 21. No. 2. Zimmern, No. 6.

7. "The lord, whose heart above rests not,
8. the lord, whose heart below rests not,
9. above and below it rests not.
10. He who has bowed me down (and) cut me off,[1]
11. on my hand has laid the fetter,
12. on my body has placed the chain.
13. The iris of my eyes he fills with tears,
14. my heart he fills with depression (and) lamentation.
15. May his pure heart rest, may the prayer address him,
16. may his heart rest in quietude!

---

[1] As there is a play here upon the assonance of the two Semitic words, *yuqaddid* and *yuqatti*, it is probable that the Semitic version is the original.

17. May the heart of his lordship rest in quietude!
18. 'O heart, turn thyself, turn thyself!' let it be said to him.
19. 'O heart, rest, rest!' let it be said to him.
20. He grants much to his heart who passes judgment on himself.[1]
21. For the quieting of his heart may the spirits of earth establish (him) when he prays.

Rev. 1. May the spirits of earth who work trouble in heaven[2] (establish him when he prays)!
2. His god has borne away the supplication: let the prayer (address him)!
3. Quieting, *or* exorcising, the cry of anguish, may thy heart be stilled!
4. O lord, the mighty priest, (Adar) the lord of the *galli*, may the prayer (address thee)!
5. O thou that speakest, lady of Nipur, may the lamentation (come before thee)!
6. O divine ruler of heaven and earth, ruler of Eridu, may the prayer (address thee)!
7. O mother of the house supreme, Dam-kina, may the lamentation (come before thee)!
8. O Merodach, lord of Babylon,[3] may the prayer (address thee)!
9. O wife of him, royal bond of heaven and earth, may the lamentation (come before thee)!
10. O messenger of life (Nebo), the god who proclaims the good name, may the prayer (address thee)!
11. O bride, the daughter of the god IP-A, may the lamentation (come before thee)!
12. O Mâtu, lord of the mountain, may the prayer (address thee)!
13. O Gubarra, lady of the field, may the lamentation (come before thee)!
14. 'Look favourably upon me!' may he say to thee.
15. 'Turn thy face toward me!' may he say to thee.
16. 'May thy heart be at rest!' may he say to thee.
17. 'May thy liver be quieted!' may he say to thee.
18. May thy heart, like the heart of a mother who has borne children, return to its place!
19. As a mother who has borne children, as a father who has begotten (them), may it return to its place!

---

[1] In the Accadian, "who judges grace."

[2] "To Anu" in the Semitic version.

[3] The description of Merodach as "lord of Babylon" indicates a period subsequent to the rise of Babylon under Khammuragas.

20. Penitential psalm, forty-five lines in number, the tablet of Mul-lil.
21. Like its original, copied and published."

VI. W.A.I. iv. 26. No. 3; 27. No. 3. Zimmern, No. 7.
1. [PRIEST.] "In lamentation is he seated,
2. in cries of anguish (and) trouble of heart,
3. in evil weeping, in evil lamentation.
4. Like doves does he mourn bitterly night and day.
5. To his merciful god like a heifer he roars.
6. Painful lamentation does he raise.
7 Before his god he prostrates his face in prayer.
8. He weeps, he has drawn near,[1] he holds not back.
9. [PENITENT.] Let me declare my doing, my doing which cannot be declared.
10. Let me repeat my word, my word which cannot be repeated.
11. O my god, let me declare my doing, my doing which cannot be declared."

VII. W.A.I. iv. 61. No. 1. Zimmern, No. 8.
6. "Sickness, a stroke . . . . (and) wasting press heavily on him; weak is (his) groaning;
7. smiting, evil, fear and oppression have bowed him down (and) stilled his lamentations.
8. He has sinned, and in anguish (*martsatus*) he weeps unto thee; his liver is darkened; he hastens to thee.
9. He is taken; he causes (his) tears to rain like a thunder-cloud; he is overpowered, and causes (his) eyelids to weep.
10. Like a shrieking bird he utters troublous cries: he declares his misery (*dulib*) with crying.
11. What can my lord's servant say and devise? May he open his mouth (for that) which I know not.
12. [PENITENT.] Many indeed are my sins I have sinned in all: may this (curse) pass away (and) depart to a place inaccessible!
13. [PRIEST.] Sin has been laid (upon him); the covering of his mouth and (eyes?) has come upon him; darkness of the face is his daylight (?); he lies prostrate (?).
14. At the gate of his sin his hands are bound; if 'he shall deliver thee' he has no knowledge.
15. He has addressed thee in prayer; may the writing of Ea give rest to thy heart!

---

[1] So Zimmern.

16. May his earnest supplication find favour with thee above; (with) groaning and casting down (he says:) 'When shall thy heart (be pacified)?'
17. Behold his painful suffering; let thy heart rest and grant unto him mercy.
18. Take his hand, forgive his sin; remove the madness and the wasting that is on him.
19. Set thy servant in thy favourable mouth,[1] and let thy majesty bathe his disease in the river.
20. (Loosen) his chain, undo his fetter: enlighten (his face); entrust him to his god who created him.
21. Give life to thy servant, let him exalt thy warlike deeds; may all mankind (magnify) thy greatness!
22. Accept his gift, receive his ransom; in a land of peace may he walk before thee!
23. With overflowing fulness let him feed thy sanctuary!
24. May the food of thy temple continue (for ever)!
25. May he pour out the oil of thy courts like water; the oil may he rain on thy threshold abundantly!
26. May he offer thee[2] the odours (?) of cedar, the finest of incense, the fatness of wheat!

Rev. 1. Look down, O lord, upon thy servant who is full of grief; let thy wind blow and forthwith[3] deliver him!
2. May he pacify thy heavy anger; strike off his bonds; let him breathe freely!
3. (Loosen) his fetter, undo his bonds! .... declare his judgment!
4. .... pity, pity his life!

. . . . . .

I. W.A.I. iv. 25.   Ritual Text.

Obv. Col. i. 9. "Its helm is of the wood of . . . .
10. Its serpent-like oar has a golden hand.
11. Its mast is pointed with turquoise.[4]
12. Seven times seven lions of Eden occupy its deck.
13. The god Kudur fills its cabin built within.
14. Its side is of cedar from the forest.

---

[1] I.e. address him favourably.

[2] Literally, "cast before thee" (*lisaŝli-ka*); comp. *islû*, "he cast away."

[3] *Zamar. Zamaru* is "to come forth;" hence "a door" is called *misar zamari*, "a bar to exit" (W. A. I. ii. 29, 51), and *zamaru* is used of the "growing" of plants and the "rising" of stars.

[4] See W. A. I. ii. 51, 17.

15. Its awning is of the palm-wood of Dilvun.
16. Carrying away the heart is the canal,
17. rejoicing its heart is the rising sun.
18. Its house, its ascent, is a mountain that gives rest to the heart.
19. The ship of the god of Eridu is destiny.
20. Dav-kina is the goddess who promises (it) life.
21. Merodach is the god who pronounces (its) good name.
22. The god who benefits the house makes it go in Eridu.
23. Nin-nangar, the bright one, the mighty workman of heaven,
24. with the pure and blissful hand has pronounced the word of life:
25. 'May the ship before thee cross the canal!
26. May the ship behind thee sail over its mouth!
27. May the heart within thee rejoicing make holiday (?) !'[1]

Col. ii. 2. Pour out on the sixth day . . . .
3. pure water (in) the temple of the lower ground . . . .
4. (Make) prostration towards the gate of the setting (sun) . . . .
5. From the temple of Borsippa take (thy) departure, and . . . .
6. his hand the gossamer (?) cloth, the white cloth (and) the fillet[2]
7. binds, and with a band (?) he covers (his) seat.
8. He heaps up the herbs and the dress; he offers the sacrificial goblet.
9. [*Recent lacuna.*] The man that is made pure, the god who created him goes a second time.
10. [*Recent lacuna.*] (When) they have ended, the god inclines over the seat.
11. [*Recent lacuna.*] Stretch the linen and tie it about the round (*sakhkharu*) cup.
12. Set it down; a second time the herbs and a mountain (?) dress
13. heap up (and) cut (on) the altar; offer the sacrificial goblet, and the robe of a herald;
14. on the left side of the man that is purified thou must bind with dark cloth, white cloth
15. (and) a fillet; on his left hand thou must bind a *barsik* dress.
16. [*Recent lacuna.*] The green corn his hand must cut.
17. [*Recent lacuna.*] Dipping (his hand in water) he says: 'O god of gold, the lusty one,
18. (it is) Ea, who verily has made the man that has been purified;
19. I have not made (him).' And the workman who has made the great wooden tablet,

---

[1] In R 204 (K 2061), 20, the Accadian *mali* is interpreted by *ruttum*.

[2] *Puśikku* (W. A. I. v. 14, 15), Aram. *pĕśiqyâ*.

20. dipping his hand in the water of the god, says: 'O Nin-igi-nangar-śir,
21. (it is) Ea who verily has made the workman,
22. I have not made (him).' At sunset the garden
23. (thou must enter, and lifting) the hand to Bel must cover his throne with linen.
24. The great wooden tablet thou must set up in the garden. At sunrise,
25. on the bank of the river, a green spot, thou must draw up pure water. Three knots
26. to Ea, the Sun-god and Merodach, thou must knot.
27. One knot to this god thou must knot.
28. Dates (and) cones (?)[1] which thou hast gathered, (with) honey and butter thou must place (saying):
29. 'Be strong, be glorious!' Three victims to Bel, Samas and Merodach, thou must sacrifice.
30. One victim to this god thou must sacrifice. Thou must offer the sacrificial goblet, but
31. not set (*tuken*) the great round cup, lifting (it) up; and upon the great round cup
32. cedar, herbs, green corn, fragments of a small trunk,

Col. iii. 1. a strong reed, the cream of abundant butter and good oil thou must place.
2. Limpid water, which thou hast set before the god, thou must raise also towards a low place,
3. and dipping (the hands therein) must say:
4. Incantation.—The day the image of the god has been made, he has caused the holy festival to be fully kept.
5. The god has risen among all lands.
6. Lift up the (nimbus of) glory, adorn thyself with heroism, O hero perfect of breast!
7. Bid lustre surround this image, establish veneration!
8. The lightning flashes! the festival appears like gold.
9. In heaven the god has been created, on earth the god has been created!
10. This festival has been created among the hosts of heaven and earth.
11. This festival has issued forth from the forest of the cedar-trees.
12. This festival is the creation of the god, the work of mankind.

---

[1] See W.A.I. ii. 42, 19. A-TIR-*tiaru* = *arusu*. *Tiyaru* is "the cedar" (W.A.I. ii. 23, 23). The determinative KU denotes "the husk of a seed" (Assyrian *kemu*).

13. Did the festival be fully kept for ever,
14. according to the command of the lusty golden god!
15. This festival is a sweet savour even when the mouth is un-opened.
16. (a pleasant taste) when food is uneaten and water un(drunk).

. . . . . .

Col. iv. 1. He has brought the pure waters within it,
2. O goddess of plants, mighty plant of Anu!
3. With his pure hands he has established thee.
4. Ea, the divine antelope has carried thee to a place of purity,
5. to a place of purity has he carried thee.
6. With his lustrous hands has he carried thee.
7. With honey and butter has he carried thee.
8. He has laid the waters of prophecy on thy mouth.
9. He has opened thy mouth in prophecy.
10. Like the god, like the place (of the god), like the heart of the god, O evil tongue!"

II. W.A.I. iv. 13. No. 3.
1. "His fist (?) he (shakes?) towards the four streets,
2. the top of his head he turns (?) towards the fountains (?) of the land.
3. Draw up ($ziriq$) the waters of prophesying at his back.
4. Cut the husk of the corn-ears (over) the gate (and) the court.
5. Evil is his face, but he may not capture.
6. In the night injure the master (?) of the house in the street.
7. Spoil, O pure one, the rancid oil;
8. spoil the acid wine!"

III. S 802.
1. ".... seven cedar-trees before you...
2. (to) Samas and Rimmon (he shall) speak thus.

3. He prays, turning back the reed, (wearing) a mountain (?) dress....

4. 'O Sun-god, the judge, (and) Rimmon, the lord of wells ($biri$)!
5. Descend, O Sun-god, the judge! descend, O Rimmon, lord of wells!
6. Descend, O Moon-god, lord of the crown! descend, O Nergal, lord of the weapon!
7. Descend, O Istar, lady of battle!
8. Descend, O Iskhara, lady of judgment!

9. Descend, O mistress of the desert, the *saśśukkat* of the great gods,
10. the beloved of Anu! descend, O lady of the great gods,
11. In my mouth his name is celebrated (MU) in whatsoever he has done;
12. and I will pray continually (*tamid*) : let there be justice!'

---

13. (He prays, taking) the cedar, bowed down (*śukkupi*) in a mountain (?) dress.

14. '(O Sun-god), the judge! O Rimmon, lord of wells!
15. I approach you in prayer.
16. (O Istar), supreme mistress, daughter of Anu!
17. (O gods), the judges!'

. . . . . .

S 718.
4. The Sun-god and Rimmon make small (?) (*izazzanu*) and . . . .
5. in whatsoever they have done I will pray continually : (let there be justice!).
6. He prays . . . .
7. 'O Sun-god, the judge! O Rimmon, (lord of wells)!'
8. He has directed the unction in . . . .
9. He has been visible on the right hand and on the left . . . .'

VI.

LITANIES TO THE GODS.

I. R 2. i. 159.

Obv. 3. "What have I done that I should bear the sin?[1]
4. To the light I have uttered the spell (*atma*), and yet I bear the sin.
5. To Nuzku, the supreme messenger of Ê-kur, I have uttered the spell, and yet I bear the sin.
6. To the Moon-god I have uttered the spell, and yet I bear the sin.
7. To the Sun-god I have uttered the spell, and yet I bear the sin.
8. To Rimmon I have uttered the spell, and yet I bear the sin.
9. To Ea I have uttered the spell, and yet I bear the sin.
10. To Merodach I have uttered the spell, and yet I bear the sin.
11. To Nebo I have uttered the spell, and yet I bear the sin.
12. To the great god and the great goddess I have uttered the spell, and yet I bear the sin.
13. To my god I have uttered the spell, and yet I bear the sin.
14. To my goddess I have uttered the spell, and yet I bear the sin.
15. To the god of my city I have uttered the spell, and yet I bear the sin.
16. To the god and goddess of my city I have uttered the spell, and yet I bear the sin.
17. To the four streets I have uttered the spell, and yet I bear the sin.
18. (To) Suqamuna I have uttered the spell, and yet I bear the sin.
19. (To) Sumaliya I have uttered the spell, and yet I bear the sin.
20. (To) the seven gods and the twin gods I have uttered the spell, and yet I bear the sin.
21. (To) the god whom I know not I have uttered the spell, and yet I bear the sin.
22. (To) .... khuya I have uttered the spell; may my sin be forgiven!"

The rest is too mutilated for translation.

---

[1] *Minâ ebus-va sertam nasaku.*

LITANIES TO THE GODS. 533

COLOPHON. 1. "(From) the hand of Di . . . .
2. in the eponymy of . . . .
3. May he have peace !"

II. Unnumbered fragment.
Obv. 1. "O hero, the illuminator of men, (the lord) of lords, the light (?) . . . .
2. hero supreme, the lord who cometh forth as leader ![1]

3. O Elimma (Mul-lil), the hero who illuminates men as man !
4. O Elimma (the chamois-god), lord supreme !
5. (O) great chief, lord of the horn, Mul-lil !
6. (O Elim)ma, lord of the god IP-A !
7. (O divine) great chief, lord of the ghost-world !
8. (O Elim)ma, master of Ê-sar(ra) !
9. (O Elim)ma, lord of the temple of the supreme heart !"

III. 79. 7-8. 28. (W.A.I. v. 52. No. 2.)
Obv. 9. "(O lord [*mulu*]) of sacrifice, may the prayer address thee ![2]
10. (O lord) of prayer, may the prayer address thee !

11. (Bless ?) the brickwork[3] of Ê-kur, the brickwork of Ê-kur !
12. O . . . . establish (RI) the temple of Mul-lil !
13. O . . . . hero, establish the temple of Nin-lil !
14. O . . . . ruler of life, establish the temple of Mul-lil !
15. O . . . . establish the temple of Nin-lil !
16. O . . . . Moon-god, establish the temple of Mul-lil !
17. O . . . . fifty, establish the temple of Mul-lil !
18. O supreme, establish (the temple of) Mul-lil !
19. O rising Sun-god, establish (it) !
20. O (thou) that comest forth (from) the gate of the temple of Erech, establish (it) !
21. O messenger of . . . . fill (it) with drops[4] of rain !
22. He fills the land with weeping . . . .
23. He has sought his place of . . . .
24. A stranger has seized the house of the oracle (*biristi*).

---

[1] (1) NER-GAL *mulu* UD-DU-NE : *mulu* . . ZU . . UD-DU-NE : NER-GAL KHU-ŚI UD-DU-NE, (2) *etillum khâidh nisi* (*bil*) *bili* . . *nu(ru?)* . . . . . : *etillum saqû : belum supû* . . . . .

[2] (*Mu-*)*lu arazu dê-rab-bi.*

[3] *Libitti*, corresponding to the Accadian *a-se-ip.*

[4] *Iśis*, rendered by *tsikhati* in W.A.I. iv. 27, 23, and *tsikhtum* in v. 22, 13.

APPENDIX VI.

25. The wine[1] is outpoured and the lamentation is outpoured.

Rev. 1. The lamentation he causes to rain like a cloud in the land.
2. The lamentation seizes the land like a cloud.
3. Like a house of sickness that is destroyed, he sits[2] in tears.
4. Like a house of sickness that is destroyed, what has happened to me?
5. The mighty shepherd's tent is (full of) sorrow and painful weeping.
6. Its broad plain is desolated (?).
7. His chariot supreme mounts the height.
8. His (horse) supreme submits to the yoke.
9. (In) this temple the beer (*sikaru*) is not outpoured,[3] its food[4] is not presented."

IV. K 4620.

3. ". . . . they leave.[5]
4. . . . . they leave the exit (*zamar*) of the lordship.
5. . . . . and they leave the exit of the prison.[6]
6. . . . . from the pure ring (*uppi*), the pure bar (*lilisi*), they go out.
7. . . . . the chain (*khalkhallati*) and the guard-room (*mandhur*) of the pure prison they leave.

8. (O lord of the gods) who inhabit thy . . . . may thy liver be appeased!
9. (O) Elimma, warrior, hero of the gods, (may thy liver be appeased)!

---

[1] In the Accadian text written MU-TUK-IN, i.e. *wüdün*.

[2] So in the Accadian text; but the Assyrian version offers the alternative renderings, "he sits" (*ittasab*) and "he lies" (*irtabits*).

[3] *Immanzi*, in the Accadian text *al-surra*.

[4] In the Assyrian version, "the pure food."

[5] *I-za-am-mu-(ru)*, in the Accadian text *munnan-tug-(a)*.

[6] *Balaggi.* In a fragmentary bilingual psalm (S 2054), referring to one "who knew not the Sun-god," we read (l. 9), "the prison of weeping he has caused her to direct" (*balag bikiti usteseru-si*); and then (ll. 10—12), ". . . well will he establish weeping for her; . . . . (in) lamentation they seat her (*napalśukhu-si; muna-durrunes*); . . . . settle the prison (*balaggu*)." *Balaggu* is a loan-word from the Accadian *balag*, expressed by an ideograph which is translated *egû*, "to surround," and *amamu*, "to bind" (W.A.I. v. 27, 10). In W.A.I. v. 32. 62—65, *tiggâ* ("a ring," from *egû*) is a synonym of *khalkhallatu* ("a chain") and *unqu*, "a ring," and is represented by *kamkammat śiparri*, "a ring of copper," and *kamkammat ubani*, "a finger-ring," preceded by the determinative of "vessel" or "copper" as well as by the Accadian *balab* (written *balag-lab*, preceded by the same determinative).

10. (O) mighty chief, lord of É-sar(ra, may thy liver be appeased)!
11. (O sovereign) supreme, mighty mountain, Mul-(lil)!
12. (O Nin-lil), mighty mother of the gods, (may thy liver be appeased)!"

V. W.A.I. iv. 67. No. 2.   Prayers.

Obv. 46. "Thou hearest the prayer, (thou) beholdest my face.
47. By day the worship of (thy) divinity, the goodness of my heart,
48. (and) the daylight thou (grantest), O Istar; the darkness thou wilt not bring back.
49. The prayer of the king is this: his happiness
50. and rejoicing bless (*dummiq*[1]) with blessing!
51. He has caused (his) men to take hold of the name of Istar and call upon it.
52. The exaltation of the king she has made like (*yumassil*) that of a god,
53. and the fear of the palace governs (*yusallidh*) the people.
54. Verily he knows that along with the god thou favourest these prayers.
55. His people and himself are circumcised (*gullubtu*[2]) unto god.
56. As for what is kept back in his heart for his god (and) his goddess,
57. is there any (*âu*) who can learn the will of the gods in heaven?
58. The counsel of the divine lord of spirits who can understand (*ikhakkim*)?
59. How can one learn the course of the god of glory (?)?
60. That which has lived and died at evening (*ina amsat*), does he renew.
61. When the head is uplifted in honour, he brings all high-mindedness[3] to shame (*ikhtapar*).
62. When the face is brought low, he exalts (*itsammur*) and brightens (it.)
63. At the opening of the light (*puridi*), I melt like honey,
64. when the openings and closings (of day) and night record their decree.[4]
65. He has troubled me and has troubled (my) body.[5]

---

[1] See W.A.I. iv. 22, 30.

[2] Or rather, perhaps, "eunuchs;" see W.A.I. ii. 24, 58.

  Tsamar.

[4] See W.A.I. v. 47, 44, where "the openings and shuttings" are explained to be "day and night."

[5] Through "want of food," according to W.A.I. v. 47, 45.

66. He prophesies and rivals their divinity.

. . . . . .

Rev. 1, 2. A fetter has he laid upon me and no bracelet.[1]
   3. His rod (*khadhru*) has destined me, a cruel (*dannat*) goad (*ziqatu*).
   4. All day long like a tyrant he pursues (me);
   5. in the hour of night he lets me not breathe freely.
   6. In the work of service my bonds are unloosed.
   7. My limbs, my extremities and my sides, belong to another.[2]
   8. In my lying down I roared like an ox.
   9. I bleated (*ubtallil*) like a sheep in my shame.[3]
  10. The scribe has torn away my aching muscle;
  11. and the augur removes[4] my laws.
  12. The diviner (*asipu*) honours not the fact of my sickness,
  13. and the augur has not given a command to my prayer.
  14. God has not helped, has not taken my hand;
  15. Istar has not pitied me, has not grasped my palms.
  16. Thy hand has inclined towards the opening of the face (*kima-khkhi*), O my prince!
  17. That I die not, the queen has conjured my tears.
  18. All my people have said that (I am) an evil-doer,
  19. and the lamb has heard my rejoicing before him.
  20. He will bring good news (*yubassiru*), his liver is bright,
  21. he . . . . during the day of all my family;
  22. upon the . . . . has their divinity had mercy."

VI. W. A. I. iv. 64. Ceremonies and Prayers.

Obv. 1. "For an evil sickness thou must bring a . . . . of medicine to the mound of the gallos-priest, sending a messenger but not approaching the man.

   2. The following ceremony must be observed.—In the night set up a green branch which has grown in a distant spot before Merodach.
   3. Pile up dates and cones, pouring out oil, and place (there) water, honey and butter.
   4. Set up a vessel containing the third of an ephah; heap up inwards (*qurbi*) and corn; place green herbs by twos.

---

[1] See W.A.I. v. 47, 60.   [2] Literally, "are strange."
[3] Or, perhaps, "distress" (*tabastanu*), from *abasu*, "to bind;" synonym *zâsinatu*.
[4] *Utassi* for *uttassi*, from *nasu*.

LITANIES TO THE GODS.

5. Offer the cup of sacrificial beer. In front of the garden (?) among the .... trees, the cedars and the palms,
6. lay (it). Spread out (*sadad*) over (it) a strong carpet. Lay (there) the herbs of the garden and the fruit of the garden.
7. Offer sacrifices. Place consecrated (?) flesh, fatty (?) flesh, roast (?) flesh.
8. Take oil with wood .... and on the middle of this oil
9. pure IM-PAR, incense (?) .... pieces of pure food, clean herbs,
10. wood of the tall tree, thorn wood, the slice of a snake,[1] SISI and SIMAN, compound together (*istenis*),
11. and lay in the midst of the oil. On the mound of the gallospriest is the god of the gods of joy. Four fire-stones,
12. four bits of gold, four crystals, and four seals (cylinders) prepare. The fire-stone, the gold,
13. the crystal and the seal-stone (must be) between the gods of joy. Plant (*sakak*) ....
14. With the dust of plants (?) in a great sacrificial cup which the god ....
15. In oil of the sherbin of Phœnicia and in the wood of .... place the cloth ....
16. Take the sick man's hand and thrice repeat this incantation (to Merodach).

---

17. Incantation.—O Merodach, lord of the world .... prince,
18. strong one, unique, mighty (*gitmalu*) ....
19. hero (*tizqaru*) supreme, who (subjugates) hostility ....
20. forceful, king of ....
21. Merodach, whose view (*paqtu*) is (extended over the world) ....
22. vision and seership (?) .... the glorious one,
23. divine son of the holy mound ....
24. the deluge of the weapon his hand (directs) ....
30. gladdener (*khâda*) of the corn and the .... creator of the wheat and the barley, renewer of the herb,
31. creator of the work of the god and the goddess, their .... art thou!
31. The dragon (*usumgal*) of the spirits of earth, the director of the spirits of heaven,
32. the omniscient lord of heaven and earth, the creator of the law (*terit*) of the universe,
33. thou art the lord, and like a crown hast thou made the tablets of the (destinies).

---

[1] Or, perhaps, "snake-leaf" (*kuda-zir*).

APPENDIX VI.

34. Thou also like the Sun-god (removest) the darkness . . . .

. . . . . .

61. My god and my goddess have taken me before the judge.
62. By the command of thy mouth may there never approach me the . . . . of bewitching and bewitchment!
63. Never may the breath of those who work charms among men approach me!
64. Never may evil dreams, signs and portents from heaven and earth approach me!
65. Never may the evil portent of city or country befall me!
65. Against the evil mouth and the evil tongue among men may thine eye preserve me (*luslim*)!
66. The medicine of the god of joy on my neck has fettered (*yuśinniqa*) all the baleful things that do me harm.
67. May it cast the evil curse and the unpropitious mouth into another place!
68. May my light shine like a fire-stone, and never may I suffer distress!

Rev. 1. May thy life make my life like a crystal, may it grant mercy!
2. O my god and my goddess, who judge me, may my land
3. be blessed like gold in the mouth of men!
4. Like a seal may my troubles be sent far away!
5. Never may the evil and unpropitious curse approach me, never may it fetter (me)!
6. In thy sight may my name and my double (*sini*) be guided aright!
7. May the medicines and the rites (?) which are established before thee put away (*lipśuśu*) all that is harmful to my image!
8. Never may the strength and anger of the god draw nigh to me!
9. May the bondage of wickedness and sin explain to the man the curse (*mamit*)!
10. May the lifting up of the hand and the invocation of the great gods
11. in thy sight, O strong one, ask for the command!
12. Like the heavens, may I be pure when enchantments befall me!
13. Like the earth, may I be bright in the time of evil witchcraft!
14. Like the midst of heaven, may I shine, may I make the multitude of my evils to fear!
15. May the green corn purify me; may the herb of Venus absolve me; may the tree-trunk take away my sin!
16. May the cup of pure water of Merodach confer a blessing!
17. May the twofold fire of the Fire-god and the Sun-god enlighten me!

LITANIES TO THE GODS.

18. By the command of Ea, the king of the deep, the god (of wisdom),
19. at the lifting up of my hand may thy heart have rest, may Merodach, the hero of the gods (give thee tranquillity)!
20. May the word of Ea be exalted, and may the queen Dav-kina (be praised)!
21. May I thy servant, such and such an one, the son of such and such an one, live; may I ....
22. May I see thy sun, may I exalt (thy head?)!
23. May I see my god ....
24. O my goddess, may thy heart speak (blessings unto me),
25. and may I, the writer, thy servant, extol the work of thy god!

26. End of spell at the uplifting of the hand to Merodach.

32. (Take) the plant of the god of joy which grows from him, the oil of the palm-stalk and the top of a palm-stalk;
33. place (them) together in oil of the sherbin of Phœnicia and with a green root; (then) anoint the man.

34. Repeat this action three times, and raise the form of the god of joy.
35. Bring forth those stones, together with the plant of the god of joy; over the middle of it say:

36. Incantation.—Thou, O god of joy, art the .... weapon of Ea and Merodach!
37. Behold the enchantment and the witchcraft that has been devised (?);
38. (hear?) O god and goddess of mankind!"

VII. W. A. I. iv. 62. No. 2. A Religious Ceremony.

Obv. 54. "The following ceremony should be performed.—Before the pure god place the foot. Set up a green branch, pure water, some grains of corn and a layer of reeds. Twice place herbs (on it).
55. Sacrifice a white lamb. Thou must present (*tudakhkha*) consecrated (?) flesh, fatty (?) flesh and roast (?) flesh.
56. Offer beer and wine. Lay a pavement of brickwork aslope. Present a sheep. Surround (*tetsen*) the entrance with *gabsu* stone.
57. The fire on the hearth and the water of the river-god thou must uplift, and must take hold (*tustakhaz*) of a feather.

58. Like a feather is one's marching perfect. Cedar-wood, sherbin-wood, scented reed, prickly grass,
59. the PAL grass and saffron (?) thou must heap up (and) offer beer and wine. This spell three times
60. thou must repeat before Istar : 'He has effected all that his (heart) conceived.' (This is) the end of the spell. She will hear the prayer.
61. As for this man, may the god, the king, the lord, the prince, the .... of the gate of the palace be at peace with him !
62. May his gods that were angry be at peace with him ! On the day he prevails like a hero he marches.
63. He shall sweep away (his enemies), shall possess the land and decree that stability be with himself. This man doubly shall the fire
64. (visit) and go straight unto his house. The impure man and the impure woman he shall never see."

INDEX OF WORDS TO THE LECTURES.[1]

A.
AB-AB, 71.
abalu (ablu), 186, 236.
abari, 128.
abgal (A.), 78.
abrik, 183.
abub, 200.
abzu (S.), 374.
addu, 138.
adî, 166.
agagu, 141.
a-gubba (A.), 286.
aharu, 47.
akitum, 261.
akkulu, 288.
a-khad (A.), 286.
akharidi, 274.
ala, alad (A.), 196, 290.
alála (A.), 248.
alam (A.), 196, 249.
alim (A.), 196.
allallu, 258.
allattum, 149.
ama (A.), 181.
amari (A.), 75.
amma (A.), 81.
amrâ, 348.
Anúna (A.), 182.
lusapi, 352.
appuna, 301.
apśi, 63, 166.
aqru, 295.
arakhu, 280.
ari (A.), 352.
aria (A.), 196.
arkhu, 72.
arlu, 83, 443.
aru, 10.
arur, arurti, 78.
asaridu, 47.
asip, ittaspu, assaputu, 51, 79, 81, 95.
asiru, 124.
asrata, 166.
asri, 301.
asundu, 285.
asurra, 125, 134, 183.
aśari (A.), 284.
aśśinnu, 81, 225.
atudu, 286.
Aua, 108.
azkaru, 68.

B.
banu, 285.
bar, barbar (A.), 149, 153.
barbarti, 289.
Baru, 151, 153.
Barqu, 265.
tabarri, 84.
batqirtu, 222.
bennâ, 184.
bînu, 245.
birit, 285.
birutu, 64.
bisbis (A.), 83, 259.
biz-biz-ene (A.), 308.
buanu, 287.
buhidu, 290.
bûti, 372.

D.
da (A.), 188.
dadil (A.), 28.
dadu, 56.
dagan (A.), 188.
dalil, dalali, 173, 352.
ludlul, 404.
dara (A.), 280.
daslum, 305.
dibiri, 372.
Dilbat (A.), 259.
DIL-ES, 82.
dim-sar (A.), 115.
dimer (S.), 143.
dime, dimma, 143.
dinânu, 94.
ditanu, 283.
dukhdhu, 84.
Dumu-zi, 232.
dunni, 128.
dupie, 185.

E.
ea (A.), 133.
edheru, 384.
edhuti, 348.
edu, 186.
edu, "only," 235.
ê-gur (S.), 67.
elim (A.), 283.
elinu, 166.
el!u, elle, 73, 81.
elmesu, 246.
ema, 82.
emu, 285.
en (A.), 52.
enu, enitu, 63, 404,
epar, 287.
epiru, 161.
epitâtu, 238.
epu, 71.
erim, erima (A.), 178, 306.
erisu, 245.
Erua, 111.
esemen (A.), 75.
essepu, 62.
etarsi, 298.
etsits, 318.

G.
gabû, 226.
galitti, 381.
gallu, 208.
gamli, 81.
gan (A.), 179.
ganni, 305.
gari, 288.
gasam (A.), 111.
gasru, 195.
ge (A.), 183.
GI-BU, 81.
gibû, 226.
gilgillum, 307.
gillati, 383.

---

[1] A. denotes Accadian, S. Sumerian.

INDEX OF WORDS TO THE LECTURES.

gingiri (A.), 265.
gipara, 384.
girśê, 244.
GIS-BAR, 180.
giskin (A.), 238.
GIS-LI-KHU-ŚI, 9.
gisme (A.), 380.
giśra (A.), 291.
gitmalu, 128.
gitmalutu, 207, 269.
gizi (A.), 32.
Gubára (A.), 211.
Gudi-bir (A.), 107, 290.
Gudua (A.), 194.
gu-enna, 296.
gugal, 128.
gur (S.), 196, 375.
gurgurru, 186.
gurum (A.), 96.
guśir (A.), 291.
guzi (S.), 94.

I.
idirtu, 71.
igaru, 68, 75.
iggillum, 132.
Igigi, 141.
ikkib, 350.
ikkil, 226.
ikrim, 226.
iltebu, 288.
innana, innína (A.), 116, 182.
ippu, 73.
irkallum, 154.
irriri, 75.
irta, 82.
isimu (A.), 141.
iśinnu, 68, 77.
isippu, isipputi, 11, 51, 62, 77.
Iskhara, 257.
issakku, 59, 183.
istaritu, 268.
ivat, 99.
izi (A.), 233.

K.
kakis, 305.
kakkul (A.), 296.
kalu, 62, 225.
kamarri, 311.
kamaśu, 62, 79.
kapar, 270.
kasum, 404.
kasdat, 363.
KA-TAR, 351.
katsati, katsuti, 62, 143.
kê, 305.
kesda (A.), 154.
kibir, 404.
kibu, 176.

kiel (A.), 145.
kigallu, 64.
kirbannu, 73.
kiriru, 357.
kiśallu, 64, 411.
kiśibu, 383.
kiśittu, 169.
kiskanu, 238.
kistu, 73, 372.
kiśu, 32.
kitsriti, 184.
kua (A.), 95.
kue (A.), 95.
kummu, 171.
kunê, 7.
kuri, 309, 321.
kurkane, 62.
kurke, 62.
kutstsur, 355.

L.
Laban (libnâti), 249.
labar, 62.
lagaru, 62.
lamaśśu, 290.
Lamga, 185.
lamma (A.), 238, 290.
li, 128.
lil, lilu, 103, 145, 281.
lilat, Lilith, 103, 145.
liu, livu, 10.
luba (A.), 321.
LUL-GIR, 404.
lulim, 284.
lu-masi, 49, 82.
lunum, 305.

M.
mad (A.), 238.
magir, 70.
makhkhu, 62.
makhru, 76.
maliki, 128.
mamit, 291, 306.
mamlu, 258.
maniti, 72.
martu, 235.
mas, masu, masi, 46, 48, 49, 82, 149.
masal, 240.
maśdi, 383.
maśkitum, 161.
Mâtu (A.), 200, 207, 281.
matsû, 223.
mazû, 296.
yumazzir, 389.
me-gal-zu (A.), 175.
mekhu, 209.
me-lul-ti, 75.
meri, mermer (A.), 202, 209.
merśi (A.), 244.

me-sag (A.), 144.
mesari, 77.
meskhirrâti, 389.
mesreti, 404.
me-te (A.), 144.
mikhrit, 166.
takhkhar, 173.
milkatu, 261.
mi-para-ki (A.), 384.
misrâta, 389.
mukhibilti, 69.
mummu, 387.
munasiku, 288.
mursamma (A.), 201.
musab, 247.
musalû, 221.
mustaldir, 384.
muśaru, 99, 245.
muttallu, 128.

N.
nabakha, 287.
Nabiu, 113.
namtabbê, 173.
nadu, nadi, 75, 224.
nadrata, 82.
nagir, 310.
naglabi, 185.
tanidi, 166.
unakkaru, 351.
nalsi, 210.
namari, namru, 9, 195.
namga, nagga (A.), 94.
nammassê, 198.
namratsit, 8, 320.
namsê, 210.
namzabi, 380.
namzitum, 296.
Nana (A.), 260.
Nangar, nagar, 67, 186.
Nannar, 157.
napakhu, 119.
napsiti, 82.
naptsu, 287.
taqqud, 311.
inattuqu, 308.
Ner (A.), 195.
Nibatu, 62.
nihi, 286.
linaha, 226.
nikaśu, 73.
nin (A.), 116, 152, 176, 254.
nindabut, 69, 70, 73, 306.
nisakku, 59, 60.
nubattu, 71.
Nunpê, 135.
nunu, 58.

P.
padhri, 185.
ipallas, 64.
papakha, 67, 68.

INDEX OF WORDS TO THE LECTURES. 543

paqata, 82.
parakku, 64, 81, 95, 237.
pasaru, 175.
pasdhi, 355.
pasisu, 61.
pateśi (A.), 59, 60.
pes (A.), 153, 258.
suplukh, 185.
pukhu, 94.
pukhur, 198.
pul, 198.
puqu, 311.

Q.
qan, 306.
QAR, 286.
qarradi, 270.
qastu, 380.
qistu, 372.
qu, 245.

R.
rahâbu, 258.
rammanu, 202.
rappu, 143, 321.
lusarsid, 166.
ribu, 141.
rimini, 96, 210.
rimka, 149.
ri'i, 270.
ritu, 161.
ritu, 238.
rits, 288.
rittu, 301.
ruha, 303.
russu, 283.

S.
sabattu, 76.
sabatu, 76.
sabat, 222.
sabis, 284.
sadakhu, 225.
sadduti, 305.
sadhakhu, 74.
sadi (A.), 321.
sadû, 407.
sagan (A.), 60, 68.
sagata, 83.
Saggil (A.), 94.
sakkanakku, 60, 68, 109.
sakparim, 309.
sakhu, 83.
Sala (A.), 210.
saladhu, 173.
Sallimmanu, 57.
salum, 372.
samkhâtu, 184.
samrata, 82.
sa-mun-śillalil (A.), 351.
sana, 81.
sar (A.), 269.

sararu, 202.
sasur, 373.
sedu, 290.
serakh (A.), 134.
sidhtum, 321.
sigaru, 75.
sindhu, 138.
sipar, sipru, 168, 369.
sipat, 138.
siptu, 63, 68, 149, 171, 318.
sitehu, 238.
sitilti, 369.
subi, 268.
sukalimtu, 356.
sulit, 174.
sulum, 76.
sumutti, 311.
sunqu, 286.
surbata, 84.
surpu, 63.
sursum, 238.
sut, 289.
sutartum, 227, 268, 281.
sutkhurat, 389.
suttu, 175.

'S.
śabba (A.), 306.
śabi, 246.
śag (A.), 372.
śagga (S.), 306.
śagi, 379.
śanaqu, 306.
śangu, 59, 61.
śar (A.), 245.
śig-śigga (A.), 285, 286.
śikhir, 81.
śila, khen-śile (A.), 173.
śimatu, 144.
śimba, śiba (A.), 245.
śippatu, 31, 384.
śuburu, 75, 185, 198, 281.
śukhal, 225.
śukkurutu, 94.
śukullu, 75.
śur (A.), 64.
śurdu, 237.

T.
tabbak, 149.
tabqirti, 321.
itakkalu, 185.
takkat, 128.
takribti, 358.
taklimu, 73.
taltal (A.), 28.
tamtu, 374.
tamtsi, 81.
tanitti, 352.
tarbatsu, 75, 161.
tarpu, 63, 143.
tarri, 404.

teraphim, 63, 143.
terit, 81.
tikpi, 82.
timi, 285.
Ti-ti-sal-lat, 27.
Titnum, 27.
tudat, 133.
tudâtu, 133.
tul, tilu, 245, 405.
turakhu, 280.
turbuhtu, 259.

TS.
tsab, 348.
tsalam, 248.
tsâtu, 169.
tsibit, 166, 287.
tsillu, 186.
tsullupu, 383.
tsurri, 185.

U.
UA, 161.
uda-kára (A.), 145.
udannis, 309.
uddanê, 151.
Ugur (A.), 196.
ukkumu, 288.
uknu, 289.
UL-BAR, 184.
UL-DUA, 169.
umasi, 301.
uniki, 286.
unut, 306.
uppidh, 222.
yuqâ, 81.
UR ("girdle," "horizon"), 118, 249.
Uras, 151.
urasu, 151.
uri, 404.
urtum, 81.
uru, 362.
Uru-ag (A.), 106.
Uru-gal (A.), 80.
uru-galli, 306.
uśa (A.), 141.
usar (A.), 125.
usues (A.), 172.
usum-gálu, usugal (A.), 199, 269.
ussabi, 95.
utuk, 107.
uz (A.), 284.
uzzu, 285.

Y.
yarakhu, 268.

Z.
zabal, 94.
zag (Dilvun), 114.

izakkû, 384.
zaninu, 161.
izarruru, 308.
ziggurrat, 237.
zikhi, 404.
zikum, zigarum, 374.
zimat, 81.
Zir-banitu, 109.
zu, 294.

zur (A.), 285.

KH.
khâdhi, 196.
khal (A.), 77.
khardatu, 274.
kharimâtu, 184.
KHAR-MES, 84.
kharran (A.), 163.

khidati, 348.
khilibu, 94.
lukhmum, 297.
yusakhnapu, 384.
khubur, 311.
khulkhul (A.), 164.
khumuntsir (A.), khun tsir, 83, 153.
khutesitiya, 305.

INDEX.

Â or Sirrida, originally a male Accadian deity representing the solar disk, became his consort, 176-9 and *notes;* bilingual hymn recited at sunset, 177-8, *notes.*

Aaron, perhaps from Assyrian *Aharu,* to send, 47, *note.*

Abel, name of, according to Oppert, 236.

Abode of the gods; beyond the Euphrates; or, according to another account, on Kharsag-kurkúra, "the mountain of the world;" its situation; famous temples named after it; reference to the words of Job and Greek legends; the proud boast of the Babylonian king; the Chaldæan Olympos; peculiar sanctity and site, 359-62; bilingual hymn refers it to Nipur; its connection with northern Babylonia; world-tree and world-mountain in relation to deities, 362-3; the idea of Hades modified; the world of the gods separated from the abode of the dead; the sky-god of Erech added to the pantheon, 363-4.

Abraham's removal to Harran, where a temple of the Moon-god rivalled that of Ur, 163.

"Abysses" or "deeps" of the great gods, large basins filled with water for purification, resembling the "sea" in the outer court of Solomon's temple, 63 and *notes.*

Accadian belief that the moon existed before the sun, the converse of the Semitic; the name of Sin most honoured in Babylonia, Assyria and the coasts of Arabia; the attributes of the Moon-god transferred to Istar, 165.

Accadian notion of the universe and the deep likened to Homer's Okeanos; the personified deity Innina assumed to have afterwards given the name to Nineveh—meaning "the god Nin," as Innana signifies "the goddess Nana;" the latter associated with Nebo at Borsippa, 116-7.

Accadian religion at first Shamanism, 19.

Accadian rule the earliest; struggles with the Semites and varying fortunes, 25.

Accadians the inventors of cuneiform writing; their language and features different from the Semites, who inherited their cult and civilisation, 5.

Accado-Sumerian, pure and unadulterated, shows the true origin and parentage of most of the hymns and magical texts; philological conclusions often verified by the texts; the dates of others inferred from the matter and style of the compositions, or references to Semitic deities, philosophical ideas, and conceptions of the divine government, 325; account of the creation in days, and its resemblance to the first chapter of Genesis, 326.

Accuracy of scribes in general, with occasional mistakes in copying, 12, 13.

Adar, the provisional reading of the name of the Assyrian war-god; occurs in the name of a god of Sepharvaim brought to Samaria by the colonists; also in the names of several Assyrian kings and one of Sennacherib's sons, 7; Adar, Ninep or Uras, also was champion of the gods, and originally a solar deity; two curious titles explained, and his relation to Mul-lil; an implacable warrior, 153-4.

Agadhé built or restored by Sargon, the founder of its celebrated library; northern Babylonia called Accad from the city; diffusion of the cult of Samas at Sippara in a Semitised form eclipsed that of Larsa; change in the language of the hymns embodying new ideas and aspirations; worship of the supreme Baal, the father and creator of the world, the one omnipotent god; hymns, 171-4.

Alála and Alála alam explained, 248-9.

Alluvium at the mouths of the Euphrates and Tigris; rate of increase and extent prove the long cult of Ea, 135.

Ana the sky, the local god of Erech; **the**

sky itself the god and creator of the visible universe; different from that of Eridu and inconsistent with the later belief, 186; the sky considered divine throughout Chaldæa, and Ana invoked in the oldest magical texts; but became a *dingir* or creator at Erech, 186-7; his cult changed by the Semites, who regarded him as Baal-Samaim; Palestine towns mentioned in the conquests of Thothmes III. called Beth-Anath and Anathoth; the daughter of a Hivite chief was called Anah or Anath; and a Horite prince Anah or Anu, 187-8; worship of the Semitic Anu carried westward about the time of Sargon, 189; confusion of Accadian Ana and Semitic Anu, 189-90; changed position when his worship assumed a more spiritual character; his heaven exalted and the refuge of the gods during the Deluge; where the spirit of Ea-bani ascended, and whence Anu assigned their places to Samas, Sin and Istar; further spiritualisation and changes; the conception rather pantheistic than monotheistic, 190-1; forces identified with him; advance of pantheism and influence of aliens on Semitic belief, 191-2.

Antiquity of Babylonian astronomy, 30.

Antiquity of Sin, "the father of the gods" according to Sargon and one of the inscriptions; called by Nabonidos the father of Samas and Istar; his temple at Ur founded by Ur-Bagas, 165-7.

Anunit, the Semitic feminine of Anúna, one of the primordial gods of Accad; identified with Istar; meaning of the masculine and feminine names; connected with Mul-lil; the Anúnas and the great gods; their place in Hades; Annunaki opposed to angels, 182-3 and *notes;* Anúnit considered a local form of Istar in the temple of Ulbar, who was addressed by Nabonidos as the mistress of battle, bearer of the bow, and the daughter of Bel; also the sister of Samas and daughter of Sin, 184.

Aráli, the world beyond the grave, described; meaning of the name, 3, 4.

Archaic names and attributes applied to Merodach in an Accadian hymn, 284.

Arks in the form of ships, containing the symbols of the gods, carried on men's shoulders, point to the earlier home on the shores of the Persian Gulf and the city of Eridu; identity of the sacred ships of Eridu and Egypt; special names; hymn in honour of the god when a new image was enthroned; its early date; the Sumerian *ship* changed into an *ark* by the Semites, 67-8.

Arteios, a mythical personage, 157.

Ashêrah the Canaanite goddess and the Babylonian Istar, 256.

Ashteroth Karnaim and the Greek legend of Astartê under the name Eurôpa, 256.

Assault of the seven wicked spirits upon the moon; flight of Samas and Rimmon; whilst Istar plotted for the sovereignty of heaven; meaning of the legend, 257-8.

Assôr the god and Assur the capital confounded and then identified; hence the city itself became divine, and all offences against each were considered alike; still the god's individuality and elemental character were retained, and he was at once the personification of the city and its Baal, or "lord;" resemblance to Yahveh in Israel, a national deity; no Assaritu by his side, like Anatu and Anu, Beltis and Bel; Istar invoked with him as an independent goddess, 126-7.

Assoros and Kissarê, the primordial heavens and earth, 249.

Assur-bani-pal defeats his brother's rebellion, and restores the sacred festivals, 354.

Assyrian religion wholly Babylonian with the sole exception of Assur as the head of the pantheon; like Yahveh in Israel, he is supreme, and king above all gods; all acts of sovereignty and conquest are done in the name of Assur, and to destroy his enemies; Babylonian deities invoked under old titles, but had lost their definiteness; Assur looked to in peril and distress; a purely local divinity at the primitive capital, but when removed to Nineveh, the new capital of a more compact kingdom from Babylonia, his worship became national; the name Assur and its meanings, 124-5; the name of the god and the country, the same, 125, *note*.

Assyrians a nation of warriors and traders rather than students; their literature an exotic, and a mere imitation of Babylonian culture, 122.

Assyrians compared physically and mentally with the Babylonians; causes of the difference; indebted to the Babylonians for literature, religion and laws; Greek and Roman indifference to Chaldæan history, 37-8.

Attributes of deities changed by the Semites to embody different conceptions, as Mul-lil and Baal or Bel; the elder and younger Bel sometimes confounded, 148-9.

Au, the goddess, the same as Zikum, confounded with Ea by Halévy, 108, *note*.

Augury and belief in the thunder as the

INDEX. 547

voice of the gods; Canaanite faith in the latter left its impress on the utterances of the Hebrews in the Psalms; the *Bath kol* of the Talmud, supernatural and prophetic messages; Accadians believed that the sounds of nature were divine voices; hymn to Mul-lil as lord of Hades, 299-301; epithets of Mul-me-sarra, Iskara, Bunene and Lagamar, 301-2.

Azag-śuga, a god, and primarily a goat, 289.

Babylon, city of, first made the capital of the country by Khammuragas, whose dynasty lasted several centuries, 18-9.

Babylonian and Assyrian modes of writing different on ordinary and religious topics; the former intelligible; the latter purposely obscure by the priests to conceal the mysteries of their worship; system of writing invented by the Accadians or proto-Chaldæans, 4, 5.

Babylonian clay tablets merely sun-dried; Assyrian baked in a kiln; British Museum collection chiefly from Nineveh; the great bulk that once stocked the libraries still buried in the mounds, 9.

Babylonian cuneiform more difficult than Assyrian, there being no official script, 13.

Babylonian literature consisted of ritual, hymns, myths, commentaries and text-books; lists of deities and their titles; descriptions of temples and images; relation and rank of the deities; also those of the neighbouring countries; sacred texts provided with keys and glosses; many of the latter now in our possession; and modern researches into the creeds and beliefs of ancient nations afford clearer ideas of their origin than were possessed by the Babylonians themselves, 16-7.

Babylonian religion; materials for its history scanty and imperfect, although the subject has attracted the attention of Rawlinson, Lenormant, Tiele and Hommel; no systematic investigation has been previously attempted; sources of information; the monuments, Old Testament, and the Greek Classics; the sculptures and inscriptions on the palace walls, and clay tablets the only reliable data; inscriptions originally pictorial, and intended to express a language different from the Semitic Babylonian and Assyrian; every character had several values, and could be used phonetically and ideographically, 3.

Babylonian religious conceptions conveyed westward illustrate the Scriptures; parallel of Sargon and Moses; both historical, but have myths and legends attached to them, 43-4.

Babylonians of the historical period believed that the ocean stream encircled the world and contained the germs of the universe; contrast of pre-historic belief in a "mountain of the world;" Babylonian cosmologies all based on the assumption that the watery abyss was the first; striking agreement with the character of the Sumerian culture-god; Ea and Oannes; worship of the deities of the deep impressed on all the cosmogonies, and carried to the west; the same general terms used by the Hebrew writer respecting "the beginning," 391-2.

Bahu probably the Gurra of Erech, the Bohu of Genesis and the Baau of Phœnicia; the Semitic Bohu, "emptiness," an unsuitable rendering of Gurra, "the watery deep;" changes and confusion of the deities by the Semites, as Bahu and Nana; Rubat the Assyrian equivalent of Gula, 262-3; made the consort of Adar by mythologists; Bahu, Â, Sala, all alike Gula; Hommel's view of her character, 264.

Bel of Nipur, the Accadian Mul-lil, absorbed the Babylonian Bel; his titles and their meanings; variations in the older and later faith, 103-4.

Bel the traditional author of the great work on astronomy and astrology, 29, *note*.

Bela, Bileam and Balaam connected by Dr. Neubauer with the chief god of Ammon; also Jeroboam and Rehoboam, 54, *note*.

Bible names and their variant forms explained, 184-5, *note*.

Bilat-ili, a title of the wife of Bel, 177.

Bil-matati, a common Semitic title of goddesses, 177.

Bit-namri, the tower of the temple of Istar, 9, *note*.

Book of Nabathæan agriculture; its description of the temple of Tammuz in Babylon, 218; probable source of the details; fragments of a tablet of the minor and foreign deities in the national pantheon; picture of religion; cylinder inscription of Cyrus, 220.

Borsippa once an independent town, now the Birs-i-Nimrod, contained the great temple of Nebo and Tasmit; the house of the seven spheres restored by Nebuchadnezzar; the tower of seven stages coloured to represent the planets, 115.

Bull-gods highly honoured; name Dapara; Merodach a primitive bull-god; the divine bulls of Ea and his wife named "the god of the field of Eden" and "the god of the house of Eden;" the winged bulls that guarded the entrance of a temple represented the genii or gods of the household; the human head and its import, as in Ea-bani; the winged divine bulls of Eridu distinct, but confounded in later times; the body-guard of the two great deities of Eridu, 290; Merodach called Gudi-bir in early astronomical literature, and regarded as the ploughman of the celestial fields or zodiacal signs; name explained on a tablet, 290-1.

"Bull of Anu" and "Bull of Rimmon," names of stars; planets regarded as sheep; the star of the "wain," "eagle," "the goddess Bahu," and "the shepherd;" the last the prototype of the Greek Boötes, 48-9.

Canaanite Ashtaroth and Anathoth, only slightly different, 194.

Captivity of the Jews in Babylon and its effects, 39-40.

Cedar essentially a tree of life; depicted on the walls of the Assyrian palaces; curious figures of cherubim on each side, standing or kneeling; sometimes human and sometimes hawk-headed, holding a cone in one hand, 241.

Chaldæan early art found at Tel-loh; spread of the worship of Tammuz northward; the native name of Tel-loh was Nin-girsu, from the god afterwards identified with Adar; after the worship of Tammuz in Sippara he was addressed as Mul-mersi, or En-Mersi, 242-3.

Chaldæan trade with India; teak, muslin; Accadian ideograph for muslin, 137-8.

Chronology, great want of; antiquity of Babylonian civilisation, and supposed era of a single monarchy ruled by the Accadians, with Ur as the capital, 17-8.

Circumcision known to the Babylonians, 83, *note*.

Clean and unclean, or distinction of lawful and unlawful food; probably refers to totemism; distinction common to Assyrians, Babylonians and Jews; the flesh of the wild-boar and ox, when forbidden; mention of the domestic pig avoided in the inscriptions, and reptiles accounted unclean, as by the Jews, 83.

Combat between Merodach and Tiamat; parallel of Michael and the great dragon; struggle with the powers of darkness, 102-3.

Comparison of the Babylonian triad who shared the great temple; local character of the religion, 120-1.

Composite animals of mythology, sometimes beneficent beings, as Oannes, the god of culture and "a pure life," described as half-man with the tail of a fish; but the majority were malignant, and against whom spells were used by the exorcist priest, 392-3.

Composite creatures the offspring of totemism; their nature and uses, 393.

Cosmology of Eridu; the watery abyss; Ea and Dav-kina; allusion to "the firmament;" Damuzi or Tammuz, 143-4.

Creation epic and its varying legends harmonised; but unmistakably materialistic; details compared with the Bible, 394-6.

Critical state of the empire before Assurbani-pal's death; Egypt lost; Babylonia clamouring for independence; the northern border threatened by semi-barbarous nations; and before the century closed, Nineveh sacked and its palaces destroyed, 11-2.

Cubit, variations of, 33, *note*.

Culture myths of Babylonia and America in relation to their primitive civilisation; questions raised; the Cushite theory of population conclusively refuted by the connection of Babylonian culture and cuneiform writing, and no traces of Egyptian theology and astronomy, 136.

Cutha legend of creation, and the curse at the end, 60.

Cyrus on the overthrow of Nabonidos, from inscription on clay cylinder; the anger of Bel and other gods as declared by the priests had been roused against him for having brought their images from the ancient sanctuaries; Nabonidos, like Saul, had been rejected from being king; Merodach had visited the deserted shrines in Sumer and Accad, and sympathised with the people's wrongs, and had chosen Cyrus, king of Elam, to the sovereignty of Chaldæa, as he had been previously hailed by the Jewish prophet; a single battle decided the struggle, and Babylon opened its gates for his triumphant entry into the city; the conqueror showed his gratitude by restoring the gods who had aided him to their ancient seats and restoring their temples; the priests in turn flattered and held him up as the favourite of the national gods, and reproached Nabonidos in the same way as Jeremiah had treated Nebuchadnezzar and the Jewish kings, 86; annalistic tablet explains why nearly the whole

INDEX. 549

population submitted at once; centralisation, civil and religious, the real causes of Nabonidos' disaster and downfal, 87-8.

Dagan or Dagon, worshipped in Harran, Phœnicia and southern Philistia; temples at Gaza, Ashdod and Beth-dagon, 188-9.

Damascius, extract from, on the primæval divinities Ana-Seir, Ki-sar, Lakhma, Lakhama, Anu, Mul-lil and Ea, 125.

David or Dod, and its connection with Dido; corroboration by Socin and Smend; worship of the supreme god under the name of Dodo and Yahveh; Dôd-i, "my beloved;" the epithet shows how national affection transferred the name of the deity to the king, 56-7.

Dav-kina or Dav-ki, the consort of Ea, personified earth, and the god Ea personified water, as elemental deities; theory of Thales, 139; the goddess of the earth at Erech; both the mother and sister of Adonis called Gingras in Cyprus; Gingiri or Gingra, the name of Istar, the feminine of *Dingir*, creator, 264-5; each Babylonian city had its own Gingira, or "creatress;" Istar became a Semitic goddess, and naturally accompanied her bridegroom Tammuz; Erech and Accad great centres of her worship, 264-5 and *notes*.

Date of the pyramid-builders; development of hieroglyphics; high culture and civilisation of the period, 33-4.

Datillu, the river of death, near the mouth of the Euphrates, beyond which Xisuthros was translated to dwell among the gods, 359.

Deities of the popular faith represented in human shape; the warlike Istar with quiver on each shoulder and bow in hand; only demons and inferior spirits or mythical personages portrayed as composite creatures, partly human and bestial; Ea has only a fish's skin thrown over his shoulders like a cloak; the monsters seen by Bêrôssos painted on the temple walls of Belos, the brood of chaos; the creation-legend of Cutha, and the creatures suckled by Tiamat; their disappearance marked the victory of light over darkness, and the gods of heaven over Titanic monsters, 277.

Descent of Istar into Hades; a mythological poem; based on Accadian materials, 221-7; curiously illustrates the Old Testament and classic authors, and in return receives light from them; explanation of particulars, 227-8; death of Tammuz (Adonis) commemorated at Gebal or Byblos every year; influence of Egyptian custom and belief; Adonis and Osiris the same; Alexandrian legend of Isis and Osiris; autumnal festival in honour of Tammuz, 230; cult changed in the west, and the god regarded as a solar deity; origin of the story; the name Accadian Dum-zi and its meanings; worshipped in Phœnicia, Cyprus, and Greece; cult modified by the Hittites, 231-6.

Difficulties in studying the religion from the mixed languages of the text, and their different dates, 6.

Dilbat the planetary name of Istar; descent, attributes, and correspondence to Nebo as the Announcer; her temple at Tel-loh called E-Ana, 259 and *notes*; her home the city of Dilbat, but Erech the real centre of her worship in historical times; common title Nana; her image recovered at the sack of Shushan; late texts distinguish Nana and Istar; Dilbat the same as 'Suttil at Borsippa, 259.

Dionysos the wine-god; his worship derived from the East, 54, *note*.

Disease usually ascribed to demoniacal possession, and expulsion necessary before recovery; pestilence and epidemics regarded with awe as a punishment from the gods; the same theory found in some of the penitential psalms; and a wide-spread calamity like the plague was held to be a minister of vengeance sent by the gods on account of sin, 309-10.

Divine names; true pronunciation carefully concealed from the uninitiated, 4.

Dog disliked by the Semites, and classed among the powers of evil; generally avoided in early art, although the Babylonians had a fine breed; Indian dog represented on terra-cotta tablets; five of Assur-bani-pal's dogs inscribed on the bas-reliefs now in the British Museum, 287-8; Babylonian dog esteemed in later times; Merodach had four divine hounds not always employed on errands of mercy; extract from legend, 288-9.

Ea, the god of the deep and the atmosphere; lord of all rivers and the supposed ocean-stream, the source of Babylonian civilisation; name not Semitic; the god of Eridu once on the shores of the Persian Gulf; early connection with Babylon, 104-5; legends from Bêrôssos and Polyhistor, 131-2; etymology of name uncertain; Lenormant's conjecture; Ea's identity with Oannes; home, duties, and how represented; shown on a gem in the British Museum; name transcribed Aos by Damascius, and may refer to the time when the inhabitants lived in pile-dwellings on the shores of the Persian Gulf, or when he had become a household deity; his symbol a serpent, compared with Zulu belief, 133-4.

Ea the demiurge addressed by many titles; invocation; creator of the black-headed race, 140-3.

Ea-bani's descent into Hades, 62-3.

Early expeditions against Cyprus and Sinai; action and re-action of the two races in forming the Babylonian religion, 34.

Edin or Eden, "garden of," according to Babylonian tradition near Eridu; bilingual hymn describing its wondrous tree, foliage, and shrine of the two (gods), 237 and *notes;* partial resemblance to the Norse Ygg-drasil; Babylonian world-tree; mystic virtues of the cedar; the work of the augur and his initiation, 240-1.

Edomite mythology illustrated by the names of the kings, Saul ('Savul), Hadad and Samlah, 181-2.

Edomite proper names derived from deities, 54.

Egibi banking records carefully preserved from the time of Nebuchadnezzar to Darius Hystaspis.

Erech the seat of Anu and Istar; the city of the choirs of festival-girls; the priests and the ministering attendants, and connected with Gisdhubar, and where the hero slew the bull created by Anu to avenge the slight of Istar; name on oldest bricks, and first called Unu-ki or Unuk, the same name as Enoch built by Cain, 184-5.

Eridu or Eriduga and Eri-zéba, not only a holy city, but anciently one of the foremost rank; its worship of Ea continued till the close of the Babylonian monarchy; the city, B.C. 3000, on the shores of the Persian Gulf, 135.

Eridu and Nipur contrasted; their different religious systems blended; inferences from geographical position, 150-1.

Erûa, Eritu and Eru, 7, *note.*

Essential distinction between Accadian and Semitic ideas of creation and descent; the first gods and spirits; evolution and growth of the Babylonian religion; resemblance of the gods to human beings who had been previously associated with animals and confounded with the old totems; deification and supernaturalism; abstraction of the gods from visible objects and creative force, 333-4; innumerable spirits controlled by creative gods representing the *Sabba;* opposed by the spirits of disease, chaos and darkness, and others, but all amenable to spells or exorcisms, 334-5.

E-Saggil, the temple of Bel-Merodach; outer courts and walled enclosure; the *ziggurat,* or "tower," and chapels intended to bring together the images and worship of Chaldæa; orientation of the great temple; like Solomon's temple, had a "holy of holies" concealed by a curtain, 64 and *notes.*

Euphrates valley the early home of the Jewish race; Ur, the birthplace of Abraham; the Tower of Babel and the dispersion of mankind; the first abode of the Canaanites and Phœnicians proved by comparative philology, 41.

E-Zida, the chapel of Nebo, where oracles were delivered to the priests at the great festivals; E-Kua, the special sanctuary of Merodach, supposed to have contained the golden statue of Bel, 95-6.

Family ideas of the gods made them human and destroyed totemism, and when carried out produced an artificial system of religion more reflective than spontaneous; cause of further changes; nomad irruptions and amalgamation of the two races also modified both religion and civilisation; absorption of the deities into Baalim and Ashtaroth; the gods of Accad transformed into the Semitic family; all outside were the servants and slaves who carried the messages of Baal everywhere; chaos, night and foreign gods considered hostile; Satan, in pure Semitic faith, an angel of the Lord, 346-7.

Fire-god partly absorbed by the Sun-god; his attributes, privileges and rank; hymn to him, 179-80; the fire-stick and its ideographs, Gibil or Kibir, and worship as Savul; afterwards considered the same as Merodach and Samas, 180-1.

Gazelle appropriated to Mul-lil of Nipur, who was specially called the gazelle-god; hence the totem of the city and god of the under-world; gazelle a peculiarly sacred animal, represented on Chaldæan cylinders both as a sacrifice and a symbol; frequently assumed the form of a goat, and became a sign of the Zodiac, 284.

Ghost-world of Nipur, beneath the earth, where the Anúnas, on a golden throne,

INDEX. 551

guarded the waters of life; results of the unification of the creeds of Nipur and Eridu, 358-9.

Gisdhubar, originally a fire-god and afterwards a Semitic solar hero, probably the prototype of Nimrod; name of three ideographs; Hommel's readings; objection and explanation, 8 and *note;* the hero of the national epic, a Babylonian conqueror as real as one of the kings, 17; falsely accused by Istar, with the help of Ea-bani, kills the bull sent by Anu to punish him; list of Istar's victims; Gisdhubar associated with deities, 248-9.

Gizeh pyramids and the development of hieroglyphics, 33.

Goat's milk used with other offerings to the gods; hymn associating the divine goat with Mul-lil, and magic formula, 285-6 and *notes.*

Hadad the supreme Baal or Sun-god; extent of his worship; adored as Rimmon at Damascus; his name occurs in the names of persons and places; and abbreviated to Dáda at Aleppo, and confounded with the Assyrian Dadu, 55-6.

Harran (Kharran) connected with Babylonian history; epithet of Mercury; temple restored by Nabonidos; figure of the god on gems and seals; restorations by Sargon, Shalmaneser and Assur-bani-pal; worship of the Moon-god once the same as in Assyria and Babylonia; ascendency of the god of Ur, 163-4.

High-priest's duties in libations to the gods; his dignity at Babylon derived from Merodach, and at Nineveh from Assur, 60-1.

Human flesh consumed by the Accadians in honour of the spirits of the dead, as in pre-historic Egypt; but such barbarous practices almost unknown to the Semites, 83-4 and *notes.*

Human shape and character of the gods contrasted with the animal-headed deities of Egypt; harmony of Semitic belief that the Creator made man in his own image; tendency of art among the two races; the winged bulls at the entrance of the temples, and the eagle-headed cherubs on each side of the sacred tree, were survivals of a time when the gods were worshipped under similar forms, proved by the written texts, 278-9.

Hymn to Bel-Merodach in the beginning of Nisan, 261-2; hymns to the Sun-god of Sippara, a clue to the relative antiquity of the rest; used daily in the service of the temple of Samas; and at sunset, sunrise, and on special occasions; all of Semitic origin, and belong to the time when Sippara and Accad were great centres of influence; internal evidence of the period when they were composed, as during the reigns of Sargon, Naram-Sin and Nebuchadnezzar; general inferences respecting the rest, 341-4; hymns used in spells implied a higher cult than mere magic; the conception of a creative deity necessarily introduced praise, adoration, and a fixed ritual; contrast with Shamanism, 355.

Incantations, exorcisms and magic, limited to the present life; Chaldæan belief in a ghost-world, or continued existence after death, under Mul-lil as lord, only vague and shadowy, 358.

Innina, perhaps the primitive Nebo of Borsippa, considered as the great deep in Accadian mythology; a curious parallel to Homer's "golden cord of Zeus," 116-7; no apparent connection with the demiurge of Borsippa and the prophet-god Nebo; explained by Accadian legends, 117-8.

Invocation of Merodach by the later kings crowned at Babylon, 109.

Irad and Jared, same name as Eridu, 185.

Irkalla, another name of Mul-gi, the lord of Hades, 154 and *note.*

Istar the only goddess who had a place by the side of Assur, 123; Istar in primitive and historical times; no Semitic etymology of name; no sign of gender, as in Beltis, Zarpanit, Anat and Tasmit; the Old Testament and Phœnician Ashtoreth; sometimes a male divinity; the Istars of Accad and Erech different, 253; Istar ceased to be the pure goddess of the evening star, and was regarded by the Semites as the goddess of fruitfulness and love; the voluptuousness and debasing character of her worship denounced by the prophets of Israel, and shocked the Greeks; diffusion of her cult and its abominable rites, 266-7; the gentler phase, when not tainted by popular frenzy, said to have had a humanising effect upon the cultivated classes; addressed in the penitential psalms as Gula, Nana and Milkat, 267-8; Accadian hymns to Istar, 268-70; the Syrian deity warlike, and worshipped by the Hittites and their disciples in Asia Minor; the Gulli and Amazons; descent of Artemis and Aphroditê; story of Semiramis; different phases of her cult, and temples at Nine-

veh and Arbela; later development as a war-goddess; also why invoked by the earlier kings; oracle sent to Esar-haddon, 274-5; Assur-bani-pal's devotion and successes, 275-7.
Isullanu, the gardener of Anu, probably the mythic prototype of Sargon, 250.

Jewish religion and Christianity; the former bound up with the fortunes of the people; its devotional utterances and prophecies; causes of its clearer views of God as the ruler of all the world; purifying effect of the captivity, 39.
Joseph; etymology of name; father of Ephraim and Manasseh; connected with an old Canaanite deity; compared with Bethel; relation to *Asip*, "a diviner," 50-2 and *notes*.

Kali, a class of priests; meaning and origin of the term, 62.
Khammuragas, the founder of a new dynasty, first made Babylon the capital, 18-9, 23-4.
Kings, like Solomon, exercised priestly functions; but distinct at Tel-loh; at first only high-priests, 59.
Kouyunjik library destroyed at the fall of Nineveh, and its buried treasures lay beneath the ruins till discovered by Sir H. C. Rawlinson, who recovered a part of the contents; Mr. Geo. Smith and Mr. H. Rassam followed, and the greater part is now in the British Museum, 12.

Laban, a god whose image once stood in the temple of Anu at Assur, 249, *note*.
Legend of seven evil spirits, 106.
Legendary poems and when composed; gloomy description of Hades, where good and bad alike flit about in darkness, and the shades of heroes sit enthroned to greet the new-comers; resemblance to the Hades of the Homeric poems; exaltation and happiness of Eabani, and reasons for Ner and Etana being retained in the regions below; growth of more spiritual ideas and the doctrine of immortality; faith enlarged, and the good yearn to live for ever "in the land of the silver sky," the true home of the gods and the blest, 365-6.
Lehman on Adrammelech and Adar-Milkat, 7, *note*.
Lenormant François on the Sacred Books of Chaldæa; contents of the two main collections; a third series consisted of penitential psalms, in many respects similar to those of the Old Testament; when composed, and order in which they were collected; use of interlinear translations, and formation of the Babylonian Bible; modification of some of Lenormant's views necessary, 315-7.
Library of Assur-bani-pal open to all; but literary age short-lived, 11.
Library of Nineveh and its contents; clay tablets and rolls of papyri chiefly copies of older works from Babylonia; it had been brought from Calah by Sennacherib, but mostly collected by Assur-banipal, "a real lover of books;" he appreciated the old texts from Erech, Ur and Babylon, 10-1.
Lilatu or Lilith, the night-demon; the name and conception passed from the Babylonians to the Jews and Idumæans, 145-6.
Lists of images and deities in the temples of Assur and Nineveh; supremacy of Assur, thrice invoked at the head of each; his name once followed by that of Istar; Assur "king of all gods;" no wife or son to share his honours; a jealous and powerful god; his worship had all the elements of a pure faith, 127-9.
Literature of Babylonia chiefly based on older compositions, as the Epic of Gisdhubar formed from earlier poems on the exploits of Hêrakles of Erech; the Descent of Istar exhibits plainly borrowed passages; the penitential psalms, hymns and magical texts, show the same traces of repetition and borrowing; clear indications of a period when the Semitic idea of a supreme Baal and a god were unknown, and only pure Shamanism prevailed, 327-8.
Local character of Ea, Merodach and Assur, 142.
Local deities, their worship, priests and temples; many cities older than Babylon, as Sippara and Ur; the local nature of Babylonian religion explains much of its history; Nabonidos' policy of centralisation resented by all classes, and reversed by Cyrus, 89-91.
Lugal-tuda, "the divine storm-bird," compared with Promètheos as a benefactor to mankind, and doomed to suffer; contrasted with the fish-god of Eridu; bilingual poem on Zu, 294-6; the old faith of totemism changed; Zu's flight; failure of the council of the gods to destroy him, and transformation into a bird, 296-9.

Magan or Magana, land of, with its mines of turquoise and copper, conquered by Naram-Sin, 31-2 and *notes*.
Magical texts and hymns connected with

INDEX. 553

particular rites and ceremonies; worship a performance with rigid adherence to particulars; inference from the texts; sometimes no traces of original; the Semitic passes into mere magic; hymn to the Sun-god, a mixture of deep feeling and debasing superstition, 319-20; hymn to remove the ban or curse; slow decay of magic and witchcraft; Accado-Sumerian language, 322-5.

Makhir, "the god of dreams;" discovery of his temple at Balawat by Mr. Rassam; its internal arrangements and contents; resemblances to the Israelitish ark; temple gates coated with embossed bronze plates, 65.

Mamit compared with the Roman Fate and Greek Atê; a terrible weapon in the hands of priestly exorcists; hymn and incantations against demoniac agency; power of the Mamit; the plague considered as heaven-inflicted for sin; fragment on the destruction of Sennacherib's army, 306-9.

Masu, hero, an epithet of several deities, specially Adar, Merodach and the Sungod; also "a scribe," or "librarian," and in astrology connected with Taurus, 47-8.

Mâtu, the god of the tempest, dreaded as the minister of Bel; one of several storm-gods, the children of the sea; his worship Semitised, and absorbing the name and attributes of Meri and Mermer, carried to Syria and Damascus, 200-2.

Medicine, and the use of clean and unclean articles of food in relation to old beliefs, 84; great work on, contains receipts for curing disease mingled with charms and spells, 317-8.

Medicine-men or exorcists, and their power over the spirits of nature, 329.

Merodach's titles, attributes and worship; description of his temple called Bêlos by the Greeks; further from Nebuchadnezzar's inscriptions; its site, name and entrance-gates; richly decorated by Nebuchadnezzar; the shrine of Zarpanit, 94-5; Merodach identified with an Accadian deity, but his attributes beneficent rather than solar; etymology of name doubtful; *Uru-dug* and *Amar-ud*, explained; pun on the latter; classed with the constellations, 106-7; becomes the head of the pantheon; Cyrus his favourite and worshipper; conception of Bel-Merodach enlarged; his place among the Greeks of Asia Minor, 108-10 and *note*.

Methuselakh and Methusael, variants of Mu-sa-ilati, 185-6, *note*.

Moses, different etymologies of name; Hebrew, Egyptian and Assyrian, 44-7.

Mystery of evil, as explained by the Accadians and Babylonians; hymn to the harmful spirits and the fire-god, 206-8 : the wind and tempest-gods little besides elemental powers; home and parentage of the spirits of the air, 208.

Moon-god of Ur distinct from that of Nipur; each Babylonian town had its own local Moon-god and forms of adoration ; in Chaldæan religion the Sun-god the offspring of the Moon-god, 155-6.

Mugheir, the site of the ancient Ur, 42.

Mul-lil, "lord of the ghost world," angry with the gods for allowing Xisuthros and his companions to escape the waters of the deluge in a ship; appeased by Ea's intercessions; excepted from the sacrifice of Xisuthros after the descent from the ark; Namtar called his beloved son, 147; ultimately a Bel or Baal, 347.

Mul-nugi, also called Irkalla; his relationship and position at Nipur and Ur, 154.

Mythological tablets; their probable date, 215.

Nabathæan legend of Tammuz and Ssabian festival, 239, *note*.

Nabonidos' discovery of the date of the reigns of Sargon and Naram-Sin, confirmed by Mr. Pinches' reading of the cylinder and other inscriptions and lists of kings; Mr. George Smith's previous supposition; method of testing the date, 23; his attempts to centralise the local cults, 91-2 and *note;* resented by all classes, 97.

Name and person inseparable among the Chaldæans; the personality liable to injury by using the name in a spell; and using the name of a deity compelled service to the priest or exorcist; secret names of the Egyptian gods; some names holy and efficacious, others of good or evil fortune; superstition about names common to both races; sacredness of the name of the god of Israel; kingly pride in the preservation of their names; those of conquered cities altered; dread of unknown deities; hymn to the creator under the names of the fifty great gods; mystical importance of names and dread of spells, 304-5.

Name of Esar-haddon changed out of affection by his father, 303-4.

Names of famous monarchs adopted by successful usurpers, 303.

Namtar, the plague-demon, and the Jewish angel of death; his messenger Isum or

Itak represented by the colossi at the entrance to a temple; Nerra and Nergal alike; legend discovered by Mr. G. Smith, 310-1; Babylon depicted suffering from the destroying angel; besieged by foes; the sword, famine and the plague let loose in the streets; Mullil's soliloquy; Merodach mourns over the doomed city; the help of other deities invoked against the nomad 'Suti; Nerra quieted, and speech of Isum; sweep of the warrior-gods westwards compared with the angel of pestilence in the time of David; different from Namtar; inference from the parallel and contrast, 311-4.

Nanak and Nanar used as names of heroes and kings, 157.

Nanar invoked as Sin; spread of the worship of Sin in southern Arabia, 164-5.

Nebo, the prophet god of Babylon and Borsippa, the patron of writing and literature; association with Istar and Nergal; special attributes and titles; his ideograph; position and rank at Borsippa, 115-6; honoured in Assyria, Babylonia, Palestine and Moab, 120.

Nebuchadnezzar's address to Merodach, 97.

Nineveh ideographically expressed by a fish; popular etymology, 57.

Nin-girsi or Tammuz, the god of Tel-loh; addressed as a shepherd; hymn or funeral dirge; a hapless Sun-god of Erech; extract from the epic of Gisdhubar, 245-8.

Nin-ki-gal, or Allat, queen of Hades, 147-8; her proper titles; dreaded in Hades; her messenger, the plague-demon, 149-50.

Nomads spread the cult of Accad north and west, proved from the names of deities in Palestine, as Nebo, Anu, Anatu and Sin, 42, *note*.

Nuzku, a solar god; his ideograph denoted "daybreak;" also "the scribes' pen;" confounded with Nebo, 118-9.

"Observations of Bel," the great work on astronomy and astrology; object, scope and contents; evidence of date, 293-4, 399-400; Accadian astronomy included a knowledge of eclipses, the formation of a calendar, invention of the Zodiac and naming of the constellations; the Semites merely added astrology; the heavenly bodies considered divine and dedicated to particular deities; some had been changed into animals by totemism; the sun was an ox, the moon a steer, and the planets sheep; the stars became symbols of deities, and a curious theological system arose; the heavens were further divided and named; Mars became Nergal, and Orion, Tammuz, 401-2.

Older Babylonian gods partly Semitic and partly Accadian adaptations, but all local, and belonging to the cities as much as the temples; analogies and differences of the Israelites and Phœnicians, 130.

Opposite characters assigned to Istar; Talmudic tale; the wife and mother of Tammuz, 250-1.

Old tablets and papyri preserved at Nineveh, 9.

Omen tablets in the British Museum, 11.

Origin of the world; the elements regarded as divine, or possessed of a divine spirit; how formed into the present order of nature; next, symbolised divine beings; this mythic view gave way to the idea that matter was created or begotten by the gods; next, matter regarded as the cause of all things, 367; cosmological theories resolved into genealogy and creation; Accadian and Semitic ideas harmonised by the assumption of a chaos and creation of the world in days; Bêrôssos' account said to have been derived from Oannes; extract from a document; transmission of the account of Bêrôssos by Alexander Polyhistor and early Christian writers, 368-70; two versions, awkwardly joined and inconsistent; the creation of monsters, animals and men, a sort of anticipation of Darwin's hypothesis, and the systems of Anaximander and Thales, 370-1; summary of a copy of a tablet made for the great temple of Cutha, 372-3; destruction of the monsters, and date of the legend, 373-4.

Ox, long honoured by mythologists, 289.

Palm and the tree of life; characteristic of Babylonia; date-wine largely used as a drink in medicine, religious ceremonies and incantations; in later belief the tree of life and tree of knowledge the same; the cedar associated with the treasures of Anu, Bel and Ea; contrast with the first part of Genesis, 241-2.

Pantheon illustrates the names of the kings Saul, David and Solomon; parallel of the names of Edomite kings, 53-5.

Papyrus titles in the colophons of Assur-bani-pal's tablets, 9-10, *note;* the reed of Magan; Accadian, gizi, 31-2, *note.*

Parsondés' legend explained by the cuneiform tablets; not a Median satrap, but the god of Ur; hymn in his honour;

INDEX. 555

language of the hymn, and the relationship of Ur and Nipur, 157-62.
Patron deities regarded as creators by their votaries, 142.
Penitential psalms and litanies; part of one by Dr. Zimmern; its language, style, and signs of a common pantheon, 336-7; development and contrast of the beliefs of the two races; the cultivated classes embraced the newer and higher views, whilst the masses clung to the old Shamanism long after magic and exorcisms had lost much of their power and sanctity; the litanies mark a new era in religious thought; Dr. Hommel points out peculiarities, use, date, and mere survivals; also dialects, 339-40; striking resemblance of some to the psalms of the Old Testament, 349-52; the two beliefs, and sin and suffering, 352.
Persian and Jewish systems compared, 90-1.
Priests' titles, classes and offices, 61-2.
Position of Samas in the hymns and inscriptions of Nabonidos; absorption of solar divinities; the Kossæan and others became his sons, and Makhir his daughter, 175 and note.
Prayer or hymn to Assur connecting him with Babylonian deities, 127-8, note.
Purification or cleansing of persons and objects important; ritual observances of anointing and washing, 61-2.

Relation of the Babylonian to his god different from the Egyptian pantheistic notion of absorption, 244.
Religion of the country first Shamanism; gradually changed, and the spirits raised to the rank of deities; hymns composed in honour of the gods, and a collection formed like the Rig-Veda, 19; the Semites introduced sun-worship and his counterpart, under various phases and names; state religion established by Khammuragas remained nearly the same till after Nebuchadnezzar's time, 19-21; the older faith held a partial footing at Nipur and Eridu a long time, 212-4.
Religion of the upper classes, priesthood and court, known from the sacred literature; that of the masses consisted chiefly of magic and incantations, 348.
Resurrection views and their origin, 40.
Rimmon or Ramânu, the supreme god of the Syrians of Damascus, identified with Hadad, and the same as on the Assyrian monuments brought to light by Mr. T. G. Pinches; extent of his worship; his ideographs, and variant names, as Dadda or Dodi, 203-4; the name used by the tribes of the Taurus and the Kolkians; possibly confused by the Edomites with the Canaanite Dôd or David; name of Ramanu never superseded by his other names, but sometimes addressed as Barqu or Barak; how his cult extended and became more national, 204-5; further changes and their causes, 209-10.
River-worship only partial, and the reason; Semitic hymn addressed to the Euphrates, 403-4.

Sabaism, or star-worship, earliest home, 396.
Sabianism of Harran in the beginning of the Christian era, only the last echo of Babylonian astro-theology, 402.
Sabbath, Accadian, like the Latin nefastus; a "rest day" in Assyrian, and a "day of rest for the heart;" in Babylonia kept every seventh day, and connected with lunar periods; differences from the Hebrew institution, 76-7.
Sacred mounds of Babylonia and the Gilgals of Palestine the sites of older structures; uses and associations; themselves divine and the habitations of the spirits of the air; Delitzsch's explanation of El-Shaddai, 407.
Sacred stones of the Semitic faith show a wide difference in the cults of the two races; each sacred stone a Bethel, the reason of its sanctity; worship of sacred stones common to all the branches of the family; famous black stone of the Kaaba and others around Mecca; Nabathæan niches in the rock for such objects; sacred stones from Sicily and Tunisia represent the worship of a triad; mythology of Byblos and the invention of Baetyli; consecration of the stone by Jacob which had served as his pillow; Palestine Bethels generally ranged in circles, or Gilgals; cones of stone, or tree trunks, and other symbols of deities mentioned in the Bible, depicted on coins and gems, 408-9; Sin of Harran shown on a gem in the British Museum; stone pillars common in Phœnician temples; two erected in Solomon's by the Tyrian workmen; account of a Bethel in the epic of Gisdhubar before the hero returns on his homeward voyage, 410.
Sacrifices and offerings nearly the same as among the Israelites; Assur-bani-pal's slaughter of caged lions, and offerings of wine over them; human sacrifices; children burnt, as in Phœnicia, 77-8; sacrifices accompanied by hymns, incantations and prayers; examples of prayers; priests' duties and service the

first night of the new year in the temple of Bel-Merodach; text and notes of ceremonial, 79-81; special dresses and ablutions necessary, 82.

Sakkanaku, a special title of the high-priest of Bel-Merodach, sometimes assumed by the kings, 109, *note.*

Saints' calendar for the intercalary month Elul; every day devoted to one or other of the gods, with certain rites and ceremonies, 70-5.

Sala and Zarpanit once the same divinity, 210; Sala of the copper hand expressly called the wife of Tammuz, the beautiful Sun-god of Eridu, 212.

Salliman, or Solomon, name of a king of Moab, 57-8.

Samas, the son of Sin, the Moon-god; the Sun-gods of Babylonia as numerous as its Moon-gods; each city had its own, 166; the Samas of Sarsa and that of Sippara described, 167-8.

Samlah, Semele, and Pen-Samlath, 54, *note.*

Sangu, name of an office nearly like the levitical, 61.

Sargon honoured alike by Accadians and Semites; myths relating to his history compared with those about Kyros, Perseus, Romulus and Remus, and Moses, 26-8; legend respecting Sargon; Sarganu, same origin as the Biblical Serug, 28, *note;* his early occupation and historical character; founded the great library at Accad; seal of his librarian; the standard works on astronomy and omens; afterwards translated by Bêrôssos; Sargon's conquest of Elam, Syria and Cyprus, proved by Cesnola's discoveries, 29-31.

Sarzec's discoveries at Tel-loh show the beginnings of Chaldæan art and writing; the latter more pictorial than cuneitic at the time, 32; statues of diorite from Magan, when the mines were held and worked by the Egyptians of the third dynasty; unit of measurement, 137.

Savul or Sawul, a Babylonian deity; name carried to Palestine and Edom, 35.

Semitic conception of religion purely local in Babylon, Canaan and Phœnicia; its Baalism in different places, so many aspects of the Sun-god, 121.

Semitic encroachments and ascendency; formation of an upper class of soldiers, traders and priests; intercourse between the Accadians and the Semitic intruders generally peaceful; the former mostly became serfs and cultivated the soil, and intermarried; edicts issued in two languages; cuneiform writing still imperfect; new values and signs invented; ideographs retained and script imitated; rivalry of the scribes in copying and compiling; rise of a mixed literary dialect and religious ideas of the two races; further influenced by dynastic changes, 35-6.

Seven a sacred number; the Chaldæan Noah's sacrifice, and use of sevens in the sacrificial vessels; the seven magic knots used by the witch; the seven anointings of the sick with oil; the sabbath or seventh day; the seven planets and demon messengers of Anu; the god of the same number; the Deluge said to have lasted seven days; the seven sheep of the hero; the seven gates of Hades; the seven zones or stones of Erech; and the seven fish-like men from the Persian Gulf, 82, *notes.*

Sex introduced into theology by the Semites, who provided every god with his female reflex, 110; want of sex in Accadian divinities a sore puzzle to the Semites from their opposite modes of thought with regard to rank and precedence, 176-7.

Shamanism and Animism explained, and use of magical texts, 330; the introduction of a moral element, rise of totemism, and the various stages of a higher cult; cosmogonic speculations and the generalisation of phenomena followed, and faith was enlarged by the belief in good and evil spirits; contrast of the two systems, and their development reviewed, 332-3.

Shinar, plains of, the earliest home of Sabianism; the astronomy and astrology of Babylonia celebrated by Greek and Latin authors, and alluded to in the Old Testament, 396-7; where astronomical observations were made long before the towers of the temples were erected for the purpose; the leading groups of the stars had been named, a calendar formed and eclipses recorded; the sun's apparent path noted and divided into twelve sections, and named from the chief constellations; the names refer to the totemistic age of the Accadian faith, 396-7; probable date of the invention of the Zodiac, 398.

Sin, name of several localities in Arabia and Moab, 42.

Sin the Moon-god never confounded with Istar in Harran, Yemen or Sinai, 256.

Sin-muballidh defeated Rim-Agu, 25-6.

Sinai quarries worked 6000 years ago; diorite statue of king Kephren, and that at Tel-loh almost similar, 33;

mountain and wilderness connected with moon-worship, 50.

Sippara pre-eminently the city of the Sun-god; its great temple E-Babára; the city and neighbourhood the original seat of Chaldæan supremacy; connected with the empire of Sargon and the story of the Deluge; legend of the buried books of Xisuthros, 168 and *note;* the Biblical Sepharvaim; Rassam's discoveries on the site; said to have been four Sipparas, but only two historical; etymology of name, 168-9; address by Nabonidos after restoring the temple, 174-5; Sippara of Anunit the twin-city; the deity the feminine of Anúna, one of the primordial gods of Accad, 182-3.

Siptu, an introductory word; its use and signification, 318 and *note.*

Sky-god of Erech and his change of position when his worship became more spiritualised; his heaven exalted, and the refuge of the gods during the deluge; where the spirit of Ea-bani ascended, and from whence Anu assigned their places to Samas, Sin and Istar; further spiritualisation and changes; the conception rather pantheistic than monotheistic, 190-1; forces identified with him; advance of pantheism, and influence of aliens on Semitic belief, 191-2.

Solomon, a divine name, proved by the inscriptions; occurs in the names of several kings, 57.

Stars worshipped as divine beings, 402-3.

Succoth-benoth, perhaps, the goddess Zarpanit, 95.

Sun-god descent in Chaldæan mythology, how explained, 155-6.

Sun-god of Nipur connected with the pig; Adar, "lord of the swine," apparently once the totem of his city, 287.

Tablet of exorcisms, and order of divine names used, 261 and *note.*

Tabula the shepherd, the double of Tammuz; Abel and Tubal-Kain, 249.

Taltal-kur-gallu, name of one of the oldest kings of Tel-loh, 29, *note.*

Tammuz, the Sun-god of Eridu, the husband of Sala of the copper hand; Tammuz, son of Ea, was the spouse of Istar, whose later husband, Rimmon, became the Syrian Sun-god, 212.

Tasmit, the wife of Nebo, helped him in his useful labours, 120.

Tebet, consecrated to Papsukal, 32-3; the goat-god, 284.

Tel-loh monuments (see Sinai quarries, 50); temple to Ana, the sky-god, erected by Gudea, 192-3 and *note.*

Temple of Bel-Merodach embellished by Nebuchadnezzar with silver and gold; its furniture, like Solomon's, of massive gold, 61-6.

Temple of Sala built by Gudea; her relation and attributes, 210-1; addressed as Gubarra in a penitential psalm; story of the goddess of the copper hand replaced by one of gold and bronze, 212.

Temples of the higher gods compared to the Capitol at Rome, 218.

Tendency to modify religious thought among the Semites; trinity of Anu, Bel of Nipur, and Ea, at the head of the pantheon; the elder Bel yielded to Bel-Merodach; vast numbers of the great gods of heaven and earth, besides minor deities of, towns and villages, and the gods of foreign countries; temples and titles also deified; three hundred spirits of heaven, and six hundred spirits of earth; force of the phrase, "lord of hosts," 216-7.

Teraphim, Assyrian tarpu, 63, *note.*

Thanksgiving days and days of humiliation specially ordered by the later kings for national affairs, 77.

Threat of Istar if refused admission into Hades, 146.

Tiamat or Tiavit, Thavatth and Heb. *t'hôm,* explained, 374.

Tiele's explanation of Istar's descent into Hades, 251.

Titnim the old Accadian name of Palestine, 202.

Totemism once common in Chaldæa evident from Gisdhubar's taunt of Istar for her treatment of Alala, the horse and the lion; epoch when each city had its totem or sacred animal; Oannes described, 279-80; ideographs of the names of the chief deities; Ea sometimes expressed by the ideograph for "antelope," in Assyrian *Turakhu,* or the Biblical Terah; other epithets derived from the antelope and "ship" used at festivals to convey Ea's image; also associated with a divine fish, 280; connected with the serpent and the goddess Innina, the correlative of Anunit; designated by the ideographs of "fish" and "enclosure," afterwards as the name of Nineveh; interchange with the snake; her parentage; temple built by Dungi, 281-2; explanation of the totems of the antelope, fish and serpent; the serpent of Edina (Edin); poetical description of Merodach's weapons, and explanation of the mythical sevens; the serpent changed into an anthropomorphic deity, the incarnation of guile and wickedness; relation to

Nina and Tiamat, 282-3; Ea, as a gazelle, had various titles; Merodach, as his son, called Asari-elim, 283-4.

Tower of Babel identified with "the illustrious mound;" Babylonian version of the building and confusion of the hostile leaders of the rebellion; use and meaning of the word "confound;" the mound in ruins before the calendar was drawn up, 406-7.

Triad of the great gods; also a secondary trinity of Samas, Sin and Istar; tendency to dualism; early Chaldæan the only genuine trinity, 193.

Triads of Accadian deities, usually male, 110.

Tsirdu or 'Sirdu, a name of Dav-kina, from the Assyrian 'Sirdu, a falcon; Sirrida, variantly written, was a title of the goddess Â; the temple and worship of Tammuz in Accad, 237.

Ur-Bagas, first-known king of united Babylonia; his monuments at Mugheir, Larsa, Warka, Niffer and Zerghul; restored temples, founded cities, and established the religion of the country, 167.

Uz, a goat, an Accadian deity, represented sitting on a throne, watching the revolution of the solar disk, holding in his hands a ring, and clad in a robe of goatskins; a similar robe put on Jacob to obtain his father's blessing, 284-5.

Vicarious punishment the limit of Accadian belief; modified and expanded by Semitic influence; epoch of the penitential psalms; later additions; a psalm or prayer, 353-5.

Water-god of Eridu took the place of the sky-god of other cities; his titles and functions, 139.

Winds specially regarded by the primitive Babylonians as spirits of good and evil; hence, both venerated and dreaded, 199-200.

Worship of mountains a survival of the days before the Chaldæan colonists descended from the mountains of the East; sacred mounds on the plains and their uses; the peak of Nizir; a temple at Calah called "the mountain of the world;" 'Sabu and Kharsak-kalama, but the most famous that of Borsippa, now called Birs-i-Nimrud; one of the sacred names of Anu derived from it, 405.

Zakmuka festival celebrated in the temple of Bel-Merodach, when the divine king seated himself in the holy place and received the homage and adoration of the rest of the gods; the temple contained a golden image of the god, and a golden table in its front; resemblance to the Jewish temple, 64-5; the festival supposed to be the same as the Sakæan; opening hymns and ceremonies, 68-9.

Zamama (Zagaga), the Sun-god of Kis; same as Adar, and symbolised by a lion, 261-2, note.

Zarpanitu, Zir-banitu, and Zir-panitu, local names of Beltis; the name pure Semitic, but she represented an older Accadian divinity; her benevolent office, 110-1; her relation to Merodach and Ea; worshipped with Lakhamun and Elagu; changes in her cult, 111-2.

Ziggurat of eight stages called the foundation-stone of heaven and earth; top chamber an observatory, 96.

Zi, or spirits, innumerable and mysterious; assigned to objects and forces of nature; the moral element unknown in Chaldæan faith; events determined by blind chance, 328.

Zikum and Zigarum or Zikúra, names of Gurra, or chaos, defined; king called Ur-Bahu, 262, note; Zikum honoured in the south as Bahu, and in the era of totemism known as "the pure heifer," 374-5; Aiôn and Protagonos; Genesis and mythological documents; the watery abyss, the primal source of the universe; Phœnician mythology; chaos and evil, 377; Zikum and Tiamat contrasted; fight between Bel and the dragon; the story compared with the first chapter of Genesis; supposed date in its present form; slightly different from the cuneiform tablets, but irreconcilable with the work of Bérossos, 387-8; comparison, and the work of the fourth day, 389-91.

www.ingramcontent.com/pod-product-compliance
Lightning Source LLC
Chambersburg PA
CBHW052110010526
44111CB00036B/1604